D0922894

A
Dictionary of
VOCAL
THEMES

by

HAROLD BARLOW
and
SAM MORGENSTERN

Crown Publishers, Inc.
NEW YORK

Copyright, 1950, by Crown Publishers, Inc.

Music
Library
ML 128
V6 B37

Printed in the United States of America

Introduction

WITH THE completion of our *Dictionary of Musical Themes,* we started on a book which would do for vocal music what *Musical Themes* did for instrumental works. It took several years of research to compile this *Dictionary of Vocal Themes,* which includes the salient and rememberable themes from operas, cantatas, oratorios, *Lieder* and art songs, as well as many miscellaneous vocal pieces not belonging to any of the above categories.

Since, in addition to the notation of the themes, this book contains the words of the music quoted, we have indexed first lines as well as titles. The reader can thereby identify a piece through its composer, title, or first line, as well as its notation.

Man has sung from the beginning of his existence, and one lifetime would not suffice to extract the themes from only those melodies which he has noted down. We were, consequently, forced to limit ourselves in some fashion or other, and decided to confine the contents of this book for the most part to those works which have been recorded here and in Europe.

The problems confronting the compiler of such a volume as this are legion. Should he include folk music? To what degree should he include popular songs? What about those works, ultra-modern ones in particular, in which a clearly defined theme is hardly discernible? Should he use original or English translations?

Having no precedent, we tried to solve these questions in what seemed to us the most practical and satisfactory manner. Folk themes and their endless variants could easily fill a book the size of this one. We therefore chose those which have been edited and arranged by composers steeped in their own national folk idiom—Bartók, Kodaly, Vaughan Williams, Warlock, Weckerlin, to name a handful—and which through recordings have become an international heritage. If a popular tune has been recorded several times by concert artists of repute, achieving thereby a kind of classical status, we have tried to include it in our book.

Operas such as *Pélleas and Mélisande, Electra* and *Salome* we omitted. Here, every vocal line is thematic or not, as you choose, and quoting them would have meant literally copying the whole score. What the general reader might remember from *Salome*—the themes from the "Dance of the Seven Veils"—is included in our first book. Most of the leitmotifs in the later Wagnerian operas appear in the orchestra rather than in the vocal line. Since these are plentifully quoted in our *Dictionary of Musical Themes,* we have used opening phrases from scenes as they are recorded. Otherwise, we would have been obliged again to quote line for line.

In such early church works as, for instance, Palestrina's *Missa Brevis* and the *Marcellus Mass* there is a constant melodic flow, any part of which could be thematic. We have quoted the opening phrases from the various sections of these Masses and the ecclesiastical motives which form their bases.

Wherever possible, we have gone to original sources for our material. All the Bach and Handel quotations were culled from the *Gesellschaft* editions. To have quoted the entire vocal output of Bach and Handel we would have had to compile two separate volumes. Here, too, our yardstick was the recorded works plus whatever we felt might be of use to the amateur, layman and professional musician. If there are any gross omissions we hope our readers will call them to our attention so that they may be included in subsequent editions.

An examination of scores of recital programs as well as record catalogues governed our choice of the songs of Schubert, who wrote close to six hundred *Lieder*. We handled Brahms, Wolf, Strauss and other great *Lieder* composers in the same manner.

Though we chose the arias and concerted numbers from operas, we did include a certain number of recitatives which are as well known as the arias which follow them.

In a limited number of songs where we felt the accompaniment theme was as important as the vocal line, if not more so, we quoted both. Thus, the eighty repetitions of the same note in the solo part of Peter Cornelius' *Ein Ton* are supplemented by their accompanying motive in the piano part. The accompaniment to Debussy's *Spleen* and the violin obbligato to Braga's *Angel's Serenade* follow immediately on their vocal themes.

Some composers, who in their lifetime may have been very prolific, are here represented by perhaps one or two songs. Time and neglect have made these composers practically obsolete, and their scores for the most part unavailable. We have, therefore, chosen a few pieces representative of their style and still occasionally heard, on the chance that some reader might recall their themes.

A few of the songs quoted here may seem unimportant to the American student. The international distribution of our *Dictionary of Musical Themes* was the basis for the inclusion of these pieces, unknown here but of interest to musicians and laymen in other lands.

Wherever possible we used original texts, though in many cases only translations were available. Of these we chose the best we could find. Because of script difficulties and the possibility of error in phonetic spelling, we used only translations of Russian texts. Here, the choice of French,

German or English was governed by the quality of the text and its adherence to the musical line.

The variety of interval combination in vocal literature is perhaps not so great as in instrumental works (what is playable is not always singable), and the reader will find a greater similarity in vocal than in instrumental themes. We came across a good deal of unconscious as well as conscious plagiarism. Though *La Paloma* is Yradier's best-known, almost only known, song, we also included his *El Areglito* because of its quasi note-for-note similarity to the "Habañera" from *Carmen*. When this obvious fact was called to Bizet's attention he frankly admitted the plagiarism, saying that he could not have invented a better theme for his "Habañera" than Yradier's.

Our own *Marines' Hymn* is, consciously or not, almost a photograph of the "Couplets des deux hommes d'armes" from Offenbach's *Geneviève de Brabant*. Though rhythmically dissimilar, the "S'io S'io dir potessi" from Handel's *Ottone* parallels the first subject of Bach's *G minor fugue* in the first book of the *Well Tempered Clavichord* and is in the same key. This is without doubt unconscious plagiarism, if plagiarism it can be called.

Of interest to readers will be the many and varied settings of the same lyrics, especially those of Heine, Goethe and Verlaine.

For the most part, we have catalogued the themes alphabetically according to categories (cantatas, *Lieder,* operas, oratorios, songs, etc.). However, in the case of some composers, we have catalogued them according to opus numbers. Mozart themes are numbered in the order of their Köchel listings.

We have proofed and re-proofed this book, yet we can only identify ourselves with the Chinese author who always included an error or two so that the reader would be flattered by recognizing it. No matter how minutely such a book is proofed some errors are bound to creep in. We shall be grateful to our readers if they call our attention to any.

A book such as this cannot be created without the help of many kind friends. First and foremost, we wish to thank Mr. Philip Miller of the Music Reference Division of the New York Public Library whose advice and aid were invaluable and constant. Mr. Miller examined our entire card index, adding a great number of works which he felt indispensable to such a book. We also wish to thank Edward Bauer, Louis Kabasakalian and Elma Alexander of his staff.

Miss Gladys Chamberlain, Director of the Music Library Branch on 58th Street, and her co-workers, Miss Mary Lee Daniels and Miss Lilly Goldberg, gave us unreservedly of their time and advice and turned over to us all the resources of their splendid collection. Misses Mildred Lorres, Heather Moon, Melva Peterson, Florence O'Neill and Margaret Quinn were also very cooperative.

We want to thank Mr. Herbert Weinstock and Mr. Ben Meiselman for the use of their scores. Dr. Hans Heinsheimer of G. Schirmer, Inc., put his entire vocal department at our disposal and Mrs. Verona Clifford, Willard Lanzillo, William Kulkman and William Terranova were more than helpful in suggesting works and supplying us with practically everything we needed in the Schirmer catalogue.

We are especially grateful to the music publishers who gave us full cooperation and assistance. However, one publisher refused to let us show the themes from certain compositions published by him. The law on the matter is not clear at this writing, and therefore there are certain entries without notation. We trust the reader will understand that these regrettable omissions were unavoidable.

Lastly, we want to thank Mr. Robert Simon of Crown Publishers for his constant advice and encouragement.

Sam Morgenstern

New York, N. Y.
September, 1950

ABT, Franz (1819-1885)

Am Neckar, am Rhein, Op. 89 — O wär' ich am Ne-ckar, O wär' ich am Rhein__ B

ute Nacht, du mein herziges Kind — All' A-bend be-vor-ch zur Ru-he geh' blick' ich hin-aus in die Nacht C

Über den Sternen ist Ruh, Op. 128, No. 1 — Ü-ber den Ster-nen ist Ruh,__ ü-ber den Ster-nen ist Ruh__ D

Wenn die Schwalben heimwärts ziehn (Agathe) — Wenn die Schwal-ben heim-wärts ziehn, wenn die Ro - sen__nicht mehr blühn E

ACQUA, Eva dell' (1856- ?)

Chanson provençale — Par les nuits sans ri-va-les, Les bel-les nuits d'é-té G

Villanelle (Copyright 1923, G. Schirmer, Inc.) — J'ai vu pas-ser l'hi-ron-del-le__ Dans le ciel pur du ma-tin: H

ADAM, Adolphe Charles (1803-1856)

Cantique pour Noël (Christmas Song) — Minuit,__ Chré-tiens,__ c'est l'heure so-len-nel-le J

Vallons de la Helvétie, from Le Chalet — Val-lons de l'Hel-vé-ti-e ob-jet de mon a-mour K

Mes amis, écoutez l'histoire, from Le Postillon de Longjumeau Act I (opera) — Mes a-mis, é-cou-tez l'his-toi-re d'un jeune et ga-lant pos-til-lon L

Si J'Etais Roi (opera) Act I — Dans le som-meil l'a-mour, je ga-ge vous fit voir M

J'i-gno-re son nom, sa nais-san-ce, lors-qu'é-per-du N

Un re-gard de ses yeux vien-drait fi-nir ma pei-ne O

Zé-pho-ris est bon ca-ma-ra-de,mais c'est un pê-cheur fort_mau-vais: P

Act II (Nemea's Aria)(A) — Des__ sou-ve-rains du ri-va-ge d'A-si-e Q

(B) — Dis un seul mot sou-dain ta cour va de-ve-nir le doux se-jour R

Vous m'ai-mez dites-vous Ah! vot-re ma-jes-té veut se jou-er i-ci S

Ah! Vous dirai-je, Maman, from Le Toreador (opera)
Folk song used by many composers, including Mozart in his Piano Variations K.265

Ah! vous di-rais-je ma-man Ce qui cau-se mon tour-ment

ADAM de la Halle (1220-1287)

Le Jeu de Robin et Marion

Ro-bin _____ m'ai-me, Ro-bin _____ m'a;

Hé! ré-veil-le toi, Ro-bin Car on em-mè-ne Ma-rot,

ADAMS, A. Emmett

The Bells of St. Mary's

ADAMS, Stephen (1844-1913)

The Holy City (A)

By permission Boosey & Hawkes, Inc., copyright owners

Last night I lay a-sleep-ing, There came a dream so fair

(B)

Je-ru-sa-lem, Je-ru-sa-lem, Lift up your gates and sing

The Midshipmite

'Twas in fif-ty-five on a win-ter's night, Cheer-i-ly, my lads, yo ho!

Nancy Lee

Of all _____ the wives as e'er you know _____ Yeo ho _____ lads, ho!

The Star of Bethlehem

It was the eve of Christ-mas, The snow lay deep and white, .

A Warrior Bold

In days of old, when knights were bold, And ba-rons held their sway

L'AFFILARD, Michel (17th-18th Cent.)

Iris

I-ris, cet-te nuit en dor-mant, _____ J'é-tais dans un ra-vis-se-ment

AHLE, Johann Georg (1650-1706)

Brünstiges Verlangen

Komm, Je-su, komm doch her zu mir, Komm her, mein Le-ben, mei-ne Zier

AIBLINGER, Johann Kaspar (1779-1867)

Jubilate Deo

Ju-bi-la-te De-o, ju-bi-la-te De-o

AICHINGER, Gregor (1564-1628)

Factus est — Fa - ctus est re-pen-te de coe-lo so — — — — — — nus — B

Regina Coeli — Re-gi-na coe - li loe-ta — — re, loe-ta — — re, al-le-lu- ja — C

Salve, Regina — Sal - ve, Re-gi - na, Ma-ter,— mi-se-ri-cor-di-ae, Vi-ta,dul-ce-do, — D

Ubi est Abel — U - bi est A - bel fra - — — — — — — ter tu - us — E

ALABIEV, Alexander Nikolaevich (1787-1851)

The Nightingale — Nach - ti - gall, O - Nach - ti - gall, san - ges - rei - che— — G

ALAIN, Albert (15th Century)

Le Paradis — Beau ciel, tu m'ap - pa - rais — Comme un lieu clair et frais — — I

ALBÉNIZ, Isaac Manuel Francisco (1860-1909)

Amor, Summa Injuria
Copyright by Salabert, Paris, N. Y. — Par - don-ne:— Quand tu m'as ai-mé — Je fus cou-pa-ble— — K

Le Paradis Retrouvé
Copyright by Salabert, Paris, N. Y. — Dans un jar-din, je ne sais où,— Sont mille oi-seaux chan-teurs— — L

Quand je te vois souffrir
Copyright by Salabert, Paris, N. Y. — Quand je te vois souf-frir— J'ou-blie les verts jar-dins,— le bleu du ciel — M

Le Refuge
Copyright by Salabert, Paris, N. Y. — J'ai re-non - cé à ce mon - de vain:Pour moi la coupe est vi-de, — N

ALBERT, Eugen d' (1864-1932)

Möchte wohl gerne ein Schmetterling sein, Op. 27, No. 2
By permission Associated Music Publishers, Inc. — Sag - te ein gol-de-ner Schmet-ter-ling zu sei-ner sil-ber-nen Frau— — P

Tiefland (opera) Prologue
By permission Associated Music Publishers, Inc. — Ich grüss' noch ein - - - mal mei - ne Ber - ge. — Q

Act 1 Traumerzählung — Zwei Va-ter-un-ser bet' ich vor dem Schlaf-en geh'n, das er-ste bet' ich — R

Wolfserzählung — Mein Le - ben wagt ich drum, ja, ja, mein— Le - ben! — S

Act 2

Hüll in die Man - til - le dich fes - ter ein,

Psyche wandelt durch Säulenhallen, from Die Toten Augen (opera)
By permission Associated Music Publishers, Inc.

Psy - che wan - delt durch Säu - len - hal - len Sü - sse Klän - ge

ALFANO, Franco (1876-   )

Dieu de Grâce (Dio Pietosa), from Resurrection (opera)
Copyright by G. Ricordi & Co., Inc.

Dieu de grâ - ce, fais qu'il vien - ne, en - fin!

ALFVEN, Hugo (1872-   )

Skogen sover
Copyright by Lundquist, Stockholm

Sko - gen so - ver.__ Strim-man- på fä - stet fläm-tar matt.__

ALNAES, Eyvind (1872-1932)

Lykken mellem to mennesker

Lyk - ken mel - lem to men - ne - sker er hver-ken-hu! el - ler

Nu brister i alle de Klofter, Op. 26, No. 2
Copyright by Hansen, Copenhagen

Nu bri - ster i al - le de klof-ter, som spraeng-te og fu - red mit sind__

ALVAREZ, F. M. (-1898)

Los Ojos Negros

Pa - ra jar - di - nes Gra - na - da__ Pa - ra mu - je-res Ma - drid

La Partida

De__ la Pa - tria los ul - ti - mos e - cos los ul - ti - mos e - cos

AMBROSE, R. S.

One Sweetly Solemn Thought

One sweet-ly sol - emn thought Comes to me o'er and o'er

ANONYMOUS

Hymn of St. Adalbert
10th century

Mo - ther and mai - den, Mo - ther of God, Bless - ed__

Alleluia—Angelus Domini
11th century

Al - le - - - - lu - ia Al - le - - - - lu - ia

Alleluia Psallat
13th century

Al - le - lu - ia psal - lat haec fa - mi - li - a__

O Miranda Dei Caritas (from Aubry's Cent Motets) 13th century

O mi - ran - da De - i ca - ri - tas

6

Leggiero invisibile

Leg-ge----ro, invi-si-bi-le Qual au--ra sui fio--re,

Parla!

Più nel dub-bio non far-mi pe-na--re,

ARENSKY, Anton (1861-1906)

But lately in dance I embraced her

But late-ly in dance I em-brac'd her

The Little Fish's Song, Op. 27, No. 1
Copyright 1944, G. Schirmer, Inc.

Ah, stay___ with___ me,___ My love-ly boy, oh,___ stay!

ARNE, Michael (1741-1786)

The Lass with the Delicate Air

Young Mol-ly, who___ lived at the foot___ of___ the___ hill,

ARNE, Thomas A. (1710-1778)

Blow, blow thou Winter Wind

Blow, blow,___ thou win-ter wind,___ Thou art not___ so un-kind___

Come Away, Death

Come, come, come a-way death, And in___ sad cy-press let me be laid

Preach not me your Musty Rules
(from Comus: a Masque)

Preach not me___ your mus-ty rules, Ye drones that mould in i-dle cell,___

Now Phoebus sinketh in the West

Now Phoe-bus sink-eth in___the West, Wel-come song and wel-come jest,

Rig-our now is gone to bed And ad-vice with___ scrup-'lous head

Orpheus with his Lute

Or-pheus with his lute, Or-pheus with his lute, with his lute_____ made___ trees.

Rule Britannia

When Brit-ain first_____ at Heav'ns com-mand

This was the char-ter, the Char-ter of the land

Rule Brit-tan-nia, Brit--tan-nia rule the waves

Tell me where is fancy bred

Tell me where is___ fan-cy___ bred,___ Or in the___ heart or in___the head?

Under the Greenwood Tree

Un-der the green-wood tree, Who loves___ to lie___ with me

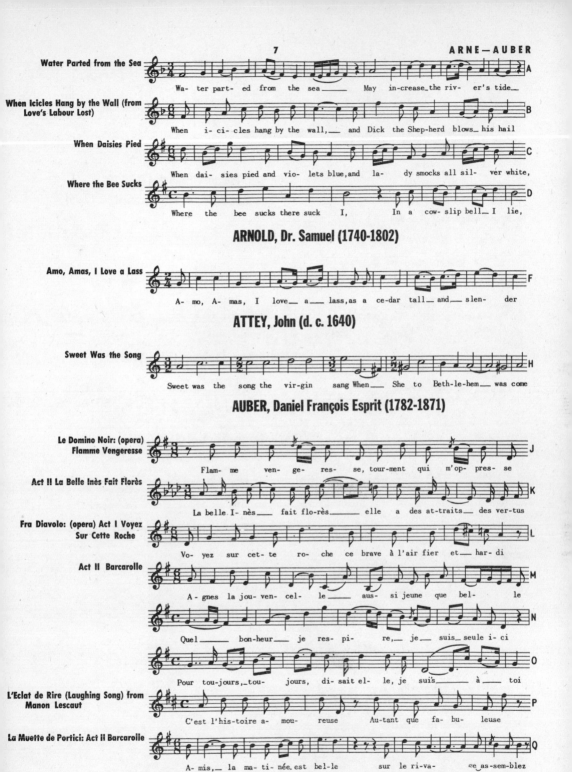

Water Parted from the Sea — A
Wa- ter part- ed from the sea___ May in-crease_the riv- er's tide___

When Icicles Hang by the Wall (from Love's Labour Lost) — B
When i- ci- cles hang by the wall,___ and Dick the Shep-herd blows_ his hail

When Daisies Pied — C
When dai- sies pied and vio- lets blue,and la- dy smocks all sil- ver white,

Where the Bee Sucks — D
Where the bee sucks there suck I, In a cow- slip bell_ I lie,

ARNOLD, Dr. Samuel (1740-1802)

Amo, Amas, I Love a Lass — F
A- mo, A- mas, I love a_ lass,as a ce-dar tall and_ slen- der

ATTEY, John (d. c. 1640)

Sweet Was the Song — H
Sweet was the song the vir- gin sang When. She to Beth-le-hem was come

AUBER, Daniel François Esprit (1782-1871)

Le Domino Noir: (opera) Flamme Vengeresse — J
Flam- me ven- ge- res- se, tour-ment qui m'op-pres- se

Act II La Belle Inès Fait Florès — K
La belle I- nès___ fait flo-rès___ elle a des at-traits___ des ver-tus

Fra Diavolo: (opera) Act I Voyez Sur Cette Roche — L
Vo- yez sur cet- te ro- che ce brave à l'air fier et_ har- di

Act II Barcarolle — M
A- gnes la jou-ven- cel- le___ aus- si jeune que bel- le

— N
Quel___ bon-heur___ je res-pi- re,___ je_ suis_ seule i- ci

— O
Pour tou-jours,_tou- jours, di-sait el- le, je suis___ à_ toi

L'Eclat de Rire (Laughing Song) from Manon Lescaut — P
C'est l'his-toire a- mou- reuse Au-tant que fa- bu- leuse

La Muette de Portici: Act II Barcarolle — Q
A- mis,_ la ma- ti- née_est bel- le sur le ri-va- ge as-sem-blez

Duet — R
A-mour sa- cré_ de la pa- tri- e, rend nous l'au-dace___

Act IV — S
Du pauvre seul a- mi fi- dè- le, de- scends_ à ma voix___

AURIC, Georges (1899-   )

Le Gloxinia
By permission Associated Music Publishers, Inc.

Je vou-drais qu'à ma fe- nê-tre Fleurisse un ten-dre glo- xi-nia;

Printemps
By permission Durand & Cie, Paris; Elkan-Vogel Co., Inc., Phila., copyright owners

Quand ce beau prin-temps je voy, J'ap-per-çoy Ra- jeu-nir la terre

BACH, Carl Philipp Emanuel (1714-1788)

(See also BACH, Philipp Emanuel)

Die Himmel rühmen des ewigen Ehre

Die Him- mel rüh- men des E- wi- gen Eh- re

Jesus in Gethsemane

Schau' hin Dort in Geth-se- ma- ne klagt, trau-ert

Der Phoenix

Der Mann, der nach den Flit- ter- wo- chen aus Lie-be küsst

BACH, Johann Christian (1735-1782)

Non è ver, from Carattaco (opera)

Non è ver, che as-si- se_in tro- no bel-le_an-cor le col- pe so- no

BACH, Johann Michael (1648-1694)

Ich weiss dass mein Erlöser lebt

Ich weiss, dass mein Er- lo-ser lebt, ich weiss dass mein Er-lo-ser lebt

BACH, Johann Sebastian (1685-1750)

CANTATAS, Church, No. 4: Christ lag in Todesbanden (Easter Cantata) No. 1

Christ lag in To-des- ban- den

No. 3

Den Tod, Den Tod, Den Tod, Den Tod, Den Tod Nie- mand zwin- gen kunnt

No. 5

Hier ist das rech- te O- ster-lamm, das rech - - - te O-ster-lamm

No. 5: Wo soll ich fliehen hin No. 5

Ver- stum-me ver-stum-me, ver- stum- me, Höl- - - len- heer,

No. 6: Bleib' bei uns No. 1

Bleib' bei uns, bleib' bei uns, den es will A - - - bend

No. 2

Hoch- ge- lob- ter Got- tes Sohn

No. 7: Christ unser Herr zum Jordan kam No. 6

Men- schen glaubt doch die- ser Gna- de

CANTATAS, Church, No. 8: Liebster Gott, wann werd' ich sterben? No. 4
A — Doch wei— chet ihr tol— len ver— geb— — —li-chen sor— gen

No. 10: Mein Seel' erhebt den Herren No. 2
B — Herr, Herr, Herr, der du stark und mäch-tig bist, der du stark und mäch-tig bist

No. 3
C — Ge-wal— — — — — — — ti-ge, Ge-wal— — — — —ti-ge stösst Gott von

No. 6
D — Sein Sa— me muss-te sich so sehr wie Sand am Meer

No.12: Weinen, Klagen, Sorgen, Zagen No. 4
E — Kreuz und Kro-ne sind ver- bun-den, Kampf und Kleinod sind ver- eint.

No. 13: Meine Seufzer, meine Thränen No. 1
F — Mei- ne Seuf-zer,mei- ne Thrä- nen kön-nen nicht zu zäh- len sein

No. 2
G — Äch— zen und er- bärm- lich wei- nen, Äch— zen,

No. 17: Wer Dank opfert, der preiset mich No. 3
H — Herr, dei- ne Gü-te reicht,so weit der Him- mel ist,

No. 5
I — Welch Ü- ber-mass der Gü- te schenkst du mir!

No. 18: Gleich wie der Regen und Schnee von Himmel No. 4
J — Mein See-len-schatz ist Got-tes Wort, Mein See-len-schatz ist Got-tes Wort

No. 20: O Ewigkeit, du Donnerwort No. 3
K — E — — — —wig-keit du machst mir ban — — — — — — — — — — ge

No. 6
L — O Mensch er- ret- te dei- ne See- le, ent-flie— — — — — — he

Part II, No. 1
M — Wacht auf, wacht auf, wacht auf, wacht auf wacht auf,wacht auf,

No. 21: Ich hatte viel Bekümmerniss No. 2
N — Ich Ich, Ich, Ich hat-te viel Be-küm-mer-niss,Ich hat-te viel Be-küm-mer-niss

No. 3
O — Seuf-zer,Thrän-en,Kum- mer, Noth,— Seuf- zer, Thrän- en, ängst-lich's

No. 5
P — Bä— che von ge-salz- nen Zäh- ren

Part II, No. 4
Q — Er- freu- e dich See- le, er- freu- e dich, Her- ze

No. 22: Jesus nahm zu sich die Zwölfe No. 2
R — Mein Je- su, zie— — — — — —he mich nach dir,

CANTATAS, Church, No. 22: Jesus nahm zu sich die Zwölfe, No. 4

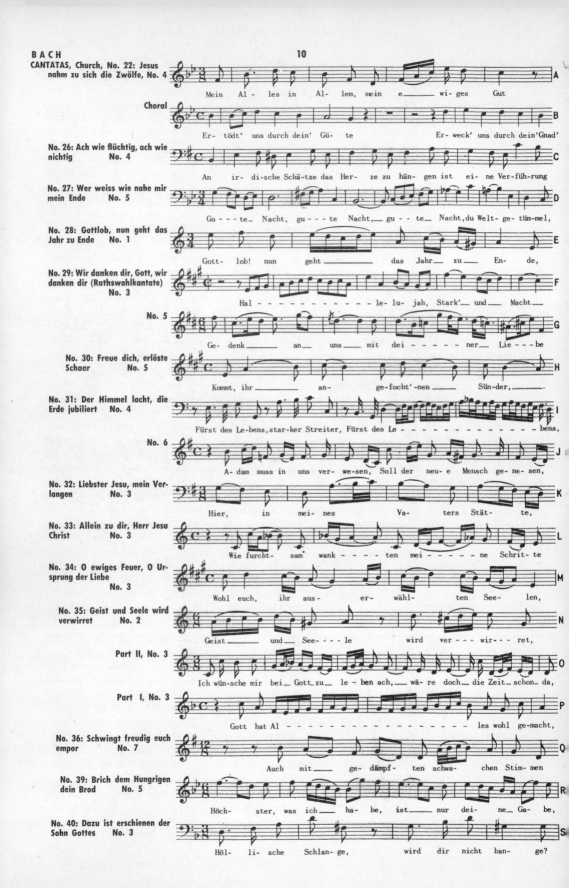

Mein Al - les in Al - lem, mein e___ wi-ges Gut A

Choral

Er- tödt' uns durch dein' Gü - te   Er- weck' uns durch dein'Gnad' B

No. 26: Ach wie flüchtig, ach wie nichtig   No. 4

An ir-di-sche Schä-tze das Her- ze zu hän- gen ist ei - ne Ver-füh-rung C

No. 27: Wer weiss wie nahe mir mein Ende   No. 5

Gu - - - te_ Nacht, gu - - -te Nacht,_ gu - te Nacht,du Welt- ge- tüm-mel, D

No. 28: Gottlob, nun geht das Jahr zu Ende   No. 1

Gott- lob! nun geht____ das Jahr zu_ En- de, E

No. 29: Wir danken dir, Gott, wir danken dir (Rathswahlkantate)   No. 3

Hal - - - - - - - - - le-lu-jah, Stark' und_ Macht_ F

No. 5

Ge-denk____ an uns___ mit dei - - - - ner Lie - - -be G

No. 30: Freue dich, erlöste Schaar   No. 5

Kommt, ihr____ an- ge-focht'-nen____ Sün-der,____ H

No. 31: Der Himmel lacht, die Erde jubiliert   No. 4

Fürst des Le-bens,star-ker Streiter, Fürst des Le - - - - - - - - - -bens, I

No. 6

A- dam muss in uns ver-we-sen, Soll der neu- e Mensch ge-ne-sen, J

No. 32: Liebster Jesu, mein Verlangen   No. 3

Hier, in mei-nes Va- ters Stät- te, K

No. 33: Allein zu dir, Herr Jesu Christ   No. 3

Wie furcht- sam wank - - - ten mei - - - ne Schrit- te L

No. 34: O ewiges Feuer, O Ursprung der Liebe   No. 3

Wohl euch, ihr aus- er- wähl- ten See- len, M

No. 35: Geist und Seele wird verwirret   No. 2

Geist____ und See- - -le wird ver - - -wir- - -ret, N

Part II, No. 3

Ich wün-sche mir bei_ Gott_ zu_ le - ben ach,_ wä- re doch_ die Zeit_ schon_ da, O

Part I, No. 3

Gott hat Al - - - - - - - - - - - - - - - les wohl ge-macht, P

No. 36: Schwingt freudig euch empor   No. 7

Auch mit____ ge- dämpf- ten schwa- chen Stim- men Q

No. 39: Brich dem Hungrigen dein Brod   No. 5

Höch- ster, was ich_ ha- be, ist____ nur dei- ne Ga- be, R

No. 40: Dazu ist erschienen der Sohn Gottes   No. 3

Höl- li-sche Schlan- ge, wird dir nicht ban- ge? S

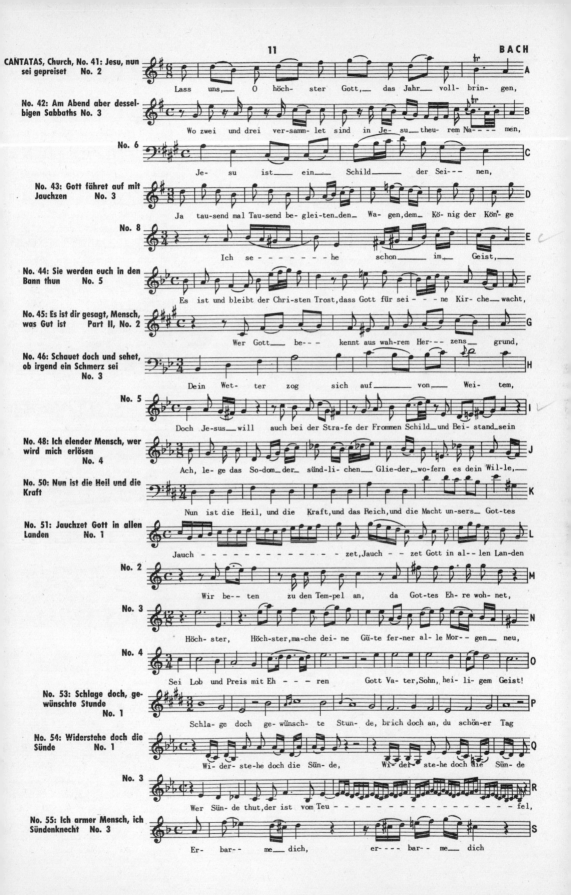

CANTATAS, Church, No. 56: Ich will
den Kreuzstab gerne tragen
No. 1

Ich will den Kreuz-stab ger-ne tra - - - - - - - - - - - - - - - gen, A

No. 3

End- lich,___ end - - - - lich wird___ mein Joch___ B

No. 57: Selig ist der Mann
No. 1

Se - - - - - - lig,-se - - - - - - lig, se - - - - - lig,se-lig ist der Mann C

No. 3

Ich wünschte___ mir den Tod,___ ich wünschte mir den Tod___ D

No. 4

Ja, ja, ich kann die Fein-de___ schla - - - - - - - - - - - - - gen, E

No. 61: Nun komm, der Heiden
Heiland   No. 3

Komm, Je- - su, Komm - - - - - - zu dei- - - ner Kir - - - che, F

No. 4

Öff- ne dich, mein gan- zes___ Her - - - ze G

No. 62: Nun komm, der Heiden
Heiland   No. 2

Be- wun-dert, O Men-schen___ dies___ gro- - -sse Ge- heim-niss, H

No. 64: Sehet, welch' eine Liebe
hat uns der Vater erzeiget
No. 5

Was die___ Welt in___ sich___ hält, I

No. 7

Von der___ Welt ver-lang'___ ich nichts,nichts, nichts,nichts, J

No. 65: Sie werden aus Saba
No. 1

Sie wer- den aus Sa- - ba Al- - - -le kom - - - - - men K

No. 2

Die Kön' ge aus Sa- ba ka- - men dar, ka - - - - men dar, L

No. 6

Nimm___ mich dir___ zu___ ei - - - gen hin M

No. 7

Ei nun,mein Gott, So fall ich dir ge- trost in dei - - - - - ne Hän- de N

No. 66: Erfreut euch, ihr Herzen
No. 3

Las- set___ dem___ Höch-sten ein Dank-lied er- schal- len O

No. 5

Ich fürch- te zwar des Gra- - -bes Fin- ster-nis- - - sen, P

Ich fürch- - te nicht,ich fürch- - te nicht des Gra- - bes Fin- - ster-nis- sen Q

No. 67: Halt' im Gedächtniss
Jesum Christ   No. 2

Mein Je- sus ist er-stan - - - den, al- lein, was schreckt mich noch? R

No. 68: Also hat Gott die Welt
geliebt   No. 2

Mein gläu- bi- - -ges Her- - ze, froh- lo- cke,___ sing',scher- ze S

13 BACH

CANTATAS, Church, No. 69: Lobe den Herrn, meine Seele No. 5 — Mein Er-lö-ser und Er-hal-ter, nimm mich stets in Hut und Wacht, — A

No. 70: Wachet, wachet, seid be-reit allezeit Part I, No. 3 — Wenn kommt der Tag aus dem wir zie-hen aus dem E-gyp-ten die-ser Welt — B

Part I, No. 5 — Lass' der Spöt-ter Zun-gen schmäh-en, es wird doch, und muss ge-sche-hen — C

Part II, No. 1 — Hebt eu-er Haupt em-por und seid ge-trost, ihr From-men, — D

Part II, No. 3 — Se-lig-ster Er-qui-ckungs-tag — E

No. 71: Gott ist mein König No. 4 — Tag und Nacht, Tag und Nacht ist dein, Tag und Nacht, Tag und Nacht, — F

No. 72: Alles nur nach Gottes Willen No. 2 (Arioso) — Herr, so du willt, so muss sich Al-les fü-gen! — G

Mit Al-lem, was ich hab' und bin Mit Al-lem was ich hab' und bin — H

No. 5 — Mein Je-sus will es thun, Er will dein Kreuz ver-sü-ssen. — I

No. 73: Herr, wie du willt, so schick's mit mir No. 4 — Herr, so du willt, Herr, so du willt, Herr, so du willt, Herr, so du willt, — J

No. 74: Wer mich liebet, der wird mein Wort halten No. 4 — Kommt! Kommt! ei-let! — K

No. 6 — Nichts kann mich er-ret-ten von höl-li-schen Ket-ten, — L

No. 75: Die Elenden sollen essen No. 3 — Mein Je-sus soll mein Al-les sein — M

No. 5 — Ich neh-me mein Lei-den mit Freu-den auf mich! — N

No. 76: Die Himmel erzählen die Ehre Gottes Part I, No. 3 — Hört, ihr Völ-ker, Got-tes Stim-me, hört, ihr Völ-ker, Got-tes Stim-me — O

Part II, No. 3 — Has-se nur, has-se mich recht, has-se nur, has-se mich recht, — P

Part II, No. 5 — Liebt, ihr Chri-sten in der That, liebt, ihr Chri-sten in der That — Q

No. 78: Jesu, der du meine Seele No. 1 — Je-su, der du mei-ne See-le, — R

No. 2 — Wir ei-len mit schwa-chen, doch em-si-gen Schrit-ten — S

CANTATAS, Church, No. 78: Jesu, der
du meine Seele, No. 4

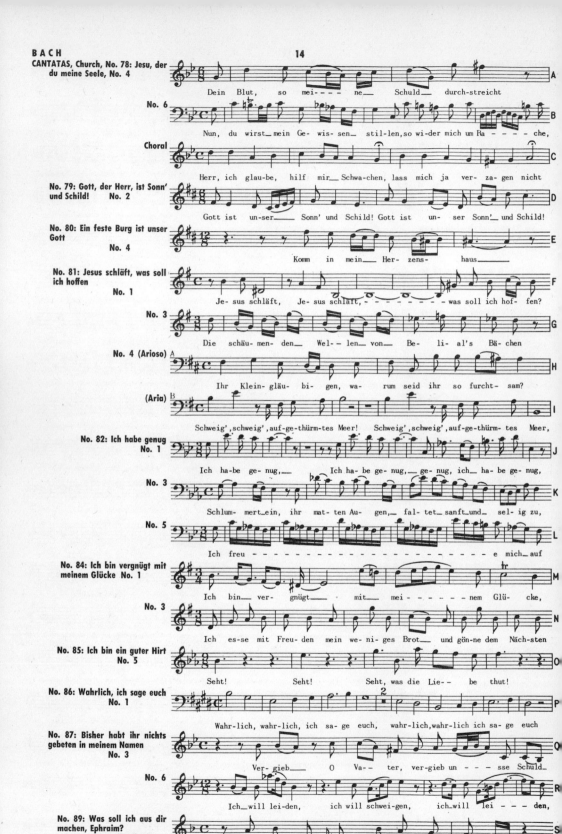

Dein Blut, so mei — — ne Schuld durch-streicht

No. 6

Nun, du wirst mein Ge- wis-sen stil-len, so wi-der mich um Ra — — — che,

Choral

Herr, ich glau-be, hilf mir Schwa-chen, lass mich ja ver-za-gen nicht

No. 79: Gott, der Herr, ist Sonn'
und Schild! No. 2

Gott ist un-ser Sonn' und Schild! Gott ist un-ser Sonn' und Schild!

No. 80: Ein feste Burg ist unser
Gott
No. 4

Komm in mein Her-zens-haus

No. 81: Jesus schläft, was soll
ich hoffen
No. 1

Je- sus schläft, Je-sus schläft, — — — — — was soll ich hof-fen?

No. 3

Die schäu-men-den Wel-len von Be- li- al's Bä-chen

No. 4 (Arioso)

Ihr Klein-gläu-bi-gen, wa-rum seid ihr so furcht-sam?

(Aria)

Schweig', schweig', auf-ge-thürm-tes Meer! Schweig', schweig', auf-ge-thürm-tes Meer!

No. 82: Ich habe genug
No. 1

Ich ha-be ge-nug, Ich ha-be ge-nug, ge-nug, ich ha-be ge-nug,

No. 3

Schlum-mert ein, ihr mat-ten Au-gen, fal-tet sanft und se- lig zu,

No. 5

Ich freu — — — — — — — — — — e mich auf

No. 84: Ich bin vergnügt mit
meinem Glücke No. 1

Ich bin ver- gnügt mit mei — — — — nem Glü-cke,

No. 3

Ich es-se mit Freu-den mein we-ni-ges Brot und gön-ne dem Näch-sten

No. 85: Ich bin ein guter Hirt
No. 5

Seht! Seht! Seht, was die Lie-- be thut!

No. 86: Wahrlich, ich sage euch
No. 1

Wahr-lich, wahr-lich, ich sa-ge euch, wahr-lich, wahr-lich ich sa-ge euch

No. 87: Bisher habt ihr nichts
gebeten in meinem Namen
No. 3

Ver- gieb O Va- ter, ver-gieb un — — — sse Schuld

No. 6

Ich will lei-den, ich will schwei-gen, ich will lei — — den,

No. 89: Was soll ich aus dir
machen, Ephraim?
No. 2

Ein un-barm-her-zi-ges Ge- rich-te

CANTATAS, Church, No. 90: Es reifet euch ein schreckliche Ende No. 3

BACH

So löschet im Ei-fer der Rä-chen-de Rich-ter — A

No. 91: Gelobet seist du, Jesus Christ No. 3

Gott, dem der Er-den-kreis zu klein, den we-der Welt noch Him-mel fas-sen, — B

No. 92: Ich hab' in Gottes Herz und Sinn No. 6

Das Brau - - - - - - - - - sen von den rauhen Win-den — C

No. 8

Mei-nem Hirten bleib' ich treu, mei-nem Hirten bleib' ich treu — D

No. 93: Wer nur den lieben Gott lässt walten No. 3

Man hal-te nur ein we-nig stil-le, wenn sich die Kreu-zes-stun-de naht, — E

No. 94: Was frag' ich nach der Welt No. 5

Die Welt kann ih-re Lust und Freud', — F

No. 95: Christus, der ist mein Leben No. 4

Ach, schlage doch bald, ach, schlage doch bald, schlage doch schlage doch — G

No. 97: In allen meinem Thaten No. 4

Ich trau - - - - - - - - e sei-ner Gna - - - den, — H

No. 6

Leg' ich mich späte nie-der, er wa - - - - - che frühe wie-der, — I

No. 8

Ihm hab ich mich er-ge-ben zu ster-ben und zu le-ben so bald — J

No. 98: Was Gott tut, das ist wohlgetan No. 1

Was Gott tut, das ist wohl-ge-than, es bleibt ge-recht sein Wil-le; — K

No. 3

Hört, ihr Au-gen, auf zu wei - - - nen, — L

No. 5

Mei-nen Je-sum lass' - - - - ich nicht, — M

No. 99: Was Gott tut, das ist wohlgetan (second version) No. 1

Was Gott thut, das ist wohl-ge-than es bleibt ge-recht sein Wil-le — N

No. 100: Was Gott tut, das ist wohlgetan (third version) No. 4

Was Gott thut, das ist wohl-ge-than, was Gott thut, was Gott thut, — O

No. 5

Was Gott thut das ist wohl - - - - ge-than! — P

No. 101: Nimm von uns, Herr, du treuer Gott No. 2

Han - - - dle nicht nach dei - - nen Rech-ten — Q

No. 102: Herr, deine Augen sehen nach den Glauben No. 3

Weh! der See-le, weh, der See-le, — R

No. 4

Ver-ach-test du den Reich - - tum sei - - - ner Gna-de — S

BACH

CANTATAS, Church, No. 122: Das neugebor'ne Kindelein   No. 2   A
O Men- schen, die ihr_ täglich sündigt, die_ ihr täglich sündigt,

No. 127: Herr Jesu Christ, whar'r Mensch und Gott   No. 3   B
Die See-- le ruht in_____ Je--- su Hän-- den,

No. 128: Auf Christi Himmelfahrt allein   No. 3   C
Auf, auf, mit hel- lem_ Schall,_____ mit, hel-lem_Schall

No. 129: Gelobet sei der Herr, mein Gott   No. 4   D
Ce- lo---bet sei_ der Herr,___ mein Gott,_ der e--wig le-- bet

Finale   E
Dem wir das_Hei- lig itzt mit Freu- den las- sen klin- gen,

No. 133: Ich freue mich in dir   No. 2   F
Ge- trost, ge-trost, ge- trost! es fasst____ ein heil'-- ger Leib

No. 3   G
Wie lieb----- lich klingt_ es in_____ den Oh--- ren!

No. 134: Ein Herz, das seinen Jesum lebend weiss   No. 2   H
Auf,auf,auf,auf, Gläu- bi- ge   Auf,Gläu-bi- ge, sin-get_die lieb-li-chen Lie-der_

No. 135: Ach Herr, mich armen Sünder   No. 3   I
Trö- ste mir, Je-- su mein_____ Ge- mü-- the

No. 5   J
Weicht_____ all'ihr Ü-bel- thä-ter,weicht!

No. 140: Wachet auf, ruft uns die Stimme   No. 1   K
Wa-- chet auf! ruft uns die Stim-----me

No. 3   L
Wann kommst du,mein Heil Ich_ kom-me,dein Theil wann kommst du, ich_kom-me.

No. 5   M
Zi-on hört die Wäch-ter sin-gen, das Herz tut ihr_vor Freu-den sprin--gen,

No. 7   N
Mein Freund_ ist_mein! Und ich_____ bin dein! Die Lie--be soll____nichts

No. 142: Uns ist ein Kind geboren   No. 2   O
Uns ist ein Kind ge- bo-ren, ein Sohn' ist_ uns ge- bo-ren,

No. 3   P
Dein Ge-burtstag ist er- schie-nen, so er-for-dert mei- ne Pflicht.

No. 144: Nimm was dein ist, und gehe hin   No. 2   Q
Mur--- re nicht, lie-ber Christ, Mur--- re nicht, lie-ber Christ.

No. 145: So du mit deinem Munde   No. 5   R
Mer- ke, mein Her- ze, be- stän- dig_ nur_ dies,

No. 146: Wir müssen durch viel Trübsal   No. 5   S
Ich sä----- e mei-ne_ Zäh--- ren mit ban--- gem Her-zen,

CANTATAS, Church,

No. 147: Herz und Mund und Tat und Leben No. 10 (Jesu, joy of man's desiring)

No. 148: Bringet dem Herrn Ehre seines Namens No. 4

No. 149: Man singet mit Freuden vom Sieg No. 4

No. 151: Süsser Trost, mein Jesus kömmt No. 1

No. 3

No. 152: Tritt auf die Glaubensbahn No. 4

No. 153: Schau', lieber Gott, wie meine Feind! No. 6

No. 154: Mein liebster Jesus ist verloren No. 1

No. 3

No. 155: Mein Gott, wie lang No. 4

No. 156: Ich stehe mit einem Fuss im Grabe No. 4

No. 159: Sehet, wir geh'n hinauf gen Jerusalem No. 4

No. 160: Ich weiss dass mein Erloser lebt No. 1

No. 161: Komm, du süsse Todesstunde No. 3

No. 167: Ihr Menschen rühmet Gottes Liebe No. 1

No. 170: Vergnügte Ruh, beliebte Seelenlust No. 1

No. 172: Erschallet, ihr Lieder No. 3

No. 4

No. 175: Er rufet seinen Schafen mit Namen No. 2

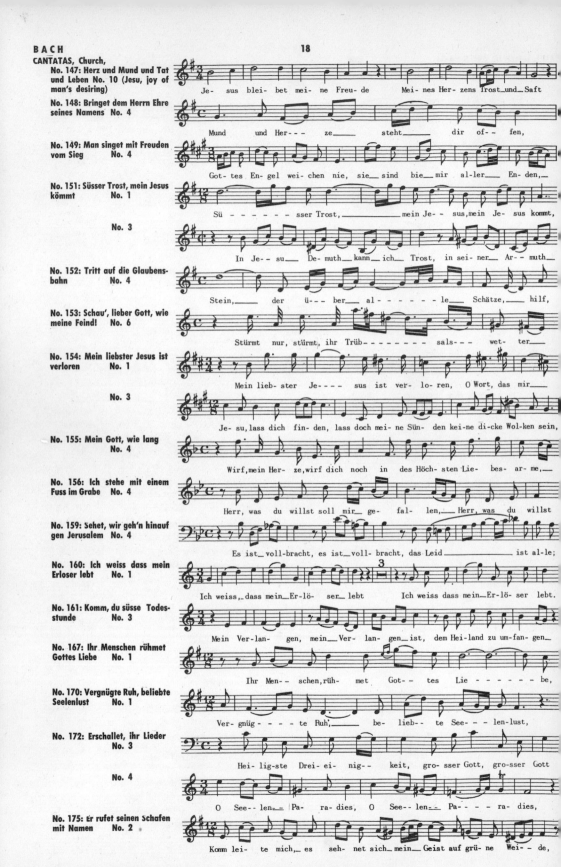

CANTATAS, Church, No. 182: Himmels-
könig, sei willkommen No. 3

Star-kes Lie-ben, star - - - - - - - - - - kes Lie-ben,

No. 4

Le- - get euch dem Hei-land un- - ter,

No. 5

Je- su, lass durch Wohl und Weh,

No. 183: Sie werden euch in den
Bann thun   No. 4

Höch - - - - - ster Trö- ster heil'- - - - ger Geist,

No. 186: Ärge dich, o Seele,
nicht   No. 8

Die Ar- men will der Herr um- - ar- men,

No. 187: Es wartet Alles auf
dich   No. 3

Du Herr, du krönst al- lein das Jahr mit dei- nem Gut,

No. 4

Da- rum sollt ihr nicht sor- gen noch sa- gen: was wer-den wir es-sen

No. 5

Gott- ver-sor- get, Gott ver-sor-get al- - - - - les Le- ben,

No. 189: Meine Seele rühmt und
preist   No. 1

Mei- ne See- le, mei-ne See- le rühmt und preist

No. 2

Denn seh' ich mich und auch mein Le-ben an, so muss mein Mund

No. 3

Gott hat sich hoch ge- se- - - - - -tzet, hoch ge-setzet und sieht auf Das

No. 5

Die- ne Gü- te, dein Er- bar- men, Dein Er-bar-men wäh-ret, Gott, zu al- ler Zeit,

No. 197: Gott ist unsere
Zuversicht   No. 3

Schlä- - - - - fert al- - - - - ler Sor- gen Kum- mer

No. 210: O holder Tag (Wedding
Cantata)   No. 3

Ru- - - het hie, mat - - - - - - - - - te Tö- - - ne,

CANTATAS, Secular
No. 158: Der Friede sei mit dir
No. 1 Recitative

Der Frie- - de sei mit dir, du ängstli- ches Ge- wis-sen!

No. 2

Welt, a- - - - de! ich bin dein mü- - de,

No. 3 Arioso

Da bleib ich, da hab' ich Vergnü- gen zu woh- - - nen,

No. 4 Choral

Hier ist das rech- te O- ster-lamm, da- von hat Gott ge- bo- ten

CANTATAS, Secular, No. 194:
Höchsterwünschtes Freudenfest
No. 3

Was des Höch- sten Glanz er- füllt, wird in kei- ne Nacht ver-hüllt,

No. 201: Der Streit zwischen
Phoebus und Pan
No. 3

Pa- tron, Pa- tron, Pa- tron, das macht der Wind, Wind, Wind, das macht der Wind!

No. 5

Mit Ver-lan-gen, mit Ver-lan-gen drück' ich deine zar - - - ten Wan-gen,

No. 202: Weichet nur
No. 1

Wei - - - - chet nur, be-trüb- - te Schat- ten

No. 2

Phö- bus eilt

No. 3

Wenn die Frühlingslüf- te strei-chen und durch bun- te Fel- der wehn,

No. 4

Sich ü- ben im lie- ben, im Scher-zen sich her- zen

No. 5 Gavotte

Se- - - het in Zu- frie- den- - - - heit

No. 205: Der Zufriedengestellte
Aeolus
No. 3

Zweig' und Aes- te, Zweig' und Ae- - -ste,

Wie will ich lus- tig la - - - - - - - - - - - chen

No. 7

Kön- nen nicht die ro-then Wan-gen, wo-mit mei- ne Früch-te pran-gen,

No. 206: Schleicht, spielende
Wellen (Birthday Cantata for
August III) No. 9

Hört doch! der sanf-ten Flö-ten Chor er-freut- - die Brust, er-götzt das Ohr,

No. 208: Was mir behagt is nur
die munt're Jagd (Birthday Cantata) No. 9 (Sheep may safely
graze)

Scha- fe kön- nen si- cher wei- den, wo ein gu- ter Hir- te wacht,

No. 211: Schweigt stille, plau-
dert nicht (Coffee Cantata)
No. 2

Hat man nicht mit sei- nen Kin-dern hun-dert tau-send Hu- de- lei!

No. 4

Ei! wie schmeckt der Cof-fee sü- sse, lieb-li- cher als tau-send Küs-se,

No. 6

Mäd-chen, die von har-ten Sin- nen, die von har- ten Sin- nen,

No. 8

Heu- te noch Heu- te noch, lie- ber Va- ter, thut es doch

No. 10

Die Ka- tze lässt das Mau- - - sen nicht, die Jung- - fern blei- ben

No. 212: Mer hahn en neue Oberkeet (Peasant Cantata)
No. 2

Mer habn en neu- e O- ber-keet an un-sern Kam- mer-herrn.

TATAS, Secular, No. 212: No. 4 hahn en neue Oberkeet (Peasant Cantata)

Ach es schmeckt doch gar zu gut, gar zu gut, wenn ein Paar recht freund-lich tut;

No. 6 — Ach Herr Schösser, geht nicht gar zu schlimm mit uns ar-men Bau-ers-leu-ten, üm,

No. 8 — Un-ser treff-lich-er lie-ber Kam-mer-herr

No. 10 — Das ist ga-lant, es spricht niemand von den ca-du-cken Scho-cken

No. 12 — Fünf-zig Tha-ler baares Geld trock'-ner Wei se zu ver-schmau-sen,

No. 14 — Klein-zschocher müs-se so zart und süs-se wie lau-ter Man-del-ker-ne sein

No. 16 — Es neh-me zehn-tau-send Du-ca-ten der Kam-mer-herr al-le Tag' ein,

No. 18 — Gieb, Schö-ne, viel Söh-ne von art'-ger Ge-stalt,

No. 20 — Dein Wach-stum sei fe-ste und la-che vor Lust

No. 22 — Und dass ihr's al-le wisst, es ist nun-mehr die Frist zu trin-ken,

No. 24 — Wir gehn nun wo der Tu-del-sack, der Tu-del-Tu-del-Tu-del Tu-del-

CHORALES: Ein feste Burg — Ein fe-ste Burg ist un-ser Gott, ein' gu-te Wehr und Waf-fen

In dulci jubilo — In dul-ci ju-bi-lo sin-get und seid froh,

Lobet den Herrn — Lo-bet den Her-ren, lo-bet den Her-ren, denn er ist sehr freund-lich,

Die Sonn' hat sich mit ihrem Glanz — Die Sonn' hat sich mit ih-rem Glanz ge-wen-det, und, was sie soll

Vater unser in Himmelreich — Va-ter un-ser im Him-mel-reich, der du uns al-le heissest gleich

Wer den lieben Gott lässt walten — Wer nur den lie-ben Gott lässt wal-ten, und hof-fet auf ihn al-le-zeit

Magnificat in D 1. Chorus — Ma-gni-fi-cat, ma-gni-fi-cat, ma-gni-fi-cat,

II. Aria — Et ex-ul-ta-vit spi-ri-tus me-us

Mass in B minor
XXIII. Dona nobis pacem

Do- - na no- - - - bis pa- - - cem, pa- - cem,

MOTETS,
No. 1 Singet dem Herrn ein
neues Lied   I A

Sin- get den Herrn

I B

Sin-get,Sin-get, Sin-get, Sin- - - - - - - - - - - - - get

II

Lo- - bet den Herrn in sei- nen Tha- ten, lo- bet ihn

III

Al- - - - - - - - - - - - les,was O- - - - - dem hat,lo-bet_den Herrn

No. 2 Der Geist hilft uns'rer
Schwachheit auf   I

Der Geist_____ hilft un-srer Schwachheit auf,

II

Der a-ber die Her- zen_ for-schet,dir weiss_was_ des Geistes Sinn sei,

III Chorale

Du hei- - li- ge Brunst, sü-sser Trost, nun hilf uns fröh-lich und ge-trost,

No. 3 Jesu, meine Freude
I

Je- su, mei-ne Freu- de, mei-nes Her-zens Wei- de, Je-su, mei- ne Zier,

II

Es ist nun nichts, nichts, nichts Ver- damm- li-ches an de-nen,

IV

Denn das Ge-setz des Geistes,der da le-ben- -dig_ma-chet in Christo Je- - -su,

V   A

Trotz, Trotz dem al- -ten|Dra- - - chen, Trotz dem al- ten Dra-chen,

B

Ihr a-ber seid nicht fleisch-lich,sondern geist- - - - - - - - - -lich

VII

So a-ber Christus in euch ist, so Christus in_____ euch ist,

VIII   A

Gu- te Nacht,_ Gu- te Nacht,_ Gu- te Nacht_ Gu- te Nacht

B

Gu- te Nacht,O We-sen, gu-te Nacht,O we-sen, Gu- te Nacht, O We- sen,

No. 5 Komm, Jesu, komm
I

Komm, komm, komm, komm. Je-su, komm. komm, Je-su,_ komm

II

Drauf schliess' ich_ mich____ in ____ dei- ne_ Hän- de

Christmas Oratorio
No. 1

Jauchzet, froh-lock-et! Auf, prei-set_die_Ta- ge! Jauch- zet!

25   BACH

Christmas Oratorio

No. 4   A
Be- rei-te dich, Zi-on, mit zärt- li- chen Trie-ben, den Schönsten,_den_ Liebsten

No. 8   B
Gro-sser Herr und star- ker Kö-nig,_ Lieb-ster Hei- land, o_ wie we-nig,

No. 15   C
Fro- - - he_ Hir- - - ten, eilt,_ ach_ ei- let,_

No. 19   D
Schla - - - - - - fe, mein Lieb- - - - - - - - - ster, ge-ni - - - sse der Ruh,_

No. 31   E
Schlie- sse, mein Her- - - ze, dies se- - li- ge Wun- - - der

No. 39   F
Flösst,_ mein Hei- land, flösst,_ dein Na- men. flösst,_ mein Hei-land,

No. 41   G
Ich will_ nur dir zu Eh-ren le - - - - - - - - - - - - - - - ben,

No. 47   H
Er-leucht' auch_ mei- - - ne_ fin- - - -stre_ Sin- - nen,

No. 57   I
Nur ein_ Wink_ von_ sei-nen Hän-den sturzt_ ohnmächt'ger Menschen Macht

No. 62   J
Nun mögt_ ihr_ stol- - zen_ Fein- - de_ schre - - cken

Easter Oratorio

No. 3   K
Kommt, ei - - - - - - - let und lau - - - - - - - fet,

No. 5   L
See- le dei- ne_ Spe- ce- rei- - - - en sol- len_ nicht mehr Myrrhen sein

No. 7   M
Sanf- te_soll mein_ To- des-kum- - - mer nur_ ein_ Schlum- - - - - mer,

No. 9   N
Sa- get, sa - - - - - - - - - - get, mir ge- - schwin- de,

John Passion

Part I No. 1 A   O
Herr, Herr, Herr, un-ser Herr - - - - - - - - - - scher

No. 1 B   P
Herr, un- ser Herr - - - - - - - - scher, un-ser Herr-scher

No. 4   Q
O gro- sse Lieb', O Lieb' ohn al- le Maa- - - sse,

No. 5   R
Dein Will' ge-scheh', Herr_Gott zu-gleich, auf Er-den wie im_Him- mel- reich;

No. 6   S
Von den_ Stri - - - cken mei-ner Sun - - den_mich zu ent-bin- den

BACH
St. John Passion

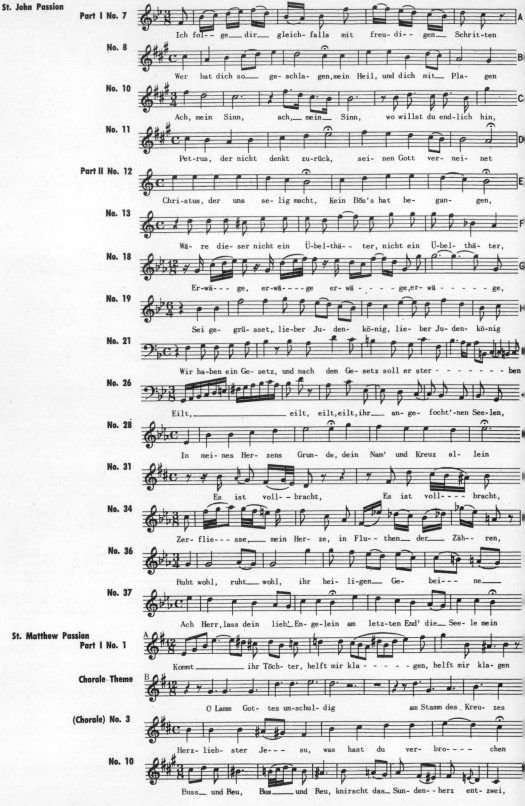

St. Matthew Passion

BACH

Part I No. 12 — A

Blu- te nur, blu- te nur blu- te nur, du lie- bes Herz,

No. 16 — B

Ich bin's, ich soll- te bü- ssen an Hän- den und an Fü- ssen

No. 17 — C

Trin- ket al - - - - le da- raus das ist mein Blut des neu- en Tes- ta- ments,

No. 19 — D

Ich will dir mein Her- - ze schen- ken, sen- - - ke dich, sen- - ke dich,

(Chorale) No. 21 — E

Er- ken- ne mich, mein Hü- ter, mein Hir- te nimm mich an

No. 26 — F

Ich will bei mei- nem Je- - - - - - - - su wa- - chen

No. 29 — G

Ger- ne will ich mich be- que- men, Kreuz und Be- cher an- zu- neh- men

(Chorale) No. 31 — H

Was mein Gott will, das g'scheh' all- zeit, sein Will' der ist der be- ste

No. 33 A — I

So ist mein Je- sus nun ge- |fan- - - - - - - - - gen,

No. 33 B — J

Sind Blitze, sind Don- ner in Wol- ken ver- - schwun- den,

No. 35 — K

O Mensch, be- wein dein Sün- - - de gross

Part II No. 36 — L

Ach - - - - - - - - - - - nun ist mein Je- sus hin, ach

(Chorale) No. 38 — M

Mir hat die Welt - - - trüg- lich ge- richt't mit Lü- gen und mit fal- schem G'dicht,

No. 41 — N

Ge- duld, Ge- duld! Ge- duld, Ge- duld!

(Chorale) No. 46 — O

Wer hat dich so ge- schla- gen, mein Heil und dich mit Pla- gen

No. 48 — P

Er bar- - - - - - - me dich, er- bar- - - me dich, mein Gott,

(Chorale) No. 49 — Q

Bin ich gleich von dir ge- wi- chen, stell' ich mich doch wie- der ein

No. 51 — R

Gebt mir mei- nen Je- - sum wie- der, Gebt mir, gebt mir mei- nen Je- sum wie- der

(Chorale) No. 55 — S

Wie wun- der- bar- lich ist doch die- se Stra- - fe! der gu- te Hir- - te lei- det

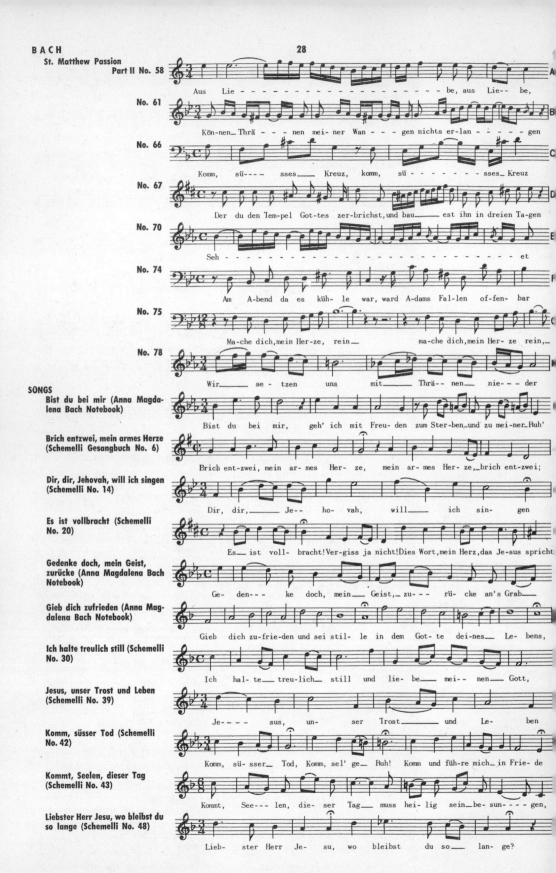

St. Matthew Passion
Part II No. 58

Aus Lie - - - - - - - - - - - be, aus Lie - - be,

No. 61

Kön-nen_Thrä - - - nen mei-ner Wan - - - gen nichts er-lan - - - gen

No. 66

Komm, sü - - - sses_ Kreuz, komm, sü - - - - - - sses_Kreuz

No. 67

Der du den Tem-pel Got-tes zer-brichst, und bau - - - est ihn in drei-en Ta-gen

No. 70

Seh - et

No. 74

Am A-bend da es küh-le war, ward A-dams Fal-len of-fen-bar

No. 75

Ma-che dich, mein Her-ze, rein_ ma-che dich, mein Her-ze rein,

No. 78

Wir_ se-tzen uns mit Thrä - - ken_ nie - - der

SONGS

Bist du bei mir (Anna Magdalena Bach Notebook)

Bist du bei mir, geh' ich mit Freu-den zum Ster-ben_und zu mei-ner_Ruh'

Brich entzwei, mein armes Herze (Schemelli Gesangbuch No. 6)

Brich ent-zwei, mein ar-mes Her-ze, mein ar-mes Her-ze,_brich ent-zwei;

Dir, dir, Jehovah, will ich singen (Schemelli No. 14)

Dir, dir,_ Je - - ho-vah, will_ ich sin - gen

Es ist vollbracht (Schemelli No. 20)

Es_ ist voll-bracht! Ver-giss ja nicht! Dies Wort, mein Herz, das Je-sus spricht

Gedenke doch, mein Geist, zurücke (Anna Magdalena Bach Notebook)

Ge-den - - - ke doch, mein_ Geist, zu - - - rü - - cke an's Grab_

Gieb dich zufrieden (Anna Magdalena Bach Notebook)

Gieb dich zu-frie-den und sei stil-le in dem Got-te dei-nes_ Le-bens,

Ich halte treulich still (Schemelli No. 30)

Ich hal-te_treu-lich still und lie-be_ mei - - nen_ Gott,

Jesus, unser Trost und Leben (Schemelli No. 39)

Je - - - sus, un - ser Trost_ und Le - ben

Komm, süsser Tod (Schemelli No. 42)

Komm, sü-sser, Tod, Komm, sel' ge-Ruh! Komm und füh-re mich_in Frie-de

Kommt, Seelen, dieser Tag (Schemelli No. 43)

Kommt, See - - - len, die-ser Tag_ muss hei-lig sein_be-sun - - - gen,

Liebster Herr Jesu, wo bleibst du so lange (Schemelli No. 48)

Lieb - ster Herr Je - su, wo bleibst du so_ lan - ge?

NGS

Mein Jesu, was für Seelenweh
(Schemelli No. 51)

Mein___ Je-su, was für See-len- weh be-fällt dich in Get- se-ma—— ne

O Jesulein süss, o Jesulein mild
(Schemelli No. 58)

O Je- su-lein süss, O Je-su-lein mild, dein's Va-ters Will'n hast du__er-füllt

Qui Tollis, from Mass in A major

Qui tollis pec-ca-ta, qui tol-lis pec-ca-ta, pec-ca-ta mun-di

So oft ich meine Tabakspfeife
(Anna Magdalena Bach Notebook)

So oft ich mei—— ne Ta——baks-pfei— fe mit gu-tem Kna——ster an-ge- füllt,

Willst du dein Herz mir schenken
(Aria di Giovanni) (Anna Magdalena Bach Notebook)

Willst du dein Herz mir schen-ken, so fang' es__ heim- lich an,

BACH, Philipp Emanuel   (see also Bach, Carl Philipp Emanuel)

Bitten

Gott, dei——— ne Gü——— te reicht___ so___ weit

Lied

Ich___ ging un- ter Er- len am küh- li- gen Bach

Passionslied

Er- for——— sche mich,___ er-fahr___ mein___ Herz,

BACH, Wilhelm Friedemann (1710-1784)

Kein Hälmlein wächst auf Erden

Kein Hälm- lein wächst auf Er- den, der Him-mel hat's be- taut

BACHELET, Alfred Georges (1864-1943)

Chère Nuit

Chè——— re nuit___ aux clar- tés___ se- rei—— nes,

BACKER-GRONDAHL, Agathe (1847-1907)

Mot Kveld, Op. 42, No. 7

Al- le de dugg- vaa-te blom-ster har sennt, So- len det siss- te God- nat

BALAKIREV, Mily Alexeivich (1837-1910)

Oh come to me!
Copyright 1911, G. Schirmer, Inc.

Oh come to me when breez-es stir the si-lent trees with lan-guid sigh-ing

BALFE, Michael William (1808-1870)

Bohemian Girl (opera)

In the gyp-sy's life you read___ the life that all would like to lead___

Bohemian Girl (opera)

I dreamt that I dwelt_ in mar- ble halls, with vas-sals and serfs at my side,_

The heart bow'd down by weight of woe, to weak-est hopes_ will_ cling

Then You'll Remember Me

When o- ther lips and o- ther_ hearts their tales of love shall tell

Trav'llers All of Ev'ry Station, from The Siege of La Rochelle (opera)

Trav'l-lers all of ev'- ry sta- tion, Trav'l-lers all of ev'ry sta-tion draw long

Come into the Garden, Maud

Come in- to the gar- den, Maud, For the black bat, Night has flown;

Excelsior

The shades of night were fall-ing fast As thro' an Al- pine vil-lage passed_

Killarney

By Kil- lar- ney's_ lakes and fells, Em'- rald isles and_ wind- ing bays

BANTOCK, Sir Granville (1868-   )

A Feast of Lanterns
By permission of Galaxy Music Corporation, N. Y., Copyright by Elkin & Co., Ltd.

In spring for sheer de-light I set the lan-terns swing-ing through the trees

The Parting
(Words by Ross)
Copyright by G. Ricordi & Co., Inc.

Oh he cam' whist-lin' up the glen,_ And, smi- lin' I gaed doon to meet him;_

BARBER, Samuel (1910-   )

The Daisies, Op. 2, No. 1
Copyright 1936, G. Schirmer, Inc.

In the scent- ed bud of the morn- ing O, when the wind- y grass

I hear an army, Op. 10, No. 3
Copyright 1939, G. Schirmer, Inc.

I_ hear_ an_ ar- my charg-ing up- on the land

A Nun Takes the Veil, Op. 13, No. 1
Copyright 1941, G. Schirmer, Inc.

I have de-sired to go where springs not fail

Sleep now, Op. 10, No. 2
Copyright 1939, G. Schirmer, Inc.

Sleep now, O sleep now O you un- qui- et heart!

Sure on this shining night, Op. 13, No. 3
Copyright 1941, G. Schirmer, Inc.

Sure on this shin- ing night of star-made shad- ows round,

With rue my heart is laden, Op. 2, No. 2
Copyright 1936, G. Schirmer, Inc.

With rue my heart is lad- en for gol-den friends I had

BARLOW, S. M. L. (1892-   )

The Cherry
Copyright by G. Ricordi & Co., Inc.

Jo- seph was an old man, an_ old man_ was he;

BARNABY, Sir Joseph (1838-1892)

Sweet and low

Sweet and low, sweet and low, wind of the wes- tern sea____

BARTLET, John (17th cent.)

Of all the birds that I do know

Of all the birds that I do know, Phil- ip my spar- row hath no peer

BARTLETT, James Carroll (1850-1929)

A Dream
Copyright by Oliver Ditson Co.
Used by permission.

Last night I was dream- ing of thee, love, was dream- ing,

BARTÓK, Béla (1881-1945)

Hungarian Folksong Settings
A gyulai kert alatt
By permission Boosey & Hawkes, Inc.,
copyright owners

A gyu- la- i kert a-latt, kert a- latt Bar-na le-gény roz-ma-rin- got a- rat

Által mennék én a Tiszán

Ál-tal-men-nék én a Ti-szán la- di-kon, la- di- kon, de la- di- kon,

Aszszonyok, Aszszonyok

Asz- szo-nyok, asz- szo- nyok, had' le- gyek tár- sa- tok,

Elindultam szép hazámbul

El- in-dul-tam szép ha- zám-bul, Hi- res kis ma- gyar-or- szág-bul.

Feketeföd
one theme

Fe-ke- te föd,____ fe-hér az én zseb-ken - - - -döm

El- ha- gyott a leg-ked-ve- sebb sze-re- tőm

Ha kimegyek arr' a magas tetőre

Ha- ki- me-gyek arr' a ma-gas te-tő- re Ta-lá-lok én sze-re-tő-re ket-tő-re.

Istenem, Istenem
one theme

Is- te-nem, Is- te- nem á-raszd meg a vi- zet Had' vi-gyen el en- gem

a pám- ka- pu já- ra;

Nem meszsze van ide kis Margitta

Nem mesz- sze van i- de kis Mar- git-ta, Hor-to-bágy-nak vi-ze kö-rül foly-ja.

Töltek a nagy erdő útját

Töl-tik a nagy er-dő út- - - - ját, Vi-szik a szé- kely ka-to- - - - nát

Vévig mentem a tárkányi sej, haj

Vé- vig men- tem a tár- ká- nyi sej, haj, nagy uc- cán;

BATESON, Thomas (1570-1630)

Cupid in a bed of roses

Cu- pid   in a bed of Ro- ses   in a bed of Ro- ses

Have I found her

Have I found her? have I found her O rich find- ing

BAX, Arnold (1883-   )

A Christmas Carol
By permission J. & W. Chester, Ltd., London, copyright pwners

There is no rose of such vir- tue   As__ is the rose_____ that bore

Cradle Song

I heard a Piper Piping
By permission Oxford Univ. Press, London, copyright owners

I heard a pi-per pi- ping the blue__ hills a- mong_____

Mater ora filium (unacc. double choir)

The White Peace
By permission J. & W. Chester, Ltd., London, copyright owners

It lies not on the sun- lit hill   Nor__ on the sun-lit plain:

BAYLY, Anselm (1719-1794)

Long, long ago

Tell me the tales that to me were so dear, Long, long a- go, Long, long a-go

BEACH, Mrs. H. H. A. (1867-1944)

Ah, Love, But a Day
Copyright by Arthur P. Schmidt Co., Boston
Used by permission.

Ah, Love, but__ a day____ And the world has changed!__

The Year's at the Spring, Op. 44, No. 1
Copyright by Arthur P. Schmidt Co., Boston
Used by permission.

The year's__at the spring,__ And day's_at the morn;__ Morn-ing's_at sev-en,

BECKER, Reinhold (1842-1924)

Frühlingszeit

Wenn   der   Früh- ling auf die Ber-- ge steigt

BEETHOVEN, Ludwig van (1770-1827)

Fidelio, Op. 72 (Opera)
Act I, No. 2

O wär' ich schon mit dir__ vereint, und dürf- te mann__ dich nen-nen!

No. 3 (Quartet)

Mir ist so wun- der-bar, es engt das Herz mir ein;

BEETHOVEN
Missa Solemnis, Op. 123
III Credo

Con sub-stan-ti-a- lem pa-tri per quem om-ni-a fac-ta sunt,

Et in-car-na-tus est de spi-ri-tu sanc- to ex Ma-ri-a vir-gi-ne,

Et vi-tam ven-tu-ri sae- - - - cu-li, a- - - -men, a- -men,

IV Sanctus

Sanc- tus Do- mi-nus, Do-mi-nus De-us Sa- - ba-oth,

Ple- ni sunt coe- li et ter-ra glo- - - - - - - - - ri-a tu-a

O- sa-na, O-sa-na in ex-cel- - - - -sis, O-sa-na, O- sa-na

V Benedictus

Be- ne-dic- - - -tus, qui ve- nit, qui ve-nit in no- mi-ne Do-mi-ni,

VI Agnus Dei

Ag- - -nus,ag- nus De-i qui tol-lis pec-ca-ta, pec-ca- ta,pec-ca-ta mun- di,

Do- - - - - - - - na no- bis pa- - - - - - - - cem,

pa- - cem, pa- - - - - - - - - - - - - - - - - - - cem,

Do- - - - na no- - bis pa- - - - - - - - - - - - - - - - - - ce

Mount of Olives, Op. 85 (oratorio)
I

Mei-ne See- le ist er- schüt-tert von den Qua-len, von den Qua-len,die mir.

II

Preist,preist des Er-lö-sers Gü- te, preist,Men-schen, sei-ne Huld

III

O Heil euch, heil euch, ihr Er- lö-sten!

III

So ru- he denn mit gan-zer Schwe-re, mit gan-zer Schwe-re auf mir

VI A

In mei-nen A- dern wüh-len ge-rech-ter Zorn und Wuth

(Chorus) B

Auf, auf! er-grei-fet den Ver- rä-ther,wei-let hier-nun län-ger nicht!

(Chorus) C

Wel-ten sin-gen, Wel- ten sin-gen, Wel-ten sin-gen Dank und Eh-re

(Chorus) D

Prei-set ihn, ihr En- gel-chö-re, laut im heil'- gen Ju-bel-ton,

SONGS:
Abendlied — A

Wenn die Son- ne nie-der- sin-ket, und der Tag zur Ruh' sich neigt

Adelaide, Op. 46 — B

Ein-sam wan- delt dein Freund im Früh- lings- gar- ten, mild von lieb-lich-en

Ah! Perfido, Op. 65 (Aria) — C

Per pie- tà, non dir- miad- di- o, non dir - - - - miad- di- o,

— D

Di- te voi, se in tan- to af-fan- no non son_ de- gna di_ pie- tà?_

Andenken — E

Ich den- ke dein,_ wenn durch den Hain der Nach-ti-gallen Ak- kor - - de schallen

An die ferne Geliebte, Op. 98, No. 1 — F

Auf dem Hü- gel sitz' ich, spä- hend in das blau- e Ne- bel- land

No. 2 — G

Wo die Ber- ge so blau aus dem ne - -bli-gen Grau schau- en her- ein,

No. 3 — H

Leich- te Seg- ler in den Hö- hen, und du Bäch- lein klein und schmal

No. 4 — I

Die- se Wol- ken in den Hö- hen, die-ser Vög-lein munt' rer Zug

No. 5 — J

Es keh-ret der Mai-en, es blü-het die Au'.Die Lüf-te,sie we-hen so mil-de,so lau,

No. 6 — K

Nimm sie_ hin denn, die- se Lie- der, die ich dir, Ge- lieb- te, sang,_

An die Geliebte — L

O dass ich dir vom stil-len Au- ge in sei-nem lie- be- vol-len Schein,

An die Hoffnung, Op. 32 — M

Die du so gern in heil'gen Näch- ten fei-erst und sanft und weich

Aus Goethe's Faust, Op. 75, No. 3 — N

Es war ein- mal ein Kö- nig, der hatt' ei- nen gros- sen Floh,

Clärchen's Song, from Egmont, Op. 84 — O

Die Trom- mel ge- rüh- ret! Das Pfeif- chen ge- spielt!

Freudvoll und leidvoll — P

Freud- voll und leid- voll, ge- dan- ken-voll sein;

Das Geheimniss — Q

Wo bluht das Blüm-chen, das nie ver-blüht? Wo strahlt das Stern- lein,

Gellert Lieder, Op. 48, No. 1 Bitten — R

Gott, dei- ne Gü- te reicht- so weit, so weit die Wol- ken ge- hen

No. 2 Die Liebe des Nächsten — S

So Je-mand spricht: Ich lie- be Gott!_ und hasst doch sei- ne Brü- der,

SONGS: Gellert Lieder, Op. 48,
No. 3 Vom Tode

Mei- ne Le- bens-zeit ver-streicht, stünd-lich eil' ich zu dem Gra- be,

No. 4 Die Ehre Gottes aus der Natur

Die Him-mel rüh- men des E- wi-gen Eh- re, ihr Schall pflanzt seinen Na-men_ fort

No. 5 Gottes Macht und Vorse-hung

Gott ist mein Lied! Er ist der Gott der Stär- ke

No. 6 Busslied

An dir al-lein, an dir hab' ich_ ge- sün-digt und ü- bel oft vor dir ge-than_

Ich liebe dich

Ich lie- be dich, so wie du mich, am A- bend und am Mor- gen,

In questa tomba oscura

In que- sta tom- ba o- scu- ra la- scia-mi ri-po- sar;

Irish Songs (voice and pianoforte trio)
The British Light Dragoons

'Twas a mar-e-chal of France, and he fain would hon-our gain,

Morning a Cruel Turmoiler Is

Mor-ning a cru- el tur-moil- er is, ban-ish- ing ease and re-pose

The Morning Air Plays on my Face

The morn- ing air_ plays on_ my face_ and, through_the gray mist peer- ing

O Harp of Erin

O harp_ of E- rin thou art now_ laid low,

O might I but my Patrick love

O might I but my Pat-rick love! My moth- er scolds se- vere-ly

Oh! Who, my dear Dermot

Oh! who, my_ dear_ Der- mot, has dared to de- ceive thee,

Once More I Hail Thee

Once more I_ hail thee, thou_ gloom- y De- cem- ber

On the Massacre of Glencoe

Oh! tell me, Har-per, where- fore_ flow_ thy way-ward notes of wail and woe

The Pulse of an Irishman

The pulse of an I- rish- man ev- er beats quick-er,when war is the sto- ry

The Return to Ulster

Once a- gain, but how_ chang'd, since my wan- d'rings be- gan

Sad and Luckless Was the Season

Sad and luck-less was the sea-son, when to court fair_ El- len flew,

The Soldier

Then, Sol- dier! come_ fill_ high the wine for we reck not of_ to- mor- row

The Soldier in a Foreign Land

The_ pip- er who sat_ on his low_ mos- sy seat

BEETHOVEN

SONGS:

Kennst du das Land (Mignon) Op. 75, No. 1

Kennst du das Land, wo die Ci-tro-nen blüh'n, im dunk-len Laub A

Der Kuss Op. 128 (ariette)

Ich war bei Chlo-en ganz al-lein, und kus-sen wollt' ich sie B

Mailied Op. 52, No. 4

Wie herr-lich_ leuch-tet_ mir_ die Na-tur,_ wie glänzt die Son-ne, C

Marmotte Op. 52, No. 7

Ich kom-me schon durch man-ches Land, a-vec que la_ mar-mot-te, D

Mit einem gemalten Band, Op. 83, No. 3

Klei-ne_ Blu-men, klei-ne Blät-ter streu-en mir mit leich-ter_ Hand_ E

Neue Liebe, neues Leben, Op. 75 No. 2

Herz, mein Herz, was soll das ge-ben? Was be-drän-get dich so sehr? F

La Partenza (Der Abschied)

Ec-co quel fie-ro i-stan--- te! Ni-ce, mia Ni-ce, ad-di-- o! G

Resignation

Lisch aus, lisch aus, mein Licht!_ was dir ge-bricht,_ das ist nun fort, H

Scotch Songs: (Op. 108 for voice and pianoforte trio)
Sally in our Alley

Of all the girls_ that are so smart there's none like pret-ty Sal-ly I

Auld Lang Syne

Should auld ac-quaintance be for-got and ne-ver brought to mind? J

Charlie is my darling

O Char-lie is my dar-ling, my dar-ling, my dar-ling K

No. 2 Sunset

The sun up-on the Weird-law hill, in Ett-rick's vale is sink-ing sweet; L

No. 3 Oh sweet were the hours

Oh! sweet were the hours, when in mirth's frol-ic throng_ M

No. 7 Bonny laddie, highland laddie

Where got ye that sil-ver moon, bon-ny lad-die,_ high-land lad-die, N

No. 8 The lovely lass of In-verness

The love-ly lass of In-ver-ness,_ nae_ joy nor plea-sure can she see; O

No. 14 O, how can I be blithe and glad

O, how can I_ be_ blithe and glad, or how can I_ gang_ brisk and braw; P

No. 16 Could this ild world have been contriv'd

Could this ill world_ have been_ con-triv'd to stand Q

No. 17 O Mary, at thy window be

O Ma-ry, at thy win-dow be, It is the wish'd, the trysted hour, R

No. 20 Faithfu' Johnie

When will you come a-gain, my_ faith-fu' Joh-nie, S

SONGS:

Scotch Songs, Op. 108 (voice and pianoforte trio)
No. 24. Again my Lyre

A- gain, my Lyre, yet once a- gain, with tears I wake

Welsh Songs: The Cottage Maid

I en- vy not the splen-dour fine that glit-ters in Sir Wat- kyn's hall

Der Wachtelschlag

Horch, wie schallt's dor-ten so lieb-lich her- vor! Fürch-te Gott!

Wonne der Wehmut, Op. 83, No. 1

Trocknet nicht, trocknet nicht Thrä-nen der e- wi-gen Lie- be!

Symphony No. 9, "Choral", Op. 125: Finale

A
Freu- de schö-ner Göt-ter- fun-ken, Toch-ter aus E- ly- si- um

B
Seid um- schlun-gen, Mil- li- o- nen! Die-sen Kuss der gan- zen Welt!

C
Freu- de, Toch-ter aus E- ly- si- um

BELLINI, Vincenzo (1801-1835)

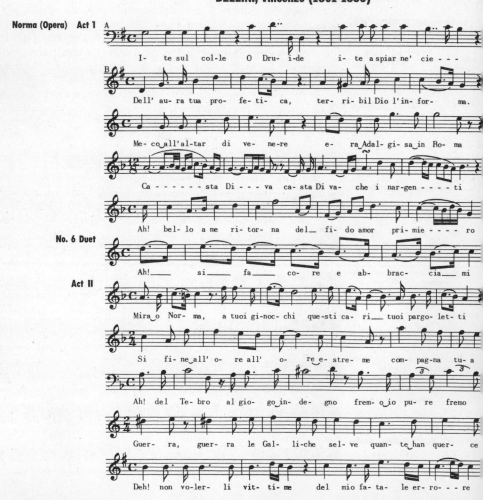

Norma (Opera)   Act 1

A
I- te sul col- le O Dru- i-de i- te a spiar ne' cie - - -

B
Dell' au-ra tua pro- fe-ti- ca, ter- ri- bil Dio l'in- for- ma.

Me- co all'al-tar di ve- ne- re e- ra Adal-gi-sa in Ro- ma

Ca - - - - - sta Di - - - va ca-sta Di va- che i nar-gen - - - - ti

Ah! bel- lo a me ri-tor- na del fi- do amor pri-mie - - - ro

No. 6 Duet

Ah! si fa co- re e ab- brac- cia- mi

Act II

Mira o Nor- ma, a tuoi gi-noc-chi que-sti ca- ri tuoi pargo-let- ti

Si fi- ne all' o- re all' o- re e-stre- me com-pag-na tu- a

Ah! del Te- bro al gio- go in-de- gno frem- o io pu- re fremo

Guer- ra, guer-ra le Gal- li-che sel- ve quan-te han quer- ce

Deh! non vo-ler- li vit- ti- me del mio fa- ta- le er-ro - - re

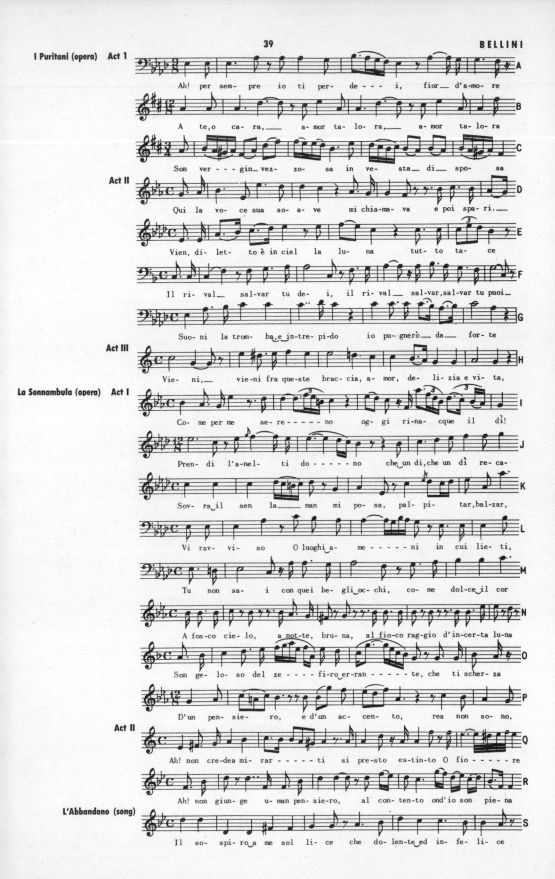

I Puritani (opera)   Act 1

Ah! per sem- pre io ti per- de—i, fior d'a-mo-re

A te, o ca-ra,___ a-mor ta-lo-ra,___ a-mor ta-lo-ra

Son ver—gin- vez- zo- sa in ve- sta___ di_ spo— sa

Act II

Qui la vo- ce sua so- a- ve mi chia-ma- va e poi spa- ri.

Vien, di- let- to è in ciel la lu- na tut-to ta- ce

Il ri- val_ sal-var tu de- i, il ri- val_ sal-var, sal-var tu puoi_

Suo- ni la trom- ba, e in-tre-pi-do io pu- gnerò___ da_ for- te

Act III

Vie- ni,_ vie-ni fra que-ste brac- cia, a- mor, de- li- zia e vi- ta,

La Sonnambula (opera)   Act I

Co- me per me se- re——no og- gi ri-na- cque il dì!

Pren- di l'a-nel- ti do——no che un dì, che un dì re- ca-

Sov- ra il sen la___man mi po- sa, pal- pi- tar, bal-zar,

Vi rav- vi- so O luoghi a- me——ni in cui lie- ti,

Tu non sa- i con quei be- gli oc- chi, co- me dol-ce il cor

A fos-co cie- lo, a not-te, bru- na, al fio-co rag-gio d'in-cer-ta lu-na

Son ge- lo- so del ze——fi-ro er-ran——te, che ti scher- za

D'un pen- sie- ro, e d'un ac- cen- to, rea non so- no,

Act II

Ah! non cre-dea mi rar——ti si pre-sto es-tin-to O fio——re

Ah! non giun- ge u- man pen-sie-ro, al con-ten-to ond'io son pie- na

L'Abbandono (song)

Il so- spi-ro a me sol li- ce che do- len-te ed in- fe- li-ce

40
BELLMAN, Carl Michael (1740-1795)

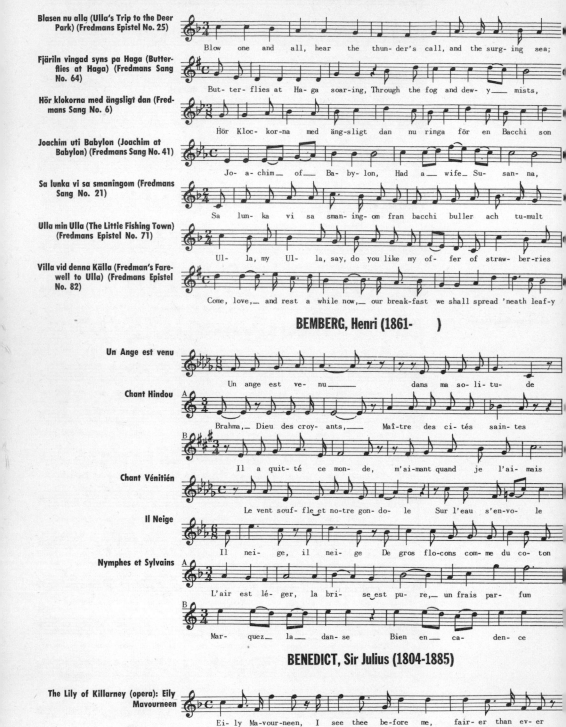

Blasen nu alla (Ulla's Trip to the Deer Park) (Fredmans Epistel No. 25)

Blow one and all, hear the thun-der's call, and the surg-ing sea;

Fjäriln vingad syns pa Haga (Butterflies at Haga) (Fredmans Sang No. 64)

But-ter-flies at Ha-ga soar-ing, Through the fog and dew-y mists,

Hör klokorna med ängsligt dan (Fredmans Sang No. 6)

Hör Kloc-kor-na med äng-sligt dan nu ringa för en Bacchi son

Joachim uti Babylon (Joachim at Babylon) (Fredmans Sang No. 41)

Jo-a-chim of Ba-by-lon, Had a wife Su-san-na,

Sa lunka vi sa smaningom (Fredmans Sang No. 21)

Sa lun-ka vi sa sman-ing-om fran bacchi buller ach tu-mult

Ulla min Ulla (The Little Fishing Town) (Fredmans Epistel No. 71)

Ul-la, my Ul-la, say, do you like my of-fer of straw-ber-ries

Villa vid denna Källa (Fredman's Farewell to Ulla) (Fredmans Epistel No. 82)

Come, love, and rest a while now, our break-fast we shall spread 'neath leafy

BEMBERG, Henri (1861-)

Un Ange est venu

Un ange est ve-nu dans ma so-li-tu-de

Chant Hindou

Brahma, Dieu des croy-ants, Maî-tre des ci-tés sain-tes

Il a quit-té ce mon-de, m'ai-mant quand je l'ai-mais

Chant Vénitién

Le vent souf-fle et no-tre gon-do-le Sur l'eau s'en-vo-le

Il Neige

Il nei-ge, il nei-ge De gros flo-cons com-me du co-ton

Nymphes et Sylvains

L'air est lé-ger, la bri-se est pu-re, un frais par-fum

Mar-quez la dan-se Bien en ca-den-ce

BENEDICT, Sir Julius (1804-1885)

The Lily of Killarney (opera): Eily Mavourneen

Ei-ly Ma-vour-neen, I see thee be-fore me, fair-er than ev-er

Act I Duet

The moon has rais'd her lamp a-bove to light the way to thee,

La Capinera (The Wren)

Col ri- tor- nar__ Del dol ce a- pril__ Tu tor- ni pur,

Carnevale di Venezia (Carnival of Venice)

O me be- a\- - -ta Ri- tor- na in Ciel l'al-bo- re

La bru- na gon- do- let- ta ap- pres- ta o Bar- ca- rol

The Gypsy and the Bird

A gyp- sy roam- ing through the mead- ows,__ Spied a lin-net

BENJAMIN, Arthur (1893-   )

Calm sea and mist

The slow_ heave of the sleep-ing sea, with pulse like mo-tion swells and falls

Hedgerow
Copyright 1925, Arthur Benjamin

The win- try winds are white; the wind seems fro- zen

The Wasp
Copyright 1925, Arthur Benjamin

Where the ripe pears droop heav- i- ly The yel- low wasp hums loud and long

BENNET, John (16th-17th cent.)

All Creatures Now

All crea-tures now are mer- ry. mer- ry, mer- ry mind- ed

Thyrsis, sleepest thou?

Thyr- sis, sleep- est thou? sleep-est thou? sleep-est thou? sleep-est thou

BERCHEM, Jachet Van (16th Cent.)

O Jesu Christe

O_ Je- su Chris- te, mi- se- re- re me- i, quum do- lo- re__

BERG, Alban (1885-1935)

Sieben frühe Lieder 1. Nacht
By permission Associated Music
Publishers, Inc.

Däm- mern Wol- ken ü- ber Nacht und Thal

2. Schilflied

Auf ge- hei- men Wal- des- pfa- de schleich ich gern im A\- - -bend-schein

3. Die Nachtigall

Das macht, es hat die Nach- ti- gall die gan- ze Nacht ge- sun- gen;

4. Traumgekrönt

Das war der Tag der wei- ssen Chry- san- the- men,

5. Im Zimmer

Herbst-son-nen-schein ___ Der lie- be A-bend blickt so still her- ein

BERG

Sieben frühe Lieder
6. Liebesode

Im Arm der Lie-be schlie-fen wir se-lig ein___

7. Sommertage

Nun zie-hen Ta-ge ü-ber die Welt,

Wozzeck (opera) Op. 7
(Three selections) I
By permission Associated Music
Publishers, Inc.

Sol-da-ten, Sol-da-ten sind schö-ne Bur----schen

II

Han-sel spann dei-ne sechs Schimmel an, Gib sie zu fressen auf's neu-

III

Rin-gel, Rin-gel Ro-sen-krantz, Rin------gel-reihn!

BERLIOZ, Hector (1803-1869)

L'Enfance du Christ, Op. 25 (oratorio)
Part I. O misère des Rois

O mi-sè-re des Rois! Ré-gner___ et ne pas vi-vre!

Part II. L'Adieu des Bergers

Il s'en va loin de___ la ter-re Où dans l'é-table il vit___ le jour

Le Repos de la Sainte Famille

Les Pé-le-rins é-tant ve-nus En un lieu de bel-le ap-pa-ren-ce

Les Nuits d'Été, Op. 7 (Songs)
No. 1 Villanelle

Quand vien-dra la sai-son nou-vel-le, Quand au-ront dis-pa-ru

No. 2 Le Spectre de la Rose

Sou-le-ve ta pau-piè-re clo-se Qu'effleu-re un son-ge

No. 4 L'Absence

Re-viens, re-viens___ ma bien ai-mé-e comme un-e fleur

La Damnation de Faust, Op. 24 (opera)
Part II. Chanson de la Puce

U-ne pu-ce gen-til-le chez un prin-ce lo-geait

Air de Roses

Voi-ci des ro-ses de cet-te nuit é-clo-ses, Sur___ ce lit en-bau-mé

Part III.

Au-tre-fois un roi de Thu-lé Qui jusqu'au tom-beau fut fi-dè-le

Mer-ci, doux cré-pus-cu-le! Oh! sois le bien-ve-nu!

Sérénade de Méphistophélès

De-vant la mai-son De ce-lui___ qui___ t'a-do-----re,

Part IV. Romance

D'a-mour l'arden-te flam-me Con-su-me-mes beaux jours.

Invocation à la nature

Na-ture im-men-se, in-pénétrable et fiè-re

Les Troyens (Opera)
Act III. Scene I
Chers Ty- ri- ens, tant de no- bles tra- vaux

Act V. Scene II
A- dieu fiè- re ci- té qu'un gé- né- reux ef- fort

I- nu- ti- les re- grets je dois quitter Car- tha- ge

En un der- nier nau- fra- ge Ah! puis- se je pé- rir

Requiem
1. Requiem aeternam
Re- qui- em ae- ter- nam, re- qui- em ae- ter- nam do- na e- is,

Te de- cet hym- nus, De- us in Si- on,

2. Dies Irae
Di- es i- rae, di- es il- la, sol- vet sae- clum,

Et i- te- rum ven- tu- rus est cum glo- ri- a

3. Quid sum miser
Quid sum mi- ser tunc dic- tu- rus

4. Rex tremendae
Rex! Rex! O rex tremendae ma- jes- ta- tis, rex tremendae ma- jes- ta- tis

5. Quaerens me
Quaerens me se- dis- ti las- sus quae- rens me,

6. Lacrymosa
La- cry- mo- sa di- es il- la,

7. Offertorium
Do- mi- ne, Do- mi- ne Je- su Chris- te!

Accompaniment

9. Sanctus
Sanc- tus, Sanc- tus, Sanc- tus, Sanc- tus,

Ho- san- na in ex- cel- sis, ho- san- na in ex- cel- sis,

10. Agnus dei
Ag- nus de- i, qui tol- lis pec- ca- ta mun- di, do- na e- is

BERNARD, Paul (1827-1879)

Ça fait peur aux oiseaux
Ne par- lez pas tant, Li- san- dre, Quand nous ten- dons nos fi- lets;

BEYDTS, Louis (1895-   )

C'est moi
Copyright 1944, Pierre Noel, Paris

Si ta marche at-tris-té- e   S'é-gare au fond d'un bois,__

Un cri

Hi-ron-delle, hi-ron-delle, Hi-ron-delle! Est-il au monde un coeur fi-dè- le?

En Arles
By permission Durand & Cie, Paris;
Eikan-Vogel Co., Inc., Phila.,
copyright owners

Dans Arle, où sont les A- lis-cams, Quand l'ombre est rou- ge

Theme in accompaniment (popular Fr. theme)

La Lyre et les Amours (Song Cycle)
No. 1 Le Bracelet
By permission Heugel & Cie, Paris,
copyright owners

A- mour en soit bé- ni!__   Le su-jet de mes voeux

No. 3 La belle esclave More

Beau mons- tre de na-tu- re,   il est vrai, ton vi-sage est noir

No. 4 Les Baisers de Dorinde

La douce ha- lei-ne des zé- phirs   Et ces eaux qui se pré- ci- pi-tent

BILLINGS, William (1746-1800)

Chester

Let ty-rants shake their i- ron__ rod And slav-'ry clank

The dying Christian's last farwell

My friends, I am go-ing a- long jour-ney__ nev-er__ to__ re-turn

Judea

A Vir- gin un- spot-ted by Proph-et fore-told

New Plymouth

O Lord our fa-thers oft have told, In__ our at- ten-tive ears__

Psalms and Fuguing Tunes:
Be Glad then, America

Be glad then A- mer- i-ca, be glad then A- mer-i-ca, shout, shout, shout

Creation

When I with__ pleas-ing won- der stand, and all__ my frame__ sur-vey,

When Jesus wept

When Je- sus wept__ the fall- ing tear in mer- cy flowed__ be-yond

The Shepherd's Carol (Shiloh)

Me- thinks I see an heav'n-ly Host of__ an- gels on the wing;

Let all__ your fears__ be ban- ished hence, Glad tid-ings I pro- claim,__

BIMBONI, Alberto (1882-   )

Sospiri miei
By permission Galaxy Music
Corporation, N. Y.

So- spi- ri mie- i an- da- te o- ve vi man- do — A

BINCHOIS, Gilles (1400-1460)

A Solis Ortu Cardine (motet)

A so- lis or - - - - tu car - - - di - - - ne _____ — C

De Plus en Plus (rondeau)

De plus en plus_____ se re- nou - - - - vel- le — D

Files a marier

Fi- les a ma- ri- er, ne vous ma- ri- ez ja ne vous ma- ri- ez ja, — E

Inter Natos Mulierum

In - - - — F

Je loe amours

Je loe a- mours et ma da- me mer- cy - - - - - - - - - - - - - - - - - e — G

Sanctus

San - - - - - - - - ctus San - - - - - - - - - ctus_____ Do- mi- nus — H

BISHOP, Sir Henry (1786-1855)

Bid me discourse

Bid me dis- course I will_ en- chant_ thine_ ear — J

The Dashing White Sergeant

If_ I_ had a beau, for a sol- dier who'd go, — K

Echo Song (arr. Frank LaForge)
Copyright 1940, G. Schirmer, Inc.

A

Some spir- it seems - - - - to play, Some spir- it seems to play!_ — L

B

Still_ I hear_____ the change- ful_ strain — M

ome Sweet Home, from Clari, or the Maid of Milan (opera)

Mid plea- sures and pal- a- ces, Though_ we may roam, — N

Lo, Here the Gentle Lark

Lo here the gen- tle lark_ wea- ry_ of_ rest — O

Love has eyes

Love's blind they say,_ O nev- er, nay_ Can words_ love's_ grace- im- part_ — P

Pretty Jane (The Bloom is on the Rye)

My pret- ty Jane, my pret- ty Jane - - - - Ah!_ nev- er, never look so shy — Q

Pretty Mocking Bird A

Liv - - - ing e - - - - cho, liv- ing e- cho, bird of_ eve,_ — R

B

Pret- ty mock- ing bird, pret- ty mock- ing bird, pret- ty pret- ty, pret- ty — S

Should he upbraid

Should he up-braid, I'll own that he pre-vail___

BIZET, Georges (1838-1875)

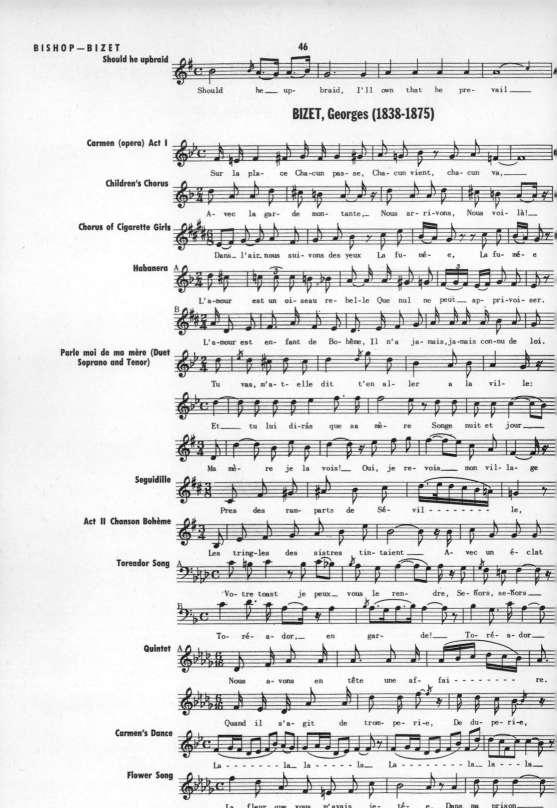

Carmen (opera) Act I

Sur la pla- ce Cha-cun pas-se, Cha- cun vient, cha-cun va,___

Children's Chorus

A- vec la gar- de mon- tante,___ Nous ar-ri-vons, Nous voi-là!

Chorus of Cigarette Girls

Dans l'air nous sui-vons des yeux La fu- mé- e, La fu-mé-e

Habanera A

L'a-mour est un oi-seau re-bel-le Que nul ne peut___ ap- pri-voi-ser.

B

L'a-mour est en- fant de Bo-hême, Il n'a ja- mais, ja-mais con-nu de loi.

Parle moi de ma mère (Duet Soprano and Tenor)

Tu vas, m'a- t- elle dit t'en al- ler a la vil- le:

Et___ tu lui di-rás que sa mè- re Songe nuit et jour___

Ma mè- re je la vois! Oui, je re- vois___ mon vil-la- ge

Seguidille

Pres des ram- parts de Sé- vil- - - - - - - le,

Act II Chanson Bohème

Les tring-les des sistres tin- taient___ A- vec un é- clat

Toreador Song A

Vo-tre toast je peux___ vous le ren- dre, Se- ñors, se-ñors

B

To- ré- a- dor, en gar- de!___ To- ré- a- dor

Quintet A

Nous a- vons en tête une af- fai- - - - - - - re.

Quand il s'a- git de trom- pe- ri-e, De du- pe-ri-e,

Carmen's Dance

La - - - - - - - la la - - - - la___ La - - - - - - - - la la - - la

Flower Song

La fleur que vous m'avais je- té- e, Dans ma prison___

Là- bas, là- bas dans la mon- ta- gne, Là-bas, là-bas

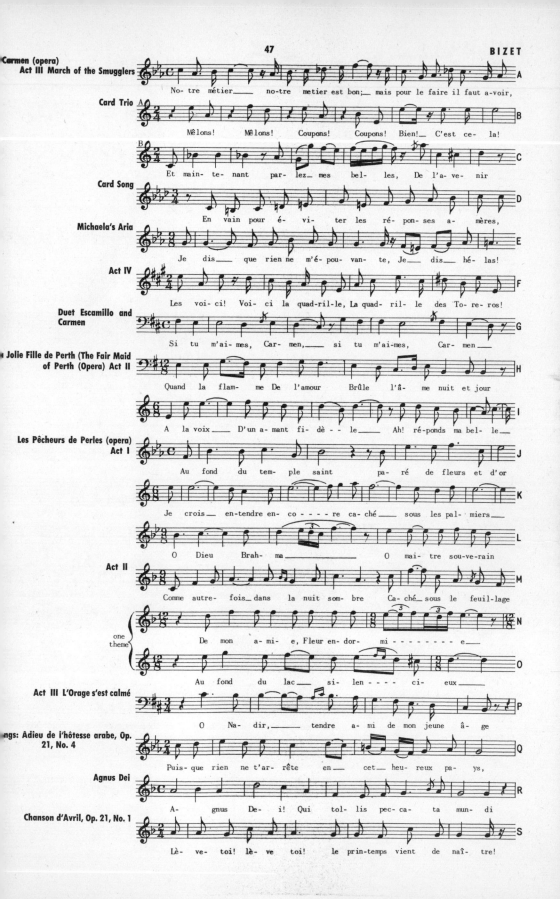

BIZET

Carmen (opera)
Act III March of the Smugglers — No-tre métier___ no-tre metier est bon;___ mais pour le faire il faut a-voir,

Card Trio — Mêlons! Mêlons! Coupons! Coupons! Bien!__ C'est ce-la!

Et main-te-nant par-lez___ mes bel-les, De l'a-ve-nir

Card Song — En vain pour é-vi-ter les ré-pon-ses a-mères,

Michaela's Aria — Je dis___ que rien ne m'é-pou-van-te, Je dis___ hé-las!

Act IV — Les voi-ci! Voi-ci la quad-ril-le, La quad-ril-le des To-re-ros!

Duet Escamillo and Carmen — Si tu m'ai-mes, Car-men,___ si tu m'ai-mes, Car-men___

Jolie Fille de Perth (The Fair Maid of Perth (Opera) Act II — Quand la flam-me De l'amour Brûle l'â-me nuit et jour

A la voix___ D'un a-mant fi-dè--le___ Ah! ré-ponds ma bel-le___

Les Pêcheurs de Perles (opera) Act I — Au fond du tem-ple saint pa-ré de fleurs et d'or

Je crois___ en-tendre en-co- - - - -re ca-ché___ sous les pal-miers___

O Dieu Brah-ma___ O mai-tre sou-ve-rain

Act II — Comme autre-fois___ dans la nuit som-bre Ca-ché___ sous le feuil-lage

one theme — De mon a-mi-e, Fleur en-dor-mi- - - - - - - -e___

Au fond du lac___ si-len- - - -ci-eux___

Act III L'Orage s'est calmé — O Na-dir,___ tendre a-mi de mon jeune â-ge

ngs: Adieu de i'hôtesse arabe, Op. 21, No. 4 — Puis-que rien ne t'ar-rête en___ cet___ heu-reux pa-ys,

Agnus Dei — A-gnus De- i! Qui tol-lis pec-ca-ta mun-di

Chanson d'Avril, Op. 21, No. 1 — Lè-ve-toi! lè-ve toi! le prin-temps vient de naî-tre!

Songs:
Ouvre ton coeur (Spanish Serenade)

La Mar- gue-rite_____ a fer- mé sa co- rol - - - le_____

Pastorale

Un jour de prin-temps_____ Tout le long d'un ver-ger_____

Vieille Chanson

Dans les bois l'a-mou-reux Myr- til A-vait pris fau- vet- te lé- gè- re

BLAND, James A. (1854-1911)

Carry me back to old Virginny
Copyright by E. B. Marks
Music Corp., N. Y.

Car- ry me back to old Vir- gin- ny There's where the cot- ton

BLANGINI, F. (1781-1841)

Care pupille

Ca- re_____ pu- pil- le tra mil- le e mil

Per valli, per boschi

Per val- li, per bo- schi cer- can-do di ni- ce sol l'- co

BLOCH, Ernest (1880-   )

Poèmes d'Automne
I. La Vagabonde
Copyright 1918, G. Schirmer, Inc.

Elle a pas- sé dans le vent d'au-tom-ne El- le che-mi-nait

II. Le Déclin

Dans le ver- ger pai- si- ble, bor- dé là- bas de peu-pli- ers

III. L'abri

J'é- cou- te la voix de mon rêve Pour al- ler à toi,

IV. Invocation

Les co- lon-nes du tem- ple s'a-ni- ment d'u- ne pa-leur plus chaude

Psalms
No. 22 (baritone and orchestra)
Copyright 1919, G. Schirmer, Inc.

E- lo- him! E- lo-him!_____ Why hast thou thus for-sa- ken me?

No. 114

Snatched a- way by Jah- veh_____ from the land where they served_____

No. 137

Re-clined_ by the wa-ters of Ba- bel,_ Our harps were hung up-on the wil-lows

BLOW, John (1649-1708)

The Self Banished

It is not that_____ I love you less, Than when_____ be- fore_____

BOATNER, Edward (1897-   )

Oh, What a beautiful city! (arr.)

Oh, what a beau-ti-ful ci-ty, Oh, what a beau-ti-ful ci-ty   A

BODENSCHATZ, Erhard (1576-1636)

Joseph, lieber Joseph mein (14th century German traditional Christmas song)

Jo-seph, lie-ber Jo-seph mein, hilf mir wie-gen mein Kin- de-lein,   C

BÖHM, Karl (1894-)

Still wie die Nacht, Op. 326, No. 27
By permission Associated Music Publishers, Inc.

Still wie die Nacht, tief wie das Meer,___ soll dei-ne Lie- be sein!___   E

Was i hab

Schö- ne Lied- le, ja die kenn i grad' drei an der Zahl   F

BOIELDIEU, François (1775-1834)

La Dame Blanche (Opera)
Act I

Ah quel plai-sir d'ê- tre sol- dat___ Ah quel plai-sir d'ê- tre sol- dat   H

Act II

Dé- jà la___ nuit, dé- jà la nuit plus som- bre sur nous ré- pand,   I

Viens gen-til- le da - - me, viens___ gen-til- le da - - me,   J

Act III Song of Georges Brown (Reverie)

Al- lons___ gai- ment re- ce-vons leur hom-ma- ge de mon nou-vel é- tat   K

BOITO, Arrigo (1842-1918)

Mefistofele (opera) Prologue
Copyright by G. Ricordi & Co., Inc.

A- ve Si- gnor,___ si-gnor de- gli an- ge- - li   M

Sal- ve Re- gi- na! s'in-nal- zi un e- co dal mon-do cie-co   N

Il bel gio- va- net- to sen vie- ne al- la fes- ta   O

Da- i cam-pi, da- i pra-ti che in- non-da_ la_ not- te,   P

Act I

Son___ lo Spi- ri- to___ che ne- ga sem- pre tut- to; l'a- stro, il fior   Q

(Duet)

Se tu mi do- ni un' o- ra di ri- po- so,   R

Fin da sta not- te, fin da sta not- te nel-l'or-gie ghiotte del mio mes-ser   S

Mefistofele (opera)
Act II Scene I Garden Scene

Ca-va-lie-ro il-lus-tre e sag-gio, co-me mai vi può al-le-tar

Sta ben al nu-bi-le cor-rer gio-con-do, in trac-cia d'i-la-ri venture

Scene II

Rid-dia-mo, rid-dia-mo! che il mon-do è ca-du-to! Rid-dia-mo, rid-dia-mo!

Act III

L'al-tra not-te in fon-do al ma-re il mio bim-bo han-no git-ta-to

(Duet)

Lon-ta-no, lon-ta-no, lon-ta-no, sui flut-ti d'un am-pio oce-à-no

Spun-ta l'au-ro-ra pal-li-do, l'ul-ti-mo di già vie-----ne

Act IV

For-ma ide-al pu-ris-si-ma del---la bel-le-za e-ter-na!

A-mo-re! mi-ste--rio ce-leste pro-fon-do! già il tempo di-le-gua

Epilogue

Guin-to sol pas-so es-tre-mo del-la più es-tre-ma e-tà,___

Nerone (opera)   **Act I**
Copyright by G. Ricordi & Co., Inc.

A not-te cu-pa, quan-do ne-gli an-tri del fu-ne---reo suol

Act II

Ec-co il ma-gi-co spec-chio in cui ri-fran-ge sua luce a-stral___

Act III

Vi-ve-te in pa-ce in con-cen-to so-a---ve d'a-mor,

BOND, Carrie Jacobs (1862-   )

I love you truly
Copyright by Boston Music Co.

I love you tru-ly, tru-ly, dear, Life with its sor-row

Just A-Wearyin' For You
Copyright by Boston Music Co.

Just a wear-y-in' for you, All the time a-feel-in' blue,

A Perfect Day
Copyright by Boston Music Co.

When you come to the end of a per-fect day and you sit a-lone

BORDES, Charles (1863-1909)

Dansons la gigue
By permission J. Hamelle Music
Publishers, Paris

Dan-sons la gi-gue J'ai-mais sur-tout ses jo-lis yeux

BORODIN, Alexander (1833-1887)

Prince Igor (opera) Prologue
Au so- leil__bril-lant gloi- re! gloi- re! Au noble I- gor, no-tre prin-ce

Act I
Je hais l'en-nui, je veux vi-vre gai-ment; I- gor pré-fè-re les ha-sards

Si l'on me trou- vait__bien di- gne D'ob-te-nir l'hon-neur__in-si- gne

Duet: Jaroslavna and Galitsky
Ah, peu m'importe à moi! Puis est-ce ton af-fai- re? J'ai pris ce qui m'a plu;

Act II
O__ fleur__ fa- né- - - - - e Ô__ fleur__ ti- - -mi- - - - de

Vladimir's Cavatina
Ah! viens, ah! viens! Viens,__ re- ponds au ten-dre ap-pel,

Igor's Aria
Hé- las! mon âme est triste A-dieu le doux re-pos En proie à mon cha-grin

Tendre é- pou- se__ bien ai- mé- e, Comme à__ toi va__

Konchak's Aria
À la Kai- a- la fut bat-tu- e Ta brave ar-mée un jour

I- gor, pour moi n'est qu'un guerrier que j'ai- me: Un cap-tif n'est jamais

Polovetsian Dance with Chorus
Va sur l'aî- le__ des doux__zé- phirs, A- é- ri- en- ne,va,__ chan-son,

Hon-neur au Khan, au chef puis-sant Ah!_____

Act IV Duet: Jaroslavna and Igor
Ah! c'est toi que j'em-bras-se. Oh! pour moi tout s'ef-fa-ce! Rê- ves,

J'ai__ cru rê- ver! mon__ Dieu, mer- ci! Est- il bien_vrai qu'ils_soit i- ci?

SONGS: A Dissonance
Thy lips say "I love thee, be-lieve me," And yet in the sound of thy voice

Flowers of Love
Where tears of my passion have fal-len, Full man- y a flow- er has sprung

The Sea
The sea toss- es and raves,__ While flinging heav'n-ward

The Sea Queen
Ah come, wea- ry one, make haste, it is eve; Thy heart is throbbing for me;

The Sleeping Beauty
Sleep, deep in fo- rest gloom, Sleep, prin- cess, ful- fil thy doom

SONGS: The Sleeping Princess

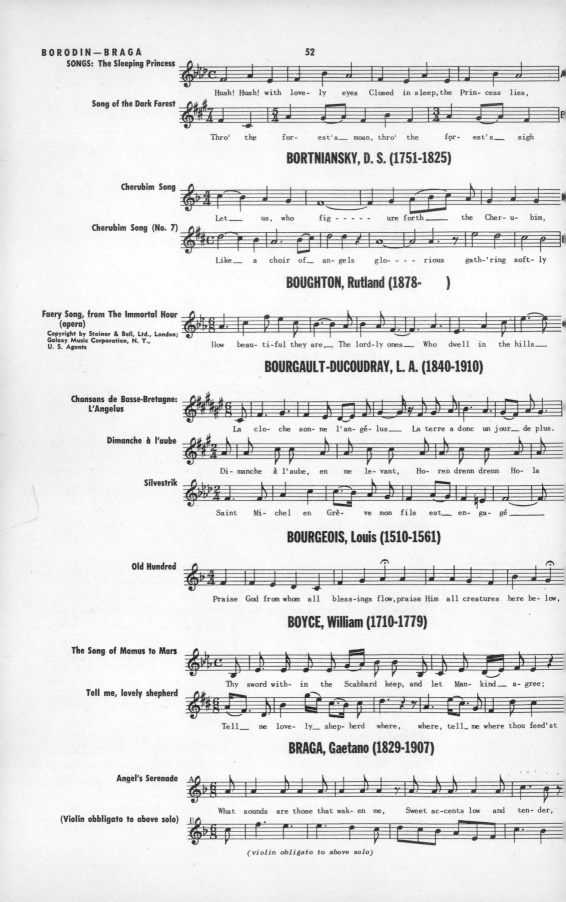

Hush! Hush! with love- ly eyes Closed in sleep, the Prin- cess lies,

Song of the Dark Forest

Thro' the for- est's_ moan, thro' the for- est's_ sigh

BORTNIANSKY, D. S. (1751-1825)

Cherubim Song

Let_ us, who fig - - - - ure forth_ the Cher- u- bim,

Cherubim Song (No. 7)

Like_ a choir of_ an- gels glo - - - rious gath-'ring soft- ly

BOUGHTON, Rutland (1878-   )

Faery Song, from The Immortal Hour
(opera)
Copyright by Stainer & Bell, Ltd., London;
Galaxy Music Corporation, N. Y.,
U. S. Agents

How beau- ti- ful they are,_ The lord- ly ones_ Who dwell in the hills_

BOURGAULT-DUCOUDRAY, L. A. (1840-1910)

Chansons de Basse-Bretagne:
L'Angelus

La clo- che son- ne l'an- gé- lus_ La terre a donc un jour_ de plus.

Dimanche à l'aube

Di- manche à l'aube, en me le- vant, Ho- ren drenn drenn Ho- la

Silvestrik

Saint Mi- chel en Grè- ve mon fils est_ en- ga- gé

BOURGEOIS, Louis (1510-1561)

Old Hundred

Praise God from whom all bless-ings flow, praise Him all creatures here be- low,

BOYCE, William (1710-1779)

The Song of Momus to Mars

Thy sword with- in the Scabbard keep, and let Man- kind_ a- gree;

Tell me, lovely shepherd

Tell_ me love- ly_ shep- herd where, where, tell_ me where thou feed'st

BRAGA, Gaetano (1829-1907)

Angel's Serenade

What sounds are those that wak- en me, Sweet ac-cents low and ten- der,

(Violin obbligato to above solo)

(violin obligato to above solo)

BRAHAM, John (1774-1856)

The Death of Nelson

O'er Nel-son's tomb with si-lent grief op-prest Bri-tan-nia mourns

'Twas__ in Tra-fal-gar's bay we saw the foe-men lay

BRAHE, May H.

Bless this House
By permission Boosey & Hawkes, Inc.,
copyright owners

Bless this house, O Lord we pray Make it safe by night and day

Down Here
By permission Boosey & Hawkes, Inc.,
copyright owners

Oh! it's quiet down here, yes as quiet as a mouse,

BRAHMS, Johannes (1833-1897)

Chorus and Solo Quartet: Songs for
Women's Chorus, 2 Horns and
Harp, Op. 17
No. 1. Es tönt ein voller Harfen-
klang

Es tönt ein vol-ler Har-fen-klang, den Lieb und Sehn-sucht schwel-len

No. 2. Lied von Shakespeare
(Come away, death!)

Komm her-bei, Komm her-bei, Tod! Und ver-senk in Cy-pres-sen

No. 3. Der Gärtner

Wo-hin ich geh und schau-e, in Feld und Wald und Tal,____

No. 4. Gesang aus Fingal

Wein' an den Fel-sen der brau-sen-den Win-de, wei-ne, O Mäd-chen

Der Gang zum Liebchen, Op. 31,
No. 3 (Quartet)

Es glänzt der Mond nie-der, Ich soll-te doch wie-der

Ein Deutsches Requiem, Op. 45 (A
German Requiem) No. 1

Se-   lig sind,   Se-lig sind, die da Leid tra-gen,

No. 2

Denn al-   les Fleisch es ist wie Gras und al-les Herr-lich-keit

So seid nun ge-dul-dig, lie---ben Brü-   der,

Die Er-lö-se-ten des Herrn wer-den wie-der kom-men

No. 3

Herr,   leh-re doch mich, dass ein En-de mit mir ha-ben muss,

Der Ge-recht-en See-len sind__ in Got-tes Hand

No. 4

Wie lieb-lich sind dei-ne Woh-nun-gen, Herr Ze------ba-oth,

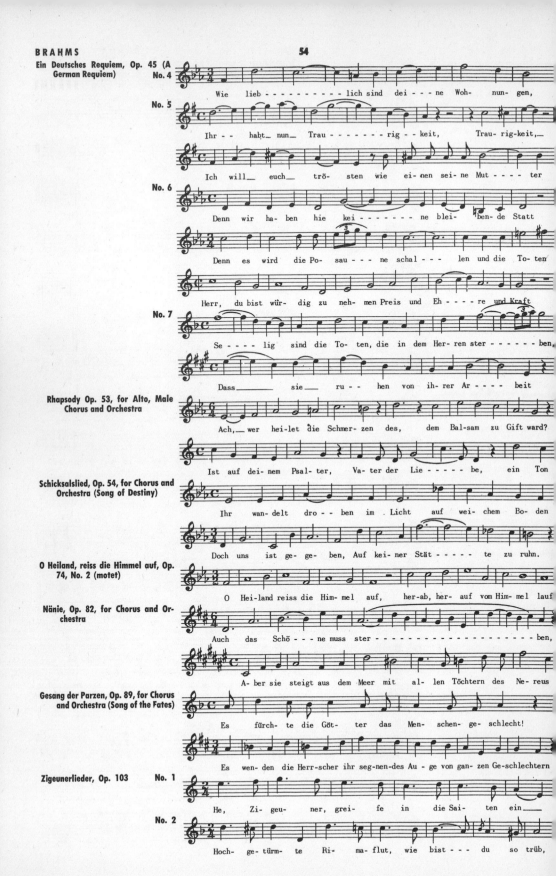

Ein Deutsches Requiem, Op. 45 (A German Requiem)

No. 4

Wie lieb - - - - - - - - - lich sind dei - - ne Woh - nun - gen,

No. 5

Ihr - - habt - nun - Trau - - - - - - rig - keit, Trau - rig - keit, - -

Ich will - euch - trö - sten wie ei - nen sei - ne Mut - - - - ter

No. 6

Denn wir ha - ben hie kei - - - - - - ne blei - ben - de Statt

Denn es wird die Po - sau - - ne schal - - - len und die To - ten

Herr, du bist wür - dig zu neh - men Preis und Eh - - - - re und Kraft

No. 7

Se - - - - lig sind die To - ten, die in dem Her - ren ster - - - - - - ben,

Dass - - - - - - - - - sie - ru - - hen von ih - rer Ar - - - - beit

Rhapsody Op. 53, for Alto, Male Chorus and Orchestra

Ach, - wer hei - let die Schmer - zen des, dem Bal - sam zu Gift ward?

Ist auf dei - nem Psal - ter, Va - ter der Lie - - - - be, ein Ton

Schicksalslied, Op. 54, for Chorus and Orchestra (Song of Destiny)

Ihr wan - delt dro - - ben im Licht auf wei - chem Bo - den

Doch uns ist ge - ge - ben, Auf kei - ner Stät - - - - te zu ruhn.

O Heiland, reiss die Himmel auf, Op. 74, No. 2 (motet)

O Hei - land reiss die Him - mel auf, her - ab, her - auf vom Him - mel lauf

Nänie, Op. 82, for Chorus and Orchestra

Auch das Schö - - - ne muss ster - - - - - - - - - - - - - - - - ben,

A - ber sie steigt aus dem Meer mit al - len Töch - tern des Ne - reus

Gesang der Parzen, Op. 89, for Chorus and Orchestra (Song of the Fates)

Es fürch - te die Göt - ter das Men - schen - ge - schlecht!

Es wen - den die Herr - scher ihr seg - nen - des Au - ge von gan - zen Ge - schlechtern

Zigeunerlieder, Op. 103

No. 1

He, Zi - geu - ner, grei - fe in die Sai - ten ein - -

No. 2

Hoch - ge - türm - te Ri - ma - flut, wie bist - - du so trüb,

geunerlieder, Op. 103   No. 3

Wisst ihr wann mein Kind- chen am al- ler- schönsten ist?   A

No. 4

Lie- ber Gott, du weisst, wie oft be- reut ich hab   B

No. 5

Brau- ner Bur- sche führt zum Tan- ze sein blau- äug- ig schö- nes Kind,   C

No. 6

Rös- lein drei- e in der Rei- he blühn so rot   D

No. 7

Kommt dir manch- mal in den Sinn, mein sü- sses Lieb   E

No. 8

Horch, der Wind_ klagt_ in den Zwei- gen_ trau- rig sacht;   F

No. 9

Weit und breit schaut Nie- mand mich an, und wenn sie mich has- sen,   G

No. 11

Ro- te A- bend- wol- ken ziehn am Fir- ma- ment_   H

dmännchen (The Little Sandman,
or, The Little Dustman), from 14
Volkskinderlieder, No. 4

Die Blü- me- lein sie schla- fen schon längst im Mon- den- schein   I

Songs and Duets:
Liebestreu, Op. 3, No. 1

O ver- senk, o ver- senk dein_ Leid, mein Kind, in die See, in die tie- fe See!"   J

In der Fremde, No. 5

Aus der Hei- mat_ hin- ter den Bli- tzen rot, da kom- men die Wol- ken her   K

Spanisches Lied, Op. 6, No. 1

In dem Schat- ten mei- ner Lo- cken schlief mir mein Ge- lieb- ter ein   L

Juchhe! No. 5

Wie ist doch die Er- de so schön, so schön! Das wis- sen die Vö- ge- lein,   M

Nachtigallen schwingen, No. 6

Nach- ti- gal- len schwin- gen lus- tig ihr Ge- fie- der   N

Treue Liebe, Op. 7, No. 1

Ein Mägd- lein sass am Mee- res- strand und blick- te voll Sehn- sucht ins Wei- te   O

Anklänge, No. 3

Hoch ü- ber stil- len Hö- - - hen stand in dem Wald ein Haus;   P

Heimkehr, No. 6

O brich nicht, Steg, du zit- terst sehr, o stürz nicht, Fels, du dräu- est schwer   Q

or dem Fenster, Op. 14, No. 1

Soll sich_ der Mond_ nicht hel- ler schei- nen   R

Ein Sonett, No. 4

Ach könnt' ich, könn- te ver- ges- sen sie, ihr schö- nes, lie- bes   S

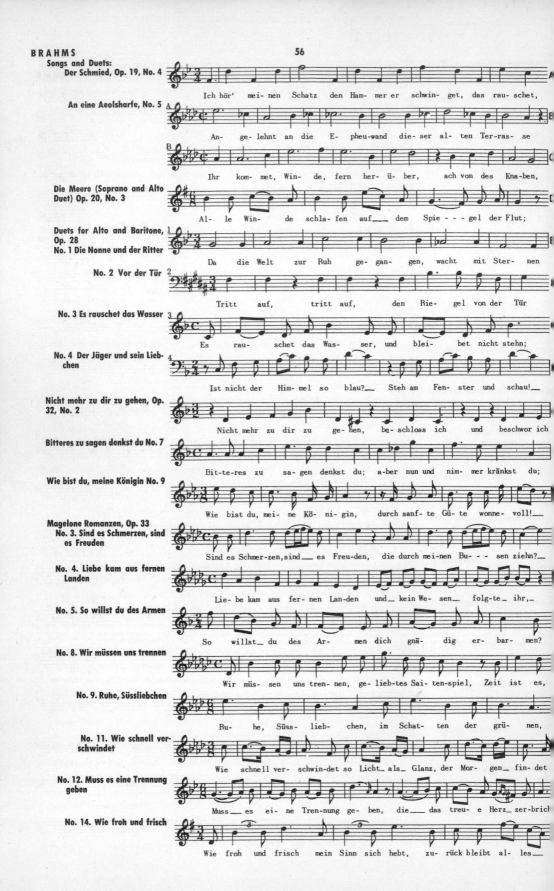

Songs and Duets:
Der Schmied, Op. 19, No. 4

Ich hör' mei- nen Schatz den Ham- mer er schwin- get, das rau- schet,

An eine Aeolsharfe, No. 5

An- ge- lehnt an die E- pheu- wand die- ser al- ten Ter- ras- se

Ihr kom- met, Win- de, fern her- ü- ber, ach von des Kna- ben,

Die Meere (Soprano and Alto Duet) Op. 20, No. 3

Al- le Win- de schla- fen auf dem Spie - - gel der Flut;

Duets for Alto and Baritone, Op. 28
No. 1 Die Nonne und der Ritter

Da die Welt zur Ruh ge- gan- gen, wacht mit Ster- nen

No. 2 Vor der Tür

Tritt auf, tritt auf, den Rie- gel von der Tür

No. 3 Es rauschet das Wasser

Es rau- schet das Was- ser, und blei- bet nicht stehn;

No. 4 Der Jäger und sein Lieb- chen

Ist nicht der Him- mel so blau? Steh am Fen- ster und schau!

Nicht mehr zu dir zu gehen, Op. 32, No. 2

Nicht mehr zu dir zu ge- hen, be- schloss ich und beschwor ich

Bitteres zu sagen denkst du No. 7

Bit- te- res zu sa- gen denkst du; a- ber nun und nim- mer kränkst du;

Wie bist du, meine Königin No. 9

Wie bist du, mei- ne Kö- ni- gin, durch sanf- te Gü- te wonne- voll!

Magelone Romanzen, Op. 33
No. 3. Sind es Schmerzen, sind es Freuden

Sind es Schmer- zen, sind es Freu- den, die durch mei- nen Bu - - sen ziehn?

No. 4. Liebe kam aus fernen Landen

Lie- be kam aus fer- nen Lan- den und kein We- sen folg- te ihr,

No. 5. So willst du des Armen

So willst du des Ar- men dich gnä- dig er- bar- men?

No. 8. Wir müssen uns trennen

Wir müs- sen uns tren- nen, ge- lieb- tes Sai- ten- spiel, Zeit ist es,

No. 9. Ruhe, Süssliebchen

Ru- he, Süss- lieb- chen, im Schat- ten der grü- nen,

No. 11. Wie schnell ver- schwindet

Wie schnell ver- schwin- det so Licht als Glanz, der Mor- gen fin- det

No. 12. Muss es eine Trennung geben

Muss es ei- ne Tren- nung ge- ben, die das treu- e Herz zer- brich

No. 14. Wie froh und frisch

Wie froh und frisch mein Sinn sich hebt, zu- rück bleibt al- les,

BRAHMS

Magelone Romanzen, Op. 33, No. 15 Treue Liebe
Treu-e Lie-be dau-ert lan-ge ü-ber-le-bet man-che, man-che Stund — A

Von ewiger Liebe, Op. 43, No. 1
Dun-kel, wie dun-kel in Wald und in Feld! A-bend schon ist es, — B

Die Mainacht, No. 2
Wann der sil-ber-ne Mond durch die Ge-sträu-che blinkt — C

An die Nachtigall, Op. 46, No. 4
Geuss nicht so laut der lieb-ent-flamm-ten Lie-der ton-rei-chen Schall — D

Botschaft, Op. 47, No. 1
We-he, Lüft-chen lind und lieb-lich um — Wan-ge der Ge-lieb-ten — E

Sonntag, No. 3
So hab ich doch die gan-ze Wo-che mein fei-nes Lieb-chen — F

O liebliche Wangen, No. 4
O lieb-li-che Wan-gen, ihr macht mir Ver-lan-gen — G

Der Gang zum Liebchen, Op. 48, No. 1
Es glänzt der mond nie-der, ich soll-te doch wie-der — H

Der Überläufer, No. 2
In den Gar-ten wol-len wir ge-hen, wo die schö-nen Ro-sen — I

Am Sonntag Morgen, Op. 49, No. 1
Am Sonn-tag Mor-gen zier-lich an-ge-tan wohl weiss ich — J

Sehnsucht, No. 3
Hin-ter — je-nen dich-ten — Wäl-dern weilst du, — K

Wiegenlied (Cradle Song), No. 4
Gu-ten A-bend, gut Nacht mit Ro-sen be-dacht — L

Wenn du nur zuweilen lächelst, Op. 57, No. 2
Wenn du nur zu-wei-len lä-chelst, nur zu-wei-len — M

Es träumte mir, No. 3
Es träum-te mir, ich sei dir teu - - - er doch zu er-wa-chen — N

Ach, wende diesen Blick, No. 4
Ach, wen-de die-sen Blick, wen-de dies An-ge-sicht! — O

Die Schnur, die Perl an Perle, No. 7
Die Schnur, die Perl an Per - - le um dei-nen Hals — P

Blinde Kuh, Op. 58, No. 1
In Fin-stern geh ich su-chen, mein Kind, wo steckst du wohl? — Q

O komme, hoide Sommernacht, No. 4
O kom-me, hol-de Som-mer-nacht, ver-schwie-gen; — R

Schwermut, No. 5
Mir ist so weh ums Herz, mir ist, als ob ich wei-nen möch-te vor Schmerz — S

BRAHMS
Songs

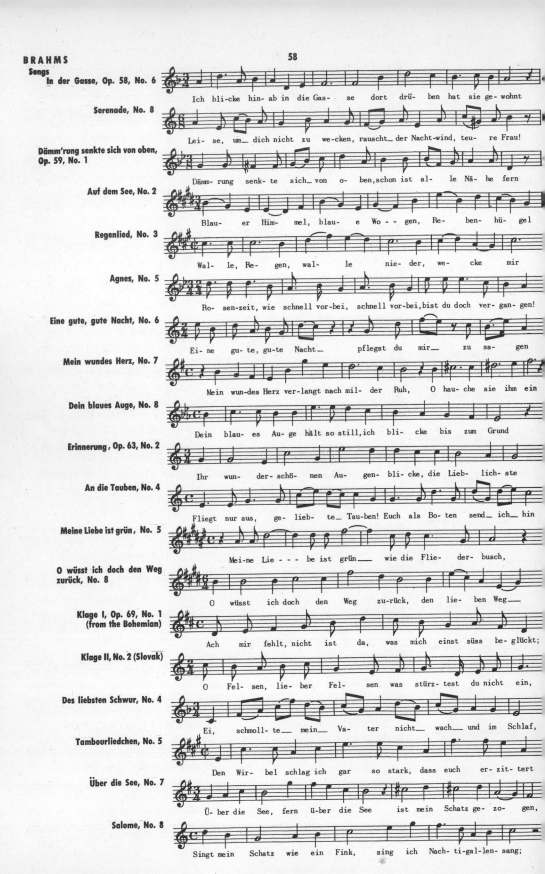

In der Gasse, Op. 58, No. 6

Ich bli-cke hin- ab in die Gas- se dort drü- ben hat sie ge- wohnt

Serenade, No. 8

Lei- se, um_ dich nicht zu we-cken, rauscht_ der Nacht-wind, teu- re Frau!

Dämm'rung senkte sich von oben, Op. 59, No. 1

Dämm- rung senk- te sich_ von o- ben, schon ist al- le Nä- he fern

Auf dem See, No. 2

Blau- er Him- mel, blau- e Wo- gen, Re- ben- hü- gel

Regenlied, No. 3

Wal- le, Re- gen, wal- le nie- der, we- cke mir

Agnes, No. 5

Ro- sen-zeit, wie schnell vor-bei, schnell vor-bei, bist du doch ver- gan- gen!

Eine gute, gute Nacht, No. 6

Ei- ne gu- te, gu-te Nacht_ pflegst du mir_ zu sa- gen

Mein wundes Herz, No. 7

Mein wun-des Herz ver-langt nach mil- der Ruh, O hau- che sie ihm ein

Dein blaues Auge, No. 8

Dein blau- es Au- ge hält so still, ich bli- cke bis zum Grund

Erinnerung, Op. 63, No. 2

Ihr wun- der- schö- nen Au- gen- bli- cke, die Lieb- lich- ste

An die Tauben, No. 4

Fliegt nur aus, ge- lieb- te_ Tau-ben! Euch als Bo- ten send_ ich_ hin

Meine Liebe ist grün, No. 5

Mei-ne Lie - - - be ist grün_ wie die Flie- der- busch,

O wüsst ich doch den Weg zurück, No. 8

O wüsst ich doch den Weg zu-rück, den lie- ben Weg_

Klage I, Op. 69, No. 1 (from the Bohemian)

Ach mir fehlt, nicht ist da, was mich einst süss be- glückt;

Klage II, No. 2 (Slovak)

O Fel- sen, lie- ber Fel- sen was stürz- test du nicht ein,

Des liebsten Schwur, No. 4

Ei, schmoll- te_ mein_ Va- ter nicht_ wach_ und im Schlaf,

Tambourliedchen, No. 5

Den Wir- bel schlag ich gar so stark, dass euch er- zit- tert

Über die See, No. 7

Ü- ber die See, fern ü-ber die See ist mein Schatz ge- zo- gen,

Salome, No. 8

Singt mein Schatz wie ein Fink, sing ich Nach- ti- gal- len- sang;

Songs

Mädchenfluch, Op. 69, No. 9

Ruft die Mut-ter, ruft die Toch-ter ü-ber drei Ge-bir-ge:

Gä-be Gott im hel-len Him-mel dass er sich er-hän-ge

Lerchengesang, Op. 70, No. 2

Ae-the-ri-sche fer-ne Stim-men, der Ler-chen himm-li-sche Grü-sse,

Es liebt sich so lieblich im Lenze, Op. 71, No. 1

Die Wel-len blin-ken und flie-ssen da-hin, es liebt sich so lieb-lich

An den Mond, No. 2

Sil - - ber-mond, mit blei-chen Strahlen pflegst du Wald und Feld zu ma-len

Geheimnis, No. 3

O Früh-lings-a-bend-däm-me-rung! O lau-es lin-des Wehn,

Willst du dass ich geh? No. 4

Auf der Hei-de weht der Wind, her-zig Kind, her-zig Kind

Minnelied, No. 5

Hol-der klingt der Vo-gel-sang, wenn die En-gel-rei - - ne,

Alte Liebe, Op. 72, No. 1

Es kehrt die dunk-le Schwal-be aus fer-nem Land zu-rück

O kühler Wald, No. 3

O küh-ler Wald wo rau-schest du, in dem mein Lieb-chen geht?

Verzagen, No. 4

Ich sitz am Stran-de der rau-schen-den See und su-che dort nach Ruh,

Sommerabend, Op. 84, No. 1

Geh schla-fen, Toch-ter, schla-fen! Schon fällt der Tau aufs Gras,

Der Kranz, No. 2

Mut-ter, hilf mir ar-men Toch-ter, sieh nur, was ein Kna-be tat

Vergebliches Ständchen, No. 4

Gu-ten A-bend, mein Schatz, Gu-ten A-bend, mein Kind,

Mondenschein, Op. 85, No. 2

Nacht liegt auf den frem-den We-gen, Kran-kes Herz und mü-de Glie-der

Mädchenlied, No. 3

Ach, und du mein küh-les Was-ser! Ach, und du mein ro-tes Rös-lein!

In Waldeseinsamkeit, No. 6

Ich sass zu dei-nen Fü-ssen in Wal-des-ein-sam-keit;

Therese, Op. 86, No. 1

Du milch-jun-ger Kna-be, wie schaust du mich an?

Feldeinsamkeit, No. 2

Ich ru-he still im ho-hen grü-nen Gras und sen-de lan-ge

59

BRAHMS

Songs
Über die Heide, Op. 86, No. 4

Ü-ber die Hei- de hal-let mein Schritt, dumpf aus der Er- de wan-dert es mit.

Todessehnen, No. 6

Ach, wer nimmt von mei-ner See-le die ge-hei- me, schwe-re Last,

Two Songs for Alto, Viola and Piano, Op. 91,
No. 1 Gestillte Sehnsucht
(also theme of viola)

In gold-nen A- bend-schein ge-tau-chet, wie fei-er-lich

Was_ lis - - - peln die Win- de, die_ Vö - - - ge - - lein?_

No. 2 Geistliches Wiegenlied
(Viola theme; old German folk tune)

Jo- sef, lie-ber Jo- sef mein, hilf mir wieg'n mein Kind-lein fein

Die ihr schwe- bet um die-se Pal-men in Nacht_ und Wind

Mit vierzig Jahren, Op. 94, No. 1

Mit vier-zig Jah-ren ist der Berg ge-stie - - - gen, wir ste-hen still

Steig auf, geliebter Schatten, No. 2

Steig auf, ge-lieb- ter Schat- ten, vor mir in to-ter Nacht

Sapphische Ode, No. 4

Ro- sen brach ich Nachts mir am dunk- len Ha - - - ge;

Kein haus, keine Heimat, No. 5

Kein Haus, Kei- ne Hei- mat, kein Weib und kein Kind,

Das Mädchen, Op. 95, No. 1

Stand das Mäd-chen, stand am Ber-ges-ab-hang, wi-der-schien der Berg

Bei dir sind meine Gedanken, No. 2

Bei dir sind mei- ne Ge- dan- ken und flat- tern, flat- tern

Der Jäger, No. 4

Mein Lieb ist ein Jä- ger, und grün ist sein Kleid,

Vorschneller Schwur, No. 5

Schwor ein jun - - ges_ Mäd-chen: Blu-men nie zu_ tra- gen,

Mädchenlied, No. 6

Am jüngsten Tag ich auf-er-steh und gleich nach mei-nem_ Lieb- sten seh

Schön war, das ich dir weihte, No. 7

Schön war, das ich dir weih- te, das gol-de- ne Ge-schmei- de

Der Tod, das ist die kühle Nacht, Op. 96, No. 1

Der Tod, das ist die küh- le Nacht, Das Le-ben ist der schwü- le Tag

Wir wandelten, No. 2

Wir wan-del-ten, wir zwei zu- sam- men Ich_ war so still

Es schauen die Blumen, No. 3

Es schau- en die Blu-men al- le zur leuch-ten-den Son- ne hin- auf;

BRAHMS

Songs

Meerfahrt, Op. 96, No. 4 — A
Mein Lieb- chen, wir sa-ssen bei sa- men trau- lich

Nachtigall, Op. 97, No. 1 — B
O Nach- ti- gall, dein sü- sser Schall, er- drin- get_ mir

Auf dem Schiffe, No. 2 — C
Ein Vö- ge- lein fliegt ü- ber den Rhein und wiegt_ die Flü- gel

Dort in den Weiden, No. 4 — D
Dort in den Wei- den steht ein Haus, da schaut die Magd zum Fen- ster 'naus!

Komm bald, No. 5 — E
Wa-rum denn war- ten von Tag zu Tag? Es blüht im Gar- ten was blü-hen mag.

Wie Melodien zieht es mir, Op. 105, No. 1 — F
Wie Me- lo- di - - en_ zieht es mir lei- se durch den Sinn

Immer leiser wird mein Schlummer, No. 2 — G
Im- mer lei- ser wird mein Schlum- mer nur wie Schlei- er

Auf dem Kirchhofe, No. 4 — H
Der Tag ging re- gen-schwer und sturm- be- wegt, ich war

Verrat, No. 5 — I
Ich stand in ei- ner lau- en Nacht an ei- ner grü- nen Lin- de

Ständchen, Op. 106, No. 1 — J
Der Mond steht ü- ber dem Ber- ge, so recht für ver- lieb- te

Es hing der Reif, No. 3 — K
Es hing der Reif im Lin- den- baum, wo- durch das Licht

Meine Lieder, No. 4 — L
Wenn mein Herz be- ginnt_ zu klin- gen und den Tö- nen

Ein Wanderer, No. 5 — M
Hier_ wo_ sich die Stra- ssen_ schei- den, wo_ nun gehn die We- ge_ hin?

Das Mädchen spricht, Op. 107, No. 3 — N
Schwal- be, sing mir_ an 'Ist's dein_ al- ter_ Mann

Maienkätzchen, No. 4 — O
Mai- en- kätz- chen er- ster Gruss, ich bre-che euch und ste- cke euch

Mädchenlied, No. 5 — P
Auf die Nacht in den Spinn-stubn, da_ sin- gen die Mäd- chen,

Vier ernste Gesänge (Four serious songs) Op. 121, No. 1 — Q
Denn es ge- het dem Men - schen_ wie dem Vieh,

No. 2 — R
Ich wand- te mich, und sa- he an al- le,

No. 3 — S
O Tod, O Tod, wie bit - - - ter, wie bit - - - ter bist du

BRAHMS
Songs and Duets:
   Vier ernste Gesänge (Four
   serious songs) Op. 121, No. 4

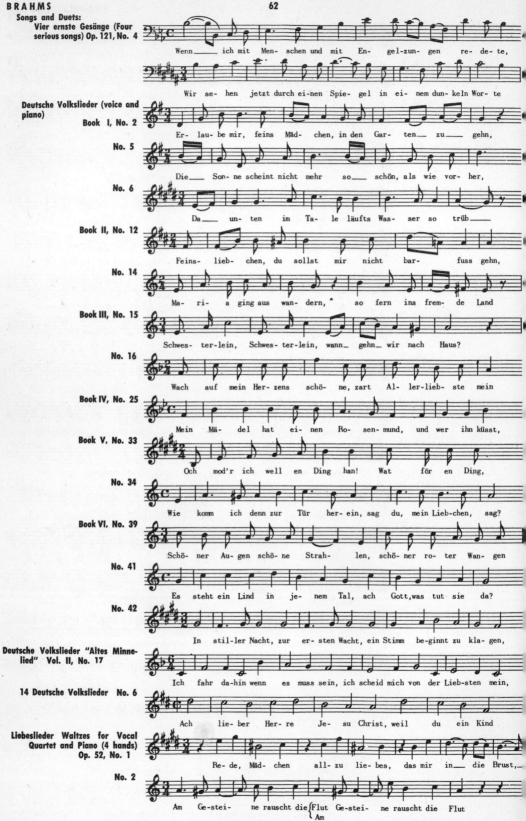

Wenn___ ich mit Men-schen und mit En-gel-zun-gen re-de-te,

Wir se-hen jetzt durch ei-nen Spie-gel in ei-nem dun-keln Wor-te

Deutsche Volkslieder (voice and piano)
   Book I, No. 2

Er-lau-be mir, feins Mäd-chen, in den Gar-ten zu___ gehn,

No. 5

Die___ Son-ne scheint nicht mehr so___ schön, als wie vor-her,

No. 6

Da un-ten im Ta-le läufts Was-ser so trüb___

Book II, No. 12

Feins-lieb-chen, du sollst mir nicht bar-___ fuss gehn,

No. 14

Ma-ri-a ging aus wan-dern, so fern ins frem-de Land

Book III, No. 15

Schwes-ter-lein, Schwes-ter-lein, wann___ gehn wir nach Haus?

No. 16

Wach auf mein Her-zens schö-ne, zart Al-ler-lieb-ste mein

Book IV, No. 25

Mein Mä-del hat ei-nen Ro-sen-mund, und wer ihn küsst,

Book V, No. 33

Och mod'r ich well en Ding han! Wat för en Ding,

No. 34

Wie komm ich denn zur Tür her-ein, sag du, mein Lieb-chen, sag?

Book VI, No. 39

Schö-ner Au-gen schö-ne Strah-len, schö-ner ro-ter Wan-gen

No. 41

Es steht ein Lind in je-nem Tal, ach Gott, was tut sie da?

No. 42

In stil-ler Nacht, zur er-sten Wacht, ein Stimm be-ginnt zu kla-gen,

Deutsche Volkslieder "Altes Minne-lied" Vol. II, No. 17

Ich fahr da-hin wenn es muss sein, ich scheid mich von der Lieb-sten mein,

14 Deutsche Volkslieder No. 6

Ach lie-ber Her-re Je-su Christ, weil du ein Kind

Liebeslieder Waltzes for Vocal Quartet and Piano (4 hands) Op. 52, No. 1

Re-de, Mäd-chen all-zu lie-bes, das mir in___ die Brust,

No. 2

Am Ge-stei- ne rauscht die {Flut Ge-stei- ne rauscht die Flut
                             {Am

Liebeslieder Waltzes, Op. 52, No. 3

O die Frau- en   O die Frau- en   wie sie Won- ne,   A

No. 4

Wie des A- bends schö- ne Rö- te   möcht ich ar- me   B

No. 5

Die grü- ne Hop- fen- ran- ke, sie schlän- gelt auf der Er- de hin   C

No. 6

Ein klei- ner, hüb- scher Vo- gel nahm den Flug zum Gar- ten hin,   D

No. 7

Wohl schön be- wandt war es vor- e- he mit mei- nem Leb- en   E

No. 8

Wenn so lind dein Au- ge mir   und so lieb - - - lich schau- et,   F

No. 9

Am Do- nau- stran- de,   Da steht ein Haus,   G

No. 10

O   wie sanft die Quel- le sich durch die Wie - se   H

No. 11

Nein, es ist nicht aus- zu- kom- men mit den Leu- ten;   I

No. 12

Schlos- ser auf! Schlos- ser auf, und ma- che Schlös- ser,   J

No. 13

Vö- ge- lein   durch- rauscht die Luft, durch- rauscht   die Luft,   K

No. 14

Sieh, wie ist die Wel - le klar,   blickt der Mond her- nie- der   L

No. 15

Nach- ti- gall, sie singt   so schön, wenn die Ster- ne   M

No. 16

Ein dun- ke- ler Schacht ist Lie- be, ein gar zu ge- fahr- li- cher Bron- nen;   N

No. 17

Nicht wand- le, mein licht;   dort aus- sen im Flur- be- reich!   O

No. 18

Es be- bet das Ge- sträu- che, ge- streift hat es im Flu- ge   P

BRETON, Tomás (1850-1923)

Jota, from La Dolores (opera)

Gran- de co- mo el mis- mo sol   Es la jo- ta   R

64

BREWER, A. Herbert (1865-1928)

The Fairy Pipers
By permission Boosey & Hawkes, Inc., copyright owners

When all the birds are gone to sleep and all the pi-pers still,

Come out! Come out! Lis-ten on the air! Up there! Down there!

BRIDGE, Frank (1879-1941)

Love Went A-Riding
Copyright by Boston Music Co.

Love_____ went a-ri - - - - ding, Love_____ went a-ri - - - - ding

O That It Were So

BRITTEN, Benjamin (1913-   )

The Ash Grove (arr.)
By permission Boosey & Hawkes, Inc., copyright owners

Down yon-der green val-ley where stream-lets__ me - - an-der

Folk Songs:
By permission Boosey & Hawkes, Inc., copyright owners

La Belle est au jardin d'amour

La belle est au jar - din d'a - mour

The Bonny Earl o Moray

Ye Hie-lands and ye Low-lands,__ O where hae ye been? They hae slain the Earl

Come you not from Newcastle

Come you not from New- cas- tle?__ Come you not there a- way?__

The foggy, foggy dew

When I was a bach-elor I lived all a-lone and worked

Heigh ho, heigh hi!

Oh I lived with my dad- dy, an ap- prent- ice was I,

Little Sir William

Eas- ter day was a ho- li- day of all days in the year

Oliver Cromwell

Ol- i- ver Crom- well lay bur-ied and dead, Hee- haw

The Plough Boy

A flax- en head- ed cow- boy, as sim-ple as may be,

Le Roi s'en va-t-en chasse

Le roi s'en va- t'en chas- se, dans le bois des_ Bour- bons__

The Sally Gardens

Down__ by the Sal- ly_ Gar- dens my__ love and I did meet,

Serenade for Tenor, Horn and Strings, Op. 31, No. 1 Pastoral (Cotton)
By permission Boosey & Hawkes, Inc., copyright owners

The Day's grown old; the faint- ing Sun Has but a lit-tle way

Serenade for Tenor, Horn and Strings, Op. 31,
No. 2 Nocturne (Tennyson)

A

The splen - - dour falls__ on cas- tle walls__ and snow- y sum- mits

No. 3 Elegy (Blake)

B

O Rose, "thou art sick; The in- vi- si-ble worm That flies__ in the night,

No. 4 Dirge (anon. 15th cent.)

C

This ae nighte, this ae nighte e- ver- y night and alle,

No. 5 Hymn (Ben Jonson)

D

Queen and hunt- ress chaste and fair___ Now the sun is laid to sleep

No. 6 Sonnet (Keats)

E

O soft__ em- balmer of the still mid-night, Shutting with care-ful fin-gers

Seven Sonnets of Michelangelo, Op. 22 Sonetto XVI
By permission Boosey & Hawkes, Inc., copyright owners

F

Si co- me nel- la pe- na e nell' in- chio- stro

XXIV

G

Spir- to ben na- to, in cui si spec- chia e ve- de

XXX

H

Veg- gio co' bei__ vo- stri oc-chi un dol- ce lu- me__

XXXI

I

A che più debb' io mai l'in-ten- sa vog- lia__ Sfo- gar con pian ti

XXXII

J

S'un casto a-mor, s'u- na pie- tà su- per- na, S'u- na for- tu- na

XXXVIII

K

Ren- de-te a gli oc-chi miei, O fon- te o fiu- me,__ ren-de- te__

LV

L

Tu sa' ch'io so, si- gnior mie, che tu sai__ Ch'i ven - - ni

BRUCH, Max (1838-1920)

Odysseus, Op. 41, No. 8
By permission Associated Music Publishers, Inc.

N

Ich wob__ dies Ge- wand mit Thrä- nen am Ta- ge

BRUCK, Arnold Von (16th Cent.)

Aus tiefer Not (4-part chorus)

P

Aus tie- fer Not schrei ich zu dir, Herr Gott, er- hör

BRUCKNER, Anton (1824-1896)

Ave Maria (chorus)
By permission Associated Music Publishers, Inc.

R

A- ve Ma- ri- a gra-ti- a ple- na Do- mi-nus te- cum

Herbstlied (chorus)

S

Durch die Wäl-der streif' ich mun-ter, wenn der Wind die Stäm- me rüt-telt,

Mass in E Minor
No. 1 Kyrie

Ky- ri- e e- le- i- son   Ky- ri- e   e- le- i- son

No. 2 Gloria in Excelsis Deo

Et in ter- ra pax ho- mi- ni- bus bo- nae vo- lun- ta- tis

No. 3 Credo in unum Deum

Pa- trem o- mni- po- ten- tem, fac- to- rem coe- li et ter- rae,

Et___ in- car- na- - tus est de Spi- ri- tu san- cto,

No. 4 Sanctus

San - - - - - - - ctus, san - - - - - - - - - -ctus, san - - - - - - - -ctus

No. 5 Benedictus

Be- ne- di- ctus, Be- ne- di- ctus be- ne- di- ctus

No. 6 Agnus Dei

Ag- nus De- i, qui tol- lis pec- ca- ta mun - - - - di

No. 7 Tota Pulchra es Maria
(Antiphon) (chorus)

To- ta pul- chra es Ma- ri- a. To- ta pul- chra es Ma- ri- a

BRUNEAU, Alfred (1857-1934)

Adieu forêt profonde, from L'Attaque
du Moulin, Op. 22 (opera)
Copyright by Choudens fils, Paris

A -dieu,___ fo- rêt pro- fon- de, a- dieu,___ géante a- mi- e,___

BUCK, Dudley (1839-1909)

Fear ye not, O Israel

Fear___ ye not, O Is- ra- el,___ nei- ther be thou still dis- may- ed

My Redeemer and my Lord
Copyright by John Church Co.
Used by permission

My Re- deem- er, My Re- deem- er and my Lord

Sunset, Op. 76, No. 4

Look off dear love a- cross the sal- low sands,

The Virgin's Lullaby
Copyright 1895, G. Schirmer, Inc.

Sleep, my Je- su sleep, my best,___ In thy lone- ly man- ger rest___

BULL, Ole (1810-1880)

Saeterjendens Söndag (The Herdgirl's
Sunday)

I gaze on the sun, it mounts in the sky, The hour soon for mass

BULLARD, Frederic Field (1864-1904)

The Stein Song
Copyright by Oliver Ditson Co.
Used by permission

Give a rouse, then, in the May- time for a life that knows no fear

The Stein Song

For it's al-ways good wea-ther, when good fel-lows get to-geth-er,

Winter Song
Copyright by Oliver Ditson Co.
Used by permission

Ho, a song by the fire! Pass the pipes, pass the bowl!

BUNGERT, August (1846-1915)

Ich hab' ein kleines Lied erdacht,
Op. 49, No. 9

Ich hab ein klei-nes Lied er-dacht und hab' es ge-sun-gen

BUONONCINI, Giovanni (1640-1703)

Deh piu a me non v'ascondete

Deh più a me nom v'as-con-de-te lu-ci va-ghe del mio sol,

Per la gloria d'adorarvi

Per la glo - - - ria d'a - - - - do-rar - - - - vi

Pupille nere

Pu-pil-le ne-re, Se voi guar-da-te, Ce-der voi fa-te,

Vado ben spesso

Va-do ben spes-so can-gian-do loco,

BURLEIGH, Harry Thacker (1866-   )

Arrangements of Negro Spirituals:
By an' By
Copyright by G. Ricordi & Co., Inc.

Oh by an' by by an' by, I'm goin' to lay down dis heavy load

Deep River

Deep riv-er, my home is o-ver Jor-dan

Go down, Moses

When Is-rael was in E-gypt's lan' Let my peo-ple go,

Go down, Mo-ses, way down to E-gypt's lan'

Hard Trials

Been a-lis'-nin' all de night long, Been a-lis'-nin' all de day

Now ain't dem hard tri-als Great trib-u-la-tion,

Heav'n, Heav'n (I got a robe)

I got a robe, You got a robe, All of God's chil-dren got a robe

I don't feel no-ways tired

I am seek-in' for a ci-ty, Hal-le-lu - - - - - ja!

Lord, I don't feel no ways tir-ed, Chil-da-ren! Oh, Glo-ry

BURLEIGH

Arrangements of Negro Spirituals:
I want to be ready

I want to be read-y I want to be read-y

Nobody Knows de Trouble I've Seen

No-bod-y knows de trou-ble I've seen, No-bod-y knows but Je-sus

Oh, Didn't It Rain

Fo'-ty days fo'-ty nights when de rain kept a-fall-in

Oh, Peter, Go ring-a dem bells

Oh, Pe-ter, go ring-a dem bells, Pe-ter, go ring-a dem bells.

Sinner, please doan let dis Harves' Pass

Sin-ner, please doan let dis har-ves' pass;_____ Sin-ner please

Swing Low Sweet Chariot

Swing low sweet char-i-ot,_____ Com-ing for to car-ry me home

Were You There?

Were you there when they cru-ci-fied my Lord?_____ Were you there

BUSCA, Padre Ludovico (17th Cent.)

Bionda, bionda Clori

Bion-da,bion-da Clo-ri bion-da Clo-ri che nel vol-to hai rac-col-to

Occhi belli

Oc-chi bel-li, non ful-mi-na-te,non ful-mi-na - - - - - - - - - - - te,

BUTTERWORTH, George (1885-1916)

A Shropshire Lad
By permission of Augener, Ltd., London

With rue my heart is lad-en For gold-en friends I had,

When the lad for long-ing sighs, Mute and dull of cheer and pale,

Oh fair e-nough are sky and plain but I know fair-er far

Bredon Hill

In sum-mer-time on Bre-don the bells they sound so clear;_____

Love- liest of trees, the cher-ry now is hung with bloom a-long the bough

Is my team plough-ing, That I was used to drive,

BUXTEHUDE, Dietrich (1637-1707)

CANTATAS:
Aperite mihi portas justitiae
(Ugrino No. 71)

A-pe- ri-te, a-pe- ri-te, a-pe- ri-te, a-pe- ri-té

CANTATAS:
- Aperite mihi portas justitiae (Ugrino No. 71) — Be- ne- dic- tus, qui ven- it, qui ve- nit qui ve- nit
- Jubilate Domino (Ugrino No. 19) — Ju- bi- la- te, Ju- bi- la- te, Ju- bi- la- te Do- mi- no,
- O fröhliche Stunden (Ugrino No. 12) — O fröh- li- che Stun-den, o fröh- li- che Zeit, es hat ü- ber wun-den,
- Singet dem Herrn (Ugrino No. 16) — Sin - - - - - - get, Sin - - - - - - get dem Her- ren__ ein_ neu-es Lied
- Was mich auf dieser Welt betrübt (Ugrino No. 71) — Was mich auf die- ser Welt be-trübt, das wäh-ret kur- ze Zeit,
- Missa Brevis (Ugrino No. 42) Kyrie — Ky- ri- e- e- lei - - - - - - - - - - - - - son
- Gloria — Et in ter- ra pax ho- mi - - - - - ni- bus

BUZZI-PECCIA, A. (1853-1943)

- Colombetta — *Copyright by G. Ricordi & Co., Inc.* — La bel- la Co- lom-bet- ta Al cal- do si ri- po- sa,
- Lolita — *Copyright by G. Ricordi & Co., Inc.* — A- mor, a- mor che lan- gue il cor,

BYRD, William (1543-1623)

MADRIGALS:
- I thought that love had been a boy (5-part madrigal) — I thought that love had been a boy, I thought that love had__ been a boy
- Lullaby, my sweet little baby — Lul- la, lul- la, Lul- la, lul- la- by, lul- la- by___
- Though Amaryllis Dance — Though A- ma- ry- lis dance in green, like fai- ry Queen
- This sweet and merry month — This sweet and mer-ry, mer-ry month, and mer-ry, mer-ry month of__ May
- Mass (five voices) I Kyrie Eleison — Ky- ri- e e- lei - - - - - - - - - - son
- II Gloria in excelsis — Et in ter- ra pax ho- mi - - - - - - - ni- bus
- III Credo — Pa- trem om- ni- po- ten- tem, fac- to- rem coe - - - - - li et ter-rae
- IV Sanctus — Sanc - - - - tus, Sanc - - - - - tus, sanc - - - - - -tus,

Four American Indian Songs, Op. 45, No. 4

The moon drops low that once soared high as an ea- gle — A

A Moonlight Song, Op. 42, No. 2
Copyright 1933, G. Schirmer, Inc.

The moon- light shim-mers thro' the vine___ That to_ my_ porch — B

CALDARA, Antonio (1670-1736)

Come raggio di sol

Co- me rag- gio di sol mi te_e se- re- no — D

Mirti, Faggi

Mir- ti, fag- gi tron- chi e fron- de — E

Selve amiche, ombrose piante

Sel- ve a- mi- che, om- bro-se pian- te, fi- do al- ber- go — F

CALLCOTT, Dr. (1766-1821)

To all you ladies now at land

To all you La- dies now at land We men at sea in- dite — H

Ye Mariners of England

Ye Ma- ri- ners of___ Eng- land that guard our na- tive seas — I

While the storm- y winds do blow,___ While the storm- y winds do blow___ — J

CAMPBELL-TIPTON, Louis (1877-1921)

The Crying of Water
Copyright 1907, G. Schirmer, Inc.

O wa- ter,___ voice of my heart___ cry- ing in_ the sand, — L

A Spirit Flower
Copyright 1908, G. Schirmer, Inc.

My heart was fro- zen e- ven as the earth_____ — M

Down through the win- ter sun- shine snow flakes came, All shim-m'ring — N

CAMPION, Thomas (1567-1620)

The Cypress curtain of the night

The cy- press cur- tain of the night is spread — P

Follow thy fair sun

Fol- low thy fair sun, un- hap- py sha- dow. Though thou — Q

Follow your saint

Fol- low your saint, fol- low with ac- cents sweet; — R

My Sweetest Lesbia

My sweet- est Les- bia, let us live and love And though the sag- er sort ... A

When to her lute Corinna sings

When to her lute Co- rin- na sings, her voice re- vives ... B

Never weather-beaten sail

Nev- er weath- er beat- en sail more will- ing bent to shore, ... C

What if a day, or a month, or a year

What if a day, or a month or a year, crown thy de- lights ... D

CAMPRA, André (1660-1744)

Charmant papillon, from Les Fêtes Vénitiennes

Char- mant pa- pil- lon dont l'ai ---- le d'or pas- se ... F

CANTELOUBE, Joseph (1879-   )

Chants d'Auvergne:
Series I,
No. 2 Baïlèro
By permission Heugel & Cie, Paris, copyright owners

Pas- tré, dè dè- laï l'a- io, a gaï-ré de boun tèn dio lou bai- lè- ro ... H

No. 3 (a)   L'aïo de Rotso

L'a- io dè rot- so te fo- ro mou- rir fi- lho- to, ... I

(b)   Ound' onoren gorda?

Ound' o- no- ren gor- da pit- chou no droou- lè- to? ... J

(c)   Obal din lou Limouzi

O- bal din lou Li- mou- zi, pit-choun' o- bal din lou Li- mou- zi ... K

Series II,
No. 2 L'Antouèno (L'Antoine)

Quond o- no- rèn o lo fiè- iro, ié! ... Quond o- no- rèn ... L

No. 5 (a) Je n'ai pas d'amie

N'aï pas ièu dè mi- o, soui qu'un pas- tou- rel ... M

(b) Lo Calhé (La Caille)

E, dio mè tu, lo cal- hé, ound as toun nîou?

Series III,
No. 1 Lo Fiolaire (La Fileuse)

Ton qu'è- rè pit-chou- nè- lo Gor- da- vè loui mou- tous,

No. 2 Passo pel prat

Lo lo lo lo lo lo lo lo lo lo lo lo lo

Pas- so pel prat bè- lo-' to Jeu pos- so- rai

No. 4 Brezaviola (Berceuse)

Soun, soun, bè- ni, bè- ni, bè- ni, soun, soun, bè- ni, bè- ni doun,

No. 5 Malurous qu'o uno fenno

Ma- lu- rous qu'o u- no fen- no, Ma- lu- rous qué n'o cat!

CAPLET, André (1878-1925)

Cinq Ballades françaises,
from La Ronde, No. 2
By permission Durand & Cie, Paris;
Elkan-Vogel Co., Inc., Phila.,
copyright owners

Si toutes les filles du monde___ vou-laient s'don-ner la main

Le Forêt
By permission Durand & Cie, Paris;
Elkan-Vogel Co., Inc., Phila.,
copyright owners

O___ Fo-rêt,___ toi___ qui vis pas-ser bien des a-mants

Les Prières
1. Oraison dominicale
By permission Durand & Cie, Paris;
Elkan-Vogel, Inc., Phila.,
copyright owners

Au nom du Père, du Fils, du Saint Esprit.___ Ain-si soit- il

2. Salutation angélique

Je vous sa-lue, Ma-ri- e, pleine de gra-ce

3. Symboles des Apôtres

Je crois en Dieu,___ le Pè- re tout puis-sant,

CAPUA, Eduardo (-1917)

Maria, Marì (Oh, Marie)
Copyright by Mills Music, Inc., N.Y.

A- ra-pe-te fe- ne-sta, fam, m'af-fac-ciz a Ma-ri- a___

O Ma-rì! O Ma- rì!___ quan-ta suon-no ca per-de pe' te___

O Sole Mio
Copyright by Boston Music Co.

Che bel- la co-sa 'na iur-na-ta'e so- le, n'a-ria se- re- na

Ma n'a-tu so- le- cchiù bel- lo ohi-ne',___ o so-le mi-o___

CARDILLO, S.

Core'ngrato
Copyright by G. Ricordi & Co., Inc.

Ca- ta- rì, Ca- ta- rì, pec-chè me di-ce-sti pa-ro-le_a-ma-re

CAREY, Henry (1690-1743)

A Pastoral

Flocks are sport - - - - ing, doves are court - - - ing

Sally in our alley: Two versions
No. 1, words by Carey
Tune "The Country Lass"

Of all the girls___ that are so smart___ there's none like pret-ty Sal-ly;

No. 2, words and music by Carey

Of___ all the girls that_are so smart, There's_none like pret-ty Sal-ly;

CARISSIMI, Giacomo (1605-1674)

A morire!

A- mo- ri- re, a mo-ri- re, a mo- ri- - re!

Deh, contentatevi

Deh, deh con- ten- ta- te- vi ch'io mi la- men- ti

Filli, non t'amo più

Fil- li non t'a- mo più e se nol cre- di a me,

L'Histoire d' Ezechias (motet for tenor)

Ob- se- cro, dó- mi- ne, me- men- to quae- so, quo mo- do

No, no, mio core

No, no, mio co- re, no! No, no! Non in- gol- far- ti!

No, no, non si speri!

No, no, non si spe- ri È mor- ta la spe- me!

Piangete, ohimè

Pian- ge- te ohi- mè, pian- ge- te, pian- ge- te ohi- mè, pian- ge- te,

Vittoria mio core!

Vit- to- ria, vit- to- ria, vit- to- ria, vit- to- ria,

Gia l'em- pia ai tuoi dan- ni Fra can- dor di sguar- di

CARPENTER, John Alden (1876-   )

Gitanjali (song cycle)
No. 1
Copyright 1914, G. Schirmer, Inc.

When I bring to you col- our'd toys, my child,___ I un- der- stand

No. 2

The sleep that flits___ on ba- by's eyes, does a- ny- bo- dy know___

The Home Road
Copyright 1932, G. Schirmer, Inc.

Sing a song of Free- dom, Fling the ban- ner high!

Serenade
Copyright 1921, G. Schirmer, Inc.

You___ were glad to- night___ And now___ you've gone a- way.___

CATALANI, Alfredo (1854-1893)

Loreley (opera)
Act I

Nel ver- de mag- gio, un dì___ dal bo- sco a___ que- sta spiag- gia

O for- ze, o for- ze re- con - - - - di- te___

Act III

Deh! deh! ti ram- men- ta___ quel dì be- a- to

La Wally (opera)
Act I

T'a- mo ben i- o! E sei dentro al mio co- re

Eb- ben? Ne an- drò lon- ta- na, come va l'e- co del- la pia cam- pa- na-

La Wally (opera)

Act III — Nè mai dun-que avro pa-ce? E da pen-sie — ri tri-sti

Act IV — M'hai sal-va-to, hai vo-lu-to obli-ar l'of-fe — sa mi-a

CAVALLI, Francesco (1602-1676)

...to chi può, from Serse (opera) — Be-a-to chi può Lon-tan del-le cor-ti Go-der quel-le sor-ti

...ell' antro magico, from Giasone (opera) — Dell' an-tro ma-gi-co Stri-den-ti car-di-ni il var-co a-pri-te-mi

Donzelle, fuggite — Don-zel-le, fug-gi-te pro-ca-ce bel-ta

CESTI, Marc'Antonio (1623-1669)

...r of Venus, from Il Pomo d'oro (opera) — Ah! quan-to è ve-ro, che il nu-do ar-cie-ro

Intorno all' idol mio — In-tor-no al-l'i-dol mi-o o spi-ra-te pur, —

CHABRIER, Emmanuel (1841-1894)

Ballade des gros Dindons — Les gros din-dons, à tra-vers champs, D'un pas so-lon-nel et tran-quil-le,

L'Île Heureuse — Dans le gol-fe aux jar-dins om-breux, — Des cou-ples blonds d'a-mants heu-reux —

Villanelle des petits canards — Ils vont, les pe-tits ca-nards, Tout au bord de la ri-viè-re

CHADWICK, G. W. (1854-1931)

Allah
Copyright by Arthur P. Schmidt Co., Boston.
By permission
Al-lah gives light in dark-ness, Al-lah gives rest in pain

Ballad of Trees and the Master
Copyright by Oliver Ditson Co.
Used by permission
In-to the woods my Mas-ter went, Clean — for spent —

The Danza, Op. 14, No. 1
Copyright by Arthur P. Schmidt Co., Boston.
By permission
If you ne-ver have danced the Dan-za — with its won-drous — rhyth-mic twirl —

Love's like a summer rose
Copyright by Arthur P. Schmidt Co., Boston.
By permission
Love's like a sum-mer rose, whose fra-grant buds un-close,

CHAMINADE, Cécile (1857-1944)

L'Anneau d'Argent

Le cher an- neau d'ar- gent que vous m'a- vez don- né,

Chanson Slave

Dans mon beau pa- ys j'a- vais un a- mi

Si J'Étais Jardinier
Copyright 1894, G. Schirmer, Inc.

Si j'é-tais jar- di- nier des cieux, Je te cueil-le- rais des é- toi-les!

CHARLES, Ernest (1895-   )

Let my song fill your heart
Copyright 1936, G. Schirmer, Inc.

Let my song fill your heart with its mel- o- dy oh so di- vine

When I Have Sung my Songs
Copyright 1934, G. Schirmer, Inc.

When I have sung my songs to you, I'll sing no more.

CHARPENTIER, Gustav (1860-   )

A Mules (after "Impressions d'Italie")

A) Les_ yeux, la belle, hé- las! tes yeux fa- rou- ches

B) C'est l'heu - - - - re_où l'amant nous con- te fol- le- ment

La Chanson de Chemin

A) Qu'est-ce qui bril- le? Une au- ber- ge Ah!_ Ah!_

B) La route est lon-gue, lon-gue, bon_ pé- le- rin._

Les Chevaux de bois

Tour- nez, tour- nez, bons che-vaux de bois,_ Tour-nez_ cent tours,

Louise (opera)
Act I
By permission Heugel & Cie, Paris,
copyright owners

O coeur a- mi! O coeur pro- mis! Hé-las! si loin,_ si près!_

De-puis long- temps j'ha-bi-tais cet-te cham- bre, sans me dou- ter, hé-las!

Act II Scene II

Oh! moi quand je suis dans la ru- e, tout mon êt- re prend com- me feu!

Act III

De puis le jour où je me suis don- né- e,

Act IV

Les pau- vres gens peu-vent-ils être heureux?_ a qui le bon D

Voir naître une en- fant, la fleur- ir des ca- res- ses,

Louise (opera) — Act IV
Res- te, re- pose-toi com- me ja-dis, toute pe- ti- te! (A)

L'en-fant ser-ait sa- ge, tout à fait sa- ge, si son pè- re vou-lait (B)

La ronde des compagnons
La cour se fleu-rit de sou-ci Com- me le front de tous ceux- ci (C)

Sérénade à Watteau
Votre âme est un pa-y-sa-ge choi-si (D)

Les Yeux de Berthe
By permission Heugel & Cie, Paris, copyright owners
Vous pou-vez mé- pri- ser les yeux les plus cé- lè- bres (E)

CHAUSSON, Ernest (1855-1899)

Amour d'antan, Op. 8, No. 2
Copyright by Salabert, Paris, N. Y.
Mon a- mour d'an-tan, vous sou-ve-nez vous? Nos coeurs ont fleu-ri (G)

Apaisement, Op. 13, No. 1
Copyright by J. Hamelle Music Publishers, Paris
La lu- ne blan- - - che luit dans le bois (H)

La Caravane, Op. 14
Copyright by J. Hamelle Music Publishers, Paris
La ca- ra-vane hu- mai- ne au Sa- ha- ra du mon- - de (I)

La Chanson Bien Douce
Copyright by Salabert, Paris, N. Y.
E- cou- tez la chan-son bien dou- ce Qui ne pleu- re (J)

Chanson d'Amour
Loin de moi, loin de moi ces lè- vres que j'a- do- re (K)

Chanson de Clown
Fuis mon â- me fuis! Je meurs sous les traits (L)

Chanson d'Ophélie
Il est mort ay- ant bien souf- fert, Ma-da- me; (M)

Chanson Perpetuelle, Op. 37
Bois fris-son-ants, ciel é- toi-lé mon bien ai-mé s'en est al-lé (N)

Le Charme, Op. 2, No. 2
Quand ton sou- ri- re me sur- prit je sen- tis fré- mir (O)

Le Colibri, Op. 2, No. 7
Le vert co- li- bri, le roi des col- li-nes, Voy- ant la ro- sée (P)

Dans le forêt du charme et de l'enchantement
Sous vos som-bres ché-ve- lu-res pe- ti-tes fées. Vous chan-tâ- tes (Q)

La Dernière Feuille, Op. 2, No. 4
Dans la fo- rêt chauve et rouil- lé- e (R)

Nanny, Op. 2, No. 1
Bois chers aux ra- miers, pleu-rez, doux feuil- la-ges, (S)

Nocturne, Op. 8, No. 1

La nuit____ é-tait pen-sive____ et____ té-né-breu- se____

Nos Souvenirs, Op. 8, No. 4

Nos sou-ve- nirs tou-tes ces cho-ses Qu'à tous les vents

Les Papillons, Op. 2, No. 3

Les pa-pil- lons cou-leur de nei- ge vo-lent par es-saims

Printemps triste, Op. 8, No. 3

Nos sen-tiers ai- més s'en vont____ re-fleu-rir____

Sérénade italienne, Op. 2, No. 5

Par-tons en bar- que sur la mer____ Pous pas-ser la nuit

Serres chaudes, Op. 24
No. 1 Serre chaude
Copyright by Salabert, Paris, N. Y.

O serre an mil-lieu des fo-rêts____ Et vos por-tes à ja-mais clo-ses!

No. 2 Serre d'ennui

O____ cet en-nui bleu dans le coeur____ a-vec la vi-si-on

No. 3 Lassitude

Ils ne sa- vent plus où se po-ser ces bai-sers,Ces lè-vres

No. 4 Fauves las

O____ les pas-si-ons____ en al- lées, Et les ri-res et les san-glots!

No. 5 Oraison

Vous sa- vez,Sei-gneur ma mi-sè- re! Voy-ez ce que je vous ap-por-te,

Les Temps de Lilas

Le temps des li- las____ et le temps des ro- ses____

CHERUBINI, Maria Luigi (1760-1842)

J'ai vu disparaître l'espoir,
from Les Abencerrages (opera)

J'ai vu dis- pa-raî-tre L'és- poir dont jo- sais me nour-rir

Guide mes pas, from Les Deux
Journées (opera)

Gui-de mes pas, ô pro-vi-den- ce! d'mon plan se-con-de

O Salutaris Hostia

O sa-lu- ta-ris, O sa-lu-ta-ris hos-ti-a qual coe-li

CHOPIN, Frédéric François (1810-1849)

Polish Songs, Op. 74
No. 1 The Maiden's Wish

Were I a sun, so high in Heav'n out-beam-ing,

Accompaniment Theme

No. 2 In Spring

Thro' the dew-y val-ley mur- mur brooks____ me- an- d'ring

Polish Songs
No. 3 Troubled Waters

Tell me an- gry flow-ing tor- rent, why so tur- bid is thy cur-rent?　A

No. 4 Bacchanal

Boys, be jol- ly, grief is fol- ly, Drink then while you can!　B

No. 5 What a young maiden loves

Stream- let lov- eth the sedg- es, bird- ling lov-eth the hedg- es,　C

No. 6 Go Thou, and haste Thee

"Go thou, and haste thee!" I mute- ly o- bey thee　D

No. 7 The Messenger

Rills are bright- ly glit-t'ring, green the banks they fol- low　E

No. 8 My Sweetheart

When an eye like fire glow- ing, And a heart no guile know- ing,　F

No. 9 A Melody

Mute and re- sign'd, for pi- ty ne'er ap- peal- ing,　G

No. 10 The Trooper before the Battle

Why so rest- ive, so un- stead- y, Thou, my trust- y steed?　H

No. 11 Two Corpses

Fond were the lov- ers, Yet ne'er their love was plight- ed　I

No. 12 My Joys

When for a mo- ment thou dost speak, my dar- ling,　J

No. 13 Melancholy

Dew in the mead - - - - - ow, mist in the val- ley　K

No. 14 The little Ring

Yet a child wert thou, O maid- en, when our faith we plight- ed　L

No. 15 The Return Home

Stran- ger in the storm swept for- est, Haste thee on, O Ri- der!　M

No. 16 Lithuanian Song

O- ver the mead- ow and home- ward I hied me,　N

No. 17 Poland's Dirge

By the storm they breast- ed Ev- 'ry leaf is wrest- ed　O

CIAMPI, Legrenzo Vincenzo (1719-1762)

e giorni son che Nina (2 different versions) (said to be by Pergolesi also)

1　Tre gior-ni son che Ni- na, che Ni- na in let- to se ne sta　Q

2　Tre gior-ni son che Ni- ra, che Ni- na, che Ni - - - na　R

CILEA, Francesco (1866-   )

Adriana Lecouvreur (opera)
Act I
Copyright by Sonzogno, Milan

I- o son' l'u- mi- le an- cel- la del Ge- nio cre- a- tor___

La dol- cis- si- ma ef- fi- gie sor- ri- den- te

Act II
O va- ga- bon- da stel- la d'O- ri- en- te non tra- mon- tar,

L'a- ni- ma ho stan- ca, e la mè- ta è lon- ta- na:

I- o son___ su- a per l'a- mor__ ch'è più for- te del- la sor- te,

Act IV
Po- ve- ri fio- ri,___ gem- me de' pra- ti, pur ie- ri na- ti,

No, la mia fron- te, che pen- sier non___ mu- ta,

L'Arlesiana (opera)
Act I
Copyright by Sonzogno, Milan

Co- me due tiz- zi ac- ce- si, dal- l'al- to del di- ru- po

Act II
Vie- ni con me sui mon- ti, go- drai va- sti o- riz- zon- ti

Anch' i- o vor- re- i dor- mir co- si,___ nel son- no al- men

Act III
Ho da- to mo- glie al pa- dre del- lo spo- so e l'ho da- ta

Sa- i che gli ho da- to a bra- ni a bra- ni l'a- ni- ma___

CIMARA, Pietro (1887-   )

Canto di Primavera
Copyright by Forlivesi, Florence

A- pri- te tut- te le fi- ne- stra al So- le

Fiocca la neve
Copyright by C. W. Homeyer, Boston

Len- ta la ne- ve fioc- ca, fioc- ca, fioc- ca___

Scherzo
Copyright by F. Bongiovanni, Bologna

U- na not- te al da- van- za- le e- ro so- la o pur non e- ro?

Stornellata Marinara
Copyright by G. Ricordi & Co., Inc.

Ah! Al- ga di ma- - re!__ Quan- do m'af- fo- sca qual- che gran do- lor

Stornello
Copyright by F. Bongiovanni, Bologna

Son co- me i chic- chi del- la me- lo- grana___

CIMAROSA, Domenico (1749-1801)

Il Matrimonio Segreto (opera)

U-di-te, tut-ti u-di-te le or- rec-chie spa-lan-ca-te

È ve- ro che in ca-sa io so-no, io son la pa-dro--na,

Pria che spun- ti in ciel___ l'au- ro-ra in ciel___ l'au- ro-ra

Bril- lar mi- sen-to il co- re, mi sen-to__ giu- bi- lar

Per-do- na- te, sig-nor mi- o, se vi lascio e fo_ par- ten-za

Se non___ ven-di-ca - - - ta con- ten-ta___ già___ so- no

CLARIBEL (1830-1896)

Come Back to Erin

Come back to Er- in, Ma- vour- neen, Ma- vour- neen

I cannot sing the old songs

I can- not sing the old songs I sang long years a- go,

CLARKE, Rebecca (1886-   )

The Seal Man
By permission Boosey & Hawkes, Inc., copyright owners

And he came by her ca- bin to the west of the road, call-ing

Shy One
By permission Boosey & Hawkes, Inc., copyright owners

Shy one, shy one, shy one of my heart, She moves___

CLARKE, Robert C. (1879-1934)

The Blind Ploughman

CLAY. Frédéric (1838-1889)

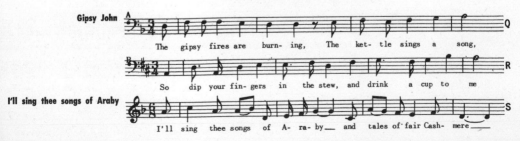

Gipsy John

The gipsy fires are burn- ing, The ket- tle sings a song,

So dip your fin- gers in the stew, and drink a cup to me

I'll sing thee songs of Araby

I'll sing thee songs of A- ra- by___ and tales of fair Cash- mere___

The Sands o' Dee

Oh! Ma- ry go, and call the cat-tle home, and call the cat-tle home

CLEMENS, Non Papa (1510-1555)

Aymer est ma vie

Ay- mer est_ ma vi- e Ay- -mer est ma_ vi- e____

COATES, Eric (1886-)

Bird Songs at Eventide

I heard you singing

Tell me where is fancy bred
By permission Boosey & Hawkes, Inc.,
copyright owners

Tell me where is fan- cy bred, Tell me where is fan- cy bred

COLERIDGE-TAYLOR, Samuel (1875-1912)

Eleänore, Op. 37, No. 6
Copyright by Novello & Co., Ltd., London

The for- est flow'rs are fad- ed all, The winds com- plain,

Life and Death

To look for thee, cry for thee, sigh for thee, un- der my breath,

Onaway! Awake, beloved!
from Song of Hiawatha, Op. 30

"On- a- way! A- wake,_ be- lov- ed!_ Thou the wild-flow'r of the fores

She rested by the Broken Brook
Copyright by Oliver Ditson Co.
Used by permission

She_ rest- ed by the Bro- ken Brook, She drank of Wear- y Well_

COOKE, Thomas Simpson (1782-1848)

Love's Ritornella

Gen- tle Zi- tel- la, whi- ther a- way? Love's Ri- tor- nel- la, list while I play

Over Hill, Over Dale

O- ver hill, o- ver dale Tho- rough brush tho- rough brier

COQUARD, Arthur (1846-1910)

Haï luli
Copyright 1899, G. Schirmer, Inc.

Je suis tris- te je m'in- qui- è- te, Je ne sais plus

Ha- ï lu- li! Ha- ï lu- li! Ha- ï lu- li!

CORNELIUS, Peter (1824-1874)

Ave Maria — B
A - - ve, a - - ve, Ma - ri - a! Gra - ti - a ple-na

r Barbier von Bagdad (The Barber of Bagdad) (comic opera)
Act I — C
Ach, das Leid hab ich er - tra-gen wie er-trag' ich nun das Glück?

— D
San- fter Schlum-mer wiegt ihn ein, lin-dert mil- de je- de Pein

Act II — E
O, hol-des Bild in En- gel- schö- ne, oft___ wenn in Träu- men

— F
So mag kein and'res Wort er- klin-gen, als das die blühnde Ro - - se

n Ton (The Monotone) Op. 3, No. 3 — G
Mir klingt ein Ton so wun-der-bar in Herz und Sin-nen im- mer dar,

— H
Accompaniment Theme

Weihnachtslieder, Op. 8 No. 1 Christbaum — I
Wie schön geschmückt der fest- li- che Raum! Die Lich- ter fun- kehn

No. 2 Die Hirten — J
Die Hir- ten wa- chen Nachts in Feld;so still und dun-kel liegt die Welt,

No. 3 Drei Könige — K
Drei Kön' - ge wan- dern aus Mor- gen-land, Ein Stern-lein führt sie

COSTELEY, Guillaume (1531-1606)

Allon, gay, gay, gay, Bergères (madrigal) — M
Al- lon, gay, gay, gay, Ber-ge- res, Al- lon, gay, al- lon, gay

Mignonne, allon voir si la Roze — N
Mi- gnon- ne, al- lon voir si la Ro- ze, Mi-gnon-ne al-lon voir

COTTRAU, Teodoro (1827-1879)

Addio a Napoli — P
Ad- dio mia bel- la Na- po- li, ad- di - o, ad- di - - o!

Santa Lucia (Neapolitan) — Q
Sul ma- re lu- ci- ca l'a- stro d'ar- gen- to

— R
Ve- ni- te al l'ag- gi- le Bar chet- ta mi - a.

COUILLART (16th Cent.)

Viri Galilaei

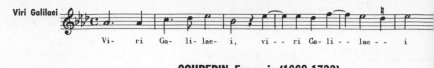

Vi - ri Ga-li-lae - i,   vi - - ri Ga-li - - lae - - i

COUPERIN, François (1668-1733)

Air Serieux (Mars 1697)

Qu'on ne me di - se plus que c'est la seule ab - sen - ce

Air Serieux (Août 1701)

Doux li - ens de mon_____ coeur, Ai - ma-bles pei - nes,

Brunete (Décembre 1711)

Ze - phi - re, mo - de - re en ces lieux L'ar-deur dont tu ca - res - - se

Ostende nobis domine, from Motets du Roy

O- sten - - - - - - - - - - - - - - - de O-sten - de no-bis, Do-mi - ne

Quatre versets d'un Motet   1.

A - dole - - scen - - tu - lus sum e - go et con - tem - ptus

2.

I - gni-tum e- lo- quium tu - um ve-he- men - - - - - - - - - - ter

3.

Ju - sti- ti - a tu- a Ju-sti-ti- a tu- a Ju-sti-ti- a in aeter - - num

4.

Qui dat ni - vem si- cut la- nam ne - - - - bulam si- cut_ ci- ne-rem

Venite exultemus Domino (motet)

Ve - ni - te e- xul - te- mus Do - mi - no ju-bi- le- mus De - o

COWARD, Noel (1899-   )

Bittersweet (operetta): I'll see you again
Copyright 1929 by Chappell & Co., Ltd. Harms, Inc. Publisher and Owner of all rights for the U. S. and Canada

I'll see you a- gain when- ev- er spring breaks through a- gain

Zigeuner
Copyright 1929 by Chappell & Co., Ltd. Harms, Inc. Publisher and Owner of all rights for the U. S. and Canada

Play to me be-neath some sum- mer moon, Zi- geu- ner

I'll follow my secret heart, from Conversation Piece (operetta)

COWLES, Eugene (1860-   )

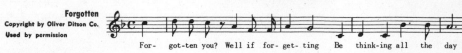

Forgotten
Copyright by Oliver Ditson Co. Used by permission

For- got-ten you? Well if for- get- ting Be think-ing all the day

CRESCENZO, Vincenzo de (1875-   )

Notte d'amore
Copyright by G. Ricordi & Co., Inc.

Lon- tan lon- ta- no Il sol scom- pa- re, Vie- ni mio amo- re,   B

Quann'a femmena vo'
Copyright by G. Ricordi & Co., Inc.

Vi- cen- zel- la tes- se- va a Fra- vo- la not- t'e ghiuorne   C

Rondine al Nido
Copyright by M V. Cardilli

Sot- to la gron- da de la tor- re an- ti- ca u- na ron- di- ne   D

Triste Maggio
Copyright by G. Ricordi & Co., Inc.

La mia ca- set- ta è tri- ste e sen- za so- le   E

CRIST, Bainbridge (1883-   )

C'est Mon Ami (old French air)
Copyright by Carl Fischer, Inc.
reprinted by permission

Ah s'il est dans vo- tre vil- la- ge, Un ber- ger   G

CROUCH, Frederick Nicholls (1808-1896)

Kathleen Mavourneen

Kath- leen Ma- vour- neen! the grey dawn is break- ing,____   I

CUI, César (1835-1918)

The Statue at Czarskoe-Selo

There stands the maid-en of stone   She has bro- ken her beau- ti- ful jar;   K

CURTIS, Ernesto de (1875-1937)

Canta pe' me

Can- ta pe me sta- not- te na can- zo- na   M

Torna a Surriento (Come back to Sorrento)
Copyright by Oliver Ditson Co.
Used by permission

Guar- da il ma- re co- mè bel- lo! spi- ra tan- ti sen- ti- men- to   N

Sen- ti co- me lie- ve sa- le dai giar- di- ni o- dor d'a- ran- ci   O

DALAYRAC, Nicholas (1753-1809)

Jeune fillette

Jeu- ne fil- let- te, pro- fi- tez des temps   Q

DAMROSCH, Walter (1862-   )

Danny Deever
Copyright by John Church Co.
Used by permission

"What are the bu- gles blow- in' for?" said Files- on- pa- rade   S

Danny Deever

For they're hang- in' Dan- ny Dee- ver, you can hear the Dead March play,

DARGOMIJSKY, Alexander (1813-1869)

I suffer

I suf- fer for I love thee from my in- most be- ing

The Lawyer's Clerk

There once was a clerk to a law- yer, So lit-tle and want-ing in grace,

The Miller

Said the mil- ler, home re- turn- ing Real- ly those are stran-ger's shoes

The Old Corporal

Chil-dren, keep step while you're march-ing! 'Ten-tion, your ri- fle hold fast!

Pretty Maiden

Oh,— pret- ty— maid- en, see the Boy - - - - ards are here!

Russalka (opera)
Act I Miller's Aria

Hey, Hey, you young ones, Hey, you— pret-ty maid-ens, I'm on to all—

Act II Olga's Song

In our street it hap-pened that a hus-band asked his wife:

Act III Cavatina

Why am I drawn to these un- hap- py shores, What is their sec- ret?

All things here re- mind me of pleas-ures long o - - ver.

Wherefore?

So full— of grief, so waste— and worn? And none— who will help th

The Worm

To my good wife I'm much in- debt- ed She taught me to be- come

DAVID, Félicien (1810-1876)

Lalla Roukh (opera)
Romance de Noureddin

Ma mai- tresse a quit- té la— ten - - - - te; Est elle al- lée

Couplets de Mirza

Si vous ne sa-vez plus— char- mer Ne vous en pre- nez—

La Perle du Bresil (opera)
Couplets de Mysoli

Char- mant— oi- seau qui sous— l'om- bra- ge

DEBUSSY, Claude (1862-1918)

Cantatas
La Damoiselle Élue

By permission Durand & Cie, Paris; Elkan-Vogel Co., Inc., Phila., copyright owners

La Da-moi- selle E- lue s'ap-puy- ait sur la bar-riè-re d'or du Ciel

DEBUSSY

La Damoiselle Élue

Au- tour d'el- le des a- mants, nou- vel- le- ment ré- u- nis,   **A**

Lorsq' au- tour de sa tê- te s'at- ta- che- ra L'au- ré- o- le,   **B**

L'Enfant Prodigue
By permission Durand & Cie, Paris;
Eikan-Vogel Co., Inc., Phila.,
copyright owners

L'an- né- e en vain chas- se l'an- né- e!   **C**

A cha- que sai- son ra- me- né- e, Leurs jeux et leurs é- bats   **D**

A- za- ël! A- za- ël Pour- quoi m'as tu quit- té- e?   **E**

Ce- pen- dant les_ soirs é- taient doux, dans la plai- ne d'or- mes plan- té- e   **F**

O temps à ja- mais éf- fa- cé,___ Où comme eux j'a- vais l'â- me pu- re   **G**

Heu- res for- tu- né- es! A- près des an- né- es   **H**

es Chansons de Charles d'Orleans
'4-part unacc.)
By permission Durand & Cie, Paris;
Eikan-Vogel Co., Inc., Phila.,
copyright owners

Dieu! qu'il la fait bon re- gar- der La gra- ci- eu- se bonne et bel- le   **I**

Dieu qu'il la___ fait bon re- gar- der   **J**

Quant j'ai ou- y le ta- bou- rin Son- ner pour s'en al- ler au may,   **K**

Y- ver, vous n'es- tes qu'un vil- lain, Y- ver, Y- ver   **L**

SONGS:
Les Angélus
By permission J. Hamelle Music
Publishers, Paris

Chlo- ches,chré- tien- nes pour les ma- ti- nes, Son- nant au coeur   **M**

Ariettes Oubliées
I
By permission Jean Jobert, Paris;
Eikan-Vogel Co., Inc., Phila.,
copyright owners

C'est l'ex- ta- se lan- gue- reu- se C'est la fa- tigue   **N**

II

Il pleu- re dans mon coeur comme il pleut dans la vil- le   **O**

III

L'om- bre des ar- -bres dans la ri- viè- re em- bru- mé- e   **P**

IV Paysages Belges—
Chevaux de Bois

Tour- nez, tour- nez, bons che- vaux de boix Tour- nez cent tours   **Q**

V Aquarelles (Green)

Voi- ci les fruits des fleurs des feuil- les et_ des bran- ches   **R**

VI Aquarelles (Spleen)

Les ro- ses é- taient tout- es rou- ges, Et les lier- res étaient tous noirs.   **S**

Ariettes Oubliées
VI Aquarelles (Spleen)

(actual theme of song)

Beau Soir
By permission Durand & Cie, Paris;
Elkan-Vogel Co., Inc., Phila.,
copyright owners

Lorsque au so-leil cou-chant les ri-viè-res sont ro-ses

La Belle au Bois Dormant

Des trous à son pour-point ver-meil, Un che-va-lier va par la

Chansons de Bilitis
I La Flûte de Pan
By permission Jean Jobert, Paris;
Elkan-Vogel Co., Inc., Phila.,
copyright owners

Pour le jour des Hy-a-cin-thies il m'a don-né u-ne sy-rin

II La Chevelure

Il m'a dit: "Cet-te nuit, j'ai rê-vé J'a-vais ta che-ve-lur

III Le Tombeau des Naïades

Le long du bois cou-vert de gi-vre, je mar-chais;

Cinq Poëmes de Baudelaire
By permission Durand & Cie, Paris;
Elkan-Vogel Co., Inc., Phila.,
copyright owners
I Le Balcon

Mè-re des sou-ve-nirs maî-tres-se des maî-tres-ses

II Harmonie du Soir

Voi-ci ve-nir les temps où vi-brant sur sa ti-ge

III Le Jet d'Eau

Tes beaux yeux sont las Pauvre a-man-te!

IV Recueillement

Sois sa-ge Ô ma dou-leur, et tiens toi plus tran-quil

V La Mort des Amants

Nous au-rons des lits pleins d'o-deurs lé-gè-res, Des di-vans pro-fonds

Deux Romances (words by P. Bourget)
By permission Durand & Cie, Paris;
Elkan-Vogel Co., Inc., Phila.,
copyright owners
1. (a) Romance
(b) Romance

L'âme é-va-po-rée et souf-fran-te L'âme dou-ce, l'âme a-do-ran-t

Voi-ci que le prin-temps, ce fils lé-ger d'A-vril

2. Les Cloches

Les feuil-les s ou-vraient sur le bord des bran-ches Dé-li-ca-te-ment

Fêtes Galantes:
First Series
1. En Sourdine
By permission Jean Jobert, Paris;
Elkan-Vogel Co., Inc., Phila.,
copyright owners

Cal-mes dans le de-mi jour Que les bran-ches hau-tes font

2. Fantoches

Sca-ra-mouche et Pul-ci-nel-la Qu'un mau-vais des-sein ras-sem-bla

3. Clair de Lune

Votre âme est un pa-y-sa-ge choi-si Que vont char-mant mas-ques

Second Series
1. Les Ingénus
By permission Durand & Cie, Paris;
Elkan-Vogel Co., Inc., Phila.,
copyright owners

Les hauts ta-lons lut-taient a-vec les lon-gues ju-pes

2. Le Faune

Un vieux fau-ne de ter-re cui-te Rit au cen-tre des bou-lin-grins,

Trois Mélodies

No. 3

L'é- che- lon- ne- ment des haies Mou- tonne à l'in- fi- ni,

DEIS, Carl (1883-   )

Come down to Kew
Copyright 1916, G. Schirmer, Inc.

Go down to Kew in li- lac time, in li- lac time

DELANNOY, Marcel (1898-   )

Le Galant Jardinier
By permission Heugel & Cie, Paris,
copyright owners

Je vais mon- ter sur la mon- ta- gne Là, j'é- lè- ve- rai un grand mur

DELBRUCK, Alfred

Un Doux Lien
Copyright 1902, G. Schirmer, Inc.

Un doux li- en nous en- la- çait tous deux, Ton bras au mien

DELIBES, Léo (1836-1891)

Arioso

Ô mer, ou- vre- toi, Lin- ceul du_ mon- de, mer pro- fon- de

Bonjour, Suzon

Bon- jour, Su- zon, ma fleur des bois!_____ Es- tu tou- jours la plus jo- li- e?

Les Filles de Cadix (Bolero)

Nous venions de voir le tau- reau, Trois gar- çons trois fil- let - - - - - - - tes,

Lakmé (opera)

Act I   A

A l'heure ac- cou- tu- mé- e Quand la plaine em- bau- mé- e

B

Blan - - - che Dour- ga,_____ Pâ - - - le Si- va_____

A1

Dô- me é- pais le_ jas- min A_ la- ro- se_ s'as- sem - - - ble

A2

Sous_ le_ dome é- pais où_ le_ blanc jas- min a_ la- ro- se_ s'as- sem - - - b

Quintet   A

Ah beaus fai- seurs de sys- te- mes, A- moureux_ du chan- ge- ment

B

Leur ver- tu bi- zar- re man- que d'ap- par- at_____

Fan- tai- si- e aux div- ins men- son- ges Tu re- viens m'é- ga- rer enc

Pour- quoi dans les grands bois ai- mé- je a m'é- ga- rer pour y pleu- rer?_____

Lakmé (opera)

Act I Duet

A — Ou- bli- er que je t'ai vu- e, Te re- dres-sant toute é- mu- e

B — C'est le Dieu de la jeu- nes- se, C'est le Dieu du prin-temps,

Act II

C — Lak- mé, ton doux re- gard se voi- le, Ton sou- ri- re s'est at-tris-té

Bell Song

D —

E — Où va- - la jeune In- dou- e Fil- le des Pa-ri- as,

F — Là- bas dans la fo- - ret plus som- bre

G — Ah! Ah! Ah! Ah! Ah! Ah! Ah! Ah! Ah! Ah! Ah! Ah! Ah! Ah!

Duet

H — Dans la fo- rêt près de nous, Se ca-che tou- te pe- ti- te,

I — Ah! c'est l'a-mour en-dor-mi Qui de son ai- le l'ef- fleu- re,

Act III

J — Sous le ciel tout é- toi- lé Le ra-mier blanc au loin s'en est al- lé

K — Ah! Viens, dans la fo-rêt pro- fon- de L'aile de l'a-mour a pas- sé

L — Tu m'as don-né le plus doux rê- ve Qu'on puisse a-voir sous notre ciel

M — Qu'au-tour de moi tout som- bre Je ne veux pas une om-bre

DELIUS, Frederick (1862-1934)

palachia (Variations on an old Slave Song) (chorus and orchestra)
By permission Boosey & Hawkes, Inc., copyright owners

O — Af- ter night has gone comes the day, the dark sha-dows will fade a-way

Cradle Song (Slumber Song)
y permission of Augener, Ltd., London

P — Das Kind- lein schlief ein Da schweb- te her- ein von En- geln

Hassan (closing chorus)
By permission Boosey &Hawkes, Inc., copyright owners

Q — We take the gold- en road to Sa- mar- kand

Indian Love Song
permission Oxford Univ. Press, London, right owners

R — I a- rise from dreams of thee in the first sweet sleep of night,

Irmeline Rose
By permission Boosey & Hawkes, Inc., copyright owners

S — There was a king in days of old and a-mongst his man-y gems

Love's Philosophy
By permission Oxford Univ. Press, London, copyright owners

The foun-tains min-gle with the riv-er, and the riv-ers with the O-cean

The Nightingale
By permission of Augener, Ltd., London

Sing, sing, Nach-ti-gall Du, sing mir ein Lied-lein le-ben-dig

To the Queen of My Heart
By permission Oxford Univ. Press, London, copyright owners

Shall we roam, my love, To the twi- -light grove, When the moon is ris-ing

DEL LEUTO, Arcangelo (16th Cent.)

Dimmi, amor

Dim-mi a-mor, dim- -mi che fa la mia ca- -ra li-ber- -tà?

DENZA, Luigi (1846-1922)

Funiculi, Funicula
Copyright by G. Ricordi & Co., Inc.

Some think___ the world is made for fun and frol-ic___ and so do I

Hark- en! Hark- en Mu- sic sounds a- far___

A May Morning

Si vous l'aviez compris
Copyright by G. Ricordi & Co., Inc.

Rien qu'au re- voir___ mur-mu-ré tout bas, En me___ ser-rant

Pour- quoi___ n'a- vez vous pas sur- pris mon se- cret

DIAZ, Eugéne (1837-1901)

Arioso, from Benvenuto Cellini (opera)

De l'art___ splen-deur im-mor- tel-le Ray- ons___ à peine en-tre-vus___

DIBDIN, Charles (1745-1814)

Tom Bowling

Here a sheer hulk, lies poor Tom Bowl-ing, the dar-ling of our___ crew,—

DOBSON, Tom (1890-1918)

Cargoes
Copyright 1920, G. Schirmer, Inc.

Quin- qui-reme of Nin-e-veh___ from dis- tant O- phir___

DOHNÁNYI, Ernest Von (1877-   )

Hungarian Folk Songs: Azok, Azok

Rain I thought it was that ran down drop by drop

Hungarian Folk Songs:
Szérettelek álnok lélek
A — Love I gave you, troth I gave you, Cru-el faith-less maid!

Valaki jár udvaromon
B — Some one I hear prowl-ing a-round knock-ing to come in.

DONATO, Baldassare (16th Cent.)

Chi la gagliarda (madrigal)
D — Chi la Gagliar-da chi la Gagliar-da Don-ne vo impa-ra-re

DONAUDY, Stefano (1879-   )

Ah, mai non cessate
Copyright by G. Ricordi & Co., Inc.
F — Ah, mai non ces-sa-te dal vo- - -stro par-lar,

Amorosi miei giorni
Copyright by G. Ricordi & Co., Inc.
G — A-mo-ro-si miei gior-ni, chi vi po-trà mai più scor-dar,

Cuor mio, cuor mio non vedi
Copyright by G. Ricordi & Co., Inc.
H — Cuor mio, cuor mio non ve-di che, quan-do a-mor ti co-glie,

Freschi luoghi, prati aulenti
Copyright by G. Ricordi & Co., Inc.
I — Fre-schi luo-ghi,—pra-ti au-len-ti, ri-ma-ne- -te sem-pre in fior;

Luoghi sereni e cari
Copyright by G. Ricordi & Co., Inc.
J — Luo-ghi se-re-ni e ca-ri, Io vi ri-tro- - -vo

O bei nidi d'amore
Copyright by G. Ricordi & Co., Inc.
K — O bei ni-di d'a-mo-re, oc-chi a mi si ca-ri,

O del mio amato ben
Copyright by G. Ricordi & Co., Inc.
L — O del mio a-ma-to ben per-du-to in-can-to!

Quando ti rivedrò
Copyright by G. Ricordi & Co., Inc.
M — Quan-do ti ri-ve-dro, in-fi-da a-man-te che mi fo-sti si ca-ra?

Se tra l'erba
Copyright by G. Ricordi & Co., Inc.
N — Se tra l'er-ba un ri-no-vel-lo bal-za e cor-re ver-so il ma-re,

Spirate pur, spirate
Copyright by G. Ricordi & Co., Inc.
O — Spi-ra-te pur,—spi-ra-te— at- -tor-no a lo—mio be-ne,

Vagliessima sembianza
Copyright by G. Ricordi & Co., Inc.
P — Va-ghis-si-ma sem-bian-za d'an-ti-ca don-na a-ma- - - -ta,

DONIZETTI, Gaetano (1797-1848)

Don Pasquale (opera)
Act I
R — Bel-la sic-co-me un an-gelo in ter-ra pel-le gri-no,—

S — Ah,— un fo-co in so-li-to mi sen-to ad-dos-so, o-mai re-sis-sti-re

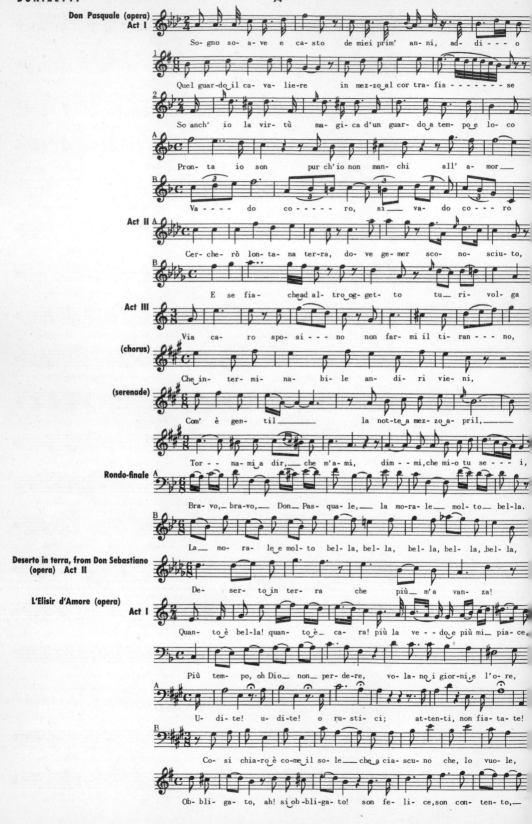

Don Pasquale (opera)
Act I

1.
So- gno so- a- ve e ca- sto de miei prim' an- ni, ad- di- - o

1.
Quel guar- do il ca- va- lie- re in mez- zo al cor tra- fis- - - - - - se

2.
So anch' io la vir- tù ma- gi- ca d'un guar- do a tem- po e lo- co

A.
Pron- ta io son pur ch'io non man- chi all' a- mor

B.
Va- - - - do co- - - - ro, si va- do co- - - ro

Act II A.
Cer- che- rò lon- ta- na ter- ra, do- ve ge- mer sco- no- sciu- to,

B.
E se fia- che ad al- tro og- get- to tu ri- vol- ga

Act III
Via ca- ro spo- si- - no non far- mi il ti- ran- - no,

(chorus)
Che in- ter- mi- na- bi- le an- di- ri vie- ni,

(serenade)
Com' è gen- til la not- te a mez- zo a- pril,

Tor- na mi a dir, che m'a- mi, dim- - mi, che mi o tu se- - - i,

Rondo-finale A.
Bra- vo, bra- vo, Don Pas- qua- le, la mo- ra- le mol- to bel- la.

B.
La mo- ra- le e mol- to bel- la, bel- la, bel- la, bel- la, bel- la,

Deserto in terra, from Don Sebastiano
(opera) Act II
De- ser- to in ter- ra che più m'a- van- za!

L'Elisir d'Amore (opera)
Act I
Quan- to è bel- la! quan- to è ca- ra! più la ve- do e più mi pia- ce,

Più tem- po, oh Dio non per- de- re, vo- la- no i gior- ni e l'o- re,

A.
U- di- te! u- di- te! o ru- sti- ci; at- ten- ti, non fia- ta- te!

B.
Co- sì chia- ro è co- me il so- le che a cia- scu- no che, lo vuo- le,

Ob- bli- ga- to, ah! si ob- bli- ga- to! son fe- li- ce, son con- ten- to,

DONIZETTI

L'Elisir d'Amore (opera)

Act I — A-di- na, cre- di- mi, te ne scon-giu- ro

Co- me Pa- ri- de vez- zo- so por- se il po- mo al-la più bel- la!

Act II — Io son ric- co e tu sei bel- la, io du- ca- ti e vez- zi hai tu

Ven- ti scu- di! E ben so- nan- - ti. Quan- do? A- des- so?

U- na fur- ti- va la- gri- ma negl' occhi suoi spun- tò

Pren- di, pren- di, per me sei li- be- ro

La Favorita (opera)

Act I — U- na ver- gi- ne, un an- giol d'a- mo- re al Si- gno- re

An- - giol ca- ro, so- a- ve, be- a- to, deh tu ve- glia

Bei rag- gi lu- cen- ti, bell' au- - re be- a- - - te,

Ah! mio be- ne mio te- so- ro, il Cie- lo t'in-vi- a, vie-ni a vien

Fia ve- ro? la- sciar- ti! e tu il chie- di a me?

Act II — Vien, Leo- no- ra, a pie- di tuo- i, ser- to e so-glio il cor,

De' ne- mi- - - ci tuoi lo sde- gno di- sfi- dar sa- prò per te,

Quan- do le so- glie pa- ter- ne var- ca- - i de- bil fan- ciul- la

In que- sto suo- lo a se- re- nar tuo cu- ra

Act III — A tan- to a- mor Leo- no- ra, il tuo ri- spon- da

O mio Fer- nan- - - - do, del- la ter- ra il tro- no

Scrit- to è in ciel il mio do- lor, su, ve- ni- te ell'è u- na fe- - sta,

Act IV — Splen- don più bel- le in ciel le stel- - le, ma lut- to or- ren- do

La Favorita (opera)
Act IV

Spir- to gen-til, ne' so-gni mie- - i bril la-sti_un dì, ma ti per-de- i

Preghiera

Pie- to - - so al par del Nu- mi, pie- to - so_____ su- per me

Vie-ni_ah vien,___ io m'ab-ban- do- no___ al- la gio-- ja____ che m'innebri

La Fille du Regiment (The Daughter of the Regiment) (opera) Act I

Au bruit de la guer- re j'ai- re- çu le jour____

A

Cha- cun le sait, cha-cun le dit le re- gi-ment___ par___ ex- cel-len-ce

B

Il est là, il est là, il est là, mor- bleu

A

De-puis l'in-stant où dans mes bras je vous re- çus___tou-te trem-blan- te

B

De cet a- veu si ten-dre non___ mon coeur en ce jour

Il faut par- tir_____ mes bons com-pag- nons d'ar-mes

Act II

Par le rang et___ par l'o- pu- len- ce en vain l'on a cru m'é-blou- ir

Sa - - - lut à la Fran- ce à mes_____ beaux__ jours___

Tous les trois ré- u- nis,quel plai-sir, mes a-mis,quel bon-heur,quel bon-heur,

Pour me rap- pro-cher__ de Ma- ri- e, je m'en-rô- lai pau- vre sol-dat

Linda di Chamounix (opera) Act I

Am- bo na- ti in que- - sta____ val- le

O lu- ce di quest' a- ni- ma de- li-zia a-mo-re_e vi- - ta

Love duet A

Per sua ma-dre an-dò una fi- glia mi-glior sor-te_a rin-trac- ciar;

Da quel dì, che t'in- con- tra- i ad a- mar__ quel dì_im-pa- ra- i

B

A con- so- lar mi_af-fre- ti- si tal gior-no de- si- a- to

Prayer

O tu che re- go- li gli_u-ma- ni_e- ven - - - - - ti,

DONIZETTI

Linda di Chamounix (opera)
Act II

Se tan-to in i- ra a-gli uo-mi-ni è l'a-mor no--stro,

Mad scene (duet)

No non è ver, men-ti-ro nò tra- dir tu non mi puo

Act III

Di tue pe-ne spar-ve il so--gno al-le gio-je a-mor ti de-sta

Lucia di Lammermoor (opera)
Act I

Cru-da, fu-ne-sta sma-nia tu m'hai sve-glia-to in pet---to

Huntsmen's Chorus

Co-me vin-ti da stan-chez-za, do-pa lun-go er-ra-re in-tor-no

La pie-ta--de in suo fa-vo-re Mi ti sen-si in-van mi det--ta

Regna-va nel si-len-zi-o al-ta la not-te e bru----na

Quan-do ra- pi-to in e-sta-si del più co-cen-te ar-do-re

Sul-la tom-ba che rin-ser-ra il tra-di-to ge-ni-to- re,

Ver-ran-no a te sul l'a- u-re i miei so-spi-ri ar-den--ti,

Act ii

Sof-fri--va nel pian-to, lan-gui---a nel do-lo--re,

Se tra-dir-mi tu po-tra-i la mia sor-te e già com-pi-ta;

Per te d'im-men-so giu-bi-lo tut-to s'av-vi va in-tor- no

Sextet

Chi mi fre-na in tal mo-men-to? Chi tron-cò del-l'i-re il cor so

E---sci, fug---gi il fu-ror che m'ac- cen-de

Act III

Qui del pa-dre an-cor re- spi-ra l'om-bra i-nul-ta e par che fre---ma

O so- le più rat-to a sor--ger t'ap-pre- sta,

Dal-le stan-ze, o-ve Lu- ci-a trat-ta a vea col suo con-sor-te

Oh qual fu-ne-sto av-ve--ni-men-to!

Lucia di Lammermoor (opera)
Act III (Mad Scene)

Al- fin son tu - - - a al-fin sei mi - - - o,

Spar- gi d'a- ma- ro pian-to il mio ter-re-stre ve - - - - lo,

Fra po- co a me ri-co-ve- rò da- rà ne-glet-to a ve - lo

Tu che a Dio spie-ga- sti l'a-li o bel-l'al-ma in-na-mo- ra- ta,

Lucrezia Borgia (opera)
Prologue

Com' è bel-lo qua-le in-can-to In quel vol-to o-ne-sto e al-te-ro

Di pe-sca-to- re i- gno- bi-le Es-ser figliuol cre-de - - - i

Act I

Vie- ni! la mia ven-det - - - -ta È me-di-ta-ta e pron - -ta

Act II

Il se- gre- to per es- ser fe-li - - - - - - - ci

M'o- di oh! m'o-di, Io non t'im-plo-ro Per vo- ler

Fra l'erbe, from La Zingara (opera)

Fan-ciul- la sui grep-pi le ca-pre e-mu- la - - - - - - - - - - - - - i

Un gior - - -no la ma - - - no mi por - - se un don-zel- lo

DOURLEN, Victor Charles (1780-1864)

Je sais attacher des rubans,
from Le Frère Philippe (opera)

Je sais at- tach-er des ru- bans, Je sais com-ment vienment

DOWLAND, John (1563-1626)

First Book of Ayres:
Awake, sweet love

A- wake, sweet love, thou art re- turned. My heart, which long

Come again! Sweet love

Come a- gain! Sweet love doth now in-vite Thy grac- es, that re-frain

Come, heavy sleep

Come, hea- vy Sleep the im-age of true Death

Go, crystal tears

Go, crys- tal tears, like to the__ morn- ing showers,

Second Book of Ayres:
Fine knacks for ladies

Fine knacks for la- dies cheap, choice, brave and new! Good pen- ny worths!

Second Book of Ayres: Flow, my tears
Flow, my tears, fall from your springs. Ex-iled for-ev-er let me mourn   A

Now cease, my wandering eyes
Now cease, my wan-d'ring eyes, strange beau-ties to ad-mire,   B

Shall I sue?
Shall I sue? Shall I seek for grace? Shall I pray? Shall I prove?   C

Now, o now I needs must part
Now, o now I needs must part, Part-ing though I ab-sent mourn   D

Say love, if thou didst ever find
Say love, if ev-er thou didst find a wo-man with a con-stant mind   E

Weep you no more, sad fountains
Weep you no more, sad foun-tains, What need you flow so fast   F

DUFAY, Guillaume (1400-1474)

Adieu m'amour
A-dieu m'a-mour, a-dieu ma joy-e   H

Alma redemptoris mater
Al-ma   I

Ave, maris Stella
A-ve,-Ma-ria Stel-la   J

Bon Jour, bon Mois
Bon jour, bon mois, bon an et bonne es-trai-ne   K

Flos Florum
Flos-flo-rum,   L

Le Jour s'endort
Le jour s'en-dort, aus-si fait la sai-son   M

...ie, from Mass (4 voices) "Se la face ay pale"
Ky-ri-e e-ley-son, Ky-ri-e e-ley-son   N

Vergine bella
Ver-gi-ne bel-la, che di sol ves-ti-ta   O

DUKAS, Paul (1865-1935)

...ce n'est pas encore, from Ariane et Barbe-Bleue Act II
By permission Durand & Cie, Paris; Elkan-Vogel Co., Inc., Phila., copyright owners
Ah! ce n'est pas en-co-re la clar-té vé-ri-ta-ble   Q

DUNHILL, Thomas (1877-   )

Cloths of Heaven, Op. 30, No. 3
...pyright Stainer & Bell, Ltd., London; Galaxy Music Corporation, N. Y., sole U. S. Agents
Had I the heaven's em-broid-ered cloths, En-wrought with gol-den   S

To the Queen of Heaven
Copyright 1926, T. F. Dunhill

Queen of heav- en, bless'd may thou be, for God- ës Son born

DUNSTABLE, John (15th Cent.)

Quam pulchra es

Quam____ pul- -chra és, et quam de- cor- ra, ca- ris- si- ma,

DUPARC, Henri (1848-1933)

Au pays où se fait la guerre
Copyright by Salabert, Paris, N. Y.

Au pa- ys où se fait la guer- - - - - re mon bel- a- mi

Chanson Triste
Copyright by Salabert, Paris, N. Y.

Dans ton coeur dort un clair de lu- ne, un doux clair de lu- ne

Élégie
Copyright by Salabert, Paris, N. Y.

Oh! ne mur- mu- rez pas son nom!__ qu'il dor- me dans l'om- bre

Extase
Copyright by Salabert, Paris, N. Y.

Sur un lys pâ- le mon coeur dort D'un som- meil doux comme la mort

L'Invitation au Voyage
Copyright by Salabert, Paris, N. Y.

Mon en- fant,__ ma sœur Songe__ a la dou- ceur D'al- ler là- bas

Lamento
Copyright by Salabert, Paris, N. Y.

Con- nais- sez vous la blan- che tom- bé Où flotte a- vec un son plain- tif

Le Manoir de Rosamunde
Copyright by Salabert, Paris, N. Y.

De sa dent soudaine__ et vo- ra- ce Comme un chien l'amour

Phidylé
Copyright by Salabert, Paris, N. Y.

A

L'herbe est molle__ au sommeil__ sous les frais peupliers,__

B

Re- po- se__ ô Phidy- lé

Sérénade Florentine
Copyright by Salabert, Paris, N. Y.

É- toi- le dont la beau- té luit__ comme un di- a- mant dans la nuit,

Soupir
Copyright by Salabert, Paris, N. Y.

Ne ja- mais la voir ni l'en- ten- dre, Ne ja- mais tout haut la nom- mer,

Testament
Copyright by Salabert, Paris, N. Y.

Pour que le vent te les ap- por- te Sur l'ai- le noi- re d'un re- mord,__

La Vague et la Cloche
Copyright by Salabert, Paris, N. Y.

U- ne fois, ter- ras- sé par un puis- sant__ breu- va- ge J'ai rê- vé__

La Vie Antérieure
Copyright by Salabert, Paris, N. Y.

J'ai long- temps ha- bi- té sous de vas- tes por- ti- ques

DUPONT, Gabriel (1878-1914)

Mandoline
Copyright 1946, G. Schirmer, Inc.

Les don-neurs de sé-ré-na-des Et les bel-les é-cou-teu-ses

DURANTE, Francesco (1684-1755)

Danza, danza, fanciulla gentile

Dan-za,__ dan-za, fan-ciul-la,__ al__ mi-o can-tar,

Vergin, tutta amor

Ver-gin, tut-ta a-mor,__ O Ma-dre di bon-ta-de, O Madre pi-a,

DVOŘÁK, Antonin (1841-1904)

The Devil and Kate, Op. 112 (opera)
Act III The Countess's Aria

Wie trau-rig rings-um öd' die Hal-len, wo-rin einst Freu-de

Dimitrij Op. 64 (opera)
Act II Dimitrij's Aria

Zdi-voké-ho ži-tí vi-ru du-še mo-je stou-hou spě-la

Act III Dimitrij's Aria

Vi-děl jsem je Xe-ni-i jsem zrel, my-slí ti-chým blahem o-po-je nou

Rusalka (opera)
Act I O lovely moon (Rusalka's Song)

Glei-ten-der Mond du, so sil-ber-zart,__ Sendest weit-hin deine Blik-ke__

Act I A strange vision (Prince's Air)

Weiss, dass ein Trug-bild du, dass wohl schwindet, wie vor der Nacht

Act II

Was im saal, in je-dem Stüb-chen heut' im Schloss für Mord-ru - - mor?

Act II Alas, alas

Hast du dir als Theil er-ko-ren,__ Im-mer wird dir Lust, nim-mer Lust und Schmerz__

Act II White flowers along the way

Blü-me-lein weiss am Wie-ges-rand, blüh-ten wohl still be-schei-den,

Act III I have golden hair

Mein, mein gold' nes Haar ist mein, mein, mein gold' nes Haar ist mein

The Sly Peasant, Op. 37 (opera)
Act I Prince's Song

Wer kann's mit Wor-ten sa-gen auch, was drinn im Her-zen

Biblical Songs, Op. 99 (duets)
No. 1 Clouds and darkness are round about
By permission Associated Music Publishers, Inc.

Clouds and dark-ness are round a-bout Him Right-eous-ness and judgment

No. 2 Lord, thou art my refuge

Lord, thou art my re-fuge and my shield, and in thy word put I my trust

No. 3 Hear my prayer, O Lord

Hear my__ prayer, O Lord, my__ God O hide__ not thy face

Univ. of California, Riverside

Biblical Songs:
No. 4 God is my Shepherd

God is my shep - - herd, I want for no - thing.

No. 5 I will sing Jehovah's praises

I will sing new songs of glad-ness, I will sing Je-ho-vah's prai-ses

No. 6 Hear my prayer, O Lord

Hear my prayer O Lord give ear un-to my cry!

No. 7 By the Waters of Babylon

By the wa-ters of Ba-by-lon, there we sat us down and wept

No. 8 Turn Thee to Me

Turn Thee to me and have mer-cy for I am de-so-late

No. 9 I will lift mine eyes up to the mountains

I will lift mine eyes up to the moun-tains,

No. 10 Sing ye a joyful song

Sing ye a joy-ful song un-to the Lord

Goin' Home, from New World Symphony, Op. 95, Largo (arr. William Arms Fisher)
Copyright 1922, Oliver Ditson Co. Used by permission.

Go-in' home, go-in' home, I'm a-go-in' home

Gypsy Songs, Op. 55
No. 1 Mein Lied ertönt

Mein Lied er-tönt, ein Lie-bespsalm, be-ginnt der Tag zu sin-ken,

No. 2 Ei, wie mein Triangel

Ei, wie mein Tri-an-gel wun-der-herr-lich läu-tet!

No. 3 Rings is der Wald so stumm

Rings ist der Wald so stumm und still, das Herz schlägt mir so ban - - ge,

No. 4 Als die alte Mutter (Songs my mother taught me)

Als die al-te Mut - - ter mich noch lehr-te sin - - - gen,

No. 5 Rein gestimmt die Saiten!

Rein ge-stimmt die Sai-ten! Bur-sche, tanz' im Krei-se!

No. 6 In dem weiten, breiten (Freer is the gypsy)

In dem wei-ten, brei-ten, luft' gen Lei-nen-klei-de

No. 7 Darf des Falken Schwinge Tatra (Cloudy heights of Tatra)

Darf des Fal-ken Schwin-ge Tat-ra-höh'n um-rau - - -schen

Lasst mich allein (Leave me alone) Op. 82, No. 1

Lasst mich al-lein in mei-nen Träu-men geh'n, stört mir die Wol-lust nicht

The Mower, Op. 73, No. 2

Nah bei Te-mes-var, dem Städt-chen mah-te Gras ein her-zig Mäd-chen

Thirteen Moravian Duets, Op. 31,
No. 1 The Fugitive

Where blue the Danube flows, far will I fly from thee Where blue the Danube fl...

No. 2 Speed thee, Birdie

Speed thee, bir-die, fly a-cross the pur-ple moun-tain

EAST, Michael (17th Cent.)

EDWARDS, Clara (Contemporary)

EDWARDS, Richard (c.1523-1566)

ELGAR, Sir Edward (1857-1934)

As torrents in summer, from King Olaf, Op. 30
By permission Novello & Co., Ltd., London

As tor-rents in sum-mer, Half dried in their chan-nels

The Dream of Gerontius
By permission Novello & Co., Ltd., London

Sanc-tus for-tis, Sanc-tus De-us De pro-fun-dis o-ro te

Praise to the ho-li-est in the height, and in the depth be praise;

O lov-ing wis-dom of our God When all was sin and shame,

Soft-ly and gen-tly dear-ly ran-somed soul

Lament, from Caractacus, Op. 35
By permission Novello & Co., Ltd., London

O my war-ri-ors, tell me tru-ly O'er the red groves where ye lie,

The Light of Life, Op. 29 (oratorio)
By permission Novello & Co., Ltd., London

Be not ex-treme, O Lord, to mark a-miss those se-cret sins

As a spi-rit didst thou pass be-fore mine eyes, I saw thee not,

Thou on-ly hast the words of life! Be pro-phet to my heart,

I am the good Shep-herd, and know my sheep, and am known by them

The Pipes of Pan
By permission Boosey & Hawkes, Inc., copyright owners

When the woods are gay in the time of June with the chest-nut flow'r and fan,

Pleading, Op. 48, No. 1
By permission Novello & Co., Ltd., London

Will you come home-ward from the hills of Dream-land, Home in the dusk,

Sea-Pictures, Op. 37
No. 1 Sea Slumber Song
By permission Boosey & Hawkes, Inc., copyright owners

Sea-birds are a-sleep, The world for-gets to weep.

No. 2 In Haven

Close-ly let me hold thy hand, Storms are sweep-ing sea and land;

No. 3 Sabbath Morning at Sea

The ship went on with so-lemn face: To meet the dark-ness on the deep,

No. 4 Where Corals Lie

The deeps have mu-sic soft and low When winds a-wake the air-y spry,

No. 5 The Swimmer

With short, sharp, vi-o-lent lights made vi-vid, To south-ward

**Coronation Ode, Op. 44, No. 6
(Trio of Pomp and Circumstance,
No. 1)**
By permission Boosey & Hawkes, Inc.,
copyright owners

**The Sun goeth down, from The King-
dom, Op. 51, No. 4 (oratorio)**
By permission Novello & Co., Ltd., London

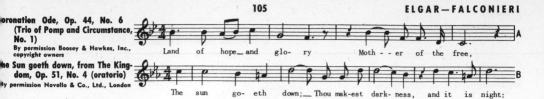

A — Land of hope_and glo- ry Moth- er of the free,

B — The sun go- eth down;_ Thou mak-est dark- ness, and it is night:

ERLEBACH, Philipp Heinrich (1657-1714)

Ihr Gedanken

Nur getrost

Schwaches Hertz

D — Ihr Ge- dan- ken, Ihr Ge- dan- ken, quält mich nicht!

E — Nur ge- trost nur ge- trost, lass al- les ge- hen,

F — Schwa- ches Hertz, du bist be- sie- get, du bist be- sie- get,

EULENBURG, Philipp zu (1847-1921)

**Rosenlieder (song cycle)
No. 1 Monatsrose**

No. 2 Wilde Rose

No. 3 Rankende Rose

No. 4 Seerose

No. 5 Weisse und rothe Rose

H — Aus des Nach-bars Haus trat mein Lieb hin-aus, hielt ein Rös-lein in der Hand

I — Bei dem Wal- des-saum im Wie- sen-hang stand am Ro- sen-strauch

J — Sagt, ihr wei-ssen Rank- rö- se-lein, Was treibt ihr am Hau-se des Lieb-chens mein?

K — Der a- bend ist still und dun-kel der See, im Schil-fe leuch-ten

L — Mein Schatz der liegt auf der Tod- ten-bahr, hat wei-sse Ro- sen

FALCONIERI, Andrea (c. 1600-1650)

Bella porta di rubini

Non più d'amore (villanella)

O Bellissimi capelli

Occhietti amati

Segui, segui dolente core

Vezzosette e care

N — Bel- la por-ta di ru- bi- ni ch'a-pri il var-co ai dol- ci ac-cen-ti,

O — Non più d'a- mo-re, Non più d'ar-do- re, Pe-ne e tor-men-ti,

P — O bel-lis-si-ma ca- pel- li, miei dol-cis-si- mi di- let- ti,

Q — Oc- chietti a- ma-ti che m'in- cen- de- te per-chè spie-ta-ti o-mai più sie-te

R — Se-gui, se-gui, do- len- te co- re, gli oc-chi fon-ti del vi-vo ar-do- re;

S — Vez- zo-set- te e ca- re pu- pi-let-te ar-den-ti, chi v'ha fat-to a- va- re

FALLA, Manuel De (1876- 1946)

El Amor Brujo (ballet)
Canciòn del amor dolido
By permission J. & W. Chester, Ltd., London, copyright owners

Yo no sé — — — — — — qué sien-to, ni sé qué me pa-sa,

Canción del fuego fatuo

Lo mis-mo que es fue-go fa-tuo, lo - - mis - mi-to es er-que-ré. —

Danza del juego de amor

Tú e-res a-quel mal gi-ta - - no, —

Las Campanas del Amanecer

Quien lo ha-bi - a de de-ci — que con o-tra la ven-di - - - - as!

Ya es-ta des pun-tan-do el dí - - - - a! Can-tad, cam-pa-nos, can-tad,

Les Colombes
Copyright by Salabert, Paris, N. Y.

Sur le co-teau, — là - bas où sont les tom-bes

Seguidilla
Copyright by E. B. Marks Music Corp., N. Y.

Un ju-pon ser-ré sur les han - - ches Un pegne é-norme à son chi-gnon —

Seven Popular Spanish Songs
No. 1 El paño moruno
By permission Associated Music Publishers, Inc.

Al pa - ño fi-no en la tien-da, Al pa - ño fi-no en la tien-da,

No. 2 Seguidilla Murciana

Cualquie-ra que el te-ja - - - - do Ten-ga de vi - - - - - drio.

No. 3 Asturiana

Por ver si me con-so-la - ba, A-rri-me-me à un pi - no ver-de de

No. 4 Jota

Di - cen que no nos que-re - mos

No. 5 Nana (Berceuse)

Duér- me-te, ni-ño, duer- me, — Duer-me, mi al-ma, —

No. 6 Canciòn

Por trai-do-res, tus o-jos, Voy á en-te-rrar los;

No. 7 Polo

Guar-do u-na - - - - - "A - - - - - - - y!" Guar-do u-na "A - - - - -

Soneto a Córdoba
By permission Oxford Univ. Press, London, copyright owners

Oh ex-cel - so mu-ro, oh to-rres co-ro-na-das De ho-nor

Tus Ojillos Negros

Yo no sé qué tie-nen tus o-ji-llos ne-gros

Mas, por o-tra par-te, son tan em-bus-te-ros

La Vida Breve
By permission Associated Music Publishers, Inc.

Vi-van los que ri - - - - - en! — Mue-ran los que llo-ran!

FARMER, John (c. 1565-c. 1600)

Fair Phyllis I saw sitting all alone

Fair Phyl-lis I saw sit-ting all a-lone   Feed-ing her flock near to the mountain

FARNABY, Giles (c. 1560-c. 1600)

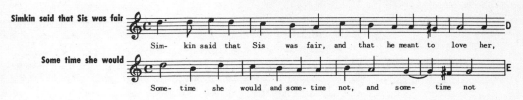

Simkin said that Sis was fair

Sim-kin said that Sis was fair, and that he meant to love her,

Some time she would

Some-time she would and some-time not, and some-time not

FAURÉ, Gabriel (1845-1924)

Dans les ruines d'une abbaye, Op. 2, No. 1
By permission J. Hamelle, Paris

Seuls tous deux, ra-vis, chant-ants, comme on s'ai - - - me;

Seule! Op. 3, No. 1
By permission J. Hamelle, Paris

Dans un bai-ser l'onde au ri-va-ge dit ses dou-leurs!

Sérénade Toscane, No. 2

O toi qui ber-ce un rêve en-chan-teur

Chanson du Pêcheur, Op. 4, No. 1
By permission J. Hamelle, Paris

Ma belle a-mi est morte Je pleurerai tou-jours!

Lydia, No. 2

Ly-di-a, sur tes roses joues Et sur ton col frais et si blanc.

Chant d'Automne, Op. 5, No. 1
By permission J. Hamelle, Paris

Bien-tôt nous plon-ge-rons dans les froi-des té-nè-bres,

L'Absent, No. 3

Sen-tiers où l'herbe se ba-lan-ce, Va-lons, côteaux, bois cheve-lus,

Tristesse, Op. 6, No. 2
By permission J. Hamelle, Paris

Av-ril est de re-tour, La pre-mière des ro-ses

Sylvie, No. 3

Si tu veux sa-voir, ma bel-le,Où s'en-vo-le à ti-re d'ai-le

Après un rêve, Op. 7, No. 1
By permission J. Hamelle, Paris

Dans un som-meil que char-mait ton i-ma-ge Je rêvais le bon-heur

Barcarolle, No. 3

Gon-do-dier du Ri-al-to mon Châ-teau,c'est la la-gu-ne

Au bord de l'eau, Op. 8, No. 1
By permission J. Hamelle, Paris

S'asseoir tous deux au bord du flot qui pas-se

La Rançon, No. 2

L'hom-me a, pour pay-er sa ran-çon Deux chaumps au tuf

Ici-Bas! Op. 8, No. 3
I- ci-bas! tous les li-las meu-rent, Tous les chants des oi-seaux sont courts

Nell, Op. 18, No. 1
By permission J. Hamelle, Paris
Ta ro-se de pour-pre a ton clair so-leil O juin, é- tin-celle en-i- vré- e,

Le Voyageur, No. 2
Voy- a- geur, où vas tu, mar- chant dans l'or vi- brant

Automne, No. 3
Au- tom- - - ne au ciel bru-meux aux ho- ri-zons na-vrants,____

Poèmes d'un Jour Op. 21 No. 1 Rencontre
By permission J. Hamelle, Paris
J'é- tais triste et pen- sif quand je t'ai ren-con- tré - - - e,

No. 2 Toujours
Vous me de- man-dez de me tai- re, De fuir loin de vous pour ja- mais,

No. 3 Adieu
Com- me tout meurt vi- te, la ro- se dé- clo- se,

Les Berceaux, Op. 23, No. 1
By permission J. Hamelle, Paris
Le long du Quai__ les grands_vaisseaux, Que la houle in-cli-ne en si-len-ce__

Notre Amour, No. 2
Notre a-mour est cho- se lé-gè- re, Com-me les par-fums que le vent prend aux

Le Secret, No. 3
Je veux que le ma-tin l'i- gno- re Le nom que j'ai dit à la nuit,

La Fée aux Chansons, Op. 27, No. 2
By permission J. Hamelle, Paris
Il é- tait u- ne Fé- e D'her- be fol- le coif- fé- e,

Aurore, Op. 39, No. 1
By permission J. Hamelle, Paris
Des jar-dins de la nuit s'en- vo-lent les é- toi - - les.

Fleur jetée, No. 2
Em- por- te ma fo-li- e au gré du vent Fleur en chan-tant cueil-li- e

Les Roses d'Ispahan, No. 4
Les ro- ses d'Is- pa- han dans leur gaî- ne de mous- se,

Noël, Op. 43, No. 1
By permission J. Hamelle, Paris
La nuit des-cend du haut des cieux, le givre au toit suspend ses fran-ges__

Nocturne, No. 2
La nuit, sur le grand mys- tè- re, entr'-ou-vre ses é- crins bleus:___

Clair de Lune, Op. 46, No. 2 (Menuet)
Vo- tre â-me est un pa- y- sa-ge choi- si qui vont char-mant mas-ques

Accomp. theme

Requiem, Op. 48 I Kyrie
By permission J. Hamelle, Paris
Ky- ri- e, Ky- ri- e, Ky- ri- e e- le- i-son Ky- ri- e e- le- i-son

FAURÉ

Requiem, Op. 48

II Offertorium — O Do- mi- ne Je- su Chris- te rex glo- ri- œ___ A

III Sanctus — Sanc- tus___ Sanc- tus___ / Sanc- tus___ Sanc- tus___ Sanc- tus- Do- mi- nus B

IV Pie Jesu — Pi- e Je- su Do- mi- ne Do- na- e- is re- qui- em C

V Agnus Dei — Ag- nus De- i qui tol- lis pec- ca- ta mun- - - - di D

VI Libera me — Li- be- ra me, Do- mi- ne___ De mor- te œ- ter- na E

VII In Paradisum — In pa- ra- di- - - sum___ De- du- cant an- ge- li___ F

Larmes, Op. 51, No. 1
By permission J. Hamelle, Paris — Pleu- rons nos cha- grins cha- cun le nô- tre U- ne lar- me tom- be G

Au Cimetière, No. 2 — Heu- reux qui meurt i- ci, Ain- si que les oi- seaux des champs___ H

Spleen, No. 3 — Il pleu- re dans mon cœur com- me il pleur sur la vil- le___ I

La Rose, No. 4 — Je di- rai la Ro- se aux plis gra- ci- eux. La Rose est le souffle em- bau- mé des Dieux, J

Dolly, Op. 56, No. 1
By permission J. Hamelle, Paris — Dol- ly,___ Ô ma mi- gnon- ne, ma ché- ri- e K

Chanson de Shylock, Op. 57
No. 1
By permission J. Hamelle, Paris — Oh! les fil- - - les!___ Ve- nez, les fil- les aux voix dou- ces! L

No. 3 Madrigal — Cel- le que j'ai- me a de beau- té Plus que Flore et plus que Po- mo- ne, M

Mandoline, Op. 58, No. 1
By permission J. Hamelle, Paris — Les don- neurs de sé- ré- na- des___ Et les bel- les é- cou- teu- ses N

En Sourdine, No. 2 — Cal- mes___ dans le de- mi- jour Que les bran- ches hau- tes font___ O

Green, No. 3 — Voi- ci des fruits, des fleurs, des feuil- les et des bran- ches___ P

C'est l'extase, No. 5 — C'est l'ex- ta- se lan- gou- reu- se, C'est la fa- ti- gue a- mou- reu- se, Q

a Bonne Chanson, Op. 61
No. 1
By permission J. Hamelle, Paris — U- ne Sainte en son au- ré- o- le, U- ne cha- te- laine en sa tour, R

No. 2 — Puis- que l'au- be gran- dit, puis- que voi- ci l'au- ro- - - - - - - re S

L'Horizon Chimérique, Op. 118, No. 3

Di- a-ne, Sé-lé- ne   lu- ne de beau métal,___ Qui re-flé-tes vers nous,   A

No. 4

Vais- seaux, nous vous au-rons ai- més en pu- re per- te;   B

En Prière
By permission J. Hamelle, Paris

Si la voix d'un en- fant peut mon-ter jus-qu'a Vous, Ô mon Pè- re   C

FAURE, Jean Baptiste (1830-1914)

Charité

Voi- ci l'hi- ver et son tris-te cor- tè- ge, Les malheur-eux souffrent beaucoup,   E

Va,___ cha- ri- té___ vier-ge pu ---- re et fé- con- de,   F

Crucifix! (duet)
By permission Heugel & Cie, Paris,
copyright owners

Vous qui pleu- rez,   ve- nez à ce Dieu, car il pleu- re   G

Les Rameaux (The Palms)

Sur nos che- mins les ra- meaux et les fleurs___   H

Ho- san- na! Gloire au Seigneur! Bé- ni ce-lui qui vient sauver le mon ----- de!   I

Sancta Maria

J'ai vu les Sé- ra- phins en son- ge Chanter dans leurs divins con-certs___   J

Vi- brez en- cor, sainte har-mo-ni- e, Vi- brez en- cor, hymne é- ternel!   K

FERRABOSCO, Alfonso (The Younger) (c. 1557- 1628)

Come, my Celia

Come, my Ce --- lia,   let us prove, while we may,   M

O eyes, o mortal stars

O eyes, O mor-tal stars, The au-thors of my harms,   N

FERRARI, Gustav (1872-)

Le Miroir
Copyright 1949, G. Schirmer, Inc.

L'o-deur de vous flot-tait dans l'air si- len-ci- eux   P

FÉVRIER, Henry (1875-)

Elle avait trois couronnes d'or
By permission Heugel & Cie, Paris,
copyright owners

Elle a-vait trois cou- ron-nes d'or.___ A qui les don-na-t-el- le?   R

L'Intruse
By permission Heugel & Cie, Paris,
copyright owners

Elle est ve- nu- e vers le palais Le soleil se le-vait   S

FIBICH, Zdenko (1850-1900)

My Moonlight Madonna
(Words by Paul Webster)
Copyright by Carl Fischer, Inc.
reprinted by permission

Where are you____ beau-ti-ful moon-light Ma-don-na____ Like the dew

Sarka, Op. 51 (opera)   Act I

Ja-ko bla-hý o-hlas do-by za-šlé vdu-še zvu-čí slo-va

Act II

Jsi krás-ná, ja-ko let-ní noc, jíž hvězd-ná zdo-ba v kšti-ci pla-ne!

(duet)

Jak jsi krás-na Cé-tiš žár jenž z na-der šle-há?

Act III

Já ne-le-kám se, smr-ti chlad-ná, muk ni sti nů____ tvých

FIELITZ, Alexander Von (1860-1930)

Eli!and, Op. 9,
No. 1 Stilles Leid
Copyright 1910, G. Schirmer, Inc.

Ei-ne stil-le Zel-le an blau-er Wel-le

No. 2 Frauenwörth

Das war ein Tag' voll Mai-en-wind, da ist____ auf blau-en

No. 3 Rosenzweige

Wohl man-chen Ro-sen-zweig brach ich von Pfa-de

No. 4 Heimliche Grüsse

O Ir-men-gard, wie schön bist du hold --- se-li-ger ist Kei-ne

No. 5 Am Strande

Mein Lieb-ling ist ein Lin-den-baum der steht am Strand;

No. 6 Kinderstimmen

Mit un-sern Fi-schern war ein Kind ge-kom-men

No. 7 Mondnacht

Ich lieg'____ an mei-nes La--gers End' und lug'__ in stille Ster-ne

No. 8 Wanderträume

O, der Al-pen blan-ke Ket-te, wie sie glänzt

No. 9 Anathema

Nun ist wohl San-ges En-de! Wie hart ich da-von schied,

No. 10 Ergebung

Ge-hor-chen ist das Er-ste! Ich hab' mich stumm ge-neigt,

Die stille Wasserrose, Op. 18, No. 1

Die stil-le Was-ser-ro-se steigt aus dem blau__ en See

Frülingslied, Op. 26, No. 1

Und ein Duf-ten zieht ü-ber die Er-den-welt,

FINCK, Heinrich (1445-1527)

Ach herzigs Herz

Ach her-zigs Herz_ mein Schmerz er-ken-nen tu, ich hab__ kein Ruh

FISCHER, Ludwig (1745-1825)

Im tiefen Keller

In tie-fen Kel-ler sitz' ich hier auf ei-nem Fass voll Re-ben,

FLÉGIER, Ange (1846-1927)

Le Cor
Copyright 1898, G. Schirmer, Inc.

J'ai-me le son du cor, le soir_ au fond des bois,_

Que de fois seul_ dans l'om-bre à mi-nuit de-meu-ré,

FLOTOW, Friedrich Von (1812-1883)

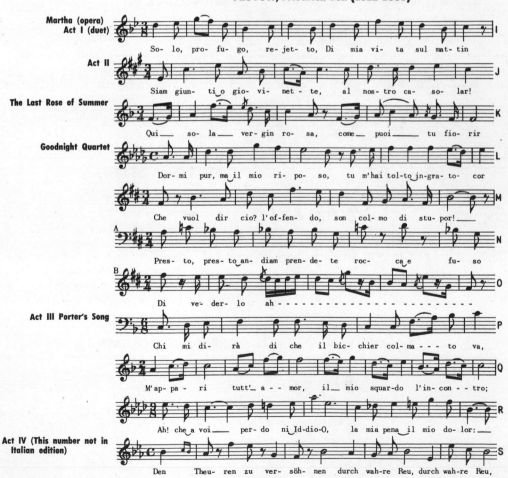

Martha (opera) Act I (duet)

So-lo, pro-fu-go, re-jet-to, Di mia vi-ta sul mat-tin

Act II

Siam giun-ti o gio-vi-net-te, al nos-tro ca-so-lar!

The Last Rose of Summer

Qui so-la ver-gin ro-sa, come_ puoi_ tu fio-rir

Goodnight Quartet

Dor-mi pur, ma il mio ri-po-so, tu m'hai tol-to in-gra-to-cor

Che vuol dir cio? l'of-fen-do, son col-mo di stu-por!

Pres-to, pres-to an-diam pren-de-te roc-ca e fu-so

Di ve-der-lo ah - - - - - - - - - - - - - - - -

Act III Porter's Song

Chi mi di-rà di che il bic-chier col-ma - - - to va,

M'ap-pa-ri tutt' a - - mor, il_ mio squar-do l'in-con - - tro;

Ah! che a voi_ per-do ni Id-dio-O, la mia pena il mio do-lor:_

Act IV (This number not in Italian edition)

Den Theu-ren zu ver-söh-nen durch wah-re Reu, durch wah-re Reu,

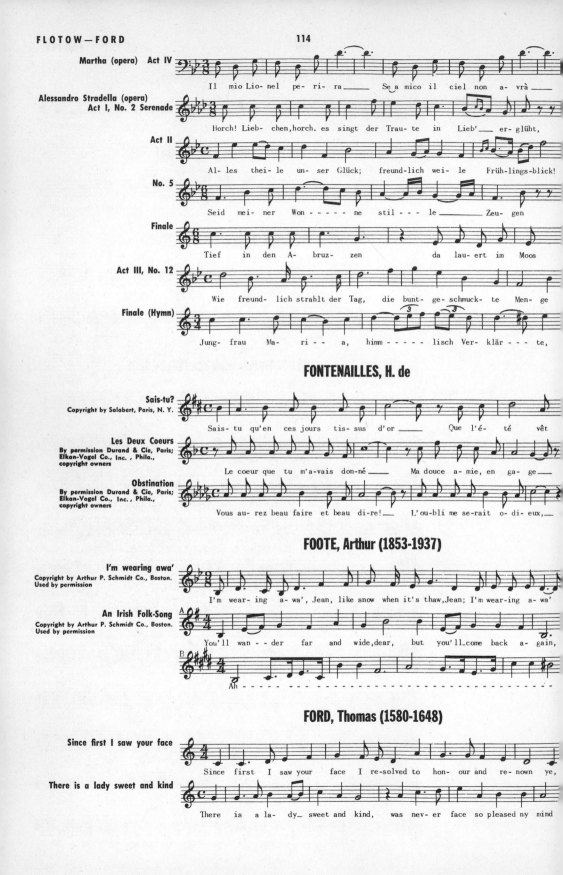

Martha (opera) Act IV

Il mio Lio- nel pe- ri- ra___ Se a mico il ciel non a- vrà___

Alessandro Stradella (opera)
Act I, No. 2 Serenade

Horch! Lieb- chen,horch. es singt der Trau- te in Lieb' er- glüht,

Act II

Al- les thei- le un- ser Glück; freund- lich wei- le Früh- lings-blick!

No. 5

Seid mei- ner Won - - - ne stil - - le Zeu- gen

Finale

Tief in den A- bruz- zen da lau- ert im Moos

Act III, No. 12

Wie freund- lich strahlt der Tag, die bunt- ge- schmuck- te Men- ge

Finale (Hymn)

Jung- frau Ma- ri- a, himm - - - - - lisch Ver- klär - - - te,

FONTENAILLES, H. de

Sais-tu?
Copyright by Salabert, Paris, N. Y.

Sais- tu qu'en ces jours tis- sus d'or___ Que l'é- té vêt

Les Deux Coeurs
By permission Durand & Cie, Paris;
Elkan-Vogel Co., Inc., Phila.,
copyright owners

Le coeur que tu m'a-vais don-né___ Ma douce a- mie, en ga- ge

Obstination
By permission Durand & Cie, Paris;
Elkan-Vogel Co., Inc., Phila.,
copyright owners

Vous au- rez beau faire et beau di-re! L'ou-bli me se-rait o- di- eux,___

FOOTE, Arthur (1853-1937)

I'm wearing awa'
Copyright by Arthur P. Schmidt Co., Boston.
Used by permission

I'm wear- ing a- wa', Jean, like snow when it's thaw,Jean; I'm wear-ing a- wa'

An Irish Folk-Song
Copyright by Arthur P. Schmidt Co., Boston.
Used by permission

A

You'll wan- -der far and wide,dear, but you'll_come back a- gain,

B

Ah - - - - - - - - - - - - -

FORD, Thomas (1580-1648)

Since first I saw your face

Since first I saw your face I re-solved to hon- our and re- nown ye,

There is a lady sweet and kind

There is a la- dy_ sweet and kind, was nev- er face so pleased my mind

FOSTER, Stephen (1826-1864)

Ah! may the red rose live alway

Ah! may the red rose live al-way, To smile 'up-on earth and sky!___ · B

Angelina Baker

'Way down on de old plan-ta-tion, Dat's where I was born, · C

An- ge-li- na Ba-ker An- ge-li- na Ba-ker's gone · D

Beautiful Dreamer

Beau-ti- ful dream- er, wake un-to me___ Star-light and dew-drops · E

Camptown Races

De Camp-town la- dies sing dis song, Doo-dah, doo-dah! · F

Come where my love lies dreaming

Come where my love lies dream-ing Dream-ing the hap-py hours a-way, · G

Gentle Annie

Thou wilt come no more, gen-tle An- nie, Like a flow'r · H

Hard Times (chorus)

T' is the song, the sigh of the wear- y; Hard times, hard times, · I

Jeanie with the light brown hair

I dream of Jea- nie with the light brown___ hair, · J

Katy Bell

Go- ing down the Sha- dy dell where the hon- ey-suck- les grow, · K

Laura Lee

Why has thy mer- ry face Gone from my side Leav- ing each cherished place · L

Little Belle Blair

We have made a grave for lit-tle Belle Blair, in the fields be-yond the town · M

Lou'siana Belle

Oh! Lou'- si- an-a's de same old state, Where Mas- sa used to dwell · N

Massa's in de cold, cold ground

Round de meadows am a ring-ing De dar-keys mourn- ful song · O

My old Kentucky Home

The sun shines bright in the old Ken-tuck- y home, · P

Nell and I

We part- ed in the spring time of life, Nell and I · Q

Nelly Bly

Nel- ly Bly! Nel- ly Bly! Bring de broom a- long, · R

Heigh, Nel- ly, Ho! Nel- ly, lis- ten, lub, to me · S

FOURDRAIN, Felix (1880-1923)

La Belle au Bois Dormant
Copyright by G. Ricordi & Co., Inc.
Comme_elle avait dor- mi cent ans Dans son lit fleu- rant la bruyère,___

Carnaval
Copyright by G. Ricordi & Co., Inc.
Car- na- val!___ joy-eux Car- na- val!___ On s'é-lan- ce

Chanson Norvégienne
Copyright by G. Ricordi & Co., Inc.
Je suis pri-se d'u- ne tris- tes - - se Qui pè- se, pè- se lour- dement

Le papillon
Copyright by G. Ricordi & Co., Inc.
Gai pa- pil- lon, pa - - - pil- lon d'or Qui t'en- vo- les rapide

FOX, Oscar J. (1879-   )

The Hills of Home
Copyright by Carl Fischer, Inc.
reprinted by permission
My prai-rie home is beau- ti-ful, but oh,___ I miss the bro- ken sky- line

The hills___ of home, the hills of home

FRANCHETTI, Alberto (1860-   )

Germania (opera)
Prologue
Copyright by G. Ricordi & Co., Inc.
Stu- den- ti! U- di- te o voi, an- ti- chi e no- vi a- mi ci

Act I
No, non chiu- der gli oc- chi va- glie ci- le- stri- ni___ co- me la- ghi,

Fe-ri- to prigio- nier, vol- li fug- gir per non mo- rir fra col- tri

FRANCK, César (1822-1890)

L'Ange Gardien
Veil- lez_ sur moi quand je m'é- veil-le Bon an- ge, puis- que Dieu_ l'a dit

Les Béatitudes (oratorio)
No. 4 Heureux les coeurs
Puis- que par- tout où nous en- traîne___ un sort fa- tal

Heu- reux les coeurs al- té- rés de jus- ti- ce

No. 8 Mater dolorosa
Moi du Sau- veur___ je suis la mè - - re; Sept glai- ves

Les Cloches du Soir
Quand les clo- ches du soir dans leur len- te vo- lé- e,

Lied
Pour moi sa main cueil- lait des ro- ses A ce buis- son___

Le Mariage des Roses

Mi- gnon- ne, sais tu com- ment S'é- pou- sent les ro- ses?

Ninon

Ni- non! Ni- non! que fais tu de la vi- e?

Nocturne

O frai- che nuit, Nuit transpar- en- te, Mys- te- re sans ob-scu-ri- té

Panis Angelicus, from Messe Solonnelle, Op. 12

Pa- nis an- ge- li-cus Fit pa- nis ho- mi-num Dat pa-nis coe-li-cus

La Procession

Dieu s'a-vance à tra- vers les champs! par les lan- des, les_ prés

Psalm 150

Lou- ez le Dieu ca- ché dans des saints ta- ber- na- cles

La Terre a tressailli, from The Redemption

La terre a tres-sail- li d'une ex- ta- se pro- fon- de

S'il est un charmant gazon

S'il est un char-mant ga- zon que le ciel ar- ro- se

Souvenance

Com- bien j'ai dou- ce sou- ve- nan- ce Du jo- li lieu

Le Vase Brisé

Le vase où meurt cet- te ver- vei- ne D'un coup d'even-tail fut fé-lé

La Vierge à la Crèche

Dans les lan- ges blancs fraîche-ment cou-sus, La_ Vierge ber- çait

FRANCK, Johann Wolfgang (17th Cent.)

Auf, auf zu Gottes Lob

Auf, auf zu Got- tes Lob, ihr hol- den Che- ru- bim

Jesus neigt sein Haupt und stirbt

Je- sus neigt_ sein_ Haupt_ und_stirbt,seht am Kreu-ze ihn ent-schlafen

Sei nur still

Sei nur_ still, sei nur_still und harr'_ auf_ Gott,er weiss alles

FRANCK, Melchior (1573-1639)

Ach treuer Gott, Herr Jesus Christ

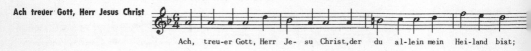

Ach, treu-er Gott, Herr Je- su Christ,der du al-lein mein Hei-land bist;

FRANZ, Robert (1815-1892)

Er ist gekommen, Op. 4, No. 7

Er ist ge- kom- men in Sturm____ und Re- gen

Aus meinen grossen Schmerzen, Op. 5, No. 1 — A
Aus mei-nen gros-sen Schmer-zen mach' ich die klei-nen Lie-der

Liebchen ist da! No. 2 — B
Blüm-lein im Gar-ten, schaut euch doch um, steht nicht so trau-rig;

Auf dem Meere, No. 3 — C
Aus den Him-mels-au-gen dro-ben fal-len zit-ternd lich-te Fun-ken

Mädchen mit dem rothen Mündchen, No. 5 — D
Mäd-chen mit dem ro-then Münd-chen, mit dem Äug-lein

Gute Nacht, No. 7 — E
Die Höh'n und Wäl-der schon stei-gen im-mer tie-fer in's A--bend-gold,

Vergessen, No. 10 — F
O ban-ger Traum, was flat-terst du mit schwar-zem Flü-gel

Wie des Mondes Abbild, Op. 6, No. 2 — G
Wie des Mon-des Ab-bild zit--tert in den wil-den Mee-res-wog-en

Bitte, Op. 9, No. 3 — H
Weil auf mir, du dunk-les Au--ge, ü--be

Für Musik, Op. 10, No. 1 — I
Nun die Schat-ten dun-. keln, Stern an Stern er-wacht.

Stille Sicherheit, No. 2 — J
Horch, wie still es wird im dun-keln Hain, Mäd-chen, wir sind sicher

Mutter, o sing' mich zur Ruh! No. 3 — K
Mut-ter, O sing'mich zur Ruh', wie auch in schö-ne-ren Stun-den,

Umsonst, No. 6 — L
Des Wal-des Sän--ger sin-gen, die ro-the Ro-se blüht,

Abschied, Op. 11, No. 1 — M
Wie schie-nen die Stern-lein so hell, so hell

Am leuchtenden Sommermorgen, No. 2 — N
Am leuch-ten-den Som--mer-mor-gen geh'ich im Gar-ten her-um

Zwei welke Rosen, Op. 13, No. 1 — O
Zwei wel-ke Ro-sen träu-men im San-de zum letz-ten Mal

Widmung, Op. 14, No. 1 — P
O dan-ke nicht für die-se Lie-der Mir ziemt es dank-bar Dir zu sein;

Du liebes Auge, Op. 16, No. 1 — Q
Du lie-bes Au-ge willst dich tau-chen in mei-nes Aug's

Abends, No. 4 — R
A--bend-lich schon rauscht der Wald aus den tief-sten Grün--den

Ständchen, Op. 17, No. 2 — S
Der Mond ist schla-fen gan-gen, die Ster-ne blin-zeln blind

Im Herbst, Op. 17. No. 6

Die Hai- de ist braun, einst blüh-te sie roth;____ die Bir- ke ist kahl,

Marie, Op. 18, No. 1

Ma- rie, am Fen-ster sit-zest du, du lie- bes sü - - - sses Kind___

Im Rhein, im heiligen Strome, No. 2

Im Rhein, im hei- li-gen Stro- me, da spie-gelt sich in den Well'n___

Die blauen Frühlingsaugen, Op. 20, No. 1

Die blau-en Frül-lungs- au - - gen schau'n aus_ dem Gras her- vor___

Das macht das dunkelgrüne Laub, No. 5

Das_ macht das dun-kel- grü- ne Laub, dass der Wald so schat-tig ist;

Im wunderschönen Monat Mai, Op. 25, No. 5

Im wun- der- schö-nen Mo- nat Mai, als al- le Knos- pen spran-gen

Lieber Schatz, sei wieder gut mir, Op. 26, No. 2

In dem Dornbusch blüht ein Rös-lein, ist ein Lust, es an- zu- sehn.

Sterne mit den gold'nen Füsschen, Op. 30, No. 1

Ster- ne mit den gold'- nen Füss- chen wan-deln dro- ben

Wonne der Wehmut, Op. 33, No. 1

Trock- net nicht,___ trock- net nicht_ Thrä-nen der e-wigen Liebe

Es ragt in's Meer der Runenstein, Op. 39, No. 2

Es ragt in's Meer der Ru- nen-stein, da sitz' ich

Wandl' ich in dem Wald des Abends, No. 4

Wandl' ich in dem Wald_ des A-bends, in dem träu- me- ri- schen Wald

Die helle Sonne leuchtet, Op. 42, No. 2

Die hel- le Son- ne leuch- tet auf's_ wei- te Meer her-nie - - - der

Es hat die Rose sich beklagt, No. 5

Es hat die Ro- se sich___ be- klagt_ dass gar zu schnell

Ach Elslein, liebes Elselein

Ach Els-lein, lie- bes El- se-lein mein, wie gern wär' ich bei dir!

Dich meiden

Dich mei- den nein,_____ ach nein!

Es taget vor dem Walde

Es ta- get vor dem Wal- de; stand auf Kä- ther- lein___

FRASER-SIMSON, Harold (1878-1944)

Vespers (Christopher Robin is saying his prayers)
Copyright 1924, E. P. Dutton & Co., Inc., N. Y.

Lit- tle boy kneels at the foot of the bed, Drops on the lit- tle hands

FRESCOBALDI, Girolamo (1583-1643)

Non mi negate, ohimè

Non mi___ ne - ga - te, ohi - mè, Lu - - mi se - re - ne,   B

Se l'Aura spira

Se l'Au - ra spi - ra tut-ta vez - - - zo-sa, La fres-ca Ro - sa ri-den-te___ stà   C

Voi partite mio Sole

Voi par - ti - te mio So - le E por-ta il vo-stro lu-me al tro-ve il gior - no;   D

FRIML, Rudolf (1881-   )

L'Amour-Toujours—l'Amour
Copyright 1922, Harms, Inc.

L'a-mour___ tou-jours___ l'a-mour,___ Love, now at last, you've found me___   F

Giannina Mia, from The Firefly (operetta)
Copyright 1912, G. Schirmer, Inc.

In my gon-do-la, love, let us glide___ O'er the drow-sy blue la-goon___   G

For___ I a - dore,___ I a-dore you Gian-ni-na mi - a   H

Give me one hour, from The White Eagle (operetta)
Copyright by Mills Music Inc., N. Y.

Give me one hour whose pas-sion re-pays The death of power,   I

Marie (operetta)
Copyright 1924 Harms, Inc.
Indian Love Call

When I'm call-ing you - - - - oo - - oo - - - oo-oo-oo!   J

Rose Marie

O Rose Ma- rie, I love you___ I'm al-ways dream-ing of you   K

Vagabond King (operetta)
Only a Rose

Song of the Vagabond

FUENLLANA, Miguel de (16th Cent.)

Paseábase el Rey moro

Pa - se - á - ba - se el rey mo - - re Por la ciu - dad   P

GABRIELI, Giovanni (1557-1612)

Benedictus

Be - - - ne - di - ctus qui ve - nit, Be - ne - di - ctus   R

Jubilate Deo

Ju - bi - la - te De - o om - - - - - nis ter - - - - - - - - - ra,   S

GADE, Niels W. (1817-1890)

Elverskud (The Erl-King's Daughter) (cantata)
Part I Oluf's Ballade

When- e'er I ride through the ten- der grove, A- glow with the sun- beams

Part III The sun now mounts the eastern sky

The sun now mounts__ the eas- tern sky, To clouds bright hues he lends

Farvel, Lille Grete

Ak, kjae- re- ste, Hr. Guld- smed jeg har kun Sorg og Saon

Knud Lavard

Herr Mag- nus han stir- ren i Vin- ter- nat- ten ud:

GALUPPI, Baldassare (1706-1785)

Adriano in Siria (opera)

E in- gra- to, lo veg- gio, ma sie- de nel so- glio, ma sie- de nel so- glio,

Pri- gio- ni- e- ra', ab- ban- do- na- ta,

Son troppo vezzose, from Enrico (opera)

Son trop- po vez-zo- se Del vol- to le ro-se, Son ca- re

GANZ, Rudolph (1877-)

A Memory
Copyright 1919, G. Schirmer, Inc.

Some- how I feel that thou__ art near, Though there is naught a-round;

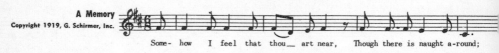

GARNIER, François (16th Cent.)

Resveillez-moy

Res- sveil-lez moy, re- sveil- lez moy mon bel a- my.__

GASPARINI, Francesco (1668-1727)

Adoramus Te, Christe (wrongly ascribed to Mozart)

Ad- o- ra - - - - - - - mus te, Chri - -ste, et be- ne- di- ci- mus__

Caro laccio, dolce nodo (cantata)

Ca- ro lac- cio, dol-ce no- do, che le- ga- sti, le - - ga- sti

Lasciar d'amarti

Lasciar d'a- mar- ti per non pe- nar, ca- ro mio be- ne,

GASTOLDI, Giovanni Giacomo (1550-1619)

Maidens fair of Mantua's city

Mai-dens fair of Man-tua's ci- ty, none so grace-ful, none so pret- ty

GEEHL, Henry E.

For you alone
Copyright by Schuberth Music Pub.
Co., Inc., N. Y.

Take thou this rose, this lit- tle ten- der rose;— B

GENTIAN, (16th Cent.)

La Loy d'Honneur

La loy d'hon- neur qui nous dict et com- man- de, D

GERMAN, Edward (1862-1936)

Charming Chloe
Copyright by Novello & Co., Ltd., London

It was the charm- ing month of May— When all— the flow'rs were fresh F

Merrie England (opera)
Act I

The Yeomen of England

Act II The English Rose

Rolling Down to Rio
Copyright by Novello & Co., Ltd., London

I nev- er sailed the A- ma- zon, I've nev- er reached— Bra- zil; K

Waltz Song, from Tom Jones
(operetta)

Who'll buy my lavender?
By permission Boosey & Hawkes, Inc.,
copyright owners

La- dies fair, I— bring to you La- ven- der with spikes of— blue M

GERSHWIN, George (1897-1937)

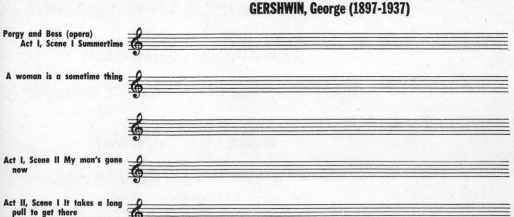

Porgy and Bess (opera)
Act I, Scene I Summertime

A woman is a sometime thing

Act I, Scene II My man's gone
now

Act II, Scene I It takes a long
pull to get there

Porgy and Bess (opera)
Act II, Scene I It takes a long pull to get there

I got plenty o' nuttin'

Buzzard Song

Bess, you is my woman now

Scene II, It ain't necessarily so

There's a boat dat's leavin' for New York

Act III, Scene III Oh, Bess, oh. where's my Bess

Oh Lawd, I'm on my way

GESUALDO, Carlo (Prince of Venosa) (1560-1613)

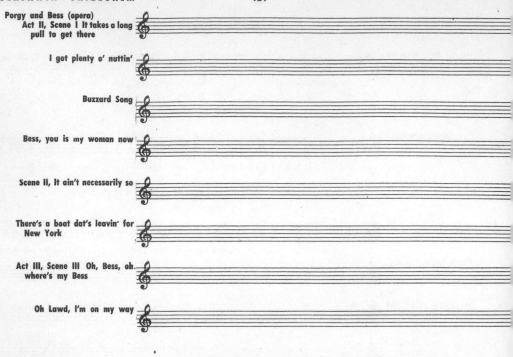

Dolcissima mia vita

Io tacerò

Moro lasso (madrigal)

Resta di darmi noia (madrigal)

GHERARDELLO, da Firenze (15th Cent.)

Tosto che l'alba; caccia

GHIZEGHEM, Hayne Van (15th Cent.)

Les grans regrets

GIANNINI, Vittorio (1903-)

Tell me, Oh blue, blue Sky
Copyright by G. Ricordi & Co., Inc.

Sum- mer has flown, the leaves are fall-ing, I hear a voice   B

GIBBONS, Orlando (1583-1625)

Ah, dear heart (madrigal)

Ah,___ dear heart__ why do you rise? The light that shines comes from your___ eyes   D

Dainty fine bird

Dain- ty fine Bird, that art en- cag- ed there   E

Hosanna to the son of David

Ho- san- na to the Son of Da- vid, of___ Da- vid   F

The Silver Swan (madrigal)

The sil- ver swan, who, liv- ing, had no note, when death ap-proached   G

What is our life? (madrigal)

What is our life?___ our___ life? A play of___ pas- sion   H

GIBBS, Cecil Armstrong (1889-)

Five Eyes, Op. 9, No. 3

In Hans' old mill his three black cats Watch the bins   J

Padraic the fidiler
Copyright 1931, A. Gibbs

Pod-raic sits in the gar- den In un- der the bright new moon___   K

Take heed, young heart
Copyright 1926, A. Gibbs

Take heed, young heart, to Time How soft his foot- fall is   L

To One Who Passed Whistling Through the Night
Copyright 1921, A. Gibbs

Some- thing hath called me, Called me from far dreams___   M

Ah   N

GILBERT, Henry F. (1868-1928)

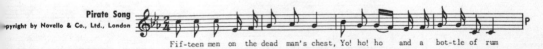

Pirate Song
Copyright by Novello & Co., Ltd., London

Fif-teen men on the dead man's chest, Yo! ho! ho and a bot-tle of rum   P

GIORDANI, Giuseppe (1744-1798)

Caro mio ben

Ca- ro mio ben, cre-di-mi al- men, sen-za di te lan - - gui-sce il cor___   R

GIORDANO, Umberto (1867-   )

Andrea Chenier (opera)
Copyright by Sonzogno, Milan

Fedora (opera)
Copyright by Sonzogno, Milan

Act I — Son ses-san-t'an-ni, o vec-chio, che tu ser-vi

Un di al-l'az-zur-ro spa-zio guardai pro-fon-do

O Pa-sto-rel-le ad-di-o, ad-di-o, ad-di-o o

Act II — Vi-ve-re in fret-ta di que-sta feb-bre ga-ja d'un go-de-re

Io non ho a-ma-to an-cor Pu-re so-ven-te nel-la vi-ta

Act III — Ne-mi-co del-la pa-tria? È vecchia fia-ba che be-a-ta-men-te

Un dì m'e-ra di gio-ia pas-sar fra gli odi e le ven-det-te.

La mam-ma mor-ta m'hanno a la por-ta del-la stan-za mi-a; mo-ri-va

Si fui sol-da-to e glo-rio-so af-fron-ta-to

Act IV — Come un bel dì di mag-gio che con bacio di ven-to

Vi-ci-no a te s'ac-que-ta l'ir-re-quie-ta a-ni-ma mi-a;

La nos-tra mor-te è il trion-fo del l'a-mor

Act I — O gran-di oc-chi lu-cen-ti di fe-de! O va-sta fron-te di me

Act II — Ve-di io pian-go ma, se pian-go, no, non è per la mia vi---ta

A-mor ti vie-ta di non a-mar

Mia ma-dre, la mia vec-chia ma-dre, so-lin-ga vi-ve

La don-na rus-sa è fem---mi-na due vol-te,

Act III — Dio di giu-sti---zia scru-ti le an-go-scie

[la sulla mia fronte, from Il Re (opera)   Act 3
Copyright by Sonzogno, Milan

Bril- la sul ---la mia fron ---te__ ri-splen --de   A

Siberia (opera)   Act I
Copyright by Sonzogno, Milan

T'in-con- trai per via! L'occhio pen-so-so e gra- ve è pe- ne- tra-to   B

Nel suo a- mo- re ri-a-ni-ma-ta la co- scien- za   C

Act II

Or ---ri- de step ---pe! Tor- ri- da l'e-sta- te!   D

Act III

Non o- di là il mar- tir d'an- go- scia fie- ra?   E

GLAZOUNOV, Alexander (1865-1936)

Romance

Wenn ich in dei-ne Au- gen seh', so schwindet all' mein Leid   G

Romance Orientale

Dans le sang brû -----le__ ar- den-te flam ---me__   H

GLIÈRE, Reinhold (1875-   )

Ah, twine no blossoms (Oh, do not wreathe) Op. 18, No. 7

Ah __twine no blos-soms fair and frag-rant To weave a-new my crown of woe,   J

[ver the Depths of the Sea, Op. 59
Copyright 1923, G. Schirmer, Inc.

O-ver- hang-ing the fath- om-less o- cean, a cliff tow- ers high   K

GLINKA, Michael (1804-1857)

Life for the Czar (Ivan Sussanin)
Act I Introduction

Fou ---dre et vent gron ---dent en vain,__ Le__ fau- con__ fran- chit__   M

Le__ doux prin- temps pa- rait Le__ beau prin- temps re- nait__   N

Rondo of Antonida

Au vil- la- ge sur la ri- viè- re, L'on__ at- tend l'ai- mé,   O

Act IV Bogdan Sobinjin's Aria

Frè- res, le froid, l'hor -----reur des__ bois pro- fonds,   P

Tris- te et__ dans l'an- gois-se,__ la fil-le at- tend, cher coeur!   Q

Sussanin's Aria

Pâle au- ro- re,__ tu vien-dras Bai- gner mes yeux las-sés   R

Russlan and Ludmilla
Act I Song of the Bard

Dort, gen Mit- ter- nacht liegt ein wüs- tes__ Land   S

Russian and Ludmilla (opera)
Act II Farlaf's Rondo

Russlan's Aria

Act III Persian Chorus

Gorisslava and Chorus

Cherubim Song

Doubt

In my blood the fire of desire burns
(Now am I all with fever shaken)

I remember

The Lark

Midnight Review

The North Star

Venetian Night (Barcarolle)

GLUCK, Christoph Willibald (1714-1787)

Alceste (opera)
Act I

Act II

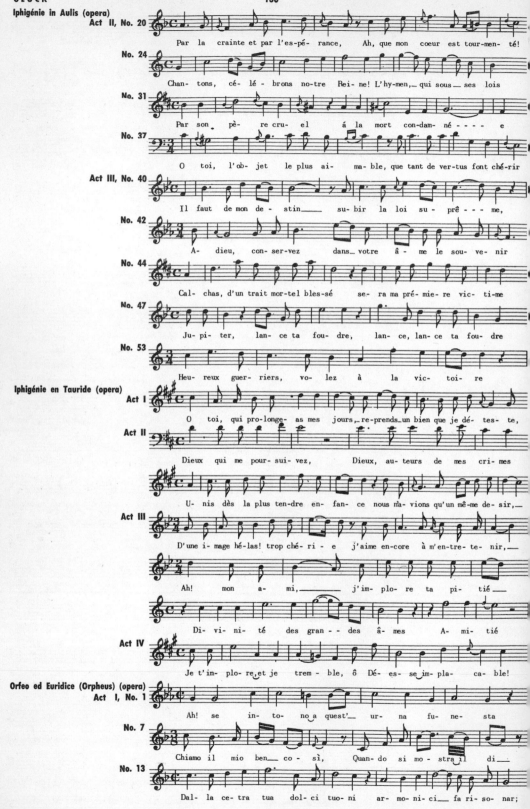

GLUCK

Iphigénie in Aulis (opera)

Act II, No. 20
Par la crainte et par l'es-pé - rance, Ah, que mon coeur est tour-men- té!

No. 24
Chan - tons, cé - lé - brons no-tre Rei-ne! L'hy-men,— qui sous— ses lois

No. 31
Par son pè - re cru-el á la mort con-dam- né - - - - e

No. 37
O toi, l'ob- jet le plus ai- ma-ble, que tant de ver-tus font ché-rir

Act III, No. 40
Il faut de mon de-stin— su-bir la loi su- prê - - - me,

No. 42
A- dieu, con- ser-vez dans— votre â- me le sou- ve- nir

No. 44
Cal- chas, d'un trait mor-tel bles-sé se- ra ma pré- mie- re vic- ti-me

No. 47
Ju- pi- ter, lan-ce ta fou- dre, lan- ce, lan-ce ta fou- dre

No. 53
Heu- reux guer-riers, vo- lez à la vic- toi- re

Iphigénie en Tauride (opera)

Act I
O toi, qui pro-longe- as mes jours,—re-prends— un bien que je dé- tes- te,

Act II
Dieux qui me pour-sui- vez, Dieux, au-teurs de mes cri- mes

U- nis dès la plus ten-dre en- fan- ce nous n'a- vions qu'un mê-me de- sir,

Act III
D'une i- mage hé-las! trop ché-ri- e j'aime en-core à m'en-tre- te- nir,

Ah! mon a- mi,— j'im- plo- re ta pi- tié

Di- vi-ni- té des gran - - des â- mes A- mi- tié

Act IV
Je t'im- plo- re,et je trem- ble, ô Dé- es- se im-pla- ca- ble!

Orfeo ed Euridice (Orpheus) (opera)

Act I, No. 1
Ah! se in- to- no a quest' ur- na fu- ne- sta

No. 7
Chiamo il mio ben— co - sì, Quan-do si mo-stra il di—

No. 13
Dal- la ce-tra tua dol-ci tuo-ni ar- mo-ni-ci fa ri- so- nar;

GLUCK

ed Euridice (Orpheus) (opera)
Act I, No. 15

Gli squar- di trat-tie - - ni, af- fre - - na gli ac- cen - - ti,

No. 17

Ad- dio, ad- dio, o miei so- spi-ri, han spe-me i miei de- si- ri;

No. 19 and 21 (chorus)

Chi mai dell' E-re-bó fra le ca- li- gi- ni sull' or- me d'Er-co-le

Act II, No. 22

Deh pla-ca- te - vi con_ me! Fu- rie, No, Fu- rie, No,

No. 23

Mi- se- ro gio- va- ne, che vuoi, che me- di- ti

No. 24

Mil- le pe - - - ne om- bre sde- gno - - - se

No. 25

Ah! qua-le in- cog- ni- to af- fet- to fle- bi- le

No. 26

Men ti- ran- ne, voi sa- re- ste al mio pian-to, al mio do- lor___

No. 32

È quest' a- si-lo a-me-no e gra-to del ri- po- so il ter-ren,___

No. 33

Che pu- ro ciel! che chia-ro sol! che mio va luce

No. 34

Vie-ni a re- gni del ri- po - - so, grande E- ro- e, te-ne- ro spo-so

Act III, No. 39 Duet

Su e con me_ vie-ni, ca- ro su e con me vie-ni,

No. 41

Che fie- ro mo- men - - - to che bar-ba-ra sor - - - te

Av_ vez-zo al con-ten- to d'un pla-ci-do ob- bli- o

No. 43

Che fa- ró sen-za Eu- ri- di - ce, do-ve an- drò senza il mio ben!

Tri- on-fi A-mo- re, e il mon-do ser-va in-tie-ro all' im-pe-ro_ del-la bel- ta

Tal di- spe- ra,_ tal af- fan- na_ d'u-na ti- ran- na

Gau- dio, gau- dio son al cuo- re que-ste pe- ne dell' a- mor

Qual pia- ce - - re, qual_ dol-cez- za l'a-mor ci ren- de,

Paris et Helena (opera)

O del mio dol-ce ar-dor___ bra-ma-to_og-get----to,

Spiag-ge_a-ma-te, o-ve ta-lo-ra l'I-dol mi-o

Un ruisselet, bien clair, from La Rencontre Imprévue (opera)

Un ruis-se-let, bien clair, bien net, Qui dans la plai-ne ri-an-te

Vieni, che poi sereno, from La Semiramide (opera)

Vie-ni che poi se-re------no, al-ta tua bel-la_in son----no

GODARD, Benjamin (1849-1895)

Nous allons partir, from Dante (opera) Act IV, Scene II

Nous al-lons par-tir___ tous deux, Par-tir___ tous deux

Berceuse, from Jocelyn (opera)

A Ca-chés dans cet a-sile où Dieu nous a con-duits

B Oh! ne t'é-veille pas en-cor___ Pour qu'un bel an-ge de ton rê-ve

La Vivandière (opéra-comique)

Viens a-vec nous pe-tit,___ Viens a-vec nous, viens!

(The Letter)

Mon p'tit gars,___ si nous t'é-cri-vons C'est pour te bien di-re sans ces-se

Chanson de Florian

Ah! s'il est dans vo-tre vil-la--ge Un ber-ger sen-si-ble

Embarquez-vous!

Em-bar-quez-vous! qu'on se dé-pè----che;

Te souviens-tu? Op. 19, No. 6

Te souviens-tu de ta pro-mes--se? Te souviens-tu des ans pas-sés?

GOETZ, Hermann (1849-1878)

Die Kraft versagt, from The Taming of the Shrew (opera)

A Die Kraft ver-sagt des Kam-pfes des Kam-pfes bin ich mü-de

B Es schwei-ge die Kla-ge In De-muth es tra----ge,

GOLDMARK, Carl (1830-1915)

The Queen of Sheba (opera)
Act I

Der Freund ist dein,___ der Freund ist dein___ der un-ter Ro--sen wei-det,

Act II

Lift thine eyes to worlds a-bove thee, to the throne___ of God most high

The Queen of Sheba (opera) Act II

Ma - gi-sche Tö - - - ne, be - rau - schen-der Duft____ kü - - - sse mich

Act III

doch eh' ich in des To-des Thal zur ew' gen Ru - he zie - he

GOMES, Antonio Carlos (Gomez) (1836-1896)

Il Guarany (opera) Act I

Gen - - - ti - le di cuo - re - - - leg - gia-dra di vi - so

Sen - to una for - za in-do-mi - ta che ognor mi trag - ge a te____

Qua - lunque via di-schiuda-si al li - be - ro tuo piè____

Act II

C'era u - na vol-ta un prin-ci - pe me-sto, pen-so-so e bel - - - - - - lo

Salvator Rosa (opera) Act I
Copyright by G. Ricordi & Co., Inc.

Mia pic - ce - rella deh! vie-ni al-lo ma - re, nel-la bar - chetta

Act II

Di spo - so di pa - dre le gio - je se - re - ne

manza (Quando nascesti tu), from Lo Schiavo (opera)

Quan - do nasces-ti tu nasciano i fior____ che il ciel baciò____

GOUBLIER, Gustave

L'Angélus de la Mer
By permission Boosey & Hawkes, Inc., copyright owners

Au loin c'est l'An - ge - lus____ c'est l'An - ge - lus qui son - ne

Le Credo du Paysan
Copyright by Jacquot & Fils, Paris

L'im men - si - té,____ les cieux, les monts, la plai - ne,____

La Voix des Chênes
Copyright by Eveillard, Paris

Quand le soleil s'en - fuit à l'ho - ri - zon,____ Se - mant la nuit

GOUDIMEL, Claude (1510-1572)

Psalm 19

Der Him - mel zahl- los Heer Er - zählt von Got - tes Ehr

Psalm 25

A toi, mon Dieu, mon____ coeur mon- te, En toi mon es - poir j'ai mis;

Psalm 123

D'où vient, Sei - gneur, que tu nous as es - pars Et si long- temps

GOUNOD, Charles François (1818-1893)

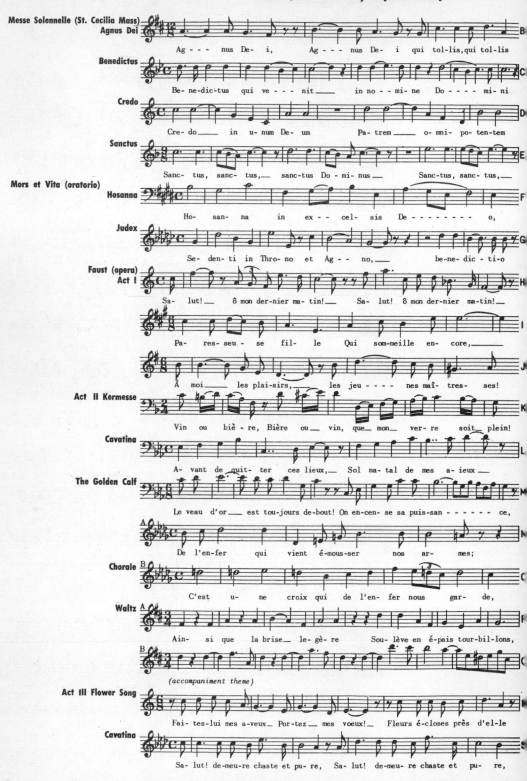

Messe Solennelle (St. Cecilia Mass)
Agnus Dei — Ag - - - nus De - i, Ag - - - nus De - i qui tol-lis, qui tol-lis

Benedictus — Be - ne-dic-tus qui ve - - - nit___ in no - - mi-ne Do - - - mi-ni

Credo — Cre-do___ in u-num De-um Pa-trem___ o-mni-po-ten-tem

Sanctus — Sanc-tus, sanc-tus,___ sanc-tus Do-mi-nus Sanc-tus, sanc-tus,___

Mors et Vita (oratorio)
Hosanna — Ho- san-na in ex - cel - sis De - - - - - - - - o,

Judex — Se - den-ti in Thro-no et Ag - - no,___ be-ne-dic-ti-o

Faust (opera)
Act I — Sa- lut!___ ô mon der-nier ma-tin! Sa- lut! ô mon der-nier ma-tin!

Pa- res-seu- se fil- le Qui som-meille en- core,___

À moi___ les plai-sirs,___ les jeu - - - - nes maî- tres- ses!

Act II Kermesse — Vin ou biè - re, Bière ou___ vin, que mon___ ver- re soit plein!

Cavatina — A- vant de quit- ter ces lieux,___ Sol na-tal de mes a-ieux___

The Golden Calf — Le veau d'or___ est tou-jours de-bout! On en-cen- se sa puis-san - - - - - - ce,

De l'en-fer qui vient é-mous-ser nos ar- mes;

Chorale — C'est u- ne croix qui de l'en- fer nous gar- de,

Waltz — Ain- si que la brise___ le-gè- re Sou- lève en é-pais tour-bil-lons,

(accompaniment theme)

Act III Flower Song — Fai- tes-lui mes a-veux___ Por-tez___ mes voeux! Fleurs é-closes près d'el-le

Cavatina — Sa- lut! de-meu-re chaste et pu- re, Sa- lut! de-meu- re chaste et pu- re,

GOUNOD

Faust (opera)
Act III The King of Thule — A
Il e-tait un Roi de Thu-lé___ Qui jus-qu'à la tom-be fi-dè - - le

Jewel Song — B
Ah! Je ris___ de me voir Si belle en ce mi-roir

Quartet — C
Pre-nez mon bras___ un mo-ment!___ Lais-sez,___ je vous en con-ju-re

Duet A — D
Lais-se-moi,___ Lais-se-moi con-tem-pler ton vi-sa-ge,

B — E
Ô nuit d'a-mour!___ ciel ra-di-eux___ Ô douces flam-mes

— F
Il m'ai-me! il m'ai-me!___ Quel trouble en mon cœur!___

Act IV — G
Il ne re-vient pas,___ Il ne re-vient pas! J'ai peur,—je fris-son-ne;

— H
Si le bon-heur___ à sou-ri-re t'in-vi-te

Scene in the church A — I
Seig-neur, daignez per-mettre à votre humble ser-van-te

B — J
Sou-viens-toi du pas-sé, quand sous l'ai-le des an-ges

Soldiers' Chorus — K
Gloire im-mor-tel-le de nos a-ieux,___ Sois nous fi-dè-le, Mou-rons comme eux___

Mephistopheles' Serenade — L
Vous qui fai-tes l'en-dor-mi-e, N'en-ten-dez-vous pas,___

Death of Valentine — M
É-cou-te-moi bien,___ Mar-gue-ri-te Ce que doit ar-ri-ver___

Act V — N
An-ges purs, an-ges ra-di-eux,___ Por-tez mon âme au sein des cieux!___

— O
Oui___ c'est toi je t'ai-me, oui, c'est toi je t'ai-me

Mireille (opera)
Act I — P
Chan-tez, chan-tez, mag-na-na-relles, Car la cueillette ai-me les chants!

Valse — Q
O lé-gère hi-ron-del - - le,___ Mes-sagè - - re fi-dè - - - le___

Act II — R
La fa-ran-do-le Joy-euse et folle En-traine au bruit des chan-sons

Chanson de Magali — S
La brise est douce et par-fu-mée___ L'oi-seau s'en-dort

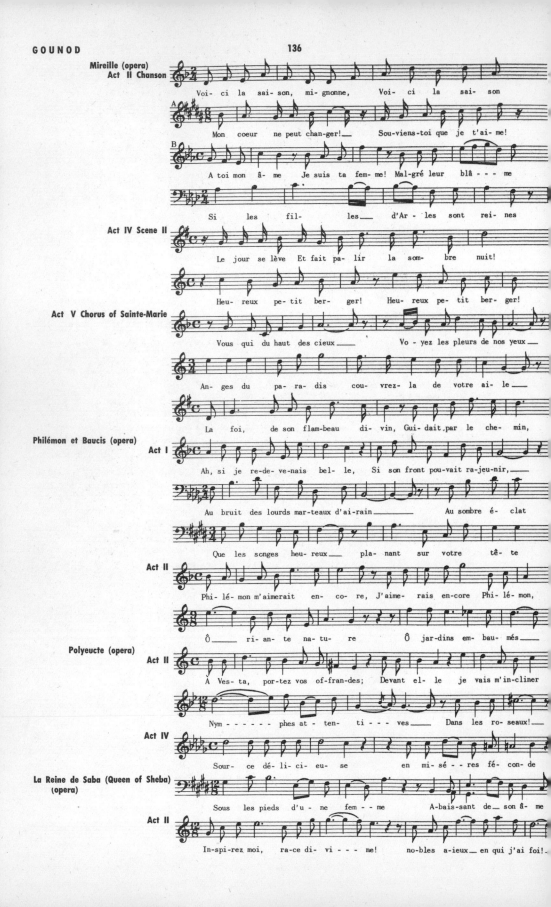

Mireille (opera)
Act II Chanson

Voi-ci la sai-son, mi-gnonne, Voi-ci la sai-son

A
Mon coeur ne peut chan-ger! Sou-viens-toi que je t'ai-me!

B
A toi mon â- me Je suis ta fem-me! Mal-gré leur blâ - - me

Si les fil- les d'Ar-les sont rei-nes

Act IV Scene II
Le jour se lève Et fait pa-lir la som- bre nuit!

Heu- reux pe-tit ber- ger! Heu-reux pe-tit ber-ger!

Act V Chorus of Sainte-Marie
Vous qui du haut des cieux Vo-yez les pleurs de nos yeux

An-ges du pa-ra-dis cou-vrez-la de votre ai-le

Philémon et Baucis (opera)
Act I
La foi, de son flam-beau di-vin, Gui-dait par le che-min,

Ah, si je re-de-ve-nais bel-le, Si son front pou-vait ra-jeu-nir,

Au bruit des lourds mar-teaux d'ai-rain Au sombre é-clat

Act II
Que les songes heu-reux pla-nant sur votre tê-te

Phi-lé-mon m'aimerait en-co-re, J'aime-rais en-core Phi-lé-mon,

Ô ri-an-te na-tu-re Ô jar-dins em-bau-més

Polyeucte (opera)
Act II
À Ves-ta, por-tez vos of-fran-des; Devant el-le je vais m'in-cliner

Nym - - - - - phes at-ten-ti - - ves Dans les ro-seaux!

Act IV
Sour-ce dé-li-ci-eu-se en mi-sé-res fé-con-de

La Reine de Saba (Queen of Sheba)
(opera)
Sous les pieds d'u-ne fem-me A-bais-sant de son â-me

Act II
In-spi-rez moi, ra-ce di-vi - - ne! no-bles a-ieux en qui j'ai foi!

GOUNOD

Reine de Saba (Queen of Sheba) (opera) Act III
Plus grand, dans son ob-scu- ri- té,___ Qu'un roi pa- ré du di-a-dè- me — A

oméo et Juliette (opera) Act I Ballade of Queen Mab
Mab, la rei- ne des__ men-son- ges, Pré-side aux son- ges, — B

"Waltz song"
Je veux vi---vre___ dans le rê---ve — C

Madrigal
Ange a- do- ra-ble, ma main cou-pa- ble Pro-fane, en l'o-sant tou-cher___ — D

Al- lons! jeu-nes gens ___ Al- lons! bel-les da- mes — E

Act II Cavatina
Ah! lè- ve- toi, so-leil!___ fais pa-lir les é- toi- les — F

Act III
Que fais tu, blan-che tour- te- rel- le, Dans ce nid de vau- tours? — G

Act IV Love duet
Nuit d'hy- mé- né--- e!___ Ô___ dou- ce nuit d'a-mour! — H

Que l'hym- ne nup- ti- al ___ suc- cède aux cris d'a- lar- mes — I

C'est là qu'après un jour vo- tre corps et votre â- me — J

A- mour,___ ra- ni- me mon cou- ra- ge, Et de mon coeur chas --- se l'ef-froi ___ — K

ma lyre immortelle, from Sappho (opera)
O- ma lyre im-mor- tel- le Qui dans les tris- tes jours___ — L

Aimons-nous!
Au fleuve le ruisseau se mêle Et le fleuve à la mer!___ — M

Au Printemps
Le printemps chas-se les hi-vers Et sou-rit dans les ar- bres verts — N

Au Rossignol
Quand ta voix cé- les- te pre-lude au si-len-ce des bel-les nuits___ — O

Ave Maria (Meditation on Bach Prelude in C, Well-tempered Clavichord, Book I, No. 1)
A- ve Ma-ri- a ___ Gra- ti-a ple- na, Do- -minus te --cum — P

Ce que je suis sans toi
Ce qu'est le lier-re sans l'or-meau. Qui fut l'ap-pui de son en- fan --- ce — Q

Le Ciel a visité la terre
Le ciel a vi-si- té la ter- re, mon bien ai- mé re-pose — R

Entreat me not to leave thee
En- treat me not to leave thee, En- treat me not to leave thee — S

Envoi de Fleurs — Si l'on veut sa- voir qui m'en- voi - - - - e ces bel- les fleurs,

La Glu — Y a- vait un fois un pauv' gas et lon lon lair- e e lon

Hymne à la Nuit — Viens, lorsque dans l'a- zur___ les as- tres ra- di- eux___

Medjé (Chanson Arabe) A — O Medjé,___ qui d'un sou- ri- re En- chainas ma li- ber- té

B — La voix___ de l'a- mour mê- me De- vrait___ te dé- sar- mer___

Nazareth — Né dans u- ne crê- che, Di- vin Ré- - demp- teur___

Oh, That We Two Were Maying — Oh, that we two were may- ing O- ver the fra- - grant grass___

O ma belle rebelle — O ma bel- le re- bel- le, Las que tu m'es cru- el- le

Où voulez-vous aller (Bacarolle) — Di- tes la jeu- ne bel- le où vou- lez vous al- ler?

Repentir (O Divine Redeemer) A — Ah! ne re- pous- se pas___ mon â- me pé- che- res- se!

B — O Di- vin Ré- demp- teur___ O Di- vin Ré- demp- teur___

Ring out, wild bells — Ring out, wild bells, to___ the wild sky___ The fly- ing cloud,

Sérénade — Quand tu chan- - - tes ber- cé- e le soir, en- tre mes bras___

Le Soir — Le soir ra- mè- ne le si- len- ce, As- sis sur ces ro- chers dé- serts,___

There is a green hill far away (Le Calvaire) A — There is a green hill far a- way,___ With- out a ci- ty wall

B — There was no oth- er good e- nough___ To pay the price

Le Vallon A — D'i- ci___ je vois la vi- e à tra- vers un nu- a- ge

B — Re- po- se- toi, mon â- me, en ce der- nier a- si- le

Venise — Dans Ve- ni- - - se la rou- ge, Pas un bateau qui bou- ge;

GRAENER, Paul (1872-1944)

Philantropisch, Op. 43 b, No. 6 — B
Ein ner-vö-ser Mensch auf ei-ner Wie-se Wä-re bes-ser ohne sie

Palmström, No. 7 — C
Palm-ström steht an ei-nem Tei-che und ent-fal-tet gross ein rotes Taschentuch

Der Page sprach, Op. 49, No. 1 — D
Mei-ne wun-der-schö-ne Kö-ni-gin, du sollst wis-sen

Der alte Herr, No. 3 — E
Kennst du nur den al-ten Her-ren der zur sel-ben Mit-tag-stunde

Der König, Op. 71, No. 3
By permission Associated Music Publishers, Inc. — F
Das war der jun-ge Kö-nig, der Kö-nig ohne Land,

Verspruch, No. 9 — G
Wir sind ein-an-der zu ge-sellt für al-le E-wig-keit,

GRAINGER, Percy (1882-   )

Brigg Fair (arr.)
Copyright by Percy Grainger — I
It was on the fift' of Au-gust, er the wea-ther fine and fair

GRANADOS, Enrique (1867-1916)

Amor y odio
Copyright by Union Musical Española — K
Pen-se que yo sa-bri-a o-cul-tar la pe-na mi-a

Callejes
Copyright by Union Musical Española — L
Dos ho-ras ha que ca-lle-je o, pe-ro no ve o

Las Currutacas modestas
Copyright by Union Musical Española — M
De-cid que da-mi se-las se ven por a-hí que luz-can a-si

El Majo discreto
Copyright by Union Musical Española — N
Di-cen que mi ma-jo es fe-o, Es po-si-ble que si

La Maja Dolorosa, No. 1
Copyright by Union Musical Española — O
¡Oh muer-te cruel ¿Por-qué tu á trai-ción

No. 2 — P
¡Ay ma-jo de mi vi-da, no no, tu no has muer-to;

No. 3 — Q
De a-quel ma-jo a-man-te que fué mi glo-ria guar-do an-he-lan-te

La Maja de Goya
Copyright by Union Musical Española — R
Yo no ol-vi da-re en mi vi-da de Go-ya la i-ma-gen

The Maiden and the Nightingale,
from Goyescas (opera) (La Maja
y el Ruiseñor)
Copyright 1915, G. Schirmer, Inc. — S
Por-qué en-tre som-bras el rui-se-ñor en-to-na su ar-mo-nio-so can-tar?

El Majo Olvidado
Copyright by Union Musical Española

Cuan-do re-cuer-des los di-as pa-sa-dos pien-sa___ en mí,

El Majo Tímido
Copyright by Union Musical Española

Lle-ga á mi re-ja y me mi-ra por la no-che un ma-jo

El Mirar de la Maja
Copyright by Union Musical Española

Por-que_es en mis o-jos___ tan hon-do_el mi-rar___

El Trá-lá-lá y el Punteado
Copyright by Union Musical Española

Es en bal-de ma-jo mí-o que si-gas ha-blan-do

GRENON, Nicolas (15th Cent.)

Je ne requier de

Je ne re-qui-er de ma----- dame_ et_ ma mi

Nova vobis gaudia

No- va vo- bis gau-di- a re- fe- ro

GRETCHANINOV, Alexander (1864-   )

The Wounded Birch, Op. 1, No. 2

By the hatch-et wound-ed, See the birch-tree lan-guish;

My Native Land (My Country) No. 4

Home -- land mine, my na-tive land! Beat-ing hoofs of hors-es,

Berceuse (Cradle Song) No. 5

Sleep, my dar - ling_ sleep, my star-ling, Bye, my ba-by, bye___

Over the Steppe, Op. 5, No. 1

Sad lies the Steppe_in its sol-i-tude Night comes on shad-ow-y wings;

Night No. 2

Stil - - le Schlaf und nächt-lich Dun-kel al-les zau-be-risch

Hushed the song of the Nightingale, Op. 20, No. 2
Copyright by Oliver Ditson Co.
Used by permission.

Hushed the song of the night-in-gale, Yon-der star fall-ing trails thro' the blue

The Captive No. 4

Je suis dans ma ca-ge dans l'om-bre gla-cée

(Children's Songs), Op. 47, No. 1 Snowflakes
By permission Associated Music Publishers, Inc.

We-het, weht ihr Flock-en-ster- ne, uns nur bleibt hübsch fer - - - - ne!___

No. 9 The Snowdrop

Im Wal-de wo Bir-ken sich drän-gen zu Hauf,___

Death (La Morte), Op. 48, No. 5
By permission Associated Music Publishers, Inc.

O mort vieux ca-pi-tai-ne, il est temps! le-vons___ l'an-cre

Ob ich gehe, ob ich stehe, Op. 120, No. 2
By permission Associated Music Publishers, Inc.

Ob ich ge-he, ob ich ste-he ob-ich ge-he, ob ich ste-he,

GRETRY, André (1741-1813)

Jugement de Midas (opera)

Doux char-me de la vi - e, Di- vi- ne mé-lo-di - e

Par___ u- ne grâ - - - ce tou-chan - te u- ne mine in-té-re-san - te

Naissantes fleurs, from Céphale et Procris (opera)

Nais - - san-tes fleurs,___ ces - - - - sez d'é- clo - - re

Plus de dépit, plus de tristesse, from Les Deux Avares (opera)

Plus de dé- pit,___ plus de tris - tes- se

Qu'il est cruel d'aimer, from Les Évènements Imprevues (opera)

Qu'il est cru- el d'ai- mer,___ D'ai- mer sans o- ser di - - re,

Richard Coeur-de-Lion (opera) Act I, No. 2

La dan- se n'est pas ce que j'ai-me, Mais c'est la fille

Duet

U- ne fiè- vre brû-lan - - te Un jour me terras- sait

Je crains de lui par- ler la nuit, J'é-cou-te trop tout ce qu'il dit

Song of Blondel

O Ri- chard, ô mon Roi! L'u- ni- vers t'a- ban- don- ne

Si l'u- ni- vers en-tier m'ou- bli- e S'il faut i- ci pas-ser ma vi- e

Serenade, from L'Amant Jaloux (opera)

Tan- dis que tout___ som- meil- le dans l'om- bre de___ la nuit___

Vous étiez ce que vous n'êtes plus, from Le Tableau Parlant (opera)

Vous é- tiez ce que vous n'ê- tes plus, Ce que vous n'ê- tes___ plus___

Zémiré et Azor (opera)

Ah, quel tour-ment d'ê- tre sen- si - - - - ble, D'a- voir un___ coeur

Du mo- ment qu'on ai- me, L'on de-vient si doux___

La fau- vet- te a - - - vec ses pe- tits___

Ro- se ché- ri - - - e, Ai- ma- ble fleur! Ro- se ché- ri - - - e

GRIEG, Edvard Hagerup (1843-1907)

To brune Øjne, Op. 5, No. 1 (Two Brown Eyes)

To bru- ne Øj- ne jeg ny- lig saa, i dem mit Hjem

Ich liebe dich (I Love Thee), Op. 5, No. 3

Du mein Ge- dan- ke, du mein Sein und Wer- den!

Vuggesang, Op. 9, No. 2

Sov min Søn, o slum- re sødt end- nu gar din Vug- ge blødt

Ausfahrt (Outward Bound), No. 4

Es war_ ei- ne dämmernde Som- mer-nacht,_ ein Schiff_ am U- - fer lag,_

Love, Op. 15, No. 2

The sun like vi-sions of love_ doth glow; he cooleth his face

The Poet's Last Song, Op. 18, No. 1

Thou Gi- ant Death O hear me high, To Spi-rit land swift fly- - ing!

Vandring i skoven No. 2

Min sø- de Brud, min un- ge Vio, min kjaer- lif hed, mit Liv

Hytten No. 3

Hvor Bøl- gen hejt_ mod ky-stens slaar en gan- ske lil- le

Herbststurm (Autumn Storm) No. 4

Im Som- mer wie war da so grün der Wald, als Zwit-schern von je-dem Zweig

Erstes Begegnen (First Meeting), Op. 21, No. 1

Des_ er- sten Se- hens Won- ne ist_ wie der Duft_ im_ Wal- de

Dein Rat ist wohl gut (Your Advice is Good) (Thanks for the Rede) No. 4

Dein Rat ist wohl gut, der mich warnt vor der Flut,

Kvad, Op. 22, No. 1

Nor- rø- na fol- ket det vil fa- re, det vil fa- re

Peer Gynt (drama with music) Solvejg's Song, Op. 23, No. 1

A

Der Win-ter mag schei-den, der Früh- ling ver-geh'n, der_ Früh-ling ver-geh'n,_

B

Ah -

Solvejg's Slumber Song, No. 2

Schlaf', du theu- er- - ster Kna- be mein! Ich will wie- gen mein Kind_

Ein Schwan (A Swan), Op. 25, No. 1

Mein Schwann, mein stil-ler, mit wei-ssem Ge-fie-der, dei-ne wonnigen

Glücksbote mein, No. 3

Glücks- bo- te mein, so nannt ich dich, ver-glich dich einem Ster-ne

Mit einer Wasserlilie, No. 4 (With a Water-Lily)

Sieh,_ Ma- rie, was ich dir brin - - - - - ge:

Am schönsten Sommerabend war's (It was a lovely summer eve) Op. 26, No. 2

Am schön- sten Som-mer- a- bend war's, ich ging durch ein ein-sam Thal,_

Hoffnung (Hope), Op. 26, No. 3
Ich möchte ju-beln in al-le Win-de doch fasst ihr wohl

Mit einer Primula Veris (With a Primrose), No. 4
Mag dir, du zar-tes Früh-lings-kind, dies er-ste Blüm-chen from-men

Den store hvide Flok (The Great White Host), Op. 30, No. 10 (baritone and male quartet)
Den sto-re hvi-de Flok vi-se, som tu sind Bjer-ge fuld of Sne,

Landkjending (Landsighting), Op. 31
Og det war O-lav Tryg-va-son, staevned o-ver Nords-jö fram

Der Frühling (Springtide), Op. 33, No. 2
Ja, noch ein-mal könnt den Win-ter ich seh'n dem Früh-lin-ge wei-chen,

Der Verwundete (The Wounded Heart), No. 3
Mein Her-ze war mit in des Le-bens streit und Wun-den hat es

An einem Bache (At the Brookside), No. 5 (Langs en Å)
Du wald, der sich her-ü-ber biegt und küsst den schwar-zen Bach

Auf der Reise zur Heimat (On the Road Home), No. 9
So seh aufs neu ich je-ne Berg und Ta-le,

Vom Monte Pincio (from Monte Pincio), Op. 39, No. 1
A-bend wie mil-de! Son-ne wie roth! Al-les er-füllt sich

Greeting, Op. 48, No. 1
Ten-der mu-sic, from my soul pour with sweet persistence;

Ein Traum (A Dream), No. 6
Mir träum-te einst ein schö-ner Traum: mich lieb-te ei-ne blon-de Maid;

Vug, o Vove, Op. 49, No. 2
Vug, o Vo-ve, med var-som Haand Baa-den, hvor-i

Spring Showers, No. 6
Sweet strains from fai-ry in-stru-ments are sound-ing

Til Norge (To Norway), Op. 58, No. 2
Du er min mor, jeg el-sker dig, der-med er al-ting sagt!

Margaretlein Lein, Op. 60, No. 1
Mar-ga-ret-lein sass spät am A-bend, der Kuckuck rief in dem grünen Tann,

Moderen synger, No. 2
Gret-chen lig-ger i Ki-ste dybt i den sor-te Muld

Im Kahne (In the Boat), No. 3
Mö-ven, Mö-ven in weis-sen Flo-cken! Son-nen-schein!

Der skreg en Fugl (There screamed a Bird), No. 4
Der skreg en Fugl o-ver ö-de Hav, langt fra Lan-de

Zur Johannisnacht (St. John's Eve), Op. 60, No. 5
Ei- ne We-ste wünsch ich von Sei- de mir, ja,— ja, von— Sei- de— mir.

Fisher's Song, Op. 61, No. 4
Ere day-light a- wak-eth, the fi-sher-man tak-eth his boat on the main

Haugtussa, Op. 67, No. 1 Det syng (Det synger)
Og vad du den Drõm og vad du den Sang sä vil du To- ner-ne gemme—

No. 2 Veslemöy (Ungmöen)
Hun er ma- ger og mörk og myg med— bru-ne og re- ne Drag,—

No. 3 Blåbaer-Li (I Blåbaer- Tuerne)
Nei se, hvor det blå- ner her! Nu vil en Hirl vi os ta- ge!

No. 4 Møte (Møde)
En stil- le Sön- dag sid-der hun i Li;— det strömmer på

No. 5 Elsk (Elskoe)
Den vil-de Gut-ten mit Sind har då- ret, som Fugl i Sna-ren jeg sid-der sa- ret;

No. 6 Killingdans (Kiddenes Dans)
A hipp og hop- pe og tipp og top- pe på den- ne— Dag;—

No. 7 Vond Dag (Ond Dag)
Hon toel-ler Dag og Stund og se- ne kvoeld til Sön-dags- tid

No. 8 Ved Gjaetle-Bekken (Ved Gjatle-Bakken)
Du ris-len- de Boek, du heis-len- de Boek, her lig-ger i Sol du så klar

A Boat on the Waves is Rocking, Op. 69, No. 1
A boat on the waves is rock- ing, There sit-ting a- lone on board—

Eros, Op. 70, No. 1
Hört mich, ihr frö- sti- gen Her - - - - zen im Nord,

Lichte Nacht (Radiant Night), No. 3
Sank nicht die Son-ne kaum erst zum Meer in duf-ti-ger däm-mernder Fer-ne,

GRIFFES, Charles Tomlinson (1884-1920)

In a Myrtle Shade, Op. 9, No. 1
Copyright 1918, G. Schirmer, Inc.
To a love- ly myr- tle bound, Blos-soms— show-'er- ing all a- round

Waikiki No. 2
Warm per- fumes like a breath from vine and tree

An Old Song Re-Sung, No. 4
I saw a ship a sail-ing, a- sail- ing, a- sail- ing,

Sorrow of Mydath, No. 5
Wear - - - y the cry— of the wind— is

A Feast of Lanterns, Op. 10, No. 5
Copyright 1917, G. Schirmer, Inc.
In Spring for sheer de-light— I set the lanterns swinging through— the trees

The Lament of Ian the Proud, Op. 11, No. 1
Copyright 1918, G. Schirmer, Inc.

What is this cry- ing___ that I hear in the wind?___

Thy Dark Eyes to Mine, No. 2

Thy dark eyes to mine, Ei- lidh,___ Lamps of de- sire!

By a lonely forest pathway
Copyright 1909, G. Schirmer, Inc.

By a lone- ly for-est path-way I am fain at eve to flee___

The Dreamy Lake
Copyright 1909, G. Schirmer, Inc.

An o- pal dream___ en- chants the lake, Where wa- ter lil- ies gent-ly lie

O'er the tarn's unruffled mirror
Copyright 1909, G. Schirmer, Inc.

O'er the tarn's un-ruf- fled mir- ror lies the moon- light's sil-ver sheen,

Time was when I in anguish lay
Copyright 1909, G. Schirmer, Inc.

Time was when I in an- guish lay, While day and night I wept;

GROTTE, Nicolas de la (16th Cent.)

Je suis amour

Je - - - - - - - - - - suis a-mour___ le grand mais- tre des dieux

GRUBER, Franz Xavier (1787-1863)

Stille Nacht, Heilige Nacht (Silent Night, Holy Night)

Stil - le Nacht, Hei- li- ge Nacht! Al- les schläft, Ein- sam wacht

GRUENBERG, Louis (1884-)

Standin' in de need of Prayer (based on a spiritual), from Emperor Jones (opera)
Copyright 1932, Cos Cob Press, Inc.

It's a- me,___ It's a- me, Oh Lawd,___ stan-din' in de need of prayer

GUARNIERI, Camargo (1907-)

Den Báu
Copyright 1947, Mercury Music Corp.
Used by permission.

Den báu den báu den col ma- ri- ol- den mi- ne- ról den,

Quebra O Côco, Menino (Break the cocoanut)
Copyright 1947, Mercury Music Corp.
Used by permission.

Fol- gue, fol-gue mi- nha gen- te, Que u-ma noi- te não é na- da

Que- bra cô- co, me- ni- na Du- ro esta! Ai com for-ca no cô- co

GUION, David W. (1895-)

All day on the Prairie (arr.)
Copyright 1930, G. Schirmer, Inc.

All day on the prai-rie in the sad-dle I ride, not e- ven a dog, boys

At the cry of the First Bird
Copyright 1924, G. Schirmer, Inc.

At the cry___ of the first bird___ they be- gan to cru-ci- fy thee

Home on the Range (Cowboy Song)
(arr.)
Copyright 1930, G. Schirmer, Inc.

Oh, give me a home where the buf-fa-lo roam, Where the deer

What shall we do with a Drunken
Sailor (arr.)
Copyright 1933, G. Schirmer, Inc.

What shall we do with a drun-ken sai-lor, What shall we do with a drun-ken sai-lor;

HAGEMAN, Richard (1882-)

At the Well
Copyright 1919, G. Schirmer, Inc.

When the two sis-ters go to fetch wa-ter They come to this spot

Christ went up into the hills
Copyright by Carl Fischer, Inc.
Used by permission

Christ went up in-to the hills a-bove, Walk-ing slow-ly

The Donkey
By permission Boosey & Hawkes, Inc.,
copyright owners

When fish-es flew and for-ests walked and figs grew up-on thorn

Do not go, my love
Copyright 1917, G. Schirmer, Inc.

Do not go, my love, with-out ask-ing my leave

Miranda
By permission Galaxy Music
Corporation, N. Y.

Do you re-mem-ber an Inn, Mi-ran - - - - - - - da,

Music I heard with you
By permission Galaxy Music
Corporation, N. Y.

Mu-sic I heard with you was more than mu-sic,

HAHN, Reynaldo (1875-)

À Chloris
By permission Heugel & Cie, Paris,
copyright owners

S'il est vrai, Chlo-ris que tu m'aimes, (Mais j'entends que tu m'aimes bi

L'Air
By permission Heugel & Cie, Paris,
copyright owners

Dans l'air s'en vont les ai-les Par le vent ca-res-sé-es

La Barcheta
By permission Heugel & Cie, Paris,
copyright owners

La no - te è be-la, Fa pres-to, o Ni-ne-ta

Chanson au Bord de la Fontaine
By permission Heugel & Cie, Paris,
copyright owners

O blan-ches co-lom-be du soir, que je vien-drai m'as-seoir

Ciboulette (operetta)
Ce n'était pas la même chose
Copyright by Salabert, Paris, N. Y.

Bien des jeu-nes gens ont vingt ans Dont la sai-son n'a pas de ro-s

Dans une charrette

C'est le prin-temps qui m'a sur-pri-se, Ce ciel trop bleu,

Moi j'm'appell' Ci-bou-let-te! Ça sonn' clair comme un' chan-son

Comme frère et soeur

Les pa-rents, quand on est bé-bé tout dé-fend-ent, dé-fend-ent, dé-fend-ent

Comm' la vie vous semble a-voir d'la dou-ceur Quand on est en-semble

HAHN

Ciboulette (operetta) — A
Nous a-vous fait un beau voy-a-ge Nous a-vons fait un beau voy-a-ge!

C'est sa banlieue — B
Y'a des ar-bres,_ des mai-sons_ Y'a l'é-glise et la mai-ri-e_

Valse — C
A-mour qui meurs, a-mour qui pas-ses, A-mour fra-gi-le,

Cimetière de Campagne — D
By permission Heugel & Cie, Paris, copyright owners
J'ai re-vu le ci-me-tiè-re du beau pa-ys d'Am-bé-rieux

Les Cygnes — E
By permission Heugel & Cie, Paris, copyright owners
Ton âme est un lac d'a-mour Dont mes dé-sirs sont les Cy-gnes

La Dernière Valse (Une Revue) — F
By permission Heugel & Cie, Paris, copyright owners
Les feuilles tom-bent, c'est l'au-tom-ne. Tu pars, tout est fi-ni

D'une prison — G
By permission Heugel & Cie, Paris, copyright owners
Le ciel est par des-sus le toit, si bleu, si cal---me

L'Énamourée — H
By permission Heugel & Cie, Paris, copyright owners
Ils se di-sent, ma co-lom-be que tu rê-ves, morte en-co-re,

En sourdine — I
Cal---mes dans le demi jour que les branches hautes font_ Pé-né-trons bien

Les Étoiles — J
By permission Heugel & Cie, Paris, copyright owners
Les cieux_ res-plen-dis-sants d'é-toi--les Aux ra-di-eux_

Fêtes Galantes — K
By permission Heugel & Cie, Paris, copyright owners
Les don-neurs de sé-ré-na---des Et les bel-les é-cou-teu---ses,_

Fumée — L
By permission Heugel & Cie, Paris, copyright owners
Com-pa-gne de l'é-ther,_ in-do-len-te_ fu-mé--e,

L'Heure Exquise — M
By permission Heugel & Cie, Paris, copyright owners
La lu-ne blan-che luit dans les bois; de cha-que bran-che Part une voix

L'Incrédule — N
By permission Heugel & Cie, Paris, copyright owners
Tu crois au marc de ca-fé,_ Au pré sa-ges, aux grands jeux_

Infidélité — O
By permission Heugel & Cie, Paris, copyright owners
Voi-ci l'or-me qui ba-lan-ce Son om---bre sur le sen-tier,

Je me metz en vostre mercy — P
By permission Heugel & Cie, Paris, copyright owners
Je me metz en vos-tre mer-cy,_ Tres bel-le, bon-ne

Lydé — Q
By permission Heugel & Cie, Paris, copyright owners
Viens, c'est le jour d'un Dieu, Pui-sons a-vec lar-gesse

Mai — R
By permission Heugel & Cie, Paris, copyright owners
De-puis un mois, chère ex-i-lé-e, Loin de mes yeux tu t'en al-las,_

Mozart (operetta) Act I — S
By permission Heugel & Cie, Paris, copyright owners
Etre a-do-ré! Pren-dre les coeurs Et les sen-tir tous qui se li-vrent,

Mozart (operetta)
Act II Letter Song

De-puis ton dé-part, mon a-mour,___ De-puis, hé-las, de si longs jours

Act III Air des Adieux

Sois cou-ra-geu- se,O ma maî-tres-se, Pen- dant que je te dis a-dieu

Nocturne
By permission Heugel & Cie, Paris, copyright owners

Sur ton sein pâ- le, mon coeur dort D'un som- meil doux___ com- me la mort.

Offrande
By permission Heugel & Cie, Paris, copyright owners

Voi- ci des fruits, des fleurs,des feuilles et des branches Et puis voi-ci mon coeur

Paysage
By permission Heugel & Cie, Paris, copyright owners

A deux pas de la mer qu'on en-tend bour-don- ner,

Paysage Triste

L'om- bre des ar- bres dans la ri-viere em-bru- mé___ meurt

Phyllis
By permission Heugel & Cie, Paris, copyright owners

De-puis neuf ans et plus___ dans l'am- pho-re scel-lé- - e

Le Plus Beau Présent
By permission Heugel & Cie, Paris, copyright owners

Tu m'as don-né un cous-sin de soi- e, Un brû-le-par-fum d'un art per- san;

Le Printemps
By permission Heugel & Cie, Paris, copyright owners

Te voi-là,___ ri- re du Prin-temps___ Les thyr-ses des li-las.

Quand je fus pris au pavillon
By permission Heugel & Cie, Paris, copyright owners

Quand je fus pris au pa-vil-lon de ma da-me très gente et bel - - le

Rêverie
By permission Heugel & Cie, Paris, copyright owners

Puisqu'i-ci vas toute â-me Donne à quel- qu'un Sa mu- si-que,sa flamme

Le Rossignol des Lilas
By permission Heugel & Cie, Paris, copyright owners

O pre-mier ros-si- gnol qui viens dans les li-las, sous ma fe- nê-tre,

Seule
By permission Heugel & Cie, Paris, copyright owners

Dans un bai-ser,l'onde,au ri- va- ge, Dit ses dou- leurs___

Si mes vers avaient des ailes

Mes vers fui-raient doux et frêles vers vo-tre jar-din si beau,

Le souvenir d'avoir chanté
By permission Heugel & Cie, Paris, copyright owners

Le sou-ve-nir d'a-voir chan-té Au so- leil,sous l'a-zur cé- les- - te,

Sur l'eau
By permission Heugel & Cie, Paris, copyright owners

Je n'en-tends que le bruit de la rive et de l'eau___

Tyndaris
By permission Heugel & Cie, Paris, copyright owners

O___ blan- che Tyn- da- ris, les Dieux me sont a- mis

HALÉVY, Jacques François (1799-1862)

La Juive (opera)
Act I

Si la ri-gneur et la ven- gean-ce leur font ha- ir___ la sain-te loi

La Juive (opera)

Act II — O Dieu, Dieu de nos pè-res, par-mi nous dé-scends!

Si tra-hi-son ou per-fi-di-e o-sait se glisser par-mi nous,

Cavatine — Dieu, que ma voix trem-blan-te s'é-lè-ve jusqu'aux cieux,

Il va ve-nir! et d'éf-froi je me sens fré-mir

Act III — Vous qui du Dieu vi-vant ou-tra-gez la puis-san-ce

Act IV — Ra-chel, quand du Seig-neur la grâ-ce tu-té-lai-re

HAMMERSCHMIDT, Andreas (1612-1675)

Sei nun wieder zufrieden — Sei nun wie-der zu-frie-den, mei-ne See-le,

HANDEL, George Frederick (1685-1759)

Arioso (cantata con stromenti) (Questionable authenticity) — Dank sei Dir, Herr, Dank sei Dir, Herr Du hast Dein

Come, let us worship, from Chandos Anthem — O come, let us wor-ship, let us wor-ship and fall down,

Di Cupido impiego — Di Cu-pi-do im-pie-go i van-ni

dolce dell' oblio (cantata for solo voice—secular) Aria — Giacchè il son-no a lei di-pin-ge la sem-bian-za del suo be-ne,

Aria — Ha' l'in-gan-no il suo di-let-to se i pen-sier mos-si d'af-fet-to

Praise of Harmony — Look down, look down, har-mo-nious Saint,

Süsse Stille — Sü-sse Stil-le, sanf-te Quel-le ru-hi-ger

Te Deum (Dettingen) — Vouch-safe, O Lord! Vouch-safe, O Lord! to keep us this day with-out sin

When thou took-est up-on thee to de-li-ver man

ODES: Alexander's Feast — Bac-chus e-ver fair and young, drink-ing days did first or-dain

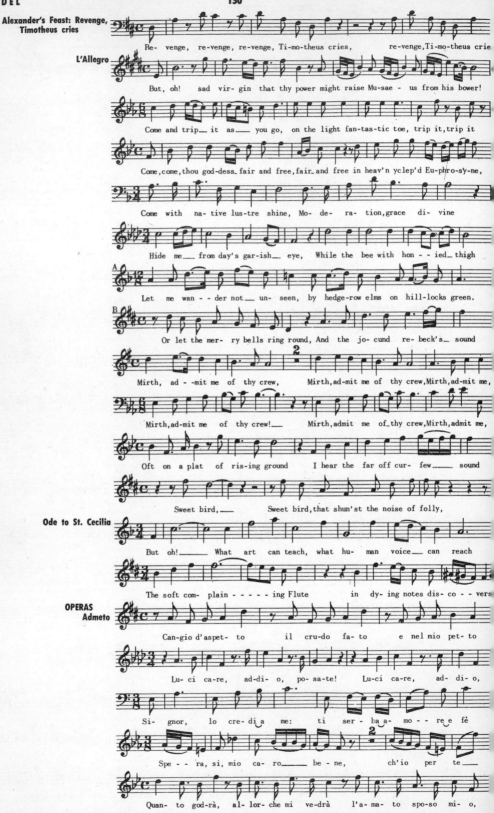

Alexander's Feast: Revenge,
Timotheus cries

Re-venge, re-venge, re-venge, Ti-mo-theus cries, re-venge, Ti-mo-theus crie

L'Allegro

But, oh! sad vir-gin that thy power might raise Mu-sae-us from his bower!

Come and trip it as you go, on the light fan-tas-tic toe, trip it, trip it

Come, come, thou god-dess fair and free, fair and free in heav'n yclep'd Eu-phro-sy-ne,

Come with na-tive lus-tre shine, Mo-de-ra-tion, grace di-vine

Hide me from day's gar-ish eye, While the bee with hon--ied thigh

Let me wan--der not un-seen, by hedge-row elms on hill-locks green.

Or let the mer-ry bells ring round, And the jo-cund re-beck's sound

Mirth, ad--mit me of thy crew, Mirth, ad-mit me of thy crew, Mirth, ad-mit me,

Mirth, ad-mit me of thy crew! Mirth, admit me of thy crew, Mirth, admit me,

Oft on a plat of ris-ing ground I hear the far off cur-few sound

Sweet bird, Sweet bird, that shun'st the noise of folly,

Ode to St. Cecilia

But oh! What art can teach, what hu-man voice can reach

The soft com-plain-----ing Flute in dy-ing notes dis-co--vers

OPERAS
Admeto

Can-gio d'aspet-to il cru-do fa-to e nel mio pet-to

Lu-ci ca-re, ad-di-o, po-sa-te! Lu-ci ca-re, ad-di-o,

Si-gnor, lo cre-di a me: ti ser-ba a-mo--re e fè

Spe--ra, si, mio ca-ro be-ne, ch'io per te

Quan-to god-rà, al-lor-che mi ve-drà l'a-ma-to spo-so mi-o,

HANDEL

Agrippina (A)
Bel pia - - ce-re__ è go- de- re fi- do a - - - mor!

(B)
Col rag-gio pla- ci- do__ del-la spe- ran- za__la__ mi- a

(C)
In- gan- na- ta u-na sol vol- ta es- ser pos-so, mà non più

(D)
Io di Ro-ma il Gio- - ve so- no,__ nè v'è già chi me- co

(E)
O - - - gni ven- - to, o - - gni ven-to ch'al por-to lo spin- ga,

Alcina (F)
Ah!__ mio__ cor! scher-ni-to se - i! Stel-le! De - i!

(G)
La boc-ca va- ga, quell' oc-chio ne- ro lo sò, t'im- pia-ga;

(H)
Mi re- - sta-no le la- gri-me, di- rei dell'al- ma i vo- ti

(I)
Sem- pli-cet-to! a don- na cre-di? a don- na cre-di?

(J)
Ver- di pra- ti, sel-ve a-me- ne, per-de - - - re-te la__ bel- ta

Al sen ti stringo e parto, from Ariodante (K)
Al sen ti strin- go e par-to al sen ti stringo e par-to,

Amadigi (L)
Ah spie- ta - - - to! e non ti muo - - - ve

Siciliana (M)
Gio - - - ja, ve- ni- te in sen;__ bril- la- te nel__ mio cor

(N)
O ren- de- te- mi il mio be- - ne, a- stri in-fi- di

(O)
Pe- na ti- ran- na io sen-to al co- re, nè spe- ro ma - i

(P)
Tu mia spe- ran- za, tu mio__ con - - for- to,

Atalanta (Q)
Ben' io sen- to l'in- gra- ta, spie- ta - - ta fu- ria a-tro-ce,

(R)
Ca - - - - - - - - - re sel-ve ca-re, ca-re sel-ve, om-bre be-a- te,

(S)
Co- me al-la tor-to- rel- la lan-gue al suo ca-ro ap-presso

OPERAS
Atalanta

Di ad I- re- ne, ti- ran- na in- fe- de- le,

La- scia ch'io par- ta so- lo, e tu ri- man- ti, oh bel- la,

M'al- lon- - ta- no, sde- gno- - se pu- pil- le,

Ri- por- tai, glo- rio- - sa pal- ma,

S'è tuo pia- cer, ch'io mo- ra va- do a mo- rir, I- re- - ne

Sof- fri in pa- ce il tuo do- lo- re, se il mio a- mor tu di- sprez- za- sti

Berenice

Si, tra i cep- pi e le ri- tor- te La mia fè ri- splen- de- rà,

No, sof- frir non può il mio a- mo- re, che non re- gni tua bel- tà,

Caro amor, from Il Pastor
Fido Act II

Ca- ro A- mor, Ca- ro A- mor, sol per mo- men- - ti

Deidàmia

Due bell' al- me in- na- mo- ra- te, ca- re, fi- de a- man- ti

Nel ri- po- so e nel con- ten- to Go- do e sen- to Lie- ve il pe- so

Se pen- si a- mor tu so- lo per vez- zo e per bel- ta

Ezio

Na- sce al bos- co in roz- - za cu- na un fe- li- ce pa- - sto- rel- la

Quan- to mai fe- li- ce sie- te, in- no- cen- ti pas- to- rel- le,

Se un bell' ar- di- - - re Può in- na- mo- rar- ti

Vi fi- - - da lo spo- - so, vi fi- - da il re- - gnan- te

Flavio

A- mor, nel mi- o pe- nar deg- - gio spe- rar,

L'ar- - mel- lin vi- ta non cu- ra se d'of- fen- de- re ha ti- mo- re

Chi può mi- ra- re e non a- - ma- re, e non a- - ma- re

OPERAS

Flavio

A

Quan - to dol - ci, quan - to ca - re son le gio - je nel mio sen,

Floridante

B

Al - - - - ma mi - a, sì, sol tu se - i la mia glo - ria, il mio di let - to,

C

A - mor com - man - da o - no - re in - vi - ta, più bel im - pe - gno

D

Finche lo strale non giun - ge al segno, pen - sier re - ga - le, no, non si sa

E

Non las - ciar Op - pres - sa del - la sor - te Pe - rir quell' alma for - te

F

Se dol - - ce m'e - ra gia vi - ver, cor mio, con te,

Giulio Cesare (Julius Caesar)

G

Da tem - pe - - - - ste il le - - gno in - fran - - - - - - - - - to,

H

Dal ful - gor di que - - sta spa - - da

I

Pian - ge - rò, pian - ge - rò la sor - te mi - a,

J

Se pie - tà di me non sen - ti giu - sto ciel, io mo - ri - rò,

K

V a - do - ro, pu - pil - le, sa - et - - te d'a - mo - - re,

Lotario

L

Già mi sem - bra al ca - - - ro av - vin - to Trar l'au - da - ce,

M

Per sal - var - ti, i - do - lo mi - o so ben i - o,

Lusinghe più care, from Alessandro

N

Lu - sin - ghe più ca - re d'A - mor ve - ri dar di

Muzio Scevola

O

Pu - pil - le sde - gno - se! sa - re - ste pie to - se,

P

Vo - la - te più dei ven - ti, mo - men - ti che scor - re - te,

Nel mondo e nell' abisso, from Riccardo

Q

Nel mon - do e nell' a - bis - so io non pa - ven - - - - - - - - to

Orlando

R

La - scia A - mor, e sie - gui Mar - te, va! com - bat - ti, com - bat - ti

S

Sor - ge in - fau sta u - na pro - cel - la, Che o - scu - rar fa il cie - lo e il mare

OPERAS
Orlando

Ottone

Partenope

Poro

Radamisto

Vagh-e pu-pil-le, no, non pian-ge-te, no,

Af-fan-ni del pen-sier, un sol mo-men-to da-te-mi pa-ce almen

Ah! tu non sai, quant' il mio cor so-spi-ra e sen-te

Del mi-nac-ciar del ven - - - - - - - - - to

Un di-sprez-za-to af-fet-to, un mi-se-ro so-spet-to

Io spe - - - ra - i, io sperai tro-var ri-po-so

S'io dir po-tes-si al mio cru-de-le la tua fe-de-le

La spe-ran-za è giun - - - - - ta in por-to

Ve-ni, o fi - - - glio! ve-ni o fi - - glio, e mi con-so-la,

Fu-ri bon - - - - - - - - - - - - - - - do spi-ra il ven-to

Sei mia gio-ja sei mio be-ne, sei mia pa-ce e mia spe-ran-za

Qual far-fal-let-ta gi-ra a quel lu-me,

Chi vi-ve a man-te sai che de-li-ra, sai che de-li-ra,

E prez-zo leg-gie-ro D'un sud-di-to il san-gue

Son con-fu-sa pa-sto-rel-la, che nel bo-sco a notte o-scu-ra,

Ca-ra spo-sa a-ma-to be-ne pren-di spe-ne

Già che mo-rir non pos-so: fu-rie che cie-co a-bis-so

Om-bra ca-ra, Om - - - - bra ca-ra di mia spo-sa

Per-fi-do! per-fi-do, di a quell' em-pio ti-ran-no

HANDEL

OPERAS
Radamisto

Qual na- ve smar- ri- ta trà sir- ti e tem- pe- sta,

Quan- do mai spie- ta- ta sor- te, spie- ta- ta sor- te,

Som- mi De- i, som- mi De- i, che scor- ge- te

Rinaldo

Ca- ra spo- sa, a- man- te ca- ra, Do- ve se- i?

Del vostro E- re- bo sull' a- ra, Col- la fa- ce del mio sdegno

Las- cia ch'io pian- ga mia cru- da sor- te,

Il Tri- cer- bero hu- mi- lia- to al mio bran- do ren- de- rò

Vò far guer- ra, e vin- cer vo- glio, e vin- cer vo- glio

Rodelinda

Con- fu- sa si mi- ri l'in- fi- da con- sor- te,

Con rau- co mor- mo- ri- o Pian- go- no al pian- to mi- o

Do- ve se- i, a- ma- to be- ne? Vie- ni, l'al- ma

L'em- pio ri- gor del fa- to vil- le- non po- trà far- mi

Ho per- du- to il ca- ro spo- so,

Mio ca- ro, be- ne! ca- ro, ca- ro! mio ca- ro be- ne!

Mor- rai sì, l'em- pia tua te- sta, già m'ap- pre- sta

Om- bre, pian- te ur- ne fu- ne- ste! Voi sa- re- ste

Pa- sto- rel- lo d'un po- ve- ro ar- men- to pur dor- me con- ten- to

Pri- gio- nie- ra hò l'al- ma in pe- na mà si bel- la

Ri- tor- na, oh ca- ro e dol- ce mio te- so- ro,

OPERAS
Rodelinda

Scas- cia- ta dal suo ni- do sen vo- la in al- tro li- do,

Spieta- ti, Io vi giu-rai, se al mio fi-glio il cor-do-na- i,

Rodrigo

Al- lor- chè sor- ge a- stro lu-cen-te,

Begl' oc- chi begl' oc- chi del mio ben,

Il dol-ce fo-co mi- o, il dol-ce fo- co mi- o

Scipione

Dim- mi, ca- ra dim-mi „tu dei mo-rir," mà oh ca-ra, non mi dir:

Ge- ne- ro- so chi sol bra- ma quel che pia-ce al ben ch'e-glia-ma

Par- to, fug-go, re-sta, e go-di de tue fro-di

Pen- sa, oh bel- la, al- la mia spe- me

Se mor-mo- ra ri-vo o fron-da, su-sur-ran ven-ti- cel-li

Son pel- le-gri- no che d'al-to ve-de il con-fi-ne del suo cam-mi-no

Tut- ta rac-col-ta an-cor nel pal-pi-tan-te cor tre-man- te ho l'al-ma,

Sento che un giusto sdegno,
from Faramondo

Sen- to che un gius-to sde- gno mi spro-na a ven-di- car- mi,

Serse (Xerxes)

Ca- ro voi sie-te all' al- ma, dol- ce voi sie-te al cor,

Del mio ca-ro ba- co a-ma- bi- le nell' im-pe- ro suo

Di- rà che a-mor per me pia- ga- to il cor non gli ha

Nè men con l'om-bre d'in-fe-del- tà vo-glio tra-di- re l'a-ni-ma

Non so se sia la spe- me, che mi so-stie-ne in vi- ta

(accompaniment)

Om- bra mai fu Di ve-ge- ta- bi-le

OPERAS
Serse (Xerxes)

A — Quel- la che tut- ta fè per me lan-guia d'a- mo- re

B — Va go - - -den-do vez-zo-so e bel-lo quel ru - scel-lo la li-ber - ta

Siroe

C — Ch'io mai vi pos- sa la-sciar d'a- ma- re

D — Deg- gio mo- ri- re o stel- le, nè all in- no- cen- za mi a

E — Ge- li- do, in o-gni ve- na scor-rer mi sen-to il san- gue:

F — Mi la- gne- rò ta-cen- do del mio de-sti-no a-va- ro,

G — Non vi piac-que in-giu-sti De- i, ch'io na-sces-si pa-sto- rel-la;

H — La sor- te mia ti- ran- na far-mi di più non può

I — Tor- ren- - te cre-sciu- to per tor- bi- da pie- na,

Sosarme

J — Ren- di'l se- re- no al ci - - - glio, Ma-dre, non pian-ger più,

K — Si, si, si, si, mi-nac-cia, e vin- ta li-ra in si gran pe- ri-glio

Tamerlano

L — A suoi pie- di pa- dre e san-gue la su- per- ba mi ve- drà,

M — Bel- la A-ste - ri- a, bel- la A-ste- ri-a il tuo cor mi di-fen-da,

N — Cor di pa-dre e cor d'a-man-te, Sal-da fe- de o-dio co- stan-te,

O — Deh! la- scia- te- mi il ne- mi- co, se to- glie-ste a me l'a-man- te

P — Em- pio, em- pio, per far-ti guer-ra, dal re-gno di sot- ter- ra

Q — Fi-glia mi- a, non pian-ger, no, no, fi-glia, no, non pian-ger,

R — For- te e lie-to a mor-te an-drei, se ce- las-si ai pen-sier mie- i

S — Nò, nò, il tuo sde- gno mi pla - - - co,

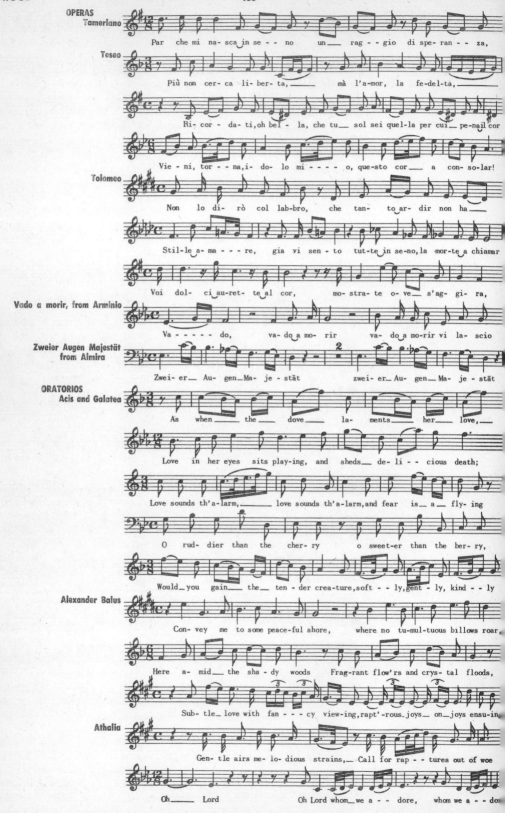

OPERAS

Tamerlano
Par che mi na-sca in se-no un rag-gio di spe-ran-za,

Teseo
Più non cer-ca li-ber-ta,___ mà l'a-mor, la fe-del-ta,___

Ri-cor-da-ti,oh bel - la, che tu___ sol sei quel-la per cui___ pe-nail cor

Tolomeo
Vie-ni, tor-na,i-do-lo mi - - - - o, que-sto cor___ a con-so-lar!

Non lo di-rò col lab-bro, che tan-to ar-dir non ha___

Stil-le a-ma-re, gia vi sen-to tut-te in se-no, la mor-te a chiamar

Vado a morir, from Arminio
Voi dol-ci au-ret-te al cor, mo-stra-te o-ve s'ag-gi-ra,

Zweier Augen Majestät from Almira
Va - - - - do, va-do a mo-rir va-do a mo-rir vi la-scio

Zwei-er__ Au-gen__Ma-je-stät zwei-er__ Au-gen__ Ma-je-stät

ORATORIOS

Acis and Galatea
As when___ the___ dove___ la-ments her___ love,

Love in her eyes sits play-ing, and sheds___ de-li - cious death;

Love sounds th'a-larm,___ love sounds th'a-larm,and fear is___ a__ fly-ing

O rud-dier than the cher-ry o sweet-er than the ber-ry,

Would__ you gain___ the__ ten-der crea-ture,soft - - ly,gent - ly, kind - - ly

Alexander Balus
Con-vey me to some peace-ful shore, where no tu-mul-tuous bil-lows roar,

Here a-mid___ the sha-dy woods Frag-rant flow'rs and crys-tal floods,

Sub-tle love with fan - - cy view-ing,rapt'-rous joys___ on__ joys ensu-in

Athalia
Gen-tle airs me-lo-dious strains,___ Call for rap - - tures out of woe

Oh___ Lord Oh Lord whom__ we a - - dore, whom we a - -do

ORATORIOS
Athalia

Will God, whose mer-cies ev-er flow   Ex-pose his chil-dren's youth to woe?

Belshazzar

Great God! who yet but dark-ly known____ Thus far hast deigned my arms to____

O sa-----cred, sacred o-ra-cles of____ truth,

Thus saith the Lord   to Cy-rus his a-noint-ed   Whose right hand I have holden

Deborah

All dan-ger dis-dain-ing, all dan-ger dis-dain-ing for bat-tle   I glow

Impious mor-tal, cease to brave__ us, Great Je-ho-vah soon__ will save__ us,

In____ the bat-tle fame____ pur-su-ing

Tears,   tears such as ten-der fa-thers shed

Esther

Al-le-lu--ja, al-le-lu------------------ja

O beau-teous Queen un-close__those eyes, My fair-est shall__not bleed,

Pluck   root and branch from out the land; Shall I the God of Is-rael   fear,

Sing songs of praise,__ bow down the knee, bow down the knee,____

Turn not, O   Queen, thy face____ a-way

Hercules

From ce-les-tial__seats de-scending, joys di-vine a-while sus-pend-ing

My fa-ther!   ah!   me-thinks I see   the sword inflict the deadly__wound

The smil-ing____ hours____ a joy-ful____ train,

The world   when__ day's ca---reer_____ is__ run

Israel in Egypt
Part I, No. 10

But as for his peo-ple,   but as for his peo-ple,

Part II, No. 17

Mo-ses   and the chil-dren of Is-rael   sung this song un-to the Lord

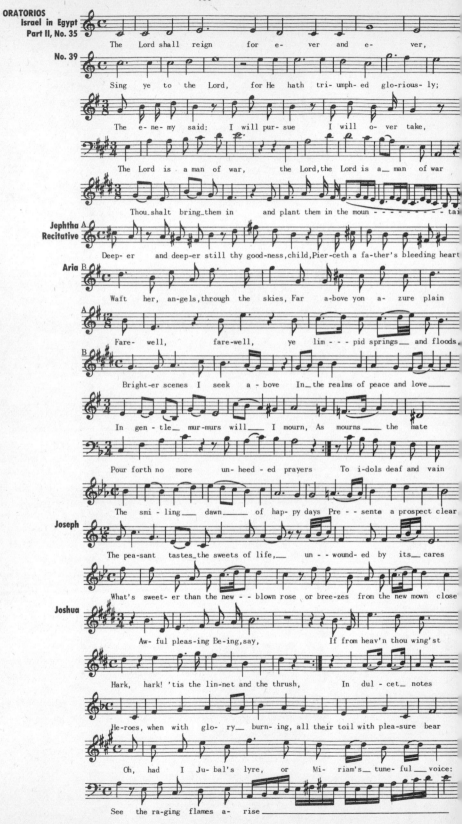

ORATORIOS
Israel in Egypt
Part II, No. 35

The Lord shall reign for e- ver and e- ver,

No. 39

Sing ye to the Lord, for He hath tri- umph- ed glo-rious- ly;

The e- ne- my said: I will pur- sue I will o- ver take,

The Lord is a man of war, the Lord, the Lord is a man of war

Thou shalt bring them in and plant them in the moun - - - - - - - - tai

Jephtha
Recitative A

Deep- er and deep-er still thy good-ness, child, Pier-ceth a fa-ther's bleeding heart

Aria B

Waft her, an-gels, through the skies, Far a-bove yon a- zure plain

A

Fare- well, fare-well, ye lim - - - pid springs and floods,

B

Bright-er scenes I seek a - bove In the realms of peace and love

In gen- tle mur-murs will I mourn, As mourns the mate

Pour forth no more un-heed - ed prayers To i-dols deaf and vain

The smi- ling dawn of hap- py days Pre - - sents a prospect clear

Joseph

The pea-sant tastes the sweets of life, un - - wound- ed by its cares

What's sweet- er than the new - - blown rose or bree-zes from the new mown close

Joshua

Aw- ful pleas-ing Be-ing, say, If from heav'n thou wing'st

Hark, hark! 'tis the lin-net and the thrush, In dul - cet notes

He-roes, when with glo- ry burn- ing, all their toil with plea-sure bear

Oh, had I Ju- bal's lyre, or Mi- riam's tune- ful voice:

See the ra-ging flames a- rise

ORATORIOS
Joshua
Shall I in Mam-re's fer-tile_ plain the remnant of my days re-main

Judas Maccabeus
No. 2
Mourn, mourn,____ mourn, ye af-flict-ed chil-dren, the re-mains

No. 9
Oh Fa - - - - ther, whose____ al- might - - y pow'r

No. 11 b
We come, we come, we come, in bright ar-ray, in bright ar-ray,

No. 22
Pi- ous or - - -gies, pi- ous_ airs, de - - - cent sor- row,____

No. 23
Fall'n is the foe Fall'n is the foe: so fall____ thy foes

No. 26
Zi- on now____ her head____ shall raise, tune your____ harps,

No. 28
Hail, hail, hail Ju- de- a,____ hap- py land, Ju- de- a,____ hap-py land,

No. 35
Arm, arm ye brave! arm, arm ye brave! a no - -ble cause, a no - - ble cause

No. 43
Call forth thy_ pow'rs, my_ soul, and_ dare the con-flict, the con-flict

No. 45
Sing un- to God and high af- fec- tions_ raise,

No. 46
Oh li- ber-ty thou choicest treasure, seat of virtue source of pleasure!

No. 51
'Tis li - - - - - - - ber-ty, dear li- ber-ty a- lone

No. 52
Hal- le- lu- jah, A- men, a- men, Hal- le- lu- ja, a- men

No. 54
Come, e- ver smil-ing li-ber-ty, come, smil-ing li-ber-ty, and with thee bring

No. 66
No, no un- hal-low'd de- sire____ our breasts shall_ in- spire,

No. 92
So ra- pid_ thy_ course is, not num- ber- less_ for- ces

No. 110
From might - - y kings he took____ the spoil, and with_ his acts_ made Judah

No. 120
How vain____ is man____ who boasts____ in fight____

Judas Maccabeus
No. 132 — The Lord work-eth won - ders

No. 136 — Sound an a-larm, sound an a-larm! your sil - ver trum-pets sound,

No. 148 — With pi-ous hearts and brave as pi-ous, Oh Si-on, we thy call at - - - tend;

No. 152 — Wise men, flat - - t'ring, may de - - - - - ceive us

No. 172 — Fa - ther of Heav'n! from Thy e-ter-nal throne, From Thy e-ter - - nal throne

No. 178 — So shall the lute and harp a-wake, and sprightly voice sweet descant run,

No. 186 — See, the con-qu'ring he - - - - - ro comes! sound the trum-pets,

No. 199 — With ho-nour let de-sert be crown'd the trum-pet ne'er in vain shall sound,

No. 210 — Oh love-ly peace, with plen-ty crown'd, oh, love-ly love-ly peace

Messiah
No. 2 — Com-fort ye, Com - - - fort ye my peo-ple,

No. 3 — Ev-'ry val - - ley, ev-'ry val - ley shall be ex-alt - ed

No. 4 — And the glo-ry, the glo-ry of the Lord, And the glo-ry, the glory of the Lord

No. 6 — But who may a-bide the day of his com-ing,

For he is like a re-fi - - - - - ner's fire

No. 7 — And he shall pu-ri-fy, and he shall purify

No. 9 — O, thou that tell-est good tid-ings to Zi - on,

No. 11 — The peo - - ple that walk - ed in dark - - - - - - - ness,

No. 12 — For un-to us a child is born, un-to us a son is giv-en,

No. 18 — Glo - ry to God, Glo - ry to God in the high - est,

ORATORIOS

Samson

Ye sons of Is-rael, now la-ment; your spear is_ broke, your bow's un-bent

Saul

Brave Jo-na-than his bow ne'er_ drew, but wing'd with death,

Fell rage and black des-pair_pos-sessed, with hor-rid sway the mon-arch's breast,

Oh_ god-like youth!_ by all_con-fess'd of hu-man race_____ the pride!

Oh Lord, whose mercies num-ber-less o'er all thy works_____ pre-vail,

Sin not, O King, a-gainst the youth Who ne'er_of-fend - - - ed_you,

Semele

End-less plea - - sure Endless plea-sure, endless love

Hence, hence, I-ris, hence a-way, I-ris, hence a-way, a-way,

Hy-men, haste, Hy-men, haste! thy torch prepare! Love al-read-y his has lighted,

Leave_ me, leave me, loath-some light! re-ceive me, re-ceive me,

Oh_____ sleep, Oh_ sleep why dost thou leave_me?

Where 'er you_walk, cool gales shall fan the glade; trees, where you sit, shall crowd

Solomon Chorus

May no rash in-tru-der dis- turb their soft hours;

What though I trace each herb and_flow'r that drinks the morning dew,

With thee th'un-sheltered moor I'd_ tread, nor once of fate_com-plain,

Susanna

Ask if yon damask rose_ be sweet, that scents the_ am-bient air?

Be-neath the cy-press gloom-y shade where silver lil-lies paint the glade

Crys-tal_streams in mur-murs_ flow-ing in mur-murs_flow--ing,

If guiltless blood be your in--tent, I here re-sign it all

ORATORIOS
Susanna

A — The parent bird in search of food a- while de-serts her cal-low brood,

B — When first__ I saw my love-ly maid, be- neath__ the cit - ron's shade

C — Ye ver-dant hills, ye balm- y vales bear wit- ness of my pain

Theodora

D — An-gels e- ver__ bright and__ fair, an-gels e- ver bright and fair, take, oh, take me,

E — As with ro- sy steps the morn ad- vanc-ing, drives the shades of night

F — De-fend her, Heaven, let an-gels spread ____

G — Lord, to__ thee, each__ night and__ day, strong in hope we sing and__ pray

The Triumph of Time and Truth

H — False, de-struc-tive ways of__ pleasure Leave, and court a no-bler__ treasure

I — Loath-some urns,__ dis-close your treas-ure, Pride and pleasure Un-veil to me

HANDL, Jacob (1550-1591)

Adoramus te, Jesu Christe

K — A- do- ra- mus te, Je- su Chris- te

Ecce quomodo montur justus

L — The right- eous, the right-eous per - - ish-eth, per- ish-eth

HANSON, Howard (1896-   )

Oh, 'tis an earth defiled, from Merry Mount (opera)
(pseud., Helen Guy Rhodes)
Copyright 1933, Harms, Inc.

N — Oh, 'tis an earth de- filed where-on we live! There is no leaf- y bow'r,

HARDELOT, Guy d' (1858-1936)

Because

I know a Lovely Garden

Sans Toi

HARRISON, Annie Fortescue (d. 1944)

In the Gloaming

In the gloam-ing o my dar-ling! When the lights are dim and low B

HARTMANN, Johann Peter (1805-1900)

Flyv, Fugl, Flyv

'Flyv, Fugl, flyv o-ver Fu-re-sø-ens Vo-ve! D

Frejas Stjerne (choral)

Kun een er Frej - - as Stjer-ne, men rundt_ den sen-der sin Glans E

Jaegersang (choral)

Snart er Nat-ten svun-den, Da-gen bry-der frem F

Jeg synge skal en Vise

Jeg syn-ge skal en Vi-se; vel-an_ jeg er_ be-red_ G

Laer mig!

Laer mig, Nat-tens Stjer-ne, at ly-de fast_ og ger--ne H

Mindnesang over de faldne

Slum-rer sødt i Sles-vigs Jord, dy-re-købt den blev ved e-der! I

Rejsen til Vinlandene (choral)

Vort Dag-waerk er til En---de; som fri og_ mun-tre Sven-de J

Sange af "Ambrosius"

Den ked-som Vin-ter gik sin Gang, den Dag saa kort, den Nat saa lang K

Studentersang (choral)

Vi er et ly-stigt Fol-ke-faerd fra al-le Ver-dens Kan-ter L

Ved Jaegerhuset

Du, som har Sorg i Sin-de gak ud i Mark og Lund, M

HARTY, Hamilton (1879-1941)

My Lagan Love (arr.)
By permission Boosey & Hawkes, Inc., copyright owners

Where Lagan stream sings lull-a-by There blows_ a li-ly fair: O

Three Irish Folksongs (arr.)
1. The Lowlands of Holland
By permission Oxford Univ. Press, London, copyright owners

The_ first night I was_ mar-ried, a_ hap-py_ hap-py bride P

2. The Faery King's Courtship

On the first day of_ May at the close of the day Q

3. The Game Played in Erin-go-Bragh

In London one day as I walked up the street, An_ im-pu-dent fel-low R

HASSLER, Leo (1564-1612)

Feinslieb, du hast mich g'fangen

Feins-lieb, du hast mich g'fan-gen mit dein zwei Aüg-lein schon

Jungfrau, dein schöne G'stalt

Jung-frau, dein schö-ne G'stalt er-frent mich sehr je länger je mehr

Mein Lieb' will mit mir kriegen

Mein Lieb' will mit mir krie-gen, hat sich ge-rist zur Schlacht

Tanzsen und Springen

Tan-zen und Sprin-gen, Sin-gen und Klin-gen, fa la la la

HATTON, John L.

Goodbye, sweetheart, goodbye

The bright stars fade, the morn is break-ing, The dew-drops pearl

Simon the Cellarer

Old Si-mon the Cel-lar-er keeps a rare store.

HAYDN, Franz Josef (1732-1809)

The Apothecary (opera)

Al-le Ta-ge, Al-le Ta-ge klop-fen, rei-ben

Sitzt Ei-nem hier im Kopf das Weh' so neh-men wir von die-sem Thee

Wo Lie-bes-göt-ter lach-ten, stürmt Hass auf Hass

Es kam ein Pa-scha aus Tür-ken-land

Die-se Püpp-chen sind nicht zu er-grün-den, sind nicht zu er-grün-den

Wie Schlei-er seh' ichs nie-der schwe-ben

Mass No. 11 (Nelson Mass)
I Kyrie

Ky-ri-e, Ky-ri-e e-lei-son Ky-ri-e e-lei-son

II Gloria

Glo-ri-a in ex-cel-sis De-o

Lau-da-mus te, be-ne-di-ci-mus te

III Qui Tollis

Qui tol-lis, qui tol-lis pec-ca-ta

HAYDN

Mass No. 11 (Nelson Mass)
IV Quoniam Tu Solus

Quo- ni- am tu so- lus so - - - - lus sanc- tus tu   A

V Credo

Cre- do in u- num De - - - um, Pa - - - - trem om- ni- po- ten - tem   B

VI Et Incarnatus

Et in- car- na- tus est de Spi- ri- tu__ san- cto   C

VII Et Resurrexit

Et, et re- sur- rex - - it ter- ti- a di - e   D

VIII Sanctus

Sanc - - - tus__ Sanc - - tus,__ san- ctus Do- mi- nus   E

IX Benedictus

Be- ne- di - ctus qui ve- nit, be- ne- di - ctus qui ve- nit   F

X Osanna

O- san- na in ex- cel - - - - - - - - - - - - - sis,   G

XI Agnus Dei

A- gnus__ De- i qui tol- lis pec- ca- ta mun- di   H

XII Dona Nobis

Do- na no- bis pa- cem pa - cem, pa - cem,   I

The Creation (Die Schöpfung)
(oratorio)   Part I, No. 6

Roll- ing in foam- ing_ bil- lows up- lift- ed, roars the boist'rous sea   J

Soft- ly purl- ing,_ glides on through si- lent vales the lim- pid brook   K

No. 8

With ver- dure clad the fields ap- pear de- lightful to__ the ra -vish'd sense__   L

No. 10

Stimmt an die Sai- ten ergreift die Leier, lasst eu- er Lob- ge- sang   M

(Same theme, text in English)

A- wake the Harp, the lyre a- wake! In shout and joy your voi- ces   N

No. 13

The hea- vens are tell- ing the glo- ry of God__   O

Part II, No. 15

On might- y_ pens up- - lift- ed_ soars_ the eagle a- loft   P

No. 18

Most beau- ti- ful ap- pear, with_ ver- dure young a- dorn'd   Q

No. 21

The cattle in herds al- rea- dy seeks his food on fields and meadows green   R

No. 22

Now heav'n in full- est glo - - - - - - - - ry_ shone__   S

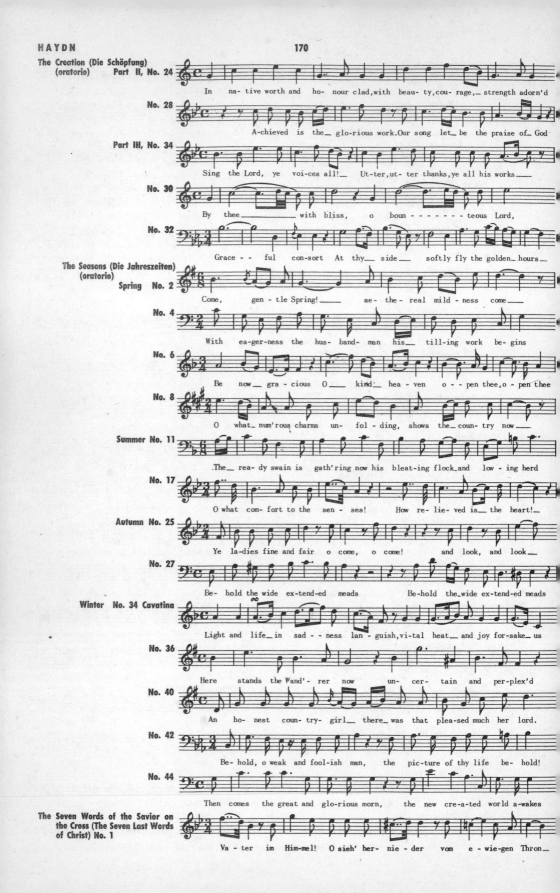

The Creation (Die Schöpfung)
(oratorio)   Part II, No. 24

In na-tive worth and ho-nour clad, with beau-ty, cou-rage, strength adorn'd

No. 28

A-chieved is the glo-rious work. Our song let be the praise of God

Part III, No. 34

Sing the Lord, ye voi-ces all! Ut-ter, ut-ter thanks, ye all his works

No. 30

By thee with bliss, o boun - - - - - - teous Lord,

No. 32

Grace - - ful con-sort At thy side softly fly the golden hours

The Seasons (Die Jahreszeiten)
(oratorio)
Spring No. 2

Come, gen - tle Spring! ae-the-real mild-ness come

No. 4

With ea-ger-ness the hus-band-man his till-ing work be-gins

No. 6

Be now gra-cious O kind hea-ven o-pen thee, o-pen thee

No. 8

O what num'rous charms un-fol-ding, shows the coun-try now

Summer No. 11

The rea-dy swain is gath'ring now his bleat-ing flock and low-ing herd

No. 17

O what com-fort to the sen-ses! How re-lie-ved is the heart!

Autumn No. 25

Ye la-dies fine and fair o come, o come! and look, and look

No. 27

Be-hold the wide ex-tend-ed meads Be-hold the wide ex-tend-ed meads

Winter No. 34 Cavatina

Light and life in sad - ness lan-guish, vi-tal heat and joy for-sake us

No. 36

Here stands the Wand'-rer now un-cer-tain and per-plex'd

No. 40

An ho-nest coun-try-girl there was that plea-sed much her lord.

No. 42

Be-hold, o weak and fool-ish man, the pic-ture of thy life be-hold!

No. 44

Then comes the great and glo-rious morn, the new cre-a-ted world a-wakes

The Seven Words of the Savior on
the Cross (The Seven Last Words
of Christ) No. 1

Va-ter im Him-mel! O sieh' her-nie-der vom e-wie-gen Thron

HAYDN

The Seven Words of the Savior on The Cross (The Seven Last Words of Christ) No. 2 — A

Ganz Er- bar-men, Gnad und Lie-be, ganz Er- bar-men, ganz Er- bar-men

No. 3 — B

Mut-ter Je-su, die du trost-los, Mutter Je- su, die_du_ trostlos,

No. 4 — C

„Wa-rum hast Du mich ver-las-sen?" Wer --- sieht hier der Gottheit Spur?

No. 5 — D

Je-sus ru - - - fet: Je-sus ru - fet ach, mich dür- stet

No. 6 — E

Es ist voll- bracht! An das Op- fer-holz ge- hef-tet,

No. 7 — F

In dei-ne Händ, O Herr, empfehl' ich mei- nen Geist, mei-nen Geist

Die Beredsamkeit — G

Freun- de, was-ser mach-et stumm, was-ser ma-chet stumm, stumm, stumm,

Deutschland über Alles (Gott erhalte Franz den Kaiser) — H

Gott er- hal-te Gott be schü- tze un-sern Kaiser

Der erste Kuss — I

Lei- se nannt ich dei - - nen Namen, und mein au-ge wart_ um dich

Die Harmonie in der Ehe — J

O wun-der-ba-re Har- mo-nie, was Er_ will, will auch_Sie

Jeder meint, das holde Kind — K

Je- der meint, das hol-de Kind, das ich mir er- wäh- le

Jeder meint, der Gegenstand — L

Je- der meint, der Ge- gen-stand, den er sich er- wäh-let

Liebes Mädchen, hör' mir zu — M

Lie- bes Mad- chen hör mir zu, öff- ne leis, das Git- ter;

Lob der Faulheit — N

Faul- heit, end-lich muss ich dir auch ein kleines Lob- leid_ bringen!

The Mermaids' Song — O

Now the_____ danc- ing sun - - beams_ play_

My Mother bids me bind my hair — P

My moth- er- bids_me bind_ my hair_with bands_of_ ros- y hue

Pensi a me — Q

Pen- si a me si fi-do a-man-te co-me_a te, sempr'io__ co-stante?

The Sailor's Song — R

High on the gid-dy_ bend-ing mast, The sea-man furls_the_ rend-ing_ sail

She never told her love — S

She ne- ver told' her love, she ne- ver told her_ love

The Spirit's Song

Hark! Hark! What I tell to thee no sor-row o'er the tomb.

Un tetto umil

Un tet----to u-mil cui cinge il fag-gio e il pin,

The Wanderer

To wan-der a-lone__ when the moon faint-ly__ beam-ing

HEAD, Michael (1900-)

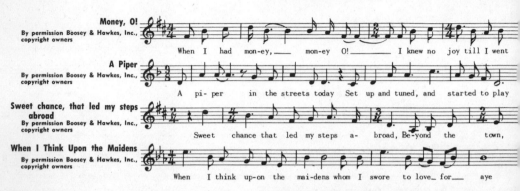

Money, O!
By permission Boosey & Hawkes, Inc., copyright owners

When I had mon-ey,__ mon-ey O!__ I knew no joy till I went

A Piper
By permission Boosey & Hawkes, Inc., copyright owners

A pi-per in the streets today Set up and tuned, and started to play

Sweet chance, that led my steps abroad
By permission Boosey & Hawkes, Inc., copyright owners

Sweet chance that led my steps a-broad, Be-yond the town,

When I Think Upon the Maidens
By permission Boosey & Hawkes, Inc., copyright owners

When I think up-on the mai-dens whom I swore to love for__ aye

HEISE, Peter (1830-1879)

Ak, hvem der Havde en Hue

Ah__ who once wore a fine bon-net with plume and bro-cade so__ gay

Arnes Sang

Ör-nen löf-ter med stoer-ke Slag o-ver de hör-e Fjel-de

Dengang jeg var Kun saa (Helligtrekongersaften)

Den-gang jeg var kun saa stor som saa, saa stor som saa__

It Rises (Det Stiger)

It ri-ses, it ri-ses, it ri-ses so high Riv-er wanders 'gainst mounta

Jylland mellem tvende Have

Jyl-land mel-lem tven-de Ha-ve som en Bu-ne-stav er lagt,

Liden Karen

Hus-ker Du i Höst, da vi hjemod fra Mar-ken gik

Woodland Stillness

Through aisles__ of birch--en for-est I led__ thee, coy__ but willing;

HENSCHEL, Sir George (1850-1934)

Morning Hymn, Op. 46, No. 1
Copyright by John Church Co. Used by permission

Soon night will pass; Through field and grass What o-dors sweet

HERBERT, Victor (1859-1924)

s in Toyland (operetta) Act II,
No. 13 Toyland
Copyright 1903, M. Witmark & Sons

Toy- land! Toy- land! Lit - tle girl and boy- land,

The Fortune Teller (operetta)
Copyright 1898, M. Witmark & Sons
Gypsy Love Song

The birds of the for-est are call-ing for thee__ and the shades, and the glades__

Slum- ber on, my lit-tle gyp-sy sweet-heart, Dream of the field and the grove

Romany Life

We have a home 'neath the for-est shade Nev- er an- y oth-er__

iss in the Dark, from Orange
Blossoms (operetta)
Copyright 1922, M. Witmark & Sons

I re- call the mad de- light of a love- ly dance__

Oh that kiss in__ the dark was__ to him just__ a lark,

Me Again, from Mlle. Modiste
(operetta)
Copyright 1915, M. Witmark & Sons

Sweet sum-mer breeze, Whis-per-ing trees, Stars shining brightly a- bove

Naughty Marietta (operetta)
Copyright 1910, M. Witmark & Sons
Ah! Sweet Mystery of Life

Ah! sweet mys-ter- y of life at last I've found thee

I'm falling in love with someone

For I'm falling in love with some- one, some one girl;__

Italian Street Song

Oh! my heart is back in Na- po- li,__ dear Na- po- li__

Zing, Zing, ziz- zy, ziz- zy, zing, zing, Boom, boom aye, Zing, Zing

'Neath the Southern Moon

'Neath the South- ern moon, Oh, love so warm and ten- der

ramp, Tramp, Tramp along the
Highway

Tramp, tramp, tramp a-long the high-way, Tramp, tramp, tramp, the road is free

litan Love Song, from Princess
at (operetta)
Copyright 1915, M. Witmark & Sons

Sweet one!__ How my heart is yearn-ing__ Ev-er__ with you to be__

The Red Mill (operetta)
Copyright 1906, M. Witmark & Sons
Because You're You

Not that I am fair, dear, Not that I am true. Not my gold- en hair, dear

Isle of Our Dreams

In the beau-ti-ful isle of our dreams, dear, there is nev-er a sorrow or pain

The Streets of New York

In old New York! In old New York! The peach crop's al- ways fine__

Alone, from Eileen (operetta)
Copyright 1917, M. Witmark & Sons

In thine arms en-fold me, my be- lov-ed! Lift thine eyes look fondly in-to mine

Waltz, from Sweethearts (operetta)
Copyright 1913, G. Schirmer, Inc.

Sweet-hearts make love their ver-y own, Sweethearts can live on love a-lone

When You're Away, from The Only Girl (operetta)
Copyright 1914, M. Witmark & Sons

When you're a-way, dear, how wear-y the lone-some hours

HERMANN, Hans (1870-1931)

Drei Wandrer, Op. 5, No. 4

Drei Wan-drer sind ge-gan--gen, und als der A-bend fiel

HEROLD, Louis (1791-1833)

Le Pré aux Clercs (opera)
Act I, No. 2

A. Le ren-dez-vous de nob-le com-pa-gni-e se don-nent tous

B. Dans la prai-ri-e fraiche et fleu-ri-e da-me jo-li-e viendra

No. 3

A. O ma ten-dre a-mi-e je suis près de toi

B. O toi de qui l'ab-sen-ce tou-jours me fait gé-mir

No. 5

Sou-ve-nir du jeune â-ge sont gravés dans mon coeur

Act II, No. 6

A. Jours de mon en-fan---ce o jours d'in-no-cen-----ce

B. Oui Mar-gue-rite en qui j'es-pè-re pro-tège u-ne pauvre

Act III

À la fleur du bel â--ge Geor-get-te cha-que jour di-sait

Perchè Tremar, from Zampa (opera)
Act III, No. 34

Per-chè tre-mar per-chè? son i-o che pre-go

HILDACH, Eugen (1849-1924)

Im Volkston

Was leuch-tet ihr Ster-ne so hell in der Nacht?

Der Lenz, Op. 19, No. 5

Die Fin-ken Schlagen, der Lenz ist da, und kei-ner kann sa-gen

Der Spielmann, Op. 15, No. 1

Du mit dei-ner Fie-del blei-be hier nicht stehn,

Wo du hingehst, Op. 8

Wo du hin--gehst, da will auch ich, auch ich hin-ge-hen

HIMMEL, Friedrich (1765-1814)

Gebet während der Schlacht

Va- ter, ich ru- fe dich! Brül- lend um- wolkt mich der Dampf

HINDEMITH, Paul (1895-   )

Eight Songs, with piano, Op. 18,
No. 2
By permission Associated Music
Publishers, Inc.

Wie Sankt Fran- cis- cus schweb'ich in - - der Luft mit bei- den Fü - - ssen

No. 4

Auf der Trep- pe sit- zen mei- ne Öhr- chen wie zwei Kätzchen die die Milch

No. 8 Trompeten

Un- ter verschnit-te-nen Wei- den wo brau- ne Kin- der spie- len

Five songs on old Texts:
Of Household Rule
By permission Associated Music
Publishers, Inc.

Es ist___ ge- - wiss ein from- - mer Mann, ein from- mer Mann,

Lady's Lament

Nun heis- sen sie mich mei- - - - - - - - - - - - - - - den

The Devil a Monk Would Be!

Ein wolf, ein wolf___ der Sün- den- angst be- wog,

True Love

Tris- tan muss- - - te oh- ne Dank Treu- e wahr'n der Kö- ni- gin

Troopers' Drinking Song

Tum- mel dich, tum-mel dich,guts Wein-lein, tum- mel dich, tum- mel dich

Frisch___ auf, gut Gsell, lass rum- mer gahn,

Das Marienleben, Op. 27,
No. 1 Geburt Maria
By permission Associated Music
Publishers, Inc.

O was muss es die En- gel ge- ko- - stet ha- ben,

Schwin- gend ver- schwie- gen sie sich und zeig- ten die Rich- tung

No. 5 Argwohn Josephs

Und der En- gel sprach___ und gab sich Müh an dem Mann

No. 7 Geburt Christi

Hät-test du der Ein- falt nicht, wie soll- te die ge-schehn___

No. 11 Pieta

Jetzt wird mein E- lend voll und na- men-los er-füllt es mich

Six Chansons
No. 1 The Doe
By permission Associated Music
Publishers, Inc.

O thou doe,_what vis-tas of sec- u- lar for-ests ap-pear in thine eyes

No. 2 The Swan

A swan is breast-ing the flow all in him-self___ en-fold- ed

Six Chansons
No. 3 Since all is passing

Since all is pass-ing, re- tain The mel- o- dies that wan-der by us

No. 4 Springtime

O song that from the sap art pour-ing and through the sounding board

No. 5 In Winter

With the win- ter, Death, gris-ly guest through the door-way steals in

No. 6 Orchard

The earth is no- where so real a pres-ence As mid thy branches, O orchard

HOLBROOKE, Joseph (1878-   )

Noden's song, from Children of Don (opera)
By permission Novello & Co., Ltd., London

Deep is my bon- dage and a dread-ful sleep__ the gods have set me

Sea King's Song, from Dylan (opera)
By permission Novello & Co., Ltd., London

The night that bounds my sub- ject spa-ces has no fierc- er gloom

HOLLMAN, J. (1852-1927)

Chanson d'Amour

Te sou- vient il des mar- ron- niers fleu- ris

HOLMÈS, Augusta (1847-1903)

Au pays
Copyright by L. Grus, Paris

Sur la route, Et gaie-ment, Sans u- - - ne crou- te!

Noël

Trois an- ges sont ve- nus ce soir M'ap-por- ter de bien

HOLST, Gustave (1874-1934)

Four Songs for Voice and Violin, Op. 35,
No. 1
By permission J. & W. Chester, Ltd., London, copyright owners
No. 2

Je- su Sweet, now will I sing to thee a song of love long- ing

My soul has nought 'but fire and ice and my bo- dy earth and wood:

No. 3

I sing of a mai- den that match-less is: King of all Kings

No. 4

My Le man is so true of love and full stead- fast

The Heart Worships
By permission Galaxy Music Corporation, N. Y., sole U. S. agents for Stainer & Bell, Ltd., London

Si- lence in Heav'n Si- lence on Earth Si- lence within

Hymn to the Waters (Choral Hymn, from the Rig-Veda)

Flow - - ing from the fir- ma- ment Forth to the o- cean.

I Love My Love (arr.)
Copyright 1917, J. Curwen
A- broad as_ I_ was walk- ing one_ eve- ning in the spring   A

Midwinter
mission Oxford Univ. Press, London,
ht owners
Our God, heaven can- not hold Him nor_ earth sus- tain   B

The Sergeant's Song
opyright by Edwin Ashdown, London
When Law- yers strive to heal a breach, and Par- sons prac- tice   C

Have I Done for My True Love
permission of Augener, Ltd., London
To- mor- row shall be my danc- ing day, I would my true_ love   D

Back O Man (melody from the German Psalter, 124th Psalm)
ermission Galaxy Music Corporation,
, sole U. S. agents for Stainer & Bell,
London
Turn back O Man, for- swear thy fool- ish ways. Old now is Earth   E

Wassail Song (arr.)
Copyright 1931, G. Holst
The was- sail, the_ was- sail through- out all the world   F

HOMER, Sidney (1864-)

Requiem, Op. 15, No. 2
Copyright 1904, G. Schirmer, Inc.
Un- der the wide and star- ry sky Dig the grave and_ let me lie.   H

A Banjo Song, Op. 22, No. 4
Copyright 1910, G. Schirmer, Inc.
I plays de ban- jo bet- ter now Dan him dat taught me do   I

Dearest, Op. 24
Copyright 1910, G. Schirmer, Inc.
Dear- est, when I am dead,_ make one last song for me   J

Sheep and Lambs, Op. 31
Copyright 1914, G. Schirmer, Inc.
All in the A- pril morn- ing A- pril airs were a- broad   K

HONEGGER, Arthur (1892-)

s" Six Poèmes de G. Apolli-aire
No. 1. A la "Santé"
Copyright by Salabert, Paris, N. Y.
Que len- te- ment passent les heu- res Com- me passe un en- ter- re- ment   M

No. 2. Clotilde
L'a- nè- mone et l'an- co- li- e Ont poussé dans le jar- din   N

No. 3. Automne
Dans le brouillard s'en vont un pa- y- san ca- gneux et son boeuf   O

No. 4. Saltimbanques
Dans la plai- ne les ba- la- dins S'e- loi- gnent au long des jar- dins   P

No. 5. L'Adieu
J'ai cueil- li ce brin de bru- yè- re L'au- tomne est mor- te   Q

No. 6. Les Cloches
Mon beau tzi- ga- ne mon a- mant É- cou- te les clo- ches qui son- nent   R

Berceuse de la Sirène
Copyright by Salabert, Paris, N. Y.
Danse a- vec nous dans le bel o- ce- an   S

Judith (opera)
Act I, No. 3 Prière
Copyright by Salabert, Paris, N. Y.

Seigneur___ Dieu de mes pères, e-cou-te-moi et viens à mon se-cours

No. 4 Cantique funèbre

Ch Béthu-li-e Béthu-lie a-ban-don-né-e nous te tendons les mai

Act II, No. 6 Incantation

Is-tar___ Is-tar___ Dé-es-se des ba-tail-les Mar-douk Mardouk

Act III, No. 11 Cantique de la bataille

Ho Ho Ho Ho___ Ho Ho Ho Ho___ Ho___

Je crie à toi___ dans le ba-taille_ Je crie à toi dans le dan-ger

No. 12 Cantinque des Vierges

Com-me le jour d'é-té met en fui-te la nuit l'É-ter-nel s'est lev

No. 13 Cantique de la victoire

Son non est Je-ho-vah___ c'est un vail-lant guerrier

Gloire au Dieu Tout Puis-sant Je-ho-vah des ar-mé-es

Mimaamaquim (Psalm 130)
Copyright by Salabert, Paris, N. Y.

Mi-ma-a-maquim que-ra-ti kha A-do-nai

4 Chansons pour voix grave
No. 1 (Tchobanian)
Copyright by Salabert, Paris, N. Y.

La douceur de tes yeux peut gue-rir___ la plus mortel-le

No. 2 (William Aguet)

Der-riè-re Marcie en fleurs je con-nais un che-min qui mè-ne jusqu'à t

No. 3 (Verlaine)

Un grand som-meil noir tom-be sur ma vi-e: Dor-mez tout es-poir

No. 4 (Ronsard)

La ter-re les eaux va bu-vant L'ar-bre la boit par sa ra-ci-ne

Le Roi David (Symphonic Psalm)
No. 2 Cantique du berger David
Copyright by E. C. Schirmer, Boston

L'É-ter-nel est mon ber-ger. Je ne suis que son a-gnea

No. 3 Psalm

Lou-é soit le Sei-gneur plein de gloi-re Le Dieu vi-vant,

No. 4 Chant de Victoire

Vi-ve Da-vid, vain-queur des Philis-tins, L'E-ter-nel l'a choi-si;

No. 7

Ah, si j'a-vais des ai-les de co-lom-be, Je vo-le-rais bien loin

No. 8 Cantique des Prophètes

L'hom-me né de la fem-me a peu de jours a vi-vre

No. 11 Psalm

L'É-ter-nel est ma lu-mière___ in-fi-ni-e

Three Psalms: 2. Psalm 140

O Dieu don- ne-moi dé-li-vran- ce de cet hom- me per- ni- ci- eux

3. Psalm 138

Il faut que de tous mes es- prits Ton los et pris,

Trois Poèmes de Claudel
No. 1 Sieste
Copyright by Salabert, Paris, N. Y.

Deux heu- res a-près di- ner Il est temps de se re- po- ser

No. 2 Le Delphinium

Tou-te pu- re comme le ciel brû- lan- te com- me le feu

No.3 Le Rendez-vous

Fo- rêt pro- fon - - - - de Il fait si som- bre

Trois poèmes de Paul Fort
No. 1 Le Chasseur Perdu en Forêt
Copyright by Salabert, Paris, N. Y.

Quand le son du cor s'en- dort, gai chas-seur ne tar- de

No. 2 Cloche du Soir

Ah! ce soir là vrai-ment tout é- tait si pai- si- ble

No. 3 Chanson de Fol

Les sor- ciers et les fées dan - - - - sent sur le cô- teau

HOOK, James (1746-1827)

Bright Phoebus

Bright Phoe-bus has mount-ed the char- iot of day

The Lass of Richmond Hill

On Rich-mond Hill there lives a lass, more bright than May- day morn,

Love's Call

Hi-ther, hi-ther, Ma- ry, hi- ther, hi- ther come

Mary of Allendale

Oh! have you seen the blush - - ing rose

With a Mile of Edinboro'

'Twas with- in a mile of Ed- in- bo- ro town

HOPKINSON, Frances (1737-1791)

Beneath a Weeping Willow's Shade

Be- neath a weep - - ing wil- low's shade, She sat and sang a- lone,

Come, Fair Rosina

Come fair Ros-i- na, come a-way, Long since stern win - - - ter's storms

My Days have been so Wondrous Free

My days have been so won - - drous free, The lit-tle birds that fly

My Generous Heart Disdains

My gen'rous heart dis- dains the slave of love to be

O'er the Hills — O'er the hills far a-way at the birth of the morn, I heard the full tone   A

The Traveller Benighted — The trav- 'ler be-night-ed and lost O'er the moun-tain pursues his lone way;   B

HORN, Charles Edward (1786-1849)

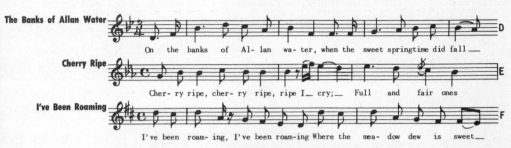

The Banks of Allan Water — On the banks of Al- lan wa-ter, when the sweet springtime did fall   D

Cherry Ripe — Cher- ry ripe, cher- ry ripe, ripe I cry;— Full and fair ones   E

I've Been Roaming — I've been roam- ing, I've been roam-ing Where the mea-dow dew is sweet   F

HORSMAN, Edward (1873-1918)

The Bird of the Wilderness
Copyright 1914, G. Schirmer, Inc.

My heart,— the bird of the wil - - der-ness   H

HUE, Georges (1858-   )

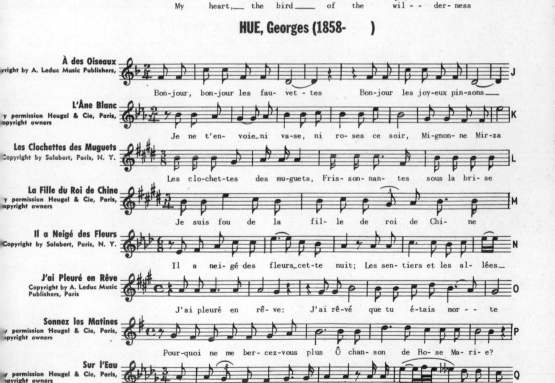

À des Oiseaux
right by A. Leduc Music Publishers,

Bon-jour, bon-jour les fau- vet- tes   Bon-jour les joy-eux pin-sons   J

L'Âne Blanc
y permission Heugel & Cie, Paris,
opyright owners

Je ne t'en- voie ni va-se, ni ro-ses ce soir, Mi-gnon-ne Mir-za   K

Les Clochettes des Muguets
Copyright by Salabert, Paris, N. Y.

Les clo-chet-tes des mu-guets, Fris- son- nan- tes sous la bri- se   L

La Fille du Roi de Chine
y permission Heugel & Cie, Paris,
opyright owners

Je suis fou de la fil- le de roi de Chi- ne   M

Il a Neigé des Fleurs
Copyright by Salabert, Paris, N. Y.

Il a nei- gé des fleurs cet-te nuit; Les sen- tiers et les al- lées   N

J'ai Pleuré en Rêve
Copyright by A. Leduc Music
Publishers, Paris

J'ai pleuré en rê- ve: J'ai rê-vé que tu é-tais mor- - te   O

Sonnez les Matines
y permission Heugel & Cie, Paris,
opyright owners

Pour-quoi ne me ber-cez-vous plus Ô chan-son de Ro-se Ma-ri- e?   P

Sur l'Eau
y permission Heugel & Cie, Paris,
opyright owners

Sur l'eau mu- si-ca- le qui pas-se U-ne ro- - - - - se se berce   Q

Tête de Femme est Légère
y permission Heugel & Cie, Paris,
opyright owners

Tê- te de femme est lé- gè- re Et tourne au-tant que plume au vent   R

HUGHES, Herbert (1882-1937)

ARRANGEMENTS:
By permission Boosey & Hawkes, Inc.,
copyright owners

A Ballynure Ballad (Antrim)

As I was goin' to Bal-ly-nure, the day I well__ re-mem-ber

I know my love (Irish tune)

I__ know my love by his way o' walk-in and I know my

I know where I'm goin' (Antrim)

I know where I'm go-in, And I know who's go-in with me

I will walk with my love (Dublin)

I once loved a boy and a bold I-rish boy who would come and would

The next market day (Ulster)

A maid goin' to Com-ber her mar-kets to larn, To sell for her mam

The Old Turf Fire

Oh, the old turf__ fire and the hearth swept clean, There is no one

She moved thro' the fair (Donegal)

My__ young love said to me__ "My_mother won't mind and my father_

HUHN, Bruno (1871-   )

Copyright by Arthur P. Schmidt Co., Boston.
Used by permission

Invictus

Out of the night that cov-ers me, Black as the pit from pole to pol

HULLAH, John Pyke (1812-1884)

Three Fishers Went Sailing

Three fish-ers went sail-ing out in-to the west

HUME; Alexander (1811-1859)

Flow Gently, Sweet Afton

Flow gent-ly, sweet__ Af-ton, a- mong thy green braes

HUMPERDINCK, Engelbert (1854-1921)

Hänsel und Gretel (opera)
Act I

A Su-sy, lit-tle Su-sy, pray what is the news?

B Cross-patch a-way, Leave me I pray! Just let me reach yo

A Bro-ther come and dance with me, both my hands I of-fer thee

B With your foot you tap, tap, tap, With your hand you clap, clap, c

Konigskinder (opera)

Act I
Va- ter! Mut- ter! Hier will ich knien!___ Bit- ten! Flehn!

Act III
Weisst noch das gro- sse Nest aus Moos und Laub ge- äst

Lie- ber Spiel-man, al- le Kin- der und ich, wir ha- ben ge- be- ten

Am Rhein
Wenn im son- - ni- gen Herb- ste die Trau- be schwillt___

Wiegenlied
Es schau-keln die Win- de das Nest in der Lin- de

HUMPHREY, Pelham (1647-1674)

I pass all my hours
I pass all my hours in a sha- dy old grove

O the sad day
O___ the sad___ day when men shall shake their heads and say

INDY, Vincent d' (1851-1931)

Madrigal dans le style ancien, Op. 4
Qui ja- mais fut de plus char-mant vi- sa- ge, De col plus blan

Mirage, Op. 56
By permission J. Hamelle Music
Publishers, Paris
De loin, tu pa-rais-sais très gran- de Et très grave aus- si

ARRANGEMENTS:
Le Roy Loys, Op. 90, No. 1
Copyright by Salabert, Paris, N. Y.
Le Roy Lo- ys est sur son pont, Ten-ant sa fille en son gi-ron.

Le Vingt-cinq d'Août, Op. 100,
No. 1
Copyright by Salabert, Paris, N. Y.
C'etait vers le vingt-cinq d'A- oût voi- ci ve- nir, sous l'vent à nous___

En Passant par la Lorraine, No. 2
En pas-sant par la Lor- rai- ne, a- vec mes sa- bots.

À La Pêche des Moules, No. 3
À la pê- che des mou- les, je ne veux plus al- ler, ma-man,

Gentil Coqu'licot, No. 4
Je des- cen- dis dans mon jar- din; Je des- cen- dis dans mon jar-di

Cadet Rousselle, No. 5
Ca- det Rous- selle a trois mai- sons qui n'ont ni pou-tres ni che- vr

Compère Guillery, No. 6
Il é- tait un p'tit hom- me, qui s'app'lait Guil-le- ry, ca-ra- b

Lied Maritime
Au loin dans la mer s'é- teint le so- leil___ et la mer est

IPPOLITOV-IVANOV, Michael (1859-1935)

Bless the Lord, O my Soul
Copyright by Boston Music Co.

Bless the Lord, O___ my soul.___ Blessed art Thou,___ O ___ Lord

Parting (Adieu)
permission J. & W. Chester, Ltd., London,
right owners

We've trod one road, long years in ev-'ry wea-ther

IRELAND, John (1879-   )

The Bells of San Marie
permission of Augener, Ltd., London

It's plea-sant in Ho- ly Ma-ry By San Ma-rie la- goon,

The Heart's Desire
By permission Boosey & Hawkes, Inc.,
copyright owners

The boys_ are up the woods_with day to fetch_the daf-fo-dils___

Hope the Hornblower
By permission Boosey & Hawkes, Inc.,
copyright owners

Hark ye, hark to the wind-ing horn, Sluggards, a-wake and front the morn!___

If there were dreams to sell
By permission Boosey & Hawkes, Inc.,
copyright owners

If there were dreams to sell,___ What would you buy?

I have twelve oxen
By permission Boosey & Hawkes, Inc.,
copyright owners

I have twelve ox- en that be fair and brown

The Lent Lily
permission of Augener, Ltd., London

'Tis spring; come out to ram- ble the hill- y brakes a- round,

The Salley Gardens
By permission Associated Music
Publishers, Inc.

Down by the sal- ley gar-dens my love and I did meet

Sea Fever
permission of Augener, Ltd., London

I must go down to the seas a-gain, to the lone- ly sea and the sky,

The Soldier
By permission Boosey & Hawkes, Inc.,
copyright owners

If I should die, think on- ly this of me: that there's some cor-ner

Vagabond
permission of Augener, Ltd., London

Dun- no a heap a- bout the what an' why

We'll to the woods no more
permission Oxford Univ. Press, London,
right owners

We'll to the woods no more, The lau-rels are all cut

ISAAC, Heinrich (1450-c. 1517)

Innsbruck, ich muss dich lassen

Inns-bruck, ich muss dich las- sen, ich fahr da- hin mein Stra- ssen

IVES, Charles (1874-   )

Ann Street

Quaint name Ann - - street. Width of same___ ten feet Bar-num's mob___

Charlie Rutlage
Copyright 1932, Cos Cob Press, Inc.

An- oth- er good cow-punch- er has gone to meet his fate,

Evening
Copyright 1932, Cos Cob Press, Inc.

Now came still Eve-ning on, and Twi-light gray had in her so- ber liv-ery

General William Booth enters into heaven
Copyright 1935, Charles Ives

Booth led bold- ly with his big bass drum (Are you washed in the blood

The Greatest Man

My teacher said us boys should write a- bout some great___ man___

Resolution

Walk- ing strong- er un- der dis- tant skies,

Two little flowers

On sun- ny days in our back yard, Two lit-tle flowers are seen

JACKSON, Marylou

Trampin' (Try'n a make Heav'n my home) (Negro spiritual) (arr.)

I'm tram- pin', tram- pin', try'n a make heav'n my home

JACOBSON, Myron

Chanson de Marie Antoinette (arr.)
Copyright 1927, Carl Fischer, Inc.
Used by permission

On dit que le plus fier c'est moi Moi pau- vre jar- di- nier

JACQUES-DALCROZE, Emile

Le Coeur de ma mie
Copyright by Jobin & Cie, Paris

Le coeur de ma mie est pe- tit, tout pe- tit, pe- tit;

JANACEK, Leos (1854-1928)

Jenufa (opera)
Act II, Scene 5
By permission Associated Music
Publishers, Inc.

Co chví - - - - la co chví - -la a já si mám- - -

Act III, Scene 12

O- de- sli Jdi ta- ke! Vsak'yčil vi- diš, že smým

JANNEQUIN, Clement (1529-1559)

A ce joly moys

A ce jo- ly moys, jo- ly moys, jo- ly moys de mays

L'Alouette

Or sus, or sus, vous dor- mez trop Ma- da- me Jo- li- et - - - - - - - - - -

Au joly jeu

Au jo- - ly, jo- ly, jo- ly jeu du pous- se- a- vant, du pous- se a- va

premier jour du joly moys de may — A

Au premier jour du jo- ly moys de may___

Au verd boys — B

Au verd boys je m'en i- ray je m'en i- ray seu- le, au verd boys,

Bataille de Marignan (La Guerre) — C

É- cou- tez, é- cou- tez é- cou- tez tous___ gentils gal - - - - - lois___

Ce moys de may — D

Ce moys de may, ce moys de may, Ce moys de may ma ver-te

Ce sont gallans — E

Ce sont gal- lans qui s'en vont res- jou- yr

Le Chant des Oiseaux A — F

Re-veil-lez- vous coeurs en- dor - mis Le___ dieu d'a-mour vous son- ne,

B — G

Les oi- seaux quand sont ra- vis, En leur chant font mer- veil- les.

Las, povre coeur — H

Las,___ po- vre coeur___ tant tu as de tri - - - - - stes - - se

Petite Nymphe folastre — I

Pe- ti- te Nym - phe fo- la- stre,Nym- phet-te que l'i-do- la-stre

Quand j'ay esté — J

Quand j'ay es- té quinze heu- res a- vec vous

Quand je boy — K

Quand je boy du vin cla- ret, Tout tour___

JARNEFELT, Armas (1869-   )

Sunnuntaina (Sunday) — M

Kau- nis Kir- kas___ nyt on aa- mu, Aa- mu ar-mas___ sun-nun-tain

JENSEN, Adolf (1837-1879)

Lehn' deine Wang', Op. 1, No. 1 — O

Lehn' dei- ne Wang an mei- ne Wang', dann flie-ssen die Trä-nen

Marie, No. 2 — P

Ma- rie, am Fen-ster sit-zest du, du lie- bes, sü- sses Kind,___

Waldesgespräch, Op. 5, No. 4 — Q

Es ist schon spät es wind schon kalt, was reit'st du ein-sam durch den Wald?

Murmuring Breezes, Op. 21, No. 4 — R

Mur - - -meln-des Lüft-chen,Blü-ten-wind, ___ der die schö-ne Welt_____

Ufer des Flusses, des Manzanares, No. 6 — S

Am U- fer des Flusses,des Man- za- na-res,Spült Lin-nen das Mäd-chen

Der Schmied, Op. 24, No. 6
Ich hör mei- nen Schatz den Ham-mer er schwin- get, das rauschet, das klin-get,

Mein Herz ist im Hochland, Op. 49, No. 1
Mein Herz ist im Hochland, mein Herz ist nicht hier! Mein Herz__ ist im Hochland

Wenn durch die Piazzetta, Op. 50, No. 3
Wenn durch die___ Piaz- zet-ta die A - - -bendluft weht, dann weisst_du

Leis' rudern hier, mein Gondolier! No. 4
Leis'_ ru- dern hier, mein__ Gon-do- lier! Die Flut vom Ru-der sprühn

Wiegenlied, Op. 53, No. 2
Süss_ und_ sacht, sach- te weh',_ Wind du vom west-li- chen Meer;_

O lass dich halten, gold'ne Stunde
O lass dich hal- ten, gold'- ne Stun- de, die nie so schön

JOHN of Fornsete (13th Cent.)

Sumer is icumen in (Reading rota)
Sum- er is i- cum- en in,__ Loud now sing cuck- oo

JOHN IV, King of Portugal (1604-1656)

Crux fidelis
Crux fi- de- lis in - - -ter om- nes

JOMMELLI, Niccolo (1714-1774)

Chi vuol comprar
Chi_ vuol com-prar la__ bel- la ca- lan- dri - - - -na

JONES, Robert (1597-1617)

Farewell, dear Love
Fare-well, dear love, since thou will needs be gone Mine eyes do show

Go to bed, sweet muse
Go to bed, sweet Muse, take thy rest, Let not thy soul be so op- prest

Love is a bable
Love, love, love, love, love is a ba- ble, love is a ba-ble

Love's god is a boy
Love's god is a boy; None but cow-herds re-gard him; His dart is a toy

My love bound me with a kiss
My love bound me with a kiss That I should no long-er stay

What if I sped?
What if I sped where I least ex- pect- ed? What shall I say?

JOSQUIN, des Prés (c. 1445-1521)

- **Allégez moy (chanson 6 voices)** — Al- le- gez moy,_____ doul- ce plai- sant bru- net - - - - te
- **Ave Maria I** — A- ve____ Ma- ri - - a Gra - - ti- a ple - - - - - na,
- **Ave Maria II** — A- ve Ma- ri - - - - - a, gra - - - - .ti-a ple - - - - - - - - na
- **Ave verum** — A- ve ve - - - rum, ve - - - - - - - rum cor- pus na - - - tum____
- **Basies moy (chanson 6 voices)** — Ba - - - - - - sies moy,_____ ba - - - - - - sies moy,
- **Coeur Langoreulx (chanson 5 voices)** — Coeur lan-go- reulx qui ne fais que____ pen- ser
- **Incessament (chanson 5 voices)** — In- ces- sa- ment____ in- ces-sa- ment____ li- vre suis
- **J'ay bien cause de lamenter (chanson 6 voices)** — A1 J'ay bien cau- se de____ la- men- ter
- A2 J'ay bien cau- se de la - - - - - - - - - men- ter
- **Je me complains (chanson 5 voices)** — Je me com- plains de mon____ a- my, de mon____ a- my
- **Kyrie of the Missa Hercules** — Ky - - - - ri- e e - - - - - le - - - - i - - - son,
- **Ma bouche rit (chanson 6 voices)** — Ma bou-che rit, ma bou- che rit et mon coeur pleu - - - - - re
- **Miserere mei, Deus** — Mi- se- re- re me- i, De - - - - - - - us,
- **N'esse pas ung grant desplaisir (chanson 5 voices)** — N'es- se pas ung grant des - - - - - - - - - plai- sir,
- **O Domine Jesu Christe** — O ____ Do - - mi- ne Je- su Chri - - - - - ste
- **Parfons regretz (chanson 5 voices)** — Par- fons re- gretz ____ et la- men- ta- ble joi - - e,
- **Plaine de dueil (chanson 5 voices)** — Plai- ne de dueil et de mé- lan- co- ly - - - e,
- **Se congié prens (chanson 6 voices)** — Se con- gié prens de mes bel- les a- mours____

Stabat Mater

Part I

Sta- bat ma- ter do- lo- ro- sa Jux- ta- cru-cem

Part II

E- ia Ma- - - - - ter fons a- - - - mo- - - - - - - - ris,

Tenez moy en voz bras (chanson 6 voices)

Te- nez moi en voz bras, Mon___ a- my, je suis___

Tu pauperum refugium

Tu pau- pe- rum re- fu- gi- um, Tu lan- - guo-rum

KAHN, Percy B.

Ave Maria
Copyright 1913, G. Schirmer, Inc.

A- ve Ma- ri- a, gra- ti- a_ ple- na

KENNEDY-Fraser, Marjory (1857-1930)

Songs of the Hebrides (arrangements)
By permission Boosey & Hawkes, Inc., copyright owners
Aillte

The Queen of Loch- lin of the brown shields Deep love gave,

An Eriskay Love Lilt

Bheir mi ò- - - - ro bhan o Bheir mi ò- - - - ro bhan

The Bens of Jura

Like wa- ter- cress ga-ther'd fresh from cool streams Thy kiss,dear love,

Bloweth the West Wind

Lad down yon- der, Ho-i- o, Keep'st thou watch_there? Ho-ro Yal- lo- vi,

A Fairy's Love Song

Why should I sit and sigh, Pu- in brack- en, pu- in brack- en,

Islay Reaper's Song

A day in the corn field I a reap- in' Cut-tin' my sheaf

Kishmul's Galley

High from the Ben a Hay- ich_ On a day of days Sea-ward I_gaz'd

Land of Heart's Desire

Land of Heart's De-sire, Isle of Youth,dear Western Isle, gleaming in sun-light!

The Mull Fisher's Love Song

O Mhairead og!___ Mhairead,my girl,___ Thy sea-blue eyes___

The Road to the Isles
A

A far croon- in is pull- in' me a- way

B

Sure, by Tummel and Lech Rannoch and Lock- a- ber I will go,

Sea Sorrow (arr. by Bantock)

Mouth of glad- ness! Mu-sic's laughter Sad that I am not be-side_thee.

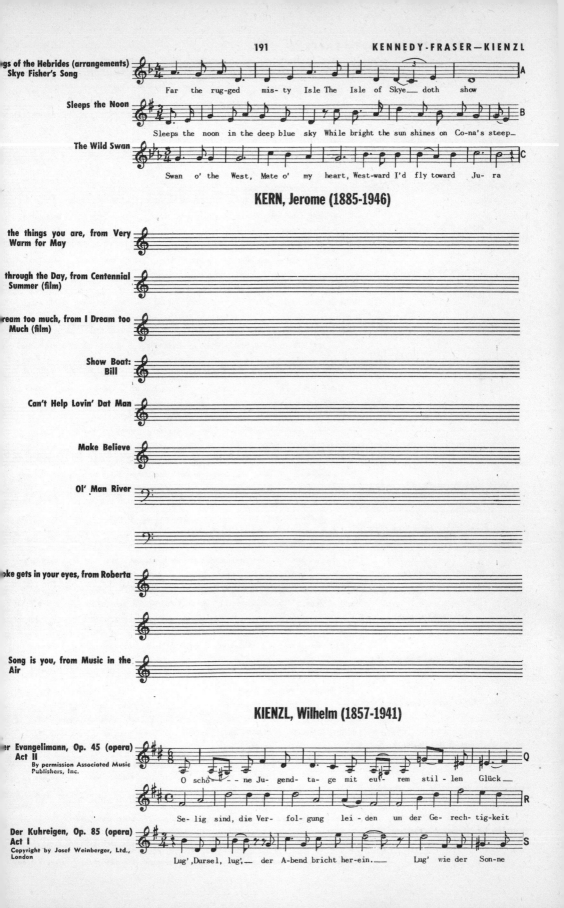

**gs of the Hebrides (arrangements)
Skye Fisher's Song**

Far the rug-ged mis-ty Isle The Isle of Skye__ doth show

A

Sleeps the Noon

Sleeps the noon in the deep blue sky While bright the sun shines on Co-na's steep__

B

The Wild Swan

Swan o' the West, Mate o' my heart, West-ward I'd fly toward Ju-ra

C

KERN, Jerome (1885-1946)

**the things you are, from Very
Warm for May**

**through the Day, from Centennial
Summer (film)**

**ream too much, from I Dream too
Much (film)**

**Show Boat:
Bill**

Can't Help Lovin' Dat Man

Make Believe

Ol' Man River

oke gets in your eyes, from Roberta

**Song is you, from Music in the
Air**

KIENZL, Wilhelm (1857-1941)

**er Evangelimann, Op. 45 (opera)
Act II**

By permission Associated Music
Publishers, Inc.

O schö— —ne Ju-gend-ta-ge mit eu— rem stil-len Glück__

Q

Se-lig sind, die Ver- fol-gung lei-den um der Ge-rech-tig-keit

R

**Der Kuhreigen, Op. 85 (opera)
Act I**

Copyright by Josef Weinberger, Ltd.,
London

Lug',Dursel, lug',__ der A-bend bricht her-ein.__ Lug' wie der Son-ne

S

Der Kuhreigen, Op. 85 (opera)
Act I

Zu __ Stras-burg auf der Schanz', da __ ging mein Trauern | an;

KILPINEN, Yrjo (1892-)

Von zwei Rosen, Op. 59, No. 3
By permission Associated Music
Publishers, Inc.

Von zwei Ro - sen duf - tet ei-ne an - ders als die and - re Ro - se,

Siehe, auch ich—lebe, Op. 59, No. 5

Al - so ihr lebt noch, al - le, al - le, ihr, am Bach ihr Wei - den

Thalatta! Op. 59, No. 6

Es stür - zen der Jugend Al - tä - re zu - sam - men,

Lieder der Liebe, Op. 60, No. 1
By permission Associated Music
Publishers, Inc.

Mein Herz ist leer, __ ich lie - - - be dich nicht mehr __

No. 2

Es ist Nacht, und mein Herz __ kommt zu dir, hält's nicht aus,

No. 3

Die - - se Ro - se von heim - li-chen Küs - - sen schwer __

No. 4

Wir sit - zen im Dun-keln. Der Vor-hang rauscht lei - - se

No. 5

Wir sind zwei Ro - sen, dar - ü - ber der Sturm fuhr und sie ab-riss.

Lieder um den Tod, Op. 62, No. 1 Vöglein Schwermut
By permission Associated Music
Publishers, Inc.

Ein schwar - zes __ Vög - lein __ fliegt ü - ber die Welt,

No. 2 Auf einem verfallenen Kirchhof

Was __ gehst du, ar - mer blei - cher Kopf, mich an Es ist kein Grund

No. 3 Der Tod und der einsame Trinker

Gu-ten A-bend, Freund! Dein Wohl! Wie geht's? __ Dein Wohl!

No. 4 Winternacht

Flok-ken-dich - te Win - ter-nacht __ Heim - kehr von der Schen - ke

No. 5 Der Säeman

Durch die Lan - de auf und ab schrei - tet weit Bau - - er Tod

No. 6 Unverlierbare Gewähr

Ei-nes gibt's dar-auf ich mich freu - - - - en darf

Vorfrühling, Op. 79, No. 3
By permission Associated Music
Publishers, Inc.

Durch ho - he Tan - nen träu-felt schon in schwinden- den Schnee das Licht.

Venezianisches Intermezzo, Op. 79, No. 4

Durch al - te Mor - mor - hal - len streift weicher Wind von Meer

Marienkirche zu Danzig im Gerüst, Op. 79, No. 7

Du Trotz des Glau - bens! Du be-helm - tes Haupt Burg Got-tes-

KJERULF, Halfdan (1815-1868)

Aftenstimmung (Twilight musing) B

The prin- cess sat high in her loft- y bow'r,

Detvar da C

Hear how the break- ers An- gri- ly lash the sand,

Ingrids Vise (Ingrid's Song) D

The fox lay low neath the birchtree root By the hea-ther, by the heather

Laengsel (Longing) E

Last night the night-in-gale woke me, When all the world was still,

Mit Hjerte og miss Lyre F

I give thee all, I can no more, Tho' poor the off'-ring be,—

Sing, Sing! G

Sing, sing Night-in-gale, sing, Sing as we watch to- geth- er,

Synnöve's Sang (Synnöve's Song) H

Grate-ful am I for the hap-py time We two, from child-hood

KNIGHT, J. P. (1812-1887)

Rock'd in the cradle of the deep J

Rock'd in the cra-dle of the deep,— I lay me down— in peace a- sleep;

KODALY, Zoltan (1882-   )

Mary Janos, Op. 15, (opera) No. 5 L

By permission Boosey & Hawkes, inc., copyright owners

Sej! verd meg Is- ten, a ki ez- tet csi- nál- ta!

No. 6 M

La— la la— la la la la la la la la la— la la la la— la la la

No. 7 N

Pi-ros al- ma le- e-sett a sár-ba Ki felve-szi nem e-sik hi- á-ba

No. 8 O

Óh,mely sok hal te-rem oz nagy Ba-la-ton bah-ha-rah-ha- ra

No. 9 P

Ti-szán in-nen Du- nán túl, túl a Ti szán, van egy esikós— nyá-jas- túl

No. 11 Q

Ku- ku- ku-kus- kám, Szállj le hoz- zám madár- kám!

No. 13 R

Ho-gyan tud- tál ró- zsám, i- de jön- ni? Ár- kot kel-tett né-ked

No. 14 S

Hej két ti- kom ta- va-li, há- rom har- mad- é- vi

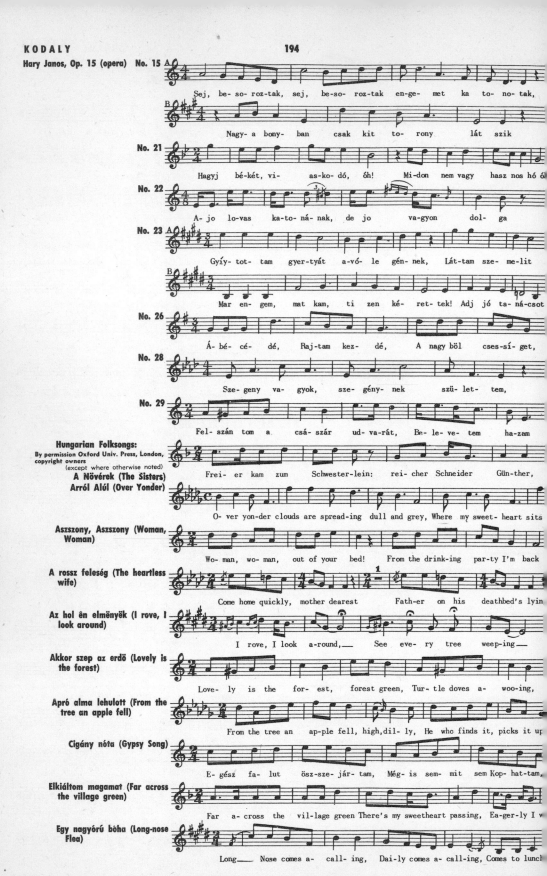

Hungarian Folksongs:

Egy kicsi madarka (Came a bird a-flying) — A
Came a bird a fly- - - - -ing To my flow- -er gar- -den

Hej, a Mohi hegy borának (Hey! The wine of Mohi)
By permission Boosey & Hawkes, Inc., copyright owners — B
Hey!___ the wine of Mo-hi vin-tage___ now costs flo-rins twen-ty

Három Árva (The Three Orphans) — C
Trudged a-long the road___ three or-phans, Way-worn, wea- ry,___

Kitrákotty mese (Tale of the clucking) — D
Once I went to mar-ket with one groat to spend, And up-on a roos-ter

Kádár Kata (Dear Mother) — E
Gyu- la-i-né, é-des a-nyám!___ En-ged-je-meg___ azt az e- gyet,

Körtéfa (The Pear Tree)
By permission Boosey & Hawkes, Inc., copyright owners — F
Still you stand, O, Peartree, As of old, green Pear Tree! Once your spreading

Kocsi, szekér (Wheelcart, barrow) — G
Wheel-cart, bar-row wheelcart, sleigh,. I'm a spin-ster, Fol-de-rol de rid-dle

Kádár István (Ballad of Stephen Kádár)
By permission Boosey & Hawkes, Inc., copyright owners — H
Once Pa- no- nia lay in dire dis- tress and pe- ril,___

Katona vagyok én (Called to serve — I
Called to serve my country all I love I'm leaving___ Sad-ly weeps my mo-ther

Kit Kéne elvenni (Which one should I marry) — J
Wise it were and time- ly ev- en now to mar- ry.

Labanc gúnydal a Kuruczra ("Labantz" mocking "Kurutz")
By permission Boosey & Hawkes, Inc., copyright owners — K
Look out, Ku- rutz, run a-way now, Rough haired Ger- mans

Megégett Rácország (All our homes)
By permission Boosey & Hawkes, Inc., copyright owners — L
All our homes___ charred ruins, Three a-lone scaped burning, One is our King's palace

Meghalok, Meghalok (Woe is me) — M
Woe is me, woe is me, so young and hale, I die. Let me for-e-ver sleep

Mónár Anna (Ballad of Annie Miller) — N
A
Come, my darling An-nie Mil- ler, Let us go forth, both to-gether,

— O
B
No, I come not, reckless Mar-tin! I won't leave my home my hus-band

Most jöttem Erdélyböl (I've just arrived) — P
Bin e-ben an- ge- langt, Aus Sie-ben- bur- gen's Land,

Öreg vagyok már én (I am old now)
By permission Boosey & Hawkes, Inc., copyright owners — Q
I am old and bold now I don't work at all now,

Puciné
By permission Boosey & Hawkes, Inc., copyright owners — R
One small loaf is all my liv- ing, This to Pu- ci- ne I'm giv-ing, Hey!

Rákoczi kesergöje (Rakoczi's Lament)
By permission Boosey & Hawkes, Inc., copyright owners — S
Hear- ken un- to me my Magyars! All my words are___ true,

Hungarian Folksongs:

Siralmas volt nekém (All my days are clouded)
By permission Boosey & Hawkes, Inc., copyright owners

All my days are cloud- ed___ Joy - - - less___ dawns___ each mor-row

Szölöhegyen keresztül (Through the vineyard)

Through the vine-yard fair Kit-ty With her bro-ther walk'd one day

Szomoru füzfänak (The weeping willow)

See the weep-ing wil-low's three and thir- ty bran- ches

Tölem a nap (Shades of eve)

Shades of eve are slow-ly fall-ing,___ No ___ re-lief

Tücsök lakodslom (Wedding of the Cricket)

Gril- le ist ein ar- mer Wicht, Möch- te sich ver- mäh- len,

Vasárnap bort inni (Sit and drink all Sunday)
By permission Boosey & Hawkes, Inc., copyright owners

Sit and drink, all___ Sun-day, Id- le rest all ___ Mon- day,

Verbunk (Recruiting)

All Hus-sars are splendid fellows Al-ways___ gay and___ chee-ry,

Virágos kenderem (All the hemp)

All the hemp lies wast- ed, far too long lay sleep- ing My be-loved

Zöld erdöben (In the forest)

Tief im Wal- de, auf der Hal- de, Tief im Wal-de auf der Hal-de

KOECHLIN, Charles (1867-   )

La Nuit
Copyright by Bordoux, Paris

Nous bé- nis- sons la dou- ce Nuit, Dont le frais bai- ser

Si tu le veux
Copyright by Boston Music Co.

Si tu le veux, ô mon a- mour, ce soir des que la fin du jour

Le Thé
Copyright by Boston Music Co.

Miss El- len, ver-sez-moi le thé___ Dans la bel- le tas- se chi-noise

Villanelle, Op. 21, No. 1
Copyright by Philippo, Paris

Le temps, l'é-ten- due et le nom- bre Sont tom- bés du noir fir-ma-ment

KOENEMAN, Theo (-1938)

When the King went forth to war, Op. 7, No. 6
By permission J. & W. Chester, Ltd., London, copyright owners

When the King went forth to war To a coun- try strange and far

KORBAY, F. (1846-1913)

**Hungarian Folksongs (arrangements):
Had a horse**

Had___ a horse, a fi- ner no one ev- er säw

But the she- riff sold him in the name of law.

The Last Hour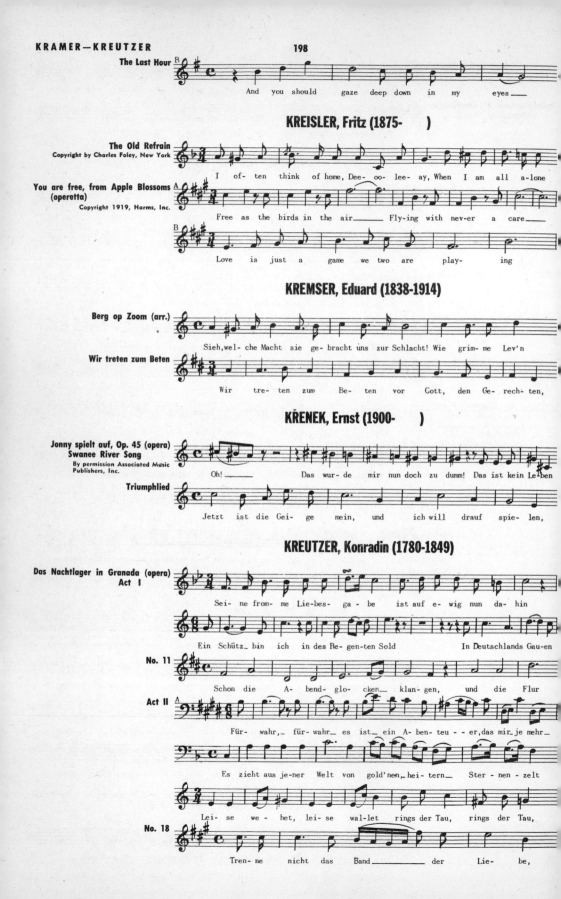

And you should gaze deep down in my eyes___

KREISLER, Fritz (1875-)

The Old Refrain
Copyright by Charles Foley, New York

I of-ten think of home, Dee-oo-lee-ay, When I am all a-lone

You are free, from Apple Blossoms (operetta)
Copyright 1919, Harms, Inc.

Free as the birds in the air___ Fly-ing with nev-er a care___

Love is just a game we two are play-ing

KREMSER, Eduard (1838-1914)

Berg op Zoom (arr.)

Sieh, wel-che Macht sie ge-bracht uns zur Schlacht! Wie grim-me Lev'n

Wir treten zum Beten

Wir tre-ten zum Be-ten vor Gott, den Ge-rech-ten,

KŘENEK, Ernst (1900-)

Jonny spielt auf, Op. 45 (opera)
Swanee River Song
By permission Associated Music Publishers, Inc.

Oh!___ Das wur-de mir nun doch zu dumm! Das ist kein Le-ben

Triumphlied

Jetzt ist die Gei-ge mein, und ich will drauf spie-len,

KREUTZER, Konradin (1780-1849)

Das Nachtlager in Granada (opera)
Act I

Sei-ne from-me Lie-bes-ga-be ist auf e-wig nun da-hin

Ein Schütz_ bin ich in des Re-gen-ten Sold In Deutschlands Gau-en

No. 11

Schon die A-bend-glo-cken_ klan-gen, und die Flur

Act II

Für-wahr,_ für-wahr_ es ist_ ein A-ben-teu--er, das mir je mehr

Es zieht aus je-ner Welt von gold'nen_ hei-tern_ Ster-nen-zelt

Lei-se we-het, lei-se wal-let rings der Tau, rings der Tau,

No. 18

Tren-ne nicht das Band___ der Lie-be,

Schäfers Sonntagslied

Das ist der Tag des Herrn, das ist der Tag des Herrn

Hobellied, from Der Verschwender (Fairy opera) Act III

Da strei- ten sich die Leut her- um oft um den Wert des Glücks

KŘIČKA, Jaroslav (1882-)

L'Albatros, Op. 14, No. 1

Tout là- haut dans le ciel pro- fond au des- sus de la va- gue,

KRIEGER, Johann Philip (1649-1725)

Die Gerechten werden weggerafft

Die Ge- rech- ten wer- den. weg- ge- rafft vor dem Un- glück,

KÜCKEN, Friedrich (1810-1882)

How Can I Leave Thee (Ach! Wie ist möglich dann)

How can I leave thee! How can I from thee part!

LA FORGE, Frank (1879-)

An einen Boten
Copyright 1909, G. Schirmer, Inc.

Wenn du zü mei'm Schat- ze kommst, sag':

Come unto these yellow sands
Copyright 1907, G. Schirmer, Inc.

Come un- to these yel - - - - - - - - - - - - - - - - low sands

Hills
Copyright by G. Ricordi & Co., Inc.

I want my hills! Hills! The trail that scorns the hol- lows

Song of the Open
Copyright by Oliver Ditson Co. Used by permission.

To your soul is it wine, As it is to mine

Take, O take those lips away
Copyright 1909, G. Schirmer, Inc.

Take, o take those lips a- way that so sweet- ly were for-sworn

LALO, Edouard (1823-1892)

Ballade à la lune

C'é- tait dans la nuit bru- ne, sur le clocher jau- ni la lu- ne

Guitare

Com- ment, disaient ils, a- vec nos na- celles fuir les al- gua- zils?

Oh, quand je dors

Oh quand je dors, viens au- près de ma cou- che!

Le Roi d'Ys (opera) Act I (Breton theme)

Les guerres sont ter- mi- né- es, Voi- ci pour nous dé- sor- mais

Le Roi d'Ys (opera)
Act I
En si-len-ce pour-quoi souf-frir? Dans mon coeur___ é-pan-che ta pei-ne!

Act II
Le sa- lut nous est pro- mis, c'est à nos seuls en- ne- mis

Ah! si j'a- vais souf-fert de la mê- me tor- tu- re,

Act III Aubade
Vai- ne-ment___ ma bien ai- mé- -e On croit me dé-ses-pé-rer

A l'au-tel j'al-lais rayon-nant___ mon amour é-tait ma pri-è-re___

L'Esclave
Cap- ti- ve et peut- ê-tre ou-bli-é- e je songe___

LAMBERT, Constant (1905-)

The Rio Grande A
By permission Oxford Univ. Press, London, copyright owners
By the Ri- o Grande___ they dance a sa- ra- bande___

B
But they dance in the ci- ty down the pub- lic squares

C
The Com- men- da- dor and Al- qua- cil___ are there on horse-back

D
The noi- - sy streets are emp- ty and hushed is the town___

E
Such a space of si- lence through the town___ to the ri-ver

LAMBERT, Frank

She is far from the land

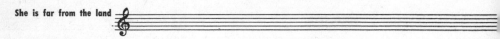

LANDINO, (Landini) Francesco (1325-1397)

Benche ora piova
Ben- che o- ra___ pio- va___ pur buon tem-po

Gram piant'agli occhi
Gram - - - - - - - - - - piant' agl'___ oc- chi

LANG, Margaret Ruthven (1867-)

Irish Love Song, Op. 22
Copyright by Arthur P. Schmidt Co., Boston. Used by permission
O, the time is long Ma- vour-neen, Till I come a-gain,

LANGE-MÜLLER, Peter Erasmus (1850-1926)

Efteraar (Autumn), Op. 61, No. 3
Copyright by Oliver Ditson Co. Used by permission.

Fa- ther, swans fly- ing- where do they go? Hence! Hence!   **B**

Skin ud, du Klare Solskin (Bright Sunshine), Op. 18, No. 4
Copyright by Oliver Ditson Co. Used by permission.

Shine bright and clear, O sun, shine, and lead us on to__ Spring   **C**

LASSEN, Eduard (1830-1904)

Allerseelen

Stell auf dem Tisch die duf- ten- den Re- se- den   **E**

Ich hatte einst ein schönes Vaterland

Ich hat- te einst ein schönes Va- ter- land;__ der Ei- chen-baum wuchs dort   **F**

Mit deinen blauen Augen

Mit dei- nen blau- en Au-- gen siehst du mich lieb- lich an__   **G**

LASSUS, Orlando de (1530-1594)

Chansons Françaises
A ce matin

A ce ma- tin ce se- rait bon- ne e-strei-- ne   **I**

Amour, donne moy payx

A- mour, A- - - - - - - - - - - - - mour, don- - ne moy payx   **J**

Bon jour, bon jour

Bon jour,_____ Bon jour, Bon jour, Bon jour, Bon jour, Bon jour   **K**

Dessus le marché d'Arras

Des- sus le mar- ché d'Ar- ras, mi- re- li, mi-- re la bon ba,   **L**

Guerir ma douleur

Gue- rir ma dou- leur_____ mon__ mal et tour- - - - ment,__   **M**

Hélas, quel jour

He- las, quel jour se- ray- je à mon_____ vou- loir   **N**

J'ay cherché la science

J'ay cher-ché la sçi- en- - - - - ce, j'ay cher-ché la sçi- en- - - - ce   **O**

Margot, labourez les vignes

Mar- got, la- bou- rez les vi- gnes, Vi- gnes, vi- gnes, vi-gno- let,   **P**

La nuit froide

La nuit froi- de et som- bre__ Cou- - - rant d'ob-scu-re om-bre   **Q**

O Mère des Amours

O Mè- re des a- mours,__ Ci- pri- ne, O gran- de dé- es- se   **R**

Tu sais, Tu sais, o gen- ti- le dé- es- se   **S**

LEGRENZI, Giovanni (1626-1690)

Che fiero costume

Che fie-ro co-stu-me d'a-li-ge-ro nu-me, che a for-za di pe-ne

LEHÁR, Franz (1870-1948)

Friederike (operetta)
Act I

Sah ein Knab' ein Rös-lein stehn, Rös-lein auf der Hei-den

Act II

O Mäd-chen, mein Mäd-chen wie lieb ich dich!

Wa-rum hast du mich wach ge-küsst? Hab nicht ge-wusst

Lie-be, se-li-ger Traum aus himm-li-schen Höh'n, du kannst nicht vergehn

Giuditta (operetta)

Du bist mei-ne Son-ne, du bist ein Traum voll sü-sser Won-ne!

Freun-de, das Le-ben ist le-bens-wert

Mei-ne Lip-pen, sie Küs-sen so heiss. Mei-ne Glie-der sind schmiegsam

Hab' ein blaues Himmelbett, from Frasquita (operetta) Act II

Schatz, ich bitt' dich, komm heut Nacht Al-les ist be-reit ge-macht.

Ein Glück dir winkt so wie noch nie, Kein Laut uns stört,

Im heimlichen Dämmer, from Eva (operetta) Act I
Copyright 1912, G. Schirmer, Inc.

Im heim-li-chen Däm-mer der sil-ber-nen Am-pel,

Wär' es auch nichts als ein Au-gen-blick, wär' es auch nichts

Das Land des Lächelns (The Land of Smiles)
Act I Immer nur lächeln

Ich tre-te ins Zim-mer, von Sehn-sucht durch-bebt.

Von Ap-fel-blü-ten ei-nen Kranz, ah

Du bist das traum-süs-se Le-ben, Du al-lein

Act II

Wer hat die Lie-be uns ins Herz ge-senkt, uns den sü-ssen Rausch

Dein ist mein gan-zes Herz! Wo du nicht bist, Kann ich nicht sein,

The Merry Widow
Act II Vilia Song

Es lebt ei- ne Vil- ja, ein Wald- mäg- de- lein,

Vil- ja, O Vil- ja, du Wald- mäg- de- lein, fass' mich und lass' mich

Act III

Lip- pen schwei-gen, 'sflü- tern Gei- gen: Hab mich lieb

Paganini (operetta) Act II

Gern hab' ich die Frau'n ge- küsst, hab' nie ge- fragt

Lie- - be, du Him- mel auf Er- den, e- - - wig be- steht

**Waltz, from The Count of Luxemburg
(operetta)**

**Was ich längst erträumte, from Der
Göttergatte**

Was ich längst er- träum- te, was ich lang ver- säum- te

**Wenn sich zwei lieben, from Der
Rastelbinder Act I**

Wenn sich zwei lie- ben, so steht's ge- schrie- ben, sind sie ein Herz,

**Der Zarewitsch (operetta)
Act I**

Ei- ner wind Kom- men der wird mich be- geh- ren

Mir ist so bang, als hielt mich ein Traum be- fan- gen

Volgalied

Hast Du dort o- ben ver- ges- sen auf mich? Es sehnt doch mein Herz

Act II

Hab' nur dich al- lein, die gan- ze Welt sollst du mir sein,

Act III Napolitana

Wa- rum hat je- der Früh- ling ach nur ei- nen Mai

**Zorika, kehre zurück, from Zigeuner-
liebe Act II**

Zo- ri- ka, Zo- ri- ka, keh- re zu- rück, lass uns zur Hei- mat

LEHMANN, Liza (1862-1918)

The Cuckoo
By permission Boosey & Hawkes, Inc.,
copyright owners

The Cuc- koo sat in the old pear tree. "Cuc- koo"

Go, lovely Rose

**In a Persian Garden (song cycle)
Ah, moon of my delight**
Copyright by Boston Music Co.

Ah, moon of my de- light that knows no wane

**Alas! that Spring should
vanish with the rose**
Copyright by G. Schirmer, Inc.

A- las! That Spring should va- nish with the Rose

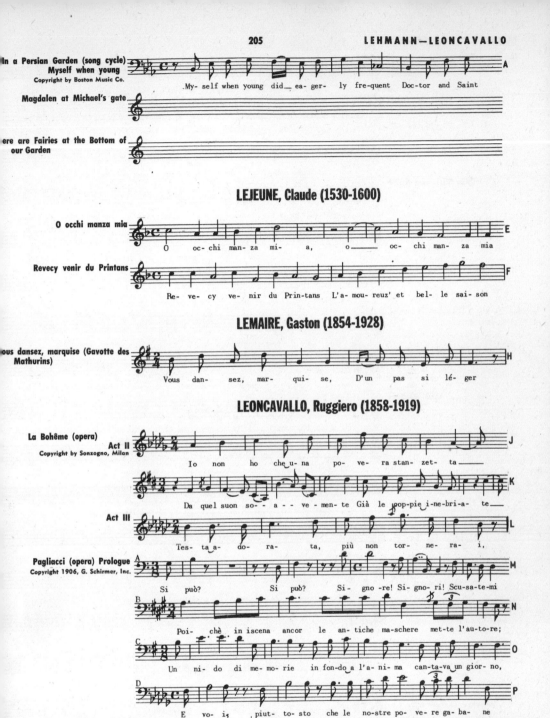

In a Persian Garden (song cycle)
Myself when young
Copyright by Boston Music Co.

...My-self when young did_ea-ger-ly fre-quent Doc-tor and Saint   A

Magdalen at Michael's gate

There are Fairies at the Bottom of our Garden

LEJEUNE, Claude (1530-1600)

O occhi manza mia

O   oc-chi man-za mi-   a,   o___ oc-chi man-za mia   E

Revecy venir du Printans

Re- ve- cy ve- nir du Prin-tans L'a- mou- reuz' et bel- le sai- son   F

LEMAIRE, Gaston (1854-1928)

Vous dansez, marquise (Gavotte des Mathurins)

Vous dan- sez, mar- qui- se, D'un pas si lé- ger   H

LEONCAVALLO, Ruggiero (1858-1919)

La Bohème (opera)
Act II
Copyright by Sonzogno, Milan

Io   non   ho che u-na   po- ve-ra stan-zet- ta___   J

Da quel suon so- a- - ve-men-te Già le cop-pie i-ne-bri-a- te   K

Act III

Tes- ta a- do- ra- ta,   più non tor- ne- ra- i,   L

Pagliacci (opera) Prologue
Copyright 1906, G. Schirmer, Inc.

Si   può?   Si può?   Si- gno- re! Si- gno- ri! Scu-sa-te-mi   M

Poi- chè in iscena ancor   le an- tiche ma-schere met-te l'au-to-re;   N

Un ni- do di me- mo- rie in fon-do a l'a-ni- ma can-ta-va un gior- no,   O

E   vo- i,   piut- to- sto   che le no-stre po- ve-re ga-ba-   ne   P

Act I

Un gran- - - de spet-ta- co- lo a ven-ti-tre o- - - - - - - - re   Q

Un tal gio- co, cre-de- te- mi   è meglio non gio-car-lo con me,   R

Bell Chorus

Din, don,_ suo-na ve- spe-ro, ra- ga- ze e gar- zon,   S

Ballatella

Stri-do- no las- sù,_   li- be-ra-men- te lan-cia-ti a vol,_   T

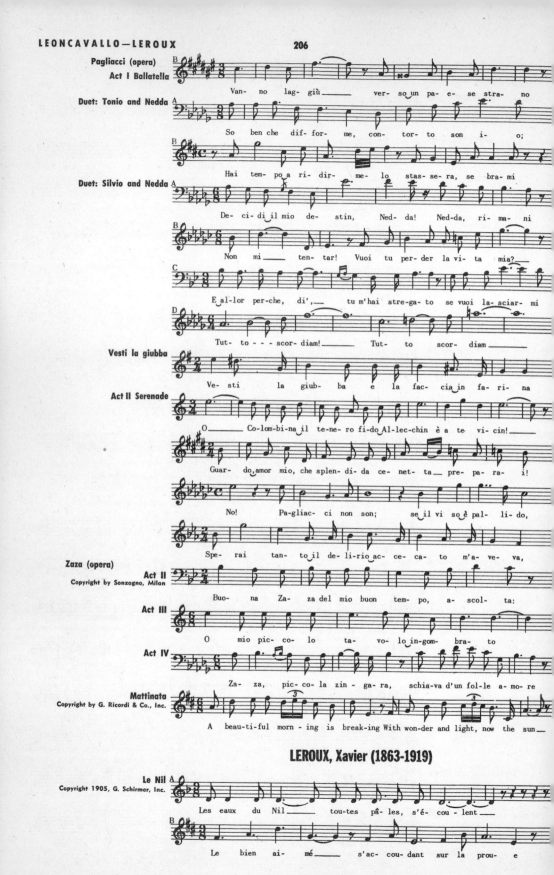

Pagliacci (opera)

Act I Ballatella

Van- no lag- giù_____ ver- so un pa- e- se stra- no

Duet: Tonio and Nedda

So ben che dif- for- me, con- tor- to son i- o;

Duet: Silvio and Nedda

Hai tem- po a ri- dir- me- lo stas- se- ra, se bra- mi

De- ci- di il mio de- stin, Ned- da! Ned- da, ri- ma- ni

Non mi_____ ten- tar! Vuoi tu per- der la vi- ta mia?

E al- lor per- che, di',_____ tu m'hai stre- ga- to se vuoi la- sciar- mi

Tut- to - - - scor- diam!_____ Tut- to scor- diam_____

Vesti la giubba

Ve- sti la giub- ba e la fac- cia in fa- ri- na

Act II Serenade

O_____ Co- lom- bi- na il te- ne- ro fi- do Al- lec- chin è a te vi- cin!_____

Guar- do, amor mio, che splen- di- da ce- net- ta_ pre- pa- ra- i!

No! Pa- gliac- ci non son; se il vi- so è pal- li- do,

Spe- rai tan- to il de- li- rio ac- ce- ca- to m'a- ve- va,

Zaza (opera)

Act II
Copyright by Sonzogno, Milan

Buo- na Za- za del mio buon tem- po, a- scol- ta:

Act III

O mio pic- co- lo ta- vo- lo in- gom- bra- to

Act IV

Za- za, pic- co- la zin- ga- ra, schia- va d'un fol- le a- mo- re

Mattinata
Copyright by G. Ricordi & Co., Inc.

A beau- ti- ful morn- ing is break- ing With won- der and light, now the sun_____

LEROUX, Xavier (1863-1919)

Le Nil
Copyright 1905, G. Schirmer, Inc.

Les eaux du Nil_____ tou- tes pâ- les, s'é- cou- lent_____

Le bien ai- mé_____ s'ac- cou- dant sur la prou- e

LEVERIDGE, Richard (c. 1670-1758)

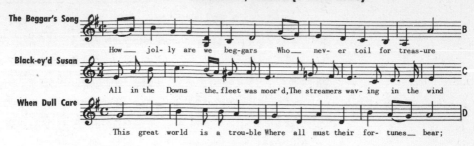

The Beggar's Song

How — jol-ly are we beg-gars Who — nev-er toil for treas-ure   **B**

Black-ey'd Susan

All in the Downs the fleet was moor'd, The streamers wav-ing in the wind   **C**

When Dull Care

This great world is a trou-ble Where all must their for-tunes — bear;   **D**

LIE, Sigund (1871-1904)

Sne (Snow)

Copyright by Oliver Ditson Co. Used by permission.

There is nought on earth so still as the snow —   **F**

LIEURANCE, Thurlow (1878-   )

the Waters of Minnetonka (Indian Love Song)

Copyright by Theodore Presser Co. Used by permission.

Moon — Deer — How near — your soul di - - - - vine —   **H**

LILLIJEBJORN, H. (1797-1875)

hen I Was Seventeen (När jag blef sjutton år) (arr.)

Four-teen years I had seem'd just to be Lit-tle maid-en so hap-py   **J**

LINLEY, William (1771-1835)

wn as white as driven snow, from "A Winter's Tale"

Lawn as white as dri-ven snow; Cy-press, black as a-ny crow;   **L**

LISZT, Franz (1811-1886)

Christus vincit, from Christus (oratorio)

Chris-tus vin-cit, Chris-tus reg-nat, Chris-tus im-pe-rat   **N**

Comment, disaient-ils

Com-ment, di-saient-ils, A-vec nos na-cel-les Fuir les al-gua-zils?   **O**

Die drei Zigeuner

Drei Zi-geu-ner fand ich ein-mal lie — — gen an ei-ner Wei - - de   **P**

Hielt der Ei-ne für sich al-lein in den Hän-den die Fie-del,   **Q**

Du bist wie eine Blume

Du — bist wie-ei-ne Blu - - me, so hold — so schön — und rein   **R**

Es muss ein Wunderbares sein

Es muss ein Wun-der-ba-res sein Um's Lie-ben zwei-er See-len   **S**

Freudvoll und Leidvoll

Freud- voll und leid- voll ge- dan- ken- voll— sein,

Ich liebe dich

Ich lie - - be dich weil ich dich lie - ben muss;—

Im Rhein, im schönen Strome

Im Rhein, im schö- nen Stro- me, Da spie- gelt sich in den Wel- len

Die Lorelei

Ich weiss nicht, was soll's be- deu- ten, dass ich so trau- rig,

Die Luft ist kühl, und es— dun- - kelt,

Mignons Lied (Kennst du das Land)

Kennst du das Land, wo die Zi- tro- nen blühn,

Missa Choralis

I Kyrie

Ky - ri- e e - le - - - - - - - i- son e- le - - - - - - - i- son

II Gloria

Glo - - - - - ri- a in ex- cel- sis De- o Et in ter- ra pax

III Credo

Cre- do in u- num De - - - um Pa- trem om- ni- po- ten - - tem

IV Sanctus

San- ctus, San- ctus, San- ctus Do- mi- nus De - - us Sa - - ba- oth

V Benedictus

Be - - - ne- di- ctus, be - - - ne- di - - - - - ctus

VI Agnus Die

A- gnus De - - - i qui tol - - lis pec- ca - ta mun- di

Nimm einen Strahl der Sonne

Nimm ei- nen Strahl der Son- ne, vom A- bend- stern das Licht,

Oh! quand je dors

Oh! quand je dors, viens au- près de ma cou- che

O Lieb (original version of Liebestraum, No. 3)

O lieb', o lieb,— so lang du lie- ben kannst—

Wieder möcht' ich dir begegnen

Wie- der möcht' ich dir be- geg- nen, Wie- der schau- en dei- nen Blick;

LOEWE, Karl (1796-1869)

Edward, Op. 1, No. 1

Dein Schwert, wie ist's von Blut so rot? Ed- ward, Ed- ward!

Ich hab' ge- schla- gen mei- nen Gei- er tot Mut - ter, Mut - ter!

Archibald Douglas, Op. 128
Denk' nicht an den al-ten Dou-glasneid, der trotzig dich be-kriegt,

Der Nöck, Op. 129, No. 2
Es tönt des Nö-cken Har-fen-schall

Tom der Reimer, Op. 135
Der Rei-mer Tho-mas lag am Bach, am Kie-sel-bach

Da sah er ei-ne blon-de Frau, die sass auf ei-nem wei-ssen Ross

Canzonetta
War schö-ner als der schön-ste Tag,

Das Erkennen
Ein Wan-der-bursch, mit dem Stab in der Hand, Kommt wie-der heim

Die nächtliche Heerschau
Nachts um die zwölf-te Stun-de ver-lässt der Tam-bour sein Grab

Der Zahn
Vic-to-ri-a! Vic-to-ri-a! Der klei-ne weis-se Zahn ist da,

LOGAN, Frederic Knight

Pale Moon
Copyright by Foster Music Co., Chicago
Out of my lodge at e-ven-tide 'Mong the sob-bing pine

LORTZING, Gustav Albert (1801-1851)

Undine (opera)
Act II
Es wohnt am See-ge-sta-de ein ar-mes Fis-cher-paar,

Act III
Va-ter, Mut-ter, Schwes-tern, Brü-der, hab' ich auf der Welt nicht mehr

O kehr' zu-rück, mein ei-tel Seh-nen ist nun ge-stillt,

Act IV
Ich war in mei-nen jun-gen Jah-ren ein feu-ri-ges, ver-lieb-tes Blut

Im Wein ist Wahr-heit nur al-lein, Im Wein ist Wahr-heit nur al-lein

Auch ich war ein Jüngling, from Der Waffenschmied (opera)
Act III
Auch ich war ein Jüng-ling mit lo-cki-gem Haar,

Der Wildschütz (opera)
Act I Duet and Chorus
A B C D, der Jung-ge-sel-len-stand tut weh, E F G H,

Act II
Fünf-tau-send Tha-ler! Fünf-tau-send Tha-ler Träum o-der wach i

Der Wildschütz (opera) Act II — Gret-chen, thrä-nen-voll, mich um Got-tes wil-len bit-tet (A)

Act III — Hei-ter-keit, und Fröh-lich-keit, ihr Göt-ter die-ses Le-bens (B)

Zar und Zimmermann (opera) Act I — Auf, Ge-sel-len, greift zur Axt und regt die nerv'-gen Ar-me (C)

A — O Sanc-ta Ju-sti-tia, ich möch-te ra-sen, ich möch-te ra-sen (D)

B — Die-se aus-drucks-vol-len Zü---ge, die-ses Aug', (E)

Act II — Le-be wohl, mein flan-drisch Mäd-chen, wi-der Wil-len muss ich fort (F)

Act III A — Heil sei dem Tag an wel-chem Du bei uns er-schie-nen "Di-del-dum (G)

B — O wie schön die Wor-te, wie schön die Wor-te flie-ssen, (H)

Sonst spielt' ich mit Scep-ter mit Kro-ne und Stern (I)

LOTTI, Antonio (1667-1740)

Crucifixus — Cru-ci-fi - - - - - - - - - - - - - - - xus, Cru-ci-fi-xus (K)

Pur dicesti — Pur di - - ce-sti, o boc - ca boc-ca bel-la, (L)

LULLY, Jean Baptiste (1632-1687)

Au clair de la lune — Au clair de la lu-ne, mon a-mi Pier-rot (N)

Alceste (opera) Prologue — Le Hé-ros que j'at-tends ne re-vien-dra-t-il pas? (O)

Act IV — Il faut pas-ser tôt ou tard, Il faut pas-ser dans ma bar-que, (P)

Amadis (opera) Act II — Dans un piè-ge fa-tal son mau-vais sort l'a-mè-ne (Q)

Bois é-pais re-dou-ble ton om-bre: Tu ne sau-rais être (R)

A-mour, que veux tu de moi? Mon coeur n'est pas fait pour toi, (S)

Amadis (opera) Act V
Fer- mez- vous pour ja- mais, mes yeux, mes tris- tes yeux

Armide (opera) Act I
Al- lez, al- lez rem- plir ma pla- ce aux lieux d'où mon mal- heur

Act II
Plus j'ob- ser- ve ces lieux, et plus je les ad- mi- re

Act III
Ah! si la li- ber- té me doit ê- tre ra- vi- e

Act IV
Que vois-je? O spec-tacle effro- ya-ble O trop funes- te sort

Cadmus et Hermione Act II
A- mour, vois quels maux tu nous fais, où sont les biens que tu pro- met's?

Act V
Belle Her- mi- o- ne, He- las! He- las! puis-je être heu- reux sans vous?

Dormons tous, from Atys (opera) Act III
Dor- mons dor- mons tous, ah! ah! Que le re- pos est

Persée (opera) Act III
A
J'ai per- du la beau- té qui me ren- dit si vai- ne

B
Je por - - te l'e- pou- vante et la mort en tous lieux.

Act V
Ô mort! Ve- nez fi- nir mon de-stin dé- plo- ra- ble

Thésée (opera) Prologue
Re- ve- nez, re- ve- nez A- mours re- ve- nez Re- ve- nez, A- mours

Que rien ne trouble i- ci Vé- nus et les a- mours

Act V
Ah! Ah! faut- il me ven- ger, En per- dant ce que j'ai - - me!

LUTHER, Martin (1483-1546)

A mighty fortress is our God (Ein feste Burg)
A might- y fort-ress is our God, A bul-wark nev-er fail - - ing

Vom Himmel hoch
Vom Him- mel hoch da Komm' ich her, ich bring' euch

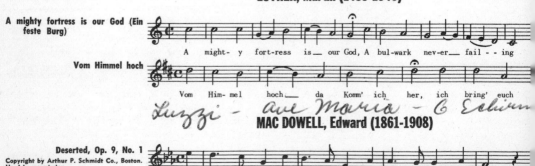

Luzzi - Ave Maria - C Schirm

MAC DOWELL, Edward (1861-1908)

Deserted, Op. 9, No. 1
Copyright by Arthur P. Schmidt Co., Boston.
Used by permission
Ye banks and braes o' bon- nie Doon, how can ye bloom sae fair!

The Blue Bell, Op. 26, No. 5
In love she fell, My shy Blue-bell, With a stroll-ing Bum- ble-Bee

Cradle Hymn, Op. 33, No. 2
Copyright by Arthur P. Schmidt Co., Boston.
Used by permission
Dor- mi Je - - - - su! dor- mi Je - su, Ma-ter ri-det

Menie, Op. 34, No. 1
Copyright by Arthur P. Schmidt Co., Boston.
Used by permission
In vain to me the cow-slips blaw, In vain to me the vi-o-lets spring

Thy beaming eyes, Op. 40, No. 3
Copyright by Arthur P. Schmidt Co., Boston.
Used by permission
Thy beam- ing eyes, Are Par- a-dise, to me, my love, to me,

The Sea, Op. 47, No. 7
One sails a-way to sea, to sea, One stands on the shore and cries

Long Ago, Op. 56, No. 1
Copyright by Arthur P. Schmidt Co., Boston.
Used by permission
Long a-go sweet-heart mine, Ros-es bloomed as ne'er be- fore,

The Swan bent low, No. 2
The Swan bent low to the Lil- y, Mid wav'- ring shad- ows green

A maid sings light, No. 3
A maid sings light, And a maid sings low, With a mer-ry, mer-ry laugh

As the gloaming shadows creep, No. 4
As the gloam - - ing shad- ows creep Through the for-est deep

Fair Springtide, Op. 60, No. 2
Copyright by Arthur P. Schmidt Co., Boston.
Used by permission
Fair Spring-tide com- eth once a- gain Stirs the sap in lone-ly trees

MAC GIMSEY, Robert (1898-)

Shadrack
Copyright 1937, Carl Fischer, Inc.
Used by special permission.
Thah was three chill - un frum nuh lan' uv Is - - ri-el Shad - - rack

MACHAUT, Guillaume De (c. 1300-1377)

De tout sui si confortée (Virelai)
De tout sui si con- for- té- e Que je-mais n'iert hoste- lé- e

Je puis trop bien (ballade)
Je - - - - - - puis trop bien ma - - - - da-me com- pa-rer

Mass
1. Kyrie
Ky- ri - - - - - e - - - - - e

2. Qui propter nos
Qui pro- pter nos ho- mi- nes,

3. Agnus Dei
A - - - - - - gnus De - - - - i
A - - - - - - gnus De - - - i

Quant Theseus (ballade)

Quant The - - - - se - - - us, Her - cu - - les et - Ja-zon

Ne quier ve - - - - oir la - - - - beau-té - - - d'Ab-sa- lon

Rose lys (rondeau)

Ro- se lys - - - - - - - - - - - printemps ver-du-re

MAHLER, Gustav (1860-1911)

Blicke mir nicht in die Lieder

Blik- ke mir - nicht in die Lie- der! Mei - ne - Au - gen -

Ich atmet' einen linden Duft

Ich at - met' ei - nen lin - den Duft Im Zim - mer stand -

Ich bin der Welt abhanden gekommen

Ich bin der Welt - - ab - - - han - den ge - kom - men

Kindertotenlieder (song cycle) No. 1
By permission Associated Music
Publishers, Inc.

Nun will die Sonn' so hell auf-geh'n als sei - kein Un - glück,

No. 2

Nun seh' ich wohl war- um so dunk- le Flam- men

No. 3

Wenn dein Müt-ter-lein tritt zur Tür her-ein und den Kopf ich dre- he,

No. 4

Oft denk ich sie sind nur aus ge- gan- gen!

No. 5

In die-sem Wet- ter, in die-sem Braus, nie hätt' ich ge- sen- det

In die- sem Wet- ter, in die-sem Saus in - die- - sem - Braus,

Des Knaben Wunderhorn (song cycle)
Des Antonius von Padua Fisch-
predigt
By permission Boosey & Hawkes, Inc.,
copyright owners

An- to- nius zur Pre- digt die Kir- che - findt - le - dig!

Das irdische Leben

Mut- ter, ach Mut- ter, es hun- gert - mich! Gib mir Brot,

Lob des hohen Verstandes

Einst- mal in ei- nem tie- fen Thal Ku- kuk und Nach- ti- gall

Rheinlegendchen

Bald - gras' ich am Nek- kar, bald gras ich am Rhein

Wer hat dies Liedlein erdacht?

Dort - o- ben am - Berg in dem hoh - - - en Haus, in dem Haus,

Wo die schönen Trompeten
blasen

Wer ist denn draussen und wer klop-fet an der mich - so - lei - - se,

MAHLER

Knaben Wunderhorn (song cycle) B — A
Wo die schönen Trompeten blasen
Das ist der Herz- al- ler-lieb- ste dein, steh auf und lass mich zu dir ein

Sieben Lieder aus letzter Zeit — B
Der Tamboursg'sell
Ich ar- mer Tam - bours- g'sell Man führt mich aus dem G'wölb —

Revelge A — C
Des Mor- gens zwi- schen drei'n und vie- ren,

B — D
Ach Bru- der, ach Bru- der, ich kann dir nicht tra- gen

Liebst du um Schönheit — E
Liebst du um Schön-heit, O nicht mich lie- be! Lie-be die Son- ne

Lied von der Erde (song cycle) A — F
By permission Boosey & Hawkes, Inc.,
copyright owners
No. 1 Das Trinklied vom Jammer der Erde
Schon winkt der Wein im gold' - -nen Po- ka- le,

B — G
Dun- kel ist das Le- ben, ist der Tod

No. 2 Der Einsame im Herbst — H
Herbst- ne- bel wal- len bläu- lich ü- berm See

No. 3 Von der Jugend A — I
Mit- ten in dem klei-nen Tei-che steht ein Pa-vil- lon aus grü- nem

B — J
In dem Häus-chen sit-zen Freun- de, schön ge-klei-det, trin-ken, plau-dern

No. 4 Von der Schönheit — K
Jun- ge Mäd- chen pflük-ken Blu-men, pflük-ken Lo-tos-blu - men an dem U-fer

No. 5 Der Trunkene im Frühling A — L
Wenn nur ein Traum das Le- ben ist war- um denn Müh' und Plag'

B — M
der Lenz ist da, sei kom- men ü- ber Nacht!

No. 6 Der Abschied — N
Die Son- ne schei- det hin-ter dem Ge- bir- ge. In al- le Tä- ler

er eines fahrenden Gesellen (song cycle) — O
No. 1
Wenn mein Schatz Hoch- zeit macht froh- li-che Hoch-zeit macht

No. 2 — P
Ging heut' mor-gens ü- ber's Feld, Tau noch auf den Grä-sern hing;

No. 3 — Q
Ich hab ein glü-hend Mes- ser, ein Mes-ser in mei-ner Brust, O weh

No. 4 — R
Die zwei blau- en Au- gen von mei-nem Schatz, die ha- ben mich

mphony No. 2: 4th movement — S
"Urlicht"
By permission Boosey & Hawkes, Inc.,
copyright owners
Der Mensch liegt in gröss- ter Noth! Der Mensch liegt in grösster Pein

Symphony No. 2, 5th movement (Chorus)

Auf- er- steh'n, ja— auf- er- steh'n, wirst du, mein Staub, nach kur- zer— Ruh!—

Symphony No. 4, 4th movement
By permission Boosey & Hawkes, Inc., copyright owners

A. Wir ge- nie- ssen die himm - - - - - - - - - - - li- schen Freu - den

B. Jo- han- nes das Lämm- lein aus- las- set, der Metz- ger He- ro- des drauf pas- set

Um Mitternacht
By permission Boosey & Hawkes, Inc., copyright owners

Um Mit - - ter- nacht hab' ich ge- wacht und auf- ge- blickt zum Him- mel

MAILLART, Louis (1817-1871)

Les Dragons de Villars (opéra-comqiue)
Act I No. 3

Ne par- le pas. Ro- se, je t'en sup- li- e, car me tra- hir

Act I No. 5

Grâce à ce vi- lain er- mi- te, a sa clo- che mau- di- te,

Act III No. 13 bis
Soldatenart (this aria by Franz Abt)

Wenn mann beim Wein sitzt, wenn man beim Wein sitzt, was ist da das Bes- t

MALOTTE, Albert Hay (1895-)

The Lord's Prayer
Copyright 1935, G. Schirmer, Inc.

Our Father,— Which art in heaven,— Hal- low- ed be— thy Name.—

Song of the Open Road
Copyright by A B C Music Corp., N. Y.

What in the world could be so sweet, As the thun- der- ing clat- ter

MANA-ZUCCA (1890-)

I love life, Op. 83
Copyright by John Chuch Co.
Used by permission

I love life— and I— want to live— and drink of life's full- nes

Rachem, Op. 60, No. 1
Copyright by John Chuch Co.
Used by permission.

A. O- vi- nu mal- ke- nu O- vi- nu O- vi- nu A- do- nai- nu

B. Wie lang wet men ins- stick- en, Wie lang wet men ins er- drick- en

MANNING, Katherine Lockhart

In the Luxembourg Gardens
Copyright 1925, G. Schirmer, Inc.

When sha- dows fall I wan- der thro' the gar- dens,

MANZOLO, Domenico (17th Cent.)

Quando tu mi guardi e ridi

Quando tu mi guar- di e ri- di, o mio be- ne, o mio co- re,

Se vedeste le piaghe

Se ve-de-ste le pia-ghe ch'io por-to nel cor,

MARCELLO, Benedetto (1686-1739)

Quella fiamma che m'accende
Recitative

Il mio bel fo-co o lon-ta-no o vi-ci-no ch'es-ser pos-si-o

Aria

Quel-la fiam-ma che m'ac - - - cen - -de

MARENZIO, Luca (1550-1599)

Già torna

Già tor-na a ral-le-grar l'a-ria e la-ter-ra

Rex Gloriae (O King of Glory)

O King of Glo-ry Lord of all pow-er, Lord of all pow'r,

Perche di pioggia

Per-che di piog - - - - gia'l ciel non si de-stil - - - - - le,

Strider faceva

Stri-der fa-ce-va le zam-po-gne a l'au - - - - - - - - - ra,

MARSCHNER, Heinrich (1795-1861)

jenem Tag, from Hans Heiling
(opera) Act I

An je-nem Tag da du mir Treu - - - - e ver-spro-chen

O lass die Treu-e nie-mals wan-ken, o lass die Treu-e

MARSHALL, Charles (1887-1927)

I Hear You Calling Me
By permission Boosey & Hawkes, Inc.,
copyright owners

I hear you call-ing me. You call'd me when the moon had veil'd her light,

MARTIN, Easthope (1887-1925)

Come to the Fair
By permission Boosey & Hawkes, Inc.,
copyright owners

The sun is a shin-ing to wel-come the day Heigh-ho! come to the fair!

MARTINI, Giovanni (1741-1816)

Plaisir d'Amour

Plai-sir d'a-mour ne du-re qu'un mo-ment; cha-grin d'a-mour

MARX, Joseph (1882-)

Ein junger Dichter denkt an die Geliebte
By permission Associated Music Publishers, Inc.

Der Mond steigt auf- wärts, ein ver- lieb- ter Träu- mer,

Hat dich die Liebe berührt
By permission Associated Music Publishers, Inc.

Hat Dich die Lie - - be be-rührt, still un-ter lär-men-dem Vol-ke

Marienlied
By permission Associated Music Publishers, Inc.

Ich se-he dich in tau-send Bil-dern Ma-ri- a lieb-lich aus-gedrückt

Nocturne
By permission Associated Music Publishers, Inc.

Süss duf-ten-de Lin-den-blü-te in quel- len-der Ju- ni-nacht,

Regenlied
By permission Associated Music Publishers, Inc.

Wo ich fer-ne des Mi- ka- ne ho-hen Gip- fel ra- gen seh,

Selige Nacht
By permission Associated Music Publishers, Inc.

Im Arm der Lie- be schie-fen wir se - - lig ein

Una gestern hat er mir Rosen gebracht
By permission Associated Music Publishers, Inc.

Und ge-stern hat er mir Ro-sen ge-bracht, Sie ha-ben ge- duf-tet

Valse de Chopin
By permission Associated Music Publishers, Inc.

Wie ein blas-ser Trop-fen Blut's färbt die Lip-pen ei-ner Kran-ken

Venetianisches Wiegenlied
By permission Associated Music Publishers, Inc.

Ni- na ni-na- na, will ich Dir sin- gen Um Mit-ter-nacht

Waldseligkeit
By permission Associated Music Publishers, Inc.

Der Wald be-ginnt zu rau- schen, den Bäu- men naht die Nacht

MASCAGNI, Pietro (1863-1945)

L'Amico Fritz (opera)
Act I
Copyright by Sonzogno, Milan

A Son po-chi fio- ri, po- ve-re vi- o- le, Son l'a-li-to d'A- pri- le,

B Noi sia - - mo fi-glie ti- mi-de e pu- di-che di pri-ma- ve-ra

La- ce-re, mi- se-ri, tan-ti bam- bi-ni lan-guia-no qua

Per voi, ghiot-to-ni i-nu- ti- li, la vi- ta è nel go- der

Act II Duetto delle ciliege

A Suzel, buon dì. D'un ga-io ro- si-gnuo- lo la vo- ce mi sve-gli

B Han del-la por-po- ra vi-vo il co- re, Son dol-ci e te- ne-re,

C Tut- to ta-ce, ep-pur tut-to al cor mi par- la; que-sta pa-ce,

Cavalleria Rusticana (opera)
Duet: Santuzza-Alfio

Tu - - rid - du, mi tol - - se, mi tol-se l'o - no - - - - - - - - - - - re,

Intermezzi

A - ve Ma - ri - - - - - a — Gra tia ple - na

Chorus

A ca-sa, a ca-sa, a- mi - ci, o - ve ci a-spet-ta-no

Brindisi A

Vi-va il vi no spu- meg- gian-te, nel bic-chie-re scin-til- lan- te

B

Vi-va il vi - - no ch'è sin - ce-ro che ci al- lieta o-gni

Addio al mamma
(Turiddu's Farewell)

Voi — do-vre-te fa - re da ma - - - - dre a San- ta,

Il Piccolo Marat (opera) Act II Duet
Copyright by Sonzogno, Milan

Va nel- la tua stan-zet-ta, Pre - - ga ed a-spet- ta—

E sempre il vecchio andazzo, from
Guglielmo Ratcliff, (opera)
Act I
Copyright by Sonzogno, Milan

E sem-pre il vec-chio an -daz-zo. Vi si cor-re a ca- val-lo

Iris (opera)
Act I inno al sole
Copyright by G. Ricordi & Co., Inc.

Son I - o! Son Io la Vi - ta! Son la Bel-tà in-fi - ni ta

A-pri la tua fi - ne-stra! For son i-o - - - - che ven-go al tuo chia-mar,

In pu- re stil- le, ga- ie scin- til- le scen- de la vi - ta!

Act II

Io pin-go, pin-go, ma'il mio pen-nel-lo in-vano stendo in-tin-go

Un dì (e - ro pic- ci- na) al tem-pio vi di un bon-zo

Or dam-mi'il brac- cio tu - o, brac-cio di ne- ve e a- vo- rio

Isabeau (opera)
Act I
Copyright by Sonzogno, Milan

Tu ch'odi lo mio gri-do scru-ta le vi- e del cie- lo —

Non co- lom-bel- le! Il do-no mi- o chiama- re vo-glio dal cie- lo

Act II A

Or so-lo in-tor- no i- na- ni- ma- te co- se

B

E pas- se- rà la vi- va cre- a-tu- ra entro il si- lenzio

Act III

Fu vi- le l'E- dit- to che vi li fè gli uo-mi- ni

Isabeau (opera) Act III
I tuo- i oc-chi! Gli a-per-ti oc-chi sol-tan-to col- pe — vo- li! —

Lodoletta (opera) Act III
Copyright by Sonzogno, Milan
Ah! ri-tro- var-la nel-la sua ca- pan-na tut- ta pian- gen- te

Flam- men, per- do- na- mi — non pian-ger più! — Son i- o!

Il Canto del Lavoro
Quan- do la la Pa- tria si chia-ma- va Ro- ma, I- ta- li- a- no,

Serenata
Co- me col ca- po sot- to la- la bian- ca —

MASSÉ, Victor (1822-1884)

Les Noces de Jeannette (opera) No. 1 Air de Jean
Qu'un au- tre se ma- ri- e, moi, je re-prends ma foi,

No. 2 Romance
Par- mi tant d'a-mou- reux — em- pressés à me plai- re,

No. 3
Ah! jar-ni-gué! Ca' n'est pas gai, le bon-homme est par- fois bru-tal.

No. 5
Cours, mon ai- guille, dans la lai- ne, ne te casse pas dans ma main!

Les voi- là, ces meubles joy-eux, les voi-là, ces meubles joy-eux

No. 6 Air du Rossignol
Au bord du che- min qui passe à ma por - - - - - - - - te

Voix lé- gè- re chan-son pas-sa- ge- re, ba-bil gra- ci- eux

Song of the Tiger, from Paul et Virginie (opera) Act I
Mid the thick li-a - - - - - - - - - - - - - - na —

MASSENET, Jules (1842-1912)

Le Cid (opera) Act I
O no-ble la - - me é-tin-ce- lan-te Pu-re comme un re-gard

Act II
Plus de tour- ments — et plus de pei- ne au jour — at-ten- du

Act III
Pleu- rez! pleu- rez mes yeux — tom- bez tris- te ro- sé- e

O sou- ve-rain, — ô ju- ge, ô pe- re, Tou-jours voi-lé —

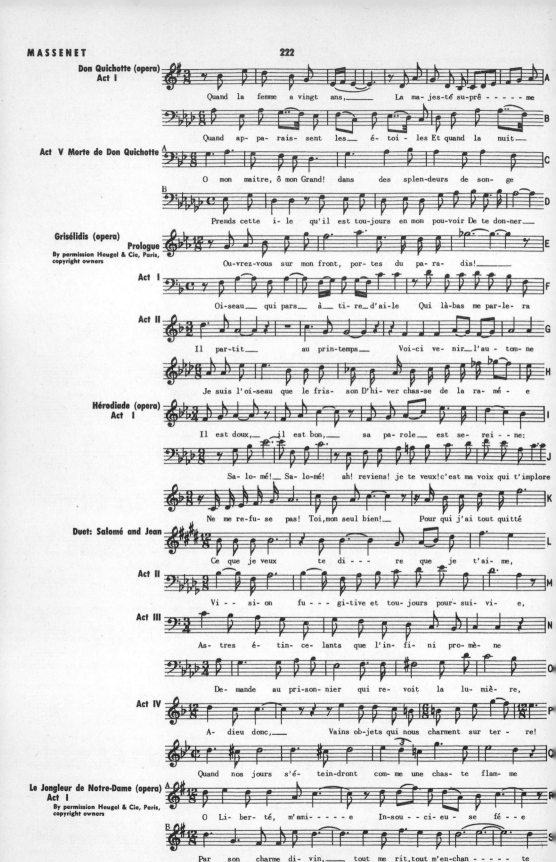

Don Quichotte (opera)
Act I

Quand la femme a vingt ans, La ma-jes-té su-prê - - - - - me

Quand ap-pa-rais-sent les é-toi-les Et quand la nuit

Act V Morte de Don Quichotte

O mon maitre, ô mon Grand! dans des splen-deurs de son-ge

Prends cette i-le qu'il est tou-jours en mon pou-voir De te don-ner

Grisélidis (opera)
Prologue

By permission Heugel & Cie, Paris,
copyright owners

Ou-vrez-vous sur mon front, por-tes du pa-ra-dis!

Act I

Oi-seau qui pars à ti-re-d'ai-le Qui là-bas me par-le-ra

Act II

Il par-tit au prin-temps Voi-ci ve-nir l'au-tom-ne

Je suis l'oi-seau que le fris-son D'hi-ver chas-se de la ra-mé-e

Hérodiade (opera)
Act I

Il est doux, il est bon, sa pa-role est se-rei - - ne:

Sa - lo-mé! Sa - lo-mé! ah! reviens! je te veux! c'est ma voix qui t'implore

Ne me re-fu-se pas! Toi, mon seul bien! Pour qui j'ai tout quitté

Duet: Salomé and Jean

Ce que je veux te di - - - re que je t'ai-me,

Act II

Vi - - si-on fu - - - gi-tive et tou-jours pour-sui-vi-e,

Act III

As-tres é-tin-ce-lants que l'in-fi-ni pro-mè-ne

De-mande au pri-son-nier qui re-voit la lu-miè-re,

Act IV

A-dieu donc, Vains ob-jets qui nous charment sur ter-re!

Quand nos jours s'é-tein-dront com-me une chas-te flam-me

Le Jongleur de Notre-Dame (opera)
Act I

By permission Heugel & Cie, Paris,
copyright owners

O Li-ber-té, m'ami - - - - e In-sou-ci-eu-se fé-e

Par son charme di-vin, tout me rit, tout m'en-chan - - - - te

Le Jongleur de Notre-Dame (opera)
Act I

Pour la Vièr - - - ge   D'a-bord voi-ci les_fleurs qu'elle ai - - me,

Act II Légende de la sauge

(orchestral theme)

Fleu - ris-sait u-ne Ro - se au__ bord__ du che-min,

Manon (opera)
Act I

Je suis_en-core   tout é-tour-di-e,   Je suis_en-core tout en-gour-di-e!

Re-gar-dez-moi bien dans les yeux!_   Je vais tout près, à la ca-ser-ne,

Ne bron-chez pas,__   Soy-ez gen-tille,__ Et n'ou-bli- ez pas

Voy- ons, Ma-non, plus de chi-mè-res, Où va ton es-prit en re-vant?_

Duet

Nous vi- vrons__ à Pa- ris, Tous les deux, Tous les deux,

accompanying figures of duet and also Letter Duet in Act II

Act II Letter Duet

J'é-cris à mon pè- re: et je trem-ble que cet- te lettre

On l'ap-pel- le Ma-non, elle eut hi- er seize ans

A- dieu, no-tre pe- ti-te ta- ble, Qui nous ré- u- nit si sou-vent!

Des Grieux's Dream

En fer-mant les yeux, je vois Là- bas__ u-ne_hum- ble re- trai- te,

Act III Scene 1

La char-man- te pro- me- na - - - - - - - - - - - - - - de

O Ro- sa-lin- de,   Il me fau-drait gra-vir le Pin-de,

Je mar- che sur tous__ les che-mins__   Aus-si bien

Gavotte

O- bé- is-sons quand leur voix ap-pel- le   Aux tendres a-mours, tou-jours,__

Pro - - - fi- tons bien de la jeu-nes- se,

Fabliau

Oui, dans_ les_ bois et dans la plai-ne Rien que_pour_ ri-re_et sans raison

Manon (opera)
Act III Scene 1

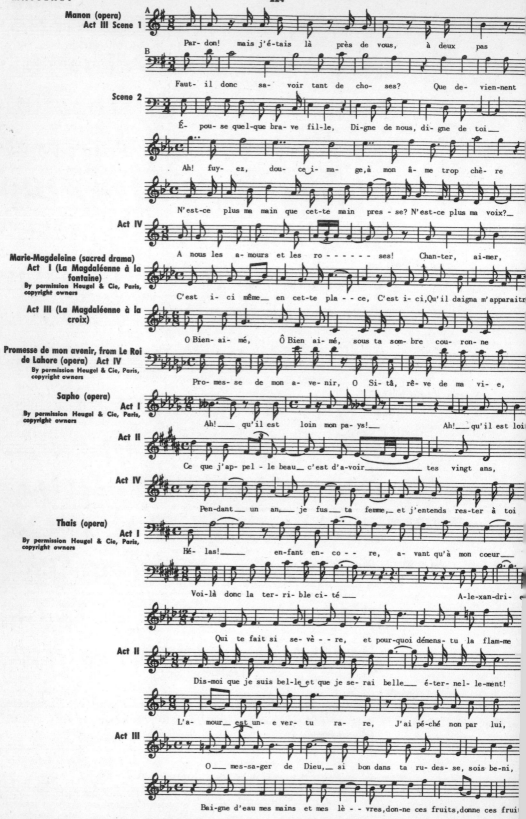

Pardon! mais j'é-tais là près de vous, à deux pas

Faut-il donc sa-voir tant de cho-ses? Que de-vien-nent

Scene 2

É-pou-se quel-que bra-ve fil-le, Di-gne de nous, di-gne de toi

Ah! fuy-ez, dou-ce i-ma-ge, à mon â-me trop chè-re

N'est-ce plus ma main que cet-te main pres-se? N'est-ce plus ma voix?

Act IV

A nous les a-mours et les ro------ses! Chan-ter, ai-mer,

Marie-Magdeleine (sacred drama)
Act I (La Magdaléenne à la fontaine)
By permission Heugel & Cie, Paris, copyright owners

C'est i-ci même en cet-te pla-ce, C'est i-ci, Qu'il daigna m'apparaîtr

Act III (La Magdaléenne à la croix)

O Bien-ai-mé, Ô Bien ai-mé, sous ta som-bre cou-ron-ne

Promesse de mon avenir, from Le Roi de Lahore (opera) Act IV
By permission Heugel & Cie, Paris, copyright owners

Pro-mes-se de mon a-ve-nir, O Si-tâ, rê-ve de ma vi-e,

Sapho (opera)
Act I
By permission Heugel & Cie, Paris, copyright owners

Ah! qu'il est loin mon pa-ys! Ah! qu'il est loi

Act II

Ce que j'ap-pel-le beau c'est d'a-voir tes vingt ans,

Act IV

Pen-dant un an je fus ta femme, et j'entends res-ter à toi

Thais (opera)
Act I
By permission Heugel & Cie, Paris, copyright owners

Hé-las! en-fant en-co-re, a-vant qu'à mon coeur

Voi-là donc la ter-ri-ble ci-té A-le-xan-dri-e

Act II

Qui te fait si se-vè--re, et pour-quoi démens-tu la flam-me

Dis-moi que je suis bel-le et que je se-rai belle é-ter-nel-le-ment!

Act III

L'a-mour est un e-ver-tu ra-re, J'ai pé-ché non par lui,

O mes-sa-ger de Dieu, si bon dans ta ru-des-se, sois be-ni,

Bai-gne d'eau mes mains et mes lè--vres, don-ne ces fruits, donne ces frui

Sérénade du Passant

Mi- gnon - - - ne, voi- ci l'A- vril! Le so- leil re- vient — d'e- xil;

Si tu veux, Mignonne

Si tu veux, Mignonne, au prin- temps Nous ver- rons fleu- rir

MAUDUIT, Jacques (1557-1627)

A la fontaine

A la fon- tai- ne je vou- drais a- vec ma bel-le al-ler jou- er,

En son temple sacré, Psalm 150

En son tem- ple sa- cré — lou- ez le grand Dieu

Si d'une petite oeillade

Si d'u- ne pe- ti- te oeil-la- de tou- te d'a-mour et de- sir

MC GILL, Josephine (1877-1919)

Duna

By permission Boosey & Hawkes, Inc.,
copyright owners

When I was a lit- tle lad with fol- ly on my lips —

MEHUL, Etienne Henri (1763-1817)

Chant du Depart

A

La vic- toire en chan- tant nous ou- vre la bar- riè- re

B

La Ré-pub- li- que vous ap- pel- le, sa- chez vaincre ou sachez pé- rir,

Champs paternels, from Joseph (opera) Act I

Champs pa- ter- nels, Hé- bron, dou- ce val-lé- e, loin de vous

Romance du barde, from Ariodant (opera) Act II

Fem- me sen- sible, en-tends tu le ra- ma- ge de ces oi- seaux

MENDELSSOHN, Felix (1809-1847)

Elijah, Op. 70 (oratorio)

No. 4

If with all your hearts ye tru- ly seek me, ye shall e- ver sure-ly find me,

No. 9

Blessed are the men who fear him, they e- ver walk in the ways of peace

No. 14

Lord God of A- bra-ham, I-saac and Is- ra- el, this day let it be known

No. 17

Is not His word — like a fire? — and like a ham-mer

No. 18

Woe, woe un-to them who for-sake Him! De- struction shall fall up- on them

St. Paul, Op. 36 (oratorio)

No. 26 — How love- ly are the mes- sen- gers that preach us the gos- pel of peace

No. 27 — I will_ sing of Thy great mer- cies, O Lord, of Thy mer- cies, O Lord,

No. 35 — O be gra- cious, ye im- mor- tals, O be gra- cious, ye im- mor- tals!

No. 40 — Be_ thou faith- ful un- to death, and I will give to thee a_ crown of life

Minnelied im Mai, Op. 8, No. 1 — Hol- der klingt der Vo- gel- sang, wenn die En- gel- rei- ne,

Erndtelied No. 4 — Es ist ein Schnit- ter, der heisst Tod, hat Ge- walt vom_ höch- sten Gott

Frühlingslied No. 6
(In Schwäbischer Mundart) — Jetzt kommt der Früh- ling, der Him- mel isch blau,_

Maienlied No. 7 — Man soll hö- ren sü- sses Sin- gen in_ den Au- en ü- ber- all

Im Grünen No. 11 — Will- kommen im Grünen! Der Him- mel ist blau, der Him- mel ist blau_

Frühlingslied, Op. 19, No. 1 — In dem Wal- de sü- sse Tö- ne sin- gen klei- ne Vö- ge- lein

Das erste Veilchen No. 2 — Als ich das er- ste Veil- chen er- blickt, wie war ich von Far- ben und Duft

Neue Liebe No. 4 — In dem Mon- den- schein im Wal- de sah ich jüngst die El- fen rei- - ten,

Gruss No. 5 — Lei- se zieht durch mein Ge- müth lieb- li- ches Ge- läu- te

Reiselied No. 6 — Brin- - get des treu'_ sten Her- - zens_ Grü- sse

Auf Flügeln des Gesanges (On Wings of Song) Op. 34, No. 2 — Auf Flü- geln des_ Ge- san- ges, Herz- lieb- chen, trag' ich dich fort,

Frühlingslied No. 3 — Es bre- chen im schal- len- den Rei- gen die Früh- lings- stim- men los,

Zuleika No. 4 — Ach um dei- ne feuch- ten Schwin- gen, West, wie sehr ich dich

Sonntagslied No. 5 — Ring- sum er- schallt im Wald und Flur viel fer- nes Glo- cken- klin- gen

Reiselied No. 6 — Der Herbst- wind rüt- telt die Bäu- me, die Nacht ist feucht und kalt;_

Minnelied, Op. 47,   No. 1

Wie der Quell so lieblich klin-get, und die Zar-ten Blu-men küsst,

Morgengruss   No. 2

Ü- ber die Ber- ge steigt schon die Son- ne, die Läm - mer-heer-de läu - tet

rühlingslied   No. 3

Durch den Wald,— den dun-keln, geht hol- de Früh - -ling-mor-gen-stun-de,

Volkslied   No. 4

Es ist be-stimmt in Got- tes Rath, dass man von Lieb-sten

Der Blumenstrauss No. 5

Sie wan-delt im Blu-men-gar-ten und mus-tert den bun - -ten Flor,—

Bei der Wiege   No. 6

Schlumm - - - re!   Schlumm- re und träu-me von kom-men-der Zeit

Der Jager Abschied, Op. 50, No. 2

Wer hat dich, du schö-ner Wald, auf-ge-baut so hoch da dro-ben?

esang (Hymn of Praise) Op. 52, No. 2

Al- les, Al- les, Al- les was O- dem hat Al- les, Al- les

No. 3

Er zäh- let uns'-re Thrä- nen in der Zeit der Noth,

No. 5

Ich har- re- te des Herrn, und er neig- te sich zu mir,

No. 6

Die Strich- e des Tod- es hat- ten uns emp- fan-gen,

Altdeutsches Lied, Op. 57, No. 1

Es ist in den Wald ge-sun-gen, wenn— ich dir mein Lei - den sa- ge

Hirtenlied   No. 2

O Win- ter, schlimmer— Win- ter, wie ist die Welt so klein!

Suleika   No. 3

Was be-deu- tet die Be- we-gung? bringt der Ost mir fro- he Kun- de?

gend, O schöne Rosenzeit, No. 4

Von al- len schö-nen Kin-dern auf der Welt— mir ei-nes doch am meisten

tianisches Gondellied   No. 5

Wenn durch— die Piaz- zet - - - ta die A- bend - luft weht,—

hied vom Wald, Op. 59, No. 3

O, Thä- ler weit o Hö- hen, O schö-ner grü- ner Wald,

achtigall   No. 4

Die Nach- ti-gall,sie war ent- fernt, der Früh-ling lockt sie wie-der

wollt' meine Lieb' ergösse sich, Op. 63, No. 1

Ich wollt'— mei-ne Lieb'— er- gös- se sich all'— in ein ein-zig Wort,

Abschiedslied der Zugvögel, Op. 63, No. 2
Wie war so schön doch Wald und Feld! Wie ist so trau-rig jetzt die Welt!

Gruss No. 3
Wo-hin ich geh', und schau-e, in Feld und Wald und Thal

Herbstlied No. 4
Ach, wie so bald ver-hal- -let der Rei-gen

O säh' ich auf der Haide dort (O wert thou in the could blast) No. 5
O säh' ich auf der Hai-de dort im Stur-me dich, im Stur-me dich!

Festgesang, Op. 68, No. 2 (male chorus) (Hark the Herald Angels sing)
Va-ter-land, in dei-nen Gau - -en brach der gold'-ne Tag einst an

Tröstung Op. 71, No. 1
Wer-de hei-ter mein Ge-mü-the und ver-giss der Angst und Pein!

An die Entfernte No. 3
Die-se Ro-se pflück' ich hier in der wei-ten Fer- -ne,

Schilflied No. 4
Auf dem Teich, dem re-gungs- lo-sen, weilt des Mon-des hol-der Glanz,

Nachtlied No. 6
Ver-gan-gen ist der lich-te Tag, von fer-ne kommt der Glo-cken Schlag;

Lauda Sion, Op. 73, No. 6
Ca- -ro ci-bus, san-guis po-tus, ma-net ta-men Christus to-tus

Der frohe Wandersmann, Op. 75, No. 1
Wenn Gott will rech-te Gunst er-wei-sen, den schickt er in die Wei-te Welt

Sonntagsmorgen, Op. 77, No. 1
Das ist der Tag des Herrn, das ist der Tag des Herrn. Ich bin al-lein

Lied aus Ruy Blas No. 3
Wo-zu der Vög-lein Chö-re be-lau-schen fern und nah?

Jagdlied Op. 84, No. 3
Mit Lust thät ich aus-rei- -ten durch ei-nen grü-nen Wald

Die Liebende schreibt, Op. 86, No. 3
Ein Blick von dei-nen Au-gen in die mei-nen

Der Mond No. 5
Mein Herz ist wie die dunk-le Nacht, wenn al-le Wi-pfel rau-schen;

Neujahrslied, Op. 88, No. 1
Mit der Freu-de zieht der Schmerz trau-lich durch die Zei-ten,

Heimkehr aus der Fremde, Op. 89, No. 4 (Son and Stranger)
Ich bin ein viel-ge-reis-ter Mann, der al-ler Län-der Tän-ze kann

Concert Aria, Op. 94 (Infelice! Gia' del mio sguardo)
Ah, ri-tor-na e-tà fe-li-ce quando ac-can-to del mio be- -ne

Die Lorely, Op. 98, No. 2 Ave Maria
Horch der A- bend- glo- cke Ton! A- ve Ma- ri- a!

Lieblingsplätzchen, Op. 99, No. 3
Wisst ihr wo ich ger- ne weil' in der A- bend- küh- le?

Wenn sich zwei Herzen scheiden, No. 5
Wenn sich zwei Her- zen schei- den, die sich der- einst ge- liebt,

Beati Mortui, Op. 115, No. 1 (male chorus)
Be- a- ti mor- tu- i in Do- mi- no mo- ri- en- tes,

Der Blumenkranz (By Celia's Arbour)
An Ce- lia's Baum in stil- - - ler Nacht

Drei Volkslieder (Three Folksongs)
No. 1 Wie kann ich froh
Wie kann ich froh und lus- tig sein? Wie kann ich geh'n mit Band und Strauss

No. 2 Abendlied
Wenn ich auf dem La- ger lie- ge, in Nacht ge- hüllt,

No. 3 Wasserfahrt
Ich stand ge- leh- net an den Mast, und zähl- te je- de Wel- le,

Hear My Prayer (Hymn)
Hear my prayer O God, in- cline thine ear! Thy- self from my pe- ti- tion

O for the wings, for the wings of a dove! Far a- way

Two Songs after Eichendorff
1. Pagenlied
Wenn die Son- ne lieb- lich schie- ne wie in Wälsch- land, lau und blau

2. Das Waldschloss
Wo noch kein Wand- rer ge- gan- gen, hoch ü- ber Jä- ger und Ross

Warnung vor dem Rhein
An den Rhein, an den Rhein, zieh nicht an den Rhein,

MENOTTI, Gian-Carlo (1911-   )

The Consul
The Empty-handed Traveler
Copyright 1950, G. Schirmer, Inc.
I'm not cry- ing for him not for us; but for John

Lullaby
I shall find for you shells and stars. I shall swim for you

Magda's Aria
To this we've come: that men with- hold the world from men

If to men, not to God, we now must pray, tell me,

What is your name? Mag- da Sor- el Age? Thir- ty three.

The Medium (opera)
Act I
Copyright 1947, G. Schirmer, Inc.

Where, oh, where___ is my new gol-den spin-dle and thread?

Mo-ther, mo-ther, are you there? Mo-ther, mo-ther, are you there?

Black Swan Song A

The sun has fallen and it lies in blood, The moon is weav-ing

B

O black swan, where, oh, where___ is my lov-er gone

Act II A

Up in the sky some one is play-ing a trom-bone and a gui-tar

B

Mon-i-ca, Mon-i-ca, dance the waltz, Mon-i-ca, Mon-i-ca, dance the waltz.

A-fraid, am I a-fraid? Madame Flo-ra a-fraid!

The Telephone A
Copyright 1947, G. Schirmer, Inc.

Hel-lo! Hel-lo? Oh Margaret, it's you, I am so glad you called,

B

And how are you? And how is John? And how is Jean? You must tell the

It all be-gan on a Sun-day, when John and I went skat-ing

Duet

Hel-lo? Hel-lo? Where are you, my dar-ling? I'm ter-ri-bly near y

MESSAGER, André (1835-1929)

Fortunio (opera)
.Act II La Maison Grise
Copyright by Choudens fils, Paris

J'ai- mais la vieil-le mai-son gri-se Où j'ai gran- di

Act III Chanson de Fortunio

Si vous croy-ez que je vais di- re Qui j'ose ai- mer

Le jour sous le soleil béni, from
Madame Chrysanthème (opera)
Act III
Copyright by Choudens fils, Paris

Le jour, sous le so-leil bé-ni,___ La nuit, sous L'é-toi-le qui rê - - - - v

Véronique (opéra-comique)
Act 1, No. 7
Copyright by Choudens fils, Paris
A

Pe-ti-te dinde: Ah! quel ou- tra-ge! Vrai-ment je suf-fo- que

B

Ah Monsieur Flo-res-tan! A nous deux main-te- nant!

Act III, No. 20

Ma foi! pour ve- nir de pro-vin-ce Le tour n'est pas trop mal,

METCALF, John W.

Absent

Copyrigrt by Artrur P. Schmidt Co., Boston.
d by permission

Some-times be-tween long shad-ows on the grass

MEYERBEER, Giacomo (1791-1864)

L'Africaine (opera)
Act I
A-dieu, mon doux ri - va - ge, a-dieu mon seule a-mour!

Pour cel-le qui m'est chè-re qui m'est chè - - re,

Act II
Sur mes ge-noux fils du so-leil, Vainqueur au champ d'a-lar - - mes

Fil-le des Rois, à toi l'hom-ma-ge à toi l'hom-ma-ge

Je vois dans la gran-de î-le, en nos jours for-tu-nés,

Act III
A-da-mas-tor, roi des va-gues pro-fon-des

Aux voi-les, aux cor-da-ges De van-cez les o-ra-ges

Act IV
Ô pa-ra-dis sor-ti de l'on - - de

Con-dui-sez- moi vers ce na-vi-re Dont le voi-le bril-le à vos yeux

L'a-voir tant a-do-ré-e Et dans ce jour fa - - tal

Dinorah (Le Pardon de Ploërmel) (opera)
Act II
De-puis lors, quand la nuit ga-gne Le vil-lage et la mon-ta-gne,

Om-bre lé-gè-re Qui suis mes pas Ne t'en va pas! non, non, non!

Act III
Le jour est le-vé, La pluie a la-vé Les cieux et la plai - - ne,

Ah! mon re-monde te ven-ge De mon fol a-ban-don

oile du Nord (opera) Act I (Finale)
Veil-le sur eux tou-jours, Mè - - - re, mè - - re,

O jours heu-reux de joie et de mi-sè - - re

La, la, la, air ché-ri la, la, la la c'est lui,

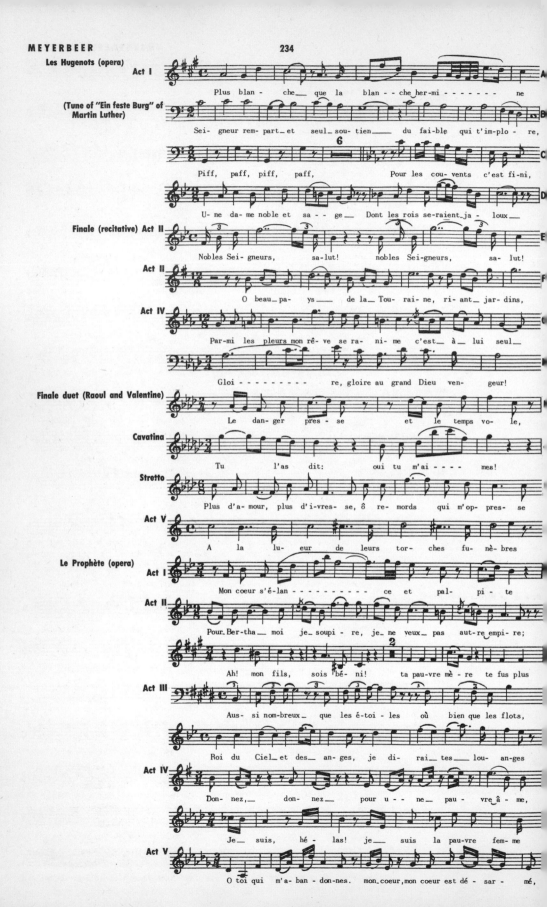

Les Hugenots (opera)
Act I
Plus blan- che_ que la blan--che her-mi------ne

(Tune of "Ein feste Burg" of Martin Luther)
Sei- gneur rem-part_ et seul sou-tien_ du fai-ble qui t'im-plo-re,

Piff, paff, piff, paff, Pour les cou-vents c'est fi-ni,

U- ne da-me noble et sa-ge_ Dont les rois se-raient ja-loux

Finale (recitative) Act II
Nobles Sei- gneurs, sa-lut! nobles Sei-gneurs, sa-lut!

Act II
O beau_ pa- ys_ de la_ Tou- rai-ne, ri-ant jar-dins,

Act IV
Par-mi les pleurs mon rê-ve se ra- ni-me c'est_ à_ lui seul

Gloi-------- re, gloire au grand Dieu ven- geur!

Finale duet (Raoul and Valentine)
Le dan-ger pres- se et le temps vo- le,

Cavatina
Tu l'as dit: oui tu m'ai---- mes!

Stretto
Plus d'a-mour, plus d'i-vres-se, ô re-mords qui m'op-pres-se

Act V
A la lu-eur de leurs tor- ches fu- nè-bres

Le Prophète (opera)
Act I
Mon coeur s'é-lan---------- ce et pal- pi-te

Act II
Pour Ber-tha_ moi je soupi- re, je ne veux_ pas aut-re empi-re;

Ah! mon fils, sois bé-ni! ta pau-vre mè-re te fus plus

Act III
Aus- si nom-breux_ que les é-toi-les où bien que les flots,

Roi du Ciel et des an-ges, je di-rai tes_ lou- an-ges

Act IV
Don-nez, don-nez_ pour u- ne pau- vre â-me,

Je_ suis, hé- las! je suis la pau-vre fem-me

Act V
O toi qui m'a-ban-don-nes, mon coeur, mon coeur est dé- sar- mé,

Robert le Diable (opera)
Act I Ballade
Ja- dis régnait en Nor-man-di-e un prin-ce no-ble et va-leu-reux,

Romance
Va!. Va!. va! dit el- le, va, mon en- fant

qu'il eut la der-niè-re pen-sé-e, la der-niè-re pen-sé-e

Act III
Quand __ je quit-tai la Nor-man-di-e un __ vieil er-mi-te de cent ans,

Évocation
Non- nes qui re-po- sez sous cet-te froi- de pier- re!

Act IV Cavatine
Ro- bert! Ro- bert! toi que j'ai- - me et qui re- çus,

Gra- ce, gra- ce,__ pour toi mê- me, pour toi mê- - me,

MEYER-HELMUND, Erik (1861-1932)

Dein gedenk' ich, Margaretha
Son- ne taucht in Mee- res-flu- then, Him-mel blitzt in letz-ten Glu-then

Das Zauberlied
Wenn dein ich denk', dann sinn ich oft

MIGNONE, Francisco (1897-)

Cantiga de ninar
Copyright by E. B. Marks Music Corp., N. Y.
Can- to bai- xi- - -nho U- ma ve-lha can- ção de ni- nar

MILAN, Luis (c. 1500-c. 1561)

Durandarte
Du- ran- dar- te du-ran- dar- te Buen ca-ba- lle- ro

Perdida tengo la color
Per- di- da ten- go la co- lor Di- ze mi- nya

MILHAUD, Darius (1892-)

L'Aurore
Copyright by Salabert, Paris, N. Y.
Quel- le dou- ce clar- té vient é- clai- rer l'O- ri- ent!

Chants Populaires Hébraiques:
IV Berceuse
By permission Heugel & Cie, Paris
copyright owners
Dors, dors, dors, __ ton pa- pa i- ra au vil- la- ge

VI Chant Hassidique
Que te di- rai- je et que te ra-con-te- rai- - - - je

Cinq Chansons de Paul Vildrac:
I Les quatre petits lions
Par- tis d'u- ne mé- na- ge- rie un jour, quatr' tout pe-tits li- ons

Cinq Chansons de Paul Vildrac:
II Poupette et Patata — A
Au beau mi-lieu de l'i-le ver-te Il y a un cha-teau de bois

III La pomme et l'escargot — B
Il y a-vait u-ne pom-me A la ci-me d'un pom-mier

IV La Malpropre — C
Un fer-mier du voi-si-na-ge Qui boit plus que de rai-son

V Le Jardinier Impatient — D
Dans son po-ta-ger ma grand mè-re m'a ré-ser-vé un pe-tit coin

Poèmes Juifs
I Chant de Nourrice — E
By permission Associated Music Publishers, Inc.
Dors, ma fleur, mon fils ché-ri pendant que je ba-lan-ce-rai ton ber-ceau;

II Chant de Sion — F
Ce n'est la ro-sée ni la pluie, ce sont mes lar-mes

III Chant du Laboureur — G
Mon es-pé-ran-ce n'est pas en-core per-due

IV Chant de la pitié — H
Dans les champs de Beth-le-em u-ne pier-re se dres-se

V Chant de resignation — I
Prends mon à-me fais en u-ne ly-re bril-lan-te

VI Chant d'amour — J
En mê-me temps que tous les bourgeons la Ro-se de mon coeur

VII Chant de forgeron — K
Près du Jourdain il y a u-ne mai-son de for-ge-ron

VIII Lamentation — L
Au ciel sept ché-ru-bins si-len-ci-eux com-me les rêves

La Tourterelle — M
By permission Durand & Cie, Paris; Elkan-Vogel Co., Inc., Phila., copyright owners
Ma co-lom-be, Ô ma tour-te-rel-le, Est-ce vous dont j'entends

Tros Poèmes de Jean Cocteau
I Fumée — N
Copyright by Ed. de la Sirene, Paris
C'est per-mis de fu-mer ga-re L'e-cu-yer de Me-dra-no

II Fête de Bordeaux — O
La ma-nège a va-peur re-gar-de s'en al-ler

III Fête de Montmartre — P
Ne vous ba-lan-cez pas si fort le Ciel est à tout le mon-de

MILLOECKER, Karl (1842-1899)

The Beggar Student (Der Bettel-student) (operetta)   No. 2 — R
Yet this he-ro all vic-to-rious whom re-vere high and low

— S
Noth-ing I have ev-er heard worse than that up-on my word, worse than that

No. 3 — T
The world to soaring ge-nius ev-er Quick re-cog-ni-tion has re-fused

The Beggar Student (Der Bettel-
student) (operetta)   No. 3

From clouds of pet-ty woe jol-li-ty breaks forth ra-diant-ly

No. 6

I've of-ten felt the pas-sion ten-der at Paris the gri-sette I knew

No. 10

I'll put the case that I were not of stock pa-tri-cian

Gasparone (operetta)
Act I No. 3

O dass ich doch der Räu-ber wä-re, ich streb-te nicht

No. 6

An-zo-let-ta sang:Komm mi-a bel-la!__ Un-ter'm Fen-ster

Act III Waltz

Er soll dein Herr sein!Wie stolz das klingt! Geltung hat's leider nur sehr bedingt

Der Arme Jonathan (operetta)
Act I, No. 5

In me__ you see_poor Jon-a-than, How shall__I bear__my life be-gun?

MOERAN, Ernest John (1894-   )

Diaphenia
By permission Boosey & Hawkes, Inc.,
copyright owners

Di - - - a-phe-nia,__ like the daf-fa-down-dil-ly,

The Sweet o' the Year
By permission of Augener, Ltd., London

When da-fo-dils be-gin to peer,with heigh!_ The do-xy o-ver the dale,

MOLLOY, J. L. (1837-1909)

The Kerry Dance

O the days of the Ker-ry danc-ing O the ring of the pi-per's tune

Love's Old Sweet Song

Once in the dear dead days be-yond re-call, When on the world

Just a song at twi-light, when the lights are low,

MONRO, George (18th Cent.)

My Lovely Celia

My love - - - ly__ Ce - lia, heav'n - - - ly fair,

MONSIGNY, Pierre Alexandre (1729-1817)

Adieu, chère Louise, from Le Déserteur
(opéra-comique)

A-dieu, chè-re Lou-i-se! Chè-re Lou-ise, a-dieu!__

Il regardait mon bouquet, from Le
Roi et le Fermier

Il re-gar-dait mon bou-quet, Sans doute il le dé-si-rait,

La sagesse est un trésor, from Rose
et Colas (opera)

La sa-gesse est un__ tré-sor,un tré-sor c'est la ges- -se

MONTEMEZZI, Italo (1875-   )

Son quarant' anni, from L'Amore dei tre re (opera) Act I
Copyright by G. Ricordi & Co., Inc.

Son quarant' an- ni che di- sce-si in questa bel-la ser-ra

MONTEVERDE, Claudio (1567-1643)

Amor (Lamento della Ninfa)

A- mor Di- ce a- mor il ciel mi- ran-do il pie fer-mò

Ardo

Ar- do Ar- do Ar- do Ar- do e scoprir ahi_ lasso

Ardo si ma non t'amo

Ar- do si ma non t'a- - - - mo_ Da un si le-al a-man- - te

Il Balletto delle Ingrate

Ahi trop- - po Ahi trop-po è du- ro cru- del sen-ten-za

Chiome d'oro

Chio-me d'oro bel the- so-ro tu mi leghi in mille mo- di_

Ch'io t'ami

Ch'io t'a- mi e t'a- mi più de la mia vi- - - - ta

Cor mio mentre vi miro

Cor mio men-tre vi mi- - - - - ro

Ecco mormora l'onde (madrigal, 5-part)

Ec- co mor- mo- ra l'on- de e tre-mo-lar le ron- de

Hor ch'el ciel e la terra (madrigal, 6-voice)

A

Hor ch'el ciel e la ter-ra el ven-to ta- ce E le fe- re e gli angeli

B

Guer-ra è il mio sta- to Guer- ra guer-ra guer-ra guer-ra guer-ra guer-ra

Lagrime d'Amante al Sepolcro dell' Amata:

In- - ce-ne-ri- te spo-glie a- va-ra tom- - ba_

II

O fiu   O fiu

Di-te-lo o fiu-mi, o fiu- mi O fiu- mi O fiu-mi e voi che udeste

III

Da- rà la notte il sol lu- me alla ter- ra Splenderà Cin- - tia il dì

IV

Ma te rac- co-glie o Nin fa ma te rac-co-glie o Nin- fa

V

O chio- me d'or ne- - ve gen-til ne- - ve gen-til_ del se- no

VI

Dun- - - que a- ma- te re- li-quie un mar di pian- to

Orfeo (opera)

Act II (Shepherds)

In que-sto pra-to a-dor-no o-gni sel-vag-gio nu-me

Qui le Na-pee vez-zo-se schie-ra sem-pre fio-ri-ta

(Orfeo)

Vi ri-cor-da o bo-schi om-bro-si Vi ri-cor-da o bo-schi om-bro-si

Lament (Orfeo)

Tu sè mor-ta se' mor-ta mia vi-ta ed io re-spi-ro

(Chorus)

Ahi ca-so a-cer-bo, Ahi fat' em - - - - pio e cru- de- le,

(Chorus)

Chi ne con-so la ahi las-si O pur chi ne con-ce-de

Act III (Orfeo)

Pos-sen - - te spir- to e for-mi-da - - - bil nu - - me

(Orfeo)

Sol tu no-bi-le Dio puoi dar-mi a- i-ta

(Orfeo)

Ahi sven-tu-ra-to a-man-te, sperar dun - que non li-ce ch'o-dan miei prie-ghi

(Chorus)

Nul-la im-pre- sa per huom si ten-ta in va - - - - no

Act IV (Prosperina)

Si-gnor quel in-fe- li-ce che per queste di morte am - - pie cam-pa-gne

(Orfeo)

Qual ho- nor di te sia de-gno mia cetra on-ni- po- ten-te,

(Chorus)

È la vir-tu-te rag-gio di ce- le- ste be-lez-za

Act V (Orfeo)

Que-sti i cam-pi di Tra-cia lo- ve pas somm'il co- re

(Orfeo and Apollo)

Sa- liam, sa- liam

(Chorus)

Van-ne Or-feo fe- li-ce a pie- no, a go- der ce- le-ste ho- no- re,

MORALES, Cristóbal de (c. 1500-1553)

O vos omnes

O vos o - - - - - - - mnes qui tran si- tis

MORLEY, Thomas (1557-c. 1603)

April is in my mistress' face
A-pril is in my Mis-tress' face, April is in my Mis-tress' face,

Dainty fine sweet nymph
Dain-ty fine sweet nymph de - light-ful, while the sun a - loft is mount-ing

Fire, fire
Fire fire, Fire, fire Fire, fire, Fire, fire, my heart

Hard by a crystal fountain
Hard by a Crys-tal fount - - - - - - - - - - - - - - - - ain

I follow, lo, the footing
I fol-low, lo, the foot-ing I fol-low, lo, the foot-ing

It was a Lover and his Lasse
It was a lov-er and his lasse with a hey, with a hoe

My bonny lass she smileth
My bon-ny lass she smil-eth When she my heart be- guil-eth

Now is the gentle season
Now is the gen-tle sea-son fresh-ly flow'r- ing

Now is the month of Maying
Now is the month of May- ing when mer-ry lads are play-ing

Shoot, false love, I care not
Shoot false love I care not, spend thy shafts, and spare not,

Since my tears and lamenting
Since___ my tears and la- ment-ing, false love breed thy con-tenting

Sing we and chant it
Sing we and chant it, While love doth grant it, Fa la la la la la la la

Sweet nymph
Sweet Nymph, come to___ thy lo-ver, to___ thy lov- er,

MOZART, Wolfgang Amadeus (1756-1791)

Bastien and Bastienne (opera) K. 50 No. 1
Mein lieb-ster Freund hat mich ver- lassen, mit ihm ist Schlaf___

No. 2
Ich geh' jetzt auf die Wei-de be - täubt und___ ganz ge-dan-ken___ leer,

No. 4
Be- fra-get mich ein zar-tes___ Kind um sein zu-künftes Glücke

No. 5
Wenn mein Ba- stien einst___ im Scherze mir ein Blüm-chen___ sonst ent-wand

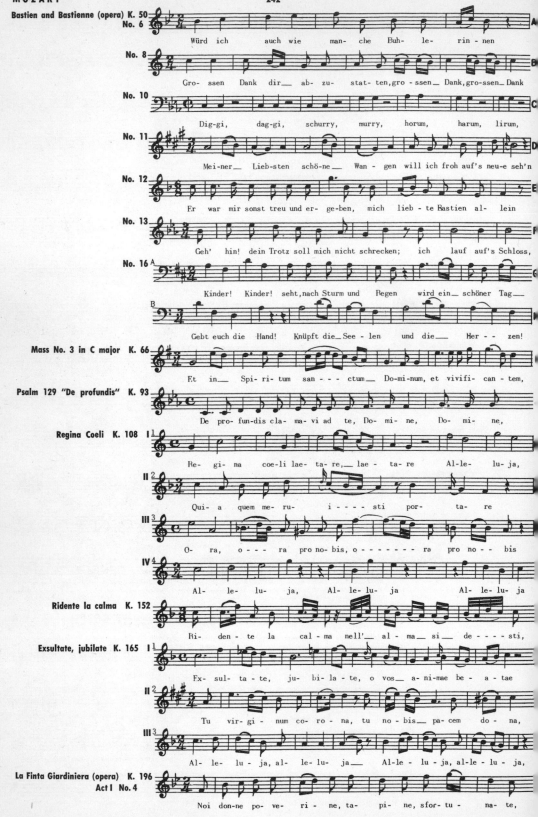

MOZART

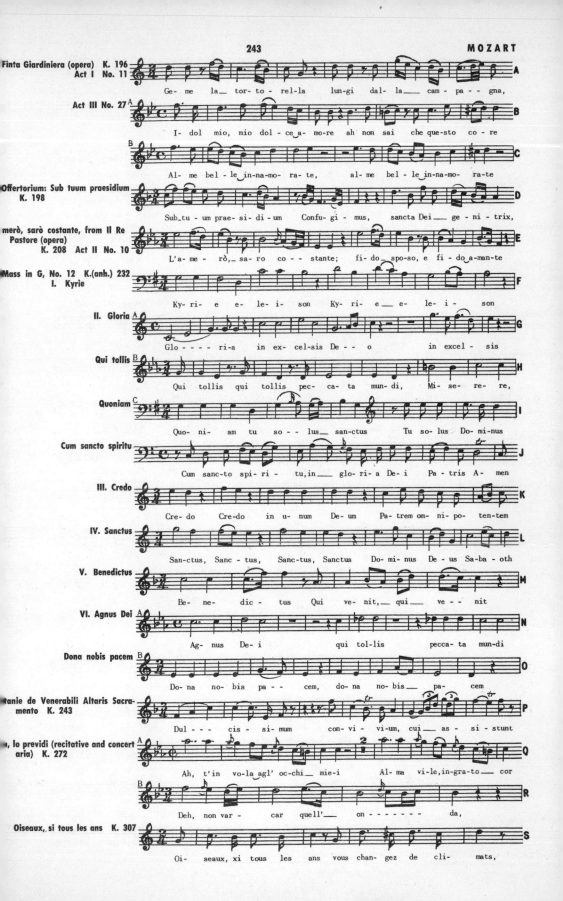

Finta Giardiniera (opera) K. 196
Act I No. 11

Ge- me la tor- to- rel- la lun- gi dal- la__ cam- pa- gna,

Act III No. 27

I- dol mio, mio dol- ce a- mo- re ah non sai che que- sto co- re

Al- me bel- le in- na- mo- ra- te, al- me bel- le in- na- mo- ra- te

Offertorium: Sub tuum praesidium
K. 198

Sub- tu- um prae- si- di- um Con- fu- gi- mus, sancta Dei__ ge- ni- trix,

merò, sarò costante, from Il Re
Pastore (opera)
K. 208 Act II No. 10

L'a- me- rò,__ sa- ro co- stante; fi- do__ spo- so, e fi- do a- man- te

Mass in G, No. 12 K.(anh.) 232
I. Kyrie

Ky- ri- e e- le- i- son Ky- ri- e e- le- i- son

II. Gloria

Glo- - - - ri- a in ex- cel- sis De- - o in excel- sis

Qui tollis

Qui tollis qui tollis pec- ca- ta mun- di, Mi- se- re- re,

Quoniam

Quo- ni- am tu so- - lus__ san- ctus Tu so- lus Do- mi- nus

Cum sancto spiritu

Cum sanc- to spi- ri- tu, in__ glo- ri- a De- i Pa- tris A- men

III. Credo

Cre- do Cre- do in u- num De- um Pa- trem om- ni- po- ten- tem

IV. Sanctus

San- ctus, Sanc- tus, Sanc- tus, Sanctus Do- mi- nus De- us Sa- ba- oth

V. Benedictus

Be- ne- dic- tus Qui ve- nit,__ qui__ ve- - nit

VI. Agnus Dei

Ag- nus De- i qui tol- lis pec- ca- ta mun- di

Dona nobis pacem

Do- na no- bis pa- - cem, do- na no- bis__ pa- cem

Litanie de Venerabili Altaris Sacra-
mento K. 243

Dul- - - cis- si- mum con- vi- vi- um, cui as- - si- stunt

..., lo previdi (recitative and concert
aria) K. 272

Ah, t'in vo- la agl' oc- chi__ mie- i Al- ma vi- le, in- gra- to__ cor

Deh, non var- car quell'__ on- - - - - - da,

Oiseaux, si tous les ans K. 307

Oi- seaux, xi tous les ans vous chan- gez de cli- mats,

Dans un bois solitaire K. 308

A

Dans un bois so-li-tai-re et som-bre je me pro-me-nais

Popoli di Tessaglia K. 316

B

Io non chie-do e-ter-ni De-i, tut-to il ciel per me se-re-no

Mass in C ("Krönungs Messe")
(Coronation Mass) K. 317
Agnus Dei

C

A- gnus De- i, a- gnus De- i, qui tol- lis pec- ca- ta,

Adoramus te K. 327

D

Ad- o- ra- mus te, Chri- ste, et be-ne-dici- mus ti-bi,

Vesperae solennes de confessor
K. 339 No. 5

E

Lau- da- te Do- mi-num o- mnes gen- tes

enlied K. 350 (K.anh. 284 f)
(attributed to Mozart. Actually
by Bernard Flies, a contemporary
of Mozart)

F

Schlafe mein Prinzchen schlaf' ein, es ruh'n nun Schäfchen und Vö- ge- lein

Komm, liebe Zither K. 341

G

Komm, lie- be Zi- ther, komm, du Freund in stil- ler Lie- be,

omeneo (opera) K. 366 Act I

H

Pa- dre! Ger- ma-ni ad-di-o voi foste io vi per-de-i

A

I

Non ho col-pa e mi con- dan- ni e mi con- dan- ni

B

J

Col-pa è vos-tra o Dei ti- ran-ni è di pe- na

K

Tut- te nel cor vi sen-to, vi sen- to, vi sen-to

L

Ve- drom- mi in-tor-no l'om-bra do-len-te, l'om-bra, l'om-bra

M

Il Pa- dre a-do- ra- to ri-tro-vo, e lo per-do

Act II

N

Se il tuo duol, se il mio de- - si- o s'in-vo-las

O

Se il pa- dre per-de- i la Patria, il ri- po- so,

P

Fuor del mar ho un mar in seno che del pri-mo è più fu-nesto

Q

I- - dol mi-o se- ri- tro-so al-tra A- man-te

Act III

R

Zef- fi- ret- ti lu- - sin- ghie- ri

S

Se co- là nè fa- ti è scrit- to

Idomeneo (opera) K. 366 Act III

D'O- re- ste, d'A- ja- ce ho in se- no i tor- men- ti D'O-re-ste

Tor - - - na la pa- ce al co- re, al co- re,

Ma che vi fece, o stelle K. 368

Spe- ra- i vi- ci- no, vi- ci- no il__ li- do,

Ma tra- por- tar__ mi sen- to,

Misera, dove son! K. 369

Ah! non son io che par- lo, Ah,__ non son__ io che par- lo

Non cu- ra il ciel ti- ra- no l'af- fan no in cui mi ve- do

A questo seno deh vieni K. 374

Or che il cie- lo a me ti ren- de, ca- ra par- te del mio cor,

Die Entführung aus dem Seraglio (The Abduction from the Seraglio) (opera)
K. 384 Act 1

Hier soll ich dich denn se- hen, Kon- stan- ze, dich, mein__ Glück__

Wer ein Lieb- chen hat ge- fun- den, das es treu und red- lich meint,

Sol- che her- ge- lauf'ne Laf - - - - - - - - - - - - - - - fen

O wie ängstlich, o wie feurig Klopft mein lie- be- vol- les Herz__

Ach ich liebte, war so glücklich, kann- te nicht der Lie- be Schmerz

Doch wie schnell schwand__ mei- ne Freude, doch wie schnell schwand meine Freude!

Act II

Durch Zärt- lich- keit und__ Schmeicheln Ge- fäl- lig- keit__ und__ Scherzen

Ich ge- he, doch rathe ich dir, den Schurken Ped- ril- lo zu mei- den

Trau- rig- keit ward mir zum Lo- se, ward mir zum Lo- se,

Mar- tern al- ler Ar- ten al- ler Ar- ten mö- gen mei- ner__ war- ten,

Wel- che Won- ne, wel- che Lust regt sich nun in mei- ner Brust

Frisch zum Kampfe! Frisch zum Streite! Nur ein fei- ger Tropf verzagt,

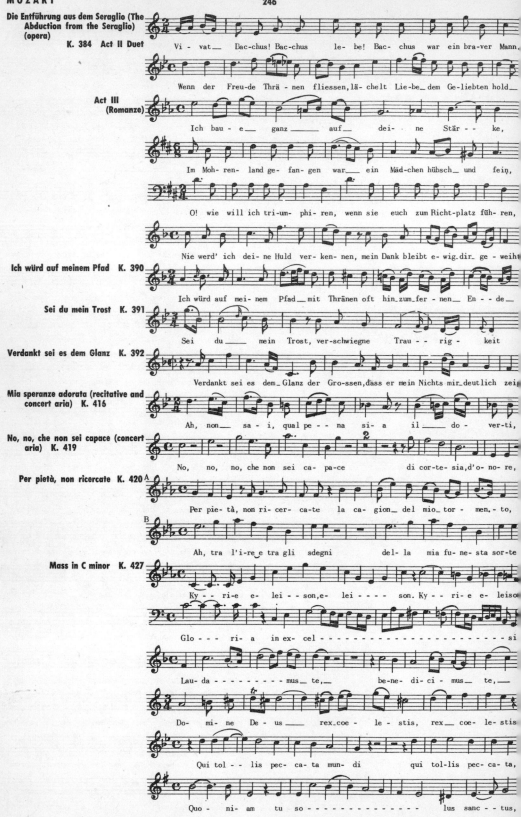

Die Entführung aus dem Seraglio (The Abduction from the Seraglio) (opera)

K. 384 Act II Duet

Vi - vat__ Bac-chus! Bac-chus le - be! Bac- chus war ein bra-ver Mann.

Wenn der Freu-de Thrä - nen fliessen, lä - chelt Lie-be_ dem Ge-liebten hold__

Act III (Romanze)

Ich bau - e__ ganz__ auf__ dei - ne Stär - - ke,

Im Moh-ren- land ge- fan-gen war__ ein Mäd-chen hübsch__ und fein,

O! wie will ich tri-um- phi - ren, wenn sie euch zum Richt-platz füh - ren,

Nie werd' ich dei - ne Huld ver- ken- nen, mein Dank bleibt e- wig dir_ ge - weiht

Ich würd auf meinem Pfad K. 390

Ich würd auf mei - nem Pfad__ mit Thränen oft hin zum fer - nen__ En - - de

Sei du mein Trost K. 391

Sei du__ mein Trost, ver-schwiegne Trau - - rig - keit

Verdankt sei es dem Glanz K. 392

Verdankt sei es dem__ Glanz der Gro-ssen, dass er mein Nichts mir_ deutlich zeig

Mia speranze adorata (recitative and concert aria) K. 416

Ah, non sa - i, qual pe - na si - a il__ do - ver-ti,

No, no, che non sei capace (concert aria) K. 419

No, no, no, che non sei ca - pa-ce di cor-te-sia, d'o - no - re,

Per pietà, non ricercate K. 420

Per pie- tà, non ri-cer- ca-te la ca- gion_ del mio tor - men, - to,

Ah, tra l'i-re e tra gli sdegni del - la mia fu-ne- sta sor-te

Mass in C minor K. 427

Ky - - ri-e e- lei - - son, e- lei - - - - son. Ky - - ri-e e- leiso

Glo - - ri- a in ex- cel - - - - - - - - - - - - - - - si

Lau-da - - - - - - - - - mus te,__ be-ne- di-ci-mus_ te,

Do - mi - ne De- us__ rex, coe - le - stis, rex_ coe - le-stis

Qui tol - - lis pec - ca-ta mun- di qui tol-lis pec-ca-ta,

Quo - ni- am tu so - - - - - - - - - - - - lus sanc - - tus,

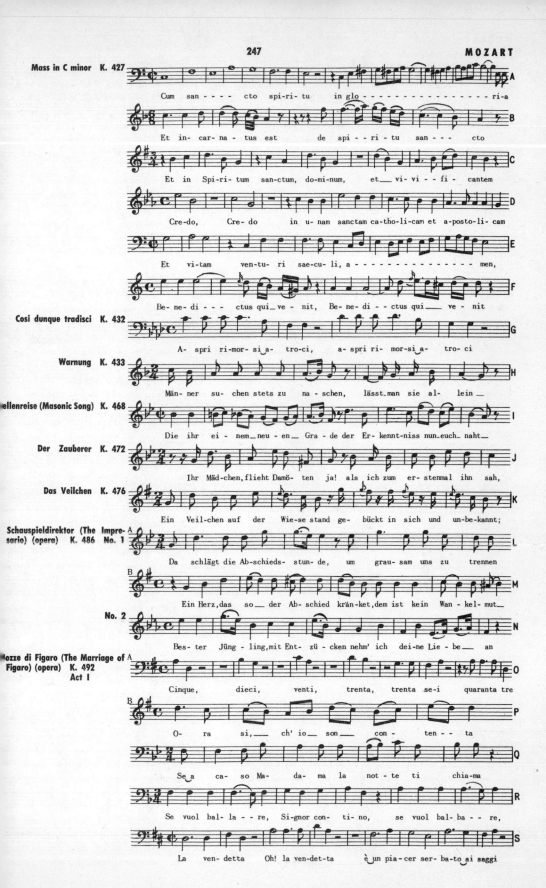

Mass in C minor K. 427

A — Cum san - - - - cto spi-ri-tu in glo - - - - - - - - - - - - - ri-a

B — Et in-car-na-tus est de spi - - ri-tu san - - - cto

C — Et in Spi-ri-tum san-ctum, do-mi-num, et__ vi-vi-fi - cantem

D — Cre-do, Cre-do in u-nam sanctam ca-tho-li-cam et a-posto-li-cam

E — Et vi-tam ven-tu-ri sae-cu-li, a - - - - - - - - - - - - - men,

F — Be-ne-di - - - ctus qui ve-nit, Be-ne-di - - ctus qui__ ve-nit

Cosi dunque tradisci K. 432

G — A-spri ri-mor-si a-tro-ci, a-spri ri-mor-si a- tro-ci

Warnung K. 433

H — Män-ner su-chen stets zu na-schen, lässt man sie al - lein__

Gesellenreise (Masonic Song) K. 468

I — Die ihr ei-nem__ neu-en__ Gra-de der Er-kennt-niss nun euch__ naht__

Der Zauberer K. 472

J — Ihr Mäd-chen, flieht Damö-ten ja! als ich zum er-stenmal ihn sah,

Das Veilchen K. 476

K — Ein Veil-chen auf der Wie-se stand ge-bückt in sich und un-be-kannt;

Schauspieldirektor (The Impresario) (opera) K. 486 No. 1

L — Da schlägt die Ab-schieds-stun-de, um grau-sam uns zu trennen

M — Ein Herz, das so__ der Ab-schied krän-ket, dem ist kein Wan-kel-mut__

No. 2

N — Bes-ter Jüng-ling, mit Ent-zü-cken nehm' ich dei-ne Lie-be__ an

Nozze di Figaro (The Marriage of Figaro) (opera) K. 492 Act I

O — Cinque, dieci, venti, trenta, trenta se-i quaranta tre

P — O-ra si, ch' io__ son con-ten - - ta

Q — Se a ca-so Ma-da-ma la not-te ti chia-ma

R — Se vuol bal-la - - re, Si-gnor con-ti-no, se vuol bal-ba - - re,

S — La ven-detta Oh! la ven-det-ta è un pia-cer ser-ba-to ai saggi

MOZART

Le Nozze di Figaro (The Marriage of Figaro) (opera) K. 492
Act I

Via re-sti ser-vi-ta, Ma-da--ma bril- lan-te!

Non so più co-sa son, co-sa fac-cio, or di fo-co o-ra sono di ghiacc

A
Co-sa sento! Tosto an-da-te, e scac-ciate il se-du-tor

B
In mal punto son qui giunto, per-do-na-te, o mio Si-gnor

Gio--va-ni lie-te, fio--ri spar-ge-te

Non più an-drai far-fal-lo-ne_a-mo-ro-so, notte e gior-no d'in-tor-no

Act II
Por-gi_a-mor qual-che ri-sto-ro al mio duo-lo,

Voi che sa-pe-te, che co-sa è_a- mor

Ve-ni-te_in-gi-noc-chia-te-vi re-sta-te fer-mo lì

A- pri-te, presto a-pri-te, a-pri-te_è la Su-san-na, sor-ti-te,

Act III A
Cru-del! per-chè fi-no-ra far----mi lan-guir co-sì?

B
Mi sen-to dal con-ten-to pie-no di gio-ja il cor,

Ve-drò mentr'io so-spi-ro fe-li-ce_un ser-vo mi-o?

Do-ve so-no i bei mo-men-ti di dol-cez-za e di pia-cer?

Sull' a-ria! Che so-a--ve zef-fi-ret--to

Bi-ce-ve-te_o pa-dron-ci-na, que-ste ro-se_e que-sti fio

A- man-ti co-stan-ti, se-gua-ci d'o-nor,

Act IV
L'ho per-du-ta, me me-schi-na! ah chi sa do-ve sa-rà!

Il ca-pro_e la_ca-pret-ta son sempre_in_a-mi-sta

MOZART

Nozze di Figaro (The Marriage of Figaro) (opera) K. 492
Act IV

A — In quegli an-ni in cui val po-co la mal pra-ti-ca ra-gion,

B — A- pre-te un po' quegli occhi uo-mini in-cauti e sciocchi!

C — Deh vie-ni non tar dar o gio- ja bel- la!

Finale

D — Pian, pia-nin! la andrò più pres-so, tem-po per-so non sa- rà

E — Pace! pa-ce! mio dol-ce te-so-ro! io co- nob-bi la vo-ce

ʼio mi scordi di te (recitative and concert aria) K. 505

F — Non te- mer a- ma-to be- - - - ne per te sem-pre,

G — Al- me bel-le, che ve-de-te le mie pe-ne in tal mo- men-to,

Alcandro, lo confesso (recitative) K. 512

H — Non so d'on-de vie-ne quel te- - ne-ro af-fetto quel moto

I — Nel se-no a de- star-mi sì fie-ri con- trasti

Mentre ti lascio, o figlia K. 513

J — Men- - - tre ti las-cio, o fi-glia, o_ fi- - glia,

K — Ti_ chie-do un sol mo- men-to, un sol mo- - men-to

Die Alte K. 517

L — Zu mei-ner Zeit, zu mei-ner Zeit be-stand noch_ Recht und Bil-lig-keit

Die Verschweigung K. 518

M — So- bald_ Da-mö-tas Clo-en_ sieht,_ so sucht_ er mit_ be-red-ten Blicken

Das Lied der Trennung K. 519

N — Die En- gel Got-tes wei-nen, wo Lie-ben-de sich tren-nen,

s Luise die Briefe ihres ungetreuen Liebhabers verbrannte K. 520

O — Er-zeugt von heisser Phan-ta-sie in ei-ner schwär-me-ri-schen Stun-de

Abendempfindung K. 523

P — A- bend ist's, die Son- ne ist ver- schwun- den,

An Chloe K. 524

Q — Wenn das Lieb' aus dei-nen blau- en, hel- len, off- nen Au-gen sieht_

Don Giovanni (Don Juan) (opera) K. 527
Act I

R — Not-te e gior-no fa- ti- car, per chi nul-la sa gra-dir

S — Ah! chi mi di- ce ma- i quel bar-ba-ro dov' e?

MOZART
Don Giovanni (Don Juan) (opera)
K. 527
Act I Catalogue Song

A — Ma - da - mi - na! Il ca - to - lo - go è que - sto,

B — Nel - la bion - da e - gli ha l'u - san - za

Gio - vi - net - te, che fa - te all'a - mo - re, che fa - te all'a - mo - re,

Ho ca - pi - to, Si - gnor, si! Si - gnor, si!

A — Là ci da - rem la ma - no, là mi di - rai di sì

B — An - diam, an - diam, mio be - ne, a ri - sto - rar le pe - ne

Ah! fug - gi il tra - di - tor! Non lo las - ciar più dir;

Or sai, che l'o - no - re ra - pi - re a me vol - se

Dal - la sua pa - ce la mia di - pen - de,

Finch'han dal vi - no cal - da la tes - ta u - na gran fes - t

A — Bat - ti, bat - ti o bel Ma - set - to, la tua po - ve - ra Zer - li - na:

B — Pa - ce, pa - ce o vi - ta mi - a! pace, pa - ce o vi - ta mi - a!

Act II

Eh via, buf - fo - ne, eh via, buf - fo - ne, non mi sec - car

Serenade

Deh vie - ni al - la fi - ne - stra o mio te - so - r

Ve - drai, ca - ri - no, se sei buo - ni - no

Ah, pie - tà! Si - gno - ri miei! Ah pie - tà, pie - tà, pie - tà, pie

Il mio te - so - ro in - tan - to an - da - te

Per que - ste tu - e ma - ni - ne, Can - di - de e te - ne - rel - le

Mi tra - dì quell' al - ma in - gra - ta, quell' al - ma in - gra - ta

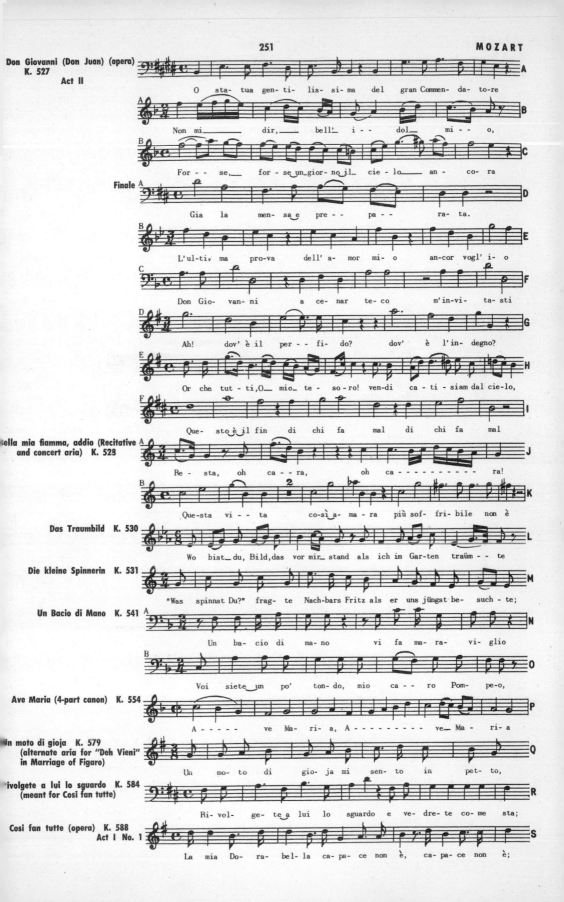

Don Giovanni (Don Juan) (opera)
K. 527
Act II

O sta- tua gen- ti- lis- si- ma del gran Commen- da- to- re

Non mi___ dir,___ bell' i -- dol mi - o,

For -- se,___ for -- se un gior- no il cie- lo___ an - co - ra

Finale

Gia la men- sa e pre -- pa -- ra - ta.

L'ul- ti- ma pro- va dell' a- mor mi - o an- cor vogl' i - o

Don Gio- van- ni a ce- nar te- co m'in- vi- ta- sti

Ah! dov' è il per -- fi- do? dov' è l'in- degno?

Or che tut- ti, O___ mio te- so- ro! ven- di ca- ti- siam dal cie- lo,

Que- sto è il fin di chi fa mal di chi fa mal

Bella mia fiamma, addio (Recitative and concert aria) K. 528

Re- sta, oh ca- ra, oh ca- - - - - - - - - ra!

Que- sta vi- ta co- sì a- ma- ra più sof- fri- bile non è

Das Traumbild K. 530

Wo bist___ du, Bild, das vor mir___ stand als ich im Gar- ten traüm -- te

Die kleine Spinnerin K. 531

"Was spinnst Du?" frag- te Nach- bars Fritz als er uns jüngst be- such- te;

Un Bacio di Mano K. 541

Un ba- cio di ma- no vi fa ma- ra- vi- glio

Voi sie- te un po' ton- do, mio ca- ro Pom- pe- o,

Ave Maria (4-part canon) K. 554

A - - - - - ve Ma- ri- a, A - - - - - - - - ve Ma- ri- a

Un moto di gioja K. 579
(alternate aria for "Deh Vieni"
in Marriage of Figaro)

Un mo- to di gio- ja mi sen- to in pet- to,

Rivolgete a lui lo sguardo K. 584
(meant for Cosi fan tutte)

Ri- vol- ge- te a lui lo sguardo e ve- dre- te co- me sta;

Cosi fan tutte (opera) K. 588
Act I No. 1

La mia Do- ra- bel- la ca- pa- ce non è, ca- pa- ce non è;

MOZART

MOZART
Cosi fan tutte (opera) K. 588
Act II No. 5

Vorrei dir, e cor non ho, e cor non ho bal- bet- tando il lab- bro va

No. 7

Al fa- to dan legge quegli oc-chi vez-zo- si; A- mor li pro-tegge

No. 11

Sma- nie im-pla- ca-bi- li, che m'a-gi-ta- te

No. 12 A

In no- mi-ni, in sol-da-ti Spe- ra- re fe-del- tà?

B

Di pa-sta si- mi- le son tut-ti quanti, son tut-ti quan-ti

No. 14

Co- me scoglio im- mo-to re- sta con-tra i venti e la tem-pesta

No. 15

Non sia-te ri- tro-si oc- chiet-ti vez-zo-si, due lam- pi amoro-si

No. 17

Un' aura a- mo- ro-sa del nos- tro te- so- ro,

Act II No. 19

U- na don-na a quin-di- ci an- ni dev' sa-per— o-gni gran mo-da;

No. 20

Pren-de- rò quel bru- net-ti-no che più le- pi-do— mi— par—

No. 21

Se- con- da-te, au- ret- - - te a- - mi- che

No. 23

Il co- re— vi— do-no bell' i-do- lo mi-o! Ma il vo-stro vo' anch' i-o!

No. 24

Ah! lo veg- gio, quell'a-ni- ma bel-la al mio pian-to re-si- ster

No. 25

Per- pie- tà— ben— mio, per- do-na all er-ror d'un al-ma aman-te

No. 26

Don-ne mie la fa-te a tan-ti e tanti a tanti e tanti a tan- ti,

No. 27 A

Tra- di- to, scher-ni- to dal per-fi-do cor dal per- fi-do cor

B

Io sen-to, che an- co- ra quest' al- - ma l'a- do- ra,

No. 28

È A- more un la-dron-cel- lo, un ser-pen-tello è A- mor

Sehnsucht nach dem Frühlinge
K. 596

Komm, lie- ber Mai und ma- - che die Bäu- me wie- der grün,

Das Kinderspiel K. 598

Wir Kin- der, wir schmecken- der_ Freu-den_ recht_ viel,

Per questa bella mano K. 612

Per que-sta bel-la ma--no, per que-sti va-ghi ra-i

Vol-gi lie-ti o fie-ri sguar-di, dim-mi pur che m'odi_o m'ami

Ave verum corpus K. 618

A- ve, a--ve, ve- rum cor-pus, na-tum de Ma-ri-a vir- gi-ne,

Die Zauberflöte (The Magic Flute) (opera) K. 620 Act I No. 2

Der Vo-gel-fän- ger bin ich ja, stets_ lus-tig,hei-sa, hop-sa-sa!

No. 3

Dies Bild-niss ist be- zau-bernd schön, wie noch kein Au-ge je ge-seh'n!

No. 4

Zum Lei- den bin ich auser-ko- ren, denn mei-ne Toch-ter feh-let mir,_

Du, du du wirst_ sie_ zu be-frei-en ge------hen,

No. 5 Quintet

Hm, Hm, Hm, Hm,_ Hm, Hm, Hm, Hm,_Hm, Hm, Hm, Hm,Hm, Hm,_Hm, Hm!

No. 7

Bei Män-nern, wel-che Lie-be fühlen,fehlt auch_ein gu- tes Her-ze nicht

Finale

Wie stark ist_ nicht_ dein_ Zau- - ber- ton!

Schnelle Fü- sse, ra-scher Mut schützt vor Feindes_List_ und_Wuth;

Das_ klinget so herr-lich das_ klin-get so schön!

Act II No. 10

O I- sis und O- si- ris,_schenket der Weisheit Geist dem_neuen Paar

No. 11

Bewah- ret euch vor Wei-ber- tü- cken,dies ist des Bun-des er- ste_ Pflicht!_

No. 13

Al- les_ fühlt der_Lie-be Freu-den, schnäbelt, tän-delt, herzt und küsst;

No. 14
Queen of the Night Aria

Der Höl-le Ra-che kocht in mei-nem Her-zen, Tod und Ver- zweiflung!

Cadenza

cadenza

No. 15

In die-sen heil'_gen Hal- len kennt man die Ra- che_ nicht,_

MOZART

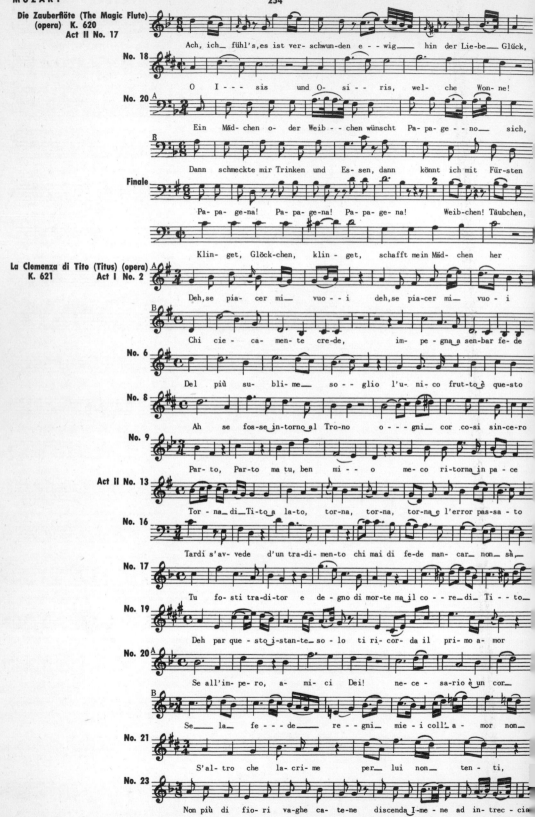

MUDARRA, Alfonso (16th Cent.)

Triste estaba el Rey David
Tris - - te es-ta - ba el rey Da-vid_____

MUSSORGSKY, Modeste (1839-1881)

Boris Godunov (opera)
Prologue Scene I Opening Chorus
Wilt thou_ leave us all un - pro-tect-ed, our_ fa - ther?

Coronation Scene (chorus)
As re-splen-dent the sun_ fills the hea-ven with glo-ry,
My soul is sad! I did not seek this charge_

Act I Scene I Pimen's Monologue
Yet one more tale the last of all these re - cords,

Scene II Varlaam's Song
Here's the tale of what hap-pened at Ka-zan,

Drunken Scene
I'll hold my tongue_ I'll hold my tongue_ Reason got plen - -ty

Act II Song of the Gnat
Once a gnat, as all gnats should, Did draw wa - ter, hew the wood

Monologue
I have a- chieved the highest 'Tis now six years that I have reign'd with peace
The hand of God, the aw- ful judge is on me,

Song of the Parrot
Our cock-a- too was play- ing with the at- tend- ants.

Clock Scene
Ah! give me air! this suf- fo- cates my soul!

Act III Scene II Polonaise
Your pro-fessed de - vo-tion, sir, I trust not, All in vain your_ sol-emn_oaths
Oh! Tzar-e- vitch, I be- seech thee, do not curse me

Act IV Scene I Revolutionary Chorus
Sirs, 'tis time we got to work, what hinders? Sirs,_ your o- pin-ion first,

Pimen's Tale A
A peace-ful her-mit of sim- ple mind, un- versed in worldly things

B
There came once at vesper hour a herds-man at my door a grey beard old and hoary
Fare-well my son I am dy-ing From now thou wilt be-gin thy rei

Boris Godunov (opera)
Act IV Scene I Farewell, my son (chorus)

Weep and mourn, ye mor-tal men,— for his life is fled— A

The Fair at Sorochinsk (opera)
Act I Revery of the Young Peasant

My heart,— why— weep-est thou? Why art— thou— pin-ing B

Sor- row, for- sake thou me!— De- spair, I bid thee go C

Act II Song of Khivria

Who would not love me, such a charm-ing love-bird, Who would not gladly D

Since the time when first I met my Bru- de- us, Bru- de- us, E

Act III Parasha's Revery and Dance

Grieve nev-er, my be-lov- ed, Griev-ing nev-er ban-ish'd sor- row F

Hi— my young and black eyed lov- er Standing up so— straight and tall. G

Khovantchina (opera)
Act II Divination by Water

Spi-rits of ne-ther worlds, Hid-den be-low the floods! Bound by a ma-gic spell, H

In shame and disgrace I be- hold— thee In exile a- lone in a dis-tant— land I

Act III Martha's Song

And by day and by night I fare O- ver mountain and mead - - ow J

Shakiltor's Aria

Ah! mal-heu- reu se Rus-si- e, mon— pa- ys cher! K

SONGS:
After the Battle

He met his death in for-eign land, in bit-ter fight-ing hand to hand, L

By the River Don

By the— Don a gar-den fair— All a-bloom— with ro- ses M

A Child's Song

In the vale, oh! in the val-ley Grows a lit-tle ber- ry, N

The Country Feast

They had opened wide the might-y doors of oak; Some on horse and some in sleds O

Cradle Song of the Poor

By-bye, by— By-bye by- bye Lower than the hum- ble way-side flow'rs P

Gathering Mushrooms

Mush- rooms brown and tall,— mus-ter'd, Mush-rooms white and small— Q

The Goat

Through a field of flow'rs en- chanting, walked a maid, her beau-ty flaunting R

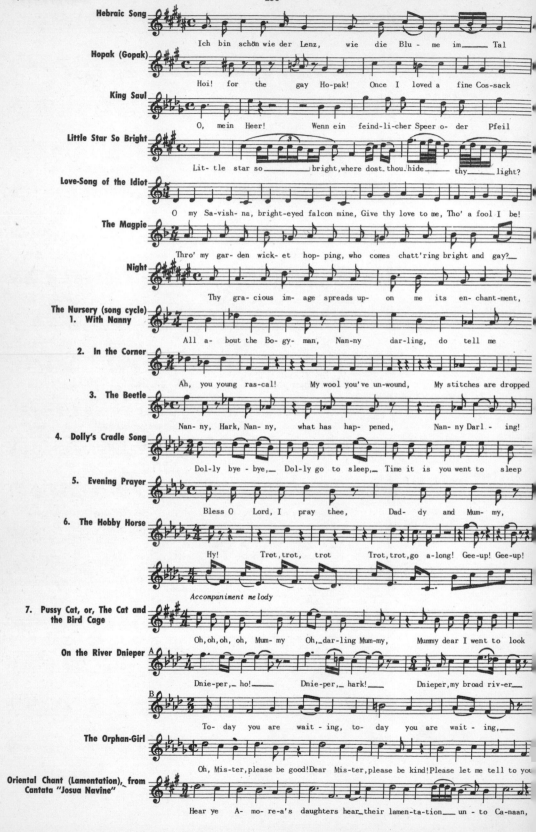

Hebraic Song
Ich bin schön wie der Lenz, wie die Blu- me im_____ Tal

Hopak (Gopak)
Hoi! for the gay Ho-pak! Once I loved a fine Cos-sack

King Saul
O, mein Heer! Wenn ein feind-li-cher Speer o- der Pfeil

Little Star So Bright
Lit- tle star so_____ bright, where dost_thou_hide_____ thy_____ light?

Love-Song of the Idiot
O my Sa-vish- na, bright-eyed falcon mine, Give thy love to me, Tho' a fool I be!

The Magpie
Thro' my gar- den wick- et hop- ping, who comes chatt'ring bright and gay?

Night
Thy gra- cious im- age spreads up- on me its en- chant-ment,

The Nursery (song cycle)
1. With Nanny
All a- bout the Bo- gy- man, Nan-ny darling, do tell me

2. In the Corner
Ah, you young ras-cal! My wool you've un-wound, My stitches are dropped

3. The Beetle
Nan- ny, Hark, Nan- ny, what has hap- pened, Nan-ny Darl - ing!

4. Dolly's Cradle Song
Dol-ly bye - bye,__ Dol-ly go to sleep,__ Time it is you went to sleep

5. Evening Prayer
Bless O Lord, I pray thee, Dad- dy and Mum- my,

6. The Hobby Horse
Hy! Trot, trot, trot Trot, trot, go a-long! Gee-up! Gee-up!

Accompaniment melody

7. Pussy Cat, or, The Cat and the Bird Cage
Oh, oh, oh, oh, Mum- my Oh,_dar-ling Mum-my, Mummy dear I went to look

On the River Dnieper A
Dnie-per,_ ho! Dnie-per,_ hark!___ Dnieper, my broad riv-er-

B
To- day you are wait- ing, to- day you are wait- ing,___

The Orphan-Girl
Oh, Mis-ter, please be good! Dear Mis-ter, please be kind! Please let me tell to you

Oriental Chant (Lamentation), from Cantata "Josua Navine"
Hear ye A- mo- re-a's daughters hear_their lamen-ta-tion_un - to Ca-naan,

MYLIUS, Wolfgang (17th Cent.)

Ein Mägdlein stund

Ein Mägd-lein stund, Wo stund es denn? Ein Mägd-lein stund

NÄGELI, Hans Georg (1773-1836)

Freut euch des Lebens

Freut euch_ des Le - - bens, weil noch_ das Lämp - chen glüht

NAGINSKI, Charles (1909-1940)

The Pasture
Copyright 1940, G. Schirmer, Inc.

I'm go - ing out to clean the pas - ture spring

Richard Cory
Copyright 1940, G. Schirmer, Inc.

When - ev - er Rich-ard Co - ry went down town

NANINI, Giovanni Maria (c.1545-1607)

Diffusa est gratia

Dif - - fu-sa est gra - - - - - - - - - - ti-a in la - bi-is, in la - - bi-is

NAPRAVNIK, Eduard (1839-1916)

Cradle Song, from Harold (opera)
Act V
Copyright 1906, G. Schirmer, Inc.

Hush thee, dear one, slumber well! Pain be gone, and grief's e- mo-tion,

NELSON, Sidney (1800-1862)

Mary of Argyle

I have heard the may is sing-ing, His love-song to the morn

NESSLER, Victor E. (1841-1900)

Behüt' dich Gott, from Der Trompeter
von Sakkingen (opera)

Das ist im Le - ben häss- lich ein ge- rich- tet,

Be- hüt' dich Gott! es wär' zu schön ge- we- sen, be- hüt dich Gott,

NEUMARK, Georg (1621-1681)

Gottestrost

Wer nur den lie- ben Gott lässt wal-ten und hof- fet

NEVIN, Ethelbert (1862-1901)

A Life Lesson
There, lit-tle girl, don't cry! They have bro-ken your doll, I know,

Little Boy Blue, Op. 12, No. 4
The lit-tle toy dog is cover'd with dust, But stur-dy and staunch he stands;

Might lak' a rose
Copyright by John Church Co.
Used by permission.
Sweetest li'-l' fel-ler, Ev'-ry bod-y knows; Dun-no what to call him,

that we two were maying, Op. 2, No. 8
Oh! that we two were may - - ing Down the stream of the soft spring breeze

One Spring Morning
One spring morn-ing, bright and fair, Tra- la- la- la- la- la- la

The Rosary
The hours I spent with thee, dear heart, are as a string of pearls to me

NICKERSON, Camille

Michieu Banjo (arr.)
Copyright by Boston Music Co.
Gar- dez pi- ti Mi- latte la, Mi- chieu Ban- jo,

NICOLAI, Karl (1810-1849)

The Merry Wives of Windsor (Die lustigen Weiber von Windsor) (opera)
Act I No. 3
Ver- füh - - - - - - - - - - rer! Wa- rum stellt ihr so

Act II No. 5
Froh- sinn und Lau- ne wür - - - zen das Le - - - - ben

Als Büb-lein klein an der Mut-ter Brust, hopp heis-sa bei Re-gen und Wind,

Act II No. 7b
Horch, die Ler-che singt im Hain, lau-sche, lausche Liebchen still,

Act III No. 11
So schweb' ich Dir Gelieb - - ter zu, so kennst Du mich, so na - hest Du,

O se- li- ge Träu- me, o sü - - - - - - sses Glück

NIEDERMEYER, Abraham Louis (1802-1861)

Le Lac
Ain- si tou-jours pous- sés vers de nou- veaux ri- va- ges

Un soir t'en sou-vient-il? nous vo- guions en si- len- ce

NIELSEN, Carl (1865-1931)

Irmelin Rose
Copyright by Hansen, Copenhagen

Se, der var en Gang en Kon- - -ge- man-gen Skat han kald- te___ sin

NIN, Joaquin (1879-   )

Classiques espagnols du chant (arr.)
Alma, sintamos (Pablo Esteve, 1730?-1792?)
By permission Associated Music Publishers, Inc.

Al- ma, sin- ta- mos! O- jos, llo- rar!

Aria de Acis y Galatea (Antonio Literes, 1680?-1755)

Si de ra-ma en ra- ma si de flor en flor

Corazón que en prisión (José Marin, 1619-1699)

Co- ra- zon que en pri- sión de res- pe- tos cau- ti___

Cloris Hermosa (Sebastian Duron, 1645?-1716?)

Gra- cio- sa mo- da e- sa que han da- do

Desengañémonos ya (José Marin, 1619-1699)

De- sen- ga- ñe- mo- nos ya; mal pa- ga- -do pen-sa- mien- - to

El jilguerito con pico de oro (Blas de Laterna, 1751-1816)

El jil- que- ti- - -to con pi- co de o- - -ro

Minué cantado (José Bassa, 1670?-1730?)

Si de A- ma- ri- lis los___ o- jos dis- pa- - - - -ran

Four Popular Spanish Songs
I Castellana (also No. 3 of Vingt chants populaires espagnols)
By permission Associated Music Publishers, Inc.

Yo me i- ba ma- dre a la ro- me- ri- a

So ell'en-ci-na en- ci- na So ell'en-ci- na Yo me i- ba mi ma- dre,

II Catalana (also No. 16 of Vingt chants populaires espagnols)

Ei- xa nit es nit de vet- lla n'ha pa- rit u- na___ don- ze- lla

A- ni- rem al camp, po- mes a cu- llir, po- me-tes cu- lli- rem

III Gallega (also No. 12 of Vingt chants populaires espagnols)

Meu a- mor meu a- mo- ri- ño Ond'es- tás que no te ve- jo

IV Asturiana (also No. 14 of Vingt chants populaires espagnols)

Fuis- ti a la siega y Col-vies- ti___ Fuis- ti a la siega y Col-vies- ti

Vingt chants populaires espagnols
I Tonada de Valdovinos
By permission Associated Music Publishers, Inc.

Sos- pi- ras- te, val- do- vi- nos La co- sa que más que- rí- a

II Cantar

Quien a- mo- res ten a- fin- que los ben___ que non he vien- to

IV Montañesa

Se- ga- ba yo a- que- lla___ tar- de

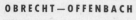

Missa super Maria Zårt Et incarnatus est

Et in- car- na____ tus est de__ Spiri-

Tsaat een meskin (No words in score)

OFFENBACH, Jacques (1819-1880)

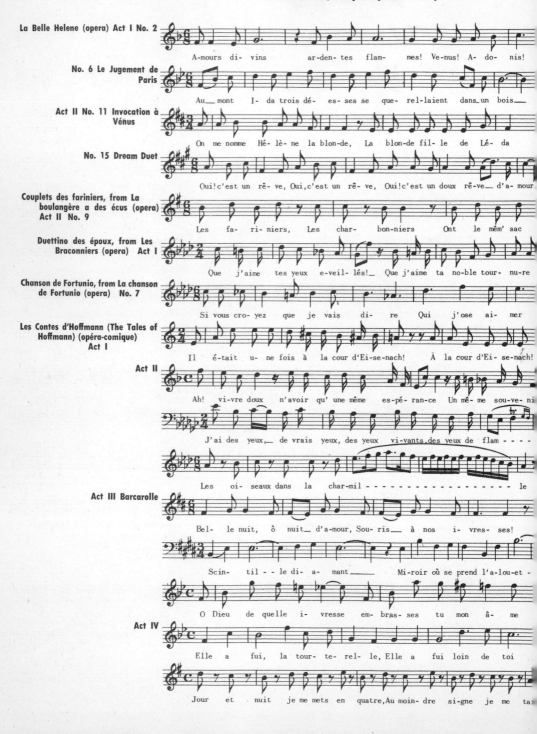

La Belle Helene (opera) Act I No. 2

A-mours di- vins ar-den- tes flam- mes! Ve-nus! A- do- nis!

No. 6 Le Jugement de Paris

Au__ mont I- da trois dé- es-ses se que- rel-laient dans un bois__

Act II No. 11 Invocation à Vénus

On me nomme Hé- lè- ne la blon-de, La blon-de fil- le de Lé- da

No. 15 Dream Duet

Oui! c'est un rê- ve, Oui, c'est un rê- ve, Oui! c'est un doux rê-ve__ d'a-mour

Couplets des fariniers, from La boulangère a des écus (opera) Act II No. 9

Les fa- ri- niers, Les char- bon-niers Ont le mêm' sac

Duettino des époux, from Les Braconniers (opera) Act I

Que j'aime tes yeux e-veil- lés!__ Que j'aime ta no-ble tour- nu-re

Chanson de Fortunio, from La chanson de Fortunio (opera) No. 7

Si vous cro- yez que je vais di- re Qui j'ose ai- mer

Les Contes d'Hoffmann (The Tales of Hoffmann) (opéra-comique) Act I

Il é-tait u- ne fois à la cour d'Ei-se-nach! À la cour d'Ei-se-nach!

Act II

Ah! vi-vre doux n'avoir qu' une même es-pé- ran-ce Un mê- me sou-ve-ni

J'ai des yeux,__ de vrais yeux, des yeux vi-vants, des yeux de flam - - - -

Les oi- seaux dans la char-mil - - - - - - - - - - - le

Act III Barcarolle

Bel- le nuit, ô nuit__ d'a-mour, Sou- ris__ à nos i- vres-ses!

Scin- til- le di- a- mant__ Mi-roir où se prend l'a-lou-et-

Act IV

O Dieu de quelle i- vresse em-bras- ses tu mon â- me

Elle a fui, la tour- te- rel- le, Elle a fui loin de toi

Jour et nuit je me mets en quatre, Au moin- dre si-gne je me tai

Contes d'Hoffmann (The Tales of Hoffmann) (opera) Act IV

A. C'est u-ne chan-son d'a-mour qui s'en-vo-le Triste ou fol-le

B. J'ai le bon-heur dans l'â-me! De-main tu se-ras ma fem-me!

C. Chère en-fant! que j'ap-pel-le Comme au-tre-fois, C'est ta mè-re,

Gendarmes' duet, from Geneviève de Brabant (opera) Act II, No. 14

D. Pro-te-ger le re-pos des vil-les

Grande Duchesse de Gérolstein (opera) Act I Couplets de sabre

E. Voi-ci le sa-bre de mon pè-re Tu vas le mettre à ton co-té

F. Voi-ci le sa-bre le sa-bre le sa-bre

Act II

G. Di-tes lui qu'on l'a re-mar-qué dis-tin-gué, Di-tes lui

Duo d'Alsace, from Lischen et Fritzchen (opera) No. 3

H. Je suis Al-sa-cien-ne, Je suis Al-sa-cien,

I. Juch-he! das Le-ben ist doch ei-ne Freu-de Juch-he!

Ronde des vignes, from Madame Favart (opera) Act I

J. Ma mère aux vi-gnes m'en voyait, Je n' sais com-ment ça s' dit

La Périchole (opera) Act I

K. Ah! quel di-ner je viens de fai-re Et quel vin

No. 7 La lettre

L. O mon cher a-mant, je te ju-re, Que je t'aim-e de tout mon coeur;

Act II

M. Que veulent di-re ces co-lè-res Et ces ges-tes de mau-vais ton

N. Mon Dieu, mon Dieu, que les hom-mes sont bê-tes,

Act III No. 17b Couplets de l'aveu

O. Tu n'est pas beau tu n'est pas riche Tu man-ques tout

O'HARA, Geoffrey (1882-)

Give a man a horse he can ride

Q. Give a man a horse he can ride, Give a man a boat he can sail

There is no death

OKEGHEM, Jean de (c. 1430-1493)

Ma Maitresse

Ma mai-tres-se et ma plus grant a my - - - - - - -

OTHMAYR, Casper (1515-1553)

Brauns-Maidelein

Mir ist ein feins brauns Mai- de-lein ge-fal- len in mein Sinn

PADILLA, José (Contemporary)

Princesita
Copyright by E. B. Marks Music Corp., N. Y.

Prin-ce-si- ta Prin-ce-si- ta la de o-jos a- zu- les

Who'll Buy My Violets (La Violetera)
Copyright 1923, Harms, Inc.

Co-mo a ves pre-cur so- ras de Pri-ma-ve - - - ra

PAISIELLO, Giovanni (1740-1816)

Déserts écartés, from Prosperine (opera)

De- serts é- car- tés som- bres lieux, Ca- chez mes sou- pirs,

Nel cor più non mi sento, from La Molinara (opera)

Nel cor più non mi sen- to bril-lar la gio- ven- tù

PALADILHE, Emile (1884-1926)

Patrie (opera)
No. 4 Air du sonneur
Copyright by Choudens fils, Paris

Ja- dis el- les chan-taient gaie- ment

No. 21 Cantabile de Rysor

Pau- vre mar-tyr obs- cur, Hum-ble hé- ros d'une heu- re

No. 22 Air de Rysor

Fuir à ja- mais fuir en- sem- ble

SONGS:
Psyché
Copyright 1911, G. Schirmer, Inc.

Je suis ja- loux, Psy- ché de tou-te la na- tu- re

Le Roitelet
Copyright 1911, G. Schirmer, Inc.

Ra- pi- de comme un rê- - ve, Vif comme un feu fol- let

Les Trois Prières

A l'heu- re où notre es-prit moins fier S'in-cli- ne comme un Roi

PALESTRINA, Giovanni Pierluigi da (1524-1594)

Hymns: I O crux ave

O crux a - - - ve, spes u- ni- ca,

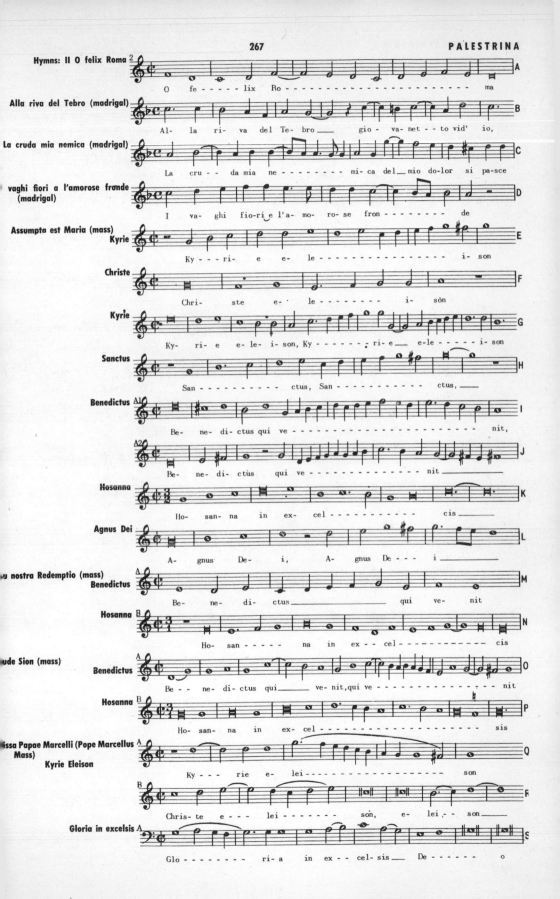

PALESTRINA **268**

Missa Papae Marcelli (Pope Marcellus Mass)
Gloria in excelsis

Qui tol- lis pec- ca- ta mun - - - - di

Credo

Cre- do in u- num De - - - - um

Sanctus

San - - - - - - - - - - - - - - ctus, San - - - - - - - - - - - ctus

Benedictus

Be- ne- dic - - - - - - - - - - - - - - - tus

O- sa- na in ex- cel- sis, O- sa - - - - - - - - na in excel - - - - - - - si

Agnus Dei

Ag - - - - nus De - i

Adoramus te Christe (motet)

A- do- ra- mus te Chri - - - - - ste, et be- ne- di- ci- mus ti- bi

Alleluia! tulerunt Dominum (motet)

Al- le- lu - - - - - ja Al- le- lu - - - - - - - - - - ja

Hodie Christus natus est (motet)

Ho- di- e Chri - - - stus na- tus est no- e no- e

Introduxit me rex in cellam (motet)

In- tro- dux- it me rex in cel- lam vi- na- ri- am

Laudate pueri Dominum (motet)

Lau- da- te pu- e- ri Do- mi- num lau- da- te

Manus tuae Domine (motet)

Ma- nus tu- ae Do - - - - - - - - - - - - - - - - mi- ne

Nunc dimittis (motet)

Nunc di- mit- tis ser - - vum tu- um, Do - - - - - - - mi- ne,

O admirabile commercium (motet)

O - - - - - ad- mi- ra- bi- le com- mer - - - - - ci- um

O bone Jesu (motet)

O bo- ne Je- su O bo- ne Je- su ex- au- di me

Paucitas dierum (motet)

Pau- ci- tas di- e- rum me- o- rum fi- ni- e- tur bre - - - - - - - vi

Regina coeli laetare (motet)

Re- gi- na coe- li lae- ta- re lae -

Sicut servus desiderat (motet)

Sic - - ut cer- vus de- si- de- rat ad fon- tes a- qua - - - - - - - - rum

Stabat mater dolorosa (motet)

Sta- bat ma- ter do - - lo- ro- sa, Juxta cru- cem la - - cry- mo- sa,

Tota pulchra es amica mea (motet)

To- ta pulchra es a- mi- ca me - - - - - - - - - - a _____ A

Tribulationes civitatum (motet) 1

Tri- bu- la- ti- o - - nes ci - - - - vi- ta- - tum au- di- vi- mus B

Peccavimus (motet) 2

Pec- ca- vi- mus pec - - - - - - - ca - - - - - vi- mus C

Vox dilecti mei (motet)

Vox vox di- le- cti me - - - - - - - - - - i Vox __ di- le- cti D

Vulnerasti cor meum (motet)

Vul- ne- ra- sti cor me - - um vul- ne- ra- sti cor me- um, E

Offertories:
Bonum est

Bo - - - - num est con- fi- te- ri _____ F

Exaltabo te, Domine

Ex- al- ta- bo- te _____ Do - - - - - - - - - - - - - - - mi- ne G

Improperium expectavit

Im - - pro- pe- ri- um ex- pe- cta- vit __ cor me - - - - - - - um, __ H

Laudate Dominum

Lau- da- te Do - - - - - - mi- num, lau- da - - te Do- mi- num __ I

Super flumina Babylonis

Su - - - per flu- mi- na Ba - - by- lon - - - - - - - - - - nis, __ J

Alma redemptoris mater (cantus firmus)

Al - - - - - - - - - - - ma Re- demp- to- ris ma - - - - - - - - ter K

Ecce, quomodo moritur justus (response)

Ec- ce quo- mo- do mo - - - ri- tur ju- stus, L

Exultate Deo

Ex- ul- ta - - - - - te De- o, ad - - ju- to- ri nos - - - - - - tro __ M

Gloria Patri

Glo- ri- a Pa- tri Et Fi- li- o, Glo- ri- a Pa- tri N

Incipit oratorio Jeremiae Prophetae (lamentation)

In- ci- pit O- ra- ti- o In- ci- pit O- ra- ti- o O

Jubilate Deo (Psalm 99)

Ju- bi- la - - - - - - - - - te De - - - - - - o P

Pueri Hebraeorum (Antiphon)

Pu - - e- ri He- brae- o- rum, He - - - - - brae- o - - - - - rum Q

PALMGREN, Selim (1878-)

Finnish Lullaby
Copyright by H. W. Gray Co.

Lit- tle songs I'll sing thee, dear- est, Lit- tle tales I bring thee, dear- est S

Summer Evening
Copyright by H. W. Gray Co.

The gol-den sun was sink-ing be-yond the hills of blue.

Summer Night (Läksin minä Kesäyönä Käymänn)

Sum-mer night in the north was glist-ning, For the day, in the

PAOLA DA FIRENZE, Don (14th Cent.)

Fra duri scogli senz' alcun governo

Fra du-ri sco-gli senz' al-cun go--ver-no

PARADIES, Pietro Domenico (1707-1791)

M'ha preso alla sua ragna

M'ha pre-so al-la sua ra-gna, m'ha pre-so al-la sua ra-gna

Quel ruscelletto

Quel ru-scel-let-to Che l'on-de chia-re Or or col ma--re

PARKER, Horatio (1863-1919)

The Lark Now Leaves His Wat'ry Nest
Copyright by John Church Co.
Used by permission

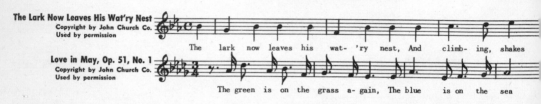

The lark now leaves his wat-'ry nest, And climb-ing, shakes

Love in May, Op. 51, No. 1
Copyright by John Church Co.
Used by permission

The green is on the grass a-gain, The blue is on the sea

PARRY, Sir Charles Herbert Hastings (1848-1918)

Armida's Garden
By permission Novello & Co., Ltd., London

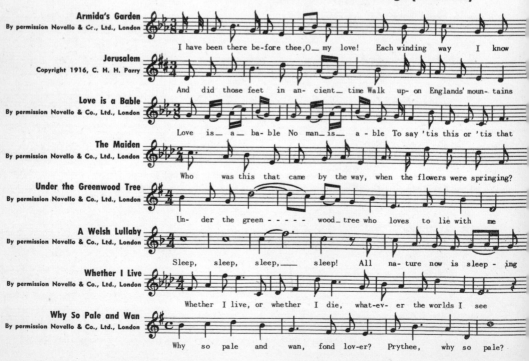

I have been there be-fore thee, O my love! Each winding way I know

Jerusalem
Copyright 1916, C. H. H. Parry

And did those feet in an-cient time Walk up-on Englands' moun-tains

Love is a Bable
By permission Novello & Co., Ltd., London

Love is a ba-ble No man is a-ble To say 'tis this or 'tis that

The Maiden
By permission Novello & Co., Ltd., London

Who was this that came by the way, when the flowers were springing?

Under the Greenwood Tree
By permission Novello & Co., Ltd., London

Un-der the green - - - - wood tree who loves to lie with me

A Welsh Lullaby
By permission Novello & Co., Ltd., London

Sleep, sleep, sleep, sleep! All na-ture now is sleep-ing

Whether I Live
By permission Novello & Co., Ltd., London

Whether I live, or whether I die, what-ev-er the worlds I see

Why So Pale and Wan
By permission Novello & Co., Ltd., London

Why so pale and wan, fond lov-er? Prythee, why so pale?

PEARSALL, R. L. (1795-1856)

In dulci jubilo

In dul-ci ju-bi-lo _____ Let us our hom-age

PEPUSCH, Johann Cristoph (1667-1752)

The Beggar's Opera (adapted by Gay; revised by Austin)

Act I

No. 2 (Air: An old woman clothed in gray)
Thro' all the employments of life Each neighbour a-bu-ses his brother,

No. 3 (Air: The Bonny Gray-eyed Morn)
'Tis wo-man that se-du-ces all man-kind, By her we first were taught

No. 4 (Air: Cold and Raw)
If an-y wench Ve-nus' gir-dle wear, Though she be ne-ver so ug-ly

No. 5 (Air: Why is your faithful slave disdained)
If love the vir-gin's heart in - - - - - - vade,

No. 6 (Air: Of all the simple things we do)
A maid is like the gol-den ore, which hath guineas in-trin-si-cal in it

No. 8 (Air: Oh London is a fine town)
Our Pol-ly is a sad slut! Nor heeds what we have taught her

No. 9 (Air: Grim King of the Ghosts)
Can Love be con-trolled by ad-vice? Will Cu-pid our mo-thers o-bey

No. 10 (Air: O Jenny, where hast thou been?)
O Pol-ly, you might have toy'd and kiss'd. By keeping men off you keep them on

No. 11 (Air: Thomas, I cannot)
I, like a ship in storms was toss'd, yet a-fraid to put in-to land

No. 12 (Air: A soldier and a sailor)
A fox may steal your hens, sir, A wench your heath and pence, sir,

No. 13 (Air: Now ponder well, ye parents dear)
O pon-der well! be not se-vere; so save a wretch-ed wife

No. 14 (Air: Pretty Parrot say)
Pretty Pol-ly, say, when I was a-way, Did your fancy never stray

No. 15 (Air: Pray, fair one be kind)
My heart was so free, It roved like the bee, till Polly my passion re-quited,

No. 16 (Air: Over the hills and far away)
Were I laid on Greenland's coast and in my arms, em-braced my lass;

No. 17 (Air: Gin thou wert my ain thing)
Oh! what pain it is to part! Can I leave thee, Can I leave thee?

Act II

No. 18 (Air: Fill every glass)
Fill ev'ry glass for wine in-spires us and fires us with courage, love and joy

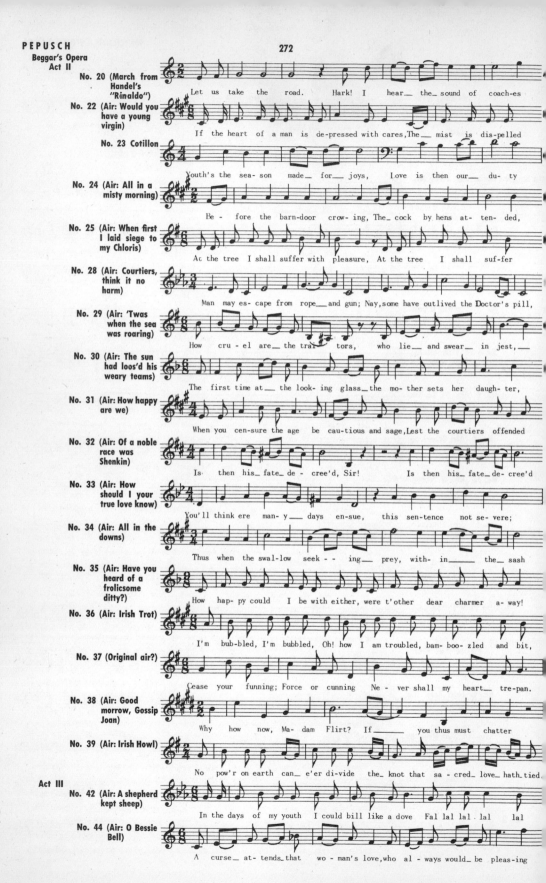

Beggar's Opera Act III

No. 45 (Air: Come, sweet lass)
Come, sweet lass, Let's ba-nish sor-row till to-mor-row, Come, sweet lass,

No. 46 (Air: The last time I went o'er the moon)
Hi-ther, dear hus-band, turn your eyes, Be-stow one glance to cheer me.

No. 47 (Air: Tom Tinker's my true love)
Which way shall I turn me how can I de-cide

No. 48 (Air: Bonny Dundee)
The charge is pre-pared; the lawyers are met,— the judges all ranged

No. 50 (Air: Happy Groves)
O cru-el, cru-el, cru-el case! Must I suf-fer this dis-grace?

(Air: Of all the girls)
Of all the friends in time of grief, when threat'ning death looks grimmer

(Air: Did you ever hear of a gallant sailor)
But can I leave my pret-ty hussies, without one tear, or ten-der sigh?

(Air: Why are mine eyes still flowing)
Their eyes, their lips, their bus— — — — — — ses

No. 51 (Air: All you that must take a leap)
Would I might be hang'd! And I would so too! To be hang'd with you

No. 52 (Air: Lumps of pudding)
Thus I stand like the Turk, with his do-xies a-round

PEREZ FREIRE, Osman

Ay, ay, ay

Copyright by E. G. Marks Music Corp., N. Y.

A só-ma te a la ven-ta-na Ay, Ay Ay pa-lo-ma del al-ma mi-a

PERGOLESI, Giovanni (1710-1736)

Ogni pena più spietata
O-gni pe-na più spie-ta-ta,— più spie-ta-ta

Se tu m'ami
Se tu m'a-mi,— se tu so-spi-ri sol per me,—

La Serva Padrona (opera) 1.
A-spet-ta-re e non ve-ni-re, sta-re a let-to e non dor-mi-re

2.
Sem-pre in con-tra-sti con te si sta con te si sta,

3.
Stiz-zo-so mio stiz-zo-so voi fa-te il bo-ri-o-so

4.
Lo co-no-sco, lo co-no-sco a que-gli och-chietti a que-gli oc-chietti

La Serva Padrona (opera)

Stabat Mater

5. A Ser-pi-na pen-se- re--te, pen-se-re-te

B Ei, mi _____ par _____ che già _____ pian pia-no

6. Son im-bro-glia- to io già, son im-bro- glia- to io già,

7. Per te ho_ io nel co-re il mar-tel-lin d'a-mo-re che mi per-cuote ognor

8. Con-ten-to tu_ sa-ra-i, sa-ra-i a- vra-i a_mor per me

1. A1 Sta-bat ma- ter do- lo- ro-------------sa

2. A2 Sta--bat ma---ter do---lo-ro----------sa

2. Cu-jus a-ni-mam ge- men-tem Con-trist-an-tem et do-len-tem

3. O quam tris-tis et af- flict-a, et af-flict-a,

4. Quae mae---re-bat___ et do---le-bat___ et do----le-bat

5. Quis est ho-mo qui non fle-ret, Christ-i ma-trem si vi-de-ret

6. Vi------dit___ su--um dul----cem__ na--tum

7. E- ia___ ma--ter, fons___ a--mo-ris, fons___ a-mo--ris

8. Fac ut ar-de-at cor me-um In a--man-do Christ-um De-um,

9. Sanct-a ma-ter, is------tud a-gas,__ is-tud__ a-gas

10. Fac ut__ por-tem Christ--i__ mor-tem Christ-i mortem,

11. In-flam-ma-tus__ et ac-cen-sus Per te,__ Vir-go--sim de-fen-sus

12. Quan- do cor-pus mo-ri-e-tur, Fac ut an-i-mae do-ne-tur

13. A- men, A---------men, A---------------men

PERI, Jacopo (1561-1633)

Euridice (opera)

Gio- i-te al can-to mio sel- ve fron-do- se; gio- i-te a-ma-ti col-li

Nel pu-ro ar-dor del__ la più bel- la stel-la Au- rea fa- cel-la

PESSARD, Emile (1843-1917)

L'Adieu du Matin
Copyright 1901, G. Schirmer, Inc.

Le ma-tin, dès que je te quit- te, Son-geant aux longs en- nuis

Requiem du Coeur
Copyright by A. Leduc Music Publishers, Paris

Mon coeur est mort! De- dans la biè- re ce__ ma- tin

PESTALOZZA, Alberto (1851-1934)

Ciribiribin

I am wait- ing here for you,_ love,_ as the eve- ning bree-zes blow

Ci- ri- bi- ri- bin, more love than mine for thee

PFITZNER, Hans (1869-   )

der Himmel darum im Lenz so blau? Op. 2, No. 2
By permission Boosey & Hawkes, Inc., copyright owners

Ist der Him- mel da- rum im Lenz so blau, weil er ü- ber die blu- mi-ge

Der Einsame, Op. 9, No. 2
By permission Boosey & Hawkes, Inc., copyright owners

Wär's dun-kel, ich läg im Wal- - de   Im Wal-de rauscht's

Gretel, Op. 11, No. 5
By permission Boosey & Hawkes, Inc., copyright owners

Vor der Tür im Son- nen-schei- ne wo das Kätz- chen sonst_ liegt_

Nachts, Op. 26, No. 2
By permission Boosey & Hawkes, Inc., copyright owners

Ich ste- he in Wal- des- schatten wie_ an des Le- bens Rand,

PIERNÉ, Gabriel (1863-1937)

L'Adieu Suprême

Lais- se- moi ché-rir ton fan- tô- me,_ Mais ne re- viens pas

Complainte des Arches de Noé
permission J. Hamelle Music Publishers,

Dans la fo- rêt les me- nui- siers; taillez les ar- ches

En Barque

Restons en- cor, Mi- gnon- ne! Ma barque est douce et bon- ne;

étaient trois petits chats blancs

Ils é- taient trois pe-tits chats blancs Tou- jours pom- pon- nés

Les Marionettes
By permission Heugel & Cie, Paris, copyright owners

Les ma-ri-on-net-tes de bois ont des ro-bes de pa-pier

Le Moulin
Copyright by Boston Music Co.

Tour-ne, tour-ne, tour-ne, mon mou-lin

Le Petit Rentier
By permission J. Hamelle Music Publishers, Paris

Il s'en est al-lé par la rou-te le pauvre homme

Serenade

Au sein des nuits tout dort L'é-toi-le brille en-cor

PIETRI, Giuseppi (1886-)

Maristella (opera)

Act I

Io co-no-sco un giar-di-no a tut-ti sco-no-sciu-to

Act II

U-no stra-no sen-so ar-ca-no pren-de il cuor!

Qui di-nan-zi all'al-ta-re giu-ro che quest' ac-cu-sa è u-na men-zogna!

PILKINGTON, Francis (d. 1638)

Care for thy Soul

Care for thy soul, care for thy soul care for thy soul

Diaphenia

Di-a-phe-ni-a like the daff-down-dil-ly, white as the sun,

Down a down

Down a down, down a down, thus Phyllis sung, By fan-cy ones op-press-ed;

Rest, sweet nymphs

Rest, sweet nymphs, let gol-den sleep Charm your star-bright-er eyes

Underneath a cypress shade

Un-der-neath a cy-press shade the Queen of love sat mourn-ing

PINSUTI, Ciro (1829-1888)

The Arrow and the Song

I shot an ar-row in-to the air, It fell to earth

Bedouin Love Song A

From the des-ert I come to thee on my A--rab shod with fire

B

Till the sun grows cold and the stars grow old

I fear no foe

I fear no foe in shin-ing ar-mour, Tho' his lance be swift

PISADOR, Diego (c. 1508-1557)

A las armas moriscote

A las ar-mas mo-ris-co- te Si las has en vo-lun- tad

PIZZETTI, Ildebrando (1880-   )

I Pastori

Set-tem - - bre, an-dia - - mo. È tem-po di mi-gra- re

O ra in ter-ra d'A- bruz-zi i miei pa- sto- ri

La madre al figlio lontano

O fi- glio, fi- glio___ in che mon-do ti tro- vi?

POLDOWSKI, (Lady Dean Paul) (1880-1932)

Columbine

permission J. & W. Chester, Ltd., London,
wright owners

Le- an-dre le sot Pier- rot qui d'un saut de pu- ce

Dansons la gigue

permission J. & W. Chester, Ltd., London,
wright owners

Dan- sons la gi- gue! j'ai-mais sur- tout ses jo-lis yeux

L'Heure Exquise

permission J. & W. Chester, Ltd., London,
wright owners

La lu- ne blan- che Luit dans les bois; de cha-que bran-che

Mandoline

permission J. & W. Chester, Ltd., London,
wright owners

Les don-neurs de sé-ré- na-des Et les bel-les é- cou- teu- ses

PONCE, M. M. (1886-   )

Estrellita

Es- tre-lli- ta del le-ja- no cie-lo Que mi- ras mi do-lor

PONCHIELLI, Amilcare (1834-1886)

La Gioconda (opera)

Act I

Fes- te! Pa- ne! fes- te! fes - - ste e pa- ne! fes-te e pa- ne!

Trio

Fi- glia che reg- gi il tre-mu- lo piè che all'a-vel — già pie- ga

Vo- ce di don-na o d'an-ge- lo le mi-e ca-te- ne ha sciol- to;

A te que- sto ro- sa- rio che le pre-ghiere a- du- na,

O gri- do di que- st'a-ni- ma___ scoppia dal gon-fio co- re

La Gioconda (opera)

Act I — O mo-nu-men----to! re-gia e bol-gia do-ga-le!

O cuor! do-no fu-ne--sto! re-tag-gio di do-lo--re.

Act II — Ho! he! ho! he! Fis-sa il ti-mo--ne! Ho! he! ho! he! Fis sa

Siam nel fon-do più pro-fon-do del-la na-ve del-la ca-la,

Pes-ca-tor af-fon-da l'es-ca, a te l'on-da sia fe-del,

Cie-lo e mar! l'e-te-res vel-lo splen-de co-me un santo altar

Duet — Deh! non tur-ba-re con ree pa-u-ra di que-sti i-stan-ti

Lag-giù nel-le neb-bie re-mo--te, lag-giù

Stel-la del ma-ri-nar! Ver-gi-ne San-ta, tu mi di-fen-di

L'a-mo co--me il ful-gor del cre-a-to, co-me l'au--ra che av-vi-va

Act III — Là tur-bi-ni e far-ne-ti-chi, la ga-ja ba-ra-on-da

Là del pa-tri---zio ve------ne-to

Già ti veg-go im-mo-ta e smor--ta

Duet — Bel-la co-sì ma-don-na, io non v'ho mai ve-du-ta

È trop-po, è trop-po or-ri-bi-le! a-ver di-nan-zi,

La ga--ia can-zo---ne, fa l'e--co lan-guir

Act IV — Sui-ci-dio! In que-sti fie-ri mo-men-ti

La Gioconda (opera)   Act IV

Eb brez- za!_ de- li- rio! So- gna- ta_ mia gio- ia!   A

accogli e calma, from Il Figliol Prodigo (opera)   Act III

Rac-cog- lie cal-ma sot- to al- la pi- a a la dol- cis- si- ma   B

POULENC, Francis (1899-)

Chantés

No. 1 Air Romantique
Copyright by Salabert, Paris, N. Y.

J'al- lais dans la cam- pagne a- vec le_ vent d'o- ra- ge   D

No. 2 Air Champêtre

Bel- le sour- ce bel- le sour-ce, je veux me rap- pe-ler sans ces-se   E

No. 3 Air Grave

Ah! fuy-ez à pré- sent, ma-lheu-reu-ses pen- sées! O co-lère, o! re-mords!   F

No. 4 Air Vif

Le tré- sor_ du ver- ger, et le jar- din en fête,   G

A sa guitarre
By permission Durand & Cie, Paris;
Elkan-Vogel Co., Inc., Phila.,
copyright owners

Ma gui- ta- re, je te chan-te, Par qui seu- le je dé- çois   H

alités

No. 1 Chanson d'Orkenise
By permission Associated Music
Publishers, Inc.

Par les por- tes d'Or- ke- ni- se veut en-trer un char- re- tier_   I

No. 2 Hotel

Ma chambre a la for- me d'u- ne ca- ge   J

No. 3 Fagnes de Wallonie

Tant_ de tris-tes- - ses plé- - ni- è- res   K

No. 4 Voyage à Paris

Ah!_ la char-man- te cho- se Quit- ter un pa- ys   L

No. 5 Sanglots

Notre a-mour est rè- glé par les cal-mes é- toi- les   M

Le Bestiaire
No. 1 Le Dromadaire
Copyright by Ed. de la Sirene, Paris

A- vec ses qua- tre dro- ma- daires_ Don Pe- dro d'Al- fa- rou- bei- ra   N

No. 2 Le Chèvre du Thibet

Les poils de cet- te chè- vre et mê- - me Ceux d'or   O

No. 3 La Sauterelle

Voi- ci la fi- ne sau-te-rel- le La nour- ri- ture_ de Saint Jean   P

No. 4 Le Dauphin

Dau- phins, vous jouez dans le mer Mais le flot est tou- jours a- mer   Q

No. 5 L'Écrevisse

In- cer-ti- tude, O! mes_ de- - lices Vous et moi nous nous en al- lons   R

No. 6 Le Carpe

Dans vos vi-viers dans vos e- tangs Car- pes que vous vi- vez long-temps!   S

Bleuet

By permission Durand & Cie, Paris;
Elkan-Vogel Co., Inc., Phila.,
copyright owners

Jeune hom-me de vingt ans__ qui as vu des choses si af-freu-ses__

C

Copyright by Salabert, Paris, N. Y.

J'ai tra-ver-sé les ponts de C C'est là que tout a com-men-cé

Chansons Gaillardes
By permission Heugel & Cie, Paris,
copyright owners
La belle jeunesse

Il faut s'ai-mer tou-jours, et ne s'é-pou-ser guè-re

Invocation aux parques

Il jure tant que je vi-vrai de vous ai-mer, Syl-vi-e

Chanson à boire

Les Rois d'E-gyp-te et de Sy-ri-e, vou-laient qu'on em-bau-mât

Chansons Villageoises
I Chansons du clair tamis
By permission Associated Music
Publishers, Inc.

Où le be-deau a pas-se Dans les pa-pa-ve-ra-cé-es

II Les gars qui vont à la fête

Les gars qui vont à la fête Ont mis la fleur au cha-peau__

III C'est le joli printemps

C'est le jo-li prin-temps qui fait sor-tir les fil-les

IV Le mendiant

Jean Mar-tin prit sa be-sa-ce Vi-ve le pas-sant

V Chanson de la fille frivole

Oh dit la fil-le fri-vo-le Que le vent y vire,

VI Le retour du sergent

Le ser-gent s'en re-vient de guer-re Les pieds gon-flés

Les Chemins de l'Amour
By permission Associated Music
Publishers, Inc.

Che-mins de mon a-mour__ Je vous cherche tou-jours__

Dans le jardin d'Anna
Copyright by Salabert, Paris, N. Y.

Cer-tes, si nous a-vions vé-cu en l'an dix-sept cent soi-xan-te

Fêtes Galantes
Copyright by Salabert, Paris, N. Y.

On voit des mar-quis sur des bi-cy-clet-tes On voit des mar-lous

Fiançailles pour rire
No. 1. La dame d'André
Copyright by Salabert, Paris, N. Y.

An-dré ne con-nait pas la da-me Qu'il prend au-jour-d'hui par la main

No. 2. Dans l'herbe

Je ne peux plus rien di-re Ni rien fai-re pour lui

No. 3. Il vole

En al-lant se cou-cher le soleil__ Se re-flète au vernis de ma ta-ble

No. 4. Mon cadavre est doux comme un gant

Mon ca-davre est doux comme un gant__ Doux comme un gant de peau gla-cé-e

No. 5. Le Violon

Couple a-mou-reux aux ac-cents mé-con-nus__

Poèmes de Ronsard
V À son page

Fais__ ra-frai-chir mon vin de sor-te qu'il passe en froi-deur un gla-çon

Tel Jour, telle Nuit No. 1.
By permission Durand & Cie, Paris;
Elkan-Vogel Co., Inc., Phila.,
copyright owners

Eon__ ne jour né - - - e j'ai re-vu qui je n'ou-blie pas

No. 2.

U-ne rui-ne co-quil-le vi-de pleu-re dans son ta-bli-er____

No. 3.

Le front comme un drapeau per-du__ Je te trâi-ne quand je suis seul__

No. 4.

U-ne rou-lot-te couverte en tui-les Le che-val mort__ un en-fant maître

No. 5.

A tou-tes bri-des toi dont la fan-tô-me

No. 6.

Une her-be pau-vre Sau- va-ge__ Ap-pa-rut dans la nei-ge

No. 7.

Je n'ai en-vie que de t'ai-mer__ Un o-rage em-plit la val-lé__

No. 8.

Fi- gu-re de for-ce brûlante et fa- rou-che Che-veux noirs

No. 9.

Nous a-vons fait la nuit____ je tiens ta main,__ je veil-le

PRAETORIUS, Michael (1571-1621)

Es ist ein Ross entsprungen (D'un arbre séculaire)

D'un ar-bre sé-cu lai-re Du vieux tronc__ d'I- sa- i

Lobet den Herren

Lo-bet den Her-ren, al-le Hei- den, prei-set sei-nen Na-men

PRESSEL, Gustav (1827-1890)

Ich sah den Wald sich färben

Ich sah den Wald sich fär-ben, die Luft war grau und stumm,

PROCH, Heinrich (1809-1878)

Air and Variations, Op. 164

Deh tor-no mio be- ne mio te-ne- ro a-mor

PROKOFIEFF, Serge (1891-   )

Alexander Nevsky, Op. 78
   Part II Song about Alexander
      Nevsky
Copyright 1945, Leeds Music Corp., N. Y.
Used by permission.

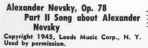

Yes, 'twas on the Riv-er Ne- va it oc- curred

Alexander Nevsky, Op. 78
Part II Song about Alexander Nevsky
Ah! how we did fight, how we rout-ed them

Part IV Arise, ye Russian people
A-rise to arms, ye Rus-sian folk, in bat-tle just, in fight to death

In our Rus-sia great, in our na-tive Rus-sia no foe shall live

Part VI Field of the Dead
I shall go a-cross the snowclad field. I shall fly a-bove the field of death

Snowdrops
Snow-drops grow on yon-der hill, Snow-drops blos-som

Snowflakes
O-ver field and plain come steal - - - - ing

PUCCINI, Giacomo (1858-1924)

La Bohême (opera)
Act I
Copyright by G. Ricordi & Co., Inc.
Nei cie-li bi-gi guar-do fu-mar dai mil-le co-mi-gno-li Pa-ri-gi

Che ge-li-αα ma-ni-na, se la la-sci ri-scal-dar. Cer-car

Ta-lor dal mio for-zie-re ru-ban tut-ti i gio-iel-li

Si Mi chia-ma-no Mi-mi, ma il mio no-me è Lu-ci-a

Mi piac-cion quel-le co-se che han si dol-ce ma-lì-a

Duet
O so-a-ve fan-ciul-la, O dol-ce vi-so

Act II Quartet
Que-sta è Mi-mi, ga-ia fio-ra-ia. Il suo ve-nir com-ple-ta

U-na cuf-fiet-ta a piz-zi, tut-ta ro-sa, ri-ca-ma-ta

Musetta's Waltz
Quan-do me'n vo' quan-do me'n vo so-let-ta per la via

Act III Mimi's Farewell
Don-de lie-ta u-scì al tuo gri-do d'a-mo-re

A-scol-ta, a-scol-ta. Le po-che ro-be a-du-na che la-sciai spar-se

Quartet
Ad-di-o dol-ce sve-glia-re Al-la mat-ti-na

La Bohême (opera)
Act IV

O Mi- mi tu più non tor- ni o gior- ni_ bel- li,

Colline's Song

Vec- chia zi- mar- ra, sen- ti, io re- sto_al pian, tu_a- scen- de- re il

So- no_an- da- ti? fin- ge- vo di dor- mi- re_ per- chè vol- li con te so- la

La Fanciulla del West (The Girl of
the Golden West) (opera) Act I
Copyright by G. Ricordi & Co., Inc.

Min- nie, dal- la mia ca- sa son par- ti- to che è là dai mon- ti

Lag- giù_ nel So- le- dad, e- ro pi- ci- na

Io non son che_u- na po- ve- ra fan- ci- ulla_

Act II

Oh, se sa- pe- ste co- me il vi- ve- re è al- le- gro!

Act III

Ch'el- la mi cre- da li- be- ro_e lon- ta- na, so- vra_u- na nuo- va via

Gianni Schicchi (opera)
Copyright by G. Ricordi & Co., Inc.

Fi- ren- ze_è come un al- be- ro fio- ri- to_ che_in piaz- za dei Si- gnori

Oh, mio bab- bi- no ca- ro, mi pia- ce_è bel- lo, bel- lo;

Mes- ser no- ta- io, pre- sto, Via da Buo- so Do- na- ti!

In_ te- sta la cap- pel- li- na! Al vi- so la pez- zo- li- na!

Madama Butterfly (opera) Act I
Copyright by G. Ricordi & Co., Inc.

Do- vun- que_al mondo lo Yan- kee va- ga- bon- do si go- de_e traf- fi- ca

A- mo- re_o gril- lo,_ dir non sa- pre- i. Cer- to co- ste- i

Spi- ra sul ma- re_e sul- la ter- ra un pri- ma- ve- ril sof- fio gio- con- do_

Io se- guo_il mio de- sti - - no e pie- na d'u- mil- tà

Bim- ba da- gli occhi pie- ni di ma- lì- a o- ra sei tut- ta mi- a

Dam- mi ch'io ba- ci le tue ma- ni ca- re_

Madama Butterfly (opera) Act I
A
Oh quan-ti oc-chi fi-si, at-ten-ti d'o-gni par-te a ri-guar- dar!

Act II Scene 1
B
Un bel dì, ve-dre-mo le-var--si un fil di fu-mo

Flower duet
C
Scuo-ti quel-la fron-da di ci-lie-gio e m'in-non-da di fior

D
Tut-ti i fior? Tut-ti i fior Tut-ti-tut-ti. Pe-sco, vio-la

Humming Chorus
E
Hum throughout

Act II Scene 2
F
Ad- di- o, fio-ri-to a-sil di le-ti-zia e d'a-mor

G
Tu? Tu? pic-co-lo Id-di- o! A-mo-re amo-re mi- o,

H
Lo so che al sue pe-ne non ci so-no con-for-ti

I
Che tua ma- dre do-vrà pren-der-ti in brac-cio

Manon Lescaut (opera)
Copyright by G. Ricordi & Co., Inc.
Act I
J
Tra voi, bel- le, bru-ne e bion- de si na-scon-de gio-vi-net- ta

K
Don- na non vi di ma i si- mi- le a que-sta!

Act II
L
In quel- le tri-ne mor-bi-de nell'al-co- va do-ra- ta

M
L'o- ra, o Tir-si, e va-ga e bel- la, Ri-de il gior-no, ri- de in-tor-no

N
Tu, tu a- mo- re? Tu? Ah mio im-men-so a- mo-re?

O
O ten-ta- tri- ce! O ten-ta- tri- ce!

P
Ah! Ma- non mi tra-di-sce il tuo fol- le pen- sier

Act III
Q
Guar-da- te, paz- zo son, guar-da- te, co- m'io pian-go e im-plo- ro

Act IV
R
Ve- di, ve-di, son io che pian- go io che im- plo- ro

S
So- la, per-du-ta, ab-ban-do- na- ta, per- du- ta,

La Rondine (opera) Act I
Copyright by Sonzogno, Milan

Chi bel so- gno di Do- ret- ta po- tè in-do- vi- nar

A

O- re dol-ci e di- vi- ne di lie-ta ba-ra- on- da

B

Fan-ciul - - la, è sboc-cia- to l'a- mo- re! Di-fen-di, di-fen-di

Senza mamma, from Suor Angelica (opera)
Copyright by G. Ricordi & Co., Inc.

Sen- za mam-ma, o bim- bo, tu sei mor- to Le tue lab- bra

Il Tabarro (opera)
Copyright by G. Ricordi & Co., Inc.

Se tu sa-pes- si gli og-get- ti stra- ni

Hai ben ra- gio- ne; me-glio non pen-sa- re pie-ga-re il ca- po

Tosca (opera) Act I
Copyright by G. Ricordi & Co., Inc.

Re- con-di-ta ar-mo- ni- a di bel-lez- ze di- ver- se!

Non la so-spi- ri la no-stra ca-set- ta

Duet

Qua- l'oc-chio al mon - - - - do può star di pa- ro

Duet

Mia ge- lo-sa! Si, lo sen- to ti tor-men- to sen-za po- sa

Te De- um Glo- ri- a Vi-va il Re! Si fe-steg-gi la vit-to-ria

Act II

Già! Mi di-con ve-nal mi di-con ve-nal,

A

Vis- si d'ar-te, vis-si d'a- mo- re, non fe-ci mai ma- le

B

Sem- pre con fe sin-ce- ra la mia pre-ghie- ra

Cantata A

Sa- le a-scen- de l'u- man can - - - - - - ti- co

B

A te que- st'in- no di glo- ria vo- li a te

Act III

E lucevan le stelle (Not beginning of aria, but most salient phrase.)

Oh! dol-ci ba-ci o lan-gui-di ca- rez- ze, mentr' io fre-men- te

O dol-ci ma- ni man-su- e-te e pu- re, o ma-ni e-le- te

A- ma- ro sol per te m'era il mo- re- re, Da te la vi- ta

Turandot (opera)
Copyright by G. Ricordi & Co., Inc.
Act I
Si-gno-re a-scol - ta! Ah si-gno-re a-scol-ta! Liù non reg-ge più! **A**

Non pian-ge-re, Liù__ Se in un lonta-no gior-no io t'ho sor-ri-so **B**

Trio (Ping, Pang and Pong)
Fer - - mo! che fai T'arre-sta! Chi sei, che fai, **C**

Non v'è in Chi - na per no- stra for- tu - na' **D**

Act II Turandot's Air
In que-sta Reg- gio, or son mil-l'an-ni e mil- le__ **E**

O prin-ci-pi, che a lun-ghe ca-ro-va-ne d'o-gni par-te del mon-do **F**

Trio (Ping, Pang and Pong)
Ad- dio, a- mo-re ad-dio,__ raz- za! Ad dio__ **G**

Act III
Nes-sun dor- ma! nes-sun dor- ma! Tu pu-re, o Prin-ci-pes- sa **H**

Tan-to a- mo - re se- gre - to e in-con-fes- sa-to, **I**

Death of Liu
Tu che di gel sei cin-to da tan-to fiam-ma vin-ta **J**

Le Villi (opera)
Copyright by G. Ricordi & Co., Inc.
Act I
If I were but like you,__ my frail for-get-me nots fair of a-zure hue__ **K**

Act II
O pure and sim- ple soul of her that was my daugh- ter,__ **L**

Back to the vanished years,__ My sor-row-ful thoughts re- turn__ **M**

PURCELL, Henry (c. 1659-1695)

h how sweet it is to love, from Tyrannic Love Act IV
Ah!__ how sweet, Ah!__ how sweet, how sweet it is to love, **O**

lia has a thousand charms, from The Rival Sisters Act II
Ce- lia has a thousand, thousand, thou - - - - - - - - - - - - - - - -sand charms, **P**

m Rosy Bowers, from Don Quixote (opera) Part III Act V
From ro- sy bowers, where sleeps__ the God__ of__ Love **Q**

Or if more in- flu- en- cing, Is__ to be brisk__ and ai- ry, **R**

nce with your trifling deity, from Timon of Athens (masque) No. 5
Hence! Hence! Hence with your trif-ling dei- ty A great - - - - - er, **S**

Music for a while, from Oedipus

Nymphs and Shepherds, from The Libertine (opera)

Retir'd from any mortal's sight, from King Richard II Act IV

Dido and Aeneas (opera) Act I

Act II

Act III

Dido and Aeneas (opera) Act III

When I am laid, am laid in earth.

With droop - - - - - ing wings, ye Cu - - pids, come

Dioclesian (opera)

What shall I do to show how much I love her?

Let us dance, let us sing, let us sing

The Fairy Queen (opera) Act III

When I have of- ten heard young maids com- plain- ing

Act IV

Next, win- ter comes slow- ly, pale, mea- ger and old,

Act V

Hark! Hark! the ech'-ing air a tri - - - - - - - umph sings

The Indian Queen (opera)

I at- tempt from Love's sick-ness to fly - - - - - in vain

Act III

Ye twice ten hun- dred de- i- ties, to whom, to whom

By the croak- ing of the toad, In their caves that make a- bode

We the spir-its of the air That of hu- man things take care,

King Arthur (opera) Act II

How blest are shep- herds, how hap- py their lass- es,

Shep-herd, shep-herd, leave de- cry-ing: Pipes are sweet on sum-mer's day

Act V

Fair-est Isle all Isles ex- cell-ing, Seat of plea- sures and of loves.

The Tempest (opera) Act II

A- rise, a-rise, ye sub - - - - - - - - - - - ter-ranean

Act III

Come un- to these yel - - - - - - - - low sands and there take hands

Full fa-thom five thy fa- ther lies; Of his bones are co - - - - rals made

Dry those eyes which are o'er- flow - - - - ing

Kind fortune smiles and she has yet in store for thee

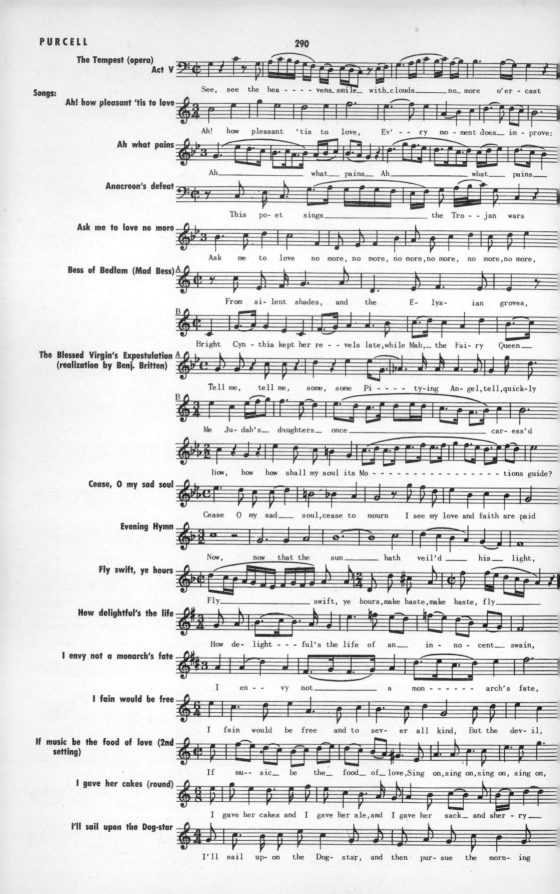

PURCELL

290

The Tempest (opera)
Act V

See, see the hea - - - - vens smile with clouds no more o'er-cast

Songs:

Ah! how pleasant 'tis to love

Ah! how pleasant 'tis to love, Ev' - ry mo-ment does im-prove:

Ah what pains

Ah what pains Ah what pains

Anacreon's defeat

This po-et sings the Tro - - jan wars

Ask me to love no more

Ask me to love no more, no more, no more, no more, no more, no more,

Bess of Bedlam (Mad Bess) A

From si-lent shades, and the E-lys-ian groves,

B

Bright Cyn-thia kept her re - - vels late, while Mab, the Fai-ry Queen

The Blessed Virgin's Expostulation A
(realization by Benj. Britten)

Tell me, tell me, some, some Pi - - - - ty-ing An-gel, tell, quick-ly

B

Me Ju-dah's daughters once car-ess'd

Iiow, how how shall my soul its Mo - - - - - - - - - - - - - - tions guide?

Cease, O my sad soul

Cease O my sad soul, cease to mourn I see my love and faith are paid

Evening Hymn

Now, now that the sun hath veil'd his light,

Fly swift, ye hours

Fly swift, ye hours, make haste, make haste, fly

How delightful's the life

How de-light - - - ful's the life of an in - no-cent swain,

I envy not a monarch's fate

I en-vy not a mon - - - - - arch's fate,

I fain would be free

I fain would be free and to sev-er all kind, But the dev-il,

If music be the food of love (2nd setting)

If mu-sic be the food of love, Sing on, sing on, sing on, sing on,

I gave her cakes (round)

I gave her cakes and I gave her ale, and I gave her sack and sher-ry

I'll sail upon the Dog-star

I'll sail up-on the Dog-star, and then pur-sue the morn-ing

Ode on St. Cecelia's Day
No. 8.
Won-drous, won-drous, won-drous won - - - drous ma - - chine,—

No. 9.
The ai - - - ry, ai - - - - - ry vi-o-lin and lof - - - ty Vi ol

No. 11.
The fife, the fife and all,all,all,all,all the har - - - - - - - - -mo ny

An Ode to Cynthia walking on Richmond Hill
On the brow_ of Rich - mond_ Hill,Which Europe scarce can par-al-lel,

Ode to Queen Mary 167 (Come ye Sons of Art)
Sound _____ the trum-pet, Sound the trum-pet

Phillis, I can ne'er forgive it
Phil-lis, I can ne'er for-give it, Nor, I think,shall e'er out-live it,

The Queen's Epicedium
A
In - cas - sum, in-cas - - - - - - - - - sum,— Les - bia,

B
En - - - - - - nym - - - phas en pas-to - - - - res!

Rejoice in the Lord alway (anthem)
Re-joice in the Lord al-ways and a- gain I say re- joice

Silvia, now your scorn give over
Sil- via, now_ your scorn.give o- ver,_ Lest you_ lose a_ faithful lov-er_

Solitude
O sol- i- tude my sweet - - - - - - - - - est choice!

The Storm
Fare- well, ye rocks,ye seas and sands,Green Nep-tune_ I _____ des-pise

Stript of their green our groves appear
Stript_ of their green our_ groves_ ap- pear, Our vales_ lie_ bur-ied_

Sweet, be no longer sad
Sweet, be no lon-ger sad, Pri-thee be wise, Recall that quick-ness

Sweet tyranness
Sweet ty- ran- ness, I now re-sign my heart,for ev-er-more 'tis thine

To thee and a lass (round)
To thee, to thee,and to a lass, that kind- ly will_ fill_ up

Turn, turn then thine eyes
Turn,_ turn_ then_ thine eyes, Turn,_ turn_ then_thine eyes,turn,_ turn,_ turn

When I a lover pale do see
When I a lo- ver pale do see Rea- dy to faint and sick-ish be,

When the cock begins to crow
When the cock be- gins to crow, the cock be- gins to crow

The Yorkshire Feast Song No. 6 — A

The pale and the pur-ple Rose that af---ter-cost so ma---ny blows,

PURCELL-COCKRANE, E. (Edward C. Purcell) (Contemporary)

Passing By — C
Copyright 1932, G. Schirmer, Inc.

There is a la-dy sweet and kind, Was nev-er face so pleas'd my mind

QUILTER, Roger (1877-)

Love's Philosophy, Op. 3, No. 1 — E
By permission Boosey & Hawkes, Inc., copyright owners

The fountains min-gle with the riv-er And the riv--ers with the o-cean;

Come away, death, Op. 6, No. 1 — F
By permission Boosey & Hawkes, Inc., copyright owners

Come a-way, come a-way death, And in sad cy-press

O mistress mine, No. 2 — G

O mis-tress mine, where are you roam-ing? O___ stay and hear

low, blow, thou winter wind, No. 3 — H

Blow, blow, thou win-ter wind, Thou art not so un-kind

To Daisies, Op. 8, No. 3 — I
By permission Boosey & Hawkes, Inc., copyright owners

Shut not so soon: The dull-eyed night has not as yet be-gun

Weep you no more, Op. 12, No. 1 — J
By permission Boosey & Hawkes, Inc., copyright owners

Weep you no more, sad foun-tains; What need you flow so fast?

Fair House of Joy, No. 7 — K

Fain would I change that note to which fond Love hath charm'd me.

Autumn Evening, Op. 14, No. 1 — L
By permission Boosey & Hawkes, Inc., copyright owners

The yel-low pop-lar leaves have strown Thy qui-et mound

Song of the Blackbird, No. 4 — M

The Night-in-gale__ has a lyre of gold, The Lark's is a cla-rion call

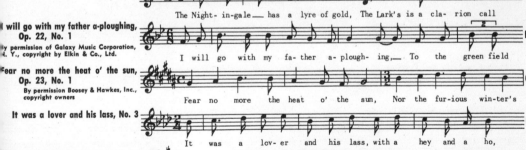

will go with my father a-ploughing, Op. 22, No. 1 — N
by permission of Galaxy Music Corporation, N. Y., copyright by Elkin & Co., Ltd.

I will go with my fa-ther a-plough-ing,__ To the green field

Fear no more the heat o' the sun, Op. 23, No. 1 — O
By permission Boosey & Hawkes, Inc., copyright owners

Fear no more the heat o' the sun, Nor the fur-ious win-ter's

It was a lover and his lass, No. 3 — P

It was a lov-er and his lass, with a hey and a ho,

Take, O take those lips away, No. 4 — Q

Take, O take those lips a-way, That so sweet-ly were for-sworn;

Hey, ho, the Wind and the Rain, No. 5 — R

When that I was and a lit-tle ti-ny boy, With hey, ho,

Go, Lovely Rose, Op. 24, No. 3 —

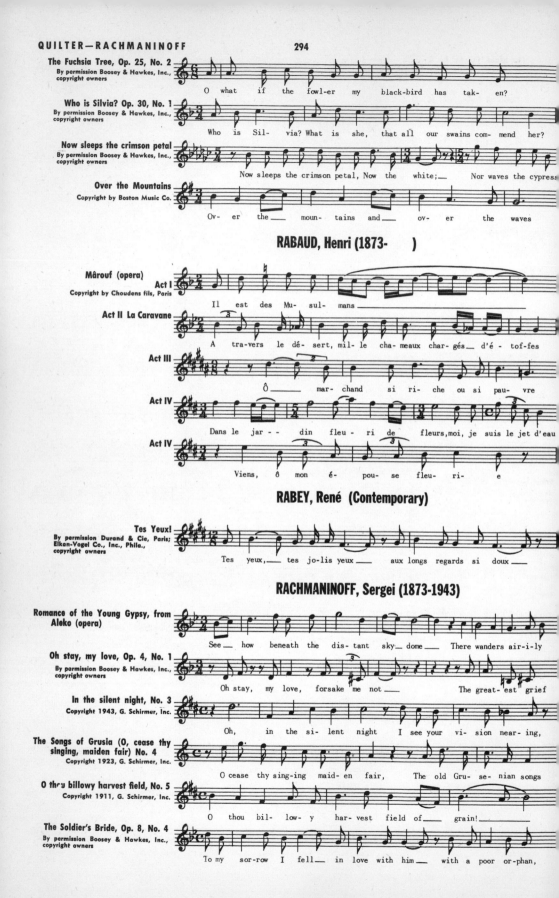

The Fuchsia Tree, Op. 25, No. 2
By permission Boosey & Hawkes, Inc., copyright owners

O what if the fowl-er my black-bird has tak-en?

Who is Silvia? Op. 30, No. 1
By permission Boosey & Hawkes, Inc., copyright owners

Who is Sil- via? What is she, that all our swains com- mend her?

Now sleeps the crimson petal
By permission Boosey & Hawkes, Inc., copyright owners

Now sleeps the crimson petal, Now the white;— Nor waves the cypress

Over the Mountains
Copyright by Boston Music Co.

Ov- er the— moun- tains and— ov- er the waves

RABAUD, Henri (1873-   )

Mârouf (opera)
Act I
Copyright by Choudens fils, Paris

Il est des Mu- sul- mans

Act II La Caravane

A tra- vers le dé- sert, mil- le cha- meaux char- gés— d'é- tof- fes

Act III

Ô— mar- chand si ri- che ou si pau- vre

Act IV

Dans le jar- - din fleu- ri de fleurs, moi, je suis le jet d'eau

Act IV

Viens, ô mon é- pou- se fleu- ri- e

RABEY, René (Contemporary)

Tes Yeux!
By permission Durand & Cie, Paris; Elkan-Vogel Co., Inc., Phila., copyright owners

Tes yeux,— tes jo-lis yeux— aux longs regards si doux

RACHMANINOFF, Sergei (1873-1943)

Romance of the Young Gypsy, from Aleko (opera)

See— how beneath the dis- tant sky— dome— There wanders air-i-ly

Oh stay, my love, Op. 4, No. 1
By permission Boosey & Hawkes, Inc., copyright owners

Oh stay, my love, forsake me not— The great- est grief

In the silent night, No. 3
Copyright 1943, G. Schirmer, Inc.

Oh, in the si- lent night I see your vi- sion near- ing,

The Songs of Grusia (O, cease thy singing, maiden fair) No. 4
Copyright 1923, G. Schirmer, Inc.

O cease thy sing-ing maid- en fair, The old Gru- se- nian songs

O thou billowy harvest field, No. 5
Copyright 1911, G. Schirmer, Inc.

O thou bil- low- y har- vest field of— grain!

The Soldier's Bride, Op. 8, No. 4
By permission Boosey & Hawkes, Inc., copyright owners

To my sor- row I fell— in love with him— with a poor or- phan,

The Island, Op. 14, No. 2
Copyright 1936, G. Schirmer, Inc.
Far out at sea an is-land lies   with gentle slopes and flow'ring masses,

Floods of Spring, No. 11
By permission Boosey & Hawkes, Inc.,
copyright owners
While yet the fields are wrapp'd in snow   The waters hear the call of spring

Fate, Op. 21, No. 1
With pil-grim's staff with wear— y gait,   With gloom— y brows

The Answer, No. 4
They won-der'd a   while: Shall our   ves- sel so   light___

Lilacs, No. 5
Copyright 1910, G. Schirmer, Inc.
Morn-ing   skies   are a- glow   where the li- lac trees blow,

How sweet the place, No. 7
How sweet the place!   Far dis - - tant gleams the riv-er in the   sun;

Sorrow in Spring, No. 12
How__ my heart aches!   yet fain would I live   now that   spring__

Christ is risen, Op. 26, No. 6
By permission Galaxy Music
Corporation, N. Y.
The Christ is ris'n__   The choirs are singing   My soul is   sad,

To the Children, No. 7
By permission Boosey & Hawkes, Inc.,
copyright owners
How oft-en   at midnight in days long since fled, Dear children

Before my window, No. 10
By permission Boosey & Hawkes, Inc.,
copyright owners
Be-fore my win- dow   stands a flow'ring cher- ry   tree,__

When yesterday we met, No. 13
By permission Boosey & Hawkes, Inc.,
copyright owners
When yes- ter- day   we   met,   her words and glances   fal-ter'd;

All things depart, No. 15
By permission Boosey & Hawkes, Inc.,
copyright owners
All things de-part— no single thing return- eth. Life hur-ries on,__

Vocalise, Op. 34, No. 14 (wordless song)
By permission Boosey & Hawkes, Inc.,
copyright owners

Daisies, Op. 38, No. 3
By permission Boosey & Hawkes, Inc.,
copyright owners
Behold, my friend, the dai - - sies sweet and ten-der   Wher-e'er I go,

Dreams, No. 5
Say,   oh   whi- ther   art bound,   rare en- chant-ment of dreams,

RADECKE, Robert (1829-1893)

Aus der Jugendzeit
Aus der Ju- gend- zeit, aus der Ju- gend- zeit klingt__ ein Lied

RAFF, Joseph Joachim (1822-1882)

Sei still
Ach, was ist Le- ben doch so schwer, wenn was du lieb__ hast

RAMEAU, Jean Philippe (1683-1764)

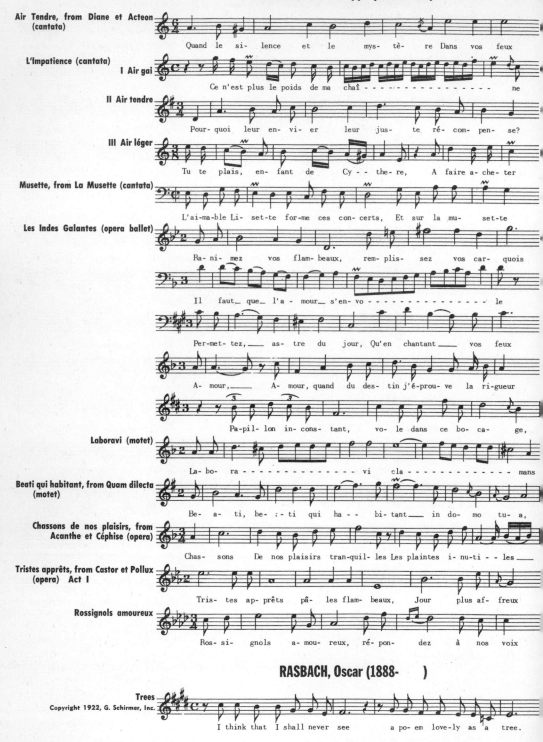

Air Tendre, from Diane et Acteon (cantata)

Quand le si- lence et le mys- tè- re Dans vos feux

L'Impatience (cantata)

I Air gai

Ce n'est plus le poids de ma chaî- - - - - - - - ne

II Air tendre

Pour- quoi leur en- vi- er leur jus- te ré- com- pen- se?

III Air léger

Tu te plais, en- fant de Cy- the- re, A faire a- che- ter

Musette, from La Musette (cantata)

L'ai- ma- ble Li- set- te for- me ces con- certs, Et sur la mu- set- te

Les Indes Galantes (opera ballet)

Ra- ni- mez vos flam- beaux, rem- plis- sez vos car- quois

Il faut_ que_ l'a- mour_ s'en- vo- - - - - - - - - le

Per- met- tez, as- tre du jour, Qu'en chantant_ vos feux

A- mour,_ A- mour, quand du des- tin j'é- prou- ve la ri- gueur

Pa- pil- lon in- cons- tant, vo- le dans ce bo- ca- ge,

Laboravi (motet)

La- bo- ra- - - - - - - - vi cla- - - - - - - - mans

Beati qui habitant, from Quam dilecta (motet)

Be- a- ti, be- a- ti qui ha- bi- tant_ in do- mo tu- a,

Chassons de nos plaisirs, from Acanthe et Céphise (opera)

Chas- sons De nos plaisirs tran- quil- les Les plaintes i- nu- ti- les

Tristes apprêts, from Castor et Pollux (opera) Act I

Tris- tes ap- prêts pâ- les flam- beaux, Jour plus af- freux

Rossignols amoureux

Ros- si- gnols a- mou- reux, ré- pon- dez à nos voix

RASBACH, Oscar (1888-   )

Trees

Copyright 1922, G. Schirmer, Inc.

I think that I shall never see a po- em love- ly as a tree.

RASI, Francesco (c. 1580-c. 1650)

Dove, misero, mai

Do- ve mi- se- ro ma- i   Spe- rar deg-gio con- for- to

Filli mia

Fil- li mi- a,   Fil- li, Fil- li____ mia dol- ce,

Filli, tu vuoi partire

Fil- li   tu vuoi par- ti- re E non vuoi__ch'io so- spi- ri

Occhi sempre sereni

Oc- chi sem- pre se- re- ni Per cui vi- vo con- ten- to,

RAVEL, Maurice (1875-1937)

Cinq melodies populaires grecques
I Chanson de la mariée
By permission Durand & Cie, Paris; Elkan-Vogel Co., Inc., Phila., copyright owners

Bé- veil-le- toi, Ré- veil-le- toi, per- drix mi- gnon- ne, Ah!

II

Là- bas, vers l'é- gli- se   Vers l'é-glise Ay- io Si- dé- ro

III

Quel ga - - - - - lant, ga- lant m'est com- pa- ra - - - ble,

IV Chanson des cueilleuses de lentisques

O - - - -   joie de mon â - - - - - - - - - - - - me,

V

Tout__ gai! gai, Ha, tout__ gai, tout gai, Ha, tout gai!

Deux Épigrammes de Clement Marot
1. D'Anne jouant de l'espinette
By permission Associated Music Publishers, Inc.

Lor-sque je voy en __ or-dre la bru-net-te Jeu - - ne en bon point,

2. D'Anne qui me jecta de la neige

An- ne par jeu me jec- ta de la nei- ge

Deux Mélodies Hebraïques
I Kaddisch
By permission Durand & Cie, Paris; Elkan-Vogel Co., Inc., Phila., copyright owners

Yith-gad- al - - - - - - weyith__ kad-dash

Yith- ba - - ra'kh.__   Wey- isch- ta - - ba'h

II l'Énigme éternelle

Frägt die Velt die al- te Ca-sche Tra la tra la la la la la__

Les grands vents venus d'outremer
By permission Durand & Cie, Paris; Elkan-Vogel Co., Inc., Phila., copyright owners

Les grands vents venus d'ou-tre- mer Pas- sent par la ville, l'hi-ver

Histoires Naturelles I Le Paon
By permission Durand & Cie, Paris; Elkan-Vogel Co., Inc., Phila., copyright owners

Il va   sûre - - ment se ma- ri- er   au- jour- d'hui.

Histoires Naturelles II Le Grillon

C'est l'heure où las d'er-rer, l'in-sec-te nè-gre re-vient

III Le Cygne

Il glis-se sur le bas-sin, comme un trai-neau blanc,

IV Le Martin-Pecheur

Ça n'a pas mor-du, ce soir mais je rap-porte une rare é-mo-tion.

V La Pintade

C'est la bossue de ma cour. Elle ne rêve que plaies à cause de sa bosse.

Manteau de fleurs
By permission J. Hamelle Music Publishers, Paris

Tou-tes les fleurs de mon jar-din sont ro-ses

Le Noël des Jouets
Copyright by Salabert, Paris, N. Y.

Le troupeau ver-ni des mou-tons Roule en tu-mul-te

Pièce en forme de Habanera (vocalise) A

B

Quatre Chants Populaires
I Chanson espagnole
By permission Durand & Cie, Paris; Elkan-Vogel, Inc., Phila., copyright owners

A-dieu, va, mon homme, a-dieu, Puisqu'ils t'ont pris pour la guer-re

II Chanson française

Jean-ne-ton où i-rons-nous gar-der,

III Chanson italienne

Pen-chée à ma fe-nê-tre, j'é-cou-te l'on-de

IV Chanson Hebraïque

Me-jer-ke, main Suhn, Me-jer-ke, main Suhn, o Mejer-ke, main Suhn

Rêves
By permission Durand & Cie, Paris; Elkan-Vogel Co., Inc., Phila., copyright owners

Un en-fant court au-tour des mar-bres U-ne voix sourd

Ronsard à son âme
By permission Durand & Cie, Paris; Elkan-Vogel, Inc., Phila., copyright owners

A-me-let-te Ron-sar-de-let-te, Mig-non-ne-let-te,

Shéhérazade
I Asie
By permission Durand & Cie, Paris; Elkan-Vogel Co., Inc., Phila., copyright owners

A1

A-sie, A-sie, A-sie,

A2

theme in accompaniment

II La Flûte enchantée A1

L'ombre est douce et mon maitre dort, Coiffe d'un bon-net co-ni-que

A2

theme in accompaniment

III L'Indifferent

Tes yeux sont doux comme ceux d'u-ne fil-le, Jeune é-tran-ger

Sainte
permission Durand & Cie, Paris; Elkan-gel Co., Inc., Phila., copyright owners

A la fe-nê-tre re-cé- lant Le san-tal vieux qui se dé- do- re   A

Sur l'Herbe
permission Durand & Cie, Paris; Elkan-gel Co., Inc., Phila., copyright owners

L'abbé di-vague Et toi, marquis, Tu mets de travers ta peruque   B

Chansons Madécasses

I

Na-han-do - - ve, o bel-le Na-han- do - -ve! l'oiseau noc- turne   C

II   A

Aoua! _____   Aoua! _____   Me- fi-ez- vous des blancs,   D

B

Du temps de nos pè-res, des blancs descen- dirent dans cette î- le,   E

III Repos

Il est doux de_ se cou-cher du-rant la chaleur sous un ar-bre touf-fu, _____   F

Don Quichotte à Dulcinée
I Chanson Romantique
permission Durand & Cie, Paris; Elkan-gel Co., Inc., Phila., copyright owners

Si vous me di-siez que la ter- re   A tant_ tour-ner_   G

II Chanson Épique

Bon Saint Mi- chel_ qui me don- nez loi-sir _____ de voir ma Da - - me   H

III Chanson à boire

Foin du bâ- tard, il- lus-tre Da- me, _____ qui pour me perdre   I

L'Enfant et les Sortilèges (opera-ballet)
Song of the clock
permission Durand & Cie, Paris; Elkan-gel Co., Inc., Phila., copyright owners

Ding, ding, ding, ding; et encor ding, ding, ding et en-cor ding   J

Song of the cup

Keng-ça- fou, Mah jong,_ Keng- ça- fou,_ Puis'kong, kong, panpa, Ça- oh- rä,   K

Song of the fire

Je ré- chauf-fe les bons, Je ré- chauf-fe les bons,   L

Lullaby

Toi, le coeur de la ro- se Toi, le par-fum du lys blanc_   M

Song of the little old man

Deux ro- bi- nets cou- lent dans un ré- ser- voir!   N

Heure Espagnole (comédie-musicale)
Scene IX Inigo's Air
permission Durand & Cie, Paris; Elkan-gel Co., Inc., Phila., copyright owners

Tant pis, ma foi, si je dé- roge! Je con-çois à l'ins-tant   O

Scene XV Gonzalve's Air

En dé- pit de cette in- hu- maine_ Je ne veux pas quit- ter   P

Scene XVII Concepción's Air

Oh! la pi- toy- able a- ven- tu- re!   Q

Trois Chansons I Nicolette
permission Durand & Cie, Paris; Elkan-gel Co., Inc., Phila., copyright owners

Ni- co- lette, à la ves- prée, S'al- lait pro- me- ner au pré,   R

II Trois beaux oiseaux du Paradis

Trois beaux oi- seaux du Pa- ra- dis, (Mon a- mi z-il est à la guer- re   S

REGER, Max (1873-1916)

Cinque canti all' antica III Ballata

Non so qual io mi vo-glia,   o vi-ver o mo-rir,

IV

Bel-la por-ta di ru-bi-ni Ch'a-pri il var-co a' dol-ci ac-cen-ti

V Canzone di re Enzo

A-mor mi fa so-ven-te Lo me-o co-re pe-na-re

E se un giorno tornasse

Copyright by G. Ricordi & Co., Inc.

E se un gior-no tor-nas-se che do-vrei dir-gli

Invito alla danza

Copyright by F. Bongiovanni, Bologna

Ma-don-na, d'un__ brac-cio so-a-ve ch'i-o cin-ga

In alto mare

Copyright by F. Bongiovanni, Bologna

E sdru-sci-to il na-vil l'i-ra del flot-te tre-gua non da.

Mattinata

Copyright by F. Bongiovanni, Bologna

Span-do-no le cam-pa-ne a la prim'al-ba l'a-ve

Nebbie

Sof-fro, lon-tan lon-ta-no Le neb-bie son-no-len-te Sal-go-no

Nevicata

Copyright by F. Bongiovanni, Bologna

Sui cam-pi e su le stra-de Si-len-zi-o-sa e lie-ve

Notte

Copyright by F. Bongiovanni, Bologna

Sul giar-di-no fan-ta-sti-co Pro-fu-ma-to di ro- sa

Pioggia

Copyright by F. Bongiovanni, Bologna

Pio-ve-a__   per le fi-ne-stra spa-lan-ca- - te

Scherzo

Copyright by F. Bongiovanni, Bologna

U-na not-te al da-van-za-le, e-ro so-la o pur non e-ro

Stornellatrice

Copyright by F. Bongiovanni, Bologna

Che mi gio-va can-tar: "Fior di be-tul-la:

Il Tramonto A

Copyright by G. Ricordi & Co., Inc.

Oh! quan-ta te-ne-ra gio-ia, che gli fè il re-spi-ro

B

Ne- ri gli oc-chi ma non ful-gi-de più

REYER, Ernest (1823-1909)

Air des colombes, from Salammbo (opera)

Copyright by Choudens fils, Paris

Oh!__   qui me don-ne-ra comme à la co-lombe des ai-les, pour fuir

Sigurd (opera) Act II

By permission Heugel & Cie, Paris, copyright owners

Et toi, Fré-ïa, dé- es- se de l'A-mour__ Belle é- pou-se

Sigurd (opera) Act II

J'ai gar-dé mon âme in-gé-nue___ A la fi-an-cée in-con-nue___

Es- prits,___ gar-diens de ces lieux vé-né-rés, sa-chez quel nom,

Sa- lut!___ splen-deur___ du jour!___ Sa-lut! astre au front pur,

Act IV

O pa- lais ra-di-eux___ de la voûte é--toi-lé- e!

RHEINBERGER, Josef (1839-1901)

Heaven the Stars now are shining

In Heav'n the stars now are shin- ing, The o- cean waves flash___

RHENÉ-BATON (1879-1940)

Berceuse
By permission Durand & Cie, Paris;
Elkan-Vogel Co., Inc., Phila.,
copyright owners

Quand l'en-fant s'en-dort dans son ber-ceau blanc, son an- ge gar-dien

pleut des petales de fleurs, Op. 14, No. 6
By permission Durand & Cie, Paris;
Elkan-Vogel Co., Inc., Phila.,
copyright owners

Il pleut___ des pe- ta- les de fleurs La flam- me

Tendresse, Op. 16, No. 5
By permission Durand & Cie, Paris;
Elkan-Vogel Co., Inc., Phila.,
copyright owners

Mets ta main sur mes yeux Je ne veux plus rien voir

RICHARD, Coeur de Lion (1157-1199)

Ja nun hons pris

Ja nun hons pris ne di- ra- sa rai- son

RICHARDSON, T. (Contemporary)

Mary

Kind, kind and gen- tle is she, Kind is my Ma- ry

RIEGO, Teresa del

Homing

O Dry Those Tears!

O dry those tears, and calm those fears, Life is not made___ for sor- row;

RIISAGER, Knudage (1897-   )

Mor Danmark
Copyright by Hansen, Copenhagen

Der er et Land, som daar-lig kan bli' me- get min- dre

RIMSKY-KORSAKOFF, Nicolai (1844-1908)

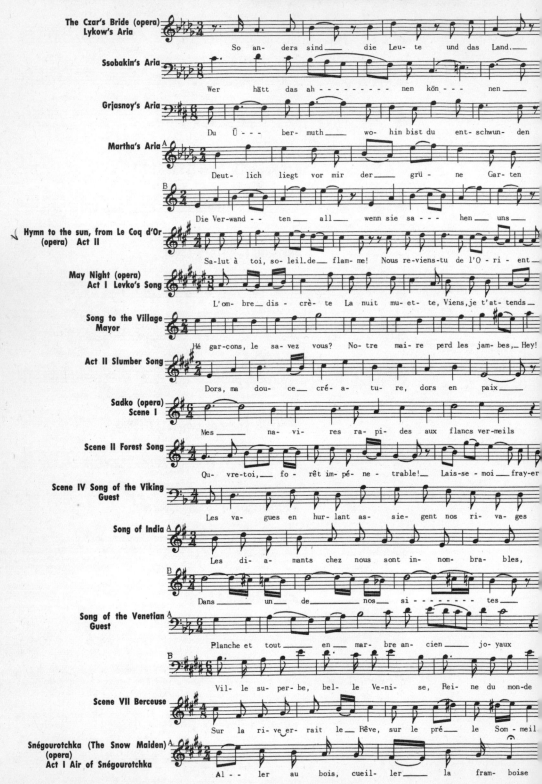

The Czar's Bride (opera) Lykow's Aria
So an-ders sind die Leu-te und das Land.

Ssobakin's Aria
Wer hätt das ah - - - - - - - - nen kön - - - nen

Grjasnoy's Aria
Du Ü - - - ber-muth wo-hin bist du ent-schwun-den

Martha's Aria A
Deut-lich liegt vor mir der grü-ne Gar-ten

B
Die Ver-wand - - ten all wenn sie sa - - - hen uns

Hymn to the sun, from Le Coq d'Or (opera) Act II
Sa-lut à toi, so-leil de flam-me! Nous re-viens-tu de l'O-ri-ent

May Night (opera) Act I Levko's Song
L'om-bre dis-crè-te La nuit mu-et-te, Viens, je t'at-tends

Song to the Village Mayor
Hé gar-cons, le sa-vez vous? No-tre mai-re perd les jam-bes, Hey!

Act II Slumber Song
Dors, ma dou-ce cré-a-tu-re, dors en paix

Sadko (opera) Scene I
Mes na-vi-res ra-pi-des aux flancs ver-meils

Scene II Forest Song
Qu-vre-toi, fo-rêt im-pé-ne-trable! Lais-se-moi fray-er

Scene IV Song of the Viking Guest
Les va-gues en hur-lant as-sie-gent nos ri-va-ges

Song of India A
Les di-a-mants chez nous sont in-nom-bra-bles,

B
Dans un de nos si - - - - - - - tes

Song of the Venetian Guest A
Planche et tout en mar-bre an-cien jo-yaux

B
Vil-le su-per-be, bel-le Ve-ni-se, Rei-ne du mon-de

Scene VII Berceuse
Sur la ri-ve er-rait le Rêve, sur le pré le Som-meil

Snégourotchka (The Snow Maiden) (opera) Act I Air of Snégourotchka A
Al - - ler au bois, cueil-ler la fram-boise

Snégourotchka (The Snow Maiden) (opera)
Act I Air of Snégourotchka
Le soir, le soir je chan - te - - rai

Arietta of Snégourotchka
Je con - nais, je con - nais,__ ma mè - - - - re,

Carnival Chorus
Les coqs chant - ent de - puis__ l'au - - ro - - - - re

Act III Song of the shepherd, Lehl
Said the thun - der to the cloud passing by, Rum-ble, grum-ble,

songs,
The Nightingale and the Rose, Op. 2, No. 2
The rose has charm'd the night-in- gale, By day and night

The Cloud and the Mountain, Op. 3, No. 3
Thro' the night a gol-den cloudlet rest-ed On a lof-ty moun-tain

A Southern Night, Op. 3, No. 6
O'er yon moun-tain-ous height Rides the Queen of the Night,

In the Georgian Hills, Op. 3, No. 8
The mists are hang- ing low a - bove the Geor-gian hills

Gonets, Op. 4
De-bout, mon gars! Sur ton che-val! Tra-ver-se bois et champs

Chanson Hébraïque, Op. 7
I sleep; my heart at break of day can__ nev-er__ sleep

Oh, if you could, Op. 39, No. 1
Hé- las! si tu pou- vais, ne fût- se qu'un in- stant,

It is not the wind blowing from the height, Op. 43, No. 2
The wind's not blow- ing from the height,__ Qui- et the evening,

The Prophet, Op. 49, No. 2
Le vrai, d'un coeur, ar-dent, cher-chant__ j'er-rais dans le dé-sert

The Maid and the Sun, Op. 50, No. 1
Far__ a- way be - yond three o- ceans

ROBERTON, Sir Hugh S. (1874-   )

All in the April evening
Copyright 1929, A. Roberton
All in the A- pril ev - - - - 'ning. A- pril airs were a- broad,

Eriskay Love Lilt (arr.)
Copyright 1915, J. Curwen & Sons
When I'm lone- ly dear white heart, Black the night or wild the sea

The Herdmaiden's Song (arr.)
Copyright by Carl Fischer, Inc. reprinted by permission
A mai- den sang sweet - ly as a bird on a tree

The Old Woman (arr.)
Copyright by Carl Fischer, Inc. reprinted by permission
As a white can- dle in a ho- ly place,__ So is the beau- ty

ROBINSON, Earl (1911-   )

Ballad for Americans
Copyright by Robbins Music Corp., N. Y.

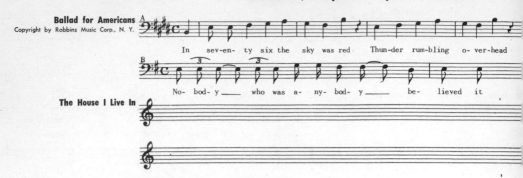

In sev-en-ty six the sky was red Thun-der rum-bling o-ver-head

No- bod- y ___ who was a- ny- bod- y ___ be- lieved it

The House I Live In

ROGERS, James H. (1857-1940)

At Parting

The sweet- est flow'r that blows ___ I give you as we part ___

The Star
Copyright 1912, G. Schirmer, Inc.

Star of me, star of me watch-ing the moth- er skies

RONALD, Sir Landon (1873-1938)

Down in the Forest, from A Cycle of Life, No. 2
By permission Boosey & Hawkes, Inc., copyright owners

Down in the for-est some-thing stirred So faint that I scarce-ly heard:

ROOT, George F. (1820-1895)

Just before the Battle, Mother

Just be- fore the bat-tle, mo- ther I am think-ing most of you

The Vacant Chair

We shall meet but we shall miss him, There will be one va-cant chair

ROPARTZ, J. Guy (1864-   )

Berceuse
Copyright by Salabert, Paris, N. Y.

O pe- tits en- fants; Voi- ci l'heure où tout bruit cesse

La Mer
Copyright by Salabert, Paris, N. Y.

Le flot, mi-roir mou- vant des cieux, S'é- veille au so- leil

ROSA, Salvator (1615-1673)

Star vicino al bell' Idol

Star vi- ci- no al bell' I- dol che s'a- ma,

Vado ben spesso

Va- do ben spes- so can- gian- do ___ lo - - - co

ROSSETER, Philip (c. 1575-1623)

If she forsake me

If she for-sake me, I must die; Shall I tell her so?

ROSSI, Francesco (17th Cent.)

Ah rendimi quel core, from Mitrane (opera)

Ah ren-di-mi quel co - - - re, Ren-di-mi quel'a-mo - - re!

Il tuo fu il mi-o pen-sie - - re   Tuo sempre il mi-o vo-le - - - re

ROSSINI, Gioacchino (1792-1868)

La Danza (Tarantella Napoletana)

Già la luna è in mez - zo al ma - - re, mam-ma mia

La la ra la ra_____ la ra la___ la ra la

The Barber of Seville (opera)
Act I

Pia - no, pia-ni-si-mo sen-za par-lar! Tut-ti con me veni-te quà,

Ec-co ri-den-te il cie - - - - - lo spun-ta la bel-la au - ro - - - ra

Serenata

Se il mio no-me sa-per voi bra-ma - - - - - - - - te,

Lar - - - go al fac-to - - tum della cit-tà;   lar-go!

All' i - dea di quel me-tal-lo por-ten-to-so on-ni-pos-sen-te

U - na vo - ce po - co fa qui nel cor mi ri-suo-no,

Io so - - - no___ do-ci-le, son ri-spet-to - - - - sa,

La ca-lum-nia è un ven-ti-cel - lo, un' au-ret-ta

duet

Dun-que io son?   tu non m'in-gan-ni?   dun-que io son la for-tu-na-ta?

Ah! tu so - - - - - lo, a-mor,_____ tu se - - - - - - - - - i,

A un Dot-tor della mia sor-te   que-ste scu-se, Si-gno-ri-na

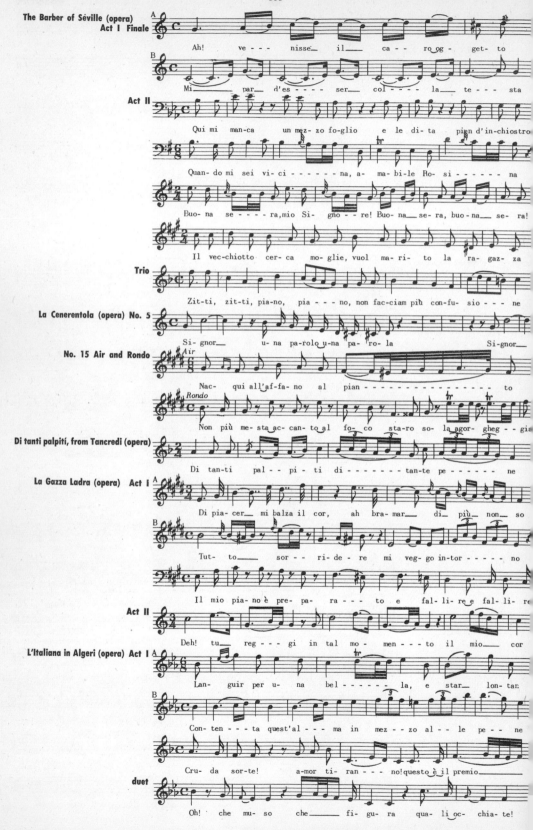

The Barber of Séville (opera)

Act I Finale — Ah! ve---nisse_ il_ ca--ro_og--get-to

Mi_ par d'es---- ser col---la_ te--sta

Act II — Qui mi man-ca un mez-zo fo-glio e le di-ta pien d'in-chiostro

Quan-do mi sei vi-ci------na, a-ma-bi-le Ro-si------na

Buo-na se----ra,mio Si-gno--re! Buo-na_ se-ra, buo-na_ se-ra!

Il vec-chiotto cer-ca mo-glie, vuol ma-ri-to la ra-gaz-za

Trio — Zit-ti, zit-ti, pia-no, pia---no, non fac-ciam più con-fu-sio--ne

La Cenerentola (opera) No. 5 — Si-gnor_ u-na pa-rolo_u-na pa--ro-la Si-gnor

No. 15 Air and Rondo — *Air* — Nac-qui all'af-fa-no al pian------to

Rondo — Non più me-sta_ac-can-to al fo-co sta-ro so-la_agor-gheg--gia

Di tanti palpití, from Tancredi (opera) — Di tan-ti pal-pi-ti di------tan-te pe------ne

La Gazza Ladra (opera) Act I — Di pia-cer_ mi balza il cor, ah bra-mar_ di più non_ so

Tut-to_ sor---ri-de-re mi veg-go in-tor------no

Act II — Il mio pia-no è pre-pa-ra---to e fal-li-re_e fal-li-re

Deh! tu_ reg---gi in tal mo-men---to il mio_ cor

L'Italiana in Algeri (opera) Act I — Lan-guir per u-na bel------la, e star_ lon-tan

Con-ten---ta quest'al---ma in mez--zo al--le pe--ne

duet — Cru-da sor-te! a-mor ti-ran---no!questo è il premio

Oh! che mu-so che_ fi-gu-ra qua-li oc-chia-te!

ROSSINI

L'Italiana in Algeri (opera) Act II — A

Per lui che a-do- ro ch'è il mio te-so-ro, più bel-la_ ren-di-mi,

B

Pen-sa al- la pat-ria e in-tre-pi-do e in-tre-pi-do

C

Qual pia - - - cer! fra pochi i-stan- ti fra pochi i- stan- ti

osè in Egitto (opera)
Invocazione — D

E- ter- no! Im- men- so! in-com-pren-si- bil Di- o!

Prayer — E

Dal tuo stel-la-to so-glio, Si- gnor ti vol- gi a noi

e ton âme si noble, from Robert
Bruce (opera) — F

Que ton â- me si no-ble, si bon-ne, Fil- le chè- re

Semiramide (opera)
Act I — G

Ah! quel gior- no o- gnor ram- men - - - - - - - - - to,

H

Ah co- me_ da quel dì, tut- to, tut-to per me_ can-gio

Act I — I

Bel rag - - - gio_ lu-sin - - - - - - - - - - - gher

B — J

Dol- ce pen- sie - - - - - - ro, di quell'i- stan - - - - - - te

Act II — K

In si bar- ba - - - ra scia- gu - - - - - - - - ra,

William Tell (opera)
Act I — L

Ah! Ma- thil- de, i- do - - - le de mon â - - me,

Bridal Chorus — M

Ciel, qui du mon - - de est la pa- ru - - re

Act II — N

Som- bre_ for- êt, dé- sert triste et_ sau- va- ge

Act III Tyrolean — O

Toi que l'oi- seau ne suivrait pas

P

Sois im- mo- bi-le, et vers la ter- re in- cline un ge- nou

Act IV — Q

A- sile hé- ré- di- tai- re, ou mes yeux s'ou- vri- rent au jour,

Stabat Mater No. 2 — R

Cu- jus a- ni- mam ge- men- tem, con- tris- tan- tem_

No. 3 — S

Quis est ho- mo qui non fle- ret, Christi ma- trem si vi- de- ret,

Stabat Mater No. 4

Pro____ pec- ca- tis su- ----- ae- gen- tis

No. 6

San- cta__ ma- ter, is- tud a- gas, cru- ci- fix- i fi- ge pla- gas,

No. 7

Fac ut por- tem Christi mor- tem pas- si- o- - nis e- jus sor- - tem,

No. 8

In- flam- ma- - - tus, in- flam- ma- tus__ et__ ac- cen- - - sus

ROUSSEAU, Jean Jacques (1712-1778)

Je vais revoir ma charmante
maîtresse, from Le Devin du
Village (opera)

Je vais re- voir ma char- man- te Mai- tres- se,

ROUSSEL, Albert (1869-1937)

Le Jardin Mouillé, Op. 3, No. 3
Copyright by Salabert, Paris, N. Y.

La croi- sée est ou- verte; il pleut Com- me mi- nu- ti- eu- se- ment

Nuit d'Automne, Op. 8, No. 2
Copyright by Salabert, Paris, N. Y.

Le cou- chant est si beau par- mi les ar- bres d'or

Invocation, No. 3
Copyright by Salabert, Paris, N. Y.

Pour que la nuit soit douce__ il fau- dra que les ro- ses

A un jeune gentilhomme, Op. 12,
No. 1
Copyright by Salabert, Paris, N. Y.

N'en- trez pas, Mon- sieur, s'il vous plaît,_ Ne bri- sez pas mes fou- gè- res,

Amoureux séparés, No. 2
Copyright by Salabert, Paris, N. Y.

Dans le roy- au- me de Yen__ un jeune ga- lant ré- si- de

Light, Op. 19, No. 1
By permission Durand & Cie, Paris;
Elkan-Vogel Co., Inc., Phila.,
copyright owners

Des lar- mes ont cou- lé__ D'un coeur se- cret et ten- dre

Sarabande, Op. 20, No. 2
By permission Durand & Cie, Paris;
Elkan-Vogel Co., Inc., Phila.,
copyright owners

Les jets d'eau dan- sent des sa- ra- ban- des

Réponse d'une épouse sage, Op. 35,
No. 2
By permission Durand & Cie, Paris;
Elkan-Vogel Co., Inc., Phila.,
copyright owners

Con- nais- sant, sei- gneur,_ mon é- tat d'é- pou- se_

Jazz dans la nuit, Op. 38
By permission Durand & Cie, Paris;
Elkan-Vogel Co., Inc., Phila.,
copyright owners

Le bal, sur le parc in- cen- dié__ jet- te ses feux

Coeur en Peril, Op. 50, No. 2
By permission Durand & Cie, Paris;
Elkan-Vogel Co., Inc., Phila.,
copyright owners

Que m'im- por- te que l'in- fan- te de Por- tu- gal__

RUBINSTEIN, Anton (1829-1894)

Der Traum, Op. 8, No. 1

Am Wie- sen- hü- gel schlum- mert ich dem brei- ten Weg

RUBINSTEIN

RUSSELL, Henry (1871-1937)

Woodman, spare that tree

Wood- man, spare that tree!__ Touch not a sin - gle__ bough!

SADERO, Geni (1891-   )

Amuri, Amuri

A- mu- ri, a- mu- - ri__ che m'ai fat- tu

Fa la nana, bambin

Fà la na- na bam- bin, Fà la na- na bel bam- bin

In mezo al Mar

In me- zo al mar ghe xe un ca- min che fu- ma__

SAINT-SAËNS, Camille (1835-1921)

O beaux rêves évanouis, from Étienne Marcel (opera) Act II
By permission Durand & Cie, Paris; Elkan-Vogel Co., Inc., Phila., copyright owners

Qui donc commande, from Henry VIII (opera) Act I
By permission Durand & Cie, Paris; Elkan-Vogel Co., Inc., Phila., copyright owners

Samson et Dalila, Op. 47 (opera) Act I
By permission Durand & Cie, Paris; Elkan-Vogel Co., Inc., Phila., copyright owners

O beaux rê- ves é- va- nouis.__ Es- pé- ran- ces tant ca- res- sé- es!

Qui donc com- man- de quand il ai- me Et quel em- pi- re

Ar- rê- tez ô mes frè- res! Et bé- nis- sez le nom de Dieu saint

Ce Dieu que vo- tre voix im- plo- re Est de- meu- ré sourd

Mau- di- te à ja- mais soit la ra- ce des en- fants d'Is- ra- ël!__

Voi- ci le prin- temps nous por- tant des fleurs__

Je viens cé- lé- brer la vic- toi- re De ce- lui qui regne en mon coeur

Prin- temps qui com- men- ce Por- tant l'és- pe- ran- ce

Act II

A- mour! viens ai- der ma fai- bles- se Ver- se le poi- son

A Mon coeur s'ouvre à ta voix, com- me s'ou- vrent les fleurs

B Ah!__ ré- ponds__ à__ ma__ ten- dres- se

Act III

Vois ma mi- sère, hé- las vois ma dé- tres- se! Pi- tié! Sei- gneur!

son et Dalila, Op. 47 (opera)
Act III

Gloire à Da-gon vain-queur! Gloire à Da-gon vain-queur! Il ai-dait

torio de Noël (Christmas Oratorio)
Op. 12 No. 2
By permission Durand & Cie, Paris;
Elkan-Vogel Co., Inc., Phila.,
copyright owners

Glo-ri-a in al-ti-si-mis De-o

No. 4

Do-mi-ne e-go cre-di-di e-go cre-di-di

No. 5

Be-ne-dic-tus, be-ne-dic-tus, be-ne-dic----tus

No. 7

Te----cum prin-ci-pi-um te-cum prin-ci-pi-um in di-e vir-tu-tis

No. 8

A-le-lu-ia, Al-le--lu-ia, Al-le-lu-ia

No. 10

Tol-li-te hos-ti-as, et a-do-ra-te Do-mi-num in a tri-o

Aimons-nous
By permission Durand & Cie, Paris;
Elkan-Vogel, Inc., Phila.,
copyright owners

Ai-mons nous et dor-mons__ Sans son-ger au res-te du mon-de

L'Attente
By permission Durand & Cie, Paris;
Elkan-Vogel Co., Inc., Phila.,
copyright owners

Monte, é-cu-reuil.__ monte au grand chê-ne, sur la bran-che des cieux

Ave Verum
By permission Durand & Cie, Paris;
Elkan-Vogel Co., Inc., Phila.,
copyright owners

A-ve A-ve ve--rum Cor-pus natum de Ma-ri-a Vir-gi-ne

Le bonheur est chose légère
By permission Durand & Cie, Paris;
Elkan-Vogel Co., Inc., Phila.,
copyright owners

Le bon-heur est cho-se lé-gè-re, Pas-sa-gè--------re

La Cloche
By permission Durand & Cie, Paris;
Elkan-Vogel Co., Inc., Phila.,
copyright owners

Seule__ en ta som-bre tour__ aux fai-tes den-te-lés

Danse Macabre
By permission Durand & Cie, Paris;
Elkan-Vogel Co., Inc., Phila.,
copyright owners

Zig et zig et zig, La mort en ca-den-ce Frap-pant u-ne tombe

Le vent d'hi-ver souffle, et la nuit est som-bre

Guitares et Mandolines
By permission Durand & Cie, Paris;
Elkan-Vogel Co., Inc., Phila.,
copyright owners

Gui-ta-res et man-do-li-nes Ont des sons qui font_ ai-mer__

Mai
By permission Durand & Cie, Paris;
Elkan-Vogel Co., Inc., Phila.,
copyright owners

Mai! les ar-bres du ver-ger Sont pou-drés de nei-ge ro-se

Mélodies Persanes, Op. 26:
Au cimetière
By permission Durand & Cie, Paris;
Elkan-Vogel Co., inc., Phila.,
copyright owners

As-sis sur cet-te blanche tom-be Ouvrons__ no-tre coeur

La Solitaire

Ô fier__ jeune__ homme, ô__ tu--eur de ga-zel-les

Nightingale and the Rose
(wordless song), from incidental
music to Parysatis
permission Durand & Cie, Paris; Elkan-
l Co., Inc., Phila., copyright owners

Le Pas d'armes du Roi Jean
By permission Durand & Cie, Paris; Elkan-Vogel Co., Inc., Phila., copyright owners

Par saint Gil - les, Viens nous en, Mon a - gi - le A - le - zan

Los aux da - mes! au roi los! Vois les flammes Des champs clos

Tournoiement
By permission Durand & Cie, Paris; Elkan-Vogel Co., Inc., Phila., copyright owners

Sans que nul - le part je sé - jour - ne Sur la pointe du gros or - teil

SALTER, Mary Turner (1856-1938)

The Cry of Rachel
Copyright 1905, G. Schirmer, Inc.

I stand in the dark, I beat on the door: Death, let me in

The Pine-Tree
Copyright 1904, G. Schirmer, Inc.

O pine-tree lone-ly stand-ing, Out-lined a-gainst the blue

SANDERSON, James

Hail to the Chief

Hail to the Chief, who in tri - umph ad - van - ces,

Heav'n send it hap-py dew, Earth lend it sap a-new

SANDERSON, Wilfrid

Until
By permission Boosey & Hawkes, Inc., copright owners

No rose in all the world un-til you came,

SARTI, Guiseppe (1729-1802)

Lungi dal caro bene

Lun-gi dal ca-ro be-ne, Vi-ve-re non pos-s'i-o

SARTORIUS, Thomas (1577-1637)

Wohlauf, ihr lieben Gäste

Wohl-auf wohl-auf, ihr lie-ben Gä - - - ste

SATIE, Erik (1866-1925)

Le Chapelier
Copyright by Salabert, Paris, N. Y.

Le cha-pe-lier s'é-ton-ne de con-sta-ter que sa mon-tre

Daphénéo
Copyright by Salabert, Paris, N. Y.

Dis-moi, Da-phé-né-o, quel est donc cet ar-bre

Je te veux
Copyright by Salabert, Paris, N. Y.

J'ai com-pris ta dé tres-se, cher a-mou-reux

Je n'ai pas de re-grets et je n'ai qu'u-ne en-vie e

La Statue de Bronze
Copyright by Salabert, Paris, N. Y.

La gre-nou-ille du jeu de tonneau S'en-nu-ie le soir   A

SCANDELLI, Antonio (1517-1580)

Ein Hennlein weiss

Ein Henn-lein-weiss ein Henn-lein weiss mit gan-zen Fleiss   C

SCARLATTI, Alessandro (1659-1725)

Chi vuole innamorarsi

Chi vuo-le in-na-mo-rar-si, Chi vuo-le in-na-ma-rar-si,   E

Già il sole dal Gange

Già il so-le dal Gan-ge, già il so-le dal Gan-ge più chia-ro,   F

O cessate di piagarmi

O ces-sa-te di pia-gar-mi, o las-cia-te-mi mo-rir   G

Ombre opache, from Correa nel peno amato (cantata)

Om-bre o-pa-che che il chia-ro-re del-la lu-ce   H

Povera pellegrina (cantata)

Po- - -ve-ra pel-le-gri-na Son io cor mio per te   I

Rugiadose, odorose

Ru-gia-do-se, o-do-ro-se, Vi-o-let-te gra-zi-o-se,   J

Se Florindo è fedele

Se Flo-rin-do è fe-de-le io m'in-na-mo-re- - -rò,   K

Sento nel core

Sen-to nel co-re cer-to do-lo-re, cer-to do-lo-re,   L

Se tu della mia morte

Se tu del-la mia mor-te a que-sta de-stra for- -te   M

Son tutta duolo

Son tut-ta duo-lo, non ho che affan-ni e mi da mor-te   N

Su, venite a consiglio

Su, su su, ve-ni-te a con-si-glio, ve-ni-te a con-siglio   O

SCARLATTI, Domenico (1685-1757)

Consolati e spera

Con-so-la-ti! e spe-ra! po-trai d'altro ogget- -to   Q

Qual farfalletta amante

Qual far-fal-let-ta a-man- - -te in vo-lo a quel-la fiam-ma   R

SCHEIN, Johann Hermann (1586-1630)

Wenn Filli ihre Liebesstrahl

Wenn Fil-le ih- re Lie- bes- strahl wirft in mein Herz

SCHILLINGS, Max von (1868-1933)

Wie wundersam, Op. 2, No. 3
By permission Associated Music Publishers, Inc.

Wie wun - - - der-sam ist dies Verlo- ren-geh'n in Lie- bes-tie- fen

SCHÖNBERG, Arnold (1874-   )

Erhebung, Op. 2, No. 3

Gieb mir dei- ne Hand, nur den Fin- ger, dann_ seh ich

Warnung, Op. 3, No. 3

Mein Hund, du,_ hat dich bloss be-knurrt und_ ich hab ihn

Hochzeitslied, No. 4

So voll und reich wand noch das Le- ben nim- mer euch sei- nen Kranz,

Geübtes Herz, No. 5

Wei-se nicht von dir mein schlichtes Herz, weil es schon so viel ge- lieb-et!

Mädchenlied, Op. 6, No. 3

Ach, wenn es nun die Mut- ter wüsst, wie du so wild mich hast ge-küsst,

Verlassen, No. 4

Im Mor- gen-grau-en schritt ich fort Ne- bel lag in den Gas- sen

Ghasel, No. 5

Ich hal-te dich in mei-nem Arm, du_ hältst die Ro-se zart_

Das Buch der hängenden Gärten, Op. 15,
No. 5
By permission Associated Music Publishers, Inc.

Sa - - get mir, auf wel-chem Pfa- de heu - te sie vor- ü- ber schrei-te,

No. 12

Wenn sich bei heil'- ger Ruh in tie- fen Mat- ten

Gurrelieder, Op. 35
Waldemar's Song
By permission Associated Music Publishers, Inc.

So tan-zen die En-gel vor Got- tes Thron nicht, wie die Welt_

Tove's Song

Nun sag ich dir zum er- sten Mal:"Kö-nig Vol-mer, ich lie- be dich!"

Waldemar's Song

Du wun- der- li- che To-ve! So reich durch dich nun bin ic

Waldtaube's Song I

Tau- ben von Gur- re Sor - - ge qualt_ mich, vom Weg

II

Weit_ flog ich, Kla- ge sucht' ich fand gar viel!_

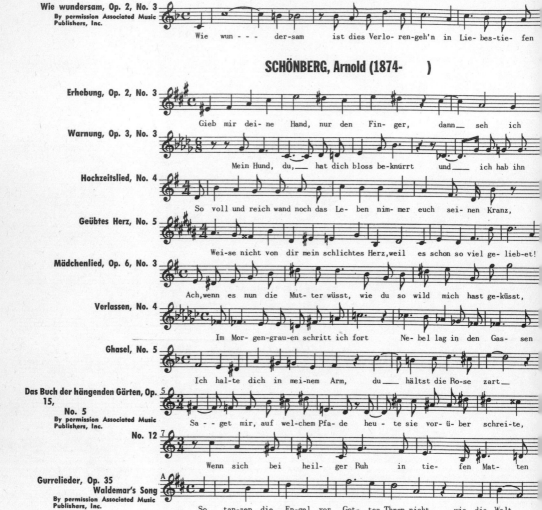

SCHUBERT, Franz (1797-1828)

Agnus Dei, from Mass in G (No. 2)
Ag- nus De- i, qui tol- lis pec- ca- ta mun- di,

Sanctus, from Mass in F
Sanc- tus, Sanc- tus Sanc- tus Do- mi- nus De- us Sa- ba- oth

Die schöne Müllerin, Op. 25 (song cycle) No. 1 "Das Wandern"
Das Wan- dern ist des Mül- lers Lust, das Wan- dern!

No. 2 Wohin?
Ich hört' ein Bäch- lein rau- schen wohl aus dem Fel- sen- quell,

No. 3 Halt!
Ei- ne Müh- le seh ich blin- ken aus den Er- len her aus

No. 4 Danksagung an den Bach
War es al- so ge- meint, mein rau- schen-der Freund? dein Sin- gen,

No. 5 Am Feierabend
Hätt' ich tau- send Ar- me zu rüh- ren! Könnt ich brau- send

No. 6 Der Neugierige
Ich fra- ge kei- ne Blu- me, ich fra- ge kei- nen Stern;

O Bäch- lein mei-ner Lie- be, wie bist du heut so stumm!

No. 7 Ungeduld
Ich schnitt' es gern in al- le Rin- den ein, ich grüb es gern

No. 8 Morgengruss
Gu- ten Mor- gen, schö-ne Mül- le- rin! Wo steckst du gleich

No. 9 Des Müllers Blumen
Am Bach viel klei- ne Blu- men stehn, aus hel- len, blau- en Au- gen sehn;

No. 10 Tränenregen
Wir sa- ssen so trau- lich bei- sam- men im küh- len Er- len-dach

No. 11 Mein!
Bäch- lein, lass dein Rau- schen sein! Rä- der, stellt euer Brau-en ein!

No. 12 Pause
Mei- ne Lau- te hab ich ge- hängt an die Wand,

No. 13 Mit dem grünen Lautenbande
Schad' um das schö- ne grü- ne Band, dass es ver- bleicht hier an der Wand,

No. 14 Der Jäger
Was sucht denn der Jä- ger am Mühl- bach hier? Bleib trot- zi- ger Jä- ger

No. 15 Eifersucht und Stolz
Wo- hin so schnell, so kraus und wild, mein lie- ber Bach?

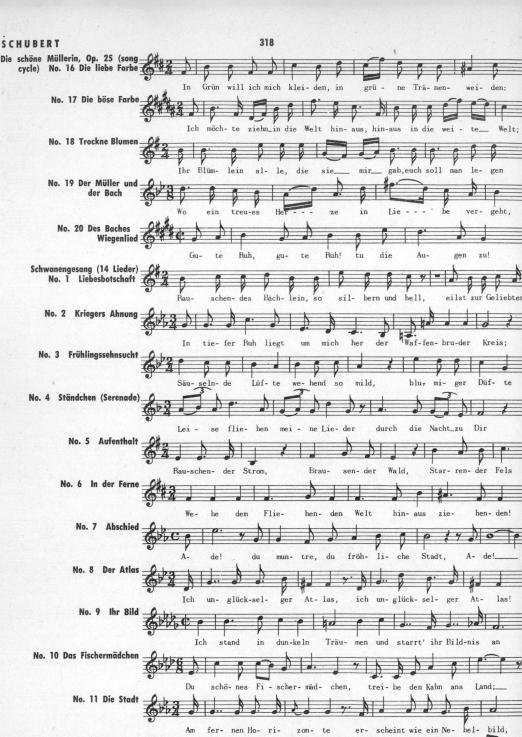

Die Winterreise, Op. 89 (song cycle)
No. 1 Gute Nacht
Fremd bin ich ein-ge-zo - - gen, fremd zieh ich wie-der aus   A

No. 2 Die Wetterfahne
Der Wind spielt mit der Wet - - ter-fah - ne   B

No. 3 Gefrorne Tränen
Ge-fror-ne Trop-fen fal-len von mei-nen Wan-gen ab: C

No. 4 Erstarrung
Ich such im Schnee ver-ge-bens nach ih-rer Trit-te Spur,   D

No. 5 Der Lindenbaum
Am Brun-nen vor dem To-re da steht ein Lin-den-baum;   E

No. 6 Wasserflut
Man-che Trän' aus mei-nen Au-gen ist ge-fal-len in den Schnee: F

No. 7 Auf dem Flusse
Der du so lus-tig rauschtest, du hel-ler, wil-der Fluss,   G

No. 8 Rückblick
Es brennt mir un-ter bei-den Soh-len, tret ich auch schon auf Eis und Schnee   H

No. 9 Irrlicht
In die tief-sten Fel-sen grün-de lock-te mich ein Irr-licht hin: I

No. 10 Rast
Nun merk ich erst, wie müd ich bin, da ich zur Ruh mich le-ge   J

No. 11 Frühlingstraum
Ich träum-te von bun-ten Blu-men, so wie sie wohl blü-hen im Mai,   K

No. 12 Einsamkeit
Wie ei-ne trü-be Wol-ke durch hei-tre Lüf-te geht,   L

No. 13 Die Post
Von der Stra-sse her ein Post-horn klingt. Was hat es,   M

No. 14 Der greise Kopf
Der Reif hat ei-nen weis-sen Schein mir ü - - - - bers Haar ge-streu-et   N

No. 15 Die Krähe
Ei-ne Krä-he war mit mir aus der Stadt ge-zo-gen,   O

No. 16 Letzte Hoffnung
Hie un da ist an den Bäu-men man-ches bun-te Blatt zu sehn,   P

No. 17 Im Dorfe
Es bel-len die Hun-de, es ras-seln die Ket-ten;   Q

No. 18 Der stürmische Morgen
Wie hat der Sturm zer-ris-sen des Him-mels grau-es Kleid!   R

No. 19 Täuschung
Ein Licht tanzt freundlich vor mir her,   ich folg ihm   S

Die Winterreise, Op. 89 (song cycle)
No. 20 Der Wegweiser

Was ver-meid ich denn die We- ge, wo die An-dern Wand-rer gehn,

No. 21 Das Wirtshaus

Auf ei-nen To-ten-ak-ker hat mich mein Weg ge-bracht

No. 22 Mut!

Fliegt der Schnee mir ins Ge-sicht, schüttl ich ihn her-un-ter

No. 23 Die Nebensonnen

Drei Son-nen sah ich am Him-mel stehn, hab lang und fest sie an-ge-sehn;

No. 24 Der Leiermann

Drü-ben hin-term Dor-fe steht ein Lei-er-mann,

Gretchen am Spinnrade, Op. 2

Mei-ne Ruh ist hin, mein Herz ist schwer; ich fin-de,

Meeres Stille, Op. 3, No. 2

Tie-fe Stil-le herrscht im Was-ser, oh-ne Re-gung ruht das Meer,

Heidenröslein, No. 3

Sah ein Knab ein Rös-lein stehn, Rös-lein auf der Hei-den,

Jägers Abendlied, No. 4

Im Fel-de schleich' ich still und wild ge-spannt

Der Wanderer, Op. 4, No. 1

Ich kom-me vom Ge-bir-ge her Es dampft das Tal

Wo bist Du, wo bist Du, mein ge-lieb-tes Land?

Wanderers Nachtlied, No. 3

Der du von dem Him-mel bist, al-les Leid und Schmerzen stillst,

Rastlose Liebe, Op. 5, No. 1

Dem Schnee, dem Re-gen, dem Wind ent-ge-gen, in Dampf der Klüf-te,

Nähe des Geliebten, No. 2

Ich den-ke dein,wenn mir der Son-ne Schimmer vom Mee-re strahlt

Das König in Thule, No. 5

Es war ein Kö-nig in Thu-le, gar treu bis an das Grab,

Memnon, Op. 6, No. 1

Den Tag hin-durch nur ein-mal mag ich spre-chen,

Am Grabe Anselmos, No. 3

Dass ich dich ver-lo-ren ha-be,Dass du nicht mehr bist,

Der Tod und das Mädchen, Op. 7, No. 3

Vor-ü-ber, ach, vor-ü-ber! geh, wil-der Kno-chen-mann

Erlafsee, Op. 8, No. 3

Mir ist so wohl, so weh' am stil-len Er-laf-see;

Die Liebe hat gelogen, Op. 23, No. 1

Die Lie- be hat ge-lo-gen, die Sor-ge las-tet schwer,___

Schwanengesang, No. 3

Wie klag ich's aus, das Ster-be-ge-fühl, das auf-lö-send

Gruppe aus dem Tartarus, Op. 24, No. 1

Horch, wie Mur-meln des em-pör-ten Mee-res wie durch hohler Felsen

Schlaflied, No. 2

Es mahnt___ der Wald, es ruft___ der Strom: "du lie--bes Büb-chen,

Romanze, Op. 26, No. 1 (from Rosamunde)

Der Voll-mond strahlt auf___ Ber-ges-höh'n, wie hab' ich dich___ ver - misst

Der Gondelfahrer, Op. 28

Es tan-zen Mond und Ster---ne den flücht'gen Gei-ster- reih'n___

Suleika II, Op. 31

Ach, um dei-ne feuch-ten___ Schwingen, West, wie sehr ich dich__ be - nei-de;

Die Forelle, Op. 32

In ei-nem Bäch-lein hel-le, da schoss in fro-her___ Eil

Nachtstück, Op. 36, No. 2

Wenn ü-ber Ber-ge sich der Ne-bel brei-tet,

Der Pilgrim, Op. 37, No. 1 (words by Schiller)

Noch in mei-nes Le-bens___ Len-ze war ich, und ich wan-dert___ aus

Der Einsame, Op. 41

Wenn mei-ne Gril-len schwir-ren, bei Nacht, am spät er-wärm-ten___ Herd,

Die junge Nonne, Op. 43, No. 1

Wie braust___ durch die Wip----fel der heu-len-de Sturm!

Nacht und Träume, No. 2

Heil'- ge Nacht,___ du sinkest nie-der nie-der wal-len auch die Träu-me,

Ellen's erster Gesang, Op. 52, No. 1 (from Scott's Lady of the Lake)

Ra--ste, Krie-ger! Krieg ist___ aus, schlaf' den Schlaf,___

Ellen's Zweiter Gesang, No. 2 (from Scott's Lady of the Lake)

Jä- ger,___ ru-he von der Jagd! Jä- ger,___ ru-he von der Jagd!

An die Leier, No. 3

A

Ich will von A-treus' Söh-nen von Kad-mus will___ ich sin-gen!

B

Doch mei-ne Sai-ten tö-nen nur Lie-be im Er-klin-gen,

Coronach, No. 4

Er ist___ uns ge-schie-den vom Berg___ und vom Wal-de

Ave Maria, No. 6

A- ve Ma-ri-----a! Jung-----frau mild,

SCHUBERT

Im Haine, Op. 56, No. 3 — A

Son- nen- strah- len durch die Tan - - nen, wie sie fal- len

Der Schmetterling, Op. 57, No. 1 — B

Wie soll ich nicht tan - - zen? es macht kei- ne Mü- he

An den Mond, No. 3 — C

Geuss, lie - - - - ber Mond, geuss dei- ne Sil- ber- flim- mer

s Mädchens Klage, Op. 58, No. 3 — D

Der Eich- wald braust, die Wol - - - ken ziehn, das Mägd - - lein sitzt

liebst mich nicht, Op. 59, No. 1 — E

Mein Herz ist zer- ris - - sen, du liebst mich nicht!

Dass sie hier gewesen! No. 2 — F

Dass der Ost- wind Düf- te hau - - - chet in die Lüf - - te,

Du bist die Ruh, No. 3 — G

Du bist die Ruh, der Frie- de mild, die Sehn- sucht du,

Lachen und Weinen, No. 4 — H

La - - chen und wei - - nen zu jeg- li- cher Stun- de

Dithyrambe, Op. 60, No. 2 — I

Nim- mer, das glaubt mir, er- schei- nen die Göt- ter, nim- mer al- lein,

Lied der Mignon I, Op. 62, No. 1 — J

Heiss mich nicht re- den, heiss mich schwei- gen denn mein Ge- heim- niss

Lied der Mignon II, No. 2 — K

So lasst mich schei- nen bis ich wer- de;

Lied der Mignon III, No. 3 — L

So lasst mich schei- nen bis ich wer- de zieht mir das wei- sse

Lied der Mignon IV, No. 4 — M

Nur wer die Sehn- sucht kennt, weiss, was ich lei- de,

d eines Schiffers an die Dioskuren, Op. 65, No. 1 — N

Di- os- ku- ren, Zwil- lings- sterne, die ihr leuch- tet mei- nen Na- chen,

Aus "Heliopolis" I, No. 3 — O

Im kal- ten, rau- hen Nor- den ist Kun- de mir ge wor- den

Der Wachtelschlag, Op. 68 — P

Ach! mir schallt's dor- ten so lieb- lich her- vor: für- chte Gott!

Auf dem Wasser zu singen, Op. 72 — Q

Mit- ten im Schimmer der spie- geln- den Wel- len gleitet, wie Schwäne,

Die Rose, Op. 73 — A — R

Es lock- te schö- ne Wär- me mich an das Licht zu wa- gen,

B — S

Was soll der mil- de A- bend? muss ich nun trau- rig fra- gen;

Über Wildemann, Op. 108, No. 1 — A
Die Win-de sau-sen am Tan-nen-hang, die Quel-len brau-sen

Todesmusik, No. 2 — B
In des To-des Fei-er- stun-de wenn ich einst von hin-nen— schei-de,

Das Lied im Grünen, Op. 115, No. 1 — C
Ins Grü- ne, ins Grü- ne, da lockt uns der Früh- ling,

Sprache der Liebe, No. 3 — D
Lass dich mit— ge-lin— den— Schlägen rüh-ren— mei-ne— zar-te Lau-te!

An die Sonne, Op. 118, No. 5 — E
Sin-ke, liebe Son-ne, sin- ke, en-de dei-nen trü- - - ben Lauf

Die Spinnerin, No. 6 — F
Als— ich— still und— ru-hig spann, oh-ne— nur zu— sto-cken

Der Hirt auf dem Felsen, Op. 129 (for soprano, clarinet and piano) A — G
Wenn— auf dem— hoch - - - - - sten Fels ich— steh',

B — H
Der Früh-ling will— kom-men, der Früh-ling mei-ne— Freud',

Das Echo, Op. 130 — I
Herz-lie- be, gu-te Mut-ter, O grol-le nicht mit mir,

Psalm, Op. 132, No. 23 — J
Gott ist mein Hirt,— mir wird nichts man - - - - geln Gott ist mein Hirt,—

Nachthelle, Op. 134 (men's chorus) — K
Die Nacht ist hei-ter und ist rein, Die Nacht ist hei-ter und ist rein

Ständchen, Op. 135 — L
Zo- gernd lei-se, Zo- gernd lei-se in des Dun-kels

Miriams Siegesgesang, Op. 136 A — M
Rührt— die Cym-bel, schlagt die— Sai-ten, lasst— den— Hall

B — N
Aus — E- gyp- - - ten vor— dem— Vol- - ke

Nachtgesang im Walde, Op. 139b (men's chorus) A — O
Sei uns stets ge-grüsst, O Nacht! a-ber dop-pelt hier im Wald,

E — P
Es regt in den Lau-ben des Wal-des sich schon,

Das Bild, Op. 165, No. 3 — Q
Ein Mäd-chen ist's, das früh und spät mir vor der See-le schwe-bet,

An die Nachtigall, Op. 172, No. 3 — R
Geuss— nicht so laut der lieb-ent- flamm-ten Lie-der ton- reichen Schall

Abendbilder — S
Still be-ginnt's im Hain zu thau-en, ru-hig webt der Dämm'-rung— Grau-en

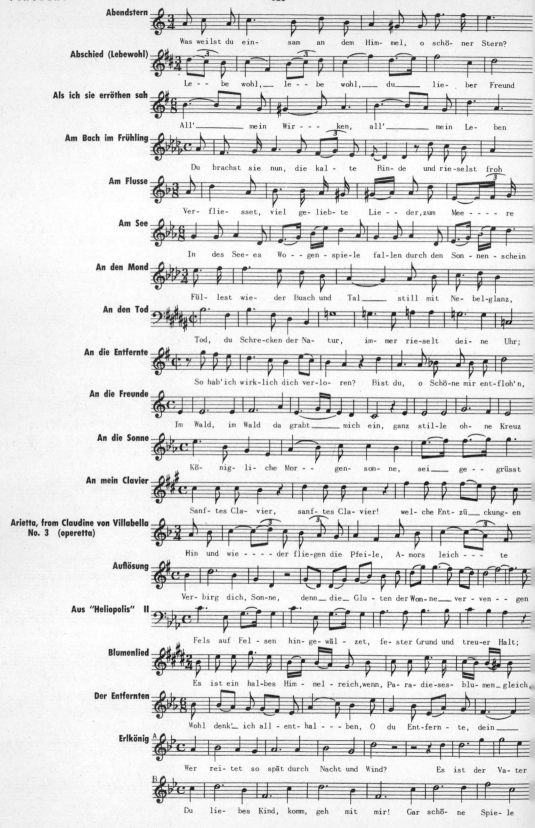

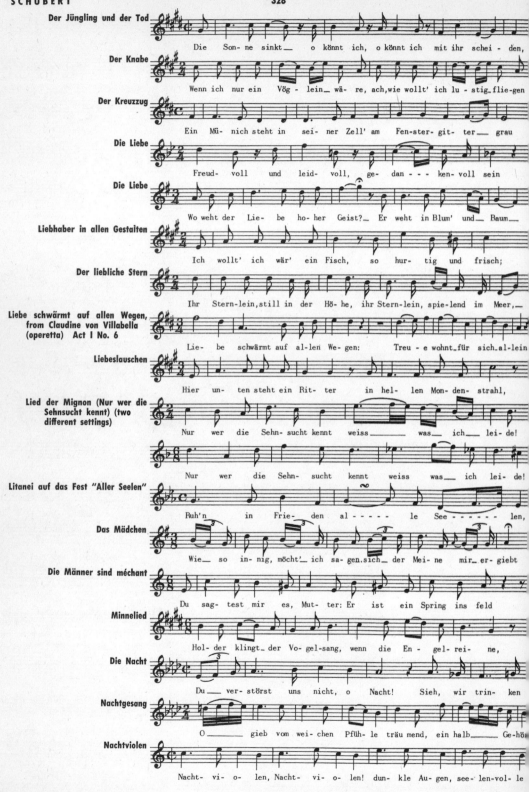

Der Jüngling und der Tod
Die Son-ne sinkt__ o könnt ich, o könnt ich mit ihr schei-den,

Der Knabe
Wenn ich nur ein Vög-lein__ wä-re, ach, wie wollt' ich lu-stig flie-gen

Der Kreuzzug
Ein Mü-nich steht in sei-ner Zell' am Fen-ster-git-ter__ grau

Die Liebe
Freud-voll und leid-voll, ge-dan---ken-voll sein

Die Liebe
Wo weht der Lie-be ho-her Geist?__ Er weht in Blum' und Baum__

Liebhaber in allen Gestalten
Ich wollt' ich wär' ein Fisch, so hur-tig und frisch;

Der liebliche Stern
Ihr Stern-lein, still in der Hö-he, ihr Stern-lein, spie-lend im Meer,__

Liebe schwärmt auf allen Wegen, from Claudine von Villabella (operetta) Act I No. 6
Lie-be schwärmt auf al-len We-gen: Treu-e wohnt__ für sich al-lein

Liebeslauschen
Hier un-ten steht ein Rit-ter in hel-len Mon-den-strahl,

Lied der Mignon (Nur wer die Sehnsucht kennt) (two different settings)
Nur wer die Sehn-sucht kennt weiss__ was ich lei-de!

Nur wer die Sehn-sucht kennt weiss was__ ich lei-de!

Litanei auf das Fest "Aller Seelen"
Ruh'n in Frie-den al----le See----len,

Das Mädchen
Wie__ so in-nig, möcht'__ ich sa-gen, sich der Mei-ne mir er-giebt

Die Männer sind méchant
Du sag-test mir es, Mut-ter: Er ist ein Spring ins feld

Minnelied
Hol-der klingt__ der Vo-gel-sang, wenn die En-gel-rei-ne,

Die Nacht
Du ver-störst uns nicht, o Nacht! Sieh, wir trin-ken

Nachtgesang
O_____ gieb vom wei-chen Pfüh-le träu-mend, ein halb__ Ge-hör

Nachtviolen
Nacht-vi-o-len, Nacht-vi-o-len! dun-kle Au-gen, see-len-vol-le

Orpheus — Wäl- ze dich hin- weg, du wil- des Feu- er!

Von der Er- - de, von der Er- de, wo die Son- - - ne,

La Pastorella — La pa- sto- rel- la al pra- - to con- - - ten- ta se- ne_____ va,

Pax vobiscum — Der Frie- de sei mit euch! das war dein Ab- schieds- se- gen

Prometheus — Be- de- cke dei- nen Him- mel, Zeus,___ mit Wol- ken- dunst

Das Rosenband — Im Früh- lings- gar- ten fand ich sie, da band ich sie

Schäfers Klagelied — Da dro- ben auf je- nem Ber- ge, da steh' ich tau- send- mal

Seligkeit — Freu- den son- der Zahl___ blüh'n_ im Him- mel's Saal___

Der Sieg — O un- be- wölk- tes Le- ben! so rein und tief und_ klar,

Ständchen (Hark, Hark, the Lark) — Horch, horch! die Lerch' im Ä- ther- blau;und Phö- bus, neu- - er- weckt,___

Thekla — Wo ich sei, und wo mich hin- ge- wen- det, als mein flücht'ger Schatte

Totengräbers Heimweh — O Mensch- heit o Le- ben! was soll's? O was soll's?

Dem Unendlichen — Wie er- hebt sich das Herz, wenn es dich, Un- end- li- cher, denkt!

Weht, Bäu- me des Le- bens, ins Har- - fen- ge- tön!

Vergissmeinnicht — Als der Früh- ling sich vom Her- zen_ der er- blüh- ten Er- de riss,

Da im wei- chen Sammt des Moo- ses sieht er, halb vom Grün ver- deckt,

Verklärung — Le- bens- fun- ke, vom Him- mel ent- glüht, der sich los- zu- win- den müht

Sanft ins_ Le- ben auf- wärts_ schwe- ben, sanft hin- schwin- den

Die Vögel — Wie lieb- lich und_ fröh- lich, zu_ schwe- ben, zu sin- gen

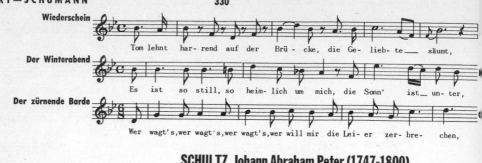

Wiederschein

Tom lehnt har- rend auf der Brü- cke, die Ge- lieb- te säumt,

Der Winterabend

Es ist so still, so heim- lich um mich, die Sonn' ist un- ter,

Der zürnende Barde

Wer wagt's, wer wagt's, wer wagt's, wer will mir die Lei- er zer- bre- chen,

SCHULTZ, Johann Abraham Peter (1747-1800)

Am Sylvester-Abend

Des Jah- res letz- te Stun- de er- tönt mit ern- stem Schlag

SCHUMANN, Clara (1819-1896)

Liebst du um Schönheit, Op. 37, No. 4

Liebst du um Schön- heit O nicht mich lie- be!

SCHUMANN, Robert (1810-1856)

Der Contrabandiste (Spanish Songs)

Ich bin der Con- tra- ban- di- ste, Weiss wohl Respect mir zu schaffen,

Morgens steh ich auf und frage, Op. 24, No. 1

Mor- gens steh' ich auf und fra- ge: Kommt fein's Lieb- chen heut'?

Es treibt mich hin, No. 2

Es treibt mich hin, es treibt mich her! Noch we- ni- ge Stun- den,

Ich wandelte unter den Bäumen, No. 3

Ich wan- del- te un- ter den Bäu- men mit mei- nem Gram al- lein

Lieb' Liebchen, No. 4

Lieb' Lieb- chen, leg's Händ- chen auf's Her- ze mein;

Schöne Wiege meiner Leiden, No. 5

Schö- ne Wie- ge mei- ner Lei- den, schö- nes Grab- mal -

Mit Myrthen und Rosen, No. 9

Mit Myr- then und Ro- sen, lieb- lich und hold,

Myrthen, Op. 25, No. 1 Widmung

A

Du mei- ne See- le, du mein Herz, du mei- ne Wonn' o du mein Schmerz,

B

Du bist die Ruh', du bist der Frie- den, du bist vom Him- mel

No. 2 Freisinn

Lasst mich nur auf mei- nem Sat- tel gel - - - ten!

No. 3 Der Nussbaum

Es grü- net ein Nuss- baum vor dem Haus, duf- tig, luf- tig brei- tet

Myrthen, Op. 25, No. 4 Jemand — A
Mein Herz ist be-trübt, ich sag' es nicht, mein Herz ist be-trübt

No. 7 Die Lotosblume — B
Die Lo-tos-blu-me äng-stigt sich vor der Son-ne Pracht,

No. 8 Talismane — C
Got-tes ist der O-ri-ent! Got-tes ist der Oc-ci-dent!

No. 9 Lied der Suleika — D
Wie, mit in-nig-stem Be-ha-gen, Lied, em-pfind' ich dei-nen Sinn!

No. 11 Lieder der Braut — E
Mut-ter, Mut-ter! Glau-be nicht, weil ich ihn lieb' al-so sehr,

No. 12 — F
Lass mich ihm am Bu-sen han-gen, Mut-ter, Mut-ter!

No. 14 Hochländisches Wiegenlied — G
Schla-fe, sü-sser klei-ner Do-nald;

No. 15 Aus den hebräischen Gesängen — H
Mein Herz ist schwer Auf! von der Wand die Lau-te,

No. 17 Zwei Venetianische Lieder — I
Leis' ru-dern hier, mein Gon-do-lier, leis', leis'!

No. 18 — J
Wenn durch die Pi-a-zet-ta die A-bend-luft weht,

No. 21 Was will die einsame Thräne? — K
Was will die ein-sa-me Thrä-ne? sie trübt mir ja den Blick.

No. 23 Im Westen — L
Ich schau ü-ber Forth, hin-ü-ber nach Nord; was hel-fen mir Nord

No. 24 Du bist wie eine Blume — M
Du bist wie ei-ne Blu-me, so hold und schön und rein;

No. 25 Aus den östlichen Rosen — N
Ich sen-de ei-nen Gruss wie Duft der Ro-sen,

No. 26 Zum Schluss — O
Hier in die-sen erd be-klomm-nen Lüf-ten, wo die Weh-mut taut,

Was soll ich sagen! Op. 27, No. 3 — P
Mein Aug' ist trüb', mein Mund ist stumm, du heissest mich re-den,

Jasminenstrauch, No. 4 — Q
Grün ist der Jas-mi-nen-strauch A-bends ein-ge-schla-fen.

Der Page, Op. 30, No. 2 — R
Da ich nun ent-sa-gen müs-sen Al-lem, was mein Herz

Der Hidalgo, No. 3 — S
Es ist so süss zu scher-zen mit Lie-dern und mit Her-zen

Der Hidalgo, Op. 30, No. 3 — Die Schö-nen von Se- vil-la, mit Fä- cher-und Man- til-la, — A

Die Kartenlegerin, Op. 31, No. 2 — Schlief die Mut-ter end-lich ein ü- ber ih-rer Haus- po-stil- le? — B

Liebesgarten, Op. 34, No. 1 — Die Lie-be ist ein Ro- sen-strauch, wo blüht er, wo blüht er? — C

Unter'm Fenster, No. 3 — Wer ist vor mei-ner Kam- mer-thür? Ich bin es, ich bin es! — D

Familien-Gemälde, No. 4 — Gross- va- ter und Gross- mut-ter, die sas-sen im Gar-ten- hag, — E

Lust der Sturmnacht, Op. 35, No. 1 — Wenn durch Berg' und Tha - - le drau-ssen Re- gen schau-ert, — F

Stirb, Lieb' und Freud, No. 2 — Zu Augs- burg steht ein ho - - - - - hes Haus — G

Wanderlied, No. 3 — Wohl- auf! noch ge-trun- ken den fun- kelnden Wein! A- de nun, ihr Lie-ben, — H

Erstes Grün, No. 4 — Du jun-ges Grün,du fri-sches Gras,wie man-ches Herz durch-dich ge-nas, — I

Auf das Trinkglas eines verstorbenen Freundes, No. 6 — Du herr- lich Glas, nun stehst du leer, Glas, das er oft — J

Wanderung, No. 7 — Wohl- auf und frisch ge- wan-dert in's un- be-kann- te Land! — K

Stille Liebe, No. 8 — Könnt'ich dich in Lie-dern prei-sen,säng ich dir das läng-ste Lied, — L

Frage, No. 9 — Wärst du nicht, heil' ger A- bend-schein! wärst du nicht, — M

Stille Thränen, No. 10 — Du bist vom Schlaf er-stan-den und wan - delst durch die Au' — N

Wer machte dich so krank? No. 11 — Dass du so krank ge-wor-den, wer hat es denn ge-macht? — O

Alte Laute, No. 12 — Hörst du den Vo- gel sin-gen? Siehst du den Blü-then-baum? — P

Sonntags am Rhein, Op. 36, No. 1 — Des Sonn- tags in der Mor- gen-stund' wie wan-dert's sich so schön — Q

Ständchen, No. 2 — Lieb- chen, was zö- gerst Du? Lieb-chen, was zö- gerst Du? — R

An den Sonnenschein, No. 4 — O Son- nen-schein, o Son- nen-schein! wie scheinst du mir in's Herz hinein, — S

Dichters Genesung, Op. 36, No. 5 — A
Und wie-der hatt' ich der Schön-sten ge-dacht, die nur in Träu-men

Liebesbotshaft, No. 6 — B
Wol-ken die ihr nach O-sten eilt, wo die Ei-ne, die Mei-ne,

Der Himmel hat eine Thräne geweint, Op. 37, No. 1 (Robt. & Clara) — C
Der Him-mel hat ei-ne Thrä-ne ge-weint, die hat sich in's Meer

Er ist gekommen, No. 2 (Robert & Clara Schumann) — D
Er ist ge-kom-men in Sturm und Re-gen, ihm schlug be-klommen

O ihr Herren, o ihr werthen, No. 3 (Robt. & Clara S.) — E
O ihr Her-ren, o ihr wer-then gros-sen rei - - - chen Her-ren all!

Flügel! Flügel! um zu fliegen, No. 8 (Robt. & Clara S.) — F
Flü- gel! Flü- gel! um zu flie-gen ü-ber Berg und Thal_

So wahr die Sonne scheinet, No. 12 (Robt. & Clara S.) — G
So wahr die Son-ne schei-net, so wahr die Wol-ke wei-net,

Liederkreis, Op. 39, No. 1 In der Fremde — H
Aus der Hei-math hin-ter den Bli-tzen rot da kom-men die Wol-ken her

No. 2 Intermezzo — I
Dein Bild-niss wun-der-se-lig hab' ich im Her-zens-grund,

No. 3 Waldesgespräch — J
Es ist schon spät_ es ist schon kalt, was reit'st du ein-sam

No. 4 Die Stille — K
Es weiss und räth es doch kei-ner, wie mir so wohl ist, so wohl!

No. 5 Mondnacht — L
Es war, als hätt'_ der Him-mel die Er-de still_ge-küsst,

No. 6 Schöne Fremde — M
Es rau-schen die Wi-pfel und schau-ern, als mach - ten zu die-ser Stund'

No. 7 Auf einer Burg — N
Ein-ge-schla-fen auf der Lau-er o-ben ist der al-te Rit-ter,

No. 8 In der Fremde — O
Ich hör die Bäch-lein rau-schen im Wal-de her und hin,

No. 9 Wehmuth — P
Ich kann wohl manch-mal sin-gen als ob ich fröh-lich sei;

No. 10 Zwielicht — Q
Dämm'- rung will die Flü- gel spreiten, schau-rig rüh-ren sich_ die Bäu-me

No. 11 Im Walde — R
Es zog ei-ne Hoch-zeit den Berg ent-lang, ich hör-te die Vö - gel

No. 12 Frühlingsnacht — S
Ü-ber'm Gar-ten durch die Lüf-te hört' ich Wan-der-vö-gel zieh'n,

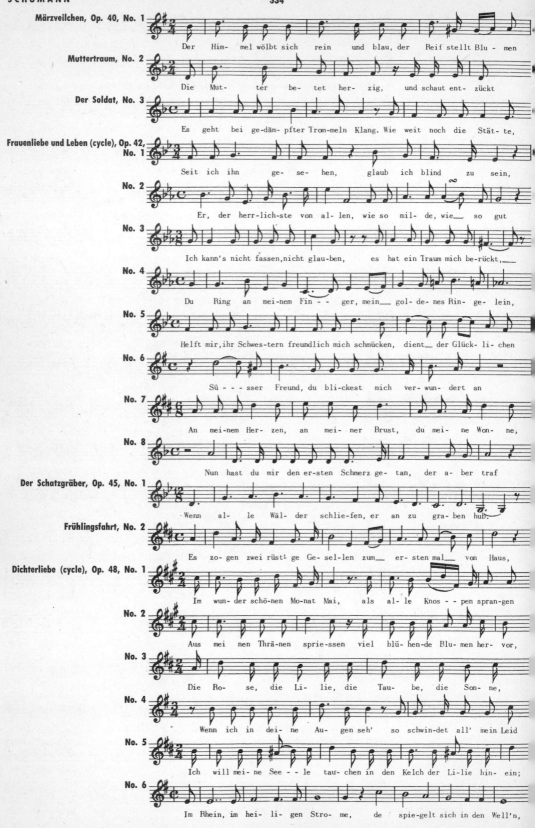

Märzveilchen, Op. 40, No. 1
Der Him- mel wölbt sich rein und blau, der Reif stellt Blu- men

Muttertraum, No. 2
Die Mut- ter be- tet her- zig, und schaut ent- zückt

Der Soldat, No. 3
Es geht bei ge- däm- pfter Trom- meln Klang. Wie weit noch die Stät- te,

Frauenliebe und Leben (cycle), Op. 42, No. 1
Seit ich ihn ge- se- hen, glaub ich blind zu sein,

No. 2
Er, der herr- lich- ste von al- len, wie so mil- de, wie_ so gut

No. 3
Ich kann's nicht fassen, nicht glau- ben, es hat ein Traum mich be- rückt,_

No. 4
Du Ring an mei- nem Fin - - ger, mein_ gol- de- nes Rin- ge- lein,

No. 5
Helft mir, ihr Schwes- tern freundlich mich schmücken, dient_ der Glück- li- chen

No. 6
Sü - - - sser Freund, du bli- ckest mich ver- wun- dert an

No. 7
An mei- nem Her- zen, an mei- ner Brust, du mei- ne Won- ne,

No. 8
Nun hast du mir den er- sten Schmerz ge- tan, der a- ber traf

Der Schatzgräber, Op. 45, No. 1
Wenn al- le Wäl- der schlie- fen, er an zu gra- ben hub.

Frühlingsfahrt, No. 2
Es zo- gen zwei rüst'- ge Ge- sel- len zum_ er- sten mal_ von Haus,

Dichterliebe (cycle), Op. 48, No. 1
Im wun- der schö- nen Mo- nat Mai, als al- le Knos - - pen spran- gen

No. 2
Aus mei- nen Thrä- nen sprie- ssen viel blü- hen- de Blu- men her- vor,

No. 3
Die Ro- se, die Li- lie, die Tau- be, die Son- ne,

No. 4
Wenn ich in dei- ne Au- gen seh' so schwin- det all' mein Leid

No. 5
Ich will mei- ne See - - le tau- chen in den Kelch der Li- lie hin- ein;

No. 6
Im Rhein, im hei- li- gen Stro- me, de spie- gelt sich in den Well'n,

Dichterliebe (cycle), Op. 48, No. 7 — A
Ich grol-le nicht, und wenn das Herz__ auch bricht. E- wig ver-lor-nes Lieb,

No. 8 — B
Und wüss-ten's die Blu-men, die klei-nen, wie tief ver-wun-det mein Herz,

No. 9 — C
Das ist ein Flö-ten und Gei- gen, Trom-pe- ten schmet-tern da- rein,

No. 10 — D
Hör' ich das Lied- chen klin-gen, das einst die Lieb-ste sang,

No. 11 — E
Ein Jüng-ling liebt ein Mäd-chen, die hat ei-nen An-dern er- wählt;

No. 12 — F
Am leuch-ten-den Som-mer-mor-gen geh ich im Gar-ten her- um

No. 13 — G
Ich hab' im Traum ge-wein- et mir träumte du lä-gest im Grab.

No. 14 — H
All-nächt-lich im Trau-me seh' ich dich, und se- he dich freund-lich

No. 15 — I
Aus al- ten Mär-chen winkt es her- vor mit weis- ser Hand,

No. 16 — J
Die al- ten, bö- sen Lie- der die Träu- me bös' und arg,

Die beiden Grenadiere (The Two Grenadiers), Op. 49, No. 1 — K
Nach Frank-reich__ zo- gen zwei Gre- na- dier', die wa-ren in Russland ge-fan-gen,

Das Paradies und die Peri, Op. 50, No. 17 — L
Schlaf' nun und ru- he in Träu- men voll Duft,

Sehnsucht, Op. 51, No. 1 — M
Ich blick'__ in mein Herz__ und ich blick'__ in die Welt,

Volksliedchen, No. 2 — N
Wenn ich früh in den Gar-ten geh, in mei-nem__ grü-nen Hut,

Blondels Lied, Op. 53, No. 1 — O
Spä- hend nach dem Ei- sen-git- ter bei des Mon-des hel-lem Schein

Loreley, No. 2 — P
Es flü-stern und rauschen die Wo-gen wohl ü- ber ihr stil - les Haus,

Der arme Peter, No. 3 — 1 — Q
Der__ Hans und die Gre- te tan-zen__ her - - um,

2 — R
In__ mei - - ner__ Brust, da sitzt__ ein__ Weh,

3 — S
Der ar- me Pe- ter wankt__ vor-bei, gar lang- sam,

Belsatzar, Op. 57
Die Mit-ter-nacht zog nä-her schon; in stum-mer Ruh' lag Ba- by- lon

Die Soldatenbraut, Op. 64, No. 1
Ach, wenn's nur der Kö- nig auch wüsst', wie wa- cker mein Schätze-lein ist!

Das verlassne Mägdelein, No. 2
Früh wann die Häh- ne krah'n eh' die Stern- lein schwin- den,

Tragödie, No. 3
1
Ent- flieh' mit mir und sei mein Weib und ruh' an mei- nem Her-zen aus!
2
Es__ fiel ein Reif in der Früh-lingsnacht, er fiel auf die zar - - - ten Blau

Die Rose stand im Thau, Op. 65, No. 1 (male chorus)
Die Ro- se stand im Thau,___ es wa- ren Per- len grau.

Melancholie, Op. 74, No. 6
Wann, wann er-scheint der Mor- gen, wann denn, wann denn!

Geständniss, No. 7
Al- so lieb' ich euch, Ge- lieb- te, dass mein Herz es nicht mag wa- gen,

Im Walde, Op. 75, No. 2 (chorus)
Es zog ei- ne Hoch-zeit den Berg ent- lang, den Berg ent- lang

Geisternähe, Op. 77, No. 3
Was weht um mei- ne Schlä- fe wie lau- e Früh-ling- luft,

Stiller Vorwurf, No. 4
In ein-sa-'men Stun- den drängt Weh- muth sich auf,

Aufträge, No. 5
Nicht so schnel-le, nicht so schnelle! wart' ein wenig, kleine Wel-le

Er und Sie, Op. 78, No. 2
Seh' ich in das stil- le Thal, wo im Son- nen- schei- ne

Ich denke dein, No. 3
Ich den- ke dein, wenn mir der Son- ne Schim- mer vom Mee- re strahlt

Wiegenlied, No. 4
Schlaf', Kind-lein, schlaf, wie du schläfst, so bist du brav!

Liederalbum für die Jugend, Op. 79, No. 1 Der Abendstern
Du lieb- li- cher Stern, du leuch- test so fern,

No. 4 Frühlingsgruss
So sei ge-grüsst viel tau- send- mal, hol- der, hol- der Früh- ling!

No. 7a Zigeunerliedchen
Un- ter__ die Sol- da - - ten__ ist ein Zi- geu- ner-bub' ge- gan- gen,

No. 7b Jeden Morgen
Je- den Mor- gen, in der Frü- he, wenn mich weckt das Ta- ges- licht,

Drei Gesänge (Hebrew Melodies) Op. 95, No. 1 Die Tochter Jephtas
Da die Hei-math, o Va-ter, da Gott von der Toch-ter

No. 2 An den Mond
Schlaf-lo-ser Son-ne, me-lan-chol-scher Stern! Dein thrän-en-voller Strahl

No. 3 Dem Helden
Dein Tag ist aus, dein Ruhm fing an, es preist des Volks Ge-sang

Nachtlied, Op. 96, No. 1
Ü-ber al-len Gi-pfeln ist Ruh', in al-len Wi-pfeln spü-rest du

Schneeglöckchen, No. 2
Die Son-ne sah die Er-de an, es ging ein mil-der Wind

Ihre Stimme, No. 3
Lass' tief in dir mich le-sen, ver-hehl auch dies mir nicht,

Himmel und Erde, No. 5
Wie der Bäu-me küh-ne Wip-fel zu des Lich-tes Hö-hen

Nur wer die Sehnsucht kennt, Op. 98a, No. 3
Nur wer die Sehn-sucht kennt, weiss was ich lei-de,

Wer nie sein Brot mit Thränen ass, No. 4
Wer nie sein Brot mit Thränen ass, wer nie die kum-mer-vol-len Näch-te

Heiss' mich nicht reden, No. 5
Heiss' mich nicht re-den, heiss' mich schweigen denn mein Ge-heim-nis

Wer sich der Einsamkeit ergiebt, No. 6
Wer sich der Ein-sam-keit er-giebt ach! der ist bald al-lein;

So lasst mich scheinen, No. 9
So lasst mich scheinen bis ich wer-de, zieht mir das weisse Kleid nicht aus!

An die Türen will ich schleichen, No. 8
An die Tü-ren will ich schlei-chen, still und sittsam will ich stehn,

Liebster, deine Worte stehlen, Op. 101, No. 2
Lieb-ster, dei-ne Wor-te steh-len aus dem Bu-sen mir das Herz

Mein schöner Stern, ich bitte dich, No. 4
Mein schö-ner Stern! ich bit-te dich, o las-se du dein heitres Licht

O Freund, mein Schirm, mein Schutz, No. 6
O Freund, mein Schirm, mein Schutz! o Freund mein Schmuck, mein Putz!

An den Abendstern, Op. 103, No. 4
Schweb' em-por am Him-mel, schö-ner A-bend-stern

Viel Glück zur Reise, Schwalben, Op. 104, No. 2
Viel Glück zur Rei-se, Schwalben! ihr eilt, ein lan-ger Zug,

Der Zeisig, No. 4
Wir sind ja, Kind, im Mai-e, wirf Buch und Heft von dir

Die Spinnerin, Op. 107, No. 4 — A

Auf dem Dorf' in den Spinn stu-ben sind lus - - tig die Mäd-chen.

Nänie, Op. 114 (women's chorus) — B

Un - ter den ro-ten Blu - men schlum-me-re, schlum-me-re,

— C

Senkt die Nacht den sanf-ten Fit - tig nie-der tönt der Zi - ther

— D

O bli-cke, wenn den Sinn dir will die Welt____ ver-wir-ren

Der Husar, tra-ra! Op. 117, No. 1 — E

Der Hu-sar, Tra - ra! was ist die Ge - fahr? Sein herz-lieb-ster Schatz

liegt der Feinde gestreckte Schaar, No. 4 — F

Da liegt__ der Feinde ge-stre-ckte Schaar, sie liegt in ihrem blutroten Blut

Frühlingslust, Op. 125, No. 2 — G

Nun ste-hen die Ro-sen in Blü-the, da wirft die Lie-be ein Netz-lein aus,

Die Meerfee, No. 3 — H

Hel - - le Sil-ber-glöck-lein klin-gen aus der Luft vom Meer;

Jung Volkers Lied, No. 4 — I

Und die mich trug im Mut-ter-arm, und die mich schwang__ in Kis-sen,

Dein Angesicht, Op. 127, No. 2 — J

Dein An-ge-sicht, so lieb und schön, das hab' ich jungst im Traum ge-seh'n,

Es leuchtet meine Liebe, No. 3 — K

Es leuch-tet mei-ne Lie - - be in ih - - rer dun-keln Pracht,

Tief im Herzen trag' ich Pein, Op. 138, No. 2 — L

Tief____ im Her - zen trag' ich Pein, muss nach aus-sen stille sein,

wie lieblich ist das Mädchen, No. 3 — M

O wie lieb-lich ist das Mäd-chen wie so schön und voll An-muth,

komanze, No. 5 — N

Flu - - ten rei-cher Eb-ro, blü - - - hen-der U - fer,

Weh, wie zornig ist das Mädchen, No. 7 — O

Weh, wie zor-nig ist das Mädchen, weh, wie zornig, weh, weh!

Hoch, hoch sind die Berge, No. 8 — P

Hoch, hoch sind die Ber - ge und steil ist der Pfad,

Provenzalisches Lied, Op. 139, No. 4 — Q

In dem Ta-len der Pro-ven-ce ist____ der Min-ne-sang entsprossen,

SCHÜTZ, Heinrich (1858-1672)

Bringt her dem Herren — S

Bringt her dem Her - ren, bringt her dem Her - ren, bringt her dem Her - - ren

Geistliche Konzerte (Psalm 40)

Erhöre mich

Ei- le mich, Gott, zu er- ret- ten Herr, mir zu hel- fen

Er- hö- re mich, er- hö- re mich, wenn ich ru- fe,

Die Furcht des Herren

Die Furcht des Her- ren Ist der Weis-heit An- fang,

O lieber Herre Gott

O lie- ber Hee- - re Gott we-cke uns auf,_ dass wir be-reit sein,

Schaffe, in mir, Gott

Schaf-fe in mir, Gott, ein rei- nes Herz und gieb mir einen neu-en,

Ich danke dem Herrn

Ich dan- ke dem Herrn von ganzem Her- zen im Rath der From- men

Ich liege und schlafe

Ich lie- ge und schla - - - - - - - - fe

Psalm 20

Der Herr er- hör dich in der Not, Sein Nam' dich wohl be- hü- te,

Psalm 74

Wie sehr lieb- lich und schö-ne, Sind doch die Woh- nung dein!

Psalm 97

Der Herr ist Kö - - - nig ü- ber all,_ Das Erd-reich sich_ des fre- ue

Psalm 121

Ich heb mein Aug- en sehn- lich auf und seh die Ber- ge

Selig sind die Toten

Se- lig sind die To- ten Se- lig sind, se-lig sin

Symphonie Sacrae Part I

Ich wer- de, ich wer- de, ich wer- de nicht ster - - - - - ben,

Part II

Herr, un-ser Herr-scher, Herr, un- ser Herr-scher, wie herrlich ist dein Nam,

SCOTT, Lady John (Alicia Ann Scott) (1810-1900)

Think on Me

When I no more be- hold thee, Think_ on me,

Annie Laurie

Max - wel-ton's braes are bon-nie, Where ear- ly fa's_ the dew,

SCOTT, Cyril (1879-)

Blackbird's Song, Op. 52, No. 3
By permission of Galaxy Music Corporation,
N. Y., copyright by Elkin & Co., Ltd.

Sweet- heart, I ne'er may know,_ Nev- er may see_

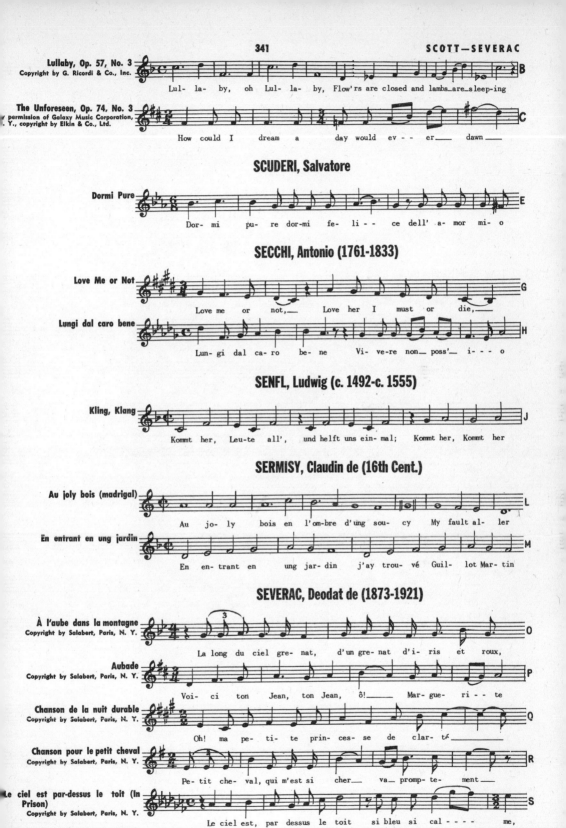

Lullaby, Op. 57, No. 3
Copyright by G. Ricordi & Co., Inc.

Lul- la- by, oh Lul- la- by, Flow'rs are closed and lambs are sleep-ing

The Unforeseen, Op. 74, No. 3
by permission of Galaxy Music Corporation, N. Y., copyright by Elkin & Co., Ltd.

How could I dream a day would ev - - er dawn

SCUDERI, Salvatore

Dormi Pure

Dor- mi pu- re dor-mi fe- li- - ce dell' a- mor mi- o

SECCHI, Antonio (1761-1833)

Love Me or Not

Love me or not, Love her I must or die,

Lungi dal caro bene

Lun- gi dal ca- ro be- ne Vi- ve-re non poss' i- - o

SENFL, Ludwig (c. 1492-c. 1555)

Kling, Klang

Kommt her, Leu-te all', und helft uns ein- mal; Kommt her, Kommt her

SERMISY, Claudin de (16th Cent.)

Au joly bois (madrigal)

Au jo- ly bois en l'om-bre d'ung sou- cy My fault al- ler

En entrant en ung jardin

En en- trant en ung jar- din j'ay trou- vé Guil- lot Mar- tin

SEVERAC, Deodat de (1873-1921)

À l'aube dans la montagne
Copyright by Salabert, Paris, N. Y.

La long du ciel gre- nat, d'un gre-nat d'i- ris et roux,

Aubade
Copyright by Salabert, Paris, N. Y.

Voi- ci ton Jean, ton Jean, ô! Mar- gue- ri- te

Chanson de la nuit durable
Copyright by Salabert, Paris, N. Y.

Oh! ma pe- ti- te prin- ces- se de clar- té

Chanson pour le petit cheval
Copyright by Salabert, Paris, N. Y.

Pe- tit che- val, qui m'est si cher va promp-te- ment

Le ciel est par-dessus le toit (In Prison)
Copyright by Salabert, Paris, N. Y.

Le ciel est, par dessus le toit si bleu si cal - - - - me,

Les Hiboux

Sous les ifs noir qui les a- bri- tent Les hi- boux se tien- nent ran- gés

Ma poupée chérie
Copyright by Salabert, Paris, N. Y.

Ma pou- pée ché- rie ne veut pas___ dor - - mir!___

SHOSTAKOVICH, Dmitri (1906-)

United Nations
Copyright 1946
Leeds Music Corp., N. Y.
Used by permission.

The sun and the stars are all ring-ing___ with song ris-ing stro

SIBELIUS, Jean (1865-)

Våren Flyktar Hastigt (Spring is Fleeting), Op. 13, No. 4
Copyright by Oliver Ditson Co.
Used by permission

Swift the spring- time pass- es yet more swift the sum- mer,

Vilse (Astray) (Verirrt), Op. 17, No. 4
By permission Associated Music Publishers, Inc.

Wir lie- fen wohl ir- re den an- dern vor- an,

Lastu lainehilla (Driftwood), No. 7
By permission Associated Music Publishers, Inc.

Span, wo- her auf Wel- len spu- ren? Ru-ne auf der Wo- ge Rük-ker

Svarta rosor (Black Roses), Op. 36, No. 1
By permission Associated Music Publishers, Inc.

Tell me what grief o- ver- comes you to- day, You that ev- er are

Säf, säf, susa (Schilfrohr, säus'le!), No. 4
By permission Associated Music Publishers, Inc.

Schilf-rohr, säus- le, Wel- le, flieh',doch sagt,wo ist jung In-ga-lill

Den första Kyssen (The First Kiss), Op. 37, No. 1
By permission Associated Music Publishers, Inc.

Zum A- bend-stern am Sil- ber- wol- ken ran- de

Var det en dröm? (Was it a dream?), No. 4
By permission Associated Music Publishers, Inc.

War___ es ein Traum___ dass Zei- ten lang Dein___ Her- zens freund ich wa

Tuol Laulaa Neitonen (A Maiden Yonder Sings), Op. 50, No. 3
Copyright by Oliver Ditson Co.
Used by permission

A mai- den yon- der___ sings Per- chance is___ dead___ her___ lov- er,

O wert thou here (Aus banger Brust), No. 4
By permission Associated Music Publishers, Inc.

The ro- ses___ blos - som___ as last year, Soft___ breezes thro' the fol- iage si

The Silent Town (Die stille Stadt), No. 5
By permission Associated Music Publishers, Inc.

A town lies in the val- ley, The pal- lid gloam- ing___ dies;

Kom nu hit, död (Come away, Death), Op. 60, No. 1 (Shakespeare)
By permission Associated Music Publishers, Inc.

Komm her-bei, komm her-bei,Tod! Ver- senk in Cy- pres- sen den Leib

Vår förnimmelser (Coming of Spring), Op. 86, No. 1
Copyright by Hansen, Copenhagen

Öf- ver drif- vans is-kri- stall blän- der so- len vär- ligt.

Blåseppan (The Anemone), Op. 88, No. 1
Copyright by Hansen, Copenhagen

Wie in der Luft du Ler-chen-schlag So willst auch Du im grü - nen_Hag

Norden (From the North), Op. 90, No. 1
Copyright by Hansen, Copenhagen

Welk___ sind die Blät - - ter,___ Eis___ deckt die Se - - en

SIBELLA, Gabriele

La Girometta (arr.)
Copyright 1919, G. Schirmer, Inc.

Chi t'ha fat-to quel-le scar-pet-te che ti stan si ben

Me l'ha fat-te lo mio A-mo-re,___ me l'ha fat-te lo mio A-mo-re

SIECZYNSKI, Dr. Rudolf

Wien, du Stadt meiner Träume

Mein Herz und mein Sinn schwärmt stets nur für Wien

Wien, Wien, nur du al-lein sollst stets die Stadt meiner Träu-me

SILCHER, Friedrich

Aennchen von Tharau

Die Lorelei

Aenn-chen von Tha-rau ist, die mir ge-fällt, sie ist mein Le-ben,

Ich weiss nicht was soll es be-deu-ten dass ich so trau-rig bin___

SINDING, Christian (1856-1941)

Moderen Synger (The mother sings)

Der Skreg un Fugl (There cried a bird)

Sylvelin, Op. 55, No. 1
Copyright 1912, G. Schirmer, Inc.

Gret-chen lies in her gloom-y bed in the wet, wet mold

There cried___ a bird in its lone - - - - - some flight

O Syl-ve-lin, God's own blessing be on you the whole day through!

SJÖBERG, C.

Tonerna

Tan-ke, hvars stri-der blott nat-ten ser___ To-ner,___

SJÖGREN, Emil (1853-1918)

Lehn' deine Wang', Op. 16, No. 5

Lehn' die-ne Wang' an mei-ne Wang' dann fliessen die Thrä-nen

SMETANA, Bedrich (1824-1884)

OPERAS

The Bartered Bride Act I
Opening Chorus

Seht am Strauch die Knos--pen___ sprin-gen! Hört die mun-tern Vö-gel___

SMETANA

The Bartered Bride
Act III

Finale

Ge-seg-net, ge-seg-net, wer liebt und auch ver-traut!

Kom-men wir ger-ne, so kom-men wir gleich, gleich, gleich,

So ist's recht, es freut uns Al-le, so ist's recht,

Dalibor Act II Love duet

Ta du-še ta tou-ha, to srd-ce, ten čar tot' lás-ky mé

Duet

Ó nev-ý-slov-né š tě-sti lá-sky

The Devil's Wall (Certova Sténa)
Act I

Stast-ná vím on přijde dnes přec mě vsr-déč-ku cos trá-nu

Ciž poz-by-la jsi ve mne ví-ry? A kdy-by můj byl kraj ten sí-rý

Tak věč-ně k to-bě ľnout rtem na rtu spo-či nout

Jen je-di-na-mě zě-ny krá-sna tvář tak do-ja-la

Act II

Kam prch-nout, kam prch-nout před je-jím tak sladkym o-brazem?

Ach, zře se to-mu pri-vy-ka Mně se to zvot-lo s nejkrásně jším

Act III

Ti-se krad-me pře-po-zor-ně špe-hům chy-trým pro-ne-snáz,

O Bo-že lá-sky Vté-to hrů-zné chvi-li mi ro-stou kří-dla

The Kiss Act I Duet

Für e-wig ver-eint treu in Lie-be ist un-ser heisses flehen

Cradle Song

Schla-fe mein Kind-lein, schlaf' ein, schla-fe ein,

Wie hell am Him-mel die Ster-ne auch steh'n, wie sanft im Mond-licht

Act II Smugglers' Chorus

Lei-se, auf-ge-passt oh-ne Ruh noch Rast; lauscht im Mor-gen-wind

If I knew how to
wipe out my fault

Zu süh-nen mei-ne gro-sse Schuld, will ich die Ge-lieb-te

Duet

Ach, ar-mer Freund, früh starb dein Gluck, schwer kehrt, was man ver-lor, zu-rück!

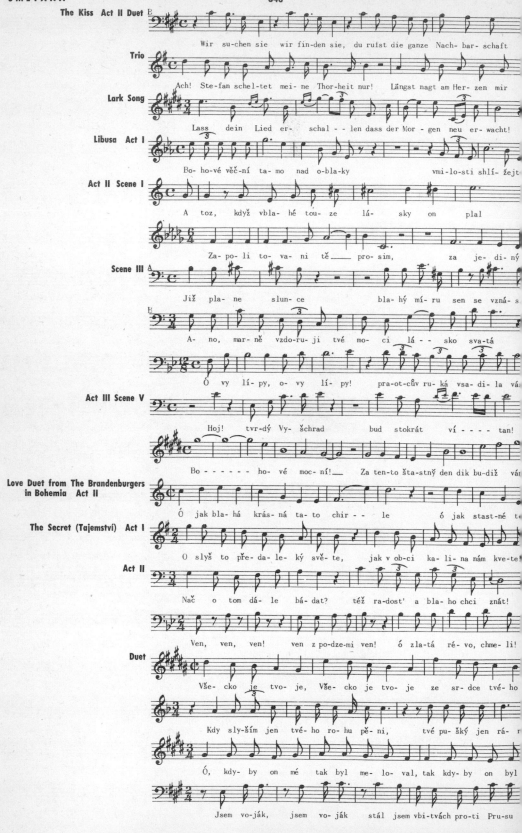

The Kiss Act II Duet

Wir su-chen sie wir fin-den sie, du rufst die ganze Nach-bar-schaft

Trio

Ach! Ste-fan schel-tet mei- ne Thor-heit nur! Längst nagt am Her- zen mir

Lark Song

Lass dein Lied er- schal - - len dass der Mor- gen neu er- wacht!

Libusa Act I

Bo- ho-vé věč-ní ta- mo nad o-bla-ky vmi-lo-sti shlí- žejt

Act II Scene I

A toz, když vbla- hé tou- ze lá- sky on plal

Za-po-li to-va-ni tě___ pro-sim, za je-di- ný

Scene III

Již pla- ne slun-ce bla- hý mí- ru sen se vzná- s.

A- no, mar- ně vzdo-ru- ji tvé mo- ci lá - - sko sva-tá

Ó vy lí- py, o- vy lí- py! pra-ot-cův ru- ká vsa-di- la vá

Act III Scene V

Hoj! tvr-dý Vy- šchrad bud stokrát ví - - - - tan!

Bo - - - - - - ho- vé moc- ní!__ Za ten-to šta-stný den dik bu-diž vá

Love Duet from The Brandenburgers
in Bohemia Act II

Ó jak bla- há krás- ná ta- to chir - - le ó jak stast-né te

The Secret (Tajemství) Act I

O slyš to pře-da- le- ký svě- te, jak v ob-ci ka- li- na nám kve-te!

Act II

Nač o tom dá- le bá- dat? též ra-dost' a bla- ho chci znát!

Ven, ven, ven! ven z po-dze-mi ven! ó zla-tá ré- vo, chme- li!

Duet

Vše- cko je tvo- je, Vše- cko je tvo- je ze sr-dce tvé-ho

Kdy sly-ším jen tvé- ho ro-hu pě- ni, tvé pu- šký jen rá- r

Ó, kdy- by on mé tak byl me-lo- val, tak kdy- by on byl

Jsem vo-ják, jsem vo- ják stál jsem vbi-tvách pro-ti Pru-su

The Secret — Act III
A — Což ta vo-da s vý-še strá-ní pa-dá,— pa-da, pa-da

The Two Widows (Dvé Vdovy) Act I
B — Ji-tro krás-né, ne-be jas-né, ky-ne nám,
C — Sa-mo-stat-né vlád-nu já vše-mi stat-ky svý-mi

Quartet
D — O ja-kou tí - - sen mé srd-ce cí - - tí, jej mám zde zří - ti,
E — Aj, viz-te lov-ce tam, jak blou-di sám a sám,

Act II
F — Kdy za-vi-tá máj, lás-ky čas, tu ob-živ-ne háj
G — Roz-hod-nu-to, u-za-vře-no, za-mit-nu-to po-stou-pe-no!
H — Ach, jak kru-tě sou-zi chlad-ný od-por ten srd-ce mé,—
I — Aj, ja-ký to kras-ny den, k ra-dos-ti jen u-stvo-řen
J — Necht' co-ko-liv mne, co-ko-liv mne zlo-bi svě-tě,

Trio
K — Co to, hol-ka, co-to, nač ta pý-cha pan-ská? vzdyt' se tan-ci pro-to

Evening Songs (Vecerni Pisne) I
L — Who's mas-ter of the gol-den strings, him you should more than hon-our,

II
M — Don't throw a-gainst the pro-phets stones! Like birds they par-don ne- ver,

III
N — I fan-cied once "pain has grown old, not to out- live to- mor- row

IV
O — Hey! what a joy-ful plea-sure to clasp a girl in danc- ing

V
P — Out of my songs— I build for thee a throne as po-ets of- ten feign

First Songs 1. Milenciny oči (My dear eyes)
Q — Nichts kann mir so ge-nü- gen, wie mei-nes Lieb-chens Blick,

2. S bohem (Goodbye)
R — Nun, wohl- an es muss ja sein le-be wohl du En-gel mein

3. Smutek Opuštěné (Sorrow of de-parture)
S — Oft am Ran-de stil-ler Flu-ten sitz' ich ein-sam da,

First Songs 4. Vyzvání (Invitation)

Pojď mil- ko,   Pojď mil- ko!   Hle sklá-ni se les ktobě néž

5. Jaro lásky

Die - ses Sai-ten-spiel der Brust, das — du hast so reich be- sai- tet

SMITH, John Christopher (1712-1795)

No more dams I'll make for fish

No   more dams — I'll make — for fish;   Nor fetch fir - ing

SPEAKS, Oley (1876-   )

Morning A
Copyright 1910, G. Schirmer, Inc.

Nev- er star was   in the sky, Win- ter winds went wail-ing by,

B

Morn- ing on the ho- ly hills, Mead- ows that en- fold the rills

On the Road to Mandalay A1
Copyright 1907, G. Schirmer, Inc.

By the old Moul-mein Pa- go- da, look- in' east- ward — to the sea

A2

Come you back to Man-da- lay, Where the old Flo-til- la lay

Sylvia
Copyright 1914, G. Schirmer, Inc.

Syl- via's hair is   like the night, Touched with glancing star- ry beams

To You

Some-   where, I know, from the blue of the sky

SPILMAN, James E.

Flow gently, sweet Afton

Flow gen- tly,   sweet — Af- ton, a- mang thy green braes

SPOHR, Ludwig (1784-1859)

As pants the Hart

As pants the Hart   for cool- ing streams When heat - ed in the chase,

The Last Judgment Part I No. 12

Lord   God of   Heav'n   and Earth, we a- dore — the

Part II No. 19

Blest are the de- part- ed   Who in the Lord are sleep - - in

Rose, softly blooming

Rose soft- ly bloom- ing formed — to — al - - lure

SPONTINI, Gaspard (1774-1851)

La Vestale (opera) Act I

Dans le sein d'un a-mi fi-dè---le

L'a-mour est un mon-stre,est un mons-tre bar-ba-re

O ma fil-le, ma fil---le, ton coeur s'é-ga-re

Act II

Toi que j'im-plo-re a-vec ef-froi re-dou-ta-ble dé-es-se

O Nu--me tu-te-lar degl' in-fe-li-ci,

Act III

Toi que je lais-se sur la ter----re, mor-tel

STANFORD, C. Villers (1852-1924)

A Carol of Bells

Ring, Christ-mas bells of Lon-don, Swing wild-ly with a will

"Greet-ings to all!" Boom the Bells of St. Paul;

Cavalier Songs No. 1

Kent-ish Sir Byng stood for his King, bid-ding the crop-head-ed

No. 2

King Charles! and who'll do him right now! King Charles!

No. 3

Boot, sad-dle, to horse and a-way! Res-cue my Cas-tle

Coelos ascendit hodie, Op. 38
By permission Boosey & Hawkes, Inc.,
copyright owners

Coe-los as-cen---dit ho-di-e Je-sus Christus Rex glo-ri-ae

Father O'Flynn

Of priests we can of-fer a charm-in' va-ri-e-ty

Breathe not his Name (Air, the Brown Maid)

Oh breathe not his name, let it sleep in the shade,

A Soft Day, Op. 140, No. 3
Copyright by Stainer & Bell, Ltd., London;
Galaxy Music Corporation, N. Y.,
agents

A soft day, thank God! A wind from the south with a hon-ey'd mouth

Songs of the Fleet, No. 5. Fare Well
Copyright by Stainer & Bell, Ltd., London;
Galaxy Music Corporation, N. Y.,
agents

Mo-ther, with un-bowed head Hear thou a-cross the sea

STANGE, Max (1856-1932)

Die Bekehrte, Op. 13, No. 1

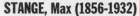

Bei dem Glanz der A -- bend- rö- the ging__ ich still

STAUB, Victor (Contemporary)

L'Heure Silencieuse
By permission Durand & Cie, Paris; Elkan-Vogel Co., Inc., Phila., copyright owners

C'est l'heu-re dis- crête__ et tran- quil-le Qu'at- tend__ pour ren-trer__

STEFFANI, Agostino (1654-1728)

Sei si caro, from Marco Aurelio (opera)

Sei si ca- ro, si vez- zo- so Hai nel vol-to un cer - to, che,

STEVENS, Richard J. S. (1757-1837)

Sigh no more, ladies

Sigh no more, la- dies, la- dies,sigh no more__

STORACE, Stephen (1763-1796)

The Pretty Creature

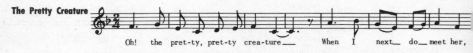

Oh! the pret-ty, pret-ty crea-ture__ When I next__ do__ meet her,

STRADELLA, Allesandro (c. 1645-1682)

Pietà, Signore (aria di chiesa)

Pie- tà, Si- gno- re, di, me do- len-te Si- gnor, pie- tà!

STRAUS, Oskar (1870-   )

OPERETTAS
The Chocolate Soldier
Copyright 1908, Ludwig Doblinger (Bernard Herzmansky)
Copyright 1909, M. Witmark & Sons
Act I My Hero

Sympathy

Waltz Dream Act. I Waltz

Come! Come! I love you on - ly, My heart is true__

Oh you lit- tle cho- co- late sol- dier man, You're__ far too sweet

My life is sweet, I hold it dear;All death is grue-some, dark and drear,

Ti- ra- la- la! Ti-ra- la-la! Tell no one! All men sus-pi-cious are,

For- give, for- give, for- give,__ Why was I there? I wished to live__

The soft sum- mer twi-light is fad- ing, I sat in the gar- den a-lone__

OPERETTAS
Waltz Dream　Act I Waltz

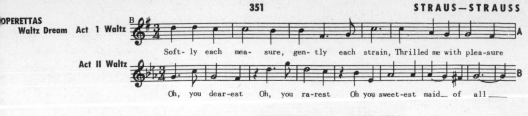

Soft-ly each mea-sure, gen-tly each strain, Thrilled me with plea-sure

Act II Waltz

Oh, you dear-est　Oh, you ra-rest　Oh you sweet-est maid_ of all __

STRAUSS, Johann (1825-1899)

OPERETTAS
Die Fledermaus (The Bat)
(Rosalinda), Op. 56
Act I No. 1

Täub-chen, das ent-flat-tert ist, stil-le mein Ver-lan-gen

Wenn ich je-nes Täub-chen wär, flie-gen könn-te hin und her,

No. 3

Eh' Du in der stil-len Kam-mer la-bo-rirst am Katz-en-jam-mer

No. 4

O je, o je, wie rührt mich dies, o je, o je, wie rührt mich dies,

No. 5 (Finale)

Trin-ke, Lieb-chen, trin-ke schnell; trin-ken macht die Au-gen hell;

Glück-lich ist, wer ver-gisst was doch nicht zu än-dern ist;

Mein Herr, was däch-ten Sie von_ mir, säss ich mit ei-nem Frem-den

Mein schö-nes gros-ses Vo-gel-haus, es ist ganz na-he hier

Act II No. 7

Ich la--de gern mir Gäs-te ein, man lebt bei mir recht_ fein,

No. 8

Mein Herr Mar-quis, ein_ Mann wie Sie, sollt' bes-ser das_ ver-steh'n

No. 10

Klän-ge ____ der_ Hei-mat, ihr weckt ____ mir das Seh-nen,

Feu-er, __ Le-bens-lust, schwellt äch-te Un-gar-brust,

No. 11 (Finale)

Im Feu-er--strom der Re-ben, tra la la la la la la la

Die Ma-je-stät wird an-er-kannt, an-er-kannt rings im Land;

Brü-der-lein, Brü-der-lein und Schwes-ter-lein __ wol-len Al-le wir sein,

Dui-du Dui-du, la la la la __ la dui-du, dui-du,

OPERETTAS
Die Fledermaus Op. 56
Act II No. 11 Finale

Mar- ian- ka, komm und tanz' me' hier! Heut ist's schon schetzko jedno mir!

Ha, welch ein Fest, wel-che Nacht voll Freud! Lie- be und wein

Act III No. 14

Spiel' ich die Un-schuld vom Lan-de, na-tür-lich im kur-zen Ge- wan-de

Wenn Sie das ge-sehn, müs-sen Sie ge-steh'n, es wär der Scha- den

Al- les_ mach'n voll Ehr-furcht mir Spa- lier; lauscht den Tö- nen_

Spiel' ich 'ne Da- me von Pa- ris, ach,_ ach,_

No. 15

Ein selt-sam A- ben-teu- er ist ge-stern mir pas- siert

Ja, ich bins, den Ihr be- tro-gen, ja, ich bins den Ihr be- tro-gen

No. 16

O Fle-der-maus, o Fle-der- maus, lass end-lich jetzt dein O- pfer aus;

Die ganze Nacht durchschwärmt,
from Waldmeister

Die gan- ze Nacht durch schwärmt ge - trun- ken und ge- lärmt.

Eine Nacht in Venedig (A night in
Venice) Act I

Dein_ Lied von Lieb und Treu- e hat ei-nen fal-schen Ton

Pel- le-gri- na ron- di-nel-la, ron-di-nel-la pel- le- gri- na

Al- le mas- kirt, Al- le mas- kirt, cos-pet- to! wie a- mu-san

Sei mir_ ge-grüsst_ du hol-des Ve- ne - - - tia,

Komm'_ in die Gon- del, mein Lieb-chen, o stei-ge doch ein,_

Act II

Treu sein, das liegt mir nicht,_ weil ich leicht den Kopf ver-lier,

Act III Lagunen
Walzer

Ach, wie so herr-lich zu schau'n_ sind all' die lieb-li-chen Frau'n_

Wie sie schmei- cheln, Lie- be heu- cheln, uns durch Thrä - nen_

Nature, from Der Lustige Krieg (The
Merry War)

Na - - ture loved she_ fair to see_ and so free, She'd be roam-ing.

The Queen's Lace Handkerchief
Act I Truffle Song

Such dish by man not oft is seen As that which once__ I tast-ed

Act II

Where the wild rose sweet-ly doth blow, There must I go;

Bright as a ray from the heav'nly heights gleam- ing,

Zigeunerbaron (The Gypsy Baron)
Act I No. 2

Als flot-ter Geist doch früh ver-waist hab ich die gan- ze Welt durch-reist

Ja das al- les auf Ehr_____ Das kann ich und noch mehr,_____

No. 3

Ja, das Schrei-ben und das Le- sen, ist__ nie mein Fach' ge- we- sen,

No. 5

Ah____ sieh da,___ ein herr-lich Frau-en- bild, das ganz mit Stau-nen

No. 6

So e- lend und so treu ist kei- ner auf Er- den

Flieh' wie du kannst und fürch- te den Zi- geu- ner

No. 7 (Finale)

Hier im die-sem Land Eu- re Wie- ge stand.__ Ach, als Kind__habt Ihr__

Um frech den Ü- ber-mut zu fröh- nen, ver- let- zet ihr den Stolz

Act II No. 8

Mein Aug' be-wacht.__ bei Tag und Nacht, dies hol- de jun- ge Blut__

Dies En- gels-ge- sicht,dies up- pi- ge Haar, dies Aug' voll Licht,

No. 9

Ha seht es winkt,__ es blinkt,__ es klingt. Ach, un- sern Bli- cken,

No. 11

Wer uns ge- traut? Ei sprich: Sag Du's!__ Der Dom- pfaff,

Und mild sang die Nach- ti- gall ihr Lied-chen in__ die Nacht,__

No. 12½

Her die Hand, es muss ja sein, lass' dein Lieb- chen fah- ren,

No. 13 (Finale)

So voll Fröh- lich-keit gibt es weit und breit__ kei- ne Stadt

Ein Für- sten- kind ein Wun-der ist ge- scheh'n, ha sie ver- dient,

Zigeunerbaron (The Gypsy Baron)
Act III No. 16

Von des Tay- o Strand wo mit star- ker Hand wir die Fein- de

"Gib Acht, es kracht" schreit mich ein Spa-nier an, schiess du nur zu,

No. 17

Hur- rah die Schlacht mit-ge-macht hab'n wir im fer- nen Land

Lus-tig oft un-ver hofft geht es auch im Krie-ge zu,

STRAUSS, Richard (1864-1948)

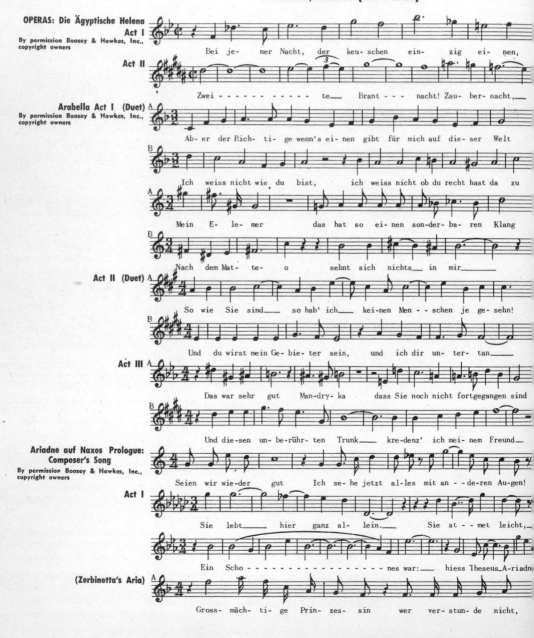

OPERAS: Die Ägyptische Helena
Act I
By permission Boosey & Hawkes, Inc.,
copyright owners

Bei je- ner Nacht, der keu-schen ein- zig ei- nen,

Act II

Zwei - - - - - - - - - te Brant - - - nacht! Zau-ber-nacht,

Arabella Act I (Duet)
By permission Boosey & Hawkes, Inc.,
copyright owners

Ab- er der Rich- ti- ge wenn's ei- nen gibt für mich auf die- ser Welt

Ich weiss nicht wie du bist, ich weiss nicht ob du recht hast da zu

Mein E- le- mer das hat so ei- nen son-der-ba- ren Klang

Nach dem Mat- te- o sehnt sich nichts in mir

Act II (Duet)

So wie Sie sind so hab' ich kei-nen Men - -schen je ge-sehn!

Und du wirst mein Ge- bie- ter sein, und ich dir un- ter-tan

Act III

Das war sehr gut Man-dry- ka dass Sie noch nicht fortgegangen sind

Und die-sen un-be-rühr-ten Trunk kre-denz' ich mei- nem Freund

Ariadne auf Naxos Prologue:
Composer's Song
By permission Boosey & Hawkes, Inc.,
copyright owners

Seien wir wie-der gut Ich se-he jetzt al-les mit an - -de-ren Au-gen!

Act I

Sie lebt hier ganz al- lein. Sie at - -met leicht,

Ein Scho - - - - - - - - - - - nes war: hiess Theseus A-riadn

(Zerbinetta's Aria)

Gross- mäch- ti- ge Prin- zes- sin wer ver-stun-de nicht,

STRAUSS

Ariadne auf Naxos (Zerbinetta's Aria)

Noch glaub' ich dem ei - nen ganz mich ge - hö - rend,

Als ein Gott kam je - - der ge - gan-gen und sein Schritt schon

Capriccio, Op. 85
By permission Boosey & Hawkes, Inc., copyright owners

Kein An - dres, das mir so im Her - - zen loht, nein, Schö - ne,

Ih - re Lie - - be schlägt mir ent-ge-gen, zart - ge-wo-ben

Du Spie - gel - bild - der ver-lieb - - ten Made - leine,

Daphne, Op. 82
By permission Boosey & Hawkes, Inc., copyright owners

O wie ger - ne blieb ich bei dir

Göt - - - ter! Bru - der im ho - hen O - lym - pos!

Wind spie - le mit mir! Se - li-ge Vö - gel woh-net in mir

Der Rosenkavalier, Op. 59
Act I Italian Serenade
By permission Boosey & Hawkes, Inc., copyright owners

Di - ri - go - ri ar - ma-to il se - no con-tro a-mor mi ri-be - llai

Da geht er hin, der auf - ge-blas-ne, schlech- te Kerl

Kann mich auch an ein Mä- del er - in-nern, die frisch aus dem Klos-ter

Die Zeit, die ist ein son- der-bar Ding, Wenn man so hin-lebt

Act II Presentation of the Rose

Mir ist die Eh - - re wi- der fah-ren dass ich der hoch

Hat ei - nen star - - - ken Ge - ruch wie Ro - - sen,

Ich kenn ihn schon recht wohl, mon Cou - sin!

Mit Ih - ren Au - gen voll Trä - - - nen kommt Sie zu mir

Herr Ca - va - lier Den mor - gi- gen A- bend hätt' i frei.

Act III Trio

Hab' mir's ge - lobt, ihn lieb zu ha-ben in der rich-ti-gen Weis',

Duet

Ist ein Traum, kann nicht wirk- lich sein dass wir zwei bei ei - nan-der sein,

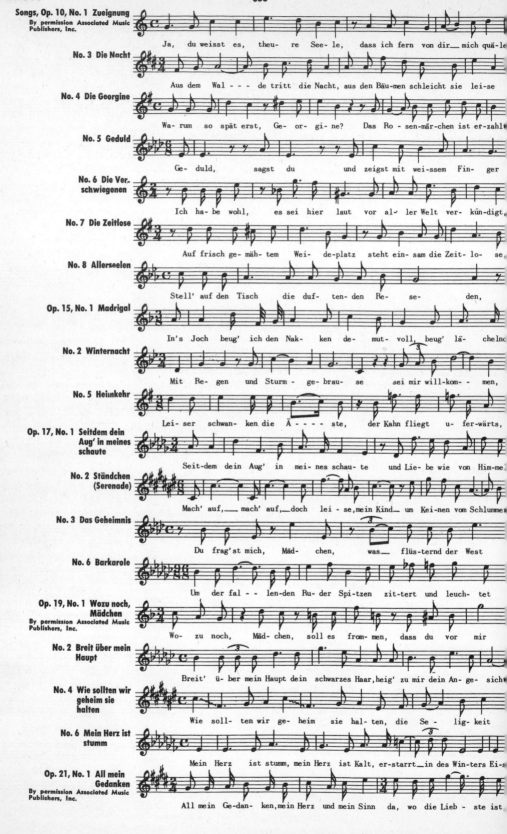

Songs, Op. 10, No. 1 Zueignung
By permission Associated Music Publishers, Inc.

Ja, du weisst es, theu- re See- le, dass ich fern von dir__ mich quä- le,

No. 3 Die Nacht

Aus dem Wal - - - de tritt die Nacht, aus den Bäu- men schleicht sie lei- se

No. 4 Die Georgine

Wa- rum so spät erst, Ge- or- gi- ne? Das Ro- sen-mär-chen ist er-zahlt

No. 5 Geduld

Ge- duld, sagst du und zeigst mit wei- ssem Fin- ger

No. 6 Die Ver-
schwiegenen

Ich ha- be wohl, es sei hier laut vor al- ler Welt ver- kün-digt,

No. 7 Die Zeitlose

Auf frisch ge- mäh- tem Wei- de-platz steht ein- sam die Zeit- lo- se,

No. 8 Allerseelen

Stell' auf den Tisch die duf- ten- den Re- se- den,

Op. 15, No. 1 Madrigal

In's Joch beug' ich den Nak- ken de- mut- voll, beug' lä- chelnd

No. 2 Winternacht

Mit Re- gen und Sturm - ge-brau- se sei mir will-kom- - men,

No. 5 Heimkehr

Lei- ser schwan- ken die Ä - - - ste, der Kahn fliegt u- fer-wärts,

Op. 17, No. 1 Seitdem dein
Aug' in meines
schaute

Seit-dem dein Aug' in mei- nes schau- te und Lie- be wie von Him-me.

No. 2 Ständchen
(Serenade)

Mach' auf,__ mach' auf,__ doch lei- se,mein Kind__ um Kei-nen vom Schlumme

No. 3 Das Geheimnis

Du frag'st mich, Mäd- chen, was__ flüs-ternd der West

No. 6 Barkarole

Um der fal - - len-den Ru- der Spi-tzen zit-tert und leuch- tet

Op. 19, No. 1 Wozu noch,
Mädchen
By permission Associated Music
Publishers, Inc.

Wo- zu noch, Mäd- chen, soll es from- men, dass du vor mir

No. 2 Breit über mein
Haupt

Breit' ü- ber mein Haupt dein schwarzes Haar,heig' zu mir dein An- ge- sicht

No. 4 Wie sollten wir
geheim sie
halten

Wie soll- ten wir ge- heim sie hal- ten, die Se- lig-keit

No. 6 Mein Herz ist
stumm

Mein Herz ist stumm, mein Herz ist Kalt, er-starrt__in des Win-ters Ei-s

Op. 21, No. 1 All mein
Gedanken
By permission Associated Music
Publishers, Inc.

All mein Ge- dan- ken,mein Herz und mein Sinn da, wo die Lieb- ste ist

ngs, Op. 21, No. 2 Du meines Her- zens Krönelein   A

Du mei-nes Her - - zens Krö- ne-lein, du bist von lau- trem Gol- de

No. 3 Ach Lieb, ich muss nun scheiden   B

Ach, Lieb, ich muss nun schei- den, geh'n ü- ber Berg und Thal,

Op. 26, No. 1 Frühlingsgedränge   C
permission Boosey & Hawkes, Inc.,
ht owners

Früh- lings- kin- der im bun- ten Ge- drän- ge; flatternde Blü- ten,

Op. 27, No. 1 Ruhe, meine Seele A   D
By permission Associated Music
Publishers, Inc.

Nicht ein Lüft-chen regt sich lei- se, sanft ent-schlummert ruht der Hain;

B   E

Ru- he, ru- he, mei- ne See- le dei- ne Stür- me gin- gen wild

No. 2 Cäcilie   F

Wenn du es wüss- test was träu- men heisst von bren-nen-den Küs- sen

No. 3 Heimliche Aufforderung   G

Auf, he- be die fun- keln-de Schaa- le em- por zum Mund,

No. 4 Morgen   H

Und mor- gen wird die Son- ne wie - - - der schei- nen

Op. 29, No. 1 Traum durch die Dämmerung   I
By permission Associated Music
Publishers, Inc.

Wei- te Wie- sen im Däm- mer-grau; die Son- ne ver-glomm,

No. 2 Schlagende Herzen   J

Ü- ber Wie- sen und Fel- der ein Kna- be ging; kling, klang

No. 3 Nachtgang   K

Wir gin- gen durch die stil- le mil- de Nacht, dein Arm in mei- nem,

Op. 31, No. 1 Blauer Sommer   L
y permission Boosey & Hawkes, Inc.
opyright owners

Ein blau- er Som- mer glanz und glu- ten-schwer geht_ ü- ber Wie- sen,

No. 3 Weisser Jasmin   M

Blei- che Blü- te, Blü- te der Lie- be, leuch- te ü- ber dem Lau- ben- dach

Op. 32, No. 1 Ich trage meine Minne vor Wonne stumm   N
By permission Associated Music
Publishers, Inc.

Ich tra- ge mei- ne Min- ne vor Won- ne stumm im Her- zen

No. 2 Sehnsucht   O

Ich ging den Weg ent-lang, der ein- sam lag den stets allein

No. 3 Liebeshymnus   P

Heil je- nem Tag, der dich ge- bo- ren, Heil ihm,

No. 4 O süsser Mai   Q

O sü- sser Mai,_ o ha- be du Er- bar-men, o sü- sser Mai,

Op. 33, No. 4 Pilgers Morgenlied   R
By permission Associated Music
Publishers, Inc.

Mor- gen- ne- bel Li- la, hül- len dei- nen Thurm ein.

Op. 36, No. 2 Für fünfzehn Pfennige   S
By permission Boosey & Hawkes, Inc.,
copyright owners

Das Mägd- lein will ein' Frei- er habn, und sollt sie'n aus der Er- de grabn,_

Songs, Op. 36, No. 3 Hat gesagt, bleibt's nicht dabei

Mein Vater hat ge-sagt ich soll das Kindlein wie-gen, wie - - - gen,

Op. 37, No. 1 Glückes genug
By permission Boosey & Hawkes, Inc., copyright owners

Wenn sanft du mir im Ar - - me schliefst,

No. 2 Ich liebe dich

Vier ad-li-ge Ros-se vo-ran un-serm Wa-gen,

No. 3 Meinem Kinde

Du schläfst und sach-te neig' ich mich ü-ber dein Bett-chen

No. 4 Mein Auge

Du bist mein Au-ge! Du durch-dringst mich ganz

Op. 39, No. 4 Befreit
By permission Boosey & Hawkes, Inc., copyright owners

Du wirst nicht wei-nen Lei-se, lei - se wirst du lä-cheln

No. 5 Lied an meinem Sohn

Der Sturm be-horcht mein Va-ter-haus, mein Herz

Op. 41a, No. 1 Wiegenlied
By permission Associated Music Publishers, Inc.

Träu - - - - - me, träu - - me du, mein süs-ses Le - - ben

No. 3 Am Ufer

Die Welt ver-stummt, dein Blut er-klingt in seinem hel-len Ab-grund

No. 5 Leise Lieder

Lei-se Lie-der sing' ich dir bei Nacht, Lie - - der, die kein sterb-blich Ohr

Op. 43, No. 2 Muttertändelei
By permission Boosey & Hawkes, Inc., copyright owners

Seht mir doch mein schö - - nes Kind, mit den gold' - - nen Zot - tel-

Op. 46, No. 4 Morgenrot
By permission Boosey & Hawkes, Inc., copyright owners

Dort wo der Mor-gen-stern her-geht und wo der Mor-gen-wind herweht,

Op. 47, No. 2 Des Dichters Abendgang

Er gehst du dich im A-bend-licht (das ist die Zeit)

Op. 48, No. 1 Freundliche Vision
By permission Boosey & Hawkes, Inc., copyright owners

Nicht im Schla-fe hab ich das ge-träumt hell am Ta-ge sah ich's

No. 2 Ich schwebe

Ich schwe-be wie auf En-gels-schwin-gen, die Er-de kaum be-rührt

No. 3 Kling

Kling! Mei-ne See-le gibt rei - nen Ton. Und ich wähn-te die Ar-me

No. 4 Winterweihe

In die-sen Win-ter-ta-gen, nun sich das Licht ver-hüllt,

No. 5 Winterliebe

Der Son-ne ent-ge-gen in Lie-bes-glu-ten wand'r ich

No. 7 Wer lieben will, muss leiden

Wer lie-ben will, muss lei - - den oh'n Lei-den, oh'n Lei-den liebt man ni

Songs, Op. 49, No. 1 Waldseligkeit
By permission Boosey & Hawkes, Inc., copyright owners

A

Der Wald be-ginnt zu rau--schen,den Bäu-men naht die Nacht:

No. 3 Wiegenliedchen

B

Bien-chen, Bien-chen, wiegt sich im Son-nen-schein

Op. 51, No. 2 Der Einsame
By permission Boosey & Hawkes, Inc., copyright owners

C

Wo ich bin, mich rings um-dun-kelt Fin-ster-nis

Op. 56, No. 1 Gefunden
By permission Associated Music Publishers, Inc.

D

Ich ging im Wal-de so für mich hin, und nichts zu su-chen,

No. 2 Blindenklage

E

Wenn ich dich fra-ge, dem das Le---ben blüht:

No. 3 Im Spätboot

F

Aus der Schiffs-bank mach' ich mei-nen Pfühl, end---lich wird

No. 4 Mit deinen blauen Augen

G

Mit dei-nen blau---en Au-gen siehst du mich lieb-lich an,

No. 5 Frühlingsfeier

H

Das ist des Früh-lings trau-ri-ge Lust! Die blü--hen-den Mäd-chen

No. 6 Die heiligen drei Könige aus Morgenland

I

Die heil'-gen drei Kön'-ge aus Mor-gen-land, sie fru-gen

Op. 68, No. 4 Als mir dein Lied erklang

J

Dein Lied er-klang! ich ha--be es ge-hört,

No. 5 Amor

K

An dem Feu------------er sass das Kind A-mor

Op. 69, No. 3 Einerlei
By permission Boosey & Hawkes, Inc., copyright owners

L

Ihr Mund ist stets der-sel------------be,

No. 5 Schlechtes Wetter

M

Das ist ein schlech-tes Wet-ter, es reg--------net und stürmt

Olympische Hymne

N

Völ---ker! Seid des Vol-kes Gä-ste, kommt durch's off-ne Tor her-ein

STRAVINSKY, Igor (1882-   )

Symphonie de Psaumes No. 1
By permission Boosey & Hawkes, Inc., copyright owners

P

E--xau-di o--ra-ti-o-nem me-am, Do--mi--ne,

Q

Quo-ni-am ad-ve-na e-go sum a------pud te

No. 2

R

Ex-pec---tans ex-pec-ta-----vi Do-mi-num

S

Et im-mi-sit in os me-um can-ti-cum nov-um

Symphonie de Psaumes No. 3

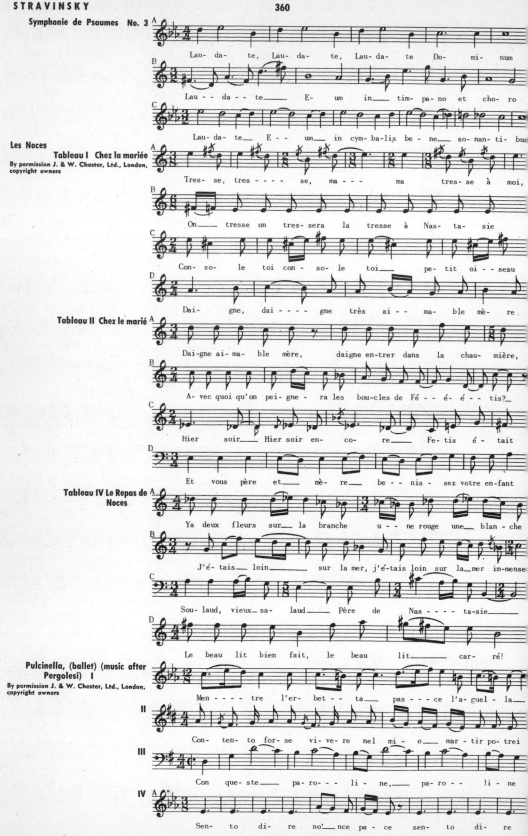

A Lau-da-te, Lau-da-te, Lau-da-te Do-mi-num

B Lau--da-te E--um in tim-pa-no et cho-ro

C Lau-da-te E--um in cym-ba-lis be-ne--so-nan-ti-bus

Les Noces

Tableau I Chez la mariée

By permission J. & W. Chester, Ltd., London, copyright owners

A Tres-se, tres----se, ma---ma tres-se à moi,

B On--tresse on tres-sera la tresse à Nas-ta-sie

C Con-so-le toi con-so-le toi__pe-tit oi--seau

D Dai--gne, dai----gne très ai--ma--ble mè--re

Tableau II Chez le marié

A Dai-gne ai-ma-ble mère, daigne en-trer dans la chau-mière,

B A-vec quoi qu'on pei-gne-ra les bou-cles de Fé--é--é--tis?

C Hier soir__Hier soir en-co--re__Fe-tis é-tait

D Et vous père et__mè--re be--nis-sez votre en-fant

Tableau IV Le Repas de Noces

A Ya deux fleurs sur__la branche u--ne rouge une__blan-che

B J'é-tais__loin__sur la mer, j'é-tais loin sur la__mer im-mense

C Sou-laud, vieux__sa-laud__Père de Nas----ta-sie__

D Le beau lit bien fait, le beau lit__car--ré!

Pulcinella, (ballet) (music after Pergolesi) I

By permission J. & W. Chester, Ltd., London, copyright owners

Men----tre l'er-bet--ta__pas---ce l'a-guel-la

II Con-ten-to for-se vi-ve-re nel mi-o__mar-tir po-trei

III Con que-ste__pa-ro--li-ne,__pa-ro--li-ne

IV A Sen--to di--re no'__nce pa-ce sen-to di--re

Pulcinella IV

Chi di - - - - se ca_____ la fem - me - na

V

U - na te fa - lanz em - pre - ce ed è ed è

VI

Pu - pil - let - te fiam - met - te_____ d'a - - mo - - - re

ur Russian Peasant Songs
I On Saints' Days at Chigisakh
ermission J. & W. Chester, Ltd., London,
right owners

On,_____ on Saints' Days_____ on Saints' Days_____ in Chi-gi-sakh

II Ovsen

Ov-sen, ov-sen, ov-sen_____ I'm a hunt-ing_the grouse,_

III The Pike

Once a pike swam out of Nov-go-rod Glo - ry!

IV Master Portly

Mas - ter Port - ly_____ tramp'- d_thro' the big tur - nip_field

Pastorale (without words)
By permission Associated Music
Publishers, Inc.

A_____ a - ou A - ou A_____ A - ou

Trois Histoires pour Enfants
I Tilimbom
ermission J. & W. Chester, Ltd., London,
right owners

Ti - lim - bom, ti - lim - bom, c'est la cloche du feu qui sonne

II Les canards, les cynges, les oies

Les ca - nards, les cy - gnes,_les oies_ qui sont ve - nus_ de Sa - voie

III Chanson de l'ours

Grin - ce, grin - ce, grin - ce patte en bou - leau_ De-dans, de-hors

STRICKLAND, Lily (1887-   )

Mah Lindy Lou
Copyright 1920, G. Schirmer, Inc.

Hon-ey_____ did you heah dat mock- in- bird sing las' night_____

My Lover is a Fisherman

Oh, my lov- er is a fish-er-man, and he sails on the big

STROZZI, Barbara (c. 1644-1664)

Amor dormiglione

A- mor, a- mor, mon dor-mir più! Su. su, su, su, Sveg- lia-te,

STULTS, R. M. (1861-1923)

The Sweetest Story Ever Told
Copyright by Oliver Ditson Co.
Used by permission

Oh, an- swer me a ques- tion, love, I pray,_____

Tell me, do you love me? Tell me soft- ly, sweet- ly, as of old,_____

SULLIVAN, Sir Arthur (1842-1900)

OPERAS
The Gondoliers Act I, No. 1

List and learn, list and learn, List and learn ye dain-ty ro-ses,

We're called gon-do-lier-i, but that's a va-ga-ry,

Thank you, gal-lant gon-do-lier-i: In a set and for-mal mea-sure

Gay and gal-lant gon-do-lier-i Take us both and hold us tight-ly

No. 3
In en-ter-prise of mar-tial kind, when there was an-y fight-ing

No. 6
I stole the Prince and brought him here, and left him gai-ly pratt-ling

No. 8
Try we life long, we can nev-er, Straighten out life's tan-gled skein,

No. 9
When a mer-ry mai-den mar-ries, Sor-row goes and plea-sure tar-ries,

No. 10
Finale
Kind sir, you can-not have the heart our lives to part

Oh, 'tis a glo-rious thing, I ween to be a reg-ular Roy-al Queen

Then a-way they go to an is-land fair That lies in a Southern sea:

Act II, No. 1
Of hap-pi-ness the ve-ry pith, In Ba-ra-ta-ria you may see:

No. 3
Take a pair of spark-ling eyes, Hid-den ev-er and a-non,

No. 5
Dance a ca-chu-cha, fan-dan-go, bo-le-ro,

Old Xe-res we'll drink Man-za-nil-la, Mon-te-ro,

No. 6
There lived a King, as I've been told, In the won-der-work-ing days of old

No. 7
In a con-tem-pla-tive fa-shion, And a tran-quil frame of mind

No. 9
On the day when I was wed-ded to your ad-mi-ra-ble sire,

SULLIVAN

OPERAS
The Gondoliers Act II, No. 10 — A
Small ti- tles and or- ders for Mayors and Re- cor- ders

No. 11 — B
I__ am a cour-tier grave and se-rious Who__ is a-bout to kiss your hand,

No. 12 Finale — C
Here is a fix un- pre- ce-den- ted! Here are a King and Queen ill-starr'd!

H. M. S. Pinafore Act I, No. 1 — D
We__ sail the o- cean blue, and our sau- cy ship's a beau-ty;

No. 2 — E
I'm called lit-tle But-ter-cup,dear lit-tle But- ter-cup,though I could never tell why

No. 3 — F
A maid-en fair to see,the pearl of min-strel-sy, A bud of blush-ing beau-ty,

No. 4 — G
I am the cap-tain of the Pin- a- fore,__and a right__ good__ cap-tain too

No. 5 — H
Then give three cheers,and one cheer more, For the har- dy cap-tain

— I
Sor-ry her lot__ who loves__too well, Hea- vy the heart__ that hopes

— J
Hea- vy the sor-row that bows__ the head, When love is a- live__

No. 8 — K
I am the mon- arch of the sea, The ru- ler of the Queen's Na- vee,

No. 9 — L
When I was a lad I serv'd a term as of- fice boy__

No. 11 — M
Re- frain, au- da- cious tar, Your suit__ from__press- ing

— N
I'd laugh my rank to scorn, in u - - nion__ ho- ly,

No. 13 — O
Fair moon to thee__ I__ sing! Bright re-gent of the hea- vens

No. 14 — P
Things are sel- dom what they seem, Skim milk mas-que- rades as cream,

— Q
Stern con- vic-tion's o'er__ him__steal-ing, That the mys-tic la- dy's__deal-ing

No. 15 — R
A sim- ple sail- or, low- ly born, un- let-ter'd and un- known,

No. 16 — S
Nev-er mind the why and where- fore, Love can lev- el ranks

OPERAS

H. M. S. Pinafore Act II, No. 17

Kind Cap-tain, I've im- por-tant in- for- ma- tion Sing hey, — A

No. 18

Care- ful- ly on tip-toe steal - ing, breathing gently as we may — B

No. 18A

For___ he him-self has said__ it, and it's great-ly to his cred- it, — C

No. 19

Fare- well, my own, Light of my life,fare- well! For crime un- known I go — D

No. 20

A ma- ny years a- go, when I was young and charm- ing, — E

No. 21

Oh joy, oh rap-ture un- for-seen,The cloud-ed sky is now se- rene — F

Iolanthe Act I, No. 1 A

Trip- ping hi- ther,trip-ping thi- ther, No- bo- dy knows why or whi-ther — G

B

We are dain- ty lit- tle fai- ries E- ver sing-ing e- ver danc-ing — H

No. 3

Good mor- row, good mo-ther___ Good mo- ther,good mor-row___ — I

No. 5

None shall part us from each o- ther,One in life and death are we: — J

No. 6 A

Bow, bow, ye low- er mid- dle class- es, Bow, bow, ye trades-men, — K

B

We are___ peers of___ high- est___ sta- tion, — L

No. 7

The Law is the true em- bo- di-ment of ev'- ry-thing that's ex- cel-lent — M

No. 8

Of all the young la-dies I know,__ This pret-ty young la-dy's the fair-est, — C

No. 10

Spurn not the no- bly born With love___ af - - fect- ed! — F

No. 12

When I went to the bar as a ve- ry young man, — C

No. 13 Finale A

When dark- ly looms the day, and all is dull and grey, — R

B

Go a- way, ma- dam; I should say, ma- dam, You dis- play, ma- dam, — S

Act II, No. 2

Stre-phon's a Mem-ber of Par- lia-ment! car-ries ev- 'ry Bill__he choos- es

OPERAS
Iolanthe Act II, No. 3 — A
When Bri- tain real- ly rul'd the waves (In good Queen Bess- 's___ time)

No. 5 — B
Oh, fool-ish fay, Think you, be-cause His brave ar-ray my bo- som thaws,

No. 7 — C
When you're lying a- wake with a dis-mal head-ache, And re- pose is ta-boo'd

No. 8 — D
He___ who shies at such a prize is___ not worth a ma- ra- ve- di,

No. 9 — E
If we're weak e- nough to tar- ry Ere we mar- ry, You___ and I,

The Mikado Act I, No. 1 — F
If you want to know who we are___ We are gen-tle-men of Ja- pan___

No. 2 — G
A wan- d'ring min- strel I a thing of shreds___ and patch-es

No. 3 — H
Our great Mi- ka- do, vir-tuous man, When he to rule our land be-gan

No. 4 A — I
Young man de-spair, Like- wise go to Yum- Yum the fair you must not woo.

B — J
And the brass will crash, and the trum- pets bray; and they'll cut a dash

No. 5 A — K
Be-hold the Lord High ex- e- cu-tion-er! A per-son-age of no- ble rank

B — L
Ta- ken from the coun- ty jail By a set of cu-rious chan-ces

No. 5a — M
As some- day it may hap-pen that a vic- tim must be found,

No. 7 — N
Three lit-tle girls from school are we, Pert as a school-girl well can be,

No. 9 — O
Were you not to Ko- ko plight- ed, I would say in ten- der tone,

No. 10 — P
I am so proud, if I al-lowed my fa- mi- ly pride To be my guide,

No. 11 Finale A — Q
The threat-en'd cloud has passed a - - way, And brightly shines the dawning day

B — R
With joy- ous shout, with joy- ous___ shout and ring- ing___ cheer

C — S
If true her tale, thy knell is rung, Pink cheek, bright eye, rose lip,

The Mikado Act I, No. 11 Finale

For__ he's go-ing to mar-ry Yum-Yum,Yum-Yum! Your an-ger pray bu-ry,

We do not heed their dis- mal__ sound, For joy reigns ev-'ry-where.

Act II, No. 1

Braid the ra- ven hair,__ Weave the sup - - - - - - ple tress,__

No. 2 A1

The sun,whose rays are all a-blaze with e- ver liv-ing glo-ry

A2

I mean to rule the earth,__ as he the sky, we real-ly know our worth__

No. 3

Bright-ly dawns our wed-ding day; Joy-ous__ hour, we give the greet-ing!

No. 4

Here's a how-de-do! If I mar-ry you, when your time has come to peris

No. 5 A

Mi- ya sa- ma, mi-ya sa-ma, On n'ma-ma no ma- ye ni

B

From ev-'ry kind of man O- be-dience I__ ex- pect

No. 6

My ob-ject all sub-lime__ I shall a-chieve in time,

No. 7 A

The cri-mi-nal cried, as he dropp'd him down, In a state of wild a-larm

B

Oh, never shall I for-get the cry,or the shriek that shriek-ed he,__

No. 8

See how the Fates their gifts al- lot, For A is hap-py B is not

No. 9

The flow- ers that bloom in the spring, Tra-la Breathe pro- mise

No. 10

Oh liv-ing I come, tell_me_ why, when hope is gone,Dost thou stay or

No. 11

On a tree by a riv-er a lit-tle tom-tit Sang__"Wil- low,

No. 12 A

There is beau- ty in the bel- low of the blast,

B

If that is so, Sing der-ry down der-ry! It's e- vi-dent ve- ry,

Patience Act I, No. 1

Twen- ty love-sick mai-dens we,__ Love-sick all a-gainst our will.

Patience Act I, No. 2 — A: I can-not tell what this love may be That com-eth to all

No. 4 — B: In a dole-ful train two and two we walk all day for we love in vain!

B — C: Through my book I seem to scan In a rapt ec-sta-tic way

No. 5 — D: When I first put this u-ni-form on, I said, as I looked in the glass

No. 6 — E: If you're anx-ious for to shine in the high aes-the-tic line

B — F: And ev-ery one will say As you walk your mys-tic way,

No. 8 — G: Pri-thee, pret-ty mai-den pri-thee, tell me true (Hey, but I'm dole-ful,

No. 9 Finale — H: Let the mer-ry cym-bals sound, Gai-ly pipe Pan-dae-an plea-sure

B — I: Now tell us, we pray you, Why thus they ar-ray you, Oh po-et,

C — J: List Re-gi-nald, while I con-fess a love that's all un-sel-fish-ness

Act II, No. 2 — K: Sil-vered is the ra-ven hair, Spread-ing is the part-ing straight,

No. 3 — L: Turn, oh turn in this di-rec-tion, Shed, oh shed a gen-tle smile

No. 4 — M: A mag-net hung in a hard-ware shop And all a-round was a lov-ing crop

No. 5 — N: Love is a plain-tive song. Sung by a suf-fering maid

B — O: Love that no wrong can cure, Love that is al-ways new,

No. 6 — P: So go to him and say to him, with com-pli-ment i-ron-i-cal

B — Q: Sing "Hey to you good-day to you" Sing "Bah to you ha! ha! to you"

No. 7 — R: You hold your-self like this, You hold your-self like that, By hook and crook

No. 8 — S: If Sa-phir I choose to mar-ry, I shall be fixed up for life;

OPERAS
Patience Act II, No. 8

No. 9

The Pirates of Penzance
Act I, No. 1

No. 2

No. 3

No. 5

No. 7

No. 8

No. 10

No. 11

No. 13

Finale

Act II, No. 1

No. 3

In that case un-pre-ce- dent- ed, Sin- gle he will live and die,

When I go out of door of da- mo- zels a score All sighing and burning,

Pour, O King, the pi- rate sher- ry, Fill, O King, the pi- rate glass!

When Fred'ric was a— lit- tle lad He— proved so brave and da- ring,

Oh bet- ter far to live— and die Un- der the brave black flag I fly

For— I am a Pi- rate King!— And it is, it is a glo- rious thing,

Climb- ing o- - ver— rock- y moun- tain, Skip- ping ri - - vu - let and fountain,

Let us gai- ly tread— the— mea - sure, Make the most of fleet- ing— pleas- ure

Oh, is there not one mai- den breast which does not feel the mo- ral beau- ty

Poor wan- d'ring one— Tho' thou hast surely strayed,— Take heart of grace,

Take heart, no dan- ger lowers, Take a - ny heart— but ours

How beau- ti- ful- ly blue the sky, The grass is ris- ing ve- ry high

Did e- ver mai- den wake from dream— of home - - ly du- ty

Now here's a first rate op- por- tu- ni- ty To get mar- ried

I am the ve- ry pat- tern of a mo- dern Ma- jor Ge- ne- ral

These chil- dren whom you see are all that I can call my own.

I'm tell- ing a ter- ri- ble sto- ry, but it does- n't di- min- ish

Oh, dry the glis- t'ning tear that dews— that mar- tial cheek!—

When the foe- man bares his steel, Ta- ran´- ta- ra, ta- ran- ta- ra

OPERAS
The Pirates of Penzance
Act II, No. 3

Go____ ye he-roes, go____ to glo-ry Though__ ye die in com-bat go--ry

No. 5

When you had left our pi-rate fold, we tried to raise our spi-rits faint.

A pa-ra-dox, a pa-ra-dox, a most in-ge-nious pa-ra-dox

No. 6

A-way, a-way___ my heart's on fire! I burn this base de-cep-tion

No. 8

Ah, leave me not to pine a-lone and de-so-late

Oh, here is love, and here is truth, and here is food for joy-ous laugh-ter

No. 10

When a fe-lon's not en-gaged in his em-ploy-ment, his em-ploy-ment,

No. 12

With cat like tread up-on our prey we steal; In si-lence dread

Come, friends, who plough the sea, truce to na-vi-ga-tion,

No. 14 Finale

Soft-ly sigh-ing to the ri--ver, Comes the lone-ly breeze___

We tri-umph now for well_we trow Your_mor-tal ca-reer's cut_short

Princess Ida Act I, No. 1

Search through-out the pa-no-ra-ma, For a sign of roy-al Ga-ma

No. 2

Now heark-en to my strict com-mand On ev'-ry hand, on ev'-ry hand

No. 3

I-da was a twelve-month old twen-ty years a-go

No. 5

We are war-riors three,__ Songs of Ga-ma Rex,__ Like most sons are we_

Bold__ and fierce and strong, ha, ha! For__ a war we burn

No. 6

If you give me your at-ten-tion, I will tell you what I am:

No. 7 Finale

P'raps if you ad-dress the la-dy most po-lite-ly, most po-lite-ly

Ex-press ive glan-ces shall be our lan-ces and pops of Sil-le-ry

OPERAS

Princess Ida Act I, No. 7 Finale

For a month to dwell in a dun-geon cell, grow-ing thin and wi-zen

Act II, No. 8

To-wards the em-py-re-an heights____ of ev'-ry kind of love,

No. 9

Migh-ty mai-den with a mis-sion, Pa-ra-gon of com-mon sense

No. 10

Oh, god-dess wise that lov-est____ light En-dow with sight

No. 11

Come might-y Must! In-e-vi-ta-ble Shall! In Thee I trust.

No. 13

I am a mai-den cold____ and state-ly Heart-less I,

No. 14

The world is but a bro-ken toy, Its plea-sures hol-low false its joy,

No. 15

A La-dy fair, of____ lin-eage high, When loved by an Ape

No. 16

The wo-man of the wis-est wit may some-times be mis-ta-ken, O!

No. 19

Would____ you know the kind____ of maid Sets____ my heart a-flame-a?

No. 22 A

When-e'er I spoke sar-cas-tic joke Re-plete with mal-ice spite-ful,

B

Oh, don't the days seem lank and long When all goes right

No. 23

I built up-on a rock, But ere De-struc-tion's hand

No. 24

When an-ger spreads his wing, and all____ seems____ dark as____ night for it,

No. 25

This hel-met, I sup-pose was meant to ward off blows, It's ve-ry hot

Ruddigore Act I, No. 1

Fair____ is Rose as bright May day, Soft____ is Rose as warm west wind,

No. 2 A

Sir Ru-pert Mur-ga-troyd His lei-sure and____ his rich-es

B

This sport____ he much en-joy'd,____ Did Ru-pert Mur-ga-troyd____

No. 3 A

If some-bo-dy there chanced to be Who loved me in a man-ner true

OPERAS
Ruddigore Act I, No. 3

No. 3: Had I the love of such_as he, Some qui-et spot he'd take_me to,

No. 4: I know a youth who loves a lit-tle maid (Hey,_but his face is a sight

No. 5: From the bri-ny sea comes_young Rich-ard, all vic- to- rious!

No. 7: If you wish in the world to ad- vance, Your_me-rits You're bound to en- hance

No. 8: The bat-tle's roar is o-ver, O my love! Em-brace thy ten- der lov- er,

No. 10: In sail-ing o'er life's o-cean wide__ Your heart_should be your on-ly guide;

No. 11: To a gar-den full of po- sies Com-eth one to ga-ther flowers,

No. 12: Wel- come,_gen-try, For_ your en- try sets our ten-der hearts a-beat-ing,

When thor-ough-ly tir-ed of be- ing ad-mir- ed By la- dies

No. 13: Oh why am I mood- y and sad? Can't guess! And why am I guil-ti-ly mad?

No. 14: You un- der-stand? Like-wise the Bride The mai-dens are ve-ry E- lat- ed

No. 15 Finale: Hail the Bride of seven - teen sum-mers: In_ fair phra-ses Hymn_her prai-ses

Leaves_in au-tumn fade and_fall Win- ter is the end of_all, Fa la la la

When I'm a bad Bart. I will tell ta-ra-did- dles! He'll tell ta- ra-did-dles

Oh, hap-py the li- ly when kiss'd by the bee; And sip-ping tran-quil-ly,

Act II, No. 2: Hap- pi-ly cou-pled are we, you see I am a jol-ly Jack Tar, my star,

No. 4: Paint- ed em- blems of_ a race__ All ac- curst in days_ of yore—

No. 5: When the night wind howls in the chim- ney cowls, and the bat in the moon-light flies

No. 7: I once was a ve-ry a- ban-doned per-son mak-ing the most of e-vil chances

OPERAS

Ruddigore Act II, No. 8

My eyes are ful-ly o-pen to my aw-ful sit-u-a-tion,

No. 10 A

There grew a lit-tle flow-er 'Neath a great oak tree

B

Sing___ hey, lack-a-day, let, the tears fall free

The Sorcerer Act I, No. 1 A

Ring forth, ye bells, with cla-rion sound, For-get your knells,

B

For to-day young A-lex-is, Young A-lex-is Point-dex-tre

No. 2 A

When he is here I sigh with plea-sure, When he is gone I sigh with grief

No. 3 A

Time was, when love and I were well ac-quain-ted,

No. 5

With heart and with voice Let us wel-come this ma-ting to the youth

No. 6 A

Oh, hap-py young heart___ Comes thy young lord a-woo-ing

No. 8

With heart and with voice let us wel-come this mat-ing

No. 9

Wel-come joy! a-dieu to sad-ness! As Au-ro-ra gilds___the___day

No. 10

All is pre-pared for seal-ing and for sign-ing, The contract has been drafted

No. 11

Love feeds on ma-ny kinds of food, I know; Some love for rank,

No. 12

My name is John Well-ing-ton Wells___ I'm a deal-er in ma-gic and spells___

No. 13 (Incantation)

Sprites of earth and air! Fiends of flame and fire! Demon souls, come

No. 14 Finale A

Eat, drink and be gay, Ba-nish all wor-ry and sor-row

B

Oh love, true love! un-world-ly, a-bid-ing, Source of all pleasure

Act II; No. 15

Hap-py are we in our lov-ing fri-vol-i-ty Hap-py and jol-ly

No. 16 A

Dear friends, take pi-ty on my lot, My cup is not of nec-tar

The Sorcerer Act II, No. 16
Oh, bit-ter joy! No words can tell How my poor—heart is blight-ed

No. 19
The fear-ful deed is done, My love is near, I go to meet my own

No. 20
Thank you for your kind-ly prof-fer, Good your heart and full your cof-fer,

Trial by Jury No. 1
Hark, the hour of ten is sound-ing; hearts with anx-ious fears are bounding

No. 2
When first my old, old love— I knew, My bo-som well'd with joy

No. 4
When I, good friends, was call'd to the bar, I'd an appe-tite fresh

No. 6
Comes the bro-ken flow-er, comes the cheat-ed maid,

No. 8
With a sense of deep e-mo-tion, I ap-proach this pain-ful case

He de-ceiv'd a girl con-fid-ing, Vows, et ce-te-ra, de-rid-ing

No. 10
Oh, gen-tle-men, lis-ten, I pray, Tho I own that my heart

No. 13
I love him, I love him, with fer-vour un-ceas-ing,

No. 14 Finale
Oh, joy un-bound-ed, with wealth sur-round-ed, The knell is sound-ed

The Yeomen of the Guard Act I, No. 1
When maid-en loves, she sits and sighs, She wan-ders to and fro;

No. 2
Tow-er war-ders, un-der or-ders, Gal-lant pike-men,

This the au-tumn of our life— This the eve-ning of— our day,

No. 3
"The screw may twist and the rack— may turn, And men may bleed

No. 5
Is life a boon? If so, it must be-fall that Death when-e'er he call

No. 7
I have a song to sing, O!— Sing me your song, O—

It is sung to the moon By a love-lorn— loon,

SULLIVAN 374

OPERAS
The Yeomen of the Guard
Act I, No. 9

I've wis- dom from the East and from the West,

No. 10

Though tear and long drawn sigh ill fit a bride__ no sad-der wife than I

No. 11

Were I thy bride, then all the world be- side were not too wide

Act II, No. 1

Night__ has spread her pall once more, and__the pris - 'ner still is free

No. 2

Oh! a pri- vate buf- foon is a light heart- ed loon,

No. 3

Here- up- on we're both a- greed, all that we two Do a- gree to

No. 4

Far from his fet- ters grim Free to de- part;__ Free both in life and l

No. 5

Strange ad- ven -ture!Mai-den wed- ded To a__ groom she'd- nev-er__ seen!

No. 7

If he's made the best use of his time,__ His twig he'll so care-ful-ly lime.

No. 8

Oh, the hap- py days of do- ing! Oh, the sigh-ing and the su-ing

No. 9

Rap- ture, rap- ture, when love's vo- ta- ry;Flushed with cap-ture,

God shall wipe away all tears, from
The Light of the World (oratorio)

God shall wipe a- way all tears from their eyes,There shall be no more de

The Golden Legend Evening Hymn

O glad- some Light of the Fa- ther im- mor - - - - - tal,

The Night is calm

The night is calm and cloud-less, And still as still__ can be

How many hired servants, from The
Prodigal Son

How ma- ny hi- red ser- vants of my fa-ther's have bread e-nou

Songs: Birds in the Night

Birds__ in the night__ that soft - - ly__ call

Ho, Jolly Jenkin, from Ivanhoe
(grand opera)

Then ho, jol- ly Jen- kin I spy a knave in drink- in

The Long Day Closes

No star is o'er the lake, Its pale watch keep- ing,

The Lost Chord

Seat- ed one day at the or- gan, I was wea- ry and ill at ease

Songs: Onward Christian Soldiers (hymn)

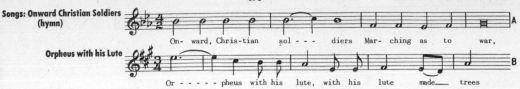

On- ward, Chris-tian sol - - - diers Mar- ching as to war,

Orpheus with his Lute

Or - - - - pheus with his lute, with his lute made__ trees

SUPPÉ, Franz von (1819-1895)

Boccaccio (operetta) No. 3

Hol-de Schö-ne, hör' die-se Tö-ne, hör' mein zärt-li-ches Lie-ber-ge-stöh-ne!

No. 6

Hab' ich nur dei-ne Lie-be, die Treu- e brauch'_ich nicht,

No. 18

Flo- renz hat schö- ne Frau-en,__ die Schön - - ste bist du

SWEELINCK, Jan Pieterzoon (1562-1621)

Hodie Christus natus est

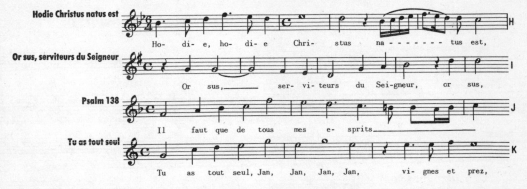

Ho- di- e, ho- di- e Chri- stus na - - - - - - - tus est,

Or sus, serviteurs du Seigneur

Or sus,___ ser- vi-teurs du Sei-gneur, or sus,

Psalm 138

Il faut que de tous mes e- sprits___

Tu as tout seul

Tu as tout seul, Jan, Jan, Jan, Jan, vi- gnes et prez,

SZULC, Joseph (1874-1935)

Clair de Lune, Op. 83, No. 1
Copyright 1920, G. Schirmer, Inc.

Votre âme est un pa- y- sa- ge choi- si Que vont char- mant

La Lune Blanche No. 8
Copyright by Salabert, Paris, N. Y.

La lu- ne blan- che luit dans le bois, de cha-que bran - che

En Sourdine No. 9

Cal- mes dans le de- mi jour, Que les bran-ches hau-tes font,

Mandoline No. 10

Les don-neurs de sé-ré- na-des et les bel-les e-cou- teu - - - - - ses

TAUBERT, Wilhelm (1811-1891)

Birdling, why sing in the forest wide

Bird- ling why sing in the for - - est wide? Say, why?

TAVERNER, John (c. 1495-1545)

Audivi

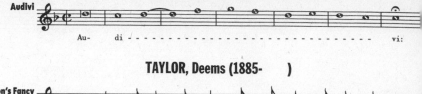

Au - di - - - - - - - - - - - - - - - - - - vi

TAYLOR, Deems (1885-)

Captain Stratton's Fancy
Copyright 1923, J. Fischer & Bro., N. Y.
Used by permission

Oh, some are fond of red wine and some are fond of white

The King's Henchman (opera) Act I
Copyright 1926, J. Fischer & Bro., N. Y.
Used by permission

Oh,___ Cae- sar, great wert thou! and___ Jul- ius was thy name!___

Act III

Nay, Mac- cus, lay him down___ What man hath met the thrust of

**May-Day Carol, Op. 15, No. 9
(transcribed)**
Copyright 1920, J. Fischer & Bro., N. Y.
Used by permission

The moon shines bright, The stars give a light, A lit-tle be-fore 'tis day

TCHAIKOVSKY, Peter Ilyich (1840-1893)

Moscow (cantata) Arioso No. 2

Ist ein Him- mels-licht, das so strahlt und blinkt durch die fin- stre Nacht.

Arioso No. 5

Wird mir, Herr mein Gott, nicht zu schwer das Kreuz, das mir auf- er- legt

**OPERAS
Adieu, forêts, from Jeanne d'Arc**

A- dieu, fo- rêts, a- dieu, près fleur- is champs d'or

**Eugene Onegin, Op. 24
Act I, No. 1**

Did'st thou not hear? how like the night- in- gale One sang by night

No. 6 Lenski's Aria

Yes, I love you, yes, I love you, Ol- ga fierce and hot,

No. 9 Letter scene A

Tho' I should die for it I've sworn now I first shall live___

B

No, ne- ver a- ny oth- er, For an- y oth- er I had loathed!

No. 11

Come, ye maid-ens all, and dance, Run while yet ye have a chance

No. 12 Onegin's Aria

If in this world a kind-ly for-tune for house-hold cares had destined me

Act II, No. 13 Waltz

Re- gale you all! Hail, hail to all beau - ty

**(Instrumental
acc. to waltz)**

Instrumental accompaniment to Waltz

OPERAS
Eugene Onegin
Act II, No. 14 — Ye who at-tend this charm-ing ball, Come and ad-mire ye one and all — A

No. 17 Lenski's Aria — How far, how far, how far ye seem be-hind me, O days of youth — B

How far — What has the com-ing day in store? Mine eyes are pow'r-less to ex-plore, — C

No. 20 — All men should once with love grow ten-der All men must once — D

Iolanthe, Op. 69 Iolanthe's Aria — Wa-rum kann-te in frü-he-ren Ta-gen we-der Thrä-nen noch Kum-mer — E

King's Aria — Wenn ich, Herr, dei-nen Zorn ent-facht wess-halb muss die-ser En-gel — F

Pique-Dame, (Queen of Spades) Op 68 Act I Herman's Arioso — Ich sche-ue mich da-nach zu fra-gen Sie ist so stolz, so schön — G

Fühl-test Du mein Lei-den, Lit-test Du mei-ne Pein — H

Tomsky's Ballade — Es rief in Ver-sailles bei der Kö-ni-gen Spiel Die Grä-fin Va-banque! — I

Duet: Lisa & Pauline — Es däm-mert, all das Licht, in dem, wir uns ge-sonnt, — J

Romance: Pauline — O Schwes-tern, klagt mit mir, O Schwes-tern, klagt mit mir — K

Act II Prince Yeletsky's Aria — Als Du zum Gat-ten mich er-ko-ren, Dich fei-er-lich mir an-ge-lobt, — L

Duet: Daphnis & Chloe — Ich ha-be Daph-nis gern, Er a-ber bleibt mir fern — M

Act III Lisa's Song — Al-les ist schla-fen ge-gan-gen, Dich nur von Haus Jagt es hin-aus — N

Tomsky's Song — Hät-ten doch die Mäd-chen Flü-gel, flö-gen ü-ber mei-nen Hü-gel, — O

Songs: Speak not, O beloved, Op. 6, No. 2 — Speak not, O be-lov-ed, O sigh not! In si-lence meet sor-row — P

Why? No. 5 — Tell me why are the ro-ses so pale? Dear-est love, — Q

None but the lonely heart (Nur wer die Sehnsucht kennt) No. 6 — None but the lone-ly heart Can know my sad-ness — R

Cradle Song, Op. 16, No. 1 — Sleep, o ba-by mine, sleep and dream, ba-by mine! — S

Songs: Linger yet, Op. 16, No. 2

Lin-ger yet! Thought of part-ing O ban-ish! Like an ar - - row

Wherefore? Op. 28, No. 3

Why did you come in dreams to me, My ab-sent love, I ne-ver for-get

Er liebt mich so sehr! No. 4

Nein, nim-mer lieb-te ich! Und doch sah ich ihn kom- men,

Kein Wort von dir, No. 5

Kein Wort von dir, der Freu- de o- der Kla- ge,

One small word, No. 6

Small head droop- ing, here you stand be- fore me

Don Juan's Serenade, Op. 38, No. 1

All Gra- na- da li - - eth qui- et In thy bal-co- ny_ ap-pear

It was in days of early spring, No. 2

It was in days of ear- ly spring, when ten- der grass was grow- ing

At the Ball, No. 3

I know not how love- ly your face is, For that,when I met you

Oh, but to hear thy voice (I wish) No. 4

Oh would but Heav'n in pi- ty grant a boon to me!

Pimpinella (Florentine Song) No. 6

Non con-tras-tar_ cogl' uo - - mi- ni, fal- lo per ca- ri- ta!

Whether Day Dawns, Op. 47, No. 3

Whe- ther day dawns_ or night sha-dows are fall- ing Whe- ther I dream

Pilgrim's Song (Benediction) No. 5

My bless- ing rest on ye, o woods, o val-leys moun- tains

Toujours à toi, No. 6 (confused with Toi seul, Op. 57, No. 6)

Que le jour bril - -le ou que l'om- bre nous cou- vre

Was I not a blade of grass in meadow green, No. 7

A

Was I not a blade of grass in mead- ow green

B

Ah. my_ heart, how hard is life to bear! Ah! my_ hear

Songs for Young People, Op. 54, No. 5 Legend

Child Je-sus in his gar-den fair Some sweet red ro- ses once had grown

No. 8 The Cuckoo

From out the ci- ty thou hast flown: Now prith- ee, what word

No. 14 Autumn

De broui-llards mo- ro- ses Les cieux sont cou- verts;

The Nightingale, Op. 57, No. 1

O Sprich wo- von die Nach- ti- gall wenn rings die Welt ver-san

Songs: All for you (T'was you alone)
Op 57, No. 6

A — Twas you a-lone e'er felt for me in sor-row Twas you a-lone

If you but knew, Op. 60, No. 3

B — If you but knew how much I suf-fer and am sigh-ing, Ah, me!

Song of the Gypsy Girl, No. 7

C — In the brush the flames are leap-ing, sparks fly up and dis-ap-pear

At the Open Window, Op. 63, No. 2

D — Wie so schwül ist es heut'! Auf das Fen-ster mit Macht! Auf die Knie

Sérénade, Op. 65, No. 1

E — Où vas-tu,souf-fle d'au-ro-re, vent de miel qui vient d'é-clo-re,

Disappointment, No. 2

F — While the sun shines in wont-ed splen-dor, the deep woods

Tears, No. 5

G — If you can bring me calm af-ter pain wreaks its pow-er

In this hour of the night, Op. 73, No. 3

H — In this hour of the night In the moon's sil-ver light

Yearning, I wait now alone (Again as before), No. 6

I — Yearn-ing I wait now a-lone,— Peace has de-part-ed

TELEMANN, George Philipp (1681-1767)

Das Frauenzimmer

K — Das Frau-en-zim---mer ver-stimmt sich im--mer

Glück

L — Das Glü-cke kömmt sel-ten per Pos-ta zu Pfer-de;

TENAGLIA, Anton Francesco (1600-16-?)

Begli occhi, mercè

N — Be-gli oc-chi,mer-cè, mer-cè,mer-cè! Be------gli oc-chi,

TESSIER, Charles (16th Cent.)

Au joli bois

P — Au jo-li bois je m'en vais, au jo-li bois— je m'en vais

THOMAS, Ambroise (1811-1896)

OPERAS
Le Caid Act I Air du Tambour Major

R — Le tam-bour ma-jor tout ga-lon-né d'or a par-tout la pom-me

S — L'a-mour, ce dieu pro-fa-ne in-ven-ta la Di-a-ne

OPERAS
Hamlet, Act I, Scene I

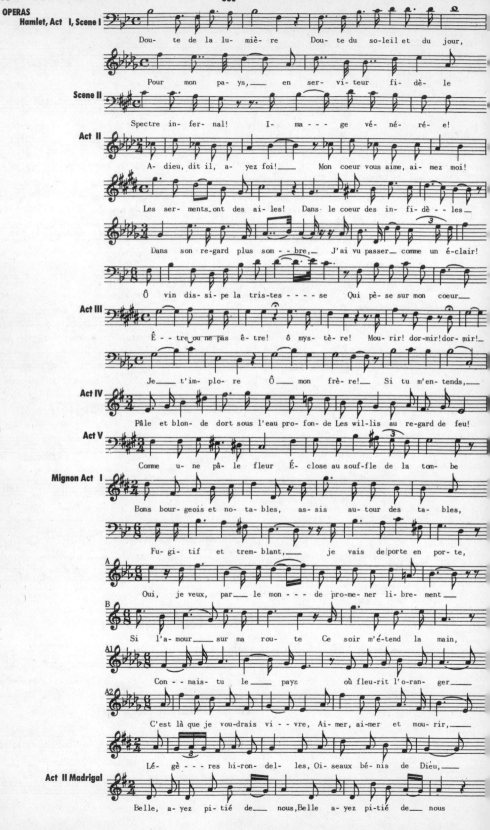

Dou- te de la lu- miè- re   Dou- te du so-leil et du jour,

Pour mon pa- ys,___ en ser-vi- teur fi- dè- le

Scene II

Spectre in- fer- nal!   I- ma- - - ge vé- né- ré- e!

Act II

A- dieu, dit il, a- yez foi!___   Mon coeur vous aime, ai- mez moi!

Les ser- ments_ont des ai- les!   Dans le coeur des in- fi- dè- - les

Dans son re-gard plus som- bre,   J'ai vu passer_ comme un é-clair!

Ô vin dis- si- pe la tris- tes- - - - se   Qui pè- se sur mon coeur___

Act III

Ê- - tre_ou ne pas ê- tre!   ô mys- tè- re!   Mou- rir! dor-mir! dor- mir!___

Je___ t'im- plo- re   Ô___ mon frè- re!   Si tu m'en- tends,___

Act IV

Pâ- le et blon- de dort sous l'eau pro-fon- de Les wil- lis au re-gard de feu!

Act V

Com- me u- ne pâ- le fleur É- close au souf-fle de la tom- be

Mignon Act I

Bons bour- geois et no- ta- bles, as- sis au- tour des ta- bles,

Fu- gi- tif et trem- blant,___ je vais de porte en por- te,

A

Oui, je veux, par le mon- - - de pro- me- ner li- bre- ment___

B

Si l'a- mour___ sur ma rou- te Ce soir m'é- tend la main,

A1

Con- - nais- tu le___ pays où fleu-rit l'o- ran- ger___

A2

C'est là que je vou- drais vi- - vre, Ai- mer, ai- mer et mou- rir,___

Lé- gè- - - res hi- ron- del- les, Oi- seaux bé- nis de Dieu,

Act II Madrigal

Belle, a- yez pi- tié de___ nous, Belle a- yez pi- tié de___ nous

OPERAS
Mignon Act II Styrienne

Je con-nais un pauvre en-fant,___ Un pauvre en-fant de Bo-hê- me___

Ah!___ la la___ la la ta___ ta la___ ral la

Me voi-ci dans son bou- doir, et je sens mon coeur

A- dieu, Mi- gnon!___ cou-ra- ge Ne pleu- re pas!

Elle est ai-mé- e Il l'aime! eh! bien! je le savais!

As- tu souffert? as- tu pleu- ré? As- tu lan-gui sans es- pé- ran- ce?

Je___ suis Ti- ta- ni- a la blon - - - - de,

Act III Berceuse

De son coeur j'ai cal-mé la fiè-vre! Un sou- ri- re doux et joy- eux

Romance

El- le ne croy- ait pas, dans sa can-deur na- ï- ve,

Ô___ prin- temps don - - ne- lui ta gout- te de___ ro-sé- e!

Le Soir (song)

La terre___ em- bra- sé- e At- tend___ la ro- sé- e

THOMAS, Christopher J. (1894-   )

O men from the fields!
Copyright 1938, Galaxy Music Corp., N. Y.

O, men from the fields! come gen- tly with- in, Tread soft- ly,

THOMÉ, Francis (1850-1909)

Sonnet d'amour
Copyright 1901, G. Schirmer, Inc.

Sous le so- leil___ qui les___ ir- ri - - se,

THOMPSON, Randall (1899-   )

Alleluia
Copyright 1940, E. C. Schirmer, Boston

Al- le- lu - ia, al- le- lu- ia, al- le- lu- ia, al- le- lu- ia,

Velvet Shoes
Copyright 1935, Harcourt, Brace

Let us walk in the white snow, In a sound - - less space

THOMSON, Virgil (1896-)

Four Saints in Three Acts
Prologue
Copyright by Arrow Music Press, N. Y.

To know to know to love her so___ Four saints pre-pare for saints

Act I

There are a great man-y per-sons___ and pla-ces near___ to-geth-er

She can have no one no one can have an-y-one___

A scene and with-ers Scene three and scene two. How can a sis-ter

Could they grow and tell it so if it was left to be to go

There can be no peace on earth with calm with calm___

They nev-er knew a-bout it green and they nev-er knew a-bout it

Act II

Can an-y-one feel an-y one mov-ing and in mov-ing can

How man-y saints are there in it There are ver-y man-y man-y saints

There are as man-y saints as there are in it.

Act III

Pi-geons on the grass a-las. Pi-geons on the grass a-las.

He asked for a dis-tant mag - pie as if they make a dif-fer-ence

There are ver-y sweet-ly ver-y sweet-ly Hen-ry

Once in a while and where and where a-round a-round

Let-ting pin in let-ting let in let in in in in in let

Variant

With wed led said with led dead said with dead led said

Act IV

Be-gin to trace be-gin to race be-gin to place be-gin and in

The Mother of Us All
Act I Scene I
Copyright by Arrow Music Press, N. Y.

Yes I was, said Su-san. You mean you are, said Anne

They be-gan to trav-el, not to trav-el you know but to go

Men are so_ con-ser-va-tive, so sel-fish so bore-some,

Do come Su-san B. An-tho-ny, do come no-bod-y no-bod-y

Scene II

Pit-y the poor_ per-se-cu-tor If mon-ey is mon-ey,

He digged a pit, he digged it deep, he digged it for his bro-ther.

Dan-iel was his fa-ther's name, fa-ther's name, fa-ther's name

Not an-y more I am not a mar-tyr an-y-more_

Hush, I hush, you hush, they hush, we hush, Hush, we hush,

Scene III

I be-lieve in pub-lic school ed-u-ca-tion

Dear Miss Con-stance Fle-tcher, it is a great plea-sure

Scene IV

If I be-lieve_ that I am right and I am_ right if they be-lieve_

We are the cho-rus of the V. I. P. Ve-ry im-por-tant per-sons

Scene V

Will they re-mem-ber that it is true that neither they, that neither you,

So beau-ti-ful. It is so beau-ti-ful to meet you here,

Act II, Scene II

I have just con-vert-ed Lil-li-an Rus-sell to the cause

Dear friends, it is so beau-ti-ful_ to meet_ you all_

That so long that the gor-geous en-sign of the re-pub-lic

Scene III

The vote, wo-men have the vote. They have it each and ev'ry one

THRANE, Waldemar (1790-1828)

Kom Kjyra (Norwegian Echo Song)

Kom Kjy- ra! Kom Kjy - ra mi! kom kjy - - ra!

TIERSOT, Julien (1857-1936)

Noel Provençal I (arr.)
By permission Heugel & Cie, Paris, copyright owners

Un flam- beau,_ Jean- nette, I- sa- bel- le! Un flam- beau

Noel Provençal II (arr.)

Guil- laume, An- toi- ne, Pier- re, Clau- de, Jac- ques, Ni- co- las_

Noel Provençal III (arr.)

Ah! quand re- vien- dra- t-il le temps, ber- ge- re? Ah!

Le Pauvre Laboreur (arr.)
By permission Heugel & Cie, Paris, copyright owners

Le pau- vre la - - bou- reur, Il _____ a bien du mal- heur

Le Retour du Marin (chanson Poitevine)
By permission Heugel & Cie, Paris, copyright owners

Quand le ma- rin re- vint de guer- re,_ Tout doux

TOMKINS, Thomas

(madrigals)

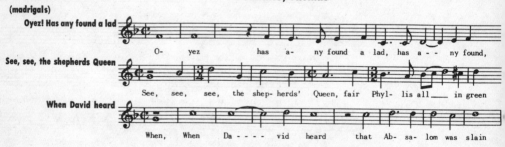

Oyez! Has any found a lad

O- yez has a- ny found a lad, has a- ny found,

See, see, the shepherds Queen

See, see, see, the shep- herds' Queen, fair Phyl- lis all _____ in green

When David heard

When, When Da - - - - vid heard that Ab- sa- lom was slain

TORELLI, Giuseppe (1650-1708)

Tu lo sai

Tu lo _____ sa- i Quan-to t'a- ma- i, Tu lo _____ sa- i,

TOSELLI, Enrico (1883-1926)

Serenade (Rimpianto)
By permission Heugel & Cie, Paris, copyright owners

Co- me un so- gno d'or scol- pi- to è nel co- re

Ma fu mol- to bre- ve in me la dol-cez- za di quel ben

TOSTI, F. Paolo (1846-1916)

L'Alba separa dalla luce l'ombra
By permission Heugel & Cie, Paris, copyright owners

L'al- ba se- pà- ra dal- la lu- ce l'om- bra_

TOSTI

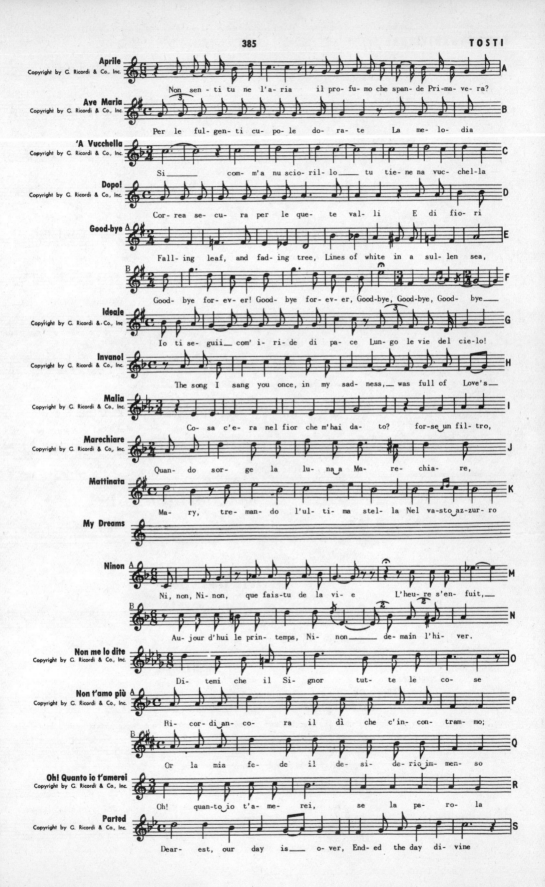

Aprile
Copyright by G. Ricordi & Co., Inc.

Non sen-ti tu ne l'a-ria   il pro-fu-mo che span-de Pri-ma-ve-ra?   A

Ave Maria
Copyright by G. Ricordi & Co., Inc.

Per le ful-gen-ti cu-po-le do-ra-te   La me-lo-dia   B

'A Vucchella
Copyright by G. Ricordi & Co., Inc.

Si___   com'ma nu scio-ril-lo___ tu tie-ne na vuc-chel-la   C

Dopo!
Copyright by G. Ricordi & Co., Inc.

Cor-rea se-cu-ra per le que-te val-li   E di fio-ri   D

Good-bye A

Fall-ing leaf, and fad-ing tree, Lines of white in a sul-len sea,   E

B

Good- bye for-ev- er! Good- bye for-ev- er, Good-bye, Good-bye, Good- bye___   F

Ideale
Copyright by G. Ricordi & Co., Inc.

Io ti se-guii___ com' i-ri-de di pa-ce Lun-go le vie del cie-lo!   G

Invano!
Copyright by G. Ricordi & Co., Inc.

The song I sang you once, in my sad-ness, was full of Love's___   H

Malia
Copyright by G. Ricordi & Co., Inc.

Co-sa c'e-ra nel fior che m'hai da-   to? for-se un fil-tro,   I

Marechiare
Copyright by G. Ricordi & Co., Inc.

Quan- do sor-ge la lu-na a Ma-re-   chia-   re,   J

Mattinata
Copyright by G. Ricordi & Co., Inc.

Ma-   ry,   tre-man-do l'ul-ti-ma stel- la Nel vasto az-zur-ro   K

My Dreams

Ninon A

Ni, non, Ni-non,   que fais-tu de la vi-e   L'heu- re s'en- fuit,___   M

B

Au- jour d'hui le prin- temps, Ni- non___ de-main l'hi-   ver.   N

Non me lo dite
Copyright by G. Ricordi & Co., Inc.

Di-temi che il Si- gnor tut-te le co- se   O

Non t'amo più A
Copyright by G. Ricordi & Co., Inc.

Ri- cor-di an-co-   ra il dì che c'in-con- tram-mo;   P

B

Or la mia fe- de il de-si- de-rio im-men-so   Q

Oh! Quanto io t'amerei
Copyright by G. Ricordi & Co., Inc.

Oh! quan-to io t'a-me-   rei,   se la pa-ro- la   R

Parted
Copyright by G. Ricordi & Co., Inc.

Dear- est, our day is___ o-ver, End- ed the day di- vine   S

Penso!
Copyright by G. Ricordi & Co., Inc.

Pen- so_al- la pri- ma vol- ta in cui vol- ge- sti

Ridonami la calma
Copyright by G. Ricordi & Co., Inc.

A- ve Ma- ri- a, per l'a- ria va_il suon d'u- na cam- pa- na

La Serenata

Vo- la, o se- re- na- ta: La mia di- let- ta_è so- la,

Sogno
Copyright by G. Ricordi & Co., Inc.

Ho so- gna- to che sta- vi_a gi- noc- chi Co- me_un san- to

L'Ultimo Canzone (The Last Song) A
Copyright by G. Ricordi & Co., Inc.

M'han det- to che do- ma- ni, Ni- na, vi fa- te spo- sa

B

Fo- glia di ro- sa,_ O fio- re d'a- ma- ran- to_

Vorrei'(Could I) A
Copyright by G. Ricordi & Co., Inc.

Vor- rei al- lor che tu pal- li- do_e mu- to pie- ghi la fron- te

B

Vor- rei_ per in- can- te- si- mi d'a- mo- re pia- na- men- te

Vorrei morir A
Copyright by G. Ricordi & Co., Inc.

Vor- rei mo- rir ne la sta- gion del l'an- no,

B

Vor- rei mo- rir, vor- rei mo- rir quan- do tra- mon- ta il so- le

TOURS, Frank E. (1877-   )

Mother o' Mine!

TOYE, Francis (1883-   )

The Inn
Copyright 1925, F. Toye

Do you re- mem- ber an inn, Mi- ran- da?

TRADITIONAL

Barbara Allen

In Scar- let town, where I was born, There was a fair maid dwel- lin'

Early one morning

Ear- ly one morn - - - ing just as the sun was ris- ing

The Holly and the Ivy

The hol- ly and the i- vy Now both are full well grown,

The Lincolnshire Poacher

When I was bound_ ap- pren - - tice, in fam- ous Lin- coln- shire,_

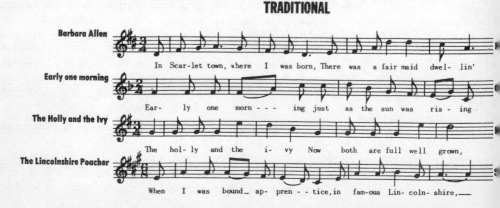

O Can Ye Sew Cushions

O can ye sew cush- ions and can ye sew sheets,

TROTERÉ, Henry (1855-1912)

In Old Madrid

Long years a- go in old Mad- rid where soft- ly sighs

TURINA, Joaquin (1882-1950)

Cantares
Copyright by Unión Musical Española

Ay!

Mas cer-ca de mi te sien-to____ cuan-do mas hu-yo de tí____

Las locas por amor
Copyright by Unión Musical Española

Te a-ma- re ____ dio-sa Ve - - - - - - - - - - - nus ____

Rima
By permission Associated Music
Publishers, Inc.

Yo soy ar- den- te yo soy mo- re- na

aeta en forma de Salve a la Virgen de la Esperanza

Dios te sal-ve, Ma-ca- re - - - - na ma-dre de los se-vi- lla- - nos

Triptico I. Farruca
Copyright by Unión Musical Española

Es- tá tu i-ma-gen que ad-mi-ro, tan pe- ga-da a mi de-se- - o

II. Cantilena

Por un a- le-gre pra-do de flo-res es-mal-ta - - - - - - to

III. Madrigal

Tus o- jos, o-jos no son, ni- ña si- no dos na- va-jos

VALDERRABANO, Enriquez de (16th Cent.)

A monte sale (Soneto)

A mon- te sa-le el a- mor_____ de la Is- la muy nom- bra-da

Señora, si te olvidaré

Se- ño- ra, si te ol-vi-da- ré La_ mi dies-tra ol vi-de à mi

VALVERDE, Joaquin (1846-1910)

Clavelitos (Carnations)
Copyright by E. B. Marks Music Corp., N. Y.

Cla- ve- li- tos a quien le doy cla- ve - - - les!____

VANDERPOOL, Frederick W. (1877-1947)

Values (Another Hour with Thee)
Copyright 1918, M. Witmark & Sons

VARNEY, Louis (1844-1908)

Valse du Colibri, from L'Amour Mouillé (comic-opera)
Copyright by Choudens fils, Paris

VAUGHAN WILLIAMS, Ralph (1872-   )

Bushes and Briars
Copyright by Novelli & Co., Ltd., London

A farmer's son so sweet
Copyright by Stainer & Bell, Ltd., London;
Galaxy Music Corporation, N. Y.,
U. S. Agents

The House of Life 1. Love-Sight
Copyright by Edwin Ashdown, London

2. Silent Noon

3. Love's Minstrels

4. Heart's Haven

5. Death in Life

6. Love's Last Gift

How can the tree but wither
By permission Oxford Univ. Press, London,
copyright owners

Linden Lea
By permission Boosey & Hawkes, Inc.,
copyright owners

Mass in G Minor I. Kyrie
Copyright 1922, J. Curwen

II. Gloria in excelsis

III. Credo

IV. A. Sanctus

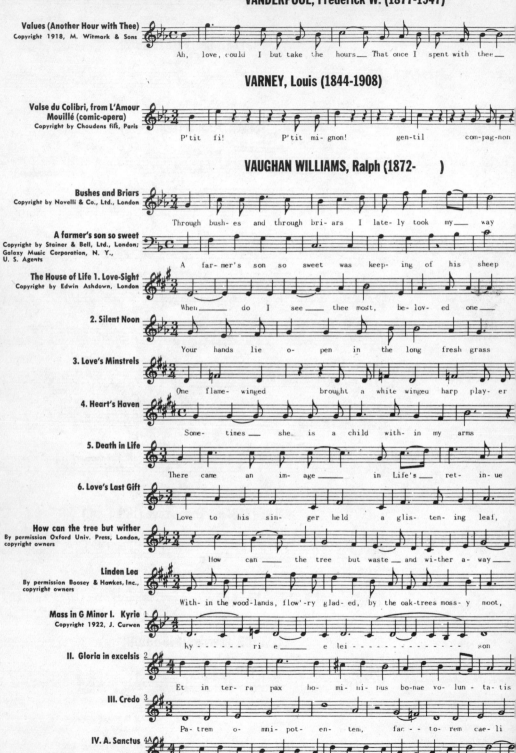

The Twilight People
By permission Oxford Univ. Press, London, copyright owners

It is a whis-per a-mong the ha---zel bush--es;

The Water Mill
By permission Oxford Univ. Press, London, copyright owners

There is a mill, an an-cient one, Brown with rain and dry with sun,

The Winter is gone
Copyright by Novello & Co., Ltd., London

The win-ter is gone and the sum-mer is come

Arrangements: Ca' the yowes
Copyright 1922, J. Curwen

Ca' the yowes, tae the knowes, Ca' them whar the hea-ther grows

The Dark Eyed Sailor
Copyright by Stainer & Bell, Ltd., London; Galaxy Music Corporation, N. Y., U. S. agents

It was a come-ly young la-dy fair, Was walk-ing out

Down in yon forest
Copyright by Stainer & Bell, Ltd., London; Galaxy Music Corporation, N. Y., U. S. agents

Down in yon for-est there stands a hall, The bells of Par-a-dise

Just as the tide was flowing
Copyright by Stainer & Bell, Ltd., London; Galaxy Music Corporation, N. Y., U. S. agents

One mor-ning in the month of May, Down by some roll-ing ri-ver

Loch Lomond
Copyright by Stainer & Bell, Ltd., London; Galaxy Music Corporation, N. Y., U. S. agents

By yon bon-ny banks and yon bon-ny braes, where the sun shines

The Springtime of the year
Copyright by Stainer & Bell, Ltd., London; Galaxy Music Corporation, N. Y., U. S. agents

As I walked out one morn-ing, in the spring-time of the year

The Turtle Dove
Copyright 1919, J. Curwen

Fare you well my dear, I must be gone, and leave you

Wassail Song
Copyright by Stainer & Bell, Ltd., London; Galaxy Music Corporation, N. Y., U. S. agents

Was- sail, Was- sail all o- ver the town

Wassail Song
Copyright by Stainer & Bell, Ltd., London; Galaxy Music Corporation, N. Y., U. S. agents

We've been a-while a- wan-der-ing A- mongst the leaves

VECCHI, Orazio (1550-1603)

Il bianco e dolce cigno

Il bian---co e dol-ce cig-no can-tan---do mo--re

Can- tan------------do, can-tan------do

VEHANEN, (1887-   )

Tuku, tuku, lampaitani (arr.) (Finnish folk tune)
By permission Galaxy Music Corporation, N. Y.

Tu- ku, tu- ku, lam- pai-ta- ni, ki- li, ki- li, ki- li- a- ni

VERACINI, Francesco (1690-1750)

Pastoral, from Rosalinda (opera)

Me- co ver- rai su quel-la, A- me-na col-li- net-ta

VERDI, Giuseppe (1813-1901)

OPERAS
Aida Act I

Ce - le - ste A - i - da, for - ma di - vi - na, mi - sti - co ser - to

Su! del Ni - lo al sa - cro li - do ac - cor - re - te, E - gi - zii e - rir,

Ri - tor - na vin - ci - tor! E dal mio lab - bro u - sci l'em - pia pa - ro - la!

L'in - sa - na pa - ro - la O nu - mi sper - de - te!

I sa - cri no - mi di pa - dre d'a - man - te

Nu - mi, pie - tà del mio sof - frir! Spe - me **non** v'ha

Finale

Pos - - - sen - - te, pos - sen - te. Ftha

Nu - me, cu - sto - de e vin - di - ce di que - sta sa - cra ter - ra

Act II, Scene I Introduction

Chi mai chi mai fra gl'inni e i plau - si er - ge al - la glo - ria il vol

Vie - ni: sul crin ti pio - va - no, Vie - ni sul crin ti pio - va - no

Ah! vie - - - ni, vie - ni a - mor mio, m'i - neb - bria,

Duet

A - mo - re a - mo - re! gau - dio tor - men - to so - a - ve eb - brez - za

A tut - ti bar - ba - ra non si mo - stro la sor - te

Scene II

Gloria al E - git - to, ad I - si - de che il sa - cro suol pro - teg - ge!

S'in - trec - ci il lo - to al lau - - - ro sul crin dei vin - ci - to - ri

Gra - - zie a - gli De - - - i ren - de - - te,

Ma tu, Re, tu si - gno - re pos - sen - te, a co - sto - ro ti vol - gi

Act III Nile Song

Oh pa - tria mia, mai più, mai più ti ri - ve - drò!

OPERAS

Aida Act III (Nile Song)

O cieli azzurri,o dolci auree native,

Ri-ve-drai le fo-re-ste imbal-sa-ma-te, le fre-sche val-li

Su, dun - - - - - - - que! sor-get-te e-gi-zie co-or-ti!

Duet

Pur ti ri-veg - - - - - - go mia dol-ce A-i - - - da

Là tra__ fo-re-ste ver-gi-ni, di fio-ri pro-fu-ma-te

Si: fug-giam da que-ste mu-ra al__ de-ser-to in-siem

Act IV Scene I Duet

Già i sa-cer-do-ti a-du-nan-si ar-bi-tri del tuo fa-to;

Ah!__ tu dei vi-ve-re! __ Sì, al-l'a-mour mio vi-vrai;

Scene II Finale

Mo-rir! si pu-ra e bel-la Mo-rir!__ per me d'a-mo-re

Ve-di? dí mor-te l'an-ge-lo radian-te a noi s'ap-pres-sa __

O ter-ra ad-di-o;ad-di-o val-le di pian-ti

Attila Act II

Dagl' im-mor-ta-li ver-ti-ci bel-li di glo-ria,

Act III Trio

Te sol,__ te sol quest' a-ni-ma a-ma im-men-so a-mo-re

Un Ballo in Maschera (The Masked Ball)
Act I Scene I

La re-ve-drà nel l'e-sta-si rag-gian-te__di pal-lo-re

Al-la vi-ta che t'ar-ri-de di spe-ran-ze e gau-dio pie-na,

Vol - - - - ta la ter-re-a __ fron-te al-le stel-le

Scene II

Re - - - dell' a-bis-so,af-fret-ta-ti, pre-ci-pi-ta per l'e-tra,

È lui è lui ne' pal-pi-ti co - - - me ri-sen-to a-des-so

Di' tu - - - se fe-de-le flut-to m'a-spet - - - - ta,

OPERAS
Un Ballo in Maschera (The Masked Ball)
Act I Scene II

È scher- zo od è fol- li - - - a sif-fatta pro-fe-zi - a

Act II

Ma dal-l'a-ri- do stelo di-vul- sa co-me a-vrò di mia ma-no

Love duet

Non sai tu che se l'a-ni-ma mi a - - - il ri-mor-so

Oh qual so-a-ve bri-vi-do l'ac-ce-so pet-to ir-ro-ra!

Ve' se di not-te qui col-la spo-sa l'in-na-mo-ra- to

Act III

Mor-rò, ma pri-ma in gra - zia deh! mi con-sen-ti al-me-no

E- ri tu che mac-chia-ve quel-l'a - - - ni-ma, la de-li-zia

Ma se m'è for-za per-der ti per sem-pre o lu-ce mi - a

(Air of the page)

Sa- per vor-res-te di che si ves-te, quan-do l'è co-sa

Don Carlos Act I

Io la vi-di e al su - - - o sor-ri-so scin-til- lar,

Act II

Dio,___ che nell' al-ma in-fon - - - de-re a-mor

Nel giar-din del bel- lo___ sa-ra-cin o-stel- lo,

Non___ pian-ger, mia com-pa - - gna, non pian-ger no,

Act IV

Dor-mi-rò sol nel man-to mio re-gal, quan-do la mia gior-na-ta

O don fa- ta- le, o don cru-del che in suo fu- ror___

O___ mia Re-gi- na, io t'im- - mo- - la-i

Per me giun- to è il dì su- pre-mo, no, mai più ci ri - - ve-drem;

Io mor - rò, ma lie-to in co-re, chè po- tei co-sì___ ser-bar

Act V

Tu che le va-ni- tà co- no-sce-sti del mon- do

OPERAS
Don Carlos Act V

I Due Foscari Act I

Act II

Act III

Ernani Act I

Act II

Act III

Act IV

S'an-cor si pian-ge in cie - - - lo pian-gi sul mio do- lo - - - re,

Dal più re-mo-to e-si-glio, sull'a- li del___ de-si - - o

Tu al ciu squardo onni-pos- sen - - - - te tut-to esul- ta o

O vec-chio cor che bat - - - - - - - ti come a'prim' an-ni in se - - - - - no

Non ma- le-dir-mi, o pro - - - - de se son del Do- ge fi - - - glio;

Al- l'in - - fe - - li-ce ve-glio con-for - - ta tu il do- lo - - - re

Que- sta dun- que è l'i-ni-qua mer-ce- de, che ser- ba- ste

Co- me ru-gia- da al co- spi-te d'un ap-pas-si-to fio - - - - - re

Ev- vi - - - va! be- viam! be- viam! Nel vi-no cer- chiam

Er- na-ni! Er-na - - - ni in-vo-la- mi all' ab-bor-ri- to am-ples- so

Tut- to___ sprez-zo___ che d'Er- na - ni non___ fa - - vel- la

Da quel dì___ che t'ho ve- du- ta bel- la co- me un pri mo a-

In- fe-li- ce! e tu cre-de- vi si bel ci- glio

Lo ve- dre - - mo, o ve- gli au-da - - ce se re- si-ster-mi

Vie - ni me- co, sol di ro - - - se in - trec-ciar ti vo' la vi - - ta,

Oh de' verd'an - - - - ni___ mie - - - - i so gui e bugiar de- lar - - - ve

Si ri- des-ti il Le- on di Ca- sti - - - glia, e d'I-be - - - ria

O som- mo Car- lo, più del tuo no- me le tue vir-tu - - di

So- lin- go, er-ran-te e mi-se-ro, Fin da prim' an-ni mie- i

OPERAS
La Forza del Destino
Act II Scene II

Act III Tarantella

Act IV

(Trio)

(chorus)

(chorus)

(soprano & chorus)

OPERAS
La Forza del Destino
Act IV

Del mon-do i ___ di-sin ___ gan-ni,

I Lombardi alla Prima Crociata
Act I

Te, ver-gin san-ta in-vo-co Sal-ve Ma-ri-a!

Act II

La mi-a le-ti-zia in-fon-de-re

Act II A

O ma-dre, dal cie-lo soc-cor-ri al mio pian-to

Act III B

Se va-no se va-no è il pre-ga-re,

Act III

Qual vo-lut-tà tra-scor-re-re sen-to di-ve-na in ve-na

Act IV Polonaise

Non fu so-gno In fon-do all' al-ma

Chorus of Pilgrims

O si-gno-re, dal tet-to na-ti-o ci chia-ma-sti

Luisa Miller Act I

Lo vi-di, e'l pri-mo pal-pi-to il cor sen-ti d'a-mo-re

Sa-cra la scel-ta è d'un con-sor-te, es-ser ap-pie-no

Il mio san-gue, la vi-ta da-re-i per ve-der-lo fe-li-ce,

Act II

Tu pu-ni-sci-mi o Si-gno-re, se t'of-fe-si,

Quan-do le se-re al pla-ci-do chia-ror d'un ciel stel-la-to

Macbeth Act II

Co-me dal ciel pre-ci-pi-ta l'om-bra più sem-pre o-scu-ra!

Act IV Coro di Profughi
Scozzesi

Pa-tria op-pres-sa! il dol-ce no-me no, di ma-dre a-ver

Ah, la pa-ter-na ma-no non vi fu scu-do o ca-ri

U-na mac-chia è qui tutt'o-ra via ti di-co,

Pie-tà, ri-spet-to, a-mo-re con-for-to a' dì ca-den-ti

Nabucodonosor
Act I Sperate, O figli A

D'E-git-to là sui lì-di E-gli a Mo-sè diè vi-ta

OPERAS

Nabucodonosor
Act I Sperate, O figli

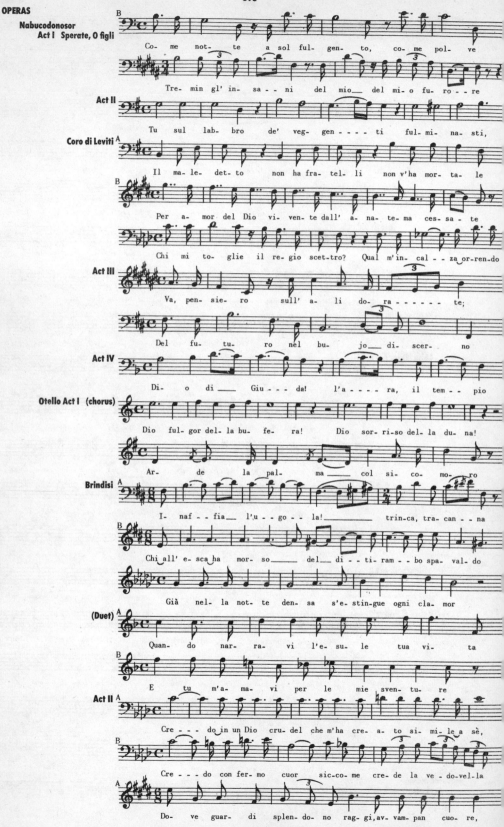

Co- me not- te a sol ful- gen- to, co- me pol- ve

Tre- min gl' in- sa- ni del mio del mio fu- ro- re

Act II

Tu sul lab- bro de' veg gen - - - - ti ful- mi- na- sti,

Coro di Leviti

Il ma- le- det- to non ha fra- tel- li non v'ha mor- ta- le

Per a- mor del Dio vi- ven- te dall' a- na- te- ma ces- sa- te

Chi mi to- glie il re- gio scet- tro? Qual m'in- cal- za or- ren- do

Act III

Va, pen- sie- ro sull' a- li do- ra - - - - - te;

Del fu- tu- ro nel bu- jo di- scer- no

Act IV

Di- o di - Giu - - da! l'a - - - - ra, il tem - - pio

Otello Act I (chorus)

Dio ful- gor del- la bu- fe- ra! Dio sor- ri- so del- la du- na!

Ar- de la pal- ma - col si- co- mo- ro

Brindisi

I- naf - - fia - l'u - - go - - la! - trin- ca, tra- can - - na

Chi all' e- sca ha mor- so - del - di - ti- ram - - bo spa- val- do

Già nel- la not- te den- sa s'e- stin- gue ogni cla- mor

(Duet)

Quan- do nar- ra- vi l'e- su- le tua vi- ta

E tu m'a- ma- vi per le mie sven- tu- re

Act II

Cre - - do in un Dio cru- del che m'ha cre- a- to si- mi- le a sè,

Cre - - do con fer- mo cuor sic- co- me cre- de la ve- do- vel- la

Do- ve guar- di splen- do- no rag- gi, av- vam- pan cuo- re,

VERDI

OPERAS
Othello Act II

A te le __ por-po-re, __ le __ per-le e gli o-stri

O - ra e per sem-pre Ad-dio sante me-mo-rie, ad dio __

The Dream

E - ra la not-te, Cas-sio dor-mi-a, gli sta-va ac-can-to

Si, pel ciel mar-mo-reo giu-ro! Per le at-tor-te fol-go-ri!

Te - sti mon __ è il Sol ch'io mi - ro, che __ m'ir-ra - dia

Act III

Dio ti gio-con-di, o spo-sa del-l'al-ma mi-a so-vra------no

Ma __ o pian-to, o duol! m'han ra-pi-to il mi-rag-gio

(Trio)

Vie - ni; l'au-la è de-ser-ta. T'i nol-tra,

Questa è una ra--gna do-ve il tuo cuor __ ca-sca,

A ter-ra sì nel li-vi-do fan-go, per-cos-sa

E un di sul mio sor-ri-so fio-ria la spe---me

Act IV Willow Song

Pian-gea __ can-tan- do nel-l'er-ma lan-da __

Prayer

Pre - ga per chi a-do-ran-do a te, si pro----stra,

Death of Othello

E tu co-me sei pal-li-da! e stan-ca, e mu-ta, e bel--la

Rigoletto Prologue

Que-sta o quel-la per me pa-ri so-no a quan-t'al---tre

Par - ti - te? Cru - de-e-le! Se-gui-re lo spo-so

Tut-to è fe-sta, tut-to è gio-ia, tut-to è fe-sta;

Act I (Duet)

Si - gnor, Va non ho nien-te Nè il chie-si A voi pre-sen-te un uom

Pa - ri sia-mo io la lin-gua, egli ha il pu-gna-le;

OPERAS
Rigoletto Act I (Duet)

(Final chorus)

Act II

(chorus)

A

B

A

B

Act III

(Quartet) A

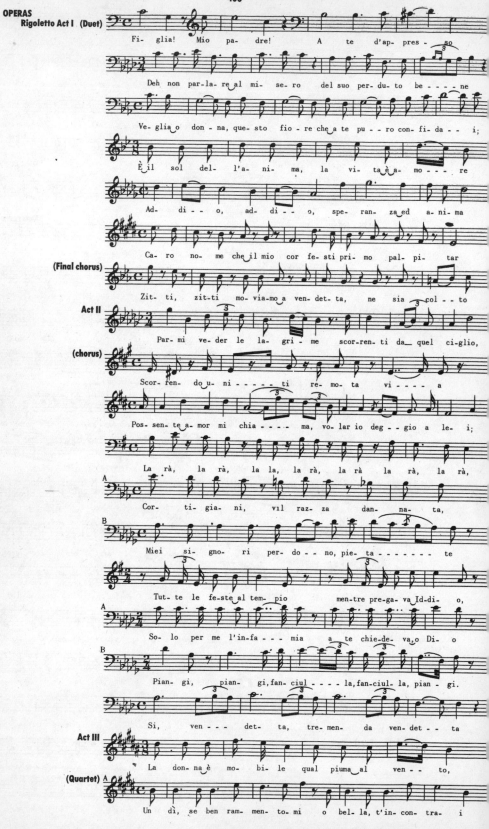

OPERAS
Rigoletto Act III (Quartet)

Bel la figlia dell'a mo re, schiavo son de'vezzi tuo i;

Ah! ah! ri do ben di core chè tai baie costan poco

In fe li ce core, cor tradi to, per angoscia non

V'ho ingannato colpevole fui l'a mai troppo

Lassu in cie lo, vicina alla madre

Simon Boccanegra Prologue

Il lacerato spirito del mesto genitore

Act I

Come in quest'o ra brunna sorridon gliastri

Figlia a tal nome io palpito qual se m'aprisse i cieli

Plebe! Patrizi! Popolo dalla feroce storia

Piango su voi sul placido raggio del vostro clivo

Act II

Sento avvampar nell'anima furente gelosia

Cielo pietoso, rendila rendila a quedo core

La Traviata Act I Brindisi

Libiamo, libiamo ne' lieti calici,

Un dì felice, eterea, mi balenaste innante

Ah, for se lui che l'anima solinga ne' tumulti,

A quel l'amor, quel l'amor ch'e palpito,

(Part 2 of Ah fors'e lui)

Sempre libera degg'io folleggiare

Act II Scene I

De miei bollenti spiriti il giovanile ardore

O mio rimor so! oh infamia! io vissi

VERDI

OPERAS

La Traviata Act II Scene I

Stri - de la vam - - - - - pa, la ___ fol - la in do - - - - mi ta

Chi del gi - ta - - no i gior - - ni ab - bel - la?

Con - dot - ta el l'era in cep - pi al su o de-stin tre - men - do

Mal reg - - gen - do all' a - - - - - spro as - sal - to,

Pe - ri gliar-ti an-cor lan - guen - - te per cam - min sel - vag - gio

Il ba - len del suo sor - ri - so d'u - - na ___ stel - la

Per me o - ra fa-ta - - - le, i tuoi mo-men - ti af-fret - ta

Finale

E deg - gio e pos - so cre - - der - lo? Ti veg - go a me d'ac-can-to!

Act III Soldiers' Chorus

Or co da di, ma fra po - co gio-che-rem ben al - tro gio - co!

Squil - li e cheg - gi la trom - - ba guer-rie-ra, chia-mi all' ar - mi

Ah si, ben mio coll' es - se - re io tuo, tu mia con-sor - te,

Di quel-la pi - - - - - ra l'or-ren - do fo - - - - - co

All' ar - mi! All' ar - mi all' ar - mi all' ar - - - mi!

Gior - ni po-ve - ri vi - ve - a, pur con - ten - ta

Act IV Scene I

D'a-mor sull' a - - li ro - se - e van-ne, sos-pir ___ do-len - - -te;

Miserere

Quel son, quel-le pre - - - ci so-len-ni, fu - ne - ste

Ah ___ che la morte o-gno - - ra è ___ tar-da nel ve - nir

Tu ve - drai che a-more in ter - ra mai del mio non fa più for - te

Mi - ra, di a-cer - be la-gri - me spar-go al tuo piedi un ri - o!

OPERAS

Il Trovatore Act IV Scene II

Si, la stan-chez-za m'op-prime, o fi- - -glio

Ai nos-tri mon-ti ri-tor-ne-re- -mo, l'an-ti-ca pa-ce

Vi-vra! Con-ten-de il giu-bi-lo i det-ti a me, Sig-no-re

I Vespri Siciliani Act II

O tu, Pa-ler-mo, ter-ra a-do-ra-ta, a-me si car-ro___

Act III

In bra-ccio alle do-vi- -zie, nel se-no__ de-gli o-nor,

Quan-do al mio sen per te par-la-va pie-tà sin-ce-ra

Act IV

Gior-no di pian- -to, di fier do- lo- -re! Men-tre l'a-mo-re

Act V Siciliana

Mer- -cè, di-let-te a-mi- -che di quoi leg-gia-dri fior;

La brez-za a-leg-gia in-tor-no a car-ez-zar-mi il vi-so e

Sacred Music:

Ave Maria (scala enigmatica)

A- ve Ma-ri- - -a, gra-ti-a ple-na,

Requiem I Requiem and Kyrie

A
Re-qui-em Re-qui-em Re-qui-em ae-ternam do-na, do-na e-is,

B
Te de-cet hym-mus, De- - - - - -us, in Si- on,

Ky- ri-e e- le- - - - - - - - - - - -i- son

II Dies Irae

A
Di-es i-rae, Di-es i- - - - - - - - - - - - - - - - - rae,

B
Tu ba mi- - - -rum___ spar- -gens___ so-num

C
Quid sum, mi- - - - -ser! tunc- -dic-tur- us

D
Rex tre-men-dae maj-es- ta- - -tis___

E
Re- - - -cor-da-re, Je- - -su pi-e Quod___ sum-cau-sa

F
In-ge-mi- -sco tam-quam re-us, Cul-pa ru-bet vul-tus me-us:

Requiem II Dies Irae
Qui ____ Ma- ri- am ab-sol vis ——— ti,

H O- ro sup-plex et ac-cli-nis, Cor con-tri-tum qua-si ci-nis,

La- cry- mo-sa di- es ___ il-la! Qua re-surg-et ex fa-vil-la

III Domine Jesu
Do —— mi- ne Do —— mi- ne Je- su Chris-te,

li- be- ra a ——— ni ——— mas

Quam o-lim A- bra-hae, quam o-lim Ab- ra-hae,

Ho ——— sti- as et pre ——— ces ___ ti-bi, Do- mi- ne

IV Sanctus (fugue for two choirs)
San- ctus, san-ctus, san- ctus, Do- mi- nus De- us ___ Sa- ba-oth,

San- ctus, san-ctus, san- ctus Do —— mi- nus Deus Sa- ba-oth

V Agnus Dei
Ag- nus De- i, A ——— gnus De- i, qui tol- lis pecca-ta mun- di,

VI Lux aeternam
Lux ae- ter- na lu- ce- at e- is Do- mi- ne

Re- qui- em ae- ter ——— nam do na e ——————— is,

et ___ lux ___ per- pe- tu- a lu—— ce- at e- is

VII Libera me
Li- be- ra me, Do- mi- ne, de mor- te ae- ter- na, ___

VIDAL, Paul (1863-1931)

Ariette
Si j'é-tais ray- on, j'i- rais, jeu- ne fil- le

Le Fidèle Coeur
Copyright 1898, G. Schirmer, Inc.
Je se- rai ta dou-ceur pro- fon- de Ta der-niè- re joie

VIDE, Jacques (15th Cent.)

Las! j'ay perdu mon espincel
Las! j'ay per- du mon es- pin ——— cel

Vit encore ce faux Dangier

Vit en-co-re ce faux Dan-gier _____

VILLA-LOBOS, Heitor (1884-)

Bachianas Brasileiras No. 5
By permission Associated Music
Publishers, Inc.

Ah _____

Tar-de u-ma nu-vem ro-sea len-ta e tran-spa-ren-te

Canção de Saudade

Ah _____

Mi- nha mae que-ri-da Tu es meu pen-sa-men-to

Estrella é lua nova (Brazilian folk
song) (arr.)
By permission Associated Music
Publishers, Inc.

Es-trel- la do céo é lu-a no-va cra-ve-ja-da

Nozani - ná (Brazilian folk song) (arr.)
By permission Associated Music
Publishers, Inc.

No- za-ri ná ô-re ku-á ku-á,___ Ka-za ê-tê

Serestas No. 1 Pobre Céga

Po-bre cé-ga, por-que cho-ram as-sim tan-to esses teus o---lhos

No. 2 O anjo da guarda

Quan- do min-ha ir-mã mor-reu (De-via ter si-do as-sim

No. 3 Canção de folha
morta

Fol- ha ca-his-te ao meu la-do La-gri-ma ver-de dos ra-mos!

No. 4 Saudades da minha
vida

Sau-da-de-do tem- po, Do tem-po__ pas- sa-do,

No. 6 No paz do outono

Na paz do ou-to-no, Gra- ve, pro-fun- da___

No. 7 Cantiguo do viuvo

A noi-te ca-in na minha al- ma, Fi-quel tris-te sem que- rer

No. 8 Canção do carreiro

Na, na! na na na na na na na na na na na na na na

No. 9 Abril

De- pols da chu-va-ra-da su- bi-ta que i-num- dou

No. 10 Desejo

Pe- la-ja-nel-la a-ber-ta eu ve- ja a lu-a pen-du-ra-da

No. 11 Redondilha

A vi-da Fin- gi-da Me cha-ma Me bei-ja Me fo-go

No. 12 Realejo

Be-a- le jo é co-mo os ou-tros são, que vao e vem___

Sino da Aldeia, Op. 87

Sino, co-ra-ção d'al-de - - - ia, Co-ra-ção

ola quebrada (Brazilian folk song) (arr.)
By permission Associated Music Publishers, Inc.

Quan-do da bri-sa no a-çoite a frô da noi-te se cur-vó

Xangô
By permission Associated Music Publishers, Inc.

Xan-gô Ô le gon-di-le O lá lá gon gon gon

VITTORIA, Tomas Luis de (c. 1535-1611)

Animan meam

A - - - ni- mam me- am di le - - - - - ctam

Ave Maria

A- ve Ma- ri - - - - - a Gra-ti- a ple-na

Caligaverunt oculi mei

Ca- li-ga- ve-runt O-cu-li me- i a fle-tu me - - o

Domine, non sum dignus

Do- mi- ne non sum dig- nus, non sum dig - - - - nus

Gaudent in coelis

Gau- dent in coe- lis a- ni- moe Sanc-to - - - - - rum,

O Domine Jesu

O Do- mi- ne Je- su Chri- ste O Do- mi- ne Je- su Chri-ste,

O magnum mysterium

O ma-gnum mys- te- ri- um et ad- mi- ra- bi- le sa-cra

O quam gloriosum

O quam glo- ri- o - - - - sum est re - - - - - gnum

O vos omnes A1

O vos om - - - nes qui tran- si- tis per vi - - - - am,

(both themes sung simultaneously) A2

O vos om- nes qui tran- si- tis per vi- am

Popule meus

Po- pu- le me-us, quid fe- ci ti- bi aut in quo con-tri-sta-vi- te

Tantum ergo

Tan- tum er- go Sa - - - cra- men- tum

Tenebrae factae sunt

Te - - ne-brae fac - - - - - tae sunt dum cru-ci-fi- xes-sent Je-sum

VIVALDI, Antonio (c. 1680-1743)

Stabat Mater I Largo

Sta- bat ma- ter do- lo-ro - - sa jux-sta cru- cem

Stabat Mater II Recitative
Cu - jus a - ni - ma ge - men-tem con - tri-stan-tem

III Andante
Pro - pec - ca - - - tis su - - - e gen - ti

IV Largo
E - ja, Ma - - ter fons a - mo - - - - - - - ris,

V Lento
Fac ut ar - - de at cor me - - - um in a - man - - do

VUILLERMOZ, Emile (1878-   )

Jardin d'amour
Copyright by Salabert, Paris, N. Y.
Quand je vais au___ jar - din, jar - din d'a - mour

WAGNER, Richard (1813-1883)

OPERAS

Der fliegende Holländer (The Flying Dutchman)
Act I Sailor's song
Mit Ge-wit-ter und Sturm aus fer-nem Meer, mein Mä- del, bin dir nah'!

A
Wie oft in Mee - res tief-sten Schlund stürzt' ich voll Sehn-sucht mich hin-ab,

B
Dich fra-ge ich, ge - pries'ner En - gel Got - - - tes

Durch Sturm und bö-sen Wind ver-schla-gen, irr' auf den Was-sern ich

Act II Spinning Chorus
Summ'___ und___ brumm', du___ gu-tes Räd - - - - - - - - - chen

Senta's Ballad
A1
Jo - ho - hoe! Jo - ho - ho - hoe! Ho - ho - hoe! Jo - - - - hoe

A2
Traft ihr das Schiff im Mee - re an; blut - rot die Se - gel,

Doch kann dem blei-chen Man - ne Er - lö-sung ein-stens noch wer - - den

Mein Herz voll Treu - e___ bis___ zum Ster - ben,

Erik's dream
Auf ho-hem Fel - sen lag' ich träu - mend, sah un-ter mir des Mee - res Flut;

Daland's Aria
Mögst du, mein Kind, den frem-den Mann will- kom - men hei - ssen;

A
Wie aus der Fer - ne längst ver-gang' ner Zei - ten

Der fliegende Holländer (The Flying Dutchman)
Act II

Wohl hub auch ich voll Sehn-sucht mei-ne Bli-cke

Love Duet

Wirst du des Va-ters Wahl nicht schel-ten? was er ver-sprach,

Ach! könn-test das Ge-schick du ah-nen, dem dann mit mir

Ver-sank ich jetzt in wun-der-ba-res Träu-men?

Act III Sailor Chorus

Steu-er-mann! Lass die Wacht! Steu-er-mann! Her zu uns

Willst je-nes Tag's du nicht dich mehr ent-sin-nen

Lohengrin Act I Elsa's Dream

Ein-sam in trü-ben Ta-gen hab' ich zu Gott ge-fleht,

Ge-grüsst du gott-ge-san-dter Held! Sei ge-grüsst, sei ge-grüsst,

Nun sei be-dankt, mein lie-ber Schwann! Zieh' durch die wei-te Flut zurück

Wenn ich im Kam-pfe für dich sie-ge willst du dass ich dein Gat-te sei?

Mein Herr und Gott, nun ruf' ich dich, dass du dem Kampf

Du kun-dest nun dein wahr Ge-richt; mein Gott und Herr,

Des rei-nen Arm gieb Hel-den-kraft; des Fal-schen Stär-ke

O fänd ich Ju-bel-wei-sen dei-nem Ruh-me gleich,

Dank, Kö-nig dir, dass du zu rich-ten kamst

Act II

Durch dich musst' ich ver-lie-ren mein Ehr', all' mein-en Ruhm

Euch Lüf-ten, die mein Kla-gen so trau-rig oft er-füllt,

Ent-weih - - - - te Got-ter Helft jetzt mei-ner Ra-che

OPERAS
Lohengrin Act II

Ge- seg- net soll sie schreiten die lang' in De- muth litt

Du Ärm- ste kannst wohl nie er- mes- sen wie zwei- fel- los

Act III Bridal Chorus

Treu- lich ge- führt zie- het da- hin wo euch der Se- gen

Das sü- sse Lied ver- hallt; wir sind al- lein, zum er- sten Mal al- lein,

Lohengrin's narration

Ath- mest Du nicht mit mir die sü- ssen Düf- te O wie so hold

In fer- nem Land un- nah- bar eu- ren Schrit- ten liegt eine Burg,

Mein lie- ber Schwan! Ach, die- se letz- te traur'- ge Fahrt

Kommt er dann heim, wenn ich ihm fern im Le- ben, dies Horn, dies Schwert,

Die Meistersinger von Nürnberg
Act I Scene I

Da zu dir der Hei - - land kam wil- lig dei- ne Tau- fe nahm,

Scene II Chorus of Apprentices

Schuh- ma- che- rei und Po- e- te- rei die lern ich da all- ei- ner- lei

A

Al- ler End' ist doch Da- vid der al - - ler ge- scheit'st

B

Das Blu - men- kränz- lein aus Sei - den fein, wird das dem Herrn Rit- ter

Scene III

Das schö- ne Fest, Jo- han- nis- tag, ihr wisst, be- geh'n wir mor- gen

Am stillen Herd in Win- ters zeit, wann Burg und Hof mir ein- ge- schneit

So rief der Lenz in den Wald, dass laut es ihn durch- hallt

Scene V A

Ja, ihr seid es; nein! Du bist es Al- les sag' ich

B

"Ein Meis- ter - - sin- ger muss es sein; nur wen ihr krönt

Act II Scene I

Jo- han- nis- tag! Jo- han- nis- tag! Blu- men und Bän- - der

Scene III Sach's Monologue A

Was duf- tet doch der Flie - - der so mild, so stark und voll

ERAS
Die Meistersinger von Nürnberg
Act II Scene III Sach's
Monologue

B   A

Len- zes Ge- bot, die_ sü- sse Noth

C   B

Dem Vo- gel, der heut' sang, dem war der Schna-bel hoch ge- wach-sen

Scene V Nightwatch-
man's Song   C

Hört, ihr Leut' und lasst euch sa-gen die Glock' hat zehn_ ge- schla- gen

Scene VI Cobbler's
Song   A   D

Je- rum! Je- rum Hal- la hal- lo he! O- ho!

B   E

Als E- va aus dem_ Pa- ra- dies vom Gott dem Herrn ver- stos-sen,

Beckmes-
ser's Song   F

"Den Tag_ seh' ich_ er- schei- nen, der mir_ wohl ge- fall'n thut

Act III Scene I David's Song   G

Am Jor- dan Sankt_ Jo- han-nes stand all_ Volk der Welt_ zu- tau- fen

H

Wahn! Wahn Ü- ber- all Wahn! wo- hin ich for-schend blick'

Scene II Prize Song   A   I

Mor- gen- lich leuch- tend_ in_ ro- si- gem Schein von Blüth und Duft

B   J

Sei euch ver- traut, welch'_ heh- res Wun- der mir ge- scheh'n

Scene iii   K

Die ich mir aus er- ko- ren, die ganz für mich ge- bo- ren,

Scene IV   L

O Sachs!_ mein Freund! du theu- rer_ Mann! Wie ich dir Ed- - lem

A   M

Die Zeu gen sind_ da, Ge- vat- ter zur_ Hand

B   N

Steh' auf Ge- sell und denk_ an_ den_ Streich

Quintet   O

Se- - lig wie_ die Son- ne mei- nes_ Glü- ckes lacht;_

Scene V   P

Sankt kris- pin,_ lo- - bet ihn!_ War gar ein hei- lig Mann,

Q

Wach' auf! es_ na- - het gen_ den Tag: ich hör'_ sin-gen im grü- nen Hag

R

Euch_ macht ihr's leicht, mir macht ihr's schwer gebt ihr mir Armen

S

Ge-schmückt mit König Da-vid's Bild, nehm ich euch auf in der Meis-ter Gild?

OPERAS

Die Meistersinger von Nürnberg
Act III Scene V

Ver- ach- tet mir die Meis- ter nicht, und ehrt mir ih- re Kunst!

Ehrt eu- re deut-schen Meis- ter, Dann bannt ihr gu- te Geis - - - - ter

Parsifal Act I Guileless fool motive

"durch Mit- leid wis- send, der rei- ne Tor, har-re sein', den ich er- kor"

Des Hai- nes Tie- re nah- ten dir nicht zahm; grüssten dich freund-lich

Vom Ba- de kehrt der Kö- nig heim; hoch steht die Son- ne

Zum letz- ten Lie- bes- mah - - le ge- rüs- tet Tag für Tag

Weh - - vol-les Er- be, dem ich ver- fal- len, ich___ einz'- ger Sün-der

Der Glau- be lebt; die Tau- be schwebt des Hei - - lands hol - der Bo- te:

"Neh- met hin mei- nen Leib, neh- met hin mein___ Blut___

Act II Flower Maidens' Waltz

A

Komm'!___ Komm'!___ Hol- der Kna- be! Komm'!___ Oh hol- der Kna- be

B

Im Lenz___ pflückt uns der Mei- ster! Wir wach - - - - - - sen___ hier___

Ihr kin- di-schen Buh- len, wei-chet von Ihm___ früh__ wel - ken-de Blu- men

Ich sah das Kind an sei- ner Mut- ter Brust,

Am- for- tas! Die Wun- de! Die Wun- de!

Act III

Wie dünkt mich doch die Au- e heut' so schön___

Amfortas' Prayer

Mein Va- ter Hoch- ge- seg - - - - ne- ter der__ Hei- den

Nur ei- ne Waf- fe taugt:___ die Wun- de schliesst, der Speer

Höch- sten Hei- les Wun- der!

Rienzi Act I

Die Frei- heit Rom's sei dies Ge-setz, ihn un-ter-than sei je- der Rö- mer,

OPERAS
Rienzi Act II
Ich sah die Stä-dte, sah das Land, ich zog ent - - lang

Act III
In sei- ner Blü- the bleicht mein Le-ben, da-hin da - - hin

Act V Rienzi's Prayer
All-mächt' ger Va- ter, blick her- ab! Hör' mich im Stau- be

Der Ring des Nibelungen
Das Rheingold
Scene I Woglinde's Song
Wei- a! Wa- ga! Wo- ge, du Wel- le, wal- le zur Wie- ge!

Scene II
Im- mer ist Un- dank Lo- ge's Lohn! Fur dich nur be- sorgt

So weit Le- ben und We- ben im Was- ser, Erd' und Luft,

Ü- ber Stock und Stein zu Thal stap- fen sie hin

Scene IV Erda's Warning
Wei- che, Wo- tan, wei- che! Fleih' des Rin- ges Fluch!

Entrance of the Gods into Valhalla
Zur Burg führt die Brü- cke leicht, doch fest eu-rem Fuss:

Wotan's Song on entrance to Valhalla
A- bend-lich strahlt der Son- ne Au- ge; in präch- ti- ger Gluth

Song of the Rhinemaidens
Rhein- gold! Rhein- gold! rei - - - - - - - nes Gold!

Die Walküre
Act I Scene III
Ein Schwert verhiess mir der Va- ter, ich fänd' es in höch-ster Noth

Der Män- ner Sip-pe sass hier im Saal, von Hun- ding zur Hoch- zeit

Finale: Love Duet
Win- ter- stür- me wi- chen dem Won- ne- mond,

Du bist der Lenz nach dem ich ver- lang- te

O süs- ses- te Won- ne! se- lig- stes Weib!

Sieg- mund heiss' ich und Sieg-mund bin ich be- zeug, es diess Schwert

Act II Scene I Call of the Walküre
Ho- jo- to- ho! Ho- jo- to- ho! hei- a- ha! hei- a- ha!

Fricka-Wotan Duet
Der al- te Sturm, die al- te Müh'! Doch Stand muss ich hier- hal- ten

OPERAS
Der Ring des Nibelungen
Die Walküre
Act II Scene I Fricka-Wotan
Duet

Scene IV

Act III Scene I

Scene II

Scene III Brunnhilde's
pleading

Wotan's farewell

Siegfried Act I Scene I

Scene II

Scene III

Act II Scene II

RAS
Der Ring des Nibelungen
Siegfried Act II   Scene III
Voice of
Forest Bird

Hei! Sieg-fried ge-hört nun der Helm und der Ring!

Lus-tig im Leid sing ich von Lie - - - - be

Act III   Scene I

Wa-che, Wa-la! Wa-la! Er-wach'!_ Aus lan-gem Schlaf

Er-da!_ Er-da!_ E - - wi-ges Weib. Aus hei-mi-scher Tie-fe

Stark ruft das Lied kräf-tig reizt der Zau-ber ich bin er-wacht

Scene III

Was ruht dort schlum-mernd im schat-ti-gen Tann Ein Ross ist's

Heil dir, Son-ne! Heil dir, Licht! Heil dir, Leuchtender Tag!

O Heil der Mut- ter, die mich ge-bar!

E - - - - - wig war ich, e - - - - wig_ bin ich

Sieg - - fried, Herr - - li-cher! Hort_ der Welt!

Götterdämmerung
"Twilight of the Gods"
Prologue: Brünnhilde & Siegfried

Zu neu-en Tha-ten theu-rer Hel-de wie liebt'ich dich,

Act I   Scene I   Hagen's Watch

Hier sitz' ich zur Wacht, wah-re den Hof, weh-re den Hal-le dem Feind.

Scene III   Waltraute's
Narrative

Ho-re mit Sinn, was ich dir sa-ge! Seit er von dir ge-schie-den,

Act II   Scene III Hagen's Call

Hoi-ho!_ Hoi-ho_ ho-ho! Ihr Gi-bichs-man-nen, wa-chet euch auf

(Chorus)

Gross Glück und Heil lacht nun dem Rhein, da Ha-gen, der Grim-me,

Scene IV

Hel-le Wehr! Hei-li-ge Waf-fe Hilf mei-nem e-wi-gen Ei-de!

Act III Scene I   Song of the
Rhinemaidens

Frau Son - - - - - ne sen - - det lich-te Strah-len;

Scene II   Siegfried's
Narration

Mi - - - me hiess ein mür-ris-cher Zwerg; in des Nei-des Zwang

OPERAS Der Ring des Niebelungen
Götterdämmerung
Act III Scene II Siegfried's
Narration

Scene III Brünnhilde's
Immolation

Tannhäuser
Act I Scene I Baccanale
(Chorus of Sirens)

Scene II

Scene III Shepherd Song

Scene IV

Act II Scene I

Scene II Elizabeth &
Tannhäuser
Duet

Scene III

Scene IV Entrance of the
Guests

OPERAS
Tannhäuser
Act II Scene IV Landgrave's Welcome

A — Gar viel und schön ward hier in die-ser Hal-le

B — Blick' ich um-her in die-sem ed-len Krei-se,

C — Auch ich darf mich so glück-lich nen-nen, zu schau'n, was, Wolf-ram, du geschaut!

D — O Him-mel! Lass' dich jetzt er-fle-hen! Gieb mei-nem Lied der wei-he

E — Dir, ho-he Lie-be, tö - - - ne be-geis-tert mein Ge-sang

Act III Scene I

F — Wohl wusst' ich hier sie im Ge-bet zu fin-den,

Pilgrims' Chorus

G — Be-glückt darf nun dich, o Hei-math, ich schau-en

Elizabeth's Prayer

H — All-mächt' ge Jung-frau, hör' mein Fle-hen! Zu dir, Ge-pries' ne,

Scene II Song to the Evening Star

I — Wie To-des-ah-nung Dämm' rung deckt die Lan-de,

J — O du mein hol-der A-bend-stern, wohl grüss' ich im-mer

Scene III Rome Narrative

K — In-brunst im Her-zen wie Kein Bü-sser noch sie je-ge-fühlt,

L — Nach Rom ge-langt' ich so zur heil'-gen Stel-le,

Tristan und Isolde
Act I   Scene I Sailor's Song

M — West-wärts schweift der Blick, ost-wärts streicht das Schiff.

Scene II

N — Herr Mo-rold zog zu Mee-re-her, in Korn-wall Zins zu haben,

Act II   Scene II Love Duet

O — O sink' her-nie-der, Nacht, O sink' her-nie-der Nacht der Lie-be

Brangäne's Warning

P — Ein - - - - - sam wa - - chend in der Nacht, wem der Traum

Scene III

Q — Wo-hin nun Tris-tan schei-det willst du, I-sol-de fol-gen?

Act III Scene I

R — Wie sie se-lig, hehr und mil-de wan-delt durch des Meer's Ge-fil-de?

Scene III Liebestod

S — Mild und lei-se wie er lä-chelt, wie das Au-ge hold er öff-net,

Songs: L'Attente

Monte, é- cu-reuil monte au grand chê- ne, Sur la bran- che des cieux

Les Deux Grenadiers A

Long- temps cap- tifs chez le Rus- se loin- tain

B

Peut- ê- tre bien qu'en ce choc meur- tri- er,

Five Wesendonck Songs
1. Der Engel

In der Kind-heit frü- hen Ta- gen hört' ich oft von En - - geln sa- gen,

2. Stehe still!

Sau- sen-des, brau-sen-des Rad der Zeit, Mes- ser du der E- wig-keit;

3. Im Treibhaus

Hoch- ge-wölb- te Blät- ter-kro- nen, Bal- da-chi- ne von Sma- ragd,

4. Schmerzen

Son- ne, wei- nest je- den A- bend dir die schö-nen Au- gen roth;

5. Träume

Sag', welch' wun- der-ba- re Träu-me hal- ten mei- nen Sinn um- fan-gen

Mignonne

Mi- gnon -ne, al-lons voir si la Ro- se qui ce ma- tin

Schlaf', holdes Kind

Schlaf hol- des Kind, ich wieg'dich in Schlum- mer,

Der Tannenbaum

Der Tan- nen-baum steht schwei-gend ein- sam auf grau- er Höh';

WALLACE, William Vincent (1812-1865)

Maritana (opera) Act I No. 4

An- gels that a-round us ho- ver, Guard us till the close of day

Act II No. 13

Yes! let me like a Sol- dier fall up- on some o- pen plain

No. 14

In hap- py mo- ments day by day, The sands of life may pass,

No. 19

There is a flow'r that bloom- eth when au- tumn leaves are shed,

Act III No. 22

Scenes that are bright- est, May charm a - - - while

WALTHER von der Vogelweide (12th-13th Cent.)

Kreuzfahrlied (Crusader's Song)
(also called Palästinalied)

Al- ler erst lebe ich mir wer- de, sit mie sün- dic

WALTON, William (1902-   )

Belshazzar's Feast (choral work)
By permission Oxford Univ. Press, London,
copyright owners

By the wa - - - - - - ters of Ba - by-lon There__ we sat down

Sing us one of the songs of Zi - on

How__ shall we sing__ the Lord's__ song, the Lord's__ song__

If I for-get thee,__ for-get__ thee

In Ba - - - - - - by-lon Belshazzar the King made a great__ feast

Bring ye the cor - - - - - - - - - - - - - net

Praise__ ye the__ god of sil - ver

Praise__ ye praise__ ye

Then sing__ a-loud to God__ our strength

Then sing, sing a-loud__ to God our strength;Make a joy-ful noise

Then__ sing,__ sing a- loud,__ Sing a-loud__

Al- le- lu- ja Al- le- lu - - - ja, al-le-lu-ja

WARD, John (16th-17th Cents.)

Hope of my heart

Hope__ of__ my heart, Hope of my__ heart O where- fore

Out from the vale

Out from__ the vale__ of deep de - - - spair, of deep de - spair

Upon a bank of roses

Up- on a bank with Ros- es set a- bout, up- on a bank

WARE, Harriet (Contemporary)

Boat Song
Copyright by John Church Co.
Used by permission

Where will you take__ me lit- tle boat, All on a sum- mer's day__

WARLOCK, Peter (1894-1930) (Philip Heseltine)

As ever I saw
By permission Boosey & Hawkes, Inc., copyright owners
She is gen-tle and al- -so wise; of all__ o-thers

Captain Stratton's Fancy
By permission of Augener, Ltd., London
Oh, some are fond of red wine and some are fond of white,

Chop Cherry
By permission J. & W. Chester, Ltd., London, copyright owners
When as the rye reach__ to the chin, and chop-cher-ry,

Corpus Christi (old English carol) (arr.)
Copyright 1921, J. Curwen
Lul- ly, lul-lay, lul-ly, lul-lay, The fau-con hath borne my make__ a-way

Fair and True
By permission Oxford Univ. Press, London, copyright owners
Love-ly kind, and kind-ly lov-ing, Such a mind were worth the mov-ing;

The Fox
By permission Oxford Univ. Press, London, copyright owners
At 'The Fox Inn' the tat-ter'd ears, the fox'-s grin

Good Ale
By permission of Augener, Ltd., London
Bring us in no brown bread__ for__ that is made of bran,

Jillian of Berry
By permission Oxford Univ. Press, London, copyright owners
For Jil-lian of Ber-ry she dwells on a hill, And she hath good beer

Passing by
By permission Oxford Univ. Press, London, copyright owners
There is a la-dy sweet and kind, Was nev-er face so pleased my mind

The Passionate Shepherd
By permission of Galaxy Music Corporation, N. Y., copyright by Elkin & Co., Ltd.
Come live with me, and__ be my love, And we will all

Piggesnie
By permission of Augener, Ltd., London
She is so pro-per and so pure, Full stead-fast, sta-ble and de-mure

Pretty Ring Time
By permission Oxford Univ. Press, London, copyright owners
It was a lov-er and his lass, With a hey and a ho

Rest, sweet Nymphs
By permission Oxford Univ. Press, London, copyright owners
Rest, sweet nymphs, let gold-en sleep Charm your star-bright-er eyes,__

Sigh no more, Ladies
By permission Oxford Univ. Press, London, copyright owners
Sigh no more, la-dies, sigh no more;__ Men were de-cei-vers ev-er.

Sleep
By permission Oxford Univ. Press, London, copyright owners
Come, sleep, and with thy sweet de-ceiv-ing Lock me in de-light a-while;

Take, O take those lips away
By permission Boosey & Hawkes, Inc., copyright owners
Take, O take__ those lips__ a-way that so sweet- -ly

Williow, willow (arr.)
By permission Oxford Univ. Press, London, copyright owners
The poor soul sat sigh-ing By a sy-ca-more tree

WEAVER, Powell (1890-   )

The Abbot of Derry
Copyright 1935, G. Schirmer, Inc.

The Ab- bot of Der- ry hates Sat- an and Sin

Moon Marketing
Copyright 1924, G. Schirmer, Inc.

Let's go to the mar- ket in the moon _____

WEBER, Carl Maria von (1786-1826)

OPERAS
Abu Hassan No. 2

Ich ge- be Gas- ter- ei- en, Mit Lied- ern und mit Tän- zen,

O Fa- ti- me, mei- ne Trau- te, die so zärt - lich zu mir spricht,

No. 5

Wird Phi- lo- me- le trau- ern, dem Kä- fig kaum ent- schlüpft,

Euryanthe Act I

Un- ter blüh'nden Man- del- bäu- men, an der Loi- re grü- nem Strand,

O mein Leid ist un- er- mes- sen, du kannst mir dein Herz ent- zieh'n

Act II

Schweigt glüh'nden Seh- nens wil- de Trie- be, ihr Au- ge sucht

We- hen mir Lüf- te Ruh, strö- men mir Düf- te zu,

O Se- lig- keit, dich fass' ich kaum, O Se- lig- keit, dich fass' ich kaum

Act III

Hier dicht am Quell wo Wei- den steh'n, die Ster- ne hell durch- schau- en,

Jaegerchor

Die Tha- le damp- fen die Hö- hen glühn!

Der Freischütz Act I

Durch die Wäl- der, durch die Au- en zog ich leich- ten Sinns da- hin!

Jetzt ist wohl ihr Fen- ster of- fen und sie horcht auf mei- nen Tritt,

Hier im ird' schen Jam- mer- thal war doch nichts als Plack und Qual

Schweig'! schweig'! da- mit dich Nie- mand warnt, schwei- ge!

Der Höl- le Netz hat dich um - garnt,

OPERAS
Der Freischütz Act I

Tri- umph!_____ die Ra- che ge- lingt!

Act II Brides-maids' Chorus

Wir win- den- dir den Jung-fern-kranz mit veil-chen- blau- er Sei- de

Kommt ein schlan- ker Bursch ge- gan- gen, blond von Lo- cken o-der braun

Lei- se, lei- se, from- me Wei- se, schwing' dich auf zum Ster-nen-krei- se

Act III

Al- les pflegt schon längst- der- Ruh'! Trau- ter Freund, wo wei-lest- du?

Romanze and Aria

Und ob die Wol- ke sie ver- hül- le, die Son- ne bleibt

Einst träum- te mein- er- sel' gen Ba- se, die Kam-mer-thür er-öff-ne sich,

Hunting Chorus

Trü- be Au-gen, Lieb-chen- tau-gen ei- nem- hol-den Bräut-chen- nicht,

Was gleicht wohl auf- Er- den dem Jä- ger-ver-gnü- gen

Oberon Act I No. 5

Von Ju- gend auf in dem Kampf- ge- fild, die Lan - - - - ze- hoch

Jetzt giesst____ sich aus ein sanft' - - rer Glanz

No. 6

Ja o Herr! mein Heil, mein- Le-ben Re- zia ist- für e - -wig dein!_

Act II No. 11 Prayer

Va- ter! Hör' mich fleh'n zu dir Va- ter Hör' mich fleh'n zu dir!

No. 12 Ocean, thou mighty monster

O- ze- an Du Un-ge- heu- er! schlan-gen-gleich hältst du um-schlun- gen

Noch seh ich die Wel- len to- ben durch- die- Nacht

Wol- ken- los strahlt jetzt die Son- ne auf die Pur- pur-wel- len nie-der

O Won - - - - - - ne! Mein Hü - - on! Zum U - - fer her- bei!_

No. 14

A- ra- bi-en, mein Hei- mat- land, du Land so teu- er mir

No. 17 Cavatina

Trau - - re, mein___ Herz, um ver-schwun- de- nes Glück!

Der kleine Fritz an seine jungen Freunde — A
Ach, wenn ich nur ein Lieb----chen hät-te, so gross wie ich

Leyer und Schwert, Op. 42, No. 2 No. 2 Lützows wilde Jagd — B
Was glänzt dort vom Wal-de im Son-nen-schein? Hör's nä-her

No. 6 Schwertlied — C
Du Schwert an mei-ner Lin-ken, was soll dein heit-res__ Blin-ken?

Schwertlied (variant) — D
Du Schwert an mei-ner Lin-ken, was soll dein hei-tres Blin-ken?

No. 7 Gebet vor der Schlacht — E
Hör uns, All-mäch-ti-ger! Hör uns, All-gü-ti-ger

Wiegenlied, Op. 13, No. 3 — F
Schlaf, Herz-ens-söhn-chen, mein Lieb-ling bist du!

WECKERLIN, Jean Baptiste (1821-1910)

Bergerettes (arrangements)
Aminte — H
Viens dans ce bo-ca-ge, belle A-min-te, Sans con-train-te

L'Amour s'envole — I
L'a-mour est un en-fant ti-mi-de, La sé-vé-ri-té

Bergère Légère — J
Ber-gè-re Lé-gè-re, Je crains tes ap-pas;__

Chantons les amours de Jean — K
Chan-tons, chan-tons les a-mours de Jean-ne, chan-tons, chan-tons

Chaque chose a son temps — L
Cha-que chose a son temps, Fil-let-te, Cha-que chose a son temps

Je connais un berger discret — M
Je con-nais un ber-ger dis-cret, qui se plaint__ et sou-pi-re,

Jeunes fillettes — A — N
Jeu-ne fil-le-te, pro-fi-tez du temps, La vi-o-let-te

B — O
Cet-te fleu-ret-te Passe en peu de temps Toute a-mou-ret-te passe

Lisette — P
En me-nant pai-tre mon trou-peau Je vis dans un bo-ca- - - - - - - ge

Maman, dites-moi — Q
Ma-man, di-tes-moi ce qu'on sent quand on ai-me,

Menuet d'Exaudet — R
Cet é-tang Qui s'e-tend dans la plai-ne, Ré-pète, au sein de ses eaux,

Le mère Bontemps — S
La mè-re Bon-temps s'en al-lait dis-ant aux fil-let-tes:

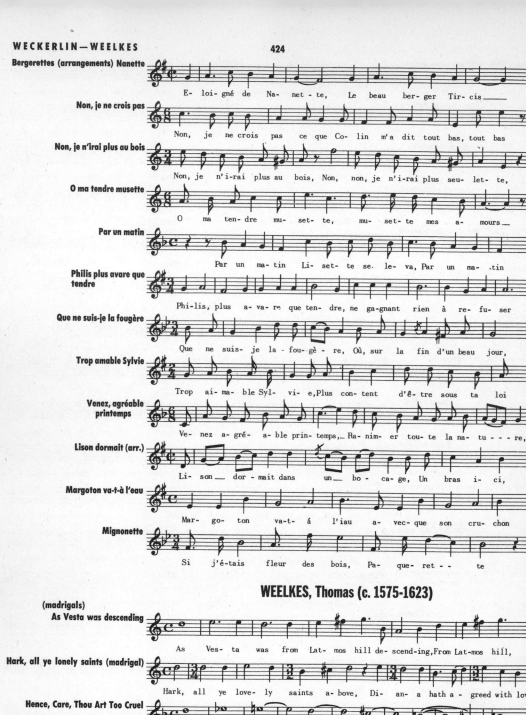

Bergerettes (arrangements) Nanette

E- loi- gné de Na- net- te, Le beau ber- ger Tir- cis

Non, je ne crois pas

Non, je ne crois pas ce que Co- lin m'a dit tout bas, tout bas

Non, je n'irai plus au bois

Non, je n'i-rai plus au bois, Non, non, je n'i-rai plus seu- let- te,

O ma tendre musette

O ma ten-dre mu-set-te, mu-set-te mes a- mours

Par un matin

Par un ma-tin Li- set-te se- le- va, Par un ma- .tin

Philis plus avare que tendre

Phi-lis, plus a-va-re que ten- dre, ne ga-gnant rien à re- fu- ser

Que ne suis-je la fougère

Que ne suis- je la-fou-gè- re, Où, sur la fin d'un beau jour,

Trop amable Sylvie

Trop ai-ma- ble Syl- vi-e, Plus con- tent d'ê- tre sous ta loi

Venez, agréable printemps

Ve- nez a-gré- a-ble prin-temps, Ra- nim- er tou-te la na- tu- - re,

Lison dormait (arr.)

Li- son dor- mait dans un bo- ca- ge, Un bras i- ci,

Margoton va-t-à l'eau

Mar- go- ton va-t- á l'iau a- vec- que son cru- chon

Mignonette

Si j'é-tais fleur des bois, Pa- que- ret- - te

WEELKES, Thomas (c. 1575-1623)

(madrigals)

As Vesta was descending

As Ves- ta was from Lat- mos hill de- scend-ing, From Lat-mos hill,

Hark, all ye lonely saints (madrigal)

Hark, all ye love- ly saints a-bove, Di- an- a hath a- greed with love

Hence, Care, Thou Art Too Cruel

Hence Care; thou art too cru - - - - el,

Lady, the birds right fairly

La- dy the birds right fair- ly, La-dy the birds right fair - - - - ly

O Care, thou wilt despatch me

O Care, thou wilt des - - - patch me, if Mu- sic do

On the Plains

On the plains Fai- ry trains were a tread- ing meas- ures,

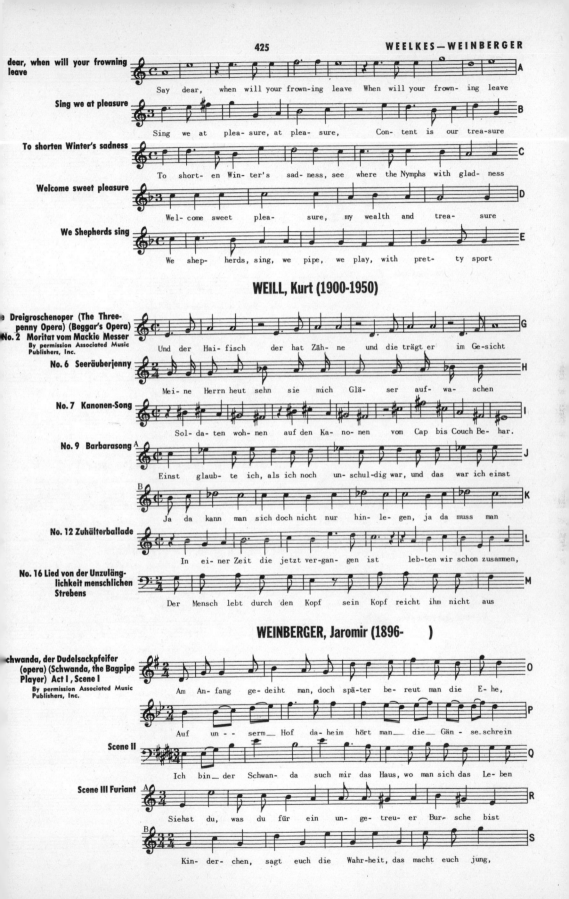

dear, when will your frowning leave

Say dear, when will your frown-ing leave When will your frown- ing leave   A

Sing we at pleasure

Sing we at plea- sure, at plea- sure, Con- tent is our trea-sure   B

To shorten Winter's sadness

To short- en Win- ter's sad- ness, see where the Nymphs with glad- ness   C

Welcome sweet pleasure

Wel- come sweet plea- sure, my wealth and trea- sure   D

We Shepherds sing

We shep- herds, sing, we pipe, we play, with pret- ty sport   E

WEILL, Kurt (1900-1950)

Dreigroschenoper (The Three-
penny Opera) (Beggar's Opera)
No. 2 Moritat vom Mackie Messer
By permission Associated Music
Publishers, Inc.

Und der Hai- fisch der hat Zäh- ne und die trägt er im Ge-sicht   G

No. 6 Seeräuberjenny

Mei- ne Herrn heut sehn sie mich Glä- ser auf- wa- schen   H

No. 7 Kanonen-Song

Sol- da- ten woh- nen auf den Ka- no- nen vom Cap bis Couch Be- har.   I

No. 9 Barbarasong A

Einst glaub- te ich, als ich noch un- schul-dig war, und das war ich einst   J

B

Ja da kann man sich doch nicht nur hin- le- gen, ja da muss man   K

No. 12 Zuhälterballade

In ei- ner Zeit die jetzt ver-gan- gen ist leb-ten wir schon zusammen,   L

No. 16 Lied von der Unzuläng-
lichkeit menschlichen
Strebens

Der Mensch lebt durch den Kopf sein Kopf reicht ihm nicht aus   M

WEINBERGER, Jaromir (1896-   )

Schwanda, der Dudelsackpfeifer
(opera) (Schwanda, the Bagpipe
Player) Act I, Scene I
By permission Associated Music
Publishers, Inc.

Am An- fang ge- deiht man, doch spä-ter be- reut man die E- he,   O

Auf un- serm Hof da-heim hört man die Gän- se schrein   P

Scene II

Ich bin der Schwan- da such mir das Haus, wo man sich das Le- ben   Q

Scene III Furiant A

Siehst du, was du für ein un- ge- treu- er Bur- sche bist   R

B

Kin- der- chen, sagt euch die Wahr-heit, das macht euch jung,   S

Schwanda, der Dudelsackpfeifer
(opera) (Schwanda, the Bagpipe
Player) Act II, Scene IV

Wie kann ich denn ver-ges-sen, was mein Lieb-stes war,

WEINGARTNER, Felix (1863-1942)

Du bist ein Kind, Op. 28, No. 12
By permission Associated Music
Publishers, Inc.

Du bist ein Kind und sollst es e-wig blei-ben;

Liebesfeier, Op. 16, No. 2

An ih-rem bun-ten Lie-der in Klet-tert die Ler- che

WERNER, H.

Haidenröslein

Sah ein Knab'_ ein Rös-lein stehn, Rös-lein auf_ der Hai-den

WERT, Giaches de (1536-1596)

Ah dolente partita (madrigal)

Ah do-len-te par-ti - - - ta! Ah fin_ del-la mia vi-ta

Un jour je m'en allai

Un jour_ je m'en al-lai, cueil-lant de vi-o-let-tes,

WESTENDORF, Thomas (Contemporary)

I'll take you home again, Kathleen

I'll take you home a-gain, Kath-leen A-cross the o-cean wild and wide_

WEYSE, Christoph Ernst Friedrich

De klare Bolger rulled, from
Sovedrikken (opera)

De Kla-re Bol-ger rul--led mod dunk--le_Af-ten lund

Gud skee Tak og Lov

Gud skee tak og Lov!_ vi saa dei--lig sov:

Han gik til Ludlams Hule, from
Ludlams Hule (opera)

Han gik til Lud-lams Hu-le i mör-ke Mi-die-nat

I Osten stiger Solen op

I O-sten sti-ger So-len op: den spre-der Guld paa Sky

Lysets Engel gaar med Glands

Ly-sets En-gel gaar med Glands gjen-nem Him-mel-por-te

Nu ringer alle Klokker mod sky

Nu rin-ger al-le klok-ker mod sky, det Ki-mier

Nu vaagne alle Guds Fugle smaa

Nu vaag-ne al-le Guds Fug-le smaa, de fly-ve fra Re-de

Teklas Sang (from Schiller's Wallenstein)

Der Eich-wald brau-set, die Wol- ken ziehn, das Mägd- lein wan- delt   A

WIDOR, Charles Marie (1845-1937)

L'Aurore, Op. 22, No. 2
permission J. Hamelle Music Publishers
is

Je ne veux pas autre chose, Op. 43, No. 1
permission J. Hamelle Music Publishers
is

Mon bras pressait, Op. 43, No. 3
permission J. Hamelle Music Publishers
is

Non Credo
permission Durand & Cie, Paris; Elkan-
gel Co., Inc., Phila., copyright owners

Nuit d'Étoiles, Op. 14, No. 1
permission J. Hamelle Music Publishers,
is

Le Plongeur, Op. 43, No. 4
permission J. Hamelle Music Publishers,
is

L'au- ro- re s'al- lu- me, L'ombre é- pais- se fuit   C

Je ne veux pas au-tre cho-se que ton sou- rire et ta voix   D

Mon bras pres-sait ta tail-le, frêle et sou-ple com-me le ro-seau,   E

Je ne crois pas que le Sa-veur soit né   Je ne crois pas,   F

Nuit d'é- toi-les, sous tes voi-les, sous ta bri- se et tes par- fums,   G

Le plon-geur, sur qui la va-gue dé-fer-le, m'a cri-é du fond   H

WILBYE, John (1574-1638)

Madrigals: Adieu, sweet Amaryllis (4-voice)

Draw on Sweet Night

Flora gave me fairest flowers (5-voice)

Lady, when I behold

Stay, Corydon thou Swain

Sweet honey-sucking bees (5-voice)

A-dieu, a- dieu, a- dieu, sweet A- ma-ril-lis! A- dieu,   J

Draw ___ on sweet night, ___ draw, ___ draw on sweet night   K

Flo- ra gave me fair-est flow-ers, Flo- ra gave me fair-est flow-ers,   L

La- dy, when I be- hold the ros- es sprout- ing   M

A1 Stay, Stay ___ Co- ry- don ___ thou swain, talk not so soon ___ of dy - - - ing,   N

A2 Stay ___ Co- ry- don thou swain, talk not so soon ___ of dy- ing   O

Sweet ho- ney- suck- ing bees, Sweet ho- ney- suck- ing bees,   P

WILLAERT, Adrian (c. 1480-1562)

Con lagrime e sospir

Con la- gri- me e so- spir ne- gan-do por- ge   R

WILSON, H. Lane

Carmena

Dance and song make glad the night

Ah! now rings a voice I know from ev'-ry voice a-part

WOLF, Hugo (1860-1903)

Abschied

Un-an-ge- klopft ein Herr tritt a-bends bei mir ein:

Der glei-chen hab' ich nie ge-sehn, all'_ mein Leb-ta- ge_ nicht ge-sehn,

Ach, des Knaben Augen

Ach, des Kna- - ben Au-gen sind mir so schön und klar er-schie- nen,

Ach, im Maien war's

Ach, im Mai-en war's, _____ im Mai- - en

Agnes

Ro-sen-zeit! wie schnell vor-bei, schnell vor-bei, bist du doch_ ge-gan-gen!

Alle gingen, Herz, zur Ruh

Al- le gin-gen, Herz, zur Ruh, al- le schla- fen, nur nicht du.

Alles endet, was entstehet

Al- les en- det, was ent-ste-het, Al- les, al- les rings ver- geh- et

Als ich auf dem Euphrat schiffte

Als ich auf dem Eu- - - phrat_ schiff- te

Anakreons Grab

Wo die Ro- se hier blüht, _ wo Re- ben um Lor-beer sich schlin-gen,

Andenken

Ich den- - ke dein _____ wenn durch_ den Hain

An den Schlaf

Schlaf! _ su- sser Schlaf! ob-wohl dem Tod, wie du, nichts gleicht, _

An die Geliebte

Wenn ich, von dei-nem An-schaun tief ge-stillt, mich stumm _____

An eine Aeolsharfe

An- ge-lehnt an die E-pheu-wand die-ser al-ten Ter- ras-se

Auch kleine Dinge

Auch klei-ne Din- ge kön- nen uns ent-zü- cken,

Auf dm grünen Balkon

Auf dem grü- nen Bal-kon mein Mäd- chen schaut nach mir durchs Git-ter-lein,

Auf ein altes Bild — In grü-ner Land-schaft Som-mer-flor bei küh-lem Was-ser Schilf — A

Auf eine Christblume No. 1 — Toch-ter des Wald's, du Li - - - li-en-ver-wan-dte, — B

No. 2 — Im Win-ter-bo-den schläft ein Blu-men-keim; der Schmet-ter-ling — C

Auf einer Wanderung — In ein freund-lich-es Städt-chen tret'ich ein in den Strassen liegt — D

Auftrag — In po-e-ti-scher E-pi-stel ruft ein des-pe-ra-ter Wicht; — E

Bedeckt mich mit Blumen — Be-deckt mich mit Blu-men, ich ster - - - - - be vor Lie-be — F

Begegnung — Was doch heut' Nacht ein Sturm ge-we-sen, bis erst der Mor-gen — G

Beherzigung — Ach, was soll der Mensch ver-lan-gen Ist es bes-ser, ruhig bleiben? — H

Bei einer Trauung — Vor lau-ter hoch-ad-li-gen zeu-gen ko-puliert man ih-rer zwei; — I

Die Bekehrte — Bei dem Glanz der A-bend-rö-te ging ich still den Wald ent-lang, — J

Benedeit die sel'ge Mutter — Be-re-deit die sel' ge Mut-ter, die so lieb - - - lich dich ge-bo-ren, — K

Bescheidene Liebe — Ich bin wie an-dre Mäd-chen nicht die, wenn sie lie-ben, — L

Biterolf — Kampf-müd und sonn-ver-brannt, fern an der Hei-den Strand, — M

Bitt' ihn, o Mutter — Bitt' ihn, o Mut-ter, bit-te den Kna-ben, nicht mehr zu zie-len — N

Blumengruss — Der Strauss, den ich ge-pflücket grü-sse dich viel tau-send-mal! — O

Cophtisches Lied No. 1 — Las-set Ge-lehr-te sich zan-ken und strei-ten, — P

No. 2 — Geh! Ge-hor-che mei-nen Win-ken, nut-ze dei-ne jun-gen Ta-ge, — Q

Dass doch gemalt all' deine Reize wären — Dass doch ge-malt all' dei-ne Rei-ze wä-ren, — R

Denk es, O Seele! — Ein Tänn-lein grü-net wo, wer weiss, im Wal-de, — S

Dereinst, dereinst, Gedanke mein

Der- einst, der- einst, Ge- dan- ke mein, wirst ru- hig sein.___

Du denkst mit einem Fädchen

Du denkst mit ei- nem Fäd- chen mich zu fan- gen,

Du milchjunger Knabe

Du milch- jun- ger Kna- be, wie siehst du mich an?

Du sagst mir dass ich keine Fürstin sei

Du sagst mir, dass ich kei- ne Für- stin sei, auch Du bist nicht

Elfenlied A

Bei Nacht im Dorf der Wäch- ter rief: El- fe

B

Was sind das hel- le___ Fen- ster- lein? Da drin wird ei- ne___ Hoch- zeit sein:

Epiphanias (Die heiligen drei König)

Die hei- li- gen drei Kö- nig mit ih- rem Stern, sie es- sen, sie trin- ken,

Er ist's

Früh- ling lässt sein blau- es___ Band, wie- der flat- tern durch die Lüf- te;

Erstes Liebeslied eines Mädchens

Was im Net- ze? Schau ein- mal! a- - ber ich___ bin ban- - - ge;

Der Feuerreiter A

Se- het ihr am Fen- ster- lein dort die ro- te Mü- tze wie- der?

B

Der so oft dem ro- ten Hahn mei- len- weit von fern ge- ro- chen,

Frage und Antwort

Fragst___ du mich, wo- her die ban- ge Lie- be mir zum Her- zen kam,

Der Freund

Wer auf den Wo- gen schlie- fe, ein sanft ge- wieg- tes Kind

Frohe Botschaft

Hielt die al- ler- schön- ste___ Her- rin einst mein Herz so eng

Frühling übers Jahr

Das Beet, schon lok- kert sich in die Höh! Da wan- ken Glöck- chen

Fühlt meine Seele

Fühlt mei- ne See- le das er- sehn- te Licht von Gott, der sie er- schuf?

Führ mich, Kind

Führ mich Kind nach Beth- le- hem! dich, mein Gott, dich wich ich sehn.

Fussreise

Am frisch ge- schmitt'- nen___ Wan- der- stab, wenn ich in der Frü- he

Ganymed

Wie im Mor- gen- glan- ze du rings mich an- glühst, Früh- ling,

Der Gärtner — A
Auf ih- rem Leib- röss- lein, so weiss wie der Schnee,

Gebet — B
Herr!_ Schi- cke was du willt, ein Lie- bes o- der Lei- des,

Geh', Geliebter, geh' jetzt — C
Geh',_ Ge- lieb- ter, geh' jetzt! Sieh, der Mor- gen däm- -mert.

Der Genesene an die Hoffnung — D
Töd- -lich grau- te mir der Mor- gen: doch schon lag mein Haupt, wie süss!

Genialisch Treiben — E
So wälz_ ich oh- ne Un- ter- lass, wie Sankt Di- o- - - - - - genes,

Gesang Weyla's — F
Du bist Orp- lid, mein Land! das fer- - - - ne leuch- tet;

Gesegnet sei das Grün — G
Ge- seg- -net sei das Grün und wer es trägt! Ein grü- nes Kleid

Gesegnet sei, durch den die Welt entstund — H
Ge- seg- net sei, durch den die Welt ent- stund;

Gesellenlied — I
"Kein Mei- ster fällt vom Him- mel". und das ist auch ein grosses Glück!

Geselle, woll'n wir uns in Kutten hüllen — J
Ge- sel- le, woll'n wir uns in Kut- ten hül- -len

Ghasél — K
Im Was- ser wogt die Li- -lie, die blan- ke, hin und her_

Gleich und Gleich — L
Ein Blu- men- glöck- -chen vom Bo- den her- vor

Grenzen der Menscheit — M
Wenn_ der ur- al- te hei- li- ge Va- ter mit ge- las- se- ner Hand

Harfenspieler No. 1 — N
Wer sich der Ein- sam- keit er- gibt, ach! der ist bald al- lein;

No. 2 — O
An die Tü- ren will_ ich schleichen, still und sitt- sam will ich stehn;

No. 3 — P
Wer nie sein Brot mit Trä- nen ass, wer nie die kum- mer- vol- len Näch- te

Heb' auf dein blondes Haupt — Q
Heb' auf dein blon- des Haupt und schla- fe nicht,_

Heimweh — R
An- ders wird die Welt mit je- dem Schritt den ich wei- - - - ter

Heimweh — S
Wer in der Frem- de will wan- dern, der muss mit der Lieb- sten gehn,

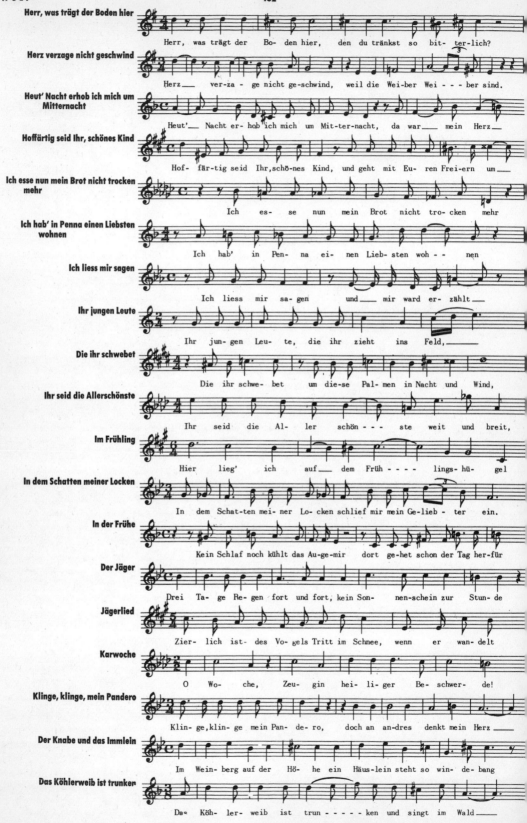

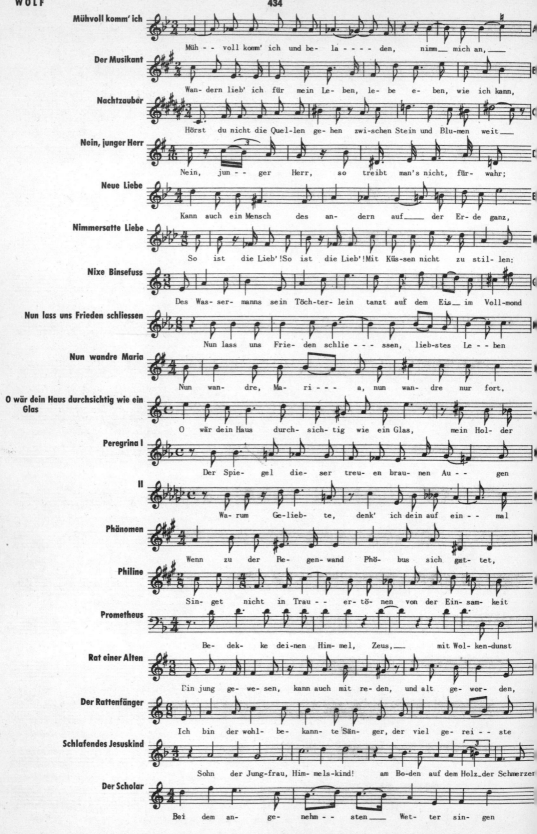

Mühvoll komm' ich

Müh - - voll komm' ich und be - la - - - den, nimm_ mich an,_

Der Musikant

Wan-dern lieb' ich für mein Le - ben, le - be e - ben, wie ich kann,

Nachtzauber

Hörst du nicht die Quel-len ge - hen zwi-schen Stein und Blu-men weit_

Nein, junger Herr

Nein, jun - - ger Herr, so treibt man's nicht, für - wahr;

Neue Liebe

Kann auch ein Mensch des an - dern auf_ der Er-de ganz,

Nimmersatte Liebe

So ist die Lieb'!So ist die Lieb'!Mit Küs-sen nicht zu stil-len:

Nixe Binsefuss

Des Was-ser-manns sein Töch-ter-lein tanzt auf dem Eis_ im Voll-mond

Nun lass uns Frieden schliessen

Nun lass uns Frie - den schlie - - ssen, lieb-stes Le - ben

Nun wandre Maria

Nun wan - dre, Ma - ri - - a, nun wan - dre nur fort,

O wär dein Haus durchsichtig wie ein Glas

O wär dein Haus durch-sich-tig wie ein Glas, mein Hol - der

Peregrina I

Der Spie - gel die - ser treu - en brau - nen Au - - gen

II

Wa - rum Ge - lieb - te, denk' ich dein auf ein - - mal

Phänomen

Wenn zu der Re - gen-wand Phö - bus sich gat - tet,

Philine

Sin - get nicht in Trau - - er-tö - nen von der Ein - sam - keit

Prometheus

Be - dek - ke dei-nen Him - mel, Zeus,_ mit Wol - ken-dunst

Rat einer Alten

Bin jung ge - we - sen, kann auch mit re-den, und alt ge - wor - den,

Der Rattenfänger

Ich bin der wohl- be - kann - te Sän - ger, der viel ge - rei - - ste

Schlafendes Jesuskind

Sohn der Jung-frau, Him - mels-kind! am Bo-den auf dem Holz_der Schmerzen

Der Scholar

Bei dem an - ge - nehm - - sten_ Wet - ter sin - gen

Treibe nur mit lieben Spott

Trei- be nur mit Lie- ben Spott, Ge- lieb- te__ mein;

Über Nacht

Ü- ber Nacht, ü- ber Nacht kommt still das Leid, und bist du er- wacht,

Um Mitternacht

Ge- las- sen stieg die Nacht__ ans Land,__ lehnt träu- mend

Und steht Ihr früh am Morgen auf

Und steht ihr früh am Mor- gen auf vom Bet- te,

Und willst du deinen Liebsten sterben sehen

Und willst du deinen Liebsten ster- ben se- hen so tra- ge nicht dein Haar

Unfall

Ich ging bei Nacht einst ü- - - ber__ Land, ein Bürsch- lein traf ich

Verborgenheit

Lass, o Welt, O lass mich sein! lo- cket nicht mit Lie- bes- ga- ben

Das Verlassene Mägdlein

Früh wann die Häh- ne krähn, eh' die Stern- lein schwin- den,

Verschling' der Abgrund

Ver- schling'__ der Ab- - - grund mei- - nes Lieb- sten Hüt- te;

Verschwiegene Liebe

Ü- ber Wip- fel und Saa- ten in den Glanz__ hin- ein

Der verzweifelte Liebhaber

Stu- die- ren will nichts brin- gen, mein Rock hält kei- nen Stich

Wanderers Nachtlied

Der du von dem Him- mel bist, al- les Leid__ und Schmer- zen stillest,

Was für ein Lied soll dir gesungen werden

Was__ für ein Lied soll dir ge- sun- gen wer- den,

Was soll der Zorn, mein Schatz

Was soll der Zorn, mein Schatz, der dich er- hitzt?

Wenn Du, mein Liebster, steigst zum Himmel auf

Wenn Du, mein Lieb- ster, steigst zum Him- mel auf,

Wenn du mich mit den Augen streifst

Wenn du mich mit den Au- gen streifst und lachst,

Wenn du zu den Blumen gehst

Wenn du zu den Blu- - men__ gehst, pflü- cke die schön- sten,

Wer rief dich denn?

Wer rief dich denn? Wer hat dich her- be- stellt? Wer hiess dich kom- men

Wer sein holdes Lieb verloren

Wer sein hol- des Lieb ver- lo- ren, weil er Lie- be nicht ver- steht,

Wiegenlied (Im Sommer)
Vom Berg hin-ab-ge-stie-gen ist nun des Ta-ges Rest;

Wiegenlied (Im Winter)
Schlaf' ein,   schlaf' ein,   schlaf' ein, mein sü-sses Kind

Wie glänzt der helle Mond
Wie glänzt der hel-le Mond so kalt und fern,

e lange schon war immer mein Verlangen
Wie lan-ge schon war im-mer mein Ver-lan-gen:

Wie soll ich fröhlich sein
Wie soll ich fröh-lich sein und la-chen gar,

Wie viele Zeit verlor ich
Wie vie-le Zeit ver-lor ich, dich zu lie-ben!

Wir haben beide lange Zeit geschwiegen
Wir ha-ben bei-de lan-ge Zeit ge-schwie-gen

Wo find' ich Trost
Ei-ne Lie-be kenn' ich die ist treu, war ge-treu so lang

Wohl denk' ich oft
Wohl denk' ich oft an mein ver-gang'nes Le-ben,

Wohl kenn' ich Euren Stand
Wohl kenn' ich Eu-ren Stand, der nicht ge-ring

Die Zigeunerin
Am Kreuz-weg da lau-sche ich wenn die Stern' und die Feu-er

Zitronenfalter im April
Grau-sa-me Früh-lings-son-ne, du weckst mich vor der Zeit,

Zum neuen Jahr
Wie heim-li-cher Wei-se ein En-ge-lein lei-se

Zur Ruh, zur Ruh!
Zur Ruh, zur Ruh, Ihr mü-den Glie-der! schliesst fest euch zu,

WOLFE, Jacques (1896-)

De Glory Road
Copyright 1928, G. Schirmer, Inc.
O de Glo-ry Road! O de Glo-ry Road! I'm gwine ter drap

Gwine to Hebb'n
Copyright 1928, G. Schirmer, Inc.
Gwine 'to Heb-b'n Gwine 'to Heb-b'n I'm gon-ter go

Short'nin Bread
Copyright 1928, Harold Flammer, Inc.
Used by permission
Put on de skil-let put on de lead Mam-my's goin' to bake

WOLFF, Erich (1874-1913)

Short'nin Bread

Mam-my's lit-tle ba-by loves short'-nin', short'-nin'

Alle Dinge haben Sprache

Al- le Din- ge ha-ben Spra- che, seit du da bist,

Aus der Ferne in die Nacht, Op. 12, No. 5

Wenn im brau-nen Ha-fen al-le Schif-fe schla-fen,

Entzücket dich ein Wunderhauch?
By permission Associated Music Publishers, Inc.

Ent- zück- et dich ein Wun- -der-hauch, der ein- zig ist

Es werde Licht!
By permission Associated Music Publishers, Inc.

Es wer- de Licht! _____ so tö- ne- te _____ der Ruf Got- tes

Fäden, Op. 13, No. 1

Vie- le Fä- - - den glei- ten zwi-schen mir _____ und dir,

Friede
By permission Associated Music Publishers, Inc.

A- bend- ru- - - - he liegt ü- ber dem Land

Horch, hörst du nicht
By permission Associated Music Publishers, Inc.

Horch hörst du nicht _____ von Him- mel her _____

Ich bin eine Harfe, Op. 13, No. 6

Ich bin ei- ne Har- fe mit gol-de- nen Sai-ten auf einsamen Gip-fel

Im Entschlafen
By permission Associated Music Publishers, Inc.

Blas- se Blü- - ten nei- gen ih- re duf- - ten- de Pracht,

Immer wieder, Op. 8, No. 3

Eh' wir uns tren-nen konn- ten, o wie hielt.mich dein_ Ge-sicht

Knabe und Veilchen, Op. 9, No. 4

Blü- he, blü- he lie- bes Veil-chen, das so lieb- - lich_ roch, _____

Märchen
By permission Associated Music Publishers, Inc.

Glaub' es mir ju-beln-de Kin-der-schar, all die schö- nen Mär-chen

Maria und der Schiffer
By permission Associated Music Publishers, Inc.

Ma- ri- a wollt' zur Kir- - - che gehn, da kam sie

Marienruf
By permission Associated Music Publishers, Inc.

Ma- ri- a, du zar- te! Du bist ein Ro- sen-gar- te,

Meine Lebenszeit verstreicht
By permission Associated Music Publishers, Inc.

Mei- ne Le- bens-zeit ver-streicht, stünd- lich eil' ich hin

Recht wie ein Leichnam
By permission Associated Music Publishers, Inc.

Recht wie ein Leich- nam wand- le ich um-her nachts zu sei-ner Tür

Soll ich denn sterben
By permission Associated Music Publishers, Inc.

Soll ich denn ster- ben, bin noch so jung? Wenn das mein Va-ter wüsst;

Ein Sonntag, Op. 17, No. 5
By permission Associated Music Publishers, Inc.

A

Von Me- lo- di- en die mich um- flie- hen bin ich im Raum um- ringt,

Spaziergang, Op. 12, No. 1

B

Ü- ber wei- te Wie- sen schweif ich wo's___ aus tau- send Kei- men bricht,___

Der süsse Schlaf
By permission Associated Music Publishers, Inc.

C

Der sü- sse Schlaf, der sonst stillt al- les wohl,

Täuscht euch, ihr Augen, nicht
By permission Associated Music Publishers, Inc.

D

Tauscht___ euch, ihr Au- gen, nicht, die Zeit ver- ge- het,

Der Trauende
By permission Associated Music Publishers, Inc.

E

Mein Mu- ter mag mi net, und kein Schatz han i net,

Viel bin ich umhergewandert
By permission Associated Music Publishers, Inc.

F

Viel bin ich um- her- ge- wan- dert, um zum Hei- le zu ge- lan- gen

Wer hat's Lieben erdacht?
By permission Associated Music Publishers, Inc.

G

Zum Ster- ben bin i ver- lie- bet in di,

Wüsst' ich nur
By permission Associated Music Publishers, Inc.

H

In der See- le ein Wach- sen und Kei- men, so viel

WOLF-FERRARI, Ermano (1876-1948)

OPERAS
Le Donne Curiose Act II
Copyright 1911, G. Schirmer, Inc.

J

Ah_____ tut- ta per te, mio be- - - - - ne

K

Il cor, il cor nel con- ten- to im- prov- vi- so

I Gioielli della Madonna (The Jewels of the Madonna) Act I
Copyright 1911, G. Schirmer, Inc.

L

Ma- don- na con so- spi- - ri, in lun- ghe ve- glie ar- den- di

M

Be- ne- di- - ci- mi tu___ Ma- dre mia buo- - - na___

Act II Serenata

N

A- pri- la, bel- la, la___ fe- ne- strel- la a- - pri la por- ta,

Lucieta e un bel nome, from I Quattro Rusteghi

O

Lu- cie- ta, Lu- cie- ta, Lu- cie- ta xe un bel no- me

Non sono buffone, from Sly
Copyright by Sonzogno, Milan

P

Non so- - - - no buf- fo- ne, io so- - - - no un po- ver uo- - mo___

The Secret of Suzanne
Copyright 1911, G. Schirmer, Inc.

Q

Oh tell me, be- lov- ed, Do you re- mem- ber Those blissful moments

R

No, I can not let you leave me I've been weep- ing, lone- ly, lone- ly

S

Oh, joy to be mus- ing with half closed eyes, to fol- low the va- pour

The Secret of Suzanne

All the world is but smoke__ and__ va - - - - - por and a puff__ of wind__

WOOD, Haydn

A Brown Bird Singing

Roses of Picardy

WOODFORDE-FINDEN, Amy (d. 1919)

Indian Love Lyrics 1. The Temple Bells
By permission Boosey & Hawkes, Inc., copyright owners

The Tem - ple bells are ring - ing, the young green corn is spring - ing,

2. Less than the Dust

Less than the dust be - neath thy cha - riot wheel___

3. Kashmiri Song

Pale hands I loved be - side the Sha - li - mar,___ Where are you now?

4. Till I Wake

When I am dy - - - ing, lean o - ver me,___

A Lover in Damascus
By permission Boosey & Hawkes, Inc., copyright owners
1. Far across the desert sands

Far, far a - cross the de - sert__ sands I hear the__ ca - mel bells

2. Where the Abana flows

Through the old ci - ty's si - - - lence___ Where the A - ba - na flows

3. Beloved in your absence

Be - lov - ed, in your ab - sence, I__ have__ told__

4. How many a lonely caravan

How ma - ny a lone - ly ca - ra - van sets out___

5. If in the great bazaars

If in the great__ ba - zaars___ They sold the gol - den stars___

6. Allah be with us

Ah, when the dark on ma - ny a heart de - scends

WOODMAN, A. Huntington

A Birthday
Copyright 1909, G. Schirmer, Inc.

My heart is like a sing - ing bird Whose nest is in a watered shoot

I am thy harp
Copyright 1907, G. Schirmer, Inc.

I am thy harp, that all un - known thou sweep - est,

YOUNG, Anthony

Phillis has such charming graces

Phil - - - - lis__ has___ such___ charm - ing__ gra - ces

YRADIER, Sebastian (1809-1865)

Areglito
(Bizet admitted using this for the
Habanera in Carmen)

Chi-ni-ta mi-a ven por a- qui que tu ya sa-bes que mue-ro por tí

si tu me quie-res di-lo que di-to y en-se-gni-di-ta

La Calesera

Ya sue-nan las cam-pa-ni-les__ Mi ca-le-se-ro ha lle-ga-o

La Paloma

Cuan- do - - - - sa-li de la Ha-ba-na val-ga- me Dios

ZONDONAI, Riccardo (1883-   )

OPERAS
Giuliano Prologue
Copyright by G. Ricordi & Co., Inc.

Non toc-che-rò mai più ar-co e sa-et-ta__ più il fo-co-la- re

Act I Love Duet

Re- i-na bel- la! Mi do-na-ste pa-ce il dì che ven- ni

Si   Qua-le vuoi,__ sa-rò. Om-bra lon-ta- no

Oc- chi so-a- vi come in sul-la se-ra

Act II

Dal- la gai - - ba fug-gi-to e il lu-si-gno- lo

Giulietta, son io, from Giulietta e
Romeo
Copyright by G. Ricordi & Co., Inc.

Giu-liet-ta! Son i- o! I- o, non mi ve-di Io che non pian-go più__

Paolo, datemi pace, from Francesca
da Rimini
Copyright by G. Ricordi & Co., Inc.

Pa-o-lo, da-te-mi pa-ce È dol-ce co-sa vi-ve-re

ZELLER, Karl (1842-1898)

OPERETTAS
Der Obersteiger

Wo__ sie war die Mül-ler- in; Zog__ es auch den Fi-scher hin

Sei nicht bös', es kann__ nicht sein,__ Sei nicht bös',

Der Vogelhändler Act I

Schenkt man sich Ro-sen in Ti-rol, Schenkt man das Herz

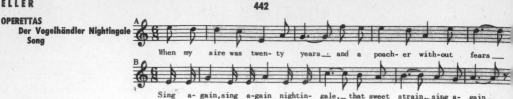

When my sire was twen-ty years — and a poach-er with-out fears —

Sing a-gain, sing a-gain nightin-gale, — that sweet strain, — sing a-gain —

HOW TO USE
THE NOTATION INDEX*

To identify a given theme, play it in the key of C (C major for major themes, C minor for minor themes) and look it up under its note sequence using the following alphabet as a guide:

A A♭ A♯ **B** B♭ B♯ **C** C♭ C♯ **D** D♭ D♯
E E♭ E♯ **F** F♭ F♯ **G** G♭ G♯

Double flats follow flats; double sharps follow sharps.

The number and letter to the right of the definition indicate the page and listing where the theme may be found in its correct key with the name of the composition and the composer. For example, 32B signifies page 32, theme B.

Trills, turns, grace notes, and embellishments are not taken into consideration here. However, it must be remembered that the appoggiatura is a regular note. In some cases the grace note may be of such nature as to give the aural impression of being a regular note, in which case the theme is indexed both with and without the grace note.

Keys are, in the main, determined by the harmonic structure of the opening bars, not by the cadence. The phrase that begins in C and goes to G is considered to be in C. Themes that may be analyzed in two keys are listed under both keys.

There are themes that defy key definition. However, if the melodic line carries a key implication of its own, if only for the first few notes, that key is used. If the theme carries no such implication, then, for the sake of convenience, the first note is assumed to be C and the rest transposed accordingly.

Each definition is carried to six places except in the case of duplication. Duplicates are continued to a point of difference. When a note is repeated many times, for space conservation an exponent is used; i.e., $GGGGGGG = G^7$.

H. B.

* Publisher's Note: The Notation Index was conceived by Harold Barlow.

C B D C F E D	167F	
C B D C F E E	234D	
C B D C G Bb	84H	
C B D F A B	118H	
C B D F E B	62B	
C B D G C B D G C B	380N	
C B D G C B D G C D	395O	
C B D G F F	43D	
C B E A G C	392H	
C B E D E C	151K	
C B E D F E	335O	
C B E D G F	42M	
C B E F G A	104G	
C B E G A G	74K	
C B Eb D G F	274F	
C B Eb Eb Eb G	433A	
C B Eb G G G	206H	
C B F A A A	413O	
C B F E C B	234A	
C B F E C G	255N	
C B F E D A	255G	
C B G A A C	142E	
C B G A B A E A	220E	
C B G A B A E D	136F	
C B G A B A G	264L	
C B G A B C	36C	
C B G A B G	85O	
C B G A C B	232I	
C B G A E E	185H	
C B G A F D	54F	
C B G A F G	7M	
C B G A G E	126S	
C B G B A A	143N	
C B G C A B	285N	
C B G D C G	335H	
C B G E D C	389O	
C B G F A G	233J	
C B G G A B	173D	
C B G G B G	353K	
C B G G F D	439S	
C Bb A A A C#	333S	
C B# A A G G	186B	
C Bb A Bb C A	16C	
C Bb A Bb C Bb	189F	
C Bb A G A C	226F	
C Bb Ab Ab G G	410B	
C Bb Ab Bb C Ab	69G	
C Bb Ab Bb G F	78G	
C Bb Ab Db	404J	
C Bb Ab G Ab F	26L	
C Bb Ab G Ab G Ab	202M	
C Bb Ab G Ab G B	10D	
C Bb Ab G Ab G F	15I	
C Bb Ab G Bb Bb	239N	
C Bb Ab G Bb C	258P	
C Bb Ab G C Bb	102E	
C Bb Ab G C C	189K	
C Bb Ab G Eb	286E	
C Bb Ab G Eb D	99A	
C Bb Ab G Eb F	138L	
C Bb Ab G F Eb Ab	353H	

C Bb Ab G F Eb D Eb F Eb	290M	
C Bb Ab G F Eb D Eb F F	194A	
C Bb Ab G F F	95A	
C Bb Ab G F G Ab Bb	268L	
C Bb Ab G F G Ab G	302O	
C Bb Ab G G Eb	28Q	
C Bb Ab G G F#	256M	
C Bb Bb A A G	25D	
C Bb Bb Ab Bb G	302Q	
C Bb Bb Bb C Bb	31N	
C Bb Bb Bb C C	89H	
C Bb Bb Bb G A	15S	
C Bb Bb C Bb G	360J	
C Bb Bb C D Eb	189S	
C Bb Bb Eb Bb F	279N	
C Bb Bb Eb Eb F	125D	
C Bb Bb G G Eb	110C	
C Bb C A Bb C	267F	
C Bb C Ab Bb C	378O	
C Bb C Ab G F	388N	
C Bb C Bb Ab Ab	440M	
C Bb C Bb Ab Bb	293F	
C Bb C Bb Ab G	234C	
C Bb C Bb C G	176K	
C Bb C Bb G Bb	360D	
C Bb C Bb G C	360J	
C Bb C D Eb D	288M	
C Bb C Eb D Bb	91D	
C Bb C Eb F Eb	376B	
C Bb C G F G	100A	
C Bb C G G G	259D	
C Bb Eb F D D	187B	
C Bb G Bb C Bb	140J	
C Bb G Bb C C	276B	
C Bb G Bb C Db	30M	
C Bb G Bb G C	294R	
C Bb G C D B	36P	
C Bb G F C Bb	286M	
C Bb G F Eb Bb	291M	
C Bb G F G F	428B	
C Bb G G Bb	299F	
C Bb G G C Bb	123K	
C Bb G G G Bb	285R	
C Bb G G G G	369P	
C C A A A G F	64N	
C C A A A G G	303J	
C C A A B A	236B	
C C A A G A	179G	
C C A A G C	66B	
C C A A G G	438A	
C C A B C E	398B	
C C A Bb C Bb	10L	
C C A C C C	389S	
C C A F A D	45G	
C C A F G F	45L	
C C A G E C	314I	
C C A G F E	346M	
C C A G G C	437R	
C C A G G F E	159C	
C C A G G F F	43H	
C C Ab Ab Ab G	211Q	

C C Ab Ab C C	281
C C Ab C B C	175
C C Ab F C D	63
C C Ab F D B	405N
C C Ab G G G	255
C C B A A A	370
C C B A A B	141
C C B A A G	329M
C C B A B A G A	137
C C B A B A G E	138M
C C B A B C	175O
C C B A B G	257C
C C B A C B	436M
C C B A D D	79I
C C B A G Bb	143
C C B A G C D D	11C
C C B A G C D E E	52M
C C B A G C D E G	375
C C B A G F E D C A	213
C C B A G F E D C C	382
C C B A G F E D F	28M
C C B Ab Ab D	412M
C C B B A A B	365
C C B B A A G	90
C C B B A C	437
C C B B A E	348C
C C B B A G	417
C C B B A# C#	232
C C B B B B	173
C C B B B Bb	313
C C B B Bb Bb	49C
C C B B C A	164
C C B B C C	289
C C B B C D E	171
C C B B C D Eb D	255
C C B B C D Eb Eb	431
C C B B C Eb	58C
C C B B G G	147
C C B Bb A G	13
C C B Bb Bb Bb	441
C C B Bb E E	159C
C C B C A A	281M
C C B C C E	327
C C B C C G	153
C C B C D A	105A
C C B C D B	29
C C B C D E D	307
C C B C D E F	349M
C C B C D Eb	168O
C C B C F D	260
C C B C G A	10C
C C B C G Eb	156
C C B D C B	88
C C B D C C	375I
C C B D C F E A	332O
C C B D C F E E	264L
C C B D F E	279A
C C B E C C	197
C C B E E D	161C
C C B Eb Eb Eb	288
C C B G A A B	351

Notation	Code	Notation	Code	Notation	Code
C Db C C Db C	65C	C E D C G G G A	296M	C E F G A E	267K
C Db Db C C F	208R	C E D C G G G G	291H	C E F G A F E D	69E
C Db Db Db Db Db	418K	C E D D A A	42R	C E F G A F E E	158O
C Db Db Eb C B	140O	C E D D C E	302I	C E F G A F G	267H
C Db E F G Ab	127H	C E D D D E	158H	C E F G A G C	271L
C D# E A G C	417E	C E D D D F	149J	C E F G A G D	103S
C D# E G C E	416F	C E D D E F	20M	C E F G A G E	90C
C E A C F E	34K	C E D D F E	244B	C E F G A G G F	45F
C E A G E D	52G	C E D E C C	51R	C E F G A G G G	269K
C E A G F A	119J	C E D E F E D	161M	C E F G B A	30E
C E A G F# G	369L	C E D E F E F	292J	C E F G C B A G F#	375J
C E A G G B	314P	C E D E F G A	274B	C E F G C B A G G	180B
C E B A G F	233R	C E D E F G F	103M	C E F G C B C	45J
C E B C C D	336N	C E D F B G	18J	C E F G C Bb	165F
C E B D C E	258N	C E D F E D D	19A	C E F G C C	143D
C E C A A C	236A	C E D F E D E	152M	C E F G C D	97S
C E C A G A	41A	C E D F E G A	169G	C E F G C E G A A	357Q
C E C B B C	129H	C E D F E G F	19L	C E F G C E G A G E	1L
C E C B C E	328R	C E D F E G G	100C	C E F G C E G A G F	210R
C E C C G G	168J	C E D G A B	152R	C E F G C F	227L
C E C E C C C	186H	C E D G B A	353I	C E F G E A B	153R
C E C E C C E	142O	C E E D C B	8I	C E F G E A G	28N
C E C E C D	222F	C E E D C E	70F	C E F G E C Ab	97O
C E C E C E C	249B	C E E D D C	43K	C E F G E C C	309R
C E C E C E F	372Q	C E E D C A	37Q	C E F G E C D	202K
C E C E F F	250H	C E E D C F	272Q	C E F G E E	18K
C E C E G E C	159E	C E E E E F	171K	C E F G E F A	420M
C E C E G E G	15A	C E E E E F	171L	C E F G E F D	152C
C E C F D G	248S	C E E E F G A	320S	C E F G E G	160C
C E C G A B A	321L	C E E E F G G	230O	C E F G F E D C D E C	241N
C E C G A B C	245D	C E E E F# G	212D	C E F G F E D C D E G	386P
C E C G A G	290D	C E E F F G	345K	C E F G F E F	162C
C E C G B A	308O	C E E F G A	212K	C E F G F G	341P
C E C G C E	16L	C E E F G G	130L	C E F G G A A C	143H
C E C G E A	160R	C E E G A A	412I	C E F G G A A G	165N
C E C G E C	168S	C E E G A G	183G	C E F G G A B	99I
C E C G E D	354S	C E E G C E	300G	C E F G G A Bb	272S
C E C G E F	403I	C E E G C F	391O	C E F G G A C	267L
C E C G E G	419G	C E E G C G	164B	C E F G G A G A	267E
C E C G G C	242H	C E E G G A	313Q	C E F G G A G F	239O
C E C G G G	22E	C E E G G C	55C	C E F G G F E D C B	152E
C E D B G G	399H	C E E G G E C C	49A	C E F G G F E D C G	107B
C E D C A A	336P	C E E G G E C D	289O	C E F G G F E D D	241G
C E D C B C	126P	C E F C E F	53M	C E F G G G A	116G
C E D C C A	109R	C E F D B C B	273H	C E F G G G C	390S
C E D C C B A B	406E	C E F D B C D	172B	C E F G G G G G A	265D
C E D C C B A F	130I	C E F D B G	246M	C E F G G G G G G	122I
C E D C C B B A A G G A	131L	C E F D C C	227H	C E F G G# A	41A
C E D C C B B A A G G F#	251C	C E F D D C	131A	C E F# G C D	282B
C E D C C C B	43O	C E F D E D	398S	C E F# G G G	407P
C E D C C C G	22F	C E F D G F	169P	C E G A A G	60F
C E D C C E D	151A	C E F E D C	291G	C E G A B C C B	362N
C E D C C E G	383N	C E F E D D	252F	C E G A B C C C B	153G
C E D C D C	138F	C E F F G B	279E	C E G A B C C C F	380L
C E D C E D	157B	C E F F G B	45N	C E G A Bb A	124D
C E D C E G F	228R	C E F F# G B	352F	C E G A C A	270M
C E D C E G G	114M	C E F G A A	341H	C E G A C C C	124H
C E D C G A	19D	C C F G A C A	83J	C E G A C C E	59D
C E D C G C	163O	C E F G A C D	53S	C E G A F D	169S
C E D C G G A	18O	C E F G A C F	53R	C E G A F G	21S
C E D C G G C	18O	C E F G A D	290F	C E G A G A	232E

Notation	Ref	Notation	Ref	Notation	Ref
C Eb G C B A	26P	C G A Bb F F	34B	C G C C# E C#	42D
C Eb G C Bb Ab G F Eb D	152A	C G A C B C	16Q	C G C D C B	287S
C Eb G C Bb Ab G F Eb G	151B	C G A D B G	54N	C G C D D E	143I
C Eb G C C Eb	161F	C G A E A G F	289Q	C G C D E C D	135K
C Eb G C D Eb	152O	C G A E A G G	247D	C G C D E C E	30S
C Eb G C E F	10S	C G A E C F	292R	C G C D E D C B	194P
C Eb G C Eb G	403O	C G A E F E D	56M	C G C D E D C D E	22P
C Eb G C G Eb	319F	C G A E F E F	216M	C G C D E D C D G	149M
C Eb G D Eb D	43N	C G A E G C	384P	C G C D E D E F E D	160Q
C Eb G F Eb C	68E	C G A F E D	71I	C G C D E D E F E E	149S
C Eb G F Eb D	44N	C G A F G C	25F	C G C D E D F	68I
C Eb G G A A	76I	C G A F G E	426N	C G C D E F E	295I
C Eb G G Eb Ab	144D	C G A G C E	292D	C G C D E F G	215P
C Eb G G F Eb	150N	C G A G C G A G C B	362H	C G C D Eb C	320E
C Eb G G G Ab	79R	C G A G C G A G C C	163S	C G C D Eb F Eb D C	101H
C Eb G G G Bb	389N	C G A G E C D	196S	C G C D Eb F Eb D Eb	285P
C Eb G G G Eb	390A	C G A G E C F	290G	C G C D Eb F G	71Q
C Eb G G G G Bb	29H	C G A G F E C	309B	C G C Db E Db	42D
C Eb G G G G C	365C	C G A G F E D C C	283E	C G C E A G	159B
C Eb G G G G G	172J	C G A G F E D C G	51M	C G C E C G	289D
C F D C B C	242D	C G A G F G F E	371O	C G C E E A	90E
C F D C C B	344F	C G A G F G F G	419J	C G C E E G	278F
C F D E A D	324L	C G A G# A C	261N	C G C E F G	81G
C F D E A D	324L	C G Ab Bb C G	105J	C G C Eb C C	32R
C F D G E C	292S	C G Ab E F G	70I	C G C Eb D B	347A
C F D G F E D	361K	C G Ab F Eb D	14A	C G C Eb D C	328K
C F E A G F	247A	C G Ab F Eb F	153F	C G C Eb F G	160S
C F E D C B	57N	C G Ab G C Ab	129S	C G C F E C	359B
C F E D C C	110G	C G Ab G Eb D	347S	C G C F E D#	393J
C F E D C# D	33R	C G Ab G F Ab	264M	C G C G C A	279Q
C F E D E C	395P	C G Ab G F Eb	281R	C G C G C Bb	281Q
C F E D E G	106F	C G Ab G G Ab	168L	C G C G C C	132D
C F E D G C	192C	C G Ab G G C	280E	C G C G C E	383C
C F Eb Eb D C	414H	C G B A E G	396K	C G C G C G	249R
C F F Ab Ab Ab	336J	C G B A Bb C G	4D	C G C G E C	326H
C F F F Ab G	340G	C G B C A F	150K	C G C G F A	351L
C F F F F F	179N	C G B C C G	162B	C G C G G G	70S
C F G Ab Eb D	32G	C G B C G B	67I	C G D C# G# D#	175Q
C F G Ab F C	347J	C G B C G B	306S	C G D E A B	205S
C F G E F D	248I	C G B F A D	392O	C G D E F G	213B
C F G E G C	409L	C G Bb A Bb G	87F	C G D Eb C G	74D
C F# G A G E	418N	C G Bb F Eb F	258J	C G D G C E	254K
C F# G G D F	8F	C G C Ab F F	163J	C G D G D G	255D
C G A A A F	269J	C G C B A F	303Q	C G D G E C	255M
C G A A B C	189D	C G C B A G A	222B	C G D G E D	346C
C G A A E F	407F	C G C B A G C	164N	C G D G Eb D	278D
C G A B A A	440H	C G C B A G G	8G	C G D G G F	156H
C G A B A G	364O	C G C B B C	150A	C G E A A C#	358E
C G A B C B	269G	C G C B C C D	20G	C G E A A F	251G
C G A B C D C B	400P	C G C B C C E	84J	C G E A D E	289L
C G A B C D C D	11L	C G C B C D	274O	C G E A G E	273A
C G A B C D E C	329A	C G C Bb Ab G F Eb D C	154J	C G E C A A	134G
C G A B C D E D	151C	C G C Bb Ab G F Eb D Eb	153S	C G E C A G	183S
C G A B C D E F	410I	C G C Bb G Bb	297M	C G E C C C	309B
C G A B C D E G E A	283A	C G C C C C	149N	C G E C C G	254P
C G A B C D E G E D	348B	C G C C D D Eb Eb	171N	C G E C D E	25N
C G A B C G	271G	C G C C D D Eb F	21N	C G E C E G C C	331C
C G A B D F	23D	C G C C D E F	13F	C G E C E G C D D	122C
C G A B E G	301F	C G C C D E G	256D	C G E C E G C D E	11C
C G A Bb A G	294F	C G C C G B	164F	C G E C E G E	382O
C G A Bb Bb G	110A			C G E C F D B	272O

Notation	Ref
D Eb Bb D Eb B	360A
D Eb C Bb Ab Ab	61H
D Eb C Bb C E	378A
D Eb C G C Eb	37O
D Eb D C B B	268O
D Eb D C B C	272J
D Eb D C D D	326R
D Eb D C D Eb	301Q
D Eb D C G Bb	438S
D Eb D C G D	405S
D Eb D D G F	269C
D Eb D Eb B C	77E
D Eb D Eb D Eb	263N
D Eb D Eb D G	55O
D Eb D Eb F G	426I
D Eb D G F D	263R
D Eb Eb D C Bb	283B
D Eb Eb F# G B	209B
D Eb F Eb D C	231K
D Eb F G Ab Bb	179B
D Eb F G G C	104H
D Eb F G G D	77H
D Eb G D Eb G	55J
D Eb G F# G C	259P
D F A E D F	283N
D F A F E D	410L
D F B C D E	416A
D F C Eb B B	221A
D F D Eb D G	54D
D F E F E D	87J
D F E F F E	22N
D F E G F A	223N
D F E G F D	381H
D F Eb D Eb D	113N
D F F F F Ab	88J
D F G A A F	144G
D F G Ab F Eb	34H
D G C Bb Ab F	54L
D G C D B C	345H
D G D D D E	91K
D G D D F F	89R
D G D E D D	159N
D G D Eb F G	208D
D G E A C F	412R
D G E C F D	247O
D G E C G D	381C
D G E E F E	76P
D G F E C G	186S
D G F E D C	125K
D G F F E F	212M
D G G A E G	47J
D G G D D E	357E
D G G D Eb C	376F
D G G G Ab Bb	106E
D G G G F G	106D
Db A A A A Db	429H
Db Db C C B	316K
Db 7	434A
D# D# D# D# E E	209S
D# D# F E E G	44C
D# E A D E G	112B
D# E E E E E E D#	303I
D# E E E E E E G	92A
D# E F G A G	375N
D# E G C G E	415J
D# E G D# E G	84O
D# G E G G A	438E
E A Ab Ab G C	82I
E A B C B A	354N
E A C# D E F	435C
E A E D B E	351B
E A E D D E	84N
E A E E E A	417N
E A E E E E	337G
E A E F G C	132P
E A F C C D	60L
E A F G E D	301E
E A G A C D	176C
E A G C B A	55B
E A G C B E	113M
E A G C D E	238F
E A G C E D	136R
E A G D C B	396E
E A G D C# D	208N
E A G E A G	104B
E A G E C A	222A
E A G E F E	51F
E A G E G C	193G
E A G E G E	352J
E A G F D B A	136J
E A G F D B G	440L
E A G F E D	137S
E A G G C F	133E
E A G G E A	187O
E A G G G F	323H
E A G G G G	370D
E B A E D C	338O
E B C C D E	322M
E B C C E B	415G
E B C D E D	265G
E B C D G E	331E
E B C E B C E	265M
E B C E B C F	174B
E B C F E D	367O
E B C G E D	380O
E B D A B G	58G
E B D C B A	348K
E B D C E A	136N
E B D C F# A	97B
E C A A B D	300C
E C A A E C	236R
E C A E C A	351S
E C A F D B	65A
E C A G C D	199H
E C A G F E	86E
E C A G G F#	353O
E C A G G G	400G
E C B A G F	107R
E C B C D E	114F
E C B D D C	321J
E C C B C A	324S
E C C B D F	60D
E C C C A A	115S
E C C C C C	358P
E C C C C D	276H
E C C C D C	101R
E C C C F E	337J
E C C D E C	194C
E C C D E E	294H
E C C D E F E	199A
E C C D E F F E	345L
E C C D E F F F	130D
E C C F F E	209F
E C C G A B	397B
E C C G F D	373N
E C C# D A B	348R
E C D B A G	66Q
E C D B D C	283F
E C D C A B	224D
E C D C E G	37R
E C D E A B	290P
E C D E C B	357J
E C D E C D	440F
E C D E E D	201B
E C D E E E	388I
E C D E E F	185M
E C D E E G	339S
E C D E F E E	308S
E C D E F E F	18I
E C D E F G A	105Q
E C D E F G E	145F
E C D E F G F E E F	27F
E C D E F G F E E F	27O
E C D E F G F E E G	26B
E C D E G A	439F
E C D G A B	270O
E C D G E C	382F
E C E A G F#	143F
E C E B A A	208M
E C E B A G	415H
E C E C C A	68F
E C E C E C	383D
E C E C E E	75K
E C E C E E	173M
E C E C F Db	258F
E C E C F E	411I
E C E C G E	150L
E C E D G C	291F
E C E Eb Cb Cb	280S
E C E F E C	404F
E C E F G D	294F
E C E F G F	290I
E C E G C# C#	328Q
E C E G E E	383Q
E C E G G F	335L
E C E G G G C	126E
E C E G G G F	317O
E C F D A G	422L
E C F D G E A B	115K
E C F D G E A G	203D
E C F G C E	149A
E C Fb Eb Cb Cb	280S

E D D C F E — 364J
E D D C G F — 233E
E D D D C C — 240B
E D D D D D — 91C
E D D D D F# — 110P
E D D E C G — 344R
E D D E D E — 331M
E D D E F G — 50I
E D D F E E — 330R
E D D F F E — 399P
E D D F F G — 73C
E D E Ab G Bb — 428O
E D E C B B — 267G
E D E C B D — 30P
E D E C D E E — 5N
E D E C D E F G A — 439K
E D E C D E F G E — 267M
E D E C D E G — 373R
E D E C E G — 236J
E D E C G A — 393I
E D E C G C — 380B
E D E C G E — 423P
E D E C G G — 237I
E D E D C A B — 223I (B)
E D E D C A C — 183N
E D E D C D C — 121H
E D E D C D E — 204E
E D E D C G — 188F
E D E E D E — 20A
E D E E E D — 62O
E D E F A F — 203N
E D E F A G E C — 270N
E D E F A G E D — 68M
E D E F B C — 171S
E D E F B G — 421K
E D E F E C — 305S
E D E F E D D — 70D
E D E F E D E C — 330Q
E D E F E D E F — 90N
E D E F E D G — 149P
E D E F F E — 228B
E D E F G F E D A — 200K
E D E F G F E D F — 152N
E D E G A G — 144O
E D E G B A — 215J
E D E G C A — 175P
E D E G E D — 260P
E D E G E E — 347P
E D E G F E D — 308I
E D E G F E F — 295S
E D F E A B — 171I
E D F E C B — 119O
E D F E D C — 154I
E D F E D D — 243K
E D F E E D — 148L
E D F G A A — 228H
E D F G A A — 349B
E D G A C E — 218H
E D G A G D — 135D
E D G C B A — 240L
E D G E E D — 339C

E D G E E F — 288S
E D G F E D C — 299S
E D G F E D E — 296F
E D G G D E — 68O
E D# D# G E D — 110E
E D# E A D F — 265K
E D# E B A G — 392N
E D# E C E F — 35H
E D# E C G F — 309A
E D# E C G F# — 309S
E D# E C G G — 98I
E D# E E D# E E C — 94K
E D# E E D# E E F — 364L
E D# E F E A — 94K
E D# E F E D C — 83E
E D# E F E D E — 264I
E D# E F E E D — 397I
E D# E F E E E — 233B
E Db E F F F — 198C
E D# E F G A — 260O
E D# E G D G — 79F
E D# E G E D# — 353F
E D# E G F D# — 265O
E D# E G F F — 373M
E D# E G F# F — 217L
E D# E G G C — 277S
E E A A A — 372R
E E A A A F — 58L
E E A A E E — 63J
E E A A G E — 310K
E E A Ab G A — 167H
E E A C D E — 83D
E E A D C# D — 356H
E E A D D E — 208B
E E A D E E — 357C
E E A E G E — 63A
E E A G E C — 213C
E E A G E E — 426A
E E A G F D — 235J
E E A G G A — 392D
E E A G G C — 1J
E E A# B C C# — 31B
E E B B C C# — 281B
E E B B C G — 347H
E E C A A G — 103F
E E C A G E — 211I
E E C B A B — 134J
E E C C E E — 385S
E E C C G G Bb — 103H
E E C C G G G — 358J
E E C D C E — 392R
E E C D E E D — 109P
E E C D E E E — 201B
E E C E C F — 351D
E E C E F G — 364I
E E C E G D — 432P
E E C F E E — 349M
E E C F E F — 1K
E E C F F E — 53O
E E C F F E — 141H
E E C F F E — 111I

E E C G A C — 147O
E E C G E E — 278N
E E C G G A E — 410M
E E C G G A G — 319S
E E C G G E E — 250I
E E C G G E E — 348A
E E C G G F — 84I
E E C G G G A — 78N
E E C G G G E — 409H
E E C G G G F# — 319S
E E D Ab E E — 208I
E E D B G G — 373O
E E D C A F — 349H
E E D C A G — 373I
E E D C B A — 431O
E E D C C C C — 385O
E E D C C C D — 328O
E E D C C D E E D — 396J
E E D C C D E E E — 204H
E E D C C E — 340M
E E D C D C A — 74I
E E D C D C B — 358O
E E D C D C D — 185I
E G D C D D — 187I
E E D C D E F — 372I
E E D C D E G — 329I
E E D C E C — 115O
E E D C E G — 97I
E E D C F F — 156O
E E D C G A — 434I
E E D C G E — 234I
E E D C G G G G F E — 371S
E E D C G G G G F F — 218I
E E D D C A — 303M
E E D D C C C — 110I
E E D D C C E — 118I
E E D D C C F — 349O
E E D D C C G C — 221I
E E D D C C G F — 332M
E E D D C G — 369S
E E D D D D — 210I
E E D D D E — 320I
E E D D F A — 334M
E E D E D E D — 142I
E E D E D E D — 366S
E E D E D E E — 154S
E E D E E E — 166I
E E D E F B — 1S
E E D E F D C — 72I
E E D E F D E — 312I
E E D E F G C — 304M
E E D E F G D — 337A
E E D E F G E — 91I
E E D E G A — 299I
E E D E G D — 101I
E E D E G E — 480S
E E D E G F E D — 120I
E E D E G F E E — 47I
E E D F E G F — 302I
E E D F E G G — 337S
E E D F F E C — 231I

Notation	Ref	Notation	Ref	Notation	Ref
G G F# F E	441I	G G G G C B B	249S	G G G G F F F F G	194D
G G F# F# F E	437C	G G G G C B C D	400S	G G G G F F F F G	196G
G G F# F# F F	279P	G G G G C B C Eb	30F	G G G G F G A	140F
G G F# F# G	364M	G G G G C B C G	367H	G G G G F G C	127E
G G F# G A A	385N	G G G G C Bb Ab Bb	387I	G G G G F G F	3N
G G F# G A B	397H	G G G G C Bb Ab G	77C	G G G G F# F	436A
G G F# G A G	368G	G G G G C Bb C	234C	G G G G F# G Bb	403A
G G F# G C	193J	G G G G C C B B	50G	G G G G F# G C	228S
G G F# G E	202A	G G G G C C B C	441N	G G G G G A A A B	283Q
G G G A A A A	351G	G G G G C C C A A	317C	G G G G G A A A E	219L
G G G A A A B B C	135M	G G G G C C C A Bb	91R	G G G G G A A A F	396D
G G G A A A B B G	280N	G G G G C C C C B	441N	G G G G G A A B	347I
G G G A A A G	86D	G G G G C C C C D	315H	G G G G G A A C	147J
G G G A B A	302E	G G G G C C E	430O	G G G G G A A D	339J
G G G A A E	114K	G G G G C C Eb	413G	G G G G G A B C C	210C
G G G A B C C A	363O	G G G G C C G	82K	G G G G G A B C D	400M
G G G A B C C C	255K	G G G G C E	228J	G G G G G A B C E	200A
G G G A B C G	418D	G G G G C Eb D C B	319D	G G G G G A B G	350P
G G G A C	115D	G G G G C Eb D C Bb	119F	G G G G G A Bb	419F
G G G A E	342R	G G G G C G A	211S	G G G G G A F	50P
G G G A F	253S	G G G G C G Bb	299N	G G G G G A G C A	238K
G G G A G E D	190N	G G G G C G G	429S	G G G G G A G C C	230P
G G G A G E E	364P	G G G G D C C C D	210G	G G G G G A G D	375A
G G G A G F E F E D	408F	G G G G D C C C G	236M	G G G G G A G E	342Q
G G G A G F E F E E	360L	G G G G D D	370F	G G G G G A G F	284R
G G G A G F E G	141Q	G G G G D E	31I	G G G G G A G G F E	360I
G G G A G F#	388Q	G G G G E C B	441S	G G G G G A G G F G	166N
G G G A G G C	306M	G G G G E C Bb	34C	G G G G G Ab Bb	287F
G G G A G G A	331N	G G G G E C C	93D	G G G G G Ab G C	432Q
G G G A G G G F	434H	G G G G E D	332D	G G G G G Ab G Eb Eb	335F
G G G A G G G G C	241H	G G G G E E E	319Q	G G G G G Ab G Eb F	132A
G G G A G G G G G	275N	G G G G E E G	319M	G G G G G Ab G F Eb	187F
G G G Ab Ab Ab Ab Bb	415L	G G G G E F D	355P	G G G G G Ab G F F	43S
G G G Ab Ab Ab Ab F#	414A	G G G G E F G	195A	G G G G G Ab G G A	175S
G G G Ab Ab Ab Ab G	231S	G G G G E G C D	395E	G G G G G Ab G G F	318P
G G G Ab Ab Ab B	133I	G G G G E G C E	225P	G G G G G Ab G G G Bb	371Q
G G G Ab Ab Ab Bb	220C	G G G G E G G	49S	G G G G G Ab G G G F	334C
G G G Ab Ab Ab G G	315G	G G G G Eb C	247G	G G G G G B A	430N
G G G Ab Ab G G	78I	G G G G Eb Eb	277H	G G G G G B G	77B
G G G Ab Ab G	233M	G G G G Eb F G Ab	297G	G G G G G Bb Eb	120P
G G G Ab Bb Ab	315G	G G G G Eb F G G F F	277K	G G G G G Bb G	406O
G G G Ab Bb Bb	280R	G G G G Fb F G G F G	71P	G G G G G C B A	197Q
G G G Ab Bb C	188C	G G G G F C	192I	G G G G G C B B	128Q
G G G Ab G F Eb	392A	G G G G F E A A	286N	G G G G G C Bb	57J
G G G Ab G F G	118I	G G G G F E A C	181H	G G G G G C C B	56F
G G G Ab G G Eb	396F	G G G G F E A G	328G	G G G G G C C C B	370I
G G G Ab G G F	268P	G G G G F E D D C	102P	G G G G G C C C C B	48O
G G G Ab G G G	318K	G G G G F E D D G	238H	G G G G G C C C C Db	40K
G G G B B	39S	G G G G F E D E	3Q	G G G G G C C D	396J
G G G B C C	65J	G G G G F E E	431S	G G G G G C C G	280Q
G G G B C D	12P	G G G G F E G F	382H	G G G G G C C E	97P
G G G B D	106M	G G G G F E G G Db	431E	G G G G G C D C	278N
G G G Bb A	341L	G G G G F E G G G	389E	G G G G G C D E	101G
G G G Bb Bb	298F	G G G G F Eb C	202O	G G G G G C E F	356L
G G G Bb C	389I	G G G G F Eb D C	247F	G G G G G C E G	372J
G G G Bb F	327A	G G G G F Eb D Eb	26E	G G G G G C G G D	358M
G G G Bb G G F	110Q	G G G G F Eb D G	392A	G G G G G C G G E	412O
G G G Bb G G G	140I	G G G G F F E E E D	261I	G G G G G D B	440Q
G G G C A	238Q	G G G G F F E E E E	69I	G G G G G D G	406L
G G G C Ab	118Q	G G G G F F F Eb	437F	G G G G G E D	427E
G G G C B A	223E	G G G G F F F F A	96A	G G G G G E F	425D

0276527

MUSIC

The Library
University of California
Riverside

JUN 3 0 2003

THIS BOOK IS DUE ON THE LAST DATE STAMPED BELOW
Books not returned on time are subject to fines according
to the Library Lending Code.
Books cannot be renewed by phone.
Books may be recalled at any time.

Music Library - (909) 787-3137
Science Library - (909) 787-3701
Tomás Rivera Library - (909) 787-3220

2/03